FOUNDATIONS OF MODERN SOCIOLOGY

With contributions
from books in the
*Foundations of
Modern Sociology
Series* by:

Joseph Ben-David
Albert K. Cohen
Amitai Etzioni
David M. Heer
Alex Inkeles
Theodore M. Mills
Wilbert E. Moore
Thomas F. O'Dea
Talcott Parsons
Patricia Sexton
Neil J. Smelser
Melvin M. Tumin

CANADIAN SECOND EDITION

FOUNDATIONS OF MODERN

sociology

METTA SPENCER

University of Toronto

With the editorial collaboration of

Alex Inkeles

Stanford University

Prentice-Hall Canada Inc.
Scarborough, Ontario

In memory of ARCHIE HANLAN

Canadian Cataloguing in Publication Data

Spencer, Metta, 1931-
   Foundations of modern sociology

Includes bibliographies and indexes.

ISBN 0-13-330027-7

1. Sociology.   2. Social history—20th century.
I. Title.

HM51.S86 1981   301   C80-094526-3

PRENTICE-HALL
FOUNDATIONS OF MODERN SOCIOLOGY SERIES
Alex Inkeles, Editor

Prentice-Hall, Inc., *Englewood Cliffs, New Jersey*
Prentice-Hall International, Inc., *London*
Prentice-Hall of Australia, Pty., Ltd., *Sydney*
Prentice-Hall of India Pvt. Ltd., *New Delhi*
Prentice-Hall of Japan, Inc., *Tokyo*
Prentice-Hall of Southeast Asia (Pte.) Ltd., *Singapore*

Printed and bound in Canada by John Deyell Company

2 3 4 5 6 JD 86 85 84 83 82

Editorial production: Janet MacLean/Tom Pendleton/
  Serena Hoffman
Design: Walter Behnke/Joe Chin
Composition: CompuScreen Typesetting Limited

PHOTO CREDITS

CONTENTS

OUTLINE

chapter 7
DEVIANCE AND CONTROL
page 181

PART TWO
Social Interaction 217

chapter 8
ORGANIZATIONS
page 219

chapter 9
SOCIAL STRATIFICATION
page 245

chapter 10
RACIAL AND ETHNIC GROUPS
page 283

PART FOUR
Changing Society   497

chapter 16
ECONOMIC LIFE

page 465

chapter 17
POPULATION AND ECOLOGY

page 499

FOREWORD, PREFACE, AND ACKNOWLEDGEMENTS

FOREWORD

For some years now Prentice-Hall and I have been working to bring the best of sociological thought and writing to a wide audience through the medium of our series on the FOUNDATIONS OF MODERN SOCIOLOGY. The series is now planned to include more than two dozen volumes covering all major areas in the field of sociology. Each book, written by an outstanding specialist, introduces a particular subfield within the discipline. The books in the series have become quite popular with both teachers and students and have enjoyed persistent and enduring support.

Over many years of teaching large lecture sections for introductory sociology, however, I was always struck by the difficulty of finding suitable introductory books—books of high quality yet effectively adapted to the needs of beginning students.

So we resolved to develop, as part of the Foundations Series, a new introductory textbook. Professor Metta Spencer, who undertook the work, brought to the task excellent advanced training, extensive research experience, and equally important, many years of teaching the introductory course.

This new text, which takes its title from the series, has more than fulfilled the goals that were set for it. The book deals with the systematic study of groups and societies. The major aspects of social life are analyzed, with special reference to the role of each aspect in the development, functioning, and change of large social systems. No other introductory text contains such a richness of material in its exposition of theoretical perspectives, in its elaboration of sociological knowledge and basic concepts, and in its description of empirical research. These qualities, linked to clear, interesting writing and strong organization, have resulted in an introductory sociology text of the highest quality.

Alex Inkeles

PREFACE

Previous editions of this book were written for North American sociology students in general. Preparing this edition has given me a chance to address the specific group of students I know best—Canadians. I had the opportunity to teach in Toronto throughout the 1970s, the decade in which Canadian sociology experienced its most exciting growth. Because of the great contributions of Canadian researchers during these years, the needs of beginning students can be served incomparably better today than even a dozen years ago. This text draws extensively upon this rich new material in an effort to convey fundamental principles and concepts in a framework that is relevant and alive to Canadian students in the 1980s. I believe that sociology should be accessible to students and connect meaningfully with their lives.

One of my friends who has taught introductory sociology for many years keeps all her letters from former students, who are now doing things like selling insurance, editing newspapers, guiding tour groups through Asia, and administering foreign aid programs. These people often make the same remark in their letters: as students they hadn't realized how much they were gaining from their sociology course, but those earlier studies now come up repeatedly in their personal life and in their work. Years later they are writing thank-you notes for the most useful course they ever took.

Sociology does not *necessarily* connect with people's lives. Indeed, it is hard work to show students how to use sociology to understand their social experiences. People talk about sociological problems every day of their lives—on subways, in court, in the dentist's waiting room, everywhere. I hope that the information in this book and the kind of perspective it provides will add value to such conversations.

It is probably impossible for an introductory course to teach students to think like sociologists. It takes a lot of courses to accomplish that. But the introductory course can give students a good start in that direction. It can at least present some basic facts about the social structure of our society. More important, a good sociology course can help students begin to develop critical independent thinking by pointing out vital issues and controversies. Facts never speak for themselves. They only speak for people who know how to assess their significance. And sociology as a discipline can provide its students with both factual information and a heightened ability to judge the *significance* of those facts.

To that end, this book focuses not only on the facts that sociologists know (and we do know a lot), but also on the arguments and debates that underlie those facts. It does no good to give students answers until they first understand the questions. Indeed, I am just as pleased when a student discovers a new problem to be puzzled over, as I am when a student provides a satisfying answer to that problem. After all, that is what sociology consists of—identifying questions, suggesting answers to those questions, and identifying new questions and problems in the suggested answers. Introductory students can begin to participate in that ongoing process of discovery too. When they do, they find that their sociological skill enhances what they have to say during the coffee break, or on the job, or almost anywhere else. Because then (and only then) does sociology truly connect with their lives.

ORGANIZATION

Each chapter is divided into three major sections: (1) a basic core section; (2) a Social Research section; and (3) a Social Policy section.

The *basic core section* of each chapter contains an orderly presentation of the major concepts and theories of the topic area of that chapter. Important sociologists past and present and the exciting controversies that sometimes swirl around them are discussed. The core section emphasizes the lasting aspects of sociology—the basic concepts and significant issues that sociologists think about.

The *Social Research: Sociologists at Work* section always appears on an orange background to set it off from the rest of the chapter. It focuses on recent empirical research in the topic area of the chapter and discusses one or more landmark studies. It emphasizes the way sociologists come to know what they know and the people and events that contributed to that store of sociological knowledge.

The *Social Policy: Issues and Viewpoints* section always appears on a gray background. This section talks about political, economic, or ethical issues about which people have to make decisions. By discussing roles that sociologists can play in shaping the world of the future, this section serves to answer questions that are sometimes raised about the "relevance" of sociology.

FEATURES

Other elements of the book have been designed to make learning more effective for students:

GLOSSARIES A glossary containing several hundred careful definitions of all important concepts is found at the end of the book for easy reference. In addition, key terms within the body of the text are printed in color, defined when they are used for the first time, and reviewed in lists of key terms at the end of each chapter. This reinforces the learning of the most important terms found in this book as well as in advanced books and courses on particular areas of sociology.

SUMMARIES Each chapter is followed by a summary that reviews the most important ideas presented in the chapter. Basic concepts are again stressed.

READING LISTS Extensive reading lists appear at the end of each chapter, with descriptive annotations to suggest potential uses of the books.

GRAPHS, CHARTS, AND TABLES Because much empirical research in the field of sociology is reported in tabular form, a selection of this type of material is included. Students are given a thorough introduction on how to read and construct tables in Chapter 2.

PHOTOGRAPHS A lively array of pictures has been chosen to provoke thought and to make points visually that could not be expressed in words.

THE REFERENCE PAPER An appendix at the end of the book is addressed to students. Its purpose is to show how to use the library and how to write a term paper.

SUPPLEMENTS

Three supplementary aids have been designed to accompany the book:

THE STUDY GUIDE AND WORKBOOK reviews the material in the textbook through presentation of chapter objectives, basic sociological concepts, and various self-administered tests. Three testing formats are used—multiple-choice, fill-in, and matching—with answers supplied for immediate feedback. Questions cover the basic core material, as well as the Social Research and Social Policy sections, and are cross-referenced to the appropriate pages of this text.

A TEST ITEM FILE includes a thousand items selected to test the student's understanding of introductory sociology. The questions, primarily multiple-choice, are referenced to the appropriate text page. Essay questions are also included.

THE INSTRUCTOR'S MANUAL outlines the basic structure of each chapter, facilitating additional lecture materials and discussion questions. Class projects and research topics are included for each chapter, as are audio-visual aids.

ACKNOWLEDGMENTS

Any textbook owes a great deal to the vast literature on which it draws, and I have drawn on the work of many outstanding scholars—from the classical theorists, like Weber, Marx, and Durkheim, to contemporary Canadian writers like Clark, Clement, and McLuhan. I also owe a special debt to the individual books in the Prentice-Hall FOUNDATIONS OF MODERN SOCIOLOGY series, from which I was able to draw freely; their editor, Alex Inkeles, has contributed to this project as well. While I want to acknowledge my debt to others, and particularly to the series authors, the final responsibility for errors or misinterpretation must rest with me.

One of the high points of writing a book comes in thanking the people who have contributed by sharing their knowledge and parts of their lives with the author. For me to do so fully would be to double the length of this book; so many magnificent colleagues and friends have helped me, and I cannot say all that I feel about their generosity, nor can I name them all. I do, however, want to include the names of both current and previous critics and staff, since their ideas and contributions are woven cumulatively into the

ongoing process of making and remaking a textbook.

This book has benefited greatly from the comments of Ralph Beals, Lawrence Felt, Paula Felt, Diane Horowitz, Leslie Howard, Nancy Howell, Brian Hull, John Kervin, Pierre Lorion, Stanford Lyman, Ted Mann, Richard Ofshe, Alice Propper, Rheta Rosen, Diana Russell, Edward Shorter, Edward Silva, John Simpson, Kenneth Walker, and Jennifer Welsh. Other people have provided useful critical reviews of various drafts of the manuscript: Mark Abrahamson, Patricia Allen, J. Cameron Coleman, Spencer Condie, Joseph E. Faulkner, Lee Frank, Richard Hall, Mark Hutter, John Klein, Thomas Koebernick, R.L. Liverman, Betty Metz, Dennis Morton, Anthony Orum, David Payne, Daisy Quarm, Elaine Smith, Ann Sundgren, and Ernest Works.

This Canadian edition has also been enhanced by the comments of Paul Anisef, Raymond Breton, J.G. Craig, Carl J. Cuneo, Ian D. Currie, Jim Curtis, John de Vries, Daniel Glenday, John Hagan, John Harp, Michael Lanphier, Alice Propper, William C. Reimer, Leroy O. Stone, Michael Sullivan, Anthony Synnott, James Teevan, and Ken Westhues. Their responses were most useful.

Students also played a major part in helping me develop the book. I distributed drafts of various chapters to several classes both in large public universities and in small private colleges. The final result is much better because of their responses to these drafts, and I thank my own students for their helpful suggestions.

Madeline Richard and Susan Robbins contributed excellent research assistance. Mary Paul and Beverley Thomas were helpful in secretarial capacities. Ann Finlayson contributed editorial suggestions.

The Prentice-Hall staff has been terrific. I am grateful to Irene Fraga for her administrative help, and to David Stirling and now Michael Murton for their co-ordination in marketing. The production has been handled admirably and pleasantly by Ann Torbert, Tom Pendleton, Walter Behnke, Serena Hoffman, Nancy Myers, Joe Chin, Arlene Vaz, and Dawn Roper.

Three editors have at different times and in different ways made an exceptional contribution to the style and organization of the manuscript—Ray Mullaney, Carolyn Smith, and Janet MacLean.

Over the years, the editorial advice and executive abilities of Alex Inkeles and Edward Stanford have made enormous contributions to this book. Now I can thank Marta Tomins and Frank Hintenberger for their own distinctive ways of helping this edition come to fruition. I am deeply grateful to all of these good people.

Our lives expand by recognizing magnificence in others, quite beyond the limiting circumstances of our relationships. And here I want to honor all that I have recognized in Ross Johnson, Jim Fisk, Susan Ingram, and in my son, Jonathan Spencer, the liveliest companion of my life.

Metta Spencer

introduction

WHAT IS SOCIOLOGY?

The social sciences
    Economics
    Political science
    History
    Geography
    Psychology
    Anthropology
    Social work
A brief historical survey
    The early sociologists
    Sociology in the United States
    Sociology in Canada
Dominant perspectives in sociology
    Evolutionism
    Structural functionalism
    The conflict model
    Symbolic interactionism
    Ethnomethodology
    Which model to choose?
Values, research, and policy

A delightful scene in an old French play features a character who becomes very pleased with himself when he finds out that he has been speaking prose all his life. You may be just as surprised to learn that you have been "speaking sociology" all your life. For example, you may have had conversations on the subject of why some youngsters become delinquent and others do not, or why there is less birth control in poor countries than in rich ones, or whether it is lonelier to live in a city than in a small town, or whether the portrayal of violence on television leads to violent actions by members of the TV audience. If so, you have discussed sociological issues. But just as some people speak prose better than others, so also some people talk about sociological issues with more knowledge than others. In this book I want to acquaint you with some of the most important contributions of people who study social relationships, that is, *sociologists*. Their field—the study of human group life—is called sociology. Its basic goal is to understand how human beings fit their activities together into a system of stable social arrangements. But this is only the beginning of a definition. We will devote this whole chapter to explaining more fully what sociology is, but first we need to know what is meant by the terms *society* and *social system*.

A society is a large, permanent, self-sufficient, self-perpetuating group of interacting people who share certain common values and beliefs. Japan is a society, and so is Canada, for example. Collectively, the members of a society perform billions of social acts during a single day. Yet the usual outcome is not total confusion but enough order to permit each person to do his or her own thing while others do theirs. Indeed, our actions generally help other people attain their goals and vice versa. The primary purpose of sociology is to explain how this happens, how the activities of individuals fit together to produce orderly collective life.

Society was here before we were born; we did not invent it. We enter social systems that are already working, and we learn how they work by participating in them. A social system is made up of the interactions of two or more people. Each person is both an actor and an object of the other's actions. Each person's actions are guided by the expected response of the other, that is, by how the other person is likely to react. Social systems may be small, made up of a mother and her baby, a rapist and his victim, or two snowmobilers passing on a narrow trail. Or they may be large, comprising the Royal Canadian Mounted Police, the Shell Oil Company, or the passengers and crew of a ship crossing the Atlantic—or an entire society.

Sociology is one of the broadest fields imaginable. Sociologists can study almost anything human beings do. What is special about sociologists is the *way* they study any given topic—the kind of questions they ask and the methods they use in trying to answer those questions. Of course sociologists experience social life personally just as other people do—they fall in love, they go to war, they work and play, and so on. But *as sociologists* they do not think of love the way a bride does, nor of war the way an admiral does, nor of work and play the way grocers and children do. In their work they think of these topics as social patterns to be explained in a scientific way, for sociology is a social science.

The social sciences

A *science* is a branch of study that is concerned with discovering and organizing facts, principles, and methods. The *natural sciences* (e.g., physics, biology, astronomy) study physical phenomena; the *social sciences* deal in a scientific way with relationships among human beings. There are several different social sciences, but the boundaries between them are very hazy. Many of the articles and books that we will discuss were written by social scientists who are not sociologists, though they might just as well have been written by sociologists. Since the different social sciences tend to cover different aspects of human relationships, a description of some of the other social sciences may help you understand what sociology is.

ECONOMICS

Economics is concerned with the production and distribution of goods and services. It deals with such factors as the flow of money and the relationship of prices to supply and demand. Few economists pay much attention to an individual's actual behavior or attitudes. Neither do they study business enterprises as social organizations. They leave such matters to the psychologist or the sociologist. Moreover, sociologists often study topics that are related to economics—for example, the social

backgrounds of businessmen and managers and the contributions of education to productivity.

Although economists have limited their horizons, they have developed a highly focused, coherent field of study. Other social scientists envy them for the precision of their terminology, the extent to which they agree on certain basic principles, and their ability to make practical suggestions for public policy.

POLITICAL SCIENCE

Traditionally, political science could be broken down into two branches—political theory and government administration. Until 30 or 40 years ago, it paid little attention to political behavior but was concerned chiefly with how to make government organizations

Sociologists can study almost anything that human beings do. Someone may be studying you right now.

Frank Siteman/Stock, Boston

efficient. Topics such as the workings of bureaucracy, the social backgrounds of political activists, and the way people acquire their political beliefs were studied by political sociologists, not political scientists.[1] However, political scientists have been turning more and more toward behavioral concerns. Today political scientists are concerned with subjects such as popular attitudes and values, the membership of radical movements, and how decisions are made in cities and bureaucracies. There is no longer any distinction between the sociologists and political scientists who study behavior.

HISTORY

Historians, as everyone knows, study the past. Sociologists are usually more interested in the present or the recent past. Historians take pride in telling us in great detail how a past event actually happened. Sociologists like to compare a set of similar events in order to find out why some of them turned out one way and some another way. A historian might study the Russian Revolution, while a sociologist might compare several different revolutions and come up with statements about which revolutionary situations lead to war and which do not, about the stages that all revolutions go through, about the outcomes of various types of revolutions, and so on. After studying fourteen revolutions, the sociologist may conclude that the rebels never win unless the government's army defects. This is a causal statement about a general class of events—the sort of statement that traditional historians avoid. To the historian each event is unique; to classify it or generalize about it is to risk distorting it. This argument is fast losing supporters, however—in fact one traditional historian whom I met recently remarked glumly that "all the historians are turning into sociologists." No doubt he exaggerated, but it is true that there are many similarities between historians and sociologists.

Some of the greatest historians have written *social* history, dealing not with kings and wars but with the less glamorous events that interest sociologists, such as changes in landowning patterns or in the relations between men and women in the family. Canadian sociology has been especially close to history, as a field. The major Canadian sociologists have devoted most of their work to explaining Canada's social development.

GEOGRAPHY

Geography is concerned with the relationship between human beings and their natural environment. Geographers usually study particular areas or particular *kinds* of areas, such as irrigated river basins or tropical forests. They may be interested in ecological problems or in the way economic systems develop in different environmental settings. Thus they may try to find out why trade routes, harbors, or markets are established in some areas and not in others, and what effect these have on their environments. Hence, geography is partly a natural science and partly a social science. While physical geographers are often interested in climate, agriculture, oceanography, soil composition, and other natural phenomena, social or cultural geographers may examine many of the same areas that sociologists are interested in, such as the logging industry or the use of milk products around the world. Urban geographers and urban sociologists sometimes work together; they may, for example, team up to study the impact of various kinds of housing on family life.

Social scientists, then, often work in very similar ways regardless of whether they were trained in economics, political science, geography, or any other social science. Canadian sociologists have tended to devote their research to the economic and political development of Canadian society. As a result, their work has been quite closely linked to the research of geographers. For example, some

George Bellerose/Stock, Boston

Geographers are social scientists who study the relationship between human society and the natural environment. They may specialize in certain kinds of environments, such as settlements around harbors. You may recognize this harbor as Hong Kong.

sociologists have focused on the growth of wheat farming in the prairie provinces while others have studied the effects of the fur trade upon the social life of Upper Canada; both topics obviously require attention to environmental factors. A major theme in Canadian sociology, again linked to geographic research, has concerned the importance of the frontier in determining the character of Canadian society.

PSYCHOLOGY

Psychology is often called the science of the mind. It deals with mental processes such as thinking, learning, remembering, and decision making. Modern psychologists also study feelings, emotions, motives, and personality.

Some experimental psychologists do bio-

logical or physiological research. It is in the area of social psychology, however, that psychology comes closest to sociology.

Some social psychologists are interested in how personality and behavior are influenced by a person's social background or by the social setting in which that person finds himself or herself. For example, Solomon Asch's studies showed that people will frequently describe a line as shorter or longer than it actually is, even while looking at it themselves, if a majority of the other people around them say that the line is shorter or longer than it actually is. Thus Asch showed that even what one sees is influenced by a *social* situation—majority pressure on a minority.[2]

Other social psychologists are especially interested in how a person's *personality* in-

7

fluences his or her social behavior. Thus studies of voting patterns have shown that Americans with rigid and intolerant personalities are more likely than other Americans to favor an isolationist foreign policy.[3]

It is often hard to see any difference between the work of researchers who were trained in sociology and that of researchers who were trained in psychology. Many people argue that social psychology should be considered a distinct field rather than a branch of sociology or psychology. However, social psychology as an area of research has not been very popular among Canadian sociologists. Rather than comparing individuals, Canadian sociologists have generally preferred to examine the ways in which regions of the country or whole social communities have developed over time.

ANTHROPOLOGY

Anthropology is as varied as sociology. It includes archaeology, physical anthropology, cultural history, many branches of linguistics, and the study of all aspects of non-industrial humanity everywhere. Like psychology, it has strong ties with the natural sciences, especially biology.

Anthropology overlaps sociology as a science of culture. *Culture*—by which we mean the system of symbols, including language and beliefs, that is shared by a particular group—is the subject matter of anthropology in the same sense that power and authority are the subject matter of political science and the production and distribution of goods is the subject matter of economics.

Anthropologists tend to study primarily primitive or nonliterate humanity, whereas sociologists study more advanced civilizations. One result of this difference is that anthropologists tend to study societies as *wholes*. If they specialize, it is usually in a particular *culture area* (e.g., Melanesia or the Arctic). Sociologists, by contrast, usually study *parts* of a society. They generally specialize in some institution, such as the family, or in some process, such as the spread of rumor. Anthropologists often live in the community they are studying, directly observing the behavior of its members or recording its customs. Sociologists, on the other hand, tend to rely on statistics and questionnaires. Finally, anthropologists study small, self-contained groups or communities, whereas sociologists study large, impersonal organizations and processes.

SOCIAL WORK

Social work is not actually a social science. It is a profession that trains its own members. However, it is often confused with sociology. When someone asks me what I do for a living, I usually reply, "Sociology." About one time in three the other person says something like, "Oh, my cousin is a social worker too."

Social work is to sociology what engineering is to physics. It is an applied field that draws upon the principles of sociology, psychology, psychoanalysis, and other social sciences, but it also uses its own set of techniques in helping people solve personal and group problems. Sociologists do research, but they almost never try to influence people directly through personal contact, as social workers do. Professors of social work also conduct research, however, and such research often overlaps that of sociologists.

A brief historical survey

Philosophers have been writing about human relationships for thousands of years. Some of them, notably Aristotle, made contributions that present-day sociologists sometimes draw upon. However, sociology as such did not exist until the late nineteenth century and was not generally included among the social sciences until 30 or 40 years ago. Most of its growth and development has occurred in the past 20 years. In fact you are about to study a very new science.

THE EARLY SOCIOLOGISTS

We usually say that Auguste Comte (1798-1857) was the first real sociologist. Comte, who coined the word *sociology*, believed that society is governed by certain "social laws" just as the physical universe is governed by certain physical laws. He wanted other scholars to join him in discovering and describing these social laws. For example, he believed that all societies passed through the same series of stages. All of the early sociologists believed this notion, and, as we will see later, they tried to identify the principles of "social evolution." Concern with social evolution was abandoned early in this century, but today there is renewed interest in this notion. Today nobody talks about social laws the way Comte did, but we continue the search for regular relationships among social patterns.

Herbert Spencer (1820-1903), like Comte, was more influential in his time than he is today. His three-volume *Principles of Sociol-*

Karl Marx

In 1818, near the border between Germany and France, a son was born to a Jewish lawyer who had officially converted to Christianity to avoid religious persecution. This boy was Karl Marx, whose political ideas later shaped history and still affect our lives. Marx hoped in his youth to become a professor. He studied philosophy at the University of Berlin, but he quickly chose the losing side in a conflict with authorities—a pattern of behavior that persisted throughout his life. By the age of 24 he was blacklisted from an academic career and had lost his first job (as newspaper editor) so he went to Paris where he studied radical politics and British economic theory. There he met his lifelong co-worker, Friedrich Engels.

In 1848 most of Europe was upset by left-wing revolts against many governments. Marx and Engels had already begun supporting radical causes; they had written the *Communist Manifesto* a short time before the revolts began. Marx was expelled from France and Germany because of radical activities and he spent most of his life in London, where he sometimes wrote for the New York *Tribune*. Engels helped support Marx's family but they were always desperately poor. In fact, at least one of his children starved and others died of diseases related to poverty. Marx was outraged by the workers' living conditions and he sought both to explain capitalism theoretically and to fight it politically. His book, *Capital*, was his most successful work, published in 1867. He died in 1883, but his works became official doctrine shaping the policies of many nations throughout the following century.

ogy, published in 1877, was the first full-scale, systematic description of sociology as a science. In it he defined sociology as the study of the family, politics, religion, social control, and industry or work. These topics are still among the primary concerns of sociologists. We will meet Spencer several times in this and later chapters.

The writer who probably had the greatest impact on sociology was Karl Marx (1818-1883), whose revolutionary activities got him thrown out of several European countries. Along with Friedrich Engels (1820-1895), Marx helped shape not only modern intellectual life but also modern history. Today many governments and political groups admire him and try to make their policies consistent with his writings.

Marx was a man with many interests and a strong sense of justice. He was upset by the misery of the working classes. He was very good at seeing connections between ideas in different fields and pulling them together. Having studied the ideas of English economic theorists, philosophers, and socialist political thinkers, he ripped them apart with savage criticism and then used the remaining shreds as the foundation of Marxism. Throughout this book you will run into various aspects of Marxism, yet they represent only a tiny fraction of Marx's writing. Marx wrote mountains of material, much of which has never been translated into English. Many sociologists disagree with him for all sorts of reasons, but most sociologists see in Marx's work both profound intelligence and deep concern for the human condition.

Two later writers share with Marx the honor of being the most influential of sociologists. They are the Frenchman Emile Durkheim (1858-1917) and the German Max Weber (1864-1920). Although they studied many of the same problems and each had many followers, neither seems to have been familiar with the other's work. They both compared different types of societies. Indeed, Durkheim, who called sociology "the science of societies,"

believed that only through such systematic comparisons can we explain complex social relationships.[4] By observing a social pattern in many different groups and circumstances, he said, we come to understand its causes and its results.

While Durkheim is best known for his comparative work on suicide, religion, and education, Weber wrote extensively on religion, various aspects of economic life (including money and the division of labor), political organization and authority, bureaucracy, class and caste, the city, and music. We will have more to say about Weber in the pages ahead.

SOCIOLOGY IN THE UNITED STATES

The real growth of sociology as a science took place in the United States. A few years ago, a weekly news magazine reported that 70 percent of the world's sociologists were American. I'm not sure where it got that figure, but it was probably fairly accurate, at least until the past decade. The rest of the world is catching up, but American publications are still being used for teaching purposes. All the American writers later mentioned are often referred to in sociology courses around the world.

The first department of sociology was established in 1893 at the University of Chicago. The American Sociological Association was formed by a group that split off from the American Economic Association in 1905. There was quite a bit of resistance to this strange new science among the more conservative private colleges in the East. Harvard did not establish a department of sociology until 1930; and as late as 1960, 5 of the nation's 20 leading liberal-arts colleges still did not offer any courses in sociology.

Members of the older and wealthier families of the East Coast cities tended to study the classics, literature, or history and to avoid sociology. As a result most of the early American sociologists came from rural rather than urban areas. Almost all the first two dozen presidents of the American Sociological Association were from rural backgrounds. A surprisingly high number were descended from ministers or were themselves trained in the ministry. They included Lester Ward, who is often called the father of American sociology.

The early European sociologists dealt mainly with theories of history or used the lives of primitive people to illustrate their ideas about evolution, religion, and society. Although similar themes and sources may be seen in the work of Ward and a few other early American sociologists, these scholars paid more attention to the severe social problems that seemed to spring up everywhere in American society. This was especially true at the University of Chicago, which for more than

Max Weber

Max Weber was born in 1864, the son of a wealthy German politician, one of the leading figures of Berlin society. Weber (pronounced Vayber) was emotionally torn by his parents' unhappy marriage. His father was heavy-handed and bullied his mother, a gentle and sensitive woman. Max went away to university, where for a while he lived up to the blustering male sex role common to Germans of his day. However, he soon moved beyond that lifestyle, possibly influenced by his mother's idealism. He was impressive to everyone who met him — handsome, independent in spirit and mind. He began by studying law but soon read widely in many other fields as well. Perhaps no one anywhere has read or remembered as much as Max Weber in the fields of economics, philosophy, linguistics — and especially world history.

By his early thirties, however, Weber quarreled with his father and threatened never to speak to him again unless he treated his mother better. Shortly after their quarrel, the father fell dead and Max suffered an emotional breakdown (perhaps from guilt) that lasted about 7 years. Unable to work, he traveled occasionally, but mostly just stared out the window, depressed. By 1904 he resumed work and over the remaining 16 years of his life he wrote astonishing amounts of important works in many fields. He is known today for works on bureaucracy, stratification, economic history, religion, and even the sociology of music. Late in his life he turned to practical politics, serving as a diplomat at the close of World War I. But in 1920, at the age of 56, he died of pneumonia, deeply respected by his many students for his personal integrity and the brilliance of his mind.

two decades (1915-1940) was almost unchallenged as the center of sociological training in America. In the living laboratory provided by the city of Chicago, they studied the slum and the ghetto, the prostitute and the juvenile delinquent, the professional criminal and the drug addict.[5]

One University of Chicago professor, Robert E. Park, had studied in Germany with a sociologist named Georg Simmel, had served as a secretary to Booker T. Washington, and had worked as a journalist. These factors all influenced his view of sociology. In his writing and teaching he imported Simmel's thought to North America. One result was increased emphasis on the study of conflict and personal relationships in urban settings. To Park, a community was an area of both cooperation and competition, much as in nature an ecological habitat is an area of cooperation and competition for the species within it. His approach became known as social ecology.

After World War I several other scholars—Charles Horton Cooley, George Herbert Mead, John Dewey, W. I. Thomas—developed an approach that came to be called the "Chicago school" of social psychology. Until that time psychologists had explained human behavior largely in terms of inborn instincts. By contrast, the Chicago school stressed the importance of social interactions in the shaping of human behavior.

During the 1930s Harvard University also became an important center of sociological thinking. The work done there was rather different from the work done in Chicago; it was more similar to European sociology. Pitirim Sorokin, a Russian refugee, influenced a number of students at Harvard, but he was outclassed in fame by a younger, rival professor named Talcott Parsons. Parsons, who had studied sociology in Germany, introduced to American scholars the ideas of Durkheim and Weber. He wrote a number of complex theoretical books that are often very difficult for undergraduates to understand. Many of his

former students, however, were so stimulated by Parsons' work that they went on to make major theoretical contributions of their own. Among them are Wilbert Moore, Robert Merton, Kingsley Davis, and Neil Smelser—names that will become familiar as you read this book. They share an approach called *structural functionalism*, about which we will have much more to say. Parsons died in 1979, just after it became apparent that his preferred approach, structural functionalism, was declining in importance. It never reached the degree of popularity among Canadian social scientists that it attained in the United States.

Especially since World War II, American sociologists have tended to use mathematical tools in their research and to obtain much of their data from questionnaires, census information, and similar sources. For about 20 years, the best place to learn these techniques was Columbia University. However, during the past 10 or 15 years, the University of Michigan has been the leading center for researchers who use mathematics and computers.

SOCIOLOGY IN CANADA

The great growth of sociology all around the world has taken place since World War II; in Canada the great period of growth has occurred even more recently, during the 1960s and 1970s. It is not possible to distinguish Canadian sociology clearly from the sociology of other countries. However, it is fair to say that *within* Canadian sociology some real differences exist between French- and English-Canadian sociologists. This is partly because French and English Canada have different intellectual roots, in Europe and the United States respectively.

Some sociological research and instruction was underway in French Canada by about 1920, first at Laval University and the University of Montreal and then later at the

University of Quebec. The inspiration for this research was primarily European, since many French Canadian scholars took their advanced training in France or some other European country before returning to teach in Quebec. European sociologists tend to focus upon the behavior of large human groups rather than on the interactions of individuals. As a result of their training, then, francophone sociologists have usually focused on such topics as economic trends, political parties, trade union movements, patterns of land ownership, or relations between Church and government. They have paid much less attention to psychological factors or the behavior of small groups such as classrooms, nuclear families, or workers on an assembly line. In keeping with this emphasis on the "macro" as opposed to "micro" level of analysis, French Canadian sociologists are said to get more

involved in discussing the abstract theoretical underpinnings of their research than most English Canadian sociologists. Anglophone sociologists supposedly discuss more down-to-earth questions related to their work; this may result from the heavy influence of American scholarship.[6]

We must immediately point out that English Canadian sociology was for a long time *itself* divided between two traditions. The first tradition was influenced by American social science and the second was largely British in origin. The American tradition was centered at McGill University, the British at the University of Toronto; these two institutions served for a long time as the centers of sociology for English Canada.[7]

It was Carl Dawson who was chiefly responsible for introducing sociology to Canada. Although occasional courses had

Carl Dawson (left) and Everett E. Hughes (right) were two early influential sociologists at McGill University.

McGill University

McGill University

been offered as early as 1910 at universities in Manitoba and the Maritimes, Canada's first real program of instruction in sociology began in 1922 under Dawson's leadership at McGill University. The program was modeled after that of the University of Chicago, the leading center of American sociology in that period. McGill's program followed the Chicago tradition by stressing the study of individuals and groups through direct, personal observation and communication. Dawson brought to McGill a number of Chicago-trained sociologists, especially Everett C. Hughes, whose book *French Canada in Transition* was the first fine sociological study of a Canadian community. Since 1936, McGill has maintained an independent sociology department of distinction.

The University of Toronto, though perhaps equally influential in the field, treated sociology quite differently than did McGill. Unlike McGill, the University of Toronto did not grant sociology the status of independent department until the 1960s; until then it was formally a part of the Department of Political Economy. Sociologists were surrounded by scholars who modeled themselves after British historians, political theorists, and economists. These scholars frankly looked down on American-style sociology; they considered it to be lacking in intellectual rigor and to be too caught up in American social issues such as poverty, delinquency, and slums.

By far the most influential social scientist at Toronto for many years was Harold A. Innis, an economic historian whose ideas will be mentioned at various points throughout this book. Innis developed a method for studying history that has come to be called the "staples approach." It is an approach that has proven particularly useful for discussing the economy of Canada. Unlike the industrialized nations of Europe and the United States, Canada has depended heavily on the "extractive" end of production; instead of the manufacture of goods and the export of finished products, the Canadian economy has largely

been based on the extraction and export of raw materials like timber, fur, ore, fish, and food grains. The "staples" approach explains Canadian development in terms of the particular staple raw materials that have been available for exploitation, as well as the other resources (such as railroads and waterways) that have determined how these staple goods could be shipped and processed. Innis's present day followers are mostly those social scientists who are concerned about Canada's failure to sustain its economic autonomy because it is so vulnerable to international corporate power. According to this view, a nation that exports raw materials has less control over its economic decisions than a nation that does more manufacturing. We shall return to this contemporary debate about Canada's independence in later chapters when we discuss Dependency Theory, a political theory that draws some of its main assumptions from Innis's "staples approach."

After Innis, S.D. Clark clearly deserves the most recognition for his long-term influence upon Canadian sociology. He assumed leadership of the sociologists at the University of Toronto in 1939 and since then he has written a number of books that generally emphasize the historical factors that make Canadian society unique. Clark has encouraged other Canadian sociologists to take the same approach, and many have done so. However, during his term as chairman of the sociology department at Toronto, there was a large influx of American-trained scholars whose interests lay neither in a historical approach nor in an overview of Canadian social development.

Any rivalry that used to exist between McGill-style and Toronto-style sociologists has disappeared long ago. Canadian sociology is now as varied as sociology in any other country; forty years ago there were hardly a dozen trained sociologists in Canada, but there are closer to a thousand today. History is still a major consideration in the research of many Canadian sociologists, despite Clark's worries to the contrary. However, many other varieties of research are now used by other sociologists. Some do surveys, and take home a briefcase full of computer print-outs to analyze every night. Others spend their time in government document libraries, poring over tables that record deaths, alcohol production, land ownership patterns, or the use of immigrants in factory work. Others fly off to Asia or Latin America at every opportunity, to study nursing homes, family-planning systems, or political parties. Sociologists' interests are so varied that it is difficult to say what approach is most "fashionable" today. In some places, particularly the University of British Columbia, York University, and the Ontario Institute for Studies in Education, a strong interest in ethnomethodology has developed in recent years. (This approach will be further discussed later in this chapter.)

The themes of Canadian sociological research are also varied. Research on the topic of Canadian unity is emphasized everywhere, both by francophone separatists and Canadian nationalists. Research on social inequality in Canada is also considered important. John Porter's book, *The Vertical Mosaic*, which deals with the unequal social opportunities of various ethnic groups in Canada, was on assigned sociology reading lists throughout Canada for about ten years. More recently, Wallace Clement and others have gained comparable attention for their research on the foreign ownership of Canadian businesses. These are only a few of the topics that command widespread attention today; in the pages ahead we shall mention many others that illustrate the exciting diversity of sociology as it is growing today in Canada and elsewhere.[8]

Harold Innis (left) and S.D. Clarke (right) had a lasting influence on sociology at the University of Toronto.

McGill University

University of Toronto

Dominant perspectives in sociology

Sociology is a science. Its task is to describe how social systems work. Every scientist carries in his or her head a model of the subject on which he or she is working—a sort of mental map of how it is put together. Shakespeare's metaphor, "All the world's a stage," is a model suggesting that people play their roles according to scripts they have memorized. A sociological model, then, is a description in general terms of the way a particular social system works. A sociologist's theories will always be based on the model that he or she believes is more accurate than any other. A theory is an explanation offered to account for a group of facts or phenomena. A model is much broader than the theories that it generates. A theory is more limited and precise, and often it can be proved wrong. A model can be called incomplete, misleading, or unproductive, but it can't be proved wrong.

The belief that diseases are caused by germs is a model on which theories about the causes of particular diseases (e.g., diphtheria or smallpox) are based. The model encourages the scientist to search for specific germs and to control particular diseases by killing the germs that cause them. The germ model has been useful in stimulating scientific discoveries, but it is not helpful to the scientist who is trying to explain illnesses that are caused by poor diet or by chemical or radiation poisoning. Therefore, while models are important, we pay a price if we hold to only one model and ignore all other possible models.

Ideally, scientists should not hold too closely to any one model and should be ready to abandon their particular picture of the world as soon as a better one comes along. In practice, however, scientists' models often become rigid and important new facts and ideas are brushed aside. A scientist will often resist any effort to replace his or her favorite model. Such resistance is especially dangerous in sociology because of the moral and political implications of sociological models. In the following pages I will describe some of the dominant points of view within sociology and the models on which they are based.

Since different schools of sociology generally fight about the merits of the models they favor, a brief introduction to these models will also serve as an introduction to the main schools of sociological thought and the controversies that have arisen within the science of sociology over the years.

The four most important models and the perspectives based on them are *evolutionism*, *structural functionalism*, the *conflict model*, and *symbolic interactionism*. For a long time the field was dominated by evolutionism. Structural functionalism developed later and was the leading model for many years, but during the past decade it has lost support as the conflict model has become more popular, especially among radical sociologists and others who focus on political processes and social upheavals. Finally, the symbolic-interactionist perspective has long held a very influential position among certain groups of sociologists but not all.

These models are not necessarily incompatible. Marx, for example, held to both an evolutionary model and a conflict model. And Durkheim was both an evolutionist and a structural functionalist. Nevertheless when sociologists get into an argument at a party or in a professional journal the debate often hinges on the differences between the models they favor. Therefore I want to sketch for you the four basic models. Each will be discussed more fully in later chapters.

EVOLUTIONISM

Beginning with Comte, all the early sociologists held to an evolutionary model of society—the belief in a law of historical progress. Comte believed that all societies go through stages of increasing complexity. This perspective, evolutionism, was generally supported by the founders of sociology—Spencer, Marx, Engels, and Durkheim. It was equally adaptable to the politics of the left and those of the right.

Social Darwinism

Spencer used the idea of evolution to block social reform and change, arguing that social evolution must follow its own slow course. This conservative outlook has been called *Social Darwinism*, and it became popular shortly after Charles Darwin published his explanation of the evolution of biological species (1859). Darwin noted that there are variations among the members of any given species of plant or animal and that every species tends to produce more offspring than the environment can support. Thus there is a struggle for existence, and within any species the individuals that are better able to cope with their environment will survive. The weaker individuals will be weeded out. This is why species change over time: The survivors in the struggle for existence pass on their superior genes to their offspring. The Social Darwinists applied this idea to human populations and came to the conclusion that competition resulted in progress because it eliminated the weaker individuals.

Emile Durkheim

Emile Durkheim was born in 1858 in eastern France, the son of a rabbi. He became a serious young scholar who turned his talents toward the scientific study of social order, soon using empirical methods and statistics to explain the forces that he believed made social events regular and predictable.

By middle age, Durkheim was in Paris, the first full-fledged professor of sociology in any French university. He was a liberal in political matters, yet also a strong nationalistic Frenchman. His work throughout his life explored the moral basis underlying society that makes order possible. His last great book, *The Elementary Forms of Religious Life*, was his most successful effort to explore this theme. In it he pointed out that religious ritual symbolizes human society and strengthens group spirit. He was not a religious person himself, but he appreciated very well the contribution that religion makes to social cohesion.

Durkheim was never a colorful personality and at the end of his life he was a deeply saddened man. His son Andre was killed as a soldier in fighting the Germans in World War I, and Durkheim never recovered from his grief. He died in 1917, but his fame has continued to grow as university students throughout the world study sociology and always learn to recognize the name of Emile Durkheim.

Marxism

At the opposite political extreme the communists Marx and Engels, who were also influenced by the evolutionary model, argued that each stage of civilization prepared the ground for the next. Each stage (or *era*) contained within itself "the seeds of its own destruction" and would be followed by a higher stage of development. Thus, according to Marx, socialism was bound to come after capitalism, but only after a revolution.

Durkheim

In each generation the leading sociologist used to come forward with a new way of classifying societies into different levels on the basis of the stage of development each society had reached. Durkheim produced a model that is still quite influential, though it is a much less sweeping version of evolutionism than those proposed by earlier sociologists. Durkheim's model showed that he was not convinced that any social changes amounted to progress toward perfection.

Durkheim did, however, believe that there was a steady historical trend toward greater specialization, that is, toward increasing division of labor.[9] He divided societies into two types on the basis of how far division of labor had progressed in the society. The first type was the small primitive or peasant community in which specialization is limited. In such a society people are bound together in close, isolated groups. Durkheim called this sort of closeness *mechanical solidarity*. Population increases are the force behind social evolution, because they cause people to specialize in different activities. As a result a new type of society is created, based on what Durkheim called *organic solidarity*. In such societies, relations are less intimate and personal, and people are linked mainly by common material interests, by contract, and by more abstract symbols.

Contemporary evolutionism

After Durkheim the evolutionary model became quite unpopular and remained so for about fifty years. However, within the past few decades a new version of this model has gained some support.[10] Contemporary evolutionists believe that the human species as a whole has gone through a number of evolutionary stages, but they do not claim that each society must go through all or most of those stages.

The new version of evolutionism suggests that the spread of industrialization is resulting in the development of similar institutions and social patterns throughout the world. This process of modernization will be discussed further in various parts of this book.

STRUCTURAL FUNCTIONALISM

Human society has often been compared to a giant organism made up of many structures, all functioning together to maintain the whole system just as our liver, lungs, kidneys, and other organs function to maintain the human body. According to this model, if you want to understand any given structure (and any regular social pattern can be seen as a structure) you must discover its function in society. These two related concepts, *structure* and *function*, were used by Spencer and Durkheim and became important in American sociology through the influence of Talcott Parsons. They gave rise to what is now known as the *structural-functional* school of sociology—or, more briefly, functionalism, that is, the belief that a social pattern is best understood in terms of its functions in a given society.

Functionalism is not incompatible with evolutionism, but most structural functionalists have studied somewhat different problems than evolutionists have. Instead of tracing the history of social patterns, they tend to look at one social pattern at one point in time in order to see how it helps maintain the society as a system. Instead of looking for the origins of a particular custom, they tend to look for its results—its functions, its contribution to the flow of social life. For example, what is the use of the painful rites in which adolescent males become fullfledged members of some primitive societies? These ceremonies do nothing pleasant or helpful for the adolescent boy who must suffer through them. However, from the functionalist's point of view they are useful training in bravery and endurance, qualities that men must have in societies that rely on hunting scarce or dangerous game for food.

Here is another example. The function of our own society's pattern (or "structure") of romantic love and courtship may be to "push" young people to become independent of their families, to take the first step toward moving away and forming their own families.

Functionalism has many critics. It is accused of trying to discover a function for every existing structure. Since it is usually possible to imagine such functions, it is easy to assume that everything that exists in a society at any given time is there because it is "functional." As a result, some functionalists have opposed any experimentation and social reform on the basis of the illogical claim that whatever exists is functional and therefore must be kept the way it is.

Every society must deal with the external environment by providing food, shelter, and protection for its members. This is one functional requisite. At some periods in our lives we can give help—at other times we must receive help. No one ever gets through life entirely on his or her own.

Red Cross Society of Canada

Functional requisites

We will save our main discussion of both evolutionism and functionalism for Chapter 19, when you will have read several examples of theories based on the two models. However, I should mention here the question that most concerns functionalists: If social life is to continue, what conditions must be met by the group? Several of Parsons' students have listed what they call the *functional requisites* of any social system.[11] I will simplify their list by grouping all the requisites under three headings: (1) the external environment, (2) the biosocial nature of humanity, and (3) the condition of collective living.

THE EXTERNAL ENVIRONMENT For a group to survive, it must be able to provide its members with food, shelter, and clothing. It must also provide care for the helpless young and protection against animal and human enemies. Many of the structures of any society are designed to serve these basic functions.

HUMANITY'S BIOSOCIAL NATURE A human group cannot survive if it fails to meet the deep inner needs of its members. The emotional, spiritual, and cultural needs of human beings are complex. All societies provide activities that allow a person to express his or her inner feelings (e.g., dance, and the arts). All societies provide special arrangements for differences in sex and age and for important events such as birth and death. Thus we have christenings, weddings, birthday parties, farewell banquets, funerals, and many other occasions to celebrate human life. Wherever there is social life there are structures or patterns of art, recreation, and religion.

COLLECTIVE LIVING Because they live in groups, men and women must consider the needs of the group as well as their own needs. Hence, they make rules and provide orderly procedures for deciding who will occupy a given site, for controlling the use of force, coordinating traffic, regulating sexual behavior, governing the exchange of goods, and so on. The invention of social organization was even more important in setting humanity apart from the animal world than the invention of tools.

The equilibrium model

A special version of the functionalist approach is the equilibrium model of society, developed most fully by Parsons. It is based on the notion of *feedback*, a term that refers to the processes by which a system regulates itself automatically. For example, a thermostat keeps the air in a house at a particular temperature. It turns the furnace on when the air becomes cooler than that temperature and turns it off when the air warms up to that temperature. The thermostat does this automatically by "feeding back" to the furnace information about the temperature in the house.

Living organisms have similar self-regulating mechanisms. For example, when you cut your finger, the blood vessels leading to the injured area immediately contract, clotting mechanisms go into action, the production of red blood cells increases, and so forth. In this way the body prevents the blood loss from the cut from upsetting its balance. The system then gradually returns to its former state.

Following this model, Parsons and others argue that society is a system with similar mechanisms for automatically regulating itself. For example, suppose that some group within a society abandons its children and fails to bring them up properly. The result might be an increase in the number of juvenile delinquents—a social nuisance. The equilibrium model suggests that the society would take corrective action—perhaps increasing its social-work services, developing community youth centers, and so on. With enough social

Eric Kroll/Taurus Photos

Is this a scene of conflict or harmony? The answer you give may depend on which sociological model you prefer—the conflict model or the functional model.

adjustment the "wounded social organism" would "heal" itself and restore its own balance.

THE CONFLICT MODEL

The strongest criticism of the equilibrium model comes from those who favor what they call the conflict model of society. It is an illusion, they say, to believe that society, especially modern society, is in a balanced state. On the contrary, societies are usually in a state of conflict. The basic condition of life is not harmony but competition among different groups for power and status. The dominant social process, therefore, is not a steady effort to restore harmony or equilibrium but an endless struggle for advantage. The equilibrium model, according to those who support the conflict approach, favors the status quo and distorts reality by screening out conflict.

Marx is the best known of the conflict theorists. Scholars who have been influenced by Marx ask such questions as, What group stands to gain from this social arrangement and what group stands to lose? How does this group maintain enough power to exploit that group? Conflict theorists assume that very few social patterns exist because they are in *everybody's* interest. Instead, they assume that whenever one group gains, a different group is likely to lose.

SYMBOLIC INTERACTIONISM

Also strongly opposed to the structural-functional model (especially its equilibrium version) are those who argue for symbolic

21

interactionism, the view that social relationships are built up through social interactions on a symbolic level, that is, through language and gestures. It is unrealistic, they claim, to picture society as an organism. Society does not contain organs; it does not feel needs, nor does it have purposes. Symbolic interactionists accuse structural functionalists of believing that individuals do not exist at all in their own right but are only parts of a large social system. According to the symbolic interactionists, only *people* have needs and purposes; only *people* act. Society is not an organism with a fixed arrangement of parts. It is not born, and it does not have a life cycle. It is not at all real in the way that people are real. Forget the mythical "social system," they say, and look at real people, at individuals acting in relation to each other. Each person tries to figure out what others are doing and adjusts his or her own behavior accordingly. People communicate about what they are planning to do, and often, though not always, they are able to make plans that fit together to make an orderly collective activity, such as playing golf or launching a rocket. They are constantly cooperating in new ways, not merely playing the fixed roles of an unchanging social system. They are always adjusting to changing conditions. Symbolic interactionism, more than most other models, tends to explain the actions of a group in terms of its members' *definition of the situation*. Its explanation of the orderliness of social relationships centers on the communication that takes place between people as they fit their actions together.

ETHNOMETHODOLOGY

Although few Canadian sociologists have specialized in social psychology, a partial exception to this pattern can be seen in the growing importance of *ethnomethodology*. This approach is closely related to symbolic interactionism but is usually considered a special approach in its own right. The name is somewhat misleading, for the distinctive thing about ethnomethodology is not its *method* of doing research, but rather the sort of question that the researcher seeks to answer. *Ethno* means "people", *ology* means "the study of", and so ethnomethodology refers to the "study of the methods that people use" in making sense of their experiences. The ethnomethodologist begins with the idea that reality is not something obvious that exists separate from any human observer. Rather, we each construct our own understanding of reality. What the researcher seeks to explain are the procedures and strategies that we all use in making sense of events. All of these procedures are so automatic that we are not aware of using them, so the researcher may have to set up unusual situations to show what we are doing. A basic point that ethnomethodologists demonstrate is that we are able to interpret events sensibly only because we *take for granted* a vast number of unquestioned assumptions. Whenever those assumptions are questioned or violated, we become confused or upset.

For example, you are reading this page from left to right and from top to bottom. Because it is a convention, you don't have to think about how to read when you pick up a book. But suppose the next page is printed so the words run from right to left and from bottom to top. How would you react to this? First you would be surprised and puzzled, and it would take you a while to figure out how to read. But you would probably smile and read on, waiting for me to explain why I had changed my way of writing. This shows one of your "methods" of making sense of the world: You assume that people have reasons for what they do and that, if you simply wait, they will clear up any confusion by accounting for their unusual behavior. If they fail to do so, you further assume that you have every right to stop them and demand an explanation. That is another of your "methods." But suppose you do have a chance to ask me why I write backward and I act as if your question makes no sense, that you have no reason to ask it.

What then? You would probably be offended and might ask one of your friends to decide which one of us was crazy. You would certainly search around for some way to explain my strange method of writing. Eventually you might conclude that this method is (a) the outcome of a printer's plan to sabotage the book as a protest against sociology or as a trade union strike tactic, or (b) a very modern, sophisticated way of writing poetry, or (c) evidence that the author is crazy, or (d) a new intelligence test designed to predict whether you are smart enough to finish university. You need to reach *some* interpretation of your experience. The way you make sense of a given situation is your "method" of interpretation.

By studying such "methods", ethnomethodologists research the ways in which people understand or create a sense of reality for themselves. Ethnomethodologists ask what assumptions people must make in order to proceed with a justifiable interpretation of their situation. Harold Garfinkel, the sociologist who founded ethnomethodology, often conducted his research by pretending to be ignorant of whatever his subjects took for granted; this exposed the nature of their necessary assumptions. Other sociologists at Canadian universities continue this sort of inquiry today.

Peter McHugh and Alan Blum, in collaboration with ethnomethodologists in other countries, have edited a book that includes essays on art and on snubbing.[12] They ask exactly what circumstances have to be taken for granted before we are warranted in regarding a thing as a piece of art. In modern art galleries you may have seen odd things called art: a heap of scrap metal, or a ladder and scrub-brush leaned against the wall, or a wad of chewing gum placed in the center of a framed canvas. What makes these objects art? After all, the very same things could be located outside the gallery and considered rubbish. McHugh and Blum conclude that, in order to be justified in calling anything art, we have to assume that the object was put together that way *intentionally*, by someone who believed himself to be creating art. An ordinary wad of gum placed on a picture through accident or absent-mindedness would not qualify as art.

How about snubbing? When someone I know pretends not to recognize me, how do I decide whether I have been snubbed or not? As Roy Turner's work demonstrates, certain circumstances have to be assumed in order to warrant the interpretation of an encounter as a snub. Suppose I think you have snubbed me; we know each other well, I have rushed up and thrown my arms around you, but you have pointedly refused to say hello to me. It is not a snub if (a) you have lost your contact lenses and can't tell me from a gorilla, or (b) you are a spy trying to hide your identity, or (c) you really don't recognize me because I have had plastic surgery and lost all my hair. One is only warranted in viewing this as a snub if it is plain that you *chose* not to return my hug as a way of saying that you don't want anything more to do with me.

These examples demonstrate the sort of questions that ethnomethodologists examine. I will not present much more ethnomethodology in this book, but at the end of the chapter you will find additional references if you want to explore the area further. Ethnomedology is an approach based on the symbolic interactionist model, about which we will have more to say in later chapters.

WHICH MODEL TO CHOOSE?

Which model is the "right" one? I can't answer this question. Societies show both conflict and harmony to varying degrees. Some institutions within a society may depend on harmony more than others. Thus, in our chapter on family life, we will find that most of the main theories are based on structural functionalism, whereas, in our chapter on politics, the Marxist theory derived from the conflict model will be more important. No single model is likely to be able to answer all our questions. Holding too firmly to evolutionism, structural functionalism, the conflict model, or symbolic interactionism will lead us off the track. We need to maintain a healthy skepticism toward each of these models, keeping in mind that any model will lead us to emphasize some facts and ignore others.

Values, research, and policy

Sociologists study the values and norms shared by members of various groups. That is, they examine people's preferences and priorities, their beliefs about duty, about right and wrong, about what is ugly or attractive, and about what ought to be done in certain situations. When sociologists study values and norms, they try to be objective and scientific about their research, not partial to one point of view over any other. However, sociologists, like other people, have values of their own. They prefer certain choices over alternative possibilities. Sometimes sociologists can influence public policy with their research findings; even the way a report is phrased can shape the way its readers think about an issue. Sociologists, therefore, may have a kind of indirect power over the course of public affairs. As a result, sociologists must ask themselves to what degree they should try to be scientifically detached and objective in their research and to what extent they should try to influence public policy by taking a strong point of view and arguing for it openly. Which aspect of the sociologist's role is more important—the scientific side or the activist, socially critical side? Should sociologists try to be neutral in describing their findings or should they let their readers know their personal beliefs? Should sociologists take sides?

There is no one "right" answer to this question. Even by choosing to do research on one subject rather than another, sociologists act according to their own values. If a question interests us enough to study it scientifically, it is usually because we think it has certain important social consequences that ought not to be overlooked; our selection of a problem is based on our personal values. Even if we try to hide our opinions, they will probably show up in the choice of words we use to discuss an issue. Moreover, good research is often carried out for the purpose of supporting some policy or other. If the research is reported fairly, it is not any less scientific because the researcher has political motives. There is nothing necessarily wrong with collecting evidence to bolster an argument. However, the misrepresentation of evidence or the distortion of facts is definitely wrong and is called "bias." No honest scientist can be satisfied with a research report that is biased or unfair. Our commitment to a particular point of view must not go so far that we fail to respect the truth or to report relevant facts.

However, facts by themselves never form the basis for public policy. Facts disclose only what *is* so—not what *ought* to be so. We decide what *ought* to be done on the basis of our system of values. Facts may *inform* our values but they do not determine them. For example, no social scientist can "prove" that Quebec should or should not separate from the rest of Canada. However, many social scientists do collect information about the probable consequences of separation, such as the expected economic outcome, the migrations of people from the province, the probable reactions of other nations, and so on. These predictions of costs and benefits can be used to support one policy or another, but the actual goals have to be established on grounds that go beyond factual evidence. Factual evidence is always weighed according to the often competing goals and values of the participants in a given situation. Thus, to a strong supporter of Canadian unity, no matter how many economic or international benefits would flow from separation, it would never be a desirable objective. A Quebec separatist, on the other hand, might even support heavy economic losses for what he considers a far more important value—the independence and survival of Québécois culture in North America.

There is a continuing disagreement among sociologists concerning whether they should write detached, neutral reports or whether they should push for the policies that they believe in. As in all other significant debates, a case can be made for both sides. In this book, we want to maintain a balance between the two opposing values—objectivity and social concern. Such a balance, we know, will be delicate at best.

SUMMARY

1. *Sociology* seeks to explain the nature of social order and disorder. A *social system* is a set of relationships among one or more people who interact.

2. A science is concerned with discovering and organizing facts, principles, and methods. Sociology is a social science dealing with human relationships. It overlaps to some degree with economics, political science, history, geography, psychology, anthropology, and social work.

3. Auguste Comte is called the "father of sociology." He and Herbert Spencer were among the early sociologists who developed the evolutionary perspective. Other influential sociologists were Karl Marx, Emile Durkheim, and Max Weber.

4. In America the center of sociological research for many years was the University of Chicago. Robert E. Park, George Herbert Mead, Charles H. Cooley, and W. I. Thomas worked there and social psychology and social ecology were developed there.

5. During the 1930s Harvard also became an important center of sociological thinking. Pitirim Sorokin and Talcott Parsons taught there and introduced from Europe an approach called *structural functionalism*.

6. Sociology has developed in Canada mostly in the past twenty years. Before then, a few sociologists worked at McGill University (especially Carl Dawson and Everett C. Hughes), and others at the University of Toronto (especially Harold Innis and S. D. Clark). The approaches differed somewhat in the two places. In addition, francophone universities have had a more European orientation toward sociology than English Canadian ones.

7. The four major models or perspectives in sociology are evolutionism, structural functionalism, the conflict model, and symbolic interactionism. Social Darwinism was one variant of evolutionism, but Marx and Durkheim were also evolutionists, at least in some ways. For a while structural functionalism, based on an image of society as an organism with interdependent parts, replaced evolutionism as a dominant perspective in sociology. The notion of functional requisites still remains important, but functionalism is otherwise declining in importance. Ethnomethodology, a branch of symbolic interactionism, is now gaining in importance in several Canadian universities.

8. Sociologists do not all agree about whether it is possible or desirable for scholars to keep their values and personal opinions distinct from their professional writing and research. In this text, we will attempt to balance objectivity and social concern.

KEY TERMS

conflict model the belief that societies are usually in a state of conflict and that the basic condition of life is competition for power and status.

evolutionism the belief in a law of historical progress; in sociology, that all societies go through stages of increasing complexity.

functionalism the belief that a social pattern is best understood in terms of its functions in a given society.

model a mental map of a subject that may be incomplete or misleading but cannot be proved wrong.

social system the stable pattern of the interactions among two or more people.

society a large, permanent, self-sufficient, self-perpetuating group of interacting people.

sociology the study of human group life.

symbolic interactionism the belief that social relationships are built up through social interactions on a symbolic level.

theory an explanation offered to account for a group of facts or phenomena; can be proved wrong.

FOR FURTHER READING

You should be familiar with a few of the professional journals in which sociological research reports are published. (You probably call them "magazines" and your librarian probably calls them "serials.") The recent copies are usually stored unbound in the library for a year or so, then bound and placed in the stacks with the books. Look for the bound copies according to the number shown in your college's card catalog. The most useful general journals are:

American Sociological Review
American Journal of Sociology
British Journal of Sociology
Canadian Review of Sociology and Anthropology
Canadian Journal of Sociology
Recherches sociographiques
Social Forces
Sociologie et societes

In addition, many specialized journals are used to present papers on particular sub-fields of sociology. It is hard to predict which of these your college may hold. Ask your librarian when you are doing further reading in a particular specialized topic.

BOOKS

HAROLD GARFINKEL, *Studies in Ethnomethodology*. Englewood Cliffs, N.J.: Prentice-Hall, 1967. Garfinkel is the sociologist most closely identified with the approach called ethnomethodology. This book is a well-known discussion of the approach. It is not particularly readable, however, except for the entertaining examples he gives. Read something from Sudnow first.

ERVING GOFFMAN, *The Presentation of Self in Everyday Life*. New York: Doubleday, 1959. Goffman is one of Canada's chief exports. He studied at the University of Toronto before moving to the United States, where he has written the most original observations of any contemporary sociologist. I will not discuss his work very thoroughly in this text, so you owe it to yourself to look at some of his books. When I first read *The Presentation of Self* I lay awake all night mentally arguing against him. I lost the argument. He writes with a marvelous dry humor.

INNIS, HAROLD A. *The Fur Trade in Canada: An Introduction to Canadian Economic History*. New Haven: Yale University Press, 1930. This is the first of Innis's contributions to Canadian social science, an important example of the "staples approach."

SIMMEL, GEORG. *Conflict*. Translated by Kurt H. Wolff. New York: Free Press, 1955. Simmel was a sociologist who influenced the Chicago School, chiefly because Robert E. Park studied with him in Europe before he taught in Chicago.

SUDNOW, DAVID, ed. *Studies in Social Interaction.* New York: The Free Press, 1972. This is an edited collection of ethnomethodological papers. An even better general introduction to the approach can be found in Wallace and Wolf.

WALLACE, RUTH and ALISON WOLF. *Contemporary Sociological Theory.* Englewood Cliffs, N.J.: Prentice-Hall, 1980. This is a clear, straightforward

discussion of social theory written for undergraduates. It introduces several sociological approaches, including ethnomethodology.

ZEITLIN, IRVING. *Rethinking Sociology.* Englewood Cliffs, N.J.: Prentice-Hall, 1973. This is an effort to put together several sociological traditions, including some that do not easily fit together, such as those founded by G. H. Mead and Karl Marx. It should not be the second sociology book you read but, say, the twentieth or thirtieth one. By then you will have something to rethink.

2

METHODS OF SOCIAL RESEARCH

"How do you know that?"

Usually when you ask people this question, you risk offending them, because you are implying that they may not really be sure of their facts. Ask a sociologist, though, and instead you risk listening all afternoon to a lengthy answer. Ordinarily an account of how a fact was established is only interesting when the fact itself is questionable or surprising. But sociologists, like all scientists, have to devise such complicated ways to establish facts that their eyes light up whenever they are invited to recount the whole tedious process.

Sociologists do not become touchy when you question the factual basis of their conclusions. They are used to defending their work; in fact, they need and enjoy such challenges. You may stir up a spirited argument by questioning a sociologist's results, but if you win the argument, he or she will probably thank you for contributing to the solution of a problem.

Sociologists, like most people, want their work to benefit society. They perform research to uncover truths that are needed by the rest of humanity. Of course, it is not always clear what knowledge the world *does* need. A researcher can spend a lifetime working on a pointless question. Worse yet, a researcher can spend a lifetime working on an important question that affects the future of millions of people but can arrive at a wrong answer because of some procedural error. After such research is published, other scholars and scientists may go on citing it for decades as evidence for their own assumptions. Faulty research can mislead thousands of other researchers and policy makers, so that their flawed judgments harm all of society.

This book exists to help you find ways of contributing to society. You can contribute something important by supporting other people in *their* attempts to contribute. Sociologists need your support. They need feedback on which questions are significant for society at this time, and they need criticism to determine whether their research is on target or wide of the mark. They *love* criticism, since it means that someone is taking their ideas seriously and "keeping them honest" by demanding rigorous reasoning and solid factual evidence.

When reading this chapter, I hope you will begin to grasp some of the problems that sociologists face when they search for the truth about social relations. If you do, you will be in a better position to support researchers in their effort to contribute to the world's storehouse of knowledge. Sociologists broadcast their ideas through the media to the world at large, but, except for the responses of a few colleagues, they have little chance to determine the effectiveness of their ideas. You help these sociologists by reading their work *critically*, so that when you act on their ideas or pass them along to others, you can also take into account their shortcomings. Of course, I want you to read and use my ideas, but I also want you to catch my mistakes and call attention to them when others read and discuss this book. Active, critical reading not only assists my contribution to society; it is a valid contribution in its own right.

In the other chapters of this book you will be looking mostly for mistakes that result from faulty theorizing, from erroneous assumptions about the subject matter. In this chapter, however, we will pay attention to the problems of method that deal with the question, "How do we know this is so?"

If I ask you how you know something you may reply that you looked it up in the dictionary, that you measured it yourself, that Ann Landers says so, or that it simply stands to reason. Sociologists account for their conclusions in exactly the same way. They support their inferences throughout as they write their research reports, mostly by explaining how they observed or measured specific events, or by citing other scholars in footnotes. If the reader doubts the writer's conclusions, he or she can then check the sources referred to in the footnotes or repeat the researcher's measurements and observations to see whether they square with the reports.

Occasionally, important studies are proved years later to be completely wrong because a skeptical reader checks the researcher's procedures and finds something amiss. In the past few years, for example, an entire field of research into organizations, the "human-relations approach," has been partly discredited because the original study that influenced all subsequent research in the field was shown to be faulty.[1] (We'll discuss this further in chapter 8.) Another example concerns the studies of twins reported a generation ago that concluded that personality and intelligence are determined by heredity far more than by social factors. Evidently these studies were completely fraudulent.[2] The "researcher" made them up out of thin air and led hundreds of genuine scholars astray until someone finally unearthed the deception. In fact, because of this fake research, British schoolchildren for many years were sorted into different-level schools at age eleven. Of course, most researchers are completely honest, but they can still make procedural mistakes. This chapter will try to show you how to catch those mistakes, either before or after they are made.

Frankly, some of this chapter will be less than thrilling. But then learning to type is also less than thrilling, even though it provides a valuable skill. It may not be clear to you that this chapter offers you another valuable skill, but, please believe me, it does. Your own life, and your usefulness as a member of society, will be greatly enhanced if you learn to read *everything* from now on with a critical eye, asking regularly whether the authors offer adequate evidence to support their conclusions. Moreover, although you may not ever read another sociology book, you will continually come across tables and research reports in popular magazines. This chapter will help you make sense, or nonsense, of what you read.

Sociology as a science

In what sense are the social sciences "scientific"? Researchers in these fields do not peer through microscopes, dissect animals, or calculate the distances between stars, but they are nonetheless scientists. They share with physical scientists the purpose of discovering and explaining regular relationships among phenomena. Science is a search for knowledge about such relationships, and scientists all try to make **generalizations** or statements that apply to whole classes of similar events. Newton was not interested in explaining why one particular apple fell to the ground; rather, he wanted to come up with a theory that would account for the tendency of all sorts of objects to fall toward the earth. So it is with the social sciences. Of course explaining a phenomenon in general terms usually allows us to explain particular cases as well.

CASE STUDIES

A **case study** is an in-depth investigation of a single case of a given phenomenon for the purpose of understanding it as fully as possible. Case studies are designed to produce clues to the explanation of a whole category of similar phenomena. But, although a case study is often a first step toward solving a puzzle, it is always necessary to go beyond the single case study and compare many different cases. Only in this way can we arrive at a general theory that covers all the particular cases.

Let's look at an example of a case study. Rex Lucas studied the feelings and behavior of two groups of men who had been trapped for a week in different areas of a coal mine.[3] He wanted to find out how the men had reacted during their ordeal. Although he was reporting only a single incident, Lucas did not look for the aspects that made it unusual, the way a reporter might have. Instead, he looked for patterns of reaction that might be generally true of human beings in similar disasters. For instance, he found that one of the two groups had been trapped in a small space where they had to interact almost constantly and maintain group morale. They banned any crying or any loss of emotional control in the presence of the group. Some of the men retreated from group pressure by sleeping or crawling away into the dark, where they could weep or talk to themselves. The other group, which was trapped in a larger area, was able to tolerate emotionalism. Notice that Lucas's study suggests that emotional control may *generally* be more necessary for groups in small spaces than for groups that have much more room.

Because it goes beyond plain description and suggests generalizations, Lucas's account is scientific research, not just good news reporting. Science is cumulative. Other researchers may try to see whether Lucas has hit upon a real generalization that explains group behavior in other, similar situations, such as a stalled elevator or a disabled submarine. To a certain extent Lucas was able to make this sort of comparison himself, since the mine explosion trapped two groups of men separately. By comparing the reactions of the two groups Lucas determined not only the one important difference between them (their control of emotionalism) but also certain similarities—such as the steps both groups went through in arriving at the decision to drink their own urine or blood in order to stay alive.

MAKING UP THEORIES AND TESTING THEM

Scientific inquiry always has two aspects— theory and research. A theory is a set of interrelated propositions. Theories attempt to explain supposed causal relationships between observable facts. A good theory will make sense of scientific facts, show how they fit together as a pattern, and allow us to predict future findings. A theory generates hypotheses, or propositions subject to future experimental testing.

Theories are not necessarily complicated. You have countless theories, just as everyone else does. Consider, for example, the theory summarized by the old saying, "Spare the rod and spoil the child," which you may or may not believe. It represents a set of interrelated propositions that run something like this:

Sometimes sociologists study one event in great detail, as for example a particular mine disaster. This is called a case study. Eventually another researcher may compare several such studies and discover a generalization that fits all of them.

United Press International

1 Children vary in how well they behave.
2 Parents vary in how strict they are in punishing children for violating parental standards of behavior; some parents spank and others do not.
3 Children inevitably sometimes misbehave while learning how to act according to parental standards.
4 Children who are not punished when they misbehave tend to continue doing so. Indeed, severe punishment, such as spanking, is the best way to make sure they correct their behavior.
5 Hence, children who have rarely been spanked are most likely to continue misbehaving. Sparing the rod spoils the child.

If you believe this theory you may act on it by paddling children at every opportunity. On the other hand, the theory yields a specific hypothesis and you may decide to test it experimentally. Suppose, for example, you are an elementary school teacher and you have certain pupils who seem to get into a lot of trouble. During your conferences with parents, you may ask how often during the past year each child was spanked. You can then keep a record and compare the answers of parents with well behaved children to the answers of those with poorly behaved children. In other words, you can conduct a genuine piece of scientific research. What will you discover? You will probably find that the theory does *not* explain your findings. Indeed, you may find that the children whose parents spared the rod behave *better* than those whose parents *used* the rod quite often. You will then need a completely different theory to account for your findings.

This is an example of empirical research, which consists of the practical activities involved in finding out whether events turn out as a hypothesis predicts. Empirical research is necessary because theory alone can go only so far. For example, Aristotle was probably the greatest scholar who ever lived, but all he knew about physics was arrived at by pure reasoning, not experimentation. He declared that the speed of a falling object was determined by its weight divided by the resistance of the air through which it fell. Heavy objects would therefore fall faster than light ones. More than 1900 years passed before anyone bothered to test the theory empirically. When Galileo dropped light and heavy objects together from the top of the tower of Pisa, he found that, contrary to Aristotle's prediction, they landed at almost the same time. Experience made it necessary to change the theory. Empirical research, then, is the practical work of collecting facts and testing theories against experience.

There is a constant interplay between theory and empirical observation, just as in ordinary life there is an interplay between our beliefs and actual events. We develop a theory to make sense of the events that we have observed empirically. The theory is a generalization expressing some supposed causal relationship between two or more phenomena (such as between weight and speed of fall or between spanking and children's conduct). From this theory, in turn, we derive new hypotheses that we go on to test empirically.

If our empirical findings do not turn out as our hypotheses predicted, we may either (1) check our procedures to make sure our empirical findings amount to a fair and accurate test of the theory or (2) try to develop a new theory and hypotheses with which to test it. We keep a theory only as long as it *works*—as long as it makes sense of known facts. Whenever new facts will not fit the theory, we must change it. This constant checking and rechecking forces us to improve our theories, and the theories, in turn, suggest additional hypotheses and procedures to test them. Without a theory, we would not know what to look for when making our empirical observations.

Until predictions about pairs of variables have been tested through observation, they are *hypotheses. After* the observations have been made, the same propositions are no longer merely hypotheses, but are *empirical generalizations,* supported by empirical evidence. Verification, however, is always tentative and subject to further checking; empirical generalizations may cease to be true in another time or place. Of course, if our hypotheses turn out to be false, we reject or change the theories that explained them.

Not all sociologists do empirical research themselves. Some stick to the work of improving theories and leave all the practical observations and calculations to others. *Theorists* are concerned mostly with making sure that the terms in a theory are used in a consistent way and that the meanings are clear and not self-contradictory. They may worry about whether Mr. Smith's theory about a given phenomenon is compatible with Ms. Brown's theory about a related phenomenon. They may be able to propose a new theory to explain a number of different studies that have not previously been seen as similar. To do this sort of work, theorists must specialize in logical reasoning. On the other hand, some sociologists specialize in the technical problems of empirical study and can tell others how to test their hypotheses by careful observation and by the use of statistical calculations. These specialists are called *methodologists*. In the rest of this chapter we will deal mainly with the concerns of this latter group.

Variables

A **variable** is a factor that varies among situations, individuals, or groups in ways that can be detected. Length, color, population size, temperature, income, sex, wisdom, and religious affiliation are examples of characteristics that may vary. A theory tries to explain why one or more variables regularly seem to influence another variable. Whatever is assumed to be the cause of a particular effect is called the **independent variable**. Whatever is assumed to be the effect is called the **dependent variable** because its value supposedly *depends* on the value of the independent variable. Both are "variable" in the sense that they can take on different values or degrees. Therefore, we can classify each particular

case by assigning a value for each of its variables. For example, each child's behavior lies somewhere between rowdy and cooperative, and parents' spanking habits vary from frequent to never. If all children behaved equally well and all parents spanked equally often, these two factors would be *constants*, not variables. In fact, as we shall see, sometimes we can make statistical comparisons while artificially holding another variable constant, or "controlling for" that variable.

Correlation and causation

If one variable causes another, its value or degree determines the value of the other. We say they "correlate" in some regular way. The more of one, the more there will be of the other. Or, in the case of negative correlations, the more of one, the *less* there will be of the other.

Here are some pairs of variables that have been thought to vary together, for which you can easily develop your own explanatory theories. In each case, the first variable is the independent variable and the second is the dependent variable.

1. The greater the **wealth**, the greater the **happiness**.

2. The more children **watch TV violence**, the more they **fight each other**.

3. The higher the **rate of unemployment**, the higher the **rate of divorce**.

4. The more **time spent on homework**, the better the **final grades**.

When we locate a genuine causal relationship, we are able to predict the value of the dependent variable by knowing the value of the independent variable. However, we can only predict a probable outcome, not a certain one. For example, if I know that you have not opened your math book all year, I can predict with considerable chance of success that you will receive a low or failing mark in math. However, once in a while I will be wrong, since homework is not the only factor that determines grades. You may be a blooming genius. You may have taken the course last

A sociologist may spend one day with the board of directors of an organisation and the next with the workers on the assembly line.

year and don't need to study again. You may cheat on the exam. Various explanations are possible.

Social researchers can statistically calculate the "correlation coefficient," or r, between two variables. This is a number that summarizes the extent to which the two vary together. It ranges between +1.0 and –1.0. If there is no consistent relationship between two variables, the correlation coefficient will be about zero. If one variable *increases* exactly at the same rate that the other one increases, the correlation coefficient will be +1.0. If one variable *decreases* exactly at the same rate as the other one increases, then r will be –1.0. However, because social behavior is so complex, a given variable is almost never caused only by one other variable; *many* variables are usually involved. As a result, sociologists hardly ever find correlation coefficients that approach either extreme. Correlations of .2 or –.3 are far more common.

Moreover, the existence of a correlation between two variables is no proof that one of them causes the other. Some other variable, correlated with them both, may be the real cause. In that case, the original correlation, though real, is *spurious* and misleading: It does not indicate a true causal relationship. Consider, for example, this statistically accurate statement that points to a spurious relationship: Single people eat more candy than married people. Why? At first glance, we might think that marriage somehow affects our appetite for sweets. But when we examine the statement closely, we realize that the single population includes children, who generally eat much more candy than adults do. Here is another example: The more fire engines at a fire, the more damage is done by the fire. Why? Not because fire engines make the blaze worse, but because extra fire engines go to fires that are *already* beyond the control of the first few engines.

In order to determine whether an apparent relationship between two variables is spurious or genuinely causal, sociologists sometimes **control** for a third variable that

35

might be causing the relationship. That is, they calculate the original correlations while holding the third variable constant or nearly so. For example, the relationship between marital status and candy consumption might be examined separately for three distinct age groups—say, people under 20, people between 20 and 45, and people over 45. We call this procedure *controlling for* age. If the relationship is spurious, the correlation between bachelorhood and candy consumption will be far closer to zero for the two age groups over 20 than it was for the whole population when age was not controlled. So, by all means, don't leap to the conclusion that one variable causes another just because the two vary together! It may. Or it may not.

Indicators

Whenever researchers set out to observe events empirically, they decide in advance what kind of observed actions or statements will represent the variables they want to measure or classify. These will be their indicators, or "operational definitions." There's a difference between conceptual definitions and operational definitions. You and I may define the concept of rowdiness in the same way, but in order to sort schoolchildren into two classes, rowdy and not-rowdy, we have to have some procedures to follow. An operational definition is one that specifies what to *do* to sort cases according to different values of the variable we are observing.

In the previously mentioned study of spanking, the indicator, or standard of sorting, for frequency of spanking was obtained by asking the parents a question and recording their answers. The indicator for the children's behavior was simply the teacher's subjective impressions. Most social scientists would not be satisfied with these rough indicators. The parents' statements and the teacher's impressions might be mistaken. Sociologists would prefer to spend time with each family counting the spankings. They would also try to personally observe and list on a chart the various types of misbehavior in the classroom.

Researchers must give careful thought to the indicators that they choose to represent particular variables. For example, consider a hypothesis that upper-class people are more likely to commit suicide than lower-class people.[4] A questionnaire would not be a good source of data for testing this hypothesis; you can't very well ask people whether or not they have committed suicide. However, other indicators are available. All governments keep records showing the number of deaths that occurred during a given period. These records usually give the cause of death and contain certain facts about the deceased person, such as sex, marital status, and occupation. It is possible to use these statistics as indicators of both the independent variable (social status) and the dependent variable (suicide rates). By studying the record of everyone who died during a given year in a particular place, one can determine whether suicides are more likely among people with high-status jobs than among those with low-status jobs. (Usually they are.) Even when using statistics, however, especially concerning a sensitive area like suicide, one must still question their accuracy.

Research: the production of knowledge

Because the subject matter of sociology is everyday life, social research is not altogether different from the kind of practical reasoning that is a necessary part of everyone's ordinary living. Most of our everyday conclusions are founded on some degree of reflection and fact-checking; this ongoing process amounts to research based on common sense. By learning to reason skilfully and to make appropriate comparisons, we become better at making sensible judgments in everyday matters. Perhaps the following dialogue and commentary will illustrate what I mean.

THE TRUTH ABOUT SWEDEN

Like many others, the following discussion weaves facts and assumptions together closely. The assumptions have to do with (a) sexual morality, (b) the definition of sex roles in the family and the work-place, and (c) political opinions of the "welfare state", in which government regulates private business and redistributes much of the country's wealth through heavy taxation and generous provision of public services and pensions. The *facts* concern the consequences of certain social policies in Sweden.

Because social scientists can seldom perform large-scale experiments with possible public policies, we have to find situations in which social and historical events have created "natural" experiments" for us to study. Sweden is a particularly interesting natural social experiment, since it has carried certain policies to a far extreme. We can learn from its experiences.

This discussion uses Sweden as a "test case" to conclude what might happen elsewhere if the same policies were adopted. Paul, like many others, has uncritically accepted certain common myths about Sweden that have reinforced his set of assumptions. In turn, those assumptions may influence his relationship with his friends, his voting choices, and many other aspects of his life. Therefore, it is important for Paul's beliefs to be tempered by factual information.

You and your cousin Paul are dozing in the park when Paul is struck by a flying frisbee. Its apologetic owners, a middle-aged Swedish couple, retrieve their plaything, leaving Paul in a bad mood and ready to express his sour opinion of Sweden.

• • •

PAUL: I hear it's a miserable place.

YOU: You do? I hear it's got more problems figured out than any other society. It sounds great to me.

PAUL: That's because you're a knee-jerk liberal. They've got a welfare state that takes care of every human need so there's no incentive for people to work or get ahead. They've carried sexual freedom so far that 98 percent of the population has sex before marriage, one baby in five is illegitimate, and pornography and prostitution are wide-open businesses. They've carried women's rights and equality so far that they've undermined the family. With all children supported by the government and with day care provided for working mothers, parents don't need each other and have no reason to stick together. No wonder the

divorce rate is so high! No wonder the suicide rate and alcoholism rate are the highest in the world! No wonder crime and drug addiction rates are so high! No wonder the Swedes are bored and lack ambition to work hard and get ahead.

YOU: Hey, hold it! Where did you hear all that?

PAUL: Where have *you* been? I'm just telling you what everyone knows. Don't you know about Sweden's high rates of suicide, alcoholism, divorce, and all the rest? They're just the natural outcome of liberal social policies. You have to expect degeneration in countries that go overboard with social welfare, sexual freedom, and women's liberation. It just figures.

YOU: I'm not a knee-jerk *anything*, but I've taken sociology and I've read a paper by Martin Schiff[5] that says you're completely wrong. So please specify the independent and dependent variables in your idiotic theory and I will demolish it, point by point.

PAUL: The *what* variables?

YOU: Independent and dependent. Causes and effects. Whatever results you're trying to account for are your dependent variables. Whatever factors you think cause them are your independent variables. So proceed.

PAUL: Oh. Well, I guess sexual freedom, the welfare state, and women's liberation are the independent variables. And alcoholism, suicide, divorce, crime, lack of ambition, and drug abuse are the dependent variables.

PAUL'S THEORY:
POSSIBLE CAUSES
- Sexual freedom
- Welfare state (a person's economic security not dependent on hard work)
- Equal rights for men and women at work and in the family

POSSIBLE EFFECTS
- Alcoholism
- Suicide
- Divorce
- Crime
- Low ambition
- Drug abuse

Paul's theory is not stated very precisely here. He has 3 independent variables, and he does not say exactly which of them is supposed to be influencing which of the 6 dependent variables. If, as Paul believes, Sweden were actually to possess all of these variables to a high degree, we still could not be sure which of them caused which. We could not even be sure of *any* causal link.

If this were a real sociological experiment we would tell Paul to state his theory more exactly and to further test it with data from several other nations besides Sweden. However, this is only a friendly discussion. Let's be generous. If we can show Paul that Sweden is high on all the independent variables but not particularly high on the dependent ones, we can still prove to him that his theory is incorrect.

YOU: Okay. Specify what you mean by "sexual freedom."

PAUL: Swedes think that sex outside of marriage is fine and dandy. They don't especially mind illegitimacy. They let their kids look at nudity and pornography. They permit legal prostitution. I call that sexual freedom, though "license" might be a better word.

YOU: Suit yourself. Part of what you say is true. They think premarital sex is fine, but that does not mean they encourage promiscuity. The acceptance of premarital sex applies to couples who are in love, not to people who are just playing around all the time. Besides, once they marry, they believe in staying faithful to

their spouses: At least 90% of Swedes have said so. So I have to qualify one of your independent variables a little. Sexual freedom in Sweden isn't as lurid as you think it is.

Paul has assumed that premarital sex leads to marital infidelity. You have offered evidence that his prediction is wrong: Swedes are high on premarital sex but not especially unfaithful after marriage. (He might have challenged your evidence, but he did not. If *I* had been there I'd have pointed out that just because 90% of Swedes *say* they believe in marital fidelity, that doesn't prove that 90% *practice* it.)

PAUL: Well, maybe not quite. But it's still the most sexually tolerant of all modern societies. Will you grant that much?

YOU: Okay. In fact, I'll agree that Sweden probably holds the highest record on all your independent variables—sexual freedom, welfare state economic policies, and equality of rights between the sexes. But it doesn't hold the record for any of the factors you are trying to explain. It doesn't have the most alcoholism, suicide, divorce, crime, lack of ambition, or drug abuse.

PAUL: You're kidding!

YOU: Nope. Swedes consume less alcohol than the people of 22 other countries. During one year when France had 46 deaths from alcoholism per 100,000 population, Sweden only had 7. The Swedish government taxes hard liquor heavily to encourage people to drink wine and beer instead. They also jail drunk drivers and revoke their licenses for 5 years, even if no accident has occurred.

PAUL: I didn't know that.

YOU: In fact, drinking has declined in Sweden since it became a welfare state. In 1830 Swedes drank 40 litres of alcohol per adult per year, but now it's only 5. And Canadians drink over 11 litres per adult per year.[6]

If the welfare state caused alcoholism, Swedes would not have cut down on drinking just as laws were passed to create their welfare state. You have eliminated *that* causal explanation. In the same way, alcoholism isn't the result of Paul's other proposed independent variables, since it *decreased* while they *increased*.

PAUL: Okay. What about divorce?

YOU: Simple. In Canada, about 25 percent of all marriages end in divorce, and in Sweden it's only 20 percent. And that's despite the fact that divorce in Sweden is automatically granted if requested by either party.

Obviously, if Swedish divorce rates are not very high, Paul's independent variables cannot lead to higher divorce rates.

PAUL: Well, all right. I guess the welfare state and sexual freedom and women's rights don't cause as much divorce as I thought. But suicide—I know for sure that Sweden tops the list of all countries for suicide.

YOU: Wrong again! It *used* to, but in the past 30 years its rates have been topped by ten other countries. Besides, there is reason to believe that Sweden's rates may be exaggerated in comparison to other countries because of collection procedures.

PAUL: How so?

YOU: Swedes tend to report suicides very truthfully and to have routine autopsies, while most other countries tend to report many suicides as "accidents". This is especially true in Catholic countries, but even Scotland, a mostly Protestant country, only reports about half its suicides. That means that Sweden may look worse compared to other countries than it actually is.

True causes and effects occur together. But, although Sweden is the world's highest nation in terms of all of the independent variables, it is not highest in terms of suicide, the dependent variable. However, Swedish suicide rates are *close* to the world's highest. Therefore, to really rule out Paul's point, you have also shown that the official rates are wrong, and that the true rates (if we knew them) would lower Sweden's suicide rate, compared to other nations. Here you haven't argued that the Swedish statistics are wrong, but that the statistics of *other countries* are wrong. You have intelligently surmised that lots of other nations would rate as high as Sweden if, like the Swedes, they told the truth in their suicide records.

YOU: There is also another factor to recognize.

Swedes have longer lives than people anywhere else and they also have one of the lowest birth rates, so they are older, on the average, than people in most other countries. Suicide is primarily committed by older people, so more Swedes are in a high-risk category than, say, Canadians are. One in every 8 Swedes is over 65 years old, as compared to one in every 9 Canadians. When you take all these factors into account, the Swedish suicide rate may be as low or lower than that of Canadians. Finally, even if the Swedish suicide rates were very high, which they aren't, they couldn't be attributed to the welfare state or sexual liberation because Swedish suicide rates were just as high before those came into being.

Here you have argued that, although the Swedish rates are actually higher than the Canadian rates, it is not fair to compare the statistics of populations that have such different age distributions. Since age is known to influence the chances of suicide, you would need to control for age before you compared Swedes to Canadians. It is mathematically possible to adjust suicide statistics to show how close the two populations would be if they had the same proportions of old people. You have suggested that this *adjusted* comparison is the appropriate one to make. And you are absolutely right.

PAUL: Okay, okay. I see you know quite a bit about Sweden. I should have read up, I guess.

YOU: What's left of your theory?

PAUL: Ambition. I don't see why anyone would bother to work hard when they can get all they need through social insurance programs. Medical care, housing, old age pensions, unemployment, child care—all sorts of things are taken care of by the Swedish government. What incentives are left for the hard worker? Or why work at all, for that matter?

YOU: I don't know *why* they should work, but I know they *do*. The Swedish standard living is the highest in Europe, so they must be fairly productive to accomplish that. And their unemployment rate is among the lowest anywhere. Lots of people even hold two jobs. And there are quite a few millionaires, despite the high taxes. Are you ready to concede defeat?

Although you had suicide statistics and divorce statistics, there is no statistical indicator to represent comparable "ambition." This makes it difficult to compare Swedes' work habits with those of workers living in societies that offer less economic security. Therefore, you have appealed to Paul's intelligence and reasoned that the Swedes must work hard or they would not be so wealthy in comparison to other countries. He seems to have accepted your reasoning since he hasn't argued the point.

PAUL: Not yet. You haven't explained away their crime rates or their high rates of drug addiction.

YOU: What's there to explain away? Sweden has crime, just as Canada and other industrialized Western states do. But Sweden has a less serious crime problem than Canada does. Most of their crime is committed by drug addicts or sometimes by prostitutes. But even their drug problem isn't as bad as in Canada. What's more, Canada's murder rate is 20 percent higher than Sweden's.[7] In the U.S., the murder rate is 500 percent higher!

PAUL: What about sex crimes? Surely with all that pornography around, there must be a lot of rapes and other sex problems, like venereal disease.

YOU: Oh, there's plenty of porn available in Sweden, but it's mostly the foreigners who keep the sex shops in business. And studies suggest that sex crimes have decreased since the legalization of pornography in Sweden and Denmark. In 1967, Sweden averaged one rape per 100,000 population, while Canada averaged 4 rapes and the U.S. averaged 12![8] The U.S. averaged nearly 11 cases of early syphilis to Sweden's 4, and its gonorrhea rate was twice as high as the rate in Sweden.

Again, you are showing that the independent and dependent variables do not vary together. The independent variables are *higher* in Sweden than in North America but the dependent variables (sex crimes and venereal disease) are *lower*. Therefore they cannot form a cause and effect relationship.

PAUL: Do you actually mean to say that Sweden's wide-open pattern of sexuality has no harmful effects? It seems to me it *must* stimulate people to do things they wouldn't otherwise do.

YOU: Some people have a different theory. They say that sexual freedom acts as a safety valve that actually decreases harmful behavior. I don't hold either theory, necessarily, but there's certainly no evidence that increases in Sweden's sexual freedom since the 1950s have led to increased marital infidelity. Of course, what happens before marriage is a different story. But even there, you have to put it into historical context. Swedes have *always*—at least for centuries—accepted premarital sex and have tended to have a liberated attitude toward women. Girls were traditionally expected to have lovers spend the night. Marriage didn't normally take place until the woman was pregnant or had given birth. So the "sexual revolution" was not such a big change in Sweden. There was never a double standard of sexual morality in Sweden. And women's incomes have always been closer to men's than they were in Canada.

PAUL: Okay, okay. You win. Sweden may be paradise on earth, for all I know. But I still don't want to go there. I guess I've just seen too many Ingmar Bergman films.

Although Paul has quite good-naturedly admitted his *factual* mistakes, he hasn't automatically changed his view of Sweden on the basis of his new information. That is probably too much to expect. But your discussion may have opened up his mind a crack wider. Nice going!

• • •

Just then a large red kite lands on your lap. Paul sails it back to its owner, a short Asian man who bows and giggles nervously.

"Dom arrigato," he says.

"Hai!" Paul replies, and then turns to you. "A Japanese. What a wonderful society that is, Japan. Now I *do* know about it. Do you realize that the Japanese . . ."

The point of this dialogue was to illustrate how valuable sociological expertise can be when discussing commonplace topics. However, research has other, more practical uses for our society. Some research takes the form of complex and long-term investigations which shape major public policies.

EVALUATIONS RESEARCH

Over the past twenty years, many government agencies have come to depend on social research as a major instrument of planning. Of course, the government has been collecting census data and economic facts for a very long time. More recently, however, it has promoted efforts to develop standardized "social indicators" for collecting data so that it can continually assess the general well-being of society.

Today, policy makers who use computers can obtain virtually instantaneous information concerning the numbers and locations of people with special needs, such as single parents, retarded adults, illiterate senior citizens, nursing home inmates, and former refugees. They can even predict the probable costs and benefits of various programs to meet these needs.

By providing basic factual information, social researchers regularly participate in long-term policy planning. It is now common for researchers to follow the progress of a new program and examine its effects. This is called *evaluations research*. Such research is often carried out by government agencies, but it is now being adopted by many private organizations as well.

Occasionally, actual local experiments are set up to test policies that are under consideration for wide-scale use. Thus researchers today examine such issues as the practicality of hospices for the dying, the effectiveness of training programs for prison inmates, the value of mutual support groups for widows and widowers, the consequences of telling adopted persons the names of their natural parents, and so on.

Practical and ethical considerations

LIMITS ON EXPERIMENTATION

In the natural sciences, researchers conduct experiments to discover new information. They may first obtain several sets of subjects, such as plants, or white rats. They then keep some of these in standard conditions, and put others through experimental treatments. Finally, the researchers compare the "treated" subjects to the "control group" to find out exactly how much change can be explained by the treatment.

Obviously, there are strict limits to the "treatments" that can be inflicted upon humans. It is unethical to treat people in ways that may injure them. In medical research, subjects may choose to undergo hazardous treatments because the benefits to humanity can be tremendous. Social experiments, however, seldom yield conclusive information so important that it justifies endangering the subject's safety.

Dangerous medical experiments also require the subject's consent. In social experiments, obtaining consent can cause certain problems when weighing results. Volunteers who are willing to be studied are often different in many ways from non-volunteers; results obtained from them might not be typical of the general population. Moreover, if the subjects are aware of being watched, they are likely to behave differently than they would if alone. Ideally, sociologists would like to watch people without their knowledge, but this too is of questionable ethics; personal privacy must be respected. I know one researcher who films people's conversations when they think they are alone. Immediately afterwards, he approaches them, tells them that the film is still in the camera, and that he will destroy it immediately if they object. If they do not object, he obtains their permission to use it in specified ways. So far, most people do not seem offended by his snooping in this manner.

There is sometimes an opposite ground for objecting to experimentation. This arises with experiments that test some new valuable service that is not yet available to the public. The issue concerns whether it is ethical to deny this service to the people who are used as the control group, who do not receive the experimental "treatment." It seems inhumane to try out a new social program with persons living on one side of the street, but not offer it to those on the other side, merely because they are needed for comparisons later on.[9]

The question of deception in general is a thorny one for sociologists. Researchers who attend events as ordinary participants know that, if they announced their intention to record and possibly publish their observations, people would behave unnaturally and would become useless as subjects. This form of deception is innocuous enough if the researchers are observing activities that are open to the public. However, when deception is used to obtain information about private, personal matters, a serious ethical question is raised.

Experimentation that causes emotional trauma also has to be questioned ethically. In Chapter 6, we will discuss a particularly important social experiment conducted by Stanley Milgram that has been criticized because it may have had lasting harmful psychological effects. The research by Zimbardo, described later in this chapter, is also ethically marginal.

Ethics committees have been established to uphold standards for all of the professional associations of social scientists. In addition, funding agencies often require that grant applications be reviewed with special attention to ethical issues. These agencies generally claim that subjects have a right to know how the results of the study will be used. Governments, and even universities, also review research proposals involving human subjects.

One of my colleagues asked his students to behave in some strange manner for a month and to report the reactions of their families and friends, who were to be kept in the dark until the experiment was over. One woman was going to paint each fingernail a different color. Another was planning to bring china, crystal, and sterling silverware to the college cafeteria and dine elegantly each lunchtime for a month. Each student had some peculiar behavior planned. Because this constituted an experiment, each plan had to be reviewed by the university's ethics committee before it could be carried out. The committee actually refused permission to a sizable number of students on the grounds that the plan might convince their families that the "researchers" were having emotional breakdowns. And, indeed, even those experiments that were approved sometimes led to unanticipated crises. The girl who painted her fingernails different colors broke her engagement because of the experiment. Her boyfriend, outraged by her bizarre behavior, forcibly removed her nail polish, whereupon she concluded that he was not the right man for her!

OBSERVATION IS NEVER NEUTRAL

Physicists have found that the very procedures needed to locate and observe tiny atomic particles actually change the location and speed of those particles. Sociologists have a parallel problem. To find out how a group of people behave when on their own, the sociologist has to infiltrate, or become part of, that group. As a group member, the sociologist must decide whether or not to go along with whatever behavior the group initiates. Sometimes this behavior is immoral or even illegal. If the sociologist complies, he or she is encouraging the behavior. If the sociologist resists, he or she is hindering the normal activity of the group. Either way, the sociologist is bound to affect the behavior of the subjects.

One famous study, *Street Corner Society*,[10] was conducted many years ago by William Whyte, a researcher who hung around a street corner in Boston with a bunch of working-class men. In the course of this study, the gang helped to stuff ballot boxes for their favorite candidate by voting several times illegally. Rather than jeopardize his relationship with the men, Whyte joined in the activity. He later felt remorse for his actions and would not advise any other young sociologist to do what he did. Nevertheless, sociologists cannot possibly keep from influencing their subjects no matter how scrupulously they refrain from expressing any opinions. As a result, it is impossible to really know how the subjects would behave if the sociologist were absent.

Sociologists constantly wonder what other people will think of the topics they have chosen and the conclusions they have reached in their research reports. Sociological research often has political connotations and a sociologist's professional colleagues can be positively vicious in their criticisms. This is as it should be; critics show that they believe social research is important and should be performed correctly. Still, ideological arguments can result in extreme discomfort and hard feelings. Only yesterday a colleague told me he would like to study the Ku Klux Klan, but he didn't think he could tolerate the "flak" it would create in his professional relationships. I quite understood his point.

CAN WE GENERALIZE?

Although researchers can only observe and describe a limited number of cases, they must try to arrive at propositions that can apply to a whole *class* of such cases. A class may include street corner gangs, riots, love affairs, or any other category of social behavior. In order to arrive at such generalizations, researchers often perform comparisons to see whether facts that apply to one case also apply to other similar ones. When researchers perform macro-sociological research, they never study a *single* case at all. Instead they may depend exclusively on statistics that apply to whole categories or classes of individual cases. Our discussion of Sweden, for instance, revolved around *rates* and *percentages*, and did not refer to any individual Swede.

Whether our data consist of observations about individuals and small groups or of statistics about large groups, we still must ask the same sort of question: Can we generalize our findings to apply to the entire population? The answer often depends on two other considerations: the *validity* of our indicators, and the *representativeness* of our subjects. Let's consider these two factors in turn.

Validity

When we discussed Sweden's suicide statistics, we pointed out that the Swedish figures are probably much closer estimates of the true rate of suicide than the figures published by many other countries. In effect, we were saying that while the Swedish statistics are fairly valid, we should not compare them to other statistics that are *not* valid.

Validity refers to the ability of an indicator to genuinely and accurately represent the variable that it is meant to represent. Suicide puts such a strain on the dead person's relatives and friends that they may prefer to hide the true cause of death. Some physicians are willing to sign a certificate showing a false cause of death. These documents become the basis for each government's statistics for its annual suicide rate. Hence documents and statistics for suicide are not always valid indicators and research that is based on them cannot be trusted.

Researchers, then, always have to ask themselves whether there is any reason to suspect that their indicators are invalid. We know, for instance, that official crime statistics are far from accurate indicators of the true amount of crime in Canada.

Questionnaires that ask simple, factual

questions are generally answered truthfully and can be assumed to validly represent real facts. For example, when we ask a person his or her sex the answer will almost certainly be valid. (Reliability, however, is a different matter from validity. **Reliability** refers to the degree of consistency obtained by repeated measurements. If I lie consistently when you ask my age, my replies will be reliable, but not valid.)

Representativeness

Representativeness refers to the extent to which the objects studied are typical of the whole class of similar cases about which we want to generalize. Obviously, if we happen to accidentally choose extremely unusual cases, then we may draw conclusions about a whole category of cases that are far from correct. Fortunately, methodologists have devised remarkably accurate ways of finding typical or representative cases for study, as well as remarkably accurate ways of estimating just *how* typical they actually are. These techniques are systems of sampling that are based on known mathematical laws of probability.

I want to describe three kinds of sampling systems. Two of them are probability samples and the other is a non-probability sample called "quota sampling." The purpose of all three systems is to obtain a number of cases for investigation that, when taken together, will adequately represent the population about which we want to generalize. Because representativeness is crucial for sample surveys, we will assume that the research is a survey,

"And what brand of iced tea mix do you use?" Consumer polls in shopping centers don't pay as much attention to selecting representative samples as do most sociological polls.

Sybil Shelton/Monkmeyer

though systematic sampling procedures can also be used for various other types of research.

A **population** is the total number of units from which one collects a limited sample of data for a survey. Surveys may be done to estimate the political opinions of the entire Canadian electorate, or, on a much smaller scale, to estimate the opinion of your neighborhood about a proposed law requiring dog owners to "stoop and scoop" when walking their pets. In the first example, the Canadian voters are the population; in the second example, the population comprises all the residents of an area around your house that you regard as your neighborhood.

Obviously, a table that summarizes data from a sample of 2000 people is much more likely to represent the general population than one that reports on a sample of 20 people. If other factors are equal, then the results of larger samples are more likely to approximate the true figures for the population. However, it is the *size* of the sample that counts, *not its proportion to the population that it represents.* If the sample is really a random one, a table showing the responses of 2000 people is equally valid whether the population from which it is drawn contains 20,000 or 20,000,000 persons! It is possible to get very good estimates of Canadian voting intentions from a sample of 2000, even though the sample represents only a small *proportion* of the Canadian population.

The basic kind of probability sample is the **random sampling**. In a random sample, all combinations of persons have an equal probability of being selected. Moreover, every individual has the same chance of being selected. Random samples can be selected by obtaining a complete listing of all population members and then using a table of random numbers or some other random device for selecting them. In practice, this is equivalent to drawing names from a hat or cards from a well shuffled deck. It is, however, a bit more exact, because pieces of paper

stick together, and shuffling is always imperfect.

It is important to recognize that random sampling does not refer to hit-or-miss sampling. One cannot obtain a random sample by interviewing the first 100 people one sees on the street corner or by accepting the first 100 telephone responses to a radio appeal. Think about the possible biases such sampling could produce. Obviously, the person who never visits the street corner or turns on a radio has no chance of being selected. In order to calculate probabilities, we must know that each person has an equal chance to be selected. To ensure this, we need some kind of listing formula and a random device for pulling names from the list.

A second kind of probability sample is the **stratified sampling**. This uses a random selection procedure *within* each of several strata or groupings of individuals. Generally, stratified samples are used to compare the responses of two or more groups. If you wanted to compare Jews with Protestants, a straight random sample of 200 persons might yield only 20 Jews and over 100 Protestants. To solve this problem, you could obtain separate lists of Protestants and Jews (the two strata) and sample 100 randomly from each list. Obviously, the principles of stratification can be extended to multiple groupings. One might subdivide the population into four strata, and select 50 cases each from white-collar Protestants, white-collar Jews, blue-collar Protestants, and blue-collar Jews.

Stratified samples ordinarily do not give every individual an equal chance of being selected. In our example, the Jews are deliberately oversampled, since we wish to obtain enough of them to compare them with the Protestants. That is, each Jew will have a higher probability of being selected than each Protestant. However, the statistician can correct for this known bias by introducing proper weights in the analysis of data.

Once a probability sample has been selected, it is essential to make sure that a very high percentage of the respondents are actually contacted and used in the survey. If, for various reasons, respondents select themselves out of the survey, then the probability nature of the sampling procedure is destroyed. Suppose, for example, that 20 percent of your respondents refused to be interviewed and another 20 percent could not be located because they were not at home. Since you would know nothing about these respondents, you would be unable to assess their probability factor in the survey. All kinds of unknown biases might creep into the study. In the case of a dog-law survey, for example, most of the dog-owners might be out walking their dogs when you call. If you give up after only one call, your sample will be unrepresentative of the neighborhood in a way that is precisely relevant to the topic of your investigation. Hence, interviewers must be politely persistent, returning to each unanswered door as many as five or six times.[11]

Finally, the third type of sample is the quota sampling. The quota sample is not a probability sample but a "purposive" sample. Rather than depending on the laws of chance to provide a representative set of cases, the quota sample directly *pursues* cases with traits that match the distribution of traits in the population. In a quota sampling, the percentage of people with a given characteristic is equal to the percentage of such people in the whole population.

Suppose a polling organization wants to estimate the support for a new expressway in a given county. The researchers might determine the percentage of voters of different age categories, different sexes, different occupations, and so on. They would set quotas for the interviewers to obtain, so that the number of women, of 20-to-30-year-olds, of skilled tradesmen, and so on would be proportional to their numbers in the whole population of the county. The quotas define exactly the sort of person the interviewer must locate. If interviewers were allowed to pick the respondents themselves, they would probably tend to pick well dressed, good-looking people

of about their own age. Such a sample would be unrepresentative.

Quota sampling allows the interviewers to replace a reluctant respondent with someone else with the same traits. However, it is not possible to calculate how likely a quota sample is to produce an accurate estimate of the true population. Moreover, lists of people with particular traits may not be accurate or readily available. For these and other reasons, probability sampling, whether random or stratified, is generally more trustworthy than quota sampling.

As you can see, researchers face various difficulties ranging from ethical considerations to the technical problems of obtaining valid indicators and representative samples. There are many more clear-cut answers to the technical questions than to the ethical questions. But that is always so: Problems that concern ethical values never have definite and objective answers, though they are probably the most important issues that we face.

Sources of sociological data

DOCUMENTS

Sociologists use many different sources of data in their search for meaningful facts. One of those sources consists of various types of documents. Conflict model sociologists often do historical research, which relies largely on documents.

Written documents include public records such as job and school records, books, newspapers, legal codes, the minutes of committee meetings, court records, voter registration lists, corporations' annual reports to their stockholders, and the like. Historians regularly use such documents in their work, and so do many sociologists. Historians often need old documents that may have been lost or destroyed or are in fragile condition because of their age, while sociologists are more likely to use recent records that are more readily available.

In addition to these public records, private, personal documents are sometimes useful sources of data. Letters, diaries, household budgets, wills, and the records in old family Bibles are documents of this sort. One imaginative researcher used his friends' Christmas card lists as data. He found that people tend to send cards to people whose social status is higher than their own and to receive cards from people whose social status is lower than their own.

In a classic study early in this century W. I. Thomas and Florian Znaniecki studied the adjustment of Polish immigrants to North America by analyzing personal documents—especially the letters they exchanged with relatives in Poland.[12]

Graphic documents include other records that are not written but contain information in a usable form—maps, films, revolutionary posters, art objects, and the like. The range of such documents is limited only by the researcher's imagination. For example, David McClelland wanted to find out when the ancient Greek trading empire covered its widest area. To do so he referred to a map that showed the sites where ancient Greek jars that once held wine and olive oil had been discovered. Because olive oil and wine were major trade products, McClelland was able to use the ages of the jars and their distribution to estimate when Greek merchants must have been traveling the greatest distances and in the greatest numbers.[13]

Philippe Ariès wrote a brilliant historical study describing the changes that took place in Europe over many centuries in the people's views of childhood and in the way children were treated.[14] Besides using public documents, such as published autobiographies, and private documents, such as diaries and letters, Ariès used the art of each period, observing the way painters had depicted children in portraits of families—how they were dressed, how adults were interacting with them, and so on.

Some types of documents do not fit neatly into the written or graphic category, and

YOU WILL WISH TO HEAR
The Famous Canadian Woman Suffrage Leader
MRS. FLORA McD. DENNISON
and
Mr. Frank Dunham
(Formerly of Colorado)
---Also---
The Liberty Loan Speaker
REV. DR. J. ELLENWOOD
at
The Final Suffrage
MASS MEETING
in
The Common Council Chamber
CITY HALL
Thursday, October 25
AT 8:00 P. M.
Presiding Officer,
MAYOR E. J. FOLEY
Vote for Woman Suffrage Amendment No. 1
NOV. 6th
Century Printing Co., Broadway, Watervliet

OISE/Women's Library

Graphic documents like this poster provide insight into social arrangements of the past.

others—such as sound recordings—belong to a special group of audiovisual documents. In fact the variety of documents available to the imaginative researcher is endless. One researcher used charts of Chicago's water pressure as data. He found that during a break between popular television programs people all over town are busy flushing toilets and drawing tap water to brew coffee, and so the water pressure drops. The amount of decrease in water pressure indicates how many viewers were deeply involved in the television program that just ended. The greatest drop in pressure occurred at the end of the season's most important football game.[15]

Tombstones are a splendid source of data. One scholar estimated the average life span of the ancient Romans from the dates on their tombstones.[16] As a careful researcher should, he thought about the problem of representa-

47

tive sampling and warned his readers that the stones do not lend themselves to perfect estimates. The poorest Romans probably died younger than wealthy Romans and couldn't afford engraved tombstones. Therefore the average life span of the whole population must have been shorter than that of the sample.

Another tombstone specialist showed how a town's cemeteries give us important clues to its patterns of social stratification. For example, in "Yankee City" a father was usually buried in the center of the family plot and the tombstones of males were usually larger than those of females. Sometimes when a family achieved prosperity and prestige, its dead members shared in its upward social

mobility by being moved to better graves in more prestigious cemeteries.[17]

The tape recorder is a very useful tool for collecting data. For example, I once wanted to find out whether the content of women's conversations was different from that of men's conversations, so I collected a lot of taped conversations—some between two females and some between two males. The typed transcripts of these tapes, in which the speakers were identified only by initials, were given to several judges, who tried to guess the sex of each person in each conversation. They might as well have flipped a coin to arrive at a guess—the two sexes could not be identified by what they talked about. However, because of the limitations of the sample, I am cautious about generalizing from these findings.

OFFICIAL STATISTICS

Governments collect a wide variety of data and publish them in statistical bulletins that are available in any good library. One of the most important sources of data for sociologists is the national census, which is taken every ten years. In Canada, it is done in years ending in 1; in the United States, in years ending in 0. An effort is made to contact every adult who is living in the country at the time and to ask a certain number of questions. At the same time, various samples of the population are asked additional questions. Researchers use the facts collected in this way to calculate tables, and those tables are printed in a number of government bulletins and other publications.

Statistics Canada (formerly the Dominion Bureau of Statistics) publishes a number of documents every year, many of which summarize data collected by various ministries in Ottawa. Each year an annual reference book, the *Canada Year Book*, is published to provide a concise summary of the facts that researchers most often need. In addition provincial governments provide reports of their own

Tombstones are an excellent source of data.

Vancouver Sun

statistics and the investigations that they have commissioned.

The *Monthly Catalog of U.S. Government Publications* is a complete index of all documents published by the U.S. government (except secret ones), as well as a list of important publications soon to be released. Canada publishes a similar index of its public documents.

Another important source of data is the *Statistical Abstract of the United States*, which is published each year. It includes summaries of facts about income, education, birth and death rates, immigration, and dozens of other topics—mostly in the form of tables.

For international statistics, sociologists often refer to publications of the United Nations and its agencies, such as UNESCO (the United Nations Education, Scientific, and Cultural Organization) and the ILO (International Labor Organization), which publish information in both French and English.

INTERVIEWS

Sometimes social scientists conduct interviews instead of going to the library for data. Whenever possible, they select certain highly informed individuals for especially detailed interviewing. Structured interviews use a standard list of questions. In unstructured interviews, the respondent is asked open-ended questions that lead to an open discussion of the topic. The interviewer may probe, ("Could you tell me a little more about that, please?"), or go off into new, unplanned topics, even though he or she usually begins with a list of topics to be covered. It doesn't matter whether the topics come up in order as long as they are eventually mentioned.

The unstructured interview is more flexible and allows the interviewer to clear up misunderstandings by changing the wording of questions. It allows for a complex discussion. However, the disadvantage of unstructured interviews is that they make it hard to compare the answers of many different re-

spondents. The questions may be worded in such different ways that each respondent understands them in a different way; as a result the answers have different meanings and may be less precise. In a structured interview each respondent is asked the same questions in the same words.

Whether the approach is structured, unstructured, or some combination of the two, the interviewer who listens to the respondent in a friendly, curious way will get the best results. The interviewer must be careful not to influence or bias the respondent by looking *too* pleased or displeased with a given response, and should never express opinions that might influence the respondent's later answers.

QUESTIONNAIRES

The structured interview depends on the use of a prepared set of questions that are read to the respondent exactly as they were written. A questionnaire is a printed list of questions given to respondents, who fill in the answers themselves, without an interviewer. You may have received questionnaires through the mail with return-addressed envelopes. This method is far cheaper for researchers than the use of interviewers. One advantage of the questionnaire is that the respondents can be anonymous. They sometimes feel more free to express unpopular opinions or reveal embarrassing facts about themselves than they would in an interview. However, about 10 percent of the population of North America cannot fill out even a simple questionnaire.[18] Thus it is not always an appropriate way of collecting data. Also, most of the time, only about half of the potential respondents return their completed questionnaires, so that the resulting sample may be quite unrepresentative. The type of questionnaire that is most likely to be returned is one that is short, interesting, and easy to fill out and return; it also helps if the questionnaire is under the letterhead of a prestigious organization.

OBSERVATION

Many studies of ongoing events can best be understood at first hand. Sometimes the researcher simply watches what is going on without getting involved in the action. This is called **detached observation**. For example, sociologists sometimes watch groups through one-way mirrors. In order to observe events more closely, however, a researcher often finds it useful to take some role within the group. This is called **participant observation**. Participant observation is generally used for symbolic interactionist research. Because this technique is so subjective, observers must continually take notes for future use and be on guard against allowing their opinions and beliefs to bias their observations. There is no such thing as pure objectivity, but some observers are more objective than others.

Scholars who use observation to get information have another problem: Their presence may influence the outcome of the events they are observing. Anthropologists have always been aware that by visiting a primitive society and talking with its members they may raise questions about things that the members have always taken for granted. This may lead to social change. Also, there may be ethical problems in either participating fully in the group's activities or refusing to participate. One cannot claim to be an impartial observer if one tries to break up the event that one went to observe. One anthropologist whom I know had been staying with a tribe at a time when it felt sure that another tribe was about to attack it with bows and arrows. Members of the anthropologist's group pleaded with him to let them use his rifle to defend themselves. He refused, but he never felt quite sure that he had done the right thing. When sociologists study criminal gangs they may have to decide whether or not to tell the police when an illegal act is being planned. Whatever decision observers make in cases like these, they can never be sure whether the events they observed would have turned out the same way if they had not been there. There are no formulas for solving these problems. They are built into the situation itself.

In the study that I am about to describe, the researchers did not have to worry about influencing the outcome of the events that they were observing. They were able to do the study with participant observation methods by taking part in celebrations before the Grey Cup game.

The Grey Cup is the championship match of the Canadian Football League, the final game of the season in which the winning team of the Western Conference plays the winners of the Eastern Conference. The game is usually played in a different city each year, and the week before the game is devoted to a boisterous public celebration in the city where the game will take place. In 1972 the game was played between the Hamilton Tiger Cats and the Saskatchewan Roughriders in Hamilton, Ontario. Sociologists Alan Listiak and John Woodard (himself a former Roughrider) were in town during that period and took the opportunity to watch the festivities. They sought to learn what purposes the celebrations served for the participants and for Canadian society in general.[19] What, if anything, is the function of Grey Cup Week? More generally, why do city officials gladly promote such events as Grey Cup Week, the Quebec Winter Carnival, or the Calgary Stampede? One obvious reason is the benefit to downtown businesses. However, there are broader sociological issues that can be examined.

According to Listiak, occasions like Grey Cup Week act as "Time Out" periods when the usual rules of behavior are relaxed and people can engage in impulsive conduct that is ordinarily unacceptable. Two justifications are generally offered for Grey Cup Week, both having to do with social integration. The first claims that Grey Cup Week integrates Canadian society by building up a Canadian identity and persuading people to think East-to-

West instead of North-to-South. National unity is reinforced when sports fans are encouraged to travel across the country to see the game. The second justification claims that Grey Cup Week promotes pride among the citizens of the host city. According to this view, Grey Cup Week supports a community's law and order in the long run by allowing for a period of short-term tension release. Grey Cup Week acts as a safety valve; a little misbehavior during Time Out is tolerated in the hope that when people get the tension out of their systems, they will settle down and be steadier citizens.

Listiak and Woodard believed that a careful observation of the Time Out week should show them who took part in the celebrations and what benefits they gained by their participation. They believed that if the Time Out genuinely served the purpose of unifying Canadian society, then the festivities would appeal almost equally to members of both the middle class and the lower class. If, on the other hand, one class celebrated more than the other, then the *whole* society would not benefit from the festival; only one particular class would benefit, possibly even at the expense of another social class.

As their method of research, Listiak and Woodard chose participant observation of six middle-class and five lower- or working-class Hamilton beer parlors and lounges. The basic investigation consisted of visits to each bar on both the Friday and Saturday evenings at the end of Grey Cup Week. Listiak and Woodard observed the clients carefully and attempted to determine how many of them were middle-class and how many were working-class. They also noted how many clients wore costumes and paraphernalia to show team support and how much noise, aggressiveness, and sexual talk or flirtation took place in each bar. After Grey Cup Week, the two researchers visited these bars several times in order to gauge the patrons' behavior on more normal evenings.

There were long line-ups to enter the middle-class bars. Almost all of the personnel and about three-quarters of the patrons wore Grey Cup costumes or at least buttons and ribbons. The Hamilton fans often wore tiger outfits and some wore hard hats, because Hamilton is an industrial town with a lunch-bucket image. Saskatchewan fans wore green and white cowboy suits or Stetson hats. The atmosphere was rowdy in the extreme. In each bar, Easterners would compete with Westerners in noise volume, as they shouted, "Yeah, Saskatchewan!", "Yeah, Hamilton!", "Gimme an 'H', gimme an 'A'", and so on. The Tiger-Cat fight song rang out every few minutes: "Oskee wee wee / Whiskey wa wa / Holy Mackinaw / Tigers / Eat 'em raw!" Football was the main topic of conversation, but sexual themes also arose; there was indiscriminate necking and sexually charged dancing. Some patrons passed out quietly from excessive drinking. Others started fights. Still others bought rounds of drinks for nearby tables of patrons, contributing to the generally festive mood.

The lower-class bars were altogether different. These were mostly beer parlors, not lounges; this meant that they could not serve hard liquor. There were no line-ups to get in. Indeed, the patrons seemed to carry on "business as usual" and the premises were only about three-quarters full. Only about one in ten customers wore any Grey Cup paraphernalia; these were only buttons and sometimes a hat, but no full costume. The few Grey Cup customers kept to themselves and were ignored or actively disliked by the regular customers. These Grey Cup clients did not engage in any of the rowdy conduct that took place in middle-class bars, but simply talked quietly and generally moved on after a couple of beers. Still, fights broke out every hour or so, often over nothing at all. Listiak and Woodard decided that these were simply the usual fights among the regular patrons of the bars. The flirting that took place was also part of the usual scene; prostitutes made contacts, left the bars with their clients, and

Ontario Ministry of Industry and Tourism

Does Grey Cup Week serve a purpose for Canadian society?

returned within the hour. The researchers were not able to determine whether the prostitutes in the working-class bars were any busier during Grey Cup Week than any other week.

Listiak concluded that the Grey Cup "Time Out" is overwhelmingly a middle-class event and not a celebration that is shared by all segments of Canadian society. Though the "Time Out" does act as an outlet for the expression of aggressive and sexual frustration, this function is limited to the middle class. According to Listiak, the middle class is much less likely to be able to express aggressive and sexual feelings openly in daily circumstances than the lower class; therefore, the middle class "needs" Time Out, as long as it does not place too much stress upon the basic values of society. Grey Cup Week is only one of the various mechanisms that strengthen the commitment of middle-class Canadians to the existing arrangements of their society.

In Chapter 9 we shall discuss the different life styles of Canadians who occupy different positions in the social ladder. The Grey Cup Week research is related to that issue. The reason for discussing it here is to demonstrate that participant observation can be carried out in commonplace settings without the need for complicated research designs.

LABORATORY EXPERIMENTS

We have already discussed some of the limitations to social experimentation. The following study[20] illustrates some of the ethical dilemmas that researchers face. Because it was producing considerable human suffering, this study had to be abandoned before it was half finished.

Social psychologists Craig Haney, W. Curtis Banks, and Philip G. Zimbardo wanted to determine the basic source of cruelty that occurs in prisons. Does this cruelty arise from the vicious *personalities* of the inmates and

52

guards or is it inherent in the very *situation* of imprisonment? To answer this question they created a mock prison. For staff and prisoners they chose, not violent or incorrigible men, but young college men selected for their outstanding personal traits. Applicants answered an ad for two weeks work and their mental, physical, and emotional traits were assessed in detail. The most stable 24 men were chosen. On a random basis, half were assigned the role of "guard" and half that of "prisoner." All were told that they would have no privacy and that some of their basic civil rights would be suspended during imprisonment.

The "Stanford County Prison" was created by removing office furniture and installing cots and signs in a university building. Real police officers then arrived unexpectedly at the prisoners' homes to "arrest," handcuff, and search them, often while curious neighbors watched. The "prisoners" were taken to the police station to be fingerprinted and blindfolded, then driven to the mock prison. At the prison, they were deloused, given numbered uniforms, photographed for a "mug shot," and placed in a cell.

"Guards" wore khaki uniforms, a whistle, a nightstick, and reflecting sunglasses that made eye contact impossible. They were told that no physical aggression was permitted but that their task was to maintain, in some unspecified way, "the reasonable degree of order within the prison necessary for its effective functioning." The guards believed that the researchers were primarily studying the behavior of prisoners.

The prisoners remained in the jail for 24 hours a day while the guards worked on three-man, 8-hour-a-day shifts, remaining at the prison only during work hours. Data analysis was based on the observation of 11 prisoners and 10 guards.

What were the results? Most prisoners became real prisoners, and the guards became real guards, unable to differentiate between their role playing and their "real selves." Within a short time, 5 prisoners had to be released because they became hysterical, became mentally unbalanced, or developed psychosomatic ailments. The others begged to be paroled. When their request was denied, they did not realize that they could simply quit their "jobs" and forfeit their pay. Like servile robots, they returned to their cells, even though they would have gladly given up the money to be "paroled" from the study. As one prisoner said later, "It was a prison to me, it *still* is a prison to me, I don't regard it as an experiment or simulation . . . I was 416. I was really my number and 416 was really going to have to decide what to do."

All the prisoners dreamed of escape or worried about their individual survival. They were not at all concerned about the welfare of the other prisoners, and rarely bothered to learn other prisoners' names or backgrounds. When they spoke of other prisoners, 85 percent of their comments were derogatory.

The guards also took their roles amazingly seriously. They quickly came to despise the prisoners they guarded. About a third of the guards became genuinely tyrannical, and enjoyed being cruel. All the guards lost considerable self-respect as they came to regard their prison roles as reflections of their true selves. To enhance their power, they redefined the prisoners' rights to eat, sleep, or go to the toilet as "privileges" that they could withhold as they pleased. Just as the prisoners became passive, the guards became aggressive and took the initiative in almost all interactions. The guards rarely referred to prisoners as individuals; they'd say "You there," rather than "Hey, Peter."

The researchers were so horrified by these results that they ended the experiment after only six days. The prisoners were enormously relieved, but the guards were disappointed. As one guard later said, "Acting authoritatively can be fun. Power can be a great pleasure."

The experimenters received a clear answer to their question. The personalities of particular guards or prisoners do not in themselves cause cruelty in prisons. Rather, the *situation* of prison life *makes over* the personalities of the people who live and work in them. This is probably true for all kinds of people, including you and me.

FIELD EXPERIMENTS

Fortunately, not all social experiments are as grim as the one at the "Stanford County Prison," nor indeed are all social experiments carried out in laboratories with paid subjects. Some of the most interesting ones have been done in public places, involving passersby. I'll describe three such studies.

Alice Isen was interested in the way people's memories are influenced by their moods.[21] She began her experiment by giving small gifts, such as nail clippers, to shoppers at a local shopping center. Apparently, such small pleasant gestures make people feel surprisingly happy. When one of Isen's associates approached the shoppers a few minutes later and asked questions about how well their cars and televisions ran, the gift recipients remembered and reported smoother running cars and televisions than the shoppers who had not been given gifts. Based on this research, Isen speculates that we file events in our memory systems according to their "emotional tone." Later, when we are in a good mood, we pull out happy memories. When in a foul mood, we remember unpleasant experiences.

The second experiment[22] was carried out by Allen Gross and Anthony Doob, who set their research both in the field and in the laboratory. First, they wanted to establish whether people are more restrained when dealing with a high-status person than with a lower-status person. (By status I mean "prestige" or "affluence." We'll discuss the term more fully in Chapter 9.) Secondly, Gross and Doob wanted to compare people's verbal responses to their actual behavior patterns; the researchers wanted to know whether people's answers in interviews are valid indicators of how they actually behave.

For the first part of the study, the researchers chose three different cars; one was a shiny, new, expensive Chrysler, the second was an old, rusty Ford, and the third was an aging, gray Rambler. They drove each of these cars to intersections on narrow streets just in time to be stopped by the traffic light. When the light turned green, they waited for a specific interval to see how many times, if at all, the driver behind them would honk. You can guess the results. When they drove the fancy Chrysler, they received far fewer honks than when they drove either of the old cars.

In the second phase of their study, Gross and Doob wrote a description of the various cars, intersections, waiting periods, and so on, and asked students whether or not they would honk their horns in similar circumstances. The results? *On paper*, the status of the car made no difference to the number of times students said they would honk their horns. Of course, there are flaws with this research design, since different people answered the questionnaire from those who were observed in their cars. Still, I am ready to believe that the findings point to a real difference between the way people say they behave and the way they actually do behave. And the research sounds like it was so much fun that I wish I'd been part of the team.

The third field experiment[23] would be easy for any class to replicate. (*Replication* is the practice of repeating a study to see whether the same results show up time after time. Unfortunately, social science experiments are rarely replicated, since researchers usually prefer to invent their own research projects.)

Various studies have established that observers tend to be more aggressive after witnessing violence than before. Jeffrey Goldstein and Robert Arms wanted to clarify whether this is connected to the outcome of the violence. Do observers become aggressive simply because they witness violence or is it because they find the outcome of the violence frustrating? For example, are spectators who have just watched a football game hostile simply because they have witnessed rough

AP Photo

In a traffic jam, do you tend to honk more at old wrecks than at new expensive cars?

physical interaction or are they more likely to become hostile if their favorite team has lost?

To answer this question, the researchers measured their respondents' hostility with a scale that had been used successfully to measure hostility in other studies. (A *scale* or index comprises a whole set of questions to measure a given attitude. Just as a whole set of math problems can test mathematical ability better than any one problem, a scale is much more comprehensive than a single question.)

Armed with clipboards and questionnaires, the researchers hailed men who were arriving at the stadium for the Army-Navy football game and asked them questions to measure their aggressiveness. After the game,

they re-interviewed the same men with the same questionnaire. As they expected, Goldstein and Arms found that the post-game responses did indicate more hostility than the pre-game responses. But they also found that those men whose preferred team had lost did not become any more hostile than those who had backed the winning team.

Finally, to obtain a control group, the researchers attended a college gymnastics meet. They interviewed the arriving and departing male spectators, just as they had done at the football game. They found that the men who witnessed the gym meet did *not* show any increase in hostility. Only when witnessing *violent*, competitive interaction, then, do spectators become more aggressive, regardless of whether they are pleased or frustrated by the outcome.

CONTENT ANALYSIS

Magazines, books, newspapers, and television programs are an important source of data about the ideas to which the public is exposed during a given period. Also, diaries and letters can be used to find out about the thoughts and experiences of individuals. With materials of this sort, sociologists use a procedure called **content analysis**, in which they study representative samples of writing from a given period or by particular individuals in order to discover common or repeated themes.

In recent years, a number of sociologists have used content analysis to demonstrate how children's books and stories present very different images of the two sexes. Because children model their behavior after that of adults, the stories they are told can produce very influential ideas about male and female abilities. In particular, little girls may lower their ambitions and try to behave according to their limited views of possible female roles. Through content analysis, a sociologist can best demonstrate how these limitations are presented to children.

One example of this research is the study

done by S. W. Pyke of 50 of the most popular books for Canadian children between the ages of three and six, and an additional random sample of 102 children's books.[24] All of these books were read by two female coders, who counted the occupations, activities, and articles or playthings for each character, page by page. According to the combined sample of books, the four most popular occupations were those of farm worker, fireman, circus worker, and criminal. The top four occupations for female characters were those of nun, witch, nurse, and maid. Women were also sometimes portrayed as teachers, circus personnel (mostly as fat ladies), and dancers.

The researchers were surprised to find that traditional sex role behaviors were not as strongly portrayed as they had expected. Although females were most often depicted as cooking and looking after children, these activities were performed by male figures over 30 percent of the time. Cleaning and sewing were, however, almost exclusively done by females, while males were generally portrayed as driving cars, fighting, doing household repairs, gardening, reading, and enjoying water sports. Remarkably, more males than females were portrayed as crying, or feeling helpless or afraid. (The authors had come to expect otherwise, based on previous research by other sociologists.)

The most prominent finding of the study was that females were portrayed as far more restricted in the variety of activities they performed. Males did a little child-care and cooking, but only *in addition to* their various activities; females didn't seem to do much but cook and sew, and were usually wearing aprons. Fictional females in these stories rarely read books or drove cars, even though real females do these things as much as males do. Pyke noted that these sex role differences were perpetuated in the stories written by women as often as in those written by men. Pyke concluded that these books are giving children an unrealistic image of the lives they may lead as adults, and that little girls, in particular, should be given more ideas about

the rich variety of activities in which they, as well as boys, may enjoyably take part.

SAMPLE SURVEYS

A *respondent* is a person who replies to a questionnaire and counts as a single case in the researcher's survey. Sample surveys usually obtain data from hundreds or thousands of respondents. We have already discussed some of the methods used in survey research: sampling, interviews, and questionnaires.

Today the analysis of all large-scale surveys involves the use of computers. Let me describe what happens to questionnaires as they are transformed first into data and then into tables and statistics for researchers. Each step in the process may involve the work of several different people. The seven main steps are as follows: (1) coding; (2) keypunching; (3) tape or disk construction; (4) programming; (5) computer processing; (6) analysis of findings; (7) writing of the research report.

Coding

Coding is the process of sorting answers into categories. Each answer is assigned a number in a codebook that the coder consults while working. For example, if the coder sees that the respondent has replied that he is male, the codebook may assign a number 1, which the coder will enter on a coding sheet in a particular spot. If the respondent is female, the coder may instead enter a 2 in that space. Every question has a particular space assigned on the coding sheet, which responds to a column on a computer card.

Keypunching

The keypunch operator receives the coding sheets when they are completed and punches one or more cards for each case. Each card has 80 columns; some of these are reserved for the case identification number and the rest are for the coded data. For example, column 5 may be the space in which the information about one's sex is punched. One hole is punched in each assigned column. In our example, a hole would be punched where the 1 or 2 was located, according to whether the respondent was male or female.

Tape or disk construction

When the keypunch operator is finished, thousands of cards may have been punched full of holes. Although the computer *could* use these cards for the production of tables or statistics, today the cards are usually used only once. The coded information is transferred into tiny spots on a magnetic tape which can be re-used many times without wearing out or falling out of sequence, as cards tend to do. Information may also be stored on a disk, which resembles a phonograph record without grooves.

Computer programming

Not many sociological researchers can do all of their own programming. A computer only runs when it is fed a program that instructs it how to proceed. The program uses certain conventions that are built into the computer system for communication purposes. Different systems are set up to work on the basis of different "languages." The programmer uses the language of the particular computer and instructs it to process the data that is contained on the tape or disk.

Computer processing

Having prepared a set of instructions on program cards, the programmer sends the tape and the program to the computer operator. The operator mounts the tape, sticks the program cards into a card-reading machine, presses a button or two, and watches the machine spew forth the most amazing products. Or, equally dramatically, the sociologist may work through a "terminal" in her office. A terminal looks much like a typewriter, but is connected through the telephone system to a distant computer. The sociologist can type some instructions without any program cards at all, and then simply wait a moment for the magical production of tables on her printer or screen. If she doesn't like what she gets, she can "interact" with the computer, as though holding a conversation with it, until the proper calculations have been made.

Analysis of findings

With all the tables and statistics prepared, there is nothing left to do but to interpret their meaning. The sociologist must draw conclusions from the material and, when necessary, obtain additional calculations to fill in a gap in the logic of her argument. For this process, there is no short cut. Computers produce calculations; the sociologist is the one who *thinks* and decides what, if anything, to make of them.

Research report writing

Writing a research report is not so different from writing a term paper, as outlined in the back of this book. In both cases, one needs to present a problem convincingly, to develop the possible theory or theories that would lead one to expect certain findings, and then to introduce the evidence in a logical way, systematically ruling out as many other interpretations of the results as possible. Through this process of eliminating false theories, the social scientist gets closer to an understanding of the truth.

Constructing and reading tables

Finally, you need to know how to construct and read simple tables. Let's invent some data for our survey on males and females. Suppose you have a theory that males are encouraged to be more financially independent and resourceful than females. We could derive this hypothesis from your theory: Young men who live with their parents are more often expected to pay for their keep than young women of the same age.

TABLE 2.1

*Payment for room and board by sex.
In raw frequencies (fictious data)*

PAY PARENTS FOR ROOM AND BOARD?	SEX		
	MALE	FEMALE	TOTAL
Yes	140	20	160
No	360	330	690
Not applicable	100	50	150
Total	600	400	1000

TABLE 2.2

*Payment for room and board by sex.
In percentages (fictitious data)*

PAY PARENTS FOR ROOM AND BOARD?	SEX	
	MALE (600)	FEMALE (400)
Yes	23.3	5.0
No	60.0	82.5
Not applicable	16.7	12.5
Total	100.0	100.0

You have obtained data from 1000 20-year-old respondents and produced a cross-tabulation. That is, you have set one variable in relation to another to find out how the various cases can be classified in terms of both variables at once. In this case, one variable is the sex of your respondent and the other is whether he or she pays for room and board. Table 2.1 shows your initial cross-tabulation. The cases who are classified as "not applicable" are those who do not live with their parents and who, therefore, probably pay for rooms elsewhere.

Notice that Table 2.1 shows, not percentage figures, but actual numbers of cases. There are 140 males who pay room and board, 330 females who do not, and so on. But the *total* number of males is different than the *total* number of females. How then can you make sense of this table?

First, you must convert the table to show percentages rather than raw frequencies. Percentages are comparable. Raw frequencies are not. To percentage, you must first decide which variable is independent and which is dependent. You can't tell this by looking at the table: Only your theory will suggest which is which. Remember that the independent variable is the one that *might be the cause of* the other. Obviously, living with one's parents and paying room and board does not affect one's sex (though it may affect one's

sex *life!*). Sex must be your *independent* variable.

Remember this rule: *Calculate percentages within categories of the independent variable.* In this case, then, you must divide each cell frequency by the column frequency. That is, divide 140 by 600, 20 by 400, 360 by 600, and so on. In this manner you produce Table 2.2.

You can now test your hypothesis by comparing the percentages in Table 2.2. In our sample, do males tend to pay room and board more than females? Round off the numbers, and you can easily see that 23 percent of males pay room and board, as contrasted to only 5 percent of females. Incidentally, our percentages in the "Not applicable" category show that males may also tend to live away from home more than females of the same age, though the difference is too small to be conclusive. In any case, of course, our figures are totally invented and reflect nothing about social reality.

Table 2.2 is one of the simplest tables that you will ever have to read. It is worth your while to learn to read more complex ones. Always *compare different categories of the same independent variable* to find the percentages that reflect a particular value of the dependent variable. In Table 2.2, *male* and *female* are the two different categories, or values, of the independent variable, sex. Yes

Punching Cards for the Computer

Many research projects use punched cards and electronic computers that produce tables and statistics very fast. The following illustration demonstrates how data can be prepared for computer processing. A questionnaire is coded according to the system that the research sets up. Each respondent (or case) will be assigned at least one computer card, and an identification number that is punched on the card. After the identification number, each item on the questionnaire is assigned to one or more columns, and the particular answer given by an individual will be shown by having a hole punched in a particular space within that column, according to the code that is estab-

lished. Later, when these cards are put through the card reading machine, they all pass over tiny wire brushes that have electrical currents passing through them. When a hole is punched in a particular spot, the current can pass through there, and the computer's memory records precisely where each card was punched. The information is then combined with data from other cards to yield complex tables or calculations. These are printed by the computer's machinery and studied by sociologists. Here you can see a brief questionnaire that has been coded and the holes that have been punched on the corresponding card.

	COLUMN NUMBER	QUESTION NUMBER	QUESTION	CODE
ID NUMBERS SEX LIVE WITH PARENTS PAY MAJOR	1–4		ID number *4265*	*4* *2* *6* *5*
	5	1	Your sex 1. Male ✓ 2. Female ____	*1*
	6	2	Do you live with your parents? 1. Yes ✓ 2. No ____	*1*
	7	3	Do you pay them room and board? 1. Yes ____ 2. No ✓ 3. Not applicable ____	*2*
		4	In what field do you plan to major in college? 1. Natural sciences ____ 2. Social sciences ____ 3. A foreign language ____ 4. History ____ 5. Engineering ✓ 6. Other ____ 7. Don't know yet ____	*5*

These are the column numbers. There are 80 columns per card.

JTC 5081

is one particular value of the dependent variable, payment for room and board. Hence, we read across the table to compare the percentages of males and females who answered *yes*. The larger the difference between these percentages, the more effect the independent variable *may* be having on the dependent variable. If the percentages were almost identical, we could be sure that the two variables, sex and payment for room and board, were not related, at least for our respondents. But the difference between 23 percent and 5 per-

cent in our table does offer some proof for your theory that males are encouraged to be more financially independent than females. Nonetheless, remember our discussion of spuriousness. The independent variable is not necessarily the cause of the results; we only believe it is the cause on theoretical grounds.

Tables are very concentrated packets of information. Sometimes even experts can take hours to interpret them. However, they do get easier with practice. So hang in there with your first few! It will definitely pay off later.

SUMMARY

1. Social researchers are scientists in that they try to arrive at generalizations. A *causal theory* is a statement that two or more different elements are regularly linked together.

2. A case study is an in-depth study of a single case of a particular phenomenon. A case study cannot serve as a basis for generalizations. One needs to compare more than one case (and preferably many) to find out how they are similar and how they are different.

3. *Theories* are generalizations that make sense of known facts. They also produce new hypotheses that, in turn, call for the collection of new evidence so that the facts can be checked empirically, that is, through experience. Thus there is a constant interplay between theory and empirical investigation.

4. Whatever a theory assumes to be a possible cause of a phenomenon is called the *independent variable*. Whatever is assumed to be its possible effect is called the *dependent variable*.

5. Social scientists do not usually observe physical phenomena; instead, they study abstract variables such as attitudes, urbanization, population size and suicide rates. They must use *indicators* to represent those variables. And they must be aware of the possibility that their indicators may not be *valid*—that they may not truly represent what they want to measure.

6. Another problem is that of obtaining representative data. We want to generalize about a whole population on the basis of the facts that we discover about a limited, but typical, *sample* of that population; if the sample is not typical, our generalizations will be incorrect.

7. Successful generalizations about regular relationships among two or more variables allow the social scientist to improve his or her *predictions*. Scientific predictions state that if X occurs then there is a high probability that Y will occur.

8. Social data come from many sources. Written and graphic *documents* and *official statistics* are often used. In addition, many researchers use *interviews* and *questionnaires*, either in small, informal studies or in large, standardized surveys that may obtain data from hundreds of thousands of respondents. Some researchers carry out *participant observation*; others do *laboratory experiments*, mostly with small groups and individuals, or *field studies* in public places. Another method of obtaining evidence is *content analysis*, in which documents, books, magazines, TV programs, and the like are studied in an attempt to find common or repeated themes.

9. After quantitative data have been collected they must be prepared for analysis. This often involves *coding* (sorting the data into categories, often giving each category a numerical value) and *keypunching* (putting the coded data on punched cards that can be read by computers). Sometimes scales or other indexes must be prepared for use as indicators of variables.

10. The researcher must often construct

and read tables. Sometimes tables are used to determine whether there is a causal relationship between two variables. If a relationship does show up, the researcher sometimes introduces *controls* to find out whether the apparent relationship is spurious. That is, two variables may be linked not because one is the cause of the other but because both are associated with some other (antecedent) variable, which is the true cause of the dependent variable. When a relationship is spurious it will be greatly reduced or will disappear in partial tables when the antecedent variable is introduced as a control.

11. When you are constructing tables, always calculate percentages *within* categories of the independent variable. When you are reading tables always compare percentages *across* categories of the independent variable.

KEY TERMS

case study an in-depth investigation of a single case of a given phenomenon.

coding the process by which raw answers are sorted into categories that can be tallied and counted.

content analysis the study of representative samples of writing from a given period or by particular individuals in order to discover common or repeated themes.

control a variable that is held constant in order to check the apparent cause-and-effect relationship between two other variables.

dependent variable a variable that is assumed to be the effect of an independent variable.

detached observation observation in which the researcher watches what is going on without getting involved.

frequency a number that shows the total of items in a given category.

generalization a statement that applies to a whole class of similar events.

hypothesis a specific prediction that may be verified by empirical findings.

independent variable a variable that is assumed to be the cause of a dependent variable.

indicator a concrete representation of an abstract variable.

participant observation observation in which the researcher takes some role within the group being observed.

population the whole number of units from which a sample is drawn.

questionnaire a printed list of questions given to respondents to answer themselves.

quota sampling sampling in which the percentage of people with a given characteristic is equal to the percentage of such people in the whole population.

random sampling sampling in which every member of the population has an equal chance of being chosen as part of the sample.

reliability the degree of consistency obtained by repeated measurements.

representativeness the extent to which the objects studied are typical of a whole class of similar cases.

stratified sampling random sampling within particular groups of individuals.

structured interview an interview that uses a standard list of questions.

theory a statement based on observed facts that

explains what is supposed to be a causal relationship between those facts.

unstructured interview an interview in which the respondent is asked questions that lead to an open and spontaneous discussion of the topic.

validity the ability of an indicator to genuinely and accurately represent the variable that it is meant to represent.

variable a characteristic that differs among situations, individuals, or groups and that can be measured.

FOR FURTHER READING

DAVIS, JAMES A. *Elementary Survey Analysis.* Englewood Cliffs, N.J.: Prentice-Hall, 1971. This little paperback does a fine job and is very readable. It is the most painless way I know to learn to understand tables and to learn why particular variables should or should not be introduced as controls.

ERICKSON, BONNIE H. and T. A. NOSANCHUK. *Understanding Data.* Toronto: McGraw-Hill Ryerson, 1977. This brings a new twist to the task of explaining social statistics at the introductory level. It is especially helpful for learning to read research reports with a critical eye. Highly recommended.

FORCESE, DENNIS P. and STEPHEN RICHER, eds. *Stages of Social Research.* Englewood Cliffs, N.J.: Prentice-Hall, 1970. This is a fine collection of

articles dealing with various aspects of research and the problems that arise during a study.

LABOVITZ, STANFORD, and ROBERT HAGEDORN. *Introduction to Social Research.* New York: McGraw-Hill, 1971. This is another slim paperback that gently leads you through the topics we have mentioned in this chapter. It is a good book to pick up and read on your own because it is simple enough to get through without a teacher's help. You can read it in an evening.

LAZARSFELD, PAUL F. and JEFFREY G. REITZ, with the collaboration of Ann K. Pasanella. *An Introduction to Applied Sociology.* New York: Elsevier Scientific Publishing, 1975. Lazarsfeld pioneered in the development of survey research and the use of tables to scientifically pinpoint factors that affect common patterns of behavior. Reitz now teaches at the University of Toronto and does research on Canadian ethnic groups.

MICHELSON, WILLIAM, ed. *Behavioral Research Methods in Environmental Design.* Stroudsburg, Pa.: Dowden, Hutchinson and Ross, 1975. This book encourages practical, useful research projects.

ONE

the individual in society

3

CULTURE

One evening not long ago I had three conversations in which the word *culture* was used, and each of the people I was talking to seemed to mean something slightly different from the others. In the first conversation I was listening to Ada, a stylish, plump blonde woman who had recently become engaged to a Muslim engineer and seemed anxious about living in the Middle East. But at one point her mood brightened and she said, "Anyway, I won't have to be constantly on a diet anymore. In Arab culture, men prefer women to be fleshy. And I certainly am that!" Ada was referring to Arab culture as a *normative system*—a set of expectations about how people should look and act.

My second conversation was with Sam, a young man who had recently spent a year abroad. He was describing the Italian family with whom he had lived in Florence. "They were so cultured!" he exclaimed. "Every dinner conversation was about Donatello or Dante or some string quartet. I wasn't used to such highbrow discussions, and I learned a lot from them." By *cultured*, Sam meant what we might call "Culture with a capital C," that is, the finest arts and traditions of a high civilization. In this sense, culture is primarily an *expressive system*.

The third conversation was with two sociologists who were arguing loudly about the Hindu taboo against eating beef. Zoltan claimed that religion was preventing India from modernizing. In India he has seen lots of scrawny cows that no longer gave milk but would provide protein if people would eat them. Karen, on the other hand, argued that a taboo against eating beef makes sense in India, where wood is so scarce that cow dung is an essential source of fuel for fires. She pointed out that even old cows sometimes have calves, and this makes them valuable because their male calves become oxen, which are essential for ploughing the fields. Furthermore, she denied that religion is the real reason why Hindus refuse to eat beef. "For one thing, there is evidence that no matter what

they claim to do, lots of Hindu farmers manage to get rid of their old cows when it is really advantageous for them to do so. Besides, religion is a cultural explanation, and I'm always suspicious of cultural explanations," she added. "I believe there is generally a good practical reason, in material terms, for a society's traditions. Many of the people may not *know* the reason, and they may tell you they are simply observing their religious customs, so you have to look at the social structure to find out the real explanation."

In making this distinction between culture and social structure, Karen meant something by the word *culture* that neither Sam nor Ada had meant. She was thinking of culture as a *system of ideas*, as a set of values that people claim to believe in but that may be quite different from what they actually do.

Thus the word *culture* has at least three somewhat different meanings. Most people use it in all three ways from time to time, but it is probably fair to say that in the humanities it is usually used to refer to an expressive system. In anthropology it is often used to refer to a normative system, but in sociology it is commonly (but not always) used to refer to a system of ideas. These meanings differ from each other only slightly, of course, but let's define **culture** as a system of ideas, values, beliefs, knowledge, and customs transmitted from generation to generation within a social group.

Elements of culture

As a biological organism, the human being compares rather poorly to a number of other beasts. We cannot swim as well as fish or run as fast as horses or kill as efficiently as tigers or swing through the trees as gracefully as monkeys. Trait by trait, we are inferior to some other animal. However, we are more flexible mentally and physically than other animals. A human being can perform more different kinds of physical activity

Japanese culture has traditionally emphasized the value of visual beauty. Their codes of artistic expression have encouraged simplicity and naturalness. You may know people who would prefer a dozen plastic daisies because they last longer. (Western values emphasize the practical side of things.)

than other animals and can take advantage of a wider range of opportunities in the natural environment. Our species has learned to control the many environments of the earth better than any other species, and we pass along this knowledge from one generation to the next by means of culture.

Probably the best-known definition of culture was proposed by an early British anthropologist, Sir Edward Tylor, who called it "that complex whole which includes knowledge, belief, art, morals, law, custom, and any other capabilities and habits acquired by man as a member of society."[1] A culture is a growing, living tradition. We each contribute a small part to the historical tradition on which our daily life is based. Over time a society develops values, symbols, folklore, myths, laws, religions, and ideals that may differ greatly from those of the people who live across the river or beyond the mountains.

SYMBOLS

Culture is made up of ideas. These ideas exist in symbolic form. A **symbol** is anything that represents something else, anything that has meaning. Language is a system of symbols. Through language, human beings are able to share their experiences and fantasies with others and even to describe their thoughts about possible future experiences. For this to happen, the words and other symbols used by the speaker must mean the same thing to the listener that they do to the speaker. Symbols must be shared for the members of a group to share a culture.

VALUES

A cultural value is something that is widely believed within a given collectivity to be desirable for its own sake. **Values** are the standards used to judge behavior and to choose among various possible goals. They are ideas that are shared by the group. When as a child you complained about having to make your bed, your parents probably justified their demand in the name of neatness, a value they taught you to take for granted.

Of course some societies value neatness more than others. Cultures differ a great deal in their emphasis on politeness, equality, self-reliance, reverence for God, democracy, and other values. Beauty is an important value to the Japanese. Masculine bravery is emphasized in Spanish culture. Politeness is stressed in Java more than in Europe or North America. Javanese personal relationships tend to be more formal than would seem "natural" to Westerners.

S. M. Lipset has argued that Canadians and, to a greater extent, Britons place less value on equality in social relationships than Americans do. He points out, for example, that Canadians are more law-abiding, and more willing to recognize the authority of police officers, than are Americans. Because Americans value equality so highly, they tend to resist regulation and they are likely to feel hostile to authority figures.[2]

NORMS

Norms are rules that tell people how to behave in particular situations. They are more specific than values and must be justified in terms of one or more values. For example, the norm against cheating on examinations is justified by a cultural value, fairness. Values are abstract ideals. But it is not enough to tell people to be guided by their love of beauty, truth, fairness, and the like. We need concrete norms as well—norms that tell us what behavior to consider fair and what unfair, what to consider beautiful and what ugly, and so on. We learn these standards of behavior as a part of our culture.

FOLKLORE

All societies, from the most primitive to the most advanced, have an oral tradition or folklore, a collection of jokes, superstitions, lullabies, old wives' tales, slang words, ghost stories, and the like. Folklore is often very old. Some children's jump-rope rhymes date back to medieval England (e.g., "I saw Esau sawing wood, And Esau saw I saw him; Though Esau saw I saw him saw, still Esau went on sawing"). You know far more folklore than you may think. How often do you break a wishbone with a friend or recite under your breath, "Thirty days hath September ..."? Myths, too, are part of folklore. What Western child does not know Santa's reindeer by name or has not received a coin from the tooth fairy? (In France a mouse performs the tooth fairy's duties.) All of these traditions are cultural.

LAW

Primitive societies maintain order by means of informal procedures and customs. Modern societies, however, more often do this by means of formal law. But laws, if they are to be obeyed, must be justified by cultural values. Speed limits, for example, are justified in the name of safety, a shared value. Thus the laws and customs of a society are part of its culture.

IDEOLOGY

An ideology is a doctrine that is used to justify a group's actions in pursuing its own interests. For example, in Chapter 1 we mentioned Social Darwinism, a theory of social evolution suggesting that the protection of weak individuals from economic competition would weaken the human population as a whole. Today most of us would call this belief an ideology. That is, it helped the rich capitalists feel less guilty about exploiting the workers for profit. (It is likely that very few Social Darwinists were poor.) Not all ideologies are complex systems of philosophy, however; they may be short phrases such as "Finders keepers, losers weepers" or "The Lord helps those who help themselves."

Three views of culture

CULTURE AS A NORMATIVE SYSTEM

Let's return now to the three conversations mentioned earlier and the three ways of looking at culture that they illustrate. Probably what comes to mind most often when social scientists think about culture is that people are expected to conform to it. This is what Ada had in mind when she happily anticipated being freed from the North American requirement that women stay slim. Every cultural system is *normative*; that is, it contains strong requirements as to what one must and must not do. The American sociologist William Graham Sumner introduced two important terms to the study of culture as a normative system. The fairly trivial norms or conventions shared by members of a society he termed folkways; the really important ethical rules he termed mores.[3]

Folkways are conventions such as style of clothing, dietary habits, and manners. If, for example, you went to school wearing the grass skirt and shark-tooth necklace of a New Guinean tribesman, you would have violated a folkway. You might have to take a lot of teasing, but you probably wouldn't be punished. One should not talk or fidget during a concert performance. One should not comb one's hair at the dinner table. One should not rip coupons out of magazines in a public library. These norms are all folkways, and a person who fails to conform to them may be thought of as thoughtless or crude, but not as a criminal or a sinner.

Mores, by contrast, are moral rules such as the prohibition of murder, theft, rape, incest, and the like. These are rules about which all the members of a society share strong feelings. Those who violate them must pay a heavy penalty. However, even mores may differ greatly from one society to another.

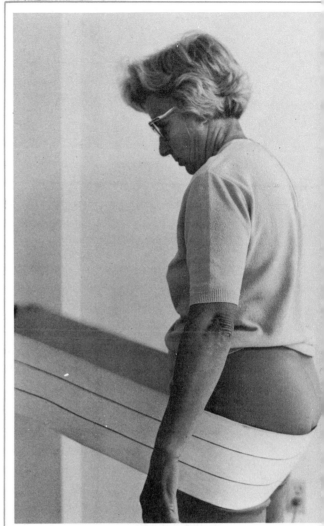

Burk Uzzle/Magnum Photos

Still trying. Western culture demands that women keep slim.

For example, in some societies adultery has been a crime punishable by death, whereas in others, such as the Inuit, a host might once have offered his guest the opportunity to have sexual relations with his wife. Failure to make such an offer might have been taken as an insult to the guest.

Social control

What happens when someone violates a norm? Some other member of the group will

69

punish the offender. The punishment helps persuade others to follow the norm that was violated. This process is called social control. The members of a group support desired forms of behavior and discourage undesired forms. They do this by means of sanctions—actions that reward conformity to norms or punish nonconformity. An icy stare and a firing squad are both social sanctions. Both are tools of social control in that people try to behave in such a way that they will not have to face either stares or a firing squad.

Most of us do not simply conform to cultural norms because they are backed up by sanctions. We usually live up to them even when nobody would know if we violated them. We do not sense norms as burdensome rules that we would like to resist. Instead, we usually want to conform to them. We make them part of our personality; we feel responsible for them, as if we had invented them ourselves. There could never be enough police officers to enforce the laws if everyone wanted to break them. Law and order are possible in a society only because most of the time people police themselves.

Cultural relativism

We have already mentioned that the norms that apply in one society may not apply in another. This is easy to grasp when reading a textbook, but it is not always so easy to accept in real life, as many anthropologists can tell you from personal experience. It's all in a day's work for field researchers to visit a warring tribe or a voodoo priestess, and these researchers use the term *culture shock* to describe the anxiety they feel while they are adjusting to the norms of other cultures. We learn in our own society not only how things are done but also how they should be done. If we learn the lesson well, we believe in it. Belief in the superiority of one's own traditions is normal.

We tend to judge other ways of life by the standards of our own group—a habit that is called ethnocentrism. For example, an ethno-

centric person may believe that Muslim men who marry several wives are "weird," "sick," "sinful," or at best "ill advised." An ethnocentric Westerner may laugh at the Hindu taboo against eating beef, and the ethnocentric Chinese may laugh at the Westerner's unwillingness to eat dogs. The ethnocentric European may be amused by the Indian custom of eating with the fingers, while the ethnocentric Indian may be embarrassed for a European who is so ill mannered as to touch food with his or her left hand. The ethnocentric person is showing a prejudice that comes from believing too much in the norms of his or her own group.

Although such prejudice is normal for people whose social world is isolated from other cultures, those who overcome it develop a broader outlook on life. Many studies have shown that highly ethnocentric people tend to be harsh, rigid, and unable to deal with ambiguity or complexity. Fortunately, education tends to reduce ethnocentrism, and the social sciences play an important role in this process because they compare different cultures as objectively as possible.

Social scientists usually avoid saying that a given tradition is "good" or "bad." Instead, they say that it is "well adapted" or "poorly adapted" to the habits and needs of a particular society. In ancient China, the feet of high-status females were kept tightly bound from early childhood. This resulted in small, deformed feet that the Chinese saw as beautiful. This practice fit in with the restrained life style idealized by many Chinese. In modern China such a practice would be unthinkable because the cultural values of the Chinese Revolution stress equality and productivity, not leisure and social status. Thus to understand a custom such as foot binding we must understand other aspects of the culture in which it is found.

The folkways and mores of various parts of the world are so different that it would be easy to conclude that there is no rule that is universally recognized by all societies. This is not the case, however. All societies frown on incest, lying, stealing, on violence within the in-group, and on failure to maintain some control over one's impulses. These standards of behavior are universal.

An anthropologist who goes to live with a remote tribe usually decides to leave his or her own morality at home as much as possible and to live by the code of the tribe. This does not mean that he or she will approve of any act performed by a member of the tribe, for there will be deviant acts there too. It does mean that the anthropologist will judge tribal behavior in terms of the tribe's normative system, not his or her own. This policy is called cultural relativism. It is based on the assumption that all cultures are equally valid and that any culture deserves respect. An act that is immoral in one culture may be moral in another. But it is meaningless to ask which culture is "right," for all are equally "right." The only way of judging a particular culture is by using standards that are themselves part of *some* culture. According to cultural relativists, any attempt to judge one culture by the standards of another is sheer ethnocentrism. This is an important issue, and we will return to it in the section on social policy at the end of this chapter.

CULTURE AS AN EXPRESSIVE SYSTEM

When my friend Sam described his Florentine hosts as "cultured" he had in mind a particular range of activities—music, literature, dance, art, and the like—that are enjoyed for their own sake, not as a means to some other end. Every society has developed a variety of practices that break the monotony of day-to-day living, providing for pageantry, collective excitement, and other meaningful experiences. Such expressive events may be stylized rituals—for example, the Japanese tea ceremony or the changing of the guard at Buckingham Palace—or periods of excitement when self-control can be relaxed—such as a bull-

Cultural relativism, if held to strictly, leaves no room for considering one society healthier than another. But what are we to think about these Hitler Youth? They may have started out like well-scrubbed Boy Scouts, but that's not how they ended up.

Wide World Photos

fight, a carnival, a drunken orgy, or a Grey Cup weekend.

Societies differ greatly in the expressive events that they encourage. When a group of young people get together to create a cultural event, they follow the traditions of their community in planning the activity, whether it is a rodeo or a chamber music concert. One community may have only a small range of simple events to choose from; another may have a wide variety of complex activities that can be mastered only after long training.

When we speak of "culture" as an expressive system we are not usually referring to such events as drunken orgies or pie-eating contests (although these are, I will grant, expressive activities of a sort). Rather, we are thinking mainly of the arts, which require a certain amount of training of the participants.

Artistic expression as a code

All art is a social experience. This may sound like a strange statement, because after all one can listen to records or paint a landscape when one is entirely alone. Some artists live like hermits and are uncomfortable at parties or club meetings. Nevertheless all art is made by human beings who are influenced by the art made by other human beings. Art is a symbolic activity, a way of communicating an inner experience. It is obvious that one must learn to paint and that learning is a social experience. But it may not be so obvious that one must also learn to *see* paintings and to *hear* music. Of course all of us can focus our eyes on a picture, but we may not get much out of it. As a way of communicating, an art form uses what we will call a code. Code making is a human activity that develops naturally in the context of social experience. You may have invented your first picture code when at the age of three you drew a circle around two dots and a U-shaped smiling mouth and called it "Mommy." Think of a code as a grammar or set of rules that may be passed along from one generation to the next. The rules for the game of chess are a code that dates back 1000 years or more. When you play the piano you can use 88 keys, no more, and when you play any given piece of music you use only certain combinations of those keys because the Western codes of musical composition rely on the use of scales, or sets of tones that we think sound pleasant together. When you hear Indian singing for the first time you may think it sounds like a cat in pain because you will not understand a code that permits the voice to slide around between tones.

A creative composer, painter, or poet is one who knows how to use his or her chosen code to the fullest. Of course only an audience that understands the code will be able to appreciate the artist's achievement. I have become somewhat familiar with Indian music and greatly enjoy it, but I still cannot tell whether a singer is performing well or poorly. I simply don't yet know the code that well. It is only through long training that we develop our own understanding and appreciation of the code.

Each period or style of art is, in a sense, a game. Just as you can play many different card games with the same deck of cards, depending on what set of rules (or code) you follow, so too there are many styles of art that can be played with the same brushes and tubes of paint. "Primitive" painters like Grandma Moses follow a code that pays little attention to perspective but requires the picture to represent something real—a landscape, perhaps, or animals or human figures. On the other hand, the code of cubism does not represent an object realistically but may present it as if it were being seen from several angles at once. The late American painter Jackson Pollock used to paint by dribbling colors straight from the can onto the canvas. The game he invented was a code that we might call "Let's-see-what-kind-of-interesting-patterns-we-can-make-with-dribbles." That's ok. Any set of rules is ok. However, some codes have more possibilities than others. Pollock went about as far with dribble art as anybody is likely to go. On the other hand, the complex and difficult styles of the Renaissance required many years of training and contained possibilities that were not exhausted by any single artist.

Publics

Every artist creates or performs for some audience. In some preindustrial societies every adult is probably able to understand and appreciate all the art that is produced in that society. Wherever culture is uniform the same artistic codes are shared by all the members of the society. However, our society is characterized by *cultural pluralism*, in which a number of very different codes are used by different artists. Consider music. We hear punk rock and Wagnerian opera, New Orleans jazz and barbershop quartets, bluegrass and concertos for oboe and kazoo. Nobody could possibly understand all those codes, so we specialize. You may say, for example, that you are "into" Led Zeppelin or (less probably) Lawrence Welk. You are then part of a particular public—a group of people who specialize in enjoying a common code of musical expression.

Some codes are harder to learn than others. *Hamlet* is harder to read than a James Bond novel. It requires more of the reader— more attention, more homework, more vocabulary, and so on. And over the years most readers who have learned to appreciate *Hamlet* have agreed that it was worth their effort.

Thus it seems fair to compare publics in terms of the complexity of the codes they understand. This is why we sometimes speak of "highbrow," "middlebrow," and "lowbrow" tastes. If you subscribe to the *New York Review of Books, Partisan Review*, or any glossy art magazine and if you often go to chamber music concerts, poetry readings, and late-night showings of film classics like *Children of Paradise*, you are a highbrow. You can make your own list of standards for middlebrows and lowbrows.

Sometimes we speak of publics as supporting either "high culture" or "popular culture." The term *popular* or *mass culture* refers to artistic codes that are not difficult to understand. Often these are products of the mass media and are enjoyed by millions of people as a form of relaxation. Magazines, TV quiz shows, and popular music are examples of popular culture.

One public may be uninterested in or even hostile to the codes understood and enjoyed by another public. Thus people who have a taste for popular culture may call the high-culture public "snobbish" or "phony." And members of the high-culture public may call popular-culture fans "uncultured." Yet people who like popular culture and mass media entertainment may be very critical of art that employs the codes that they understand; for example, they may recognize the difference between a good James Bond novel and a bad one. To do that is to be "cultured" according to that particular code.

Instead of calling people "uncultured," some people think it is more polite to refer to them as "culturally deprived." This unfortunate term implies that the "deprived" group or person is a clod who cannot do or appreciate anything that is excellent. Of course the understanding and enjoyment of great music, literature, drama, ballet, and so on is a splendid human achievement. If you have had an opportunity to learn how to conduct symphonies, you are very lucky. Furthermore, if familiarity with the codes of high cultures is a gift that some people receive, then obviously other people are deprived of it, and I suppose it is fair to call them "culturally deprived." However, some "deprived" people are brilliantly creative in the codes with which they *are* familiar. Much primitive art, for example, is marvelous. Thus to be "deprived" of high culture is not necessarily to be uncultured. Not at all.

The culturally sophisticated person is familiar with a variety of different codes of expression. This familiarity enriches his or her experience and adds to the pleasures of daily life. We are not underplaying the importance of high culture when we add that popular culture is ok too. In short, great art is great, but other things are all right too.

CULTURE AS A SYSTEM OF IDEAS

When you hear the word *culture* you will probably be correct 90 percent of the time if you interpret it as referring to normative and/or expressive traditions. However, you should be aware that sociologists sometimes use the term in a narrower sense, as Karen was using it in her argument with Zoltan about the Indian taboo against eating beef.

When we speak of the culture of a group, we have in mind both its customary *practices* and the *ideas* that guide those practices. We don't normally need to distinguish the practices from the ideas. However, some sociologists do make this distinction. Talcott Parsons, for instance, believed that a culture is a world view acquired by a person as a member of his or her society—the system of ideas, the symbols that enable him or her to interpret the world meaningfully. Culture gives us an idea of our place in history, our relationship to nature, to a God or gods, and to the universe. It stresses some values over others, thereby providing the principles on which a specific set of social patterns is based. Parsons distinguished between the culture and the social system, or the roles and *actual practices* that exist among members of social groups. Thus he would be careful to distinguish between the *role* of a painter (which is part of the social system) and the painter's *knowledge* about art (which is part of the cultural system). The social system is what people do; the cultural system is the set of ideas that they share.

Obviously there is a close relationship between the two systems. The culture controls and shapes the social system. People form relationships and organizations that are guided by the general values and ideas that they all share.

Culture and social structure

The process through which the culture influences the social system is called institutionalization. It translates general values into the specific norms that directly govern the actions of the members of a group. For example, one of the values or ideas shared by members of Western culture today is a high regard for intellectual or logical ability. As a result, we have institutionalized certain prac-

tices for the purpose of creating and maintaining intellectual ability as widely as possible. These practices are carried out in schools and universities. And within the university we have institutionalized a number of specific norms of behavior, such as the requirement that you do your own work without cheating. Most of our everyday activities are institutionalized aspects of our roles. These activities are part of the social system and can be distinguished from our values and ideas, which are part of the cultural system.

Many, if not most, sociologists agree with Parsons that the social system is controlled by the cultural system—that people live largely according to their ideas about what is desirable and good. Not all sociologists do agree to this, however. Some point out, quite sensibly, that we can't always live up to our ideals. The conditions in which we live do not always give us the chance to meet those standards. These sociologists therefore look for what they call "structural" explanations for social events, that is, the opportunities and limitations that people have to adjust to. When people are trying to solve a problem they ask such questions as, What materials are available? Who is around to help us? Are they willing to cooperate? If not, do we have ways of forcing them to help? What would we have to give up if we used all our time and materials to carry out this project? Will this solution create worse problems for us in the long run? And so on. To answer such questions you don't worry about the cultural system. Rather, you are concerned with the social system that *now exists*—the *social structure*—and with the opportunities for and limitations on future action contained in that structure. This is the point that Karen was insisting on when she claimed that Hindus have good practical reasons for prohibiting the slaughter of cows for beef. Zoltan, on the other hand, thought this particular norm could be explained by the cultural system of India—the Hindu religion.[4]

In that particular argument, I tend to agree

with Karen that Indian society might lose more than it would gain if Hindus gave up the taboo on beef. But on the broader issue, I cannot agree with either Karen or Zoltan. Of course the cultural system shapes the social system. And of course it does not completely determine the social system. There is often a conflict between what people want to do and what they have the opportunity to do. I think that people try to act on the basis of their ideas, or culture, but their opportunities are limited by reality, which includes the existing social structure.

Institutionalization is the bridge linking the cultural system and the social system. Our beliefs and ideas shape our actions. It is by establishing regular patterned ways of doing things (i.e., institutionalizing a practice) that we turn our shared ideas into shared habits, customs, organizations, and so on. These common shared arrangements constitute the social system or the social structure (for most purposes the two terms can be used interchangeably). Through institutionalization our cultural system shapes our social system.

Technology

Every society institutionalizes certain practical techniques for controlling its environment. This is technology. We can define technology as the institutionalized application of knowledge to control nature for human uses. It includes the skills, materials, methods, and social structures that make it possible for us to maintain a given standard of living. Primitive tribes have a very simple technology. But modern societies, with a cultural system that includes knowledge about physics, physiology, and the like, have institutionalized a number of social structures to control nature by building dams, splitting atoms, repairing heart valves, and so forth. The worldwide telephone system is one example of modern technology. It involves the regular use of technical knowledge in the

social relations of millions of people every day. Thus the cultural system (which includes such knowledge as the principles of electronic engineering) has been institutionalized, creating a complex social structure—the telephone system.

Technology differs from expressive systems such as the arts, religion, and sports in this way: It improves and develops. It is cumulative. This is not so with the arts. Many cave paintings would be praised as great works of art even if they were painted today. However, the technology of cave dwellers was far simpler than that of even the least developed twentieth-century nations. The dif-

It's easy to tell whether a new product works better than the old one. Technology keeps improving, but does technology improve a society? How do you suppose photography has made this African tribesman's life different from his grandfather's?

Jerry Frank/DPI

ference is that painting is primarily an expressive activity. Within any type of art some works will be better than others. When it comes to rock operas, I think *Godspell* is superior to *Tommy*. However, rock operas do not become better and better as more are written. If a good one is written, other composers will not necessarily learn from it and write better ones. Composing as a skill does not make steady progress the way technology does. Indeed, it is harder to judge expressive cultural forms than it is to judge technology. Artistic standards are more open to disagreement—for example, you may think *Tommy* is better than *Godspell*.

With technology we are on firmer ground, for we judge technology in terms of *efficiency*. Technology is used to satisfy some human need, and it is usually possible to tell whether a new method is more efficient than the old one. The old method will usually be replaced by the new one. This is not necessarily true for expressive activities such as art, religion, sports, or drama. After Pablo Picasso and Henri Matisse had radically changed the style of modern painting, many painters, such as Andrew Wyeth, went right on painting realistic landscapes that were almost 100 years "out of date" but still had great artistic value. In contrast, when the Sabin polio vaccine came into use production of the older Salk vaccine almost stopped.

Although new methods replace old ones, it often happens that a method that seemed to be an improvement turns out to have harmful side effects that were not foreseen. Indeed, some people believe humankind will be destroyed by the side effects of our technological "improvements." Jacques Cousteau's divers report, for example, that marine life, poisoned by industrial waste products, is declining in all of the world's oceans. From one point of view this is because technology has developed too fast, but from another point of view it is because technology has not developed fast *enough*. We must work as fast as possible to find new methods of recycling industrial wastes, and we must create new political in-

stitutions that will force industry to use the new recycling methods. Thus technological progress creates new problems that call for new technological solutions. Some people are so upset by this fact that they have been saying, in effect, "Stop the world, I want to get off!" However, the world's population is now too large to allow us all to retreat from technological problems by returning to a simpler life style, churning our own butter, grinding our own flour, traveling on horseback, and so forth. For most of us the solution will have to involve more technology, not less.

The term **cultural lag** is sometimes used to explain social problems, such as pollution, that arise because of a time lag between a technological change and the social and cultural changes that the technological change requires. This term was introduced by William F. Ogburn, who suggested that technological changes tend to occur quickly and to cause new situations that require normative changes in social relationships.[5] Because we are slow to change our norms, problems often occur during the lag time. Perhaps the best example of Ogburn's point is the current "population explosion." Technological methods of limiting (i.e., postponing) deaths are in use, but in many places old norms discourage the use of new methods of limiting births. As a result, populations are growing at a disastrous rate in many areas. Culture lag is one example of a society's failure to maintain integration among its structures.

Cultural integration and diversity

Norms are built up by many people, usually over a long period. They have to fit together to form a workable system for all the members of a society. If we each made up our own rules, the social system would quickly break down, for we would not see all the ways in which our actions affect others. A society is a unified collectivity, and the lives of its members are interdependent. Thus its folkways, mores, and values have to be compatible. We say that the parts of a society need to be *functionally integrated*. Anthropologists who study distant cultures have gathered surprising evidence that primitive cultures are integrated systems. These researchers have shown how the change of one minor custom can have far-reaching and unforeseen effects on the social and cultural system. Consider the following example.

The Yir Yoront tribe used to live in a barren part of Australia, using a technology as primitive as that of any society on earth.[6] The Yir Yoront used a Stone Age technology; in fact they treated their stone tools with great reverence. To them, a stone ax was a rare and marvelous object to be cared for by a few respected high-ranking tribesmen. The ax played a part in certain religious ceremonies, in which it was a symbol of the group's ancestry. The tool could also be used for nonreligious tasks and was one of the tribe's most valuable objects. When a man needed the ax he would ask one of the tribal leaders for permission to use it. Only if the leader thought he was worthy would he be given that permission. Thus the rarity of the valuable tool made permission to use it a privilege and a method of social control.

Then white people came, bringing with them modern technology—steel axes. Even in the middle of the desert a tribesman could easily get a steel ax from a trader or missionary. These axes were far more efficient than the old stone ax. But the effects of this change were not all good. It undercut social control and respect for tradition. No longer could the old men keep the youth in line by refusing to let them use an ax. Those of higher rank lost their control over those of lower rank. The structure of authority within the tribe became confused and great tension resulted.

In the early days of anthropology field researchers usually described societies in terms of a list of culture traits. A **culture trait** is the smallest unit of culture. I have already mentioned several examples: the tooth fairy,

the custom of eating with knives and forks, the use of stone axes, Santa's reindeer, and so on. It was assumed that these traits were independent of one another and that each could be "grafted" onto a different culture without changing any of its other traits. The early researchers would not have foreseen any difficulty in "grafting" the use of steel axes onto tribal culture. Gradually, however, social scientists became aware that the traits of a given culture often fit together and reinforce each other. This is what we mean by *cultural integration*.

A given rule may perform a vital but unrecognized function in maintaining the whole system—so much so that unforeseen problems arise if it is changed. The norms governing the use of an ax may be, at the same time, rules by which manliness is rewarded, political authority is recognized, and loyalty to the society is expressed. Many anthropologists today are so impressed by the cultural integration of the societies they visit that they are opposed to almost any influence on those societies from the outside world.

However, it is not always true that a whole society shares the same cultural beliefs, values, and norms. Although the various cultural elements of a given society often fit together very well, the extent of cultural integration differs from one society to another. Modern societies are particularly likely to show much cultural diversity. In North America, for example, we have a great variety of groups with different cultures and life styles. There are ethnic communities in which life goes on the way it did in the "old country" and deviant communities that support theft, drug use, or sexual fetishes. There are unusual religious communities, astrological societies, nudist camps, prohibitionist groups, and so on. These groups are based on different **subcultures**. Their members share values and ideas that differ from those of the wider society of which they are a part.

The word **counterculture** has come into the language since the 1960s. It refers to a subculture (such as that of hippies or dropouts) that included a core of beliefs and traits that differed from those of the wider culture of Western society. However, it wasn't just *different* from the "straight" or mainstream culture; it was *in opposition to* that culture. Its members countered the "straight" culture by looking scruffy, using drugs, believing in

During the 60's many people were upset with the direction of Western culture. To show their contempt for the culture they lived in they painted their faces and wore weird clothes. This was a way of loudly saying, "I don't want to be a part of this culture!" This was a counterculture.

Teresa Zabala/Palmer

astrology and the tarot, experimenting with unusual sexual relationships, living on yogurt and sunflower seeds, selling candles and beads on the sidewalk, and the like. The ideas that were common to the counterculture included belief in natural foods, enlightenment through drugs, and communal living. It claimed not to value achievement, materialistic success, or competition.

What influences culture?

Many theories have been proposed to explain why cultures differ so greatly from one society to another. I will mention three types of theory: racial, geographical, and technological. They are all, at best, partial explanations of cultural variation, and they are not necessarily incompatible. It is possible that all three could play a role in the development of a given culture. Even so, all three theories taken together still would not explain many differences between cultures. Two societies in similar geographical settings, whose people are of the same racial stock, share the same language, and have similar technological skills, may still be very different in terms of culture. Culture seems to be free to develop in a number of different directions. Hence, the best we can hope to do is to point out some of the factors that influence the development of culture. Unfortunately, most of the theories that have been proposed throughout history cannot even do that. Racism is one such theory.

RACE AND CULTURE

The confusion between race and culture has had a harmful influence on the history of ideas. Human beings inherit certain physical traits (e.g., skin color and facial features) that mark them as "Caucasian," "Asian," and so on. These traits are passed from parents to offspring by tiny genes that are found in all living cells. Until recently, many people believed—

and a few still do—that cultural traits are transmitted in the same way. On this basis they decided that some human populations are born to greatness while others are doomed to fail. Hitler, for example, claimed that the German people were destined by their genetic superiority to rule Europe, if not the world.

The flaw in this theory is obvious. The genetic traits of breeding populations are far more stable than their cultural traits. For example, the genetic explanation cannot explain why the Italians, who built and ruled the Roman Empire, now live in one of the poorer countries of Europe and rule nobody but themselves.

I could list hundreds of similar examples. The Indian descendants of the Mayas live in poverty in Yucatan in the very shadow of the huge stone temples built by their ancestors. China had the most brilliant civilization on earth during the T'ang Dynasty (A.D. 618–907). If the Chinese people were "cultured" because of their heredity, why did that civilization flower and then wither? The racial explanation of cultural variation is clearly mistaken. Yet racism is such an important issue that we will discuss it further in Chapter 10.

GEOGRAPHY AND CULTURE

The geographical theory, also widely held, explains cultural traits in terms of the society's physical setting. This theory is not entirely false, but it is very limited. It was popular 30 or 40 years ago, when it was widely noted that all the most technologically advanced cultures of the world were found in places with temperate climates.[7] Is there something stimulating about mild weather? The argument seems valid at first, but it is not supported by historical evidence. Most of today's leading industrial societies are found in the temperate zone, but the lost civilizations of ancient times were located in areas with a wide range of climates.

The physical setting does not determine

what a culture *will* become, but it sets limits on what it *can* become. Thus Arctic tribes don't dance in grass skirts. People have to keep warm, and they have to use whatever materials are available. Still, within these limits they could develop many different ways of dancing. The environment contains both opportunities and limitations, but even a rich environment does not guarantee that a society will develop an advanced culture. Thus the California Indians lived in one of the most hospitable environments on the earth, but they were among the most primitive tribes of North America. Culture must work with Mother Nature, but she does not draw its design.

Moreover, as technology improves, the influence of nature decreases. Technology overcomes the limitations of nature so that there are more opportunities than there were before. For example, though people in the Arctic might never have invented hula dancing in grass skirts, they may take up such dancing if they live in well-heated brick houses.

TECHNOLOGY AND CULTURE

Sociologists sometimes distinguish between two aspects of technology—ideas and social practices. Some writers argue that the ideas (i.e., the culture) are shaped by the technological practices (i.e., the social structure). Let's look at three writers who take this position: Karl Marx, Harold Innis, and Marshall McLuhan.

Marx: technology and ideology

Marx's philosophy is called *historical materialism* because it assumes that history is determined by the material circumstances that people face—especially the necessity of earning bread.[8] Marx believed that the social structure (the technological practices) of a group determines its culture. That is, people do what they have to do in order to survive.

Then they think up ideals to justify what they do. These ideals are really ideologies.

The technology of producing food, clothes, shelter, and other necessities is the basic factor in any social group. This is the true basis of its social structure. People who own the means of production (land, livestock, factories, etc.) form the ruling class. Naturally, they try to justify their dominant position, and they support teachers, writers, priests, and politicians as long as these people produce ideas that support their position. These ideas are the culture of the society, but to Marx they were simply ideologies. For example, religion teaches workers to be humble. It tells them to look for their reward in the next life, not in this one. Thus religion is ideology, and so are politics, literature, philosophy, art, and all the other aspects of culture. Through ideology the ruling class hoodwinks the workers and keeps them in line.

Marx distinguished between those social institutions that handle basic economic production and those that handle cultural matters. The latter he called the *superstructure*. The educational system, the religious, legal, and political institutions are all part of the superstructure. Marx believed that whatever happened in the superstructure depended entirely on what happened in the institutions that handled economic production. Historical changes were always determined by bread-and-butter issues, not by abstract ideals or noble values. And for that matter, when you look below the surface, even the abstract ideals are invented to protect some group's bread-and-butter interests—or so Marx believed. Thus the economic structure—the technology of production—determines culture. Marxists still assume that this is the case.

Innis and McLuhan: communication and culture

Marx's position is not the only materialist interpretation of culture. Many non-Marxist theorists also focus on the influence of tech-

nology on culture. Let's look at two more recent materialist theorists, Harold Innis and Marshall McLuhan, who both stress the technology of communication rather than the technology of production.

Innis, an economic historian, showed that the culture of a society is greatly influenced by the nature of the media through which the culture is communicated.[9] In particular, he emphasized the differences between societies that depend on oral communication and those that use writing. The human voice has certain physical characteristics that put limits on *preliterate* (i.e., oral) societies. First, because of the voice's short range, members of a group must be close together to communicate with one another. Second, because sound is not permanent, an oral society is "time bound." A verbal event happens in a moment and is gone. It cannot be recaptured except in the memory of its hearers, and memory distorts reality. According to Innis, people whose culture is oral cannot keep accurate records. In speaking of past events they are more free to invent. As a result such societies do not separate history from myth. Their stories are imaginative and illogical.

Writing changes all this. Written communications are permanent and are not distorted by memory. A *literate* group (one that uses writing) can spread out over a large area and still maintain its identity and its political coordination. Bureaucratic empires become possible. Reason replaces traditional sacred authority. Members of a literate society can check documents against other historical records. Their standards of judgment can become more objective and consistent. The culture of a literate society becomes critical, logical, and empirical.

The distinction between preliterate and literate societies is such an important one that many of these observations had been made by other writers. Innis, however, found that even small technological improvements in the media of communication often had great historical impact. For instance, the cost, durabil-

FIGURE 3.1

In these drawings, from about 2800 years ago, the first line shows the inscription as originally written; it is read from right to left, as has been the custom in Semitic languages. In the second line the same message is reversed so as to read from left to right. The next line translates the Semitic letters into the modern alphabet. The fourth line includes the unwritten vowels to show pronunciation, and the final one is the English translation.

1. (Semitic inscription, right to left)
2. (Semitic inscription, reversed)
3. ʾN K · M S c · B N · K M S M L D · M L K · M ʾ B
4. ʾANᵒKⁱ MᵉShᵃᶜ BᵉN KᵃMᵒShMᵃLD MᵉLᵉK MᵒʾAB
5. I Mesha son-of Kamoshmald king-of Moab

Source: ''The Evolution of a Writing System,'' from *The Human Adventure* by G. H. Pelto. © Copyright 1962 by Macmillan Publishing Co., Inc.

ity, and portability of writing materials are important technological factors. Thus as papyrus replaced clay tablets and was itself replaced by parchment and then by paper, the number and kinds of written documents multiplied and culture spread more rapidly. Without paper, the development of printing would not have been possible.

McLuhan calls one of his own books a "footnote" to some of Innis' writings.[10] His more famous work, *Understanding Media* (1964),[11] explores the cultural effects of different communications media even further. This book stimulated much debate.

McLuhan sees the media as extensions of the human body. Just as a crowbar extends the power of the human arm, so too media can extend the power of human senses. A telescope and a movie camera both extend the power of the human eye. The telescope allows it to see things that are far away, and the movie camera allows it to see things that are distant in both space and time—World War I battles or the peak of Mount Everest, for example. We can see the world and communicate with others in new ways by using tech-

nological inventions, but by doing so we change ourselves too.

Consider the members of a preliterate society. They use all their senses, but a lot of their attention is directed toward hearing, for it is almost their only means of contact with the thoughts of others. Now suppose these people learn to read. They then learn by using their eyes rather than their ears. It's as if literacy enlarges one's eyes and shrinks one's ears.

In addition, literacy takes people out of the real world and into the world of books. As McLuhan points out, these two worlds are quite different. He asks us to suppose that we are looking at a red, white, and blue flag with stars and stripes on it. Then someone takes it down and puts in its place a piece of paper on which are written the words *American flag*. The words cannot fully replace the real flag.

A nonliterate person experiences his or her culture as a large number of impressions that bombard the senses all at once in no logical order. These impressions are associated with mythical ideas, fantastic images, and magical symbols. A literate person, on the other hand, experiences culture through words read one at a time. These words must be strung together in a logical order, and they are a poor substitute for real objects.

We read a book with detachment. It does not affect us as deeply as contacts with real people. But McLuhan goes further, claiming that a literate society is *generally* more detached, critical, and rational than a nonliterate one. He believes that by reading books we develop mental habits that we carry over into the real world.

For better or worse, literate culture is about to become a thing of the past, according to McLuhan. Modern electronic media are changing the world. We are entering a "post-literate" era. Television counteracts some of the effects of literacy. It forces people to use their ears as well as their eyes. It pours out a simultaneous, nonsequential, illogical flood of impressions that demand the active participation of the viewer. A television viewer must become involved with the people who appear on the screen, real people who live all over the world. People around the globe are linked together by the electronic extensions of the human nervous system—telephones, television, tape recorders, and so forth. The logical thought and careful reasoning of literate humanity decline in the culture of post-literate humanity and are replaced by a renewed tendency to use myths and symbolic imagery.

These, then, are McLuhan's main ideas. They have been criticized widely, and McLuhan does not bother to defend them very seriously. Instead, he views these ideas as something that he has been playing with, and he invites us to play with them too.

SOCIAL RESEARCH: *Sociologists at Work*

MONEY FOR CANADIAN CULTURAL PROJECTS

Someday I want to conduct a survey to find out the most popular topics of party-time conversation in Canada. I have a hunch that one of the top ten subjects will concern the definition of "Canadian culture."

Does Canada have a culture of its own? If not, why not? And how important is it to create one? Of course, every group of people shares *some* culture; otherwise they could not understand each other or act together. But is there anything unique that Canadians share beyond what is shared by members of other Western societies? In particular, do Canadians simply "borrow" American culture without producing anything special of their own? What symbols represent Canada?

You may have struggled with one aspect of this question when trying to select a nice gift for a foreigner that will remind him or her of Canada. The Dutch give wooden shoes, tulips, and long clay pipes. The Swiss give cuckoo clocks; the Irish, tweed caps; the Mexicans, painted tin soldiers; the Australians, boomerangs. But what represents Canada? Mounties, yes. But you can't buy and gift-wrap a mountie.

The problem of selecting presents is, by itself, a small matter but it points to similar problems in other areas. Who are the outstanding contemporary Canadian painters, and how many people know their pictures when they see them? (The Group of Seven and Emily Carr are no longer contemporary.) How popular are Canadian magazines and how do they differ in content from American ones? What, if anything, is special about Canadian television? How about Canadian movies? Do Canadian singers, actors, and dancers have to move to New York or Hollywood to gain the fame they deserve?

Questions of this kind are widely discussed, and the general opinion is that Canadian culture is simply not supported or appreciated as much as it should be. It is agreed that, in a strong modern society, independent mass media and artistic productions should flourish. Why this largely fails to happen is not obvious.

S. M. Crean has studied the question in some detail. In her book, *Who's Afraid of Canadian Culture?*, she points out many of the economic and political factors that tend to weaken Canadian culture.[12] As an ardent nationalist, she is plainly urging the government to protect local products from overwhelming foreign competition. Cultural products, like any other goods or services, cost money. Thus their existence is responsive to the market forces of supply and demand. Crean's research focuses on the way that government policies affect those market forces.

Whose idea of Canadian culture is this?

Ontario Ministry of Industry and Tourism

The Canada Council is an example of such a government policy. Since 1945, the federal government has maintained a system of direct assistance to support artists, scholars, and performing groups, such as operas or ballet companies. Such artists as poets, composers, or playwrights can seldom earn their living from their crafts. The Canada Council was created in 1957 as a funding agency to support the work of the most promising creative producers. (We should point out that universities also support such activities by offering teaching jobs that leave several months of the year free for creative work.)

Obviously there will always be more applicants for such grants than there is money to go around. The Canada Council's annual budget exceeds $50 million; half of this is spent in grants for the humanities and half for the arts. Crean points out that the Canada Council's policy concentrates on funding top professionals. She would prefer the money to be divided into small amounts and shared among a great many ordinary people who will never become internationally recognized superstars. The superstars are not likely to employ local Canadian themes in their work; rather, they play to a sophisticated international audience that compares each new novel, symphony, or painting to Hemingway, Beethoven, or Picasso, without regard to whether it says anything special about Canada. A major ballet company, for instance, may be less likely to create a truly new Canadian dance than a high school gymnastics coach in Fredericton or a YWCA dance director in Nanaimo. The present funding system, however, does not encourage these lesser known artists. As Crean describes it, Canada offers caviar to a few instead of strawberry jam to everyone. This promotes an "Official Culture" that does not reflect the interests of most ordinary people.

Funding policy is not the only hindrance to Canadian culture. Once a product has been created, it still has to compete in an international market for the chance to be distributed. As the film industry demonstrates, this economic reality can be a considerable obstacle.

The National Film Board was established in 1939 and has since produced an abundance of excellent short films. However, the NFB was not supposed to produce films for commercial distribution. Canadian performers had to go to Hollywood to get acting jobs. Eventually some NFB-trained filmmakers began to try their hand at feature films. In Quebec this began in the 1940s; in English

Canada, however, feature films were not made until the mid-1960s when the government began to encourage film-making. For a few years the prospects seemed good. *Goin' Down the Road, Paperback Hero*, and *The Apprenticeship of Duddy Kravitz* were all highly successful films that seemed to herald the development of a big Canadian film industry. At the end of the 1970s, however, the industry was still floundering. Why? Crean suggests that insufficient attention was paid to distributing the films. The Canadian Film Development Corporation had helped finance nearly 200 films but few of the moviegoers in Canada had ever seen one.

A large proportion of the movie theatres in Canada (especially in urban areas) are controlled by two chains, Famous Players and Odeon. Both of these companies have regular commitments to film production companies abroad, and it is not necessarily to their advantage to show Canadian films. No law requires theatres to show any quota of Canadian content. The government has been reluctant to regulate the business dealings of the film industry, both out of respect for the principle of free enterprise and because such regulations, like censorship, interfere with the moviegoer's freedom of choice. Most people just want to see a good movie; its national origin is of secondary importance.

The same goes for books. Canadian book publishers always live dangerously: The competition with foreign publishers makes their business uncomfortably risky. This is not because the market for books is so small, in absolute terms. Over $300 million is spent for English-language books in Canada every year. If Canadians spoke a peculiar language that no other people understood, this would constitute a good-sized market that could support a publishing industry quite handsomely. The problem is that Canada is a small part of the English-speaking world, and maintains a policy of freely importing books published elsewhere. Canada publishes about 2500 books per year, while the United Kingdom publishes 33,000 and the United States about 37,000.[13] The production of books in Canada is generally more expensive than in countries with larger populations; because a printing of a Canadian book has to be smaller in output than an ordinary printing of an American or British book, the cost is 20 or 25 percent higher.

In English Canada, buyers for libraries and schools, eager to cut costs, frequently order their books directly from publishers. This used to be the case in Quebec, where business was lost to publishing companies in France. In order to support the local book trade, the government enacted regulations requiring purchases for libraries and schools to be made through regular booksellers. This enabled the book stores to display a whole array of French Canadian publications to entice browsers; as a result buyers selected more books than they had when equally exposed to local and foreign marketing pressures.[14] Crean would like to see similar governmental support offered to Canadian publishers throughout English Canada. She also offers strong advice on ways to preserve Canadian culture in other domains, including broadcasting, the arts, film, dance, and education. Some of her opinions will be further considered in our discussion of social policy later in the chapter.

POPULAR CULTURE AND THE MASS MEDIA

In any heterogeneous society (i.e., one with a variety of subgroups), there is likely to be conflict among different cultural publics. North American society is no exception. At times such conflicts enter the political arena. One such conflict concerns whether the government should uphold specific cultural standards. For example, it might do so through censorship, through power to grant or withhold broadcasting licenses, or by means of subsidies to struggling artists and cultural groups such as opera companies.

People who would like more government support for "high" culture usually give one or both of the following reasons: (1) High culture deserves special treatment simply because of its excellence, and/or (2) popular culture is often harmful to society and therefore should not be encouraged. Of course these two arguments are quite separate. You can accept one without accepting the other.

Herbert Gans has studied the evidence for the second argument and has concluded that it is largely mistaken.[15] He believes that the mass media offer many more benefits than dangers. What are those "dangers," anyway? Various critics of popular culture see different ones. Some fear that psychological disturbances and even sex crimes may be caused by pornography. Some are concerned about the wasteful, materialistic attitudes that are encouraged by advertising. Others are offended by the commercials themselves. Some are concerned

Massage parlors and pornography theaters are seen by many as a threat to the quality of Western culture.

about the effects of watching violence. Some are worried that people may model their lives on those of their favorite stars. Finally, many critics are particularly concerned about the power of journalists and TV newscasters to influence public opinion through biased reporting.

Gans' general conclusion—and he admits that it is a personal one—is that there is no cause for alarm. People are not helpless victims of the media who believe everything they see on the TV screen. Media audiences are usually groups—families, dating couples, and so on—who choose programs that are consistent with their own values and opinions. They have a chance to argue against the statements they hear or even to decide to turn off the TV or cancel a magazine subscription. Sensible adults learn to "discount" claims made in the media, especially when those claims are intended to persuade or influence the reader or viewer—as is obviously true of political speeches and advertising.

By and large, people do not accept news reports uncritically, but TV newscasts still have a lot of influence on the political "agenda." That is, the media report certain events and not others, and what they report determines what becomes a matter of public debate. It does not, however, determine the answers that will come out of the political process.[16] Nor does political advertising have a major impact on the outcome of elections. The only reason for concern about such advertising is that all the candidates or issues do not always have equal access to the media, and media ads often make some difference when elections are close.

Gans believes that many observers have probably overestimated the influence of the media on manners and morals. He sees no reason to believe that many adults, or even teenagers, model their lives or base their choices of dates or spouses on their favorite performers. Instead, people base their choices of TV programs and reading matter on their own values.

There is no doubt that good advertising leads to higher sales, but whether this is socially harmful or not is a question to which there is no clear answer.

We will give this matter more attention later in the book, but for now we may simply note that most people in Western societies do not seem to mind advertising. I find many ads obnoxious, but sometimes I am glad to be informed about something that I would otherwise have missed.

The pornography issue is a complicated one. Erotic movies definitely arouse sexual feelings for a while. However, the U.S. Commission on Obscenity and Pornography found that the use of erotic materials cannot be shown to have long-term effects. Danish law has permitted unlimited display of pornography for several years without an increase in sex crimes.[17] On the other hand, in areas where massage parlors, "skin flicks," and other pornographic performances are located, crime, drunkenness, drug abuse, and prostitution commonly increase. Often other businesses leave because the area becomes so sleazy. The legal action involved in closing massage parlors is often long and fruitless. Some cities have responded to the problem with

zoning laws, which do not prohibit such places but require them to be several blocks apart so that no area decays because of their presence.

Finally, we must think about the very important issue of violence on TV and in movies. By now it is clear that at least some people are affected at least some of the time by watching violence. Laboratory evidence shows that violent films stimulate aggressive behavior by youths immediately after watching them, but there is no evidence of long-term effects. Several recent studies, including one sponsored by the U.S. Surgeon General's Advisory Committee (1972)[18] and one directed by Judy LaMarsh for the Canadian government (1977), have concluded that television viewing and violent behavior are linked.

However, not all people are equally affected by TV violence. Girls do not respond with aggression. Emotionally disturbed people apparently are affected more than stable people. Gans believes that TV violence cannot be a very strong influence on the amount of violence that occurs in the general

The controversy continues over the way and the extent to which television influences its viewers, but there can be no doubt that it does enthrall them.

Jean-Claude Lejeune/Stock, Boston

population, for the amount of violent crime has actually decreased during the years since TV came into widespread use.[19] Nor is there any theoretical reason to think that the media are a major influence on violence. Police records show that the poor are more violent than the rich, which is what most of us would predict. Poverty is obviously a major and steady source of frustration. Moreover, studies of children indicate that parents and peers have more

influence on a child's behavior than the TV set. Thus although the mass media no doubt play a very important role in influencing public life, at their worst they are probably not as harmful as some people have feared. There is some basis for concern about TV violence, however, since it does affect the behavior of males, the poor, children, and emotionally unstable people. In Chapter 10 we will discuss other issues relating to the mass media.

SOCIAL POLICY:
Issues and Viewpoints

To some extent, sociologists can be scientific and neutral in their discussion of culture. However, after reflecting upon certain topics, even sociologists must arrive at a point of view. Sociologists can inform people about some of the facts surrounding those views, but the issues can never be settled simply on the basis of fact alone. I want to mention three of the issues that Canadians in general (and sociologists especially) must at some point come to terms with. (1) How does cultural relativism apply to contacts between developed and underdeveloped societies? (2) How far should the government go in supporting Canadian culture when it is in competition with alternative products from other societies? (3) Should public policy favor high culture or popular culture?

CULTURAL RELATIVISM AND ETHICS

You will recall that cultural relativism is the belief that any society's practices must be judged only in terms of its own cultural values. Many social scientists take this position at the beginning of their careers but later move away from it. It is hard to maintain. Few relativists, for example, could bring themselves to eat human flesh if it were offered to them by a cannibalistic host, even if that practice happened to be acceptable in the society they were visiting.

Today most scholars, while they admit that their judgments are imperfect and that there could be no perfection anyway, recognize that it is impossible to avoid making judgments about other cultures. We do have to decide what to support and what to oppose. Cultural relativism arose in reaction to the arrogance of Europeans who looked down on primitive societies. However praiseworthy it may have been originally, since World War II this policy has come to be recognized as socially irresponsible. As Erich Fromm has pointed out in his analysis of Nazism, it is possible for whole societies to be "sick"—to have perverted values, to carry out policies that they may later feel ashamed of. Relativism does not allow the scholar to view such societies as "sick." A relativist is bound to accept genocide as valid if it is a true cultural ideal in the society, or cannibalism, sexism, racism, or anything else.

From an aesthetic point of view, some groups offer fewer expressive forms than other groups do. A relativistic outlook would not allow us to conclude that one group is "culturally impoverished" compared to another. But in some cases that is a reasonable conclusion.

Moreover, from a technological point of view, it is obvious that not all cultures are equally advanced. Although all societies value life and health and comfort, they are not equally able to attain these benefits. Therefore many social scientists have abandoned the effort to remain neutral toward foreign cultures. They now work actively to modernize underdeveloped countries. Modernization requires changes in values and life styles. Some researchers in poor societies try to persuade people to boil their drinking water and to plant new strains of rice seed.

However, a few relativists still view such activities as a form of "cultural imperialism" that threatens the society's cultural integrity. They point to the Yir Yoront as an example of what happens when a society imports a foreign technology. And, indeed, the spread of industrialization and Western ideas through education, tourism, and exposure to Western media does progressively undermine regional traditions. To my mind, modernization is, on balance, a good thing. To yours it may not be.

PROTECTING CANADIAN CULTURE

The research by S. M. Crean that we discussed earlier was intended to support a very definite point of view about political policy. Crean argues passionately for a preservation of Canadian culture

Should the Canadian government support expensive international stars or grass-roots performers like these?

Ontario Ballet Theatre

against forces that are mainly American and capitalist. She would gladly establish quotas requiring people who trade in cultural products to support Canadian producers. Crean is strongly committed to one particular value and rejects possible alternative values, though these could also be defended with reasonable arguments.

The belief in the importance of Canadian cultural products can interfere with the pursuit of alternative values, such as artistic excellence, free enterprise, artistic liberty, and freedom of the press. Canadian society evidently prizes the value of extended access to, and choice from, a variety of cultural products. Canada could imitate certain other societies and place a high tariff on foreign films, books, and shows so that most people would choose the cheaper domestic product over the expensive import. Canada could also adopt tough copyright laws that would make foreign competitors insecure about entering the Canadian market. Or worse, Canada could protect its own culture by banning foreign materials that challenge the ideas that officials want to protect, much as Iron Curtain countries search visitors and confiscate books that they don't want in the country. Some combination of these policies might protect Canadian products, but the public would vigorously protest the infringement on its freedom and the government would soon yield to public pressure. Obviously, Canadians do not value their own culture above *all* other values.

You may feel that Canadians simply don't value their own culture *enough* relative to other concerns, and that more should be done to insulate and give financial support to the creative people who are contributing their ideas to Canadian society. You may also believe that there should be a more democratic orientation in funding new productions. Should the few major opera, ballet, and theatre companies sink or swim on the strength of their box office receipts alone? Should local amateur organizations and new artists be funded instead? Does it matter whether regional artists ever gain fame outside their own small Canadian towns? Or, alternatively, is it important for Canadian dancers, actors, and singers to be recognized around the world, and to win international prizes at such events as the Cannes Film Festival? Should the health of Canadian culture be measured by its vigor at the grass roots level or by the international celebrity of its stars?

There are no firm answers to such questions.

There are only opinions, and you have a right to your own, just as Crean does to hers. And if your opinion is important to you, you have a right to work toward its acceptance by others, particularly those who make official policy.

HIGH VERSUS POPULAR CULTURE

Which public should control the mass media? At present the government does not involve itself much in this issue but simply lets the law of supply and demand determine the outcome. This means, in practice, that popular culture is well served while high culture, which appeals to smaller audiences, is not well served. Commercial success requires large audiences.

I would prefer greater diversity. I'd like to see every public enjoy its own television programs, records, plays, books, movies, and newspapers. I certainly don't think high culture should dominate the media. In general, the public does not need to be protected from its own popular taste. The problem is that sometimes the TV channels are all showing soap operas or quiz shows and there is no choice between popular culture and high culture.

Smaller publics with special interests (e.g. ethnic groups) deserve access to their own cultural products, and we would all be enriched if this were made possible. Herbert Gans, among other writers, supports a policy of cultural pluralism instead of uniformity. All groups—intellectuals, workers, minorities, and so on—should be able to find cultural products that suit their needs and tastes. For every culture is a living human tradition that deserves the respect of others.

SUMMARY

1. A *culture* consists of a system of ideas, values, beliefs, and knowledge that is passed from one generation to the next within a social group. The term is sometimes applied to a system of norms or obligations. Sometimes it refers to an expressive system, especially the arts. And sometimes sociologists think of "culture" as distinct from the social system or structure. In that sense the culture is a set of ideas that the social system tries to live up to by institutionalizing specific practices.

2. Culture is communicated largely through symbols. A *symbol* is anything that stands for something else. A culture includes values, norms, folklore, law, and ideology. A *value* is something that is widely believed to be desirable or worthwhile for its own sake. A *norm* is a rule prescribing how to behave in particular situations. Primitive societies have informal ways of enforcing their norms, but

modern societies use written laws. *Folklore* consists of myths, jokes, superstitions, songs, stories, and the like. An *ideology* is a set of beliefs that enable a group to justify (at least to its own members) what it is doing.

3. *Technology* consists of the use of knowledge in an institutionalized way to control nature for practical purposes. It differs from expressive forms of symbolic activity in that it normally improves and develops over time. Technology is judged on the basis of efficiency, while expressive forms are judged by aesthetic standards, which are more subjective than the standard of efficiency.

4. There is a tendency for cultures to be *functionally integrated*; that is, the parts of any given cultural system tend to fit together. However, in modern societies there is much cultural diversity, and many different subcultures may be found within the same society.

5. Several different theories have been proposed to explain, in part, why cultures differ so greatly from one society to another.

The racial theory is based on the mistaken notion that some cultures are more advanced than others because their members inherit a high level of ability in their genes. Another theory holds that cultural differences are due to differences in geographical factors, including climate. This theory has also been shown to have little validity. Technological factors are the basis for certain other theories, especially those of Marx, Innis, and McLuhan. Marx thought technology produced changes in the basic structure of society. Culture, on the other hand, was part of the "superstructure." That is, it depended on the basic structure—the economic arrangements. McLuhan and Innis pointed out how technology of

communication influences the culture of a given society and even the personality traits of people who belong to it.

The Innis-McLuhan version of the technology theory simply points out that the kind of media used to communicate messages (e.g., clay tablets or television) determines how a person will experience the act of communicating. Reading is a very different experience from watching television, and so people who mostly read probably differ psychologically and culturally from people who mostly watch television. The reading culture is very logical and critical; the television culture is more likely to participate actively in the communication process.

KEY TERMS

code a grammar or set of rules that may be passed along from one generation to the next.

counterculture a subculture (such as that of hippies and dropouts) that is opposed to the conventional culture of the wider society.

cultural relativism the assumption that all cultures are equally valid and that any culture deserves respect.

cultural lag a term used to explain social problems that arise because there is a time lag between a technological change and the social and cultural changes required by that change.

culture a system of ideas, values, beliefs, knowledge, and customs transmitted from generation to generation within a social group.

culture trait the smallest unit of culture.

ethnocentrism the tendency to judge other ways of life by the standards of one's own group.

folklore a society's oral tradition (its collection of jokes, superstitions, lullabies, old wives' tales, slang words, ghost stories, etc.)

folkways the trivial norms or conventions shared by members of a society.

ideology a doctrine used to justify a group's actions in pursuing its own interests.

institutionalization the process through which culture influences the social system; the development of structures to carry out the shared values of the society.

mores a society's important ethical rules.

norm a rule that tells members of a society how to behave in particular situations.

public a group of people who share a particular code and an interest in a given issue or tradition.

sanction an action that rewards conformity to norms or punishes nonconformity.

social control the process by which members of a group support desired forms of behavior and discourage undesired forms.

social system the roles and actual practices that exist among members of a social group.

subculture a group whose members share values and ideas that differ from those of the wider society.

symbol anything that represents something else, i.e., anything that has meaning.

technology the institutionalized application of knowledge to control nature for human uses.

value a standard used by members of a society to judge behavior and to choose among various possible goals.

FOR FURTHER READING

BELSHAW, CYRIL S. *The Sorcerer's Apprentice.* Toronto: Pergamon Press, 1976. This book deals with the predicament of social researchers in villages of the Third World, who often witness the brutalizing effects of government policies on the local societies. One has to discover how to be a researcher and use power too. Belshaw has a deep understanding of such administrative problems.

BENEDICT, RUTH. *Patterns of Culture.* Boston: Houghton Mifflin, 1934. A classic in anthropology, this is pleasant to read too. It pursues the relationship between character-type (personality) and culture, drawing on American Indian tribes to illustrate the great diversity of cultural patterns. Small and delightful.

ELKIN, FREDERICK. *Rebels and Colleagues: Advertising and Social Change in French Canada.* Montreal: McGill-Queens University Press, 1973. This is an unusual study of the interplay between social change (here the Quiet Revolution) and the people who consciously try to influence public opinion. Sometimes advertising tricks backfire, sometimes they work.

GRUNEAU, R. S. and J. G. ALBINSON. *Canadian Sport: Sociological Perspectives.* Don Mills, Ont.: Addison-Wesley, 1976. There is a whole area of sociology, not yet well-developed but definitely growing, that analyzes sports and recreation. This is a new contribution to that field.

HARRIS, MARVIN. *Cannibals and Kings: The Origins of Cultures.* New York: Random House, 1977. Harris is an amazingly provocative writer. He tries to explain all kinds of anthropological problems in terms of material necessities—such as the necessity of all human beings to obtain protein. For some it is easy, for others difficult—depending on the natural environment. I will let you imagine how he ties cannibalism and the political evolution of monarchy into this theme. No, don't just imagine. Read it.

LORIMER, JAMES and MYFANWY PHILLIPS. *Working People: Life in a Downtown City Neighborhood.* Toronto: James Lewis and Samuel, 1971. This is a descriptive account of life in a working-class neighborhood of Toronto.

MCLUHAN, MARSHALL. *Understanding Media: The Extensions of Man.* New York: McGraw-Hill, 1965. McLuhan is the fellow Woody Allen had hidden behind the posters at the theatre in *Annie Hall*. This is the book they were arguing about in the ticket line.

THEODORE ROSZAK. *Where the Wasteland Ends: Politics and Transcendence in Postindustrial Society.* Garden City, N.Y.: Doubleday, 1972. I am a great admirer of Roszak (except sometimes). He discusses the new Western cultural forms that derive from Eastern religions, and has an unusually keen awareness of their value to modern people, who are supposed to be so objective and scientific.

RUTHERFORD, PAUL. *The Making of the Canadian Media.* Toronto: McGraw-Hill Ryerson, 1977. This is useful as an introductory history of the major newspapers in various regions of Canada. However, it is too limited to show the impact of such influential organizations as the National Film Board or the CBC.

SUMNER, WILLIAM GRAHAM. *Folkways.* New York: New American Library, 1960. First published, 1907. This is Sumner's most famous book, still popular in paperback. I have never read it straight through, but I have dipped in here and there for a chapter or two. It lends itself to that sort of reading.

4

SOCIALIZATION

Biological factors in socialization
The family and early socialization
    Family structure and child
       development
    Learning language and ideals
    Socialization in subcultures
Socialization through the life cycle
    Anticipatory socialization
    Socialization in adulthood
    Resocialization
Three views of socialization
    Durkheim on moral authority
    Piaget on moral reasoning
    Freud on repression
Social Research: Sociologists at Work
Social Policy: Issues and Viewpoints

What was the last beverage you drank? Milk? Coffee? Beer? Why did you choose that beverage? Because you needed it? Where did that "need" come from? Is it a basic part of your makeup? Clearly the need for *some* sort of liquid is a basic need of all human beings. But the preference for one particular beverage is shaped by experience. Your "need" for coffee or beer has been learned through your relationships with coffee drinkers and beer drinkers. If you had grown up in a different society you might dislike both.

What about milk? Milk drinking must be basic to human nature, for we are all mammals. That is true, but in many societies adults never drink milk. What happens to their "need" for milk as they grow up? Do they substitute an artificial need for a natural need when they begin choosing tea instead of milk? Are some needs natural and others artificial? What about blood? Members of some African tribes drink cow's blood with great pleasure. If you had grown up in such a tribe you would too.

You are born with a few basic, unspecific needs, but as you grow to adulthood in a particular society you develop a great many specific needs. We say that general needs are *channeled* by social experience. Your need for liquid may be channeled away from milk toward tea. It may even be channeled toward more and more specific preferences—away from oolong tea and toward Darjeeling tea, for example.

The Karimojong tribe of Uganda rarely slaughter their cattle for meat, but they obtain protein from them anyway—by drinking blood and milk. A thong is tightened around the cow's neck to make its jugular vein stand out a little, then an arrow is shot into the vein. When 4 to 8 pints of blood have been taken, the thong is released and the blood stops flowing.

Africapix

Adult needs and motives develop largely out of the individual's experience of social interaction. However, it does not make sense to ask an adult which of his or her preferences are basic and which have been channeled by his or her social experience. People feel as strongly about their acquired needs as they do about the basic ones out of which the acquired ones develop.

The channeling process begins in early infancy and continues throughout life, even when one is not aware that it is taking place. For example, one study observed the development of infants' preferences for different kinds of juice. Nurses offered the babies both orange and tomato juice several times, always allowing the children to choose between the two drinks. Fairly soon it became clear that each child was beginning to choose the juice that the nurse herself preferred.[1] The nurses had no intention of influencing the children, but social interaction always has an effect on the participants whether it is intended or not. The channeling process ordinarily prepares a person to fit comfortably into the community and take part in its affairs. Through socialization we learn to need the things that our community can provide for us and not to need other things. This is usually a good thing; a North American child who developed a strong need to drink cow's blood, for example, would be quite a misfit.

"All the world's a stage" wrote Shakespeare, "and all the men and women merely players." This is pure sociology. A social system is organized according to a script that all of its members have learned. For example, we know roughly how people have to behave in order to create the collective activity that we call a bank. We do not spread a picnic lunch on the floor of the bank lobby or hunt Easter eggs behind the tellers' windows because those actions would not follow the script; in fact they would disrupt the performance.

All the participants in a collective activity have particular **roles** to play. These roles form a system. The teller's role and the customer's role are interdependent aspects of a collective activity. Each requires something from the other.

Role performances are guided by norms. Thus if a bank teller ignores a customer and spends ten minutes gossiping with a friend, he or she is violating a norm. The teller is supposed to wait on the customer, not chat with a friend, so the customer has a right to get huffy. The term *norm* usually means "average," as when we say that a girl is shorter than the norm for her age. In sociology, however, norms do not simply define behavior that is "typical" of people who play a given role; rather, they refer to behavior that is obligatory. Norms define how roles *ought* to be performed.

Role conflict (or role strain) is the awkward situation in which a person occupies two roles governed by conflicting norms. It may be impossible, or possible only at great cost, to conform to all of those norms. Generally, social groups try to prevent role conflict by keeping people from occupying positions in which there is an obvious "conflict of interests." For example, universities discourage professors from dating their students because the role of lover conflicts with the role of grader of term papers.

An **institution** is a complex system of roles organized around some central activity or social need. Institutions are the main building blocks of a society. Examples include courts, schools, churches, hospitals, prisons, and the like. The number of institutions and their degree of specialization vary from one society to another. Highly developed societies have many specialized institutions characterized by extreme division of labor with each part performing a narrow range of tasks.

Socialization is the process of learning the rules of behavior for a given social group as well as acquiring the motivation to perform properly. But through socialization people acquire not only culturally prescribed needs and motivations but also many other aspects of personality. They acquire language, knowledge and skills, commitments to particular norms and values, and the ability to perform in many role relationships.

Socialization is the process through which people come to *want* to do what they *must* do. That is, a society has patterns and traditions that can survive only if its new members learn

"All the world's a stage." Which of these acts have you played?

UPI

them and accept them. Thus the social system is the context within which the personality system must take shape. I want to discuss three important aspects of socialization: (1) the biological factors that human beings inherit and that affect their ability to learn and perform, (2) the family setting and its part in early learning, and (3) the continuing importance of socialization throughout the life cycle.

Biological factors in socialization

We often wonder whether a particular behavior pattern was acquired through socialization or whether it is dictated by the body's basic needs. This sort of question arises when we study universal human traits. For example, is every human being *born* with a natural tendency to fight? Or do we *learn* to fight through socialization? (If fighting is social in origin, perhaps a different way of socializing children might eliminate war.) We may also ask how many of the traits that distinguish males from females are *biological* in origin and how many result from the different *social* experiences of males and females. Do human females *inherit* the tendency to protect their infants, or is this tendency *learned*? Few such questions have been answered satisfactorily, but a new field, called *sociobiology*, specializes in research on such topics. Seldom has any new field of study made so many enemies so quickly! A great many people, including some social scientists, are unwilling to believe that *any* behavior pattern is determined by biological factors. One reason is that this would imply that human beings have no more freedom of choice than other animals. Moreover, some feminists object to the idea that biological factors are responsible for, say, the attachment between mothers and their babies, for the quality of a person's sexual experience, or for the tendency of males to dominate females.

The social scientists who mistrust the biological explanation of behavior are often scholars who recall similar research that proved to be fruitless in the past. Two generations or so ago many psychologists were interested in listing the "instincts" of human beings. This turned out to be useless because we now know that human behavior is not predetermined the way animal behavior seems to be; therefore the notion of "instinct" can hardly apply to human beings the way it applies to lower animals. Birds have an instinct to fly south, but we have to learn to read road maps when we want to take a trip. This is one reason that the human infant is dependent on its family for so long. It takes 15 or 20 years for a child to become socialized because so much more than instinct is involved in human behavior. In any case a new interest in these issues has emerged during the past five or ten years, and sociobiologists are studying them.

Besides looking for species-wide (universal) biologically based patterns of behavior, we sometimes wonder whether biology is responsible for the differences between individuals or between groups. When we talk of "biologically" determined traits we usually mean genetic traits—traits that are determined by the genes that are contained in the cells of the body. These traits are obviously permanent. No scientist has yet been able to change your genes. But of course not all "biological" influences are genetic. The environment has important influences on the biological organism, and these influences may or may not be permanent. For example, we may ask questions about an individual's prenatal environment. Did the mother eat a balanced diet when she was pregnant? What medicines did she take? Was her hormone system balanced? Many other biological factors are not genetic but environmental. Some children may be unusually sensitive to certain chemicals that are commonly added to food, and become jumpy and distracted when they eat them. Some people's moods may be influenced by the balance of positive and negative ions in the air. However, here we are concerned only with *genetic* factors that may influence behavior.

Which is the more important influence on behavior: heredity or the social environment? This is a very tricky question, and I want to point out why. Let me give you an analogy: Is skin color determined more by heredity or by the environment? The answer has to be that it depends on whom you are comparing. If you are trying to explain the variations in skin color among, say, the white children in an average classroom, you will probably conclude that heredity is mostly responsible for whatever differences you find. Some kids have olive skin and some are pale—they are born that way. Now suppose that half of the children in the class are black and half are white. Again, most of the variation in skin color is clearly due to heredity. But suppose we are considering a class in which there are no black children but in which half of the children have been to the beach and are deeply tanned while half have stayed indoors and are pale. Obviously most of the variation among the members of that class would be caused by environmental, not genetic, differences.

By the same token, since personality traits are influenced both by heredity and by the environment, in a particular group hereditary factors may explain most of the variations for a given trait. But if we look at a different group we may find that environmental factors explain most of the variations among its members. A careful scientist would not say, for example, that "intelligence is mostly hereditary," but might say that "within a great many groups, though not all groups, most of the variation in intelligence is due to heredity." There is no doubt that genetic factors are important influences on intelligence as well as on other aspects of personality.

We have other evidence of this. For example, identical twins have identical genes, and indeed, their intelligence scores are usually almost identical. Fraternal twins (not identical) have genes that are no more similar

than those of any pair of nontwin siblings, and their scores on IQ tests are usually about as far apart as those of any other pair of nontwin siblings. Similar genes make for similar intelligence—usually—unless something quite unusual has happened in the social or physical environment that had a strong impact on one twin but not on the other. For example, if one twin has experienced a serious vitamin deficiency or brain injury or has been greatly disadvantaged in his or her social relationships, these environmental differences will make for a big IQ difference between the twins.

Heredity may explain many other differences in the abilities and personality traits of individuals. Even mental illness seems to be influenced by hereditary factors. That is, some people seem to inherit a tendency toward schizophrenia. Whether they actually become schizophrenic or not probably depends on other factors as well, but those factors are not yet understood by scientists. The social situation is certainly among those factors, but no one knows just how important it is. Its importance may differ for different people. For example, one person's genes may create such a strong tendency toward schizophrenia that she will have a breakdown in a situation of very mild stress. Another person's genes may create only a slight tendency toward schizophrenia, but a situation of stress may become so severe that he breaks down anyway. But this is only speculation. Scientists don't really understand these processes yet. The point I want to make is that behavioral variations among individuals may be due to genetic factors in many cases.

Finally, let us ask whether behavior differences between *groups* may be due to genetic differences. The answer depends on what kinds of group you are comparing. Males and females? No doubt many behavioral differences are influenced by hormones, which we know men and women produce in different amounts. We will return to this issue later. How about social classes? Are the differences between the life styles of the upper class and the lower class caused by genetic factors? No—or maybe to a tiny extent. Perhaps the upper class includes a slightly higher percentage of individuals who have inherited a gift for, say, sports, singing, or mechanical tinkering that has enabled them to get rich. And perhaps the lower class includes a slightly higher percentage of individuals with a genetic handicap that keeps them from winning out in the competition for jobs. But these genetic differences between social classes cannot explain the differences between their life styles.[2] To account for these differences we have to understand that different classes have different subcultures. And we have to understand much more about the structural factors involved—such as job discrimination and unequal opportunities of all kinds.

What about differences in behavior between, say, Christians and Jews? Or between Asians, blacks, and whites? Or between English Canadians and French Canadians? Can we explain any difference between their patterns of behavior in terms of genetic differences? No. Any genetic difference would certainly be minor compared to the strength of cultural tradition. And culture is passed from one generation to the next through the socialization process, not through genes. I mentioned this issue in Chapter 3 and must return to it again in Chapter 14. But the basic answer to the question of whether differences in groups' behavior are due to genetic differences is very simple: No.

The family and early socialization

Because it is so obvious that the quality of a young child's experience is a crucial factor in his or her later development, most research on socialization has focused on the impact of different family arrangements on child development. Psychologists have discovered in the laboratory what everybody knew already—that "tender loving care," or good parenting, is the most important element in an infant's experience. A baby becomes attached to someone (usually its mother) by about the sixth month of life and goes into deep mourning if it is separated from her even for a few days. There is evidence that the lack of such a close relationship for a long period leaves permanent scars on the personality. At first children who are deprived of their mothers cry a lot; then they gradually withdraw from any human relationship. Often they seem unaffected by close contact with human beings. When they become adults, their inability to care deeply about others may take the form of superficial, exploitive attitudes toward other people. Of course it is not just the mother who is important to the child. The entire family serves as the context in which abilities and values are

Are people born with a natural tendency to fight or do they learn fighting? Sometimes people can't distinguish between their "natural impulses" and their learned patterns of behavior.

AP Photo

Photo Trends

Moments like this give babies a fund of inner good feelings to draw on throughout life. They are able to love themselves inwardly, like Mommy loved them.

learned. And the structure of the family is an important factor in the child's development.

FAMILY STRUCTURE AND CHILD DEVELOPMENT

Although North Americans are generally aware of the population explosion as a world problem and are willing to limit the size of their families, sometimes this willingness is mixed with regret. You may share the feelings of a young woman I know who said, a little sadly, "It's too bad my kids won't have the warmth and fun of growing up in a big, rollicking family."

Don't worry. Research suggests that big families offer less, in general, to children than small families do. Children from smaller families tend to do better in school, show greater motivation to achieve, and score higher on intelligence tests, even within the same social class.[3] And the fun and warmth? Well, children from small families are at least as well

adjusted, if not better adjusted, than those from larger families.[4] Possibly this is because they get less physical punishment.[5] And probably it is also because their parents can give them more attention than they would if they had more children.[6]

Besides, when most families are small, a higher percentage of children have the chance to be the first child in the family. And first-born children are lucky. They are usually bigger than later-born children of the same age and adults are more likely to talk with them. They receive more warmth from their parents in the early years than their younger brothers and sisters do. Firstborns are usually models of their siblings and sometimes dominate them. However, parents dislike such domination and are likely to punish the first-born for it.[7] In any case firstborns are far more likely to be successful in later life than their siblings. This is not because they are more intelligent but because they are more likely to be oriented toward adults and adult-approved activities such as schoolwork.[8]

LEARNING LANGUAGE AND IDEALS

One of the family's most vital contributions to the child is help in learning to use language. The child who has more chances to talk with adults gets more intellectual stimulation than a child who spends more time talking with peers. Children brought up in orphanages and other institutions are more backward in their speech than in any other area.[9] It seems that even infants need the stimulation of adult speech. It is probably because they are around adults more often that firstborns and children from small families do better than other children, by and large.

Not only must the child learn speech in the family; he or she must also internalize the values of the wider group. **Internalization** means making those values part of one's personality so that they become one's own rules, not rules imposed by others. For ex-

100

Peter Menzel/Stock, Boston

Lucky kids. Children in small families have advantages over children in large families.

ample, a child who has internalized the norm forbidding theft will not ordinarily *consider* stealing. Internalization does not require any special attention by adults—it happens as a matter of course in the normal family setting. Many parents used to think they needed to provide moral teaching for their children, in Boy Scout meetings, Sunday school, or the like. However, research has shown that children who have been trained in such programs are no more honest than those who have not received this kind of training.[10] Parents who start teaching morality early and are strict with their children do not have greater success than other parents in teaching their children moral standards.

What does count then? Not moral lectures but close relationships. You and I learned our values by interacting with the people who were important to us. We noticed not just what they said but what they *did* in situations involving choices between different values. And our relatives, because they were dearer to us, probably had a greater influence on our lives than strangers and authorities such as clergyman and teachers.

Most of us have internalized our parents' values. They have become part of our personalities. Later in life we may react against them, try to overcome them, or even organize our life style around the goal of opposing them. Yet even then those parental values will always be there inside us, always significant, because of those early bonds of affection.

SOCIALIZATION IN SUBCULTURES

Socialization can be stressful, especially if the values that one learns differ from those of other people in the social environment. This situation is sometimes faced by children whose parents belong to unusual groups with special viewpoints or lifestyles, whether they are religious sects, immigrant communities, or people with unusual convictions, such as nudists, vegetarians, or communists in an ordinary Canadian town. When the demands of family and friends do not fit together, the child has to find some way of adjusting to the conflict. This may create a period of emotional stress.

Consider, for example, the Mennonite children of Waterloo County, Ontario. The Mennonites, like the Hutterites and Amish, are a religious sect that came to North America generations ago to escape from persecution. They hold to an old-fashioned way of rural life, though certain branches of their group have modernized somewhat. In Waterloo County, Mennonites have three branches: traditional, transitional, and progressive.

The traditional Mennonites refuse to use radios, telephones, cars, or electrical appliances. They are dedicated farmers and like to spend their money to buy more land so their children can be farmers too. They wear very plain clothes and drive horses and buggies. The second, transitional group has taken to driving cars with the chrome painted black, and they do use phones, tractors, and electricity. However, children past the age of fourteen are not allowed to go to school, because their ideas may become too modern. Finally, the progressive group has moved much further toward modernity. They behave much the way other Canadians elsewhere behave, using modern technology and sending their children to school as long as they want to go.

The children of these three Mennonite branches tend to adapt somewhat differently in their social relationships. Minako Kurokawa has studied 460 Mennonite children and their mothers.[11] She points out that parents who have conflicts in their own value systems are likely to be especially inconsistent in the treatment of their children. Presumably, the transitional Mennonite parents have more conflicts within their own values than either the progressive or the traditional Mennonites. And indeed, the study showed that this group of parents, who were in transition from old-fashioned to modern customs, were strict but inconsistent in disciplining their children. What effect did this have on their children?

Emotional disturbances can be obvious or hidden, that is, overt or covert. Overt problems are obvious; children behave aggressively, lie, throw temper tantrums, and get into trouble with police or neighbors. Children who hide their emotional problems do things like sucking their thumbs, soiling their pants, having nightmares, and getting particular illnesses. The children of progressive Mennonite parents had a considerable amount of freedom; when they experienced problems, they showed their emotional difficulties overtly by acting up. The children of the transitional group seemed more troubled than any other Mennonite youngsters, and their problems were covert; they had nervous and physical disorders but did not misbehave overtly. Children with covert disturbances tend to have more feelings of guilt and inadequacy than other children.

Nevertheless, it is important to realize that people who live through periods of stress are not necessarily worse off for it in the long run. Some of the greatest contributions to society have been made by people whose childhoods were troubled and who eventually came to terms with their lives in healthy ways. Most Mennonite children turn out all right, whatever branch is responsible for their socialization, whether their upbringing is stressful or easy.

Brantford Expositor

When a group's values differ from those of the society at large, its children have to make some difficult choices.

Socialization through the life cycle

Childhood is only the first stage of our socialization. Each new stage of life puts us into new situations, and at each new stage we take on new roles. And to perform any new role we must understand the skills it requires, as well as our expectations of others and theirs of us when we play that role. Educational institutions have been set up to provide the background knowledge that we need when we play our various roles. But important though they are, schools can do only so much to prepare us. We must learn the roles themselves through experience and by watching role models. Some of this learning we must do as we go along, but we try to do some of it in advance.

ANTICIPATORY SOCIALIZATION

We must have at least some understanding of a wide variety of roles, if only because we must interact with the butcher, the baker, the candlestick maker, and all the rest. But when there is a chance that we may play a particular role ourselves at some future time we usually try to learn a lot about it. This is called **anticipatory socialization**. We try out various roles in our imagination to see how they feel.

103

And we look for role models—people who are already playing the roles that we expect to play, or people whom we admire. Role models are particularly important to young people, who often develop an intense curiosity about some famous person whom they would like to resemble. (For me it was Ingrid Bergman; I used to practice a Swedish accent in private.) Adults are not as given to hero worship as youths, but they too sometimes feel a need for anticipatory socialization. Thus a woman who is planning her first Caribbean cruise may read etiquette books and travel magazines so that she can appear sophisticated while playing her new role.

SOCIALIZATION IN ADULTHOOD

One obvious difference between childhood and adulthood is the fact that adults usually have more chances to choose what roles they will play and to arrange for their own socialization. This can be a heavy responsibility when one is preparing for a difficult role, such as that of physician. In one study, Blanche Geer and Howard Becker found that medical students took their training very seriously and were upset when they found that no matter how hard or how long they studied they couldn't possibly learn everything that they might someday need to know. And nobody could possibly tell them with any certainty what they should study thoroughly and what they could skip or go over lightly. Their uncertainty made for painful anxiety, and one way in which they coped with this anxiety was by forming close relationships with their classmates. By checking their guesses against those of other students, they collectively developed some idea of the subjects they should study most thoroughly. Sometimes their standards conflicted with those of their professors, but they protected themselves from feeling guilty or inadequate by developing these informal standards and trying to live up to them.[12]

A lot of adult socialization cannot be done in advance but has to be done on the job. You simply feel your way through new situations, paying attention to how other people react, and hope for the best. Consider parenthood, for example. No matter how well you try to prepare for it, you still have to improvise to meet unexpected situations. Indeed, it makes almost as much sense to say that the baby socializes the father into his role as a parent as it does to say that the father socializes the baby. Certainly infants keep their parents informed about how they are feeling and parents take that information seriously.

At each stage of the life cycle we look ahead and vaguely plan for the next stage. We can hardly imagine the stages that are far in the future, and sometimes we even forget how far we have already come. Most societies have ceremonies that mark the transition from one stage to another. These are called *rites of passage*. They include such events as christenings, confirmations, Bar Mitzvahs, weddings, retirement banquets, farewell parties, and funerals. In many primitive societies, young boys have to undergo painful initiation rites similar to (or worse than) the "hazings" that new fraternity members sometimes have to go through in North American colleges. These rites remind us of the passing of time so that we will update our self-image to match the society's views about what we can appropriately do or expect others to do. We may forget to update our self-image unless we are prodded by others, for we do not feel any different than we did thirty years before. Only our bodies seem to keep changing. In her study of aging, Simone de Beauvoir mentions what any middle-aged person has experienced—the shock one feels when one passes a mirror unexpectedly, the surprise or even denial that one's body actually is the way it appears to be. One might say, "Oh well, it's only a bad day. Tomorrow I will look like myself again." But not so. And eventually, at some point during middle age, we stop measuring our lives in terms of how many years have gone by since we were born and begin counting the years we probably have left.

Thus people must be socialized, whether they are willing or not, for the roles that they must play in the middle and later stages of their lives. Women shopping together may ask each other, "Do you think I'm too old to wear a two-piece swimsuit?" Men playing golf may compare notes on buying a retirement condominium in Florida. This is socialization too, no less so than the doll play of little girls.

Your first ceremonial celebration may have been a christening or a birth. Every community has some way of symbolically welcoming its members.

Ann Hagen Griffiths/DPI

RESOCIALIZATION

Not all adult socialization experiences are pleasant. Certain organizations exist for the purpose of **resocializing** an adult whose previous socialization was inadequate. Prisons are the best example of such organizations. They are not very successful, however, in that many of their "graduates" continue to behave in ways that the society disapproves of.

Erving Goffman has studied organizations whose purpose is resocialization. He calls these places total institutions because the person who is being resocialized must spend almost all of his or her time in them. They include the army, prisons, mental hospitals, convents, and boarding schools—all places where batches of recruits are herded from one activity to another according to a fixed schedule. The whole institution is designed to teach a person new roles, skills, or values. The resocialization process aims for uniformity, not individuality: new recruits often are not allowed to see their friends or relatives for several weeks after entering the institution. Their heads may be shaved; they may be dressed in ugly uniforms and made to do degrading jobs such as cleaning toilets. Only after they have shown that they are ready to conform to the demands of the organization are they gradually given full status as members. As a reward they receive an "identity kit"—the clothing, cosmetics, equipment, and services that one needs if one is going to put together the kind of personal identity and appearance that one wants to show to others.[13]

Three views of socialization

In our study of socialization theories, we will discuss three writers who studied human nature and the process of becoming civilized. They are Emile Durkheim, Jean Piaget, and Sigmund Freud.

DURKHEIM ON MORAL AUTHORITY

Durkheim's view is the one that has most influenced sociologists' ideas about socialization. Unfortunately, however, Durkheim's understanding of psychological processes was probably his weakest point. As we will see, his discussion of social learning leaves much to be desired.

For many years, Durkheim was a professor of both sociology and education, but today the teaching methods he recommended are seen as old-fashioned, rigid, and repressive. He believed that moral education was the teacher's main responsibility, and moral education (or socialization) meant impressing society's norms upon the young person in such a way that they became part of his or her personality. The educator's dominant characteristic is moral authority.

Just as the priest is the interpreter of his god, the teacher is the interpreter of the great moral ideas of his time and of his country. Let him be attached to these ideas, let him feel all their grandeur, and the authority which is in them, and of which he is aware, cannot fail to be communicated to his person and to everything that emanates from him. ... It is this respect which, through word and gesture, passes from him to the child.[14]

Durkheim viewed the child as a blank sheet of paper on which society writes. His advice to the teacher seems a bit heavy-handed to present-day educators. He compared the process of education to hypnosis, in that

(1) The child is naturally in a state of passivity quite comparable to that in which the hypnotic subject is found artificially placed. His mind yet contains only a small number of conceptions able to fight against those which are suggested to him; his will is still rudimentary. Therefore he is very suggestible. For the same reason, he is very susceptible to the force of example, very much inclined to imitation. (2) The ascendancy that the teacher naturally has over his pupil, because of the superiority of his experience and of his culture, will naturally give to his influence the efficacious force that he needs.[15]

For the sake of this high goal, Durkheim believed, the teacher must have a compelling will and must be consistent. "For authority implies confidence, and the child cannot have confidence in anyone whom he sees hesitating, shifting, going back on his decisions."[16]

PIAGET ON MORAL REASONING

The Swiss psychologist Jean Piaget has contributed more than any other social scientist to our understanding of the development of children's thinking. Piaget opposed Durkheim's view of socialization in his best-known book, *The Moral Judgment of the Child.*[17] He agreed with Durkheim that morality is a product of social experience, but he disagreed with Durkheim's view of how it all comes about. To demonstrate his own point of view, Piaget conducted research that consisted mostly of asking Swiss children to teach him how to play marbles. The goal was to get the children to explain the rules of the game to him so that he could find out how they reasoned about such matters as fair play. He found that younger and older children usually have quite different ideas about rules.

The young children had a viewpoint that Piaget called **moral realism**. They believed that rules either had existed forever or had been laid down by God or some other authority figure. When Piaget asked the children whether it would still be a fair game of marbles if they agreed to change one of the rules, the child of 5 or 6 would usually say no. The authority of the rules was never questioned. Even so, the young child did not fully understand the rules and broke them all the time.

Young children also insisted on obeying the letter of the law, not the spirit of the law. Good behavior consisted of following rules exactly, whatever the situation. For example, Piaget asked children to judge which child was more naughty, a child who stole a ribbon to wear or a child who stole a roll worth twice as much to give to a hungry friend. Young children were far more likely than older ones to say that the theft of the roll was more serious because it cost more. Young moral realists have many of the attitudes that Durkheim believed were desirable. In particular, they have boundless respect for the authority of adults. In fact the child assumes that whatever decision an adult makes must be just and proper. This attitude Piaget called *unilateral respect* because the child does not expect the adult to have equal respect for him or her. The judgments of adults are not questioned.

By the age of 8 or 9 a child is usually beginning to develop a more sophisticated form of reasoning about rules and obligations, an attitude that Piaget called the **morality of**

cooperation. By perhaps 10 or 12, most children are able to reason in this way. A child develops this ability through experiences such as the settling of disputes in games of marbles to the satisfaction of all players. Rules at this stage are rational, produced by argument, rather than fixed, absolute principles. In their games, children at this age are, indeed, more interested in disputes and complicated rule changes than in the physical skills needed to play the game. They actually follow the rules more closely than ever now that they see them as agreements among themselves. Moreover, they tend to be milder in punishing those who break the rules. They choose forms of punishment that are designed to show offenders how they have hurt others or caused them to withdraw their trust. Their responses, then, are designed to restore unity to the group, not just as punishment for its

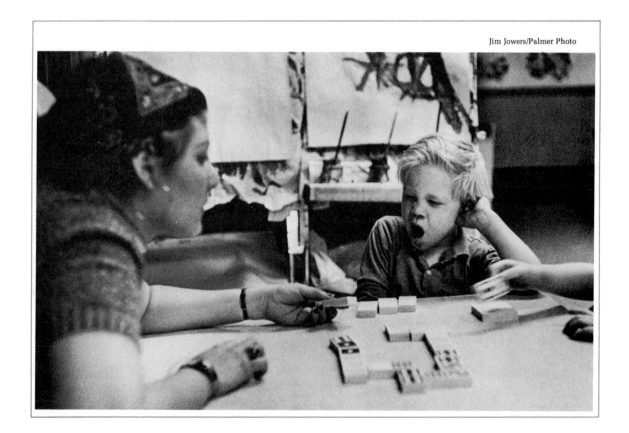
Jim Jowers/Palmer Photo

own sake. This is concern for the spirit of law, for reciprocity and equality. Piaget believes that it develops out of *mutual* as opposed to *unilateral* respect.

It is on this point that he specifically disagrees with Durkheim. Durkheim's advice smacks of moral realism. The child is expected to be hypnotically compelled by the strong will of the teacher, who is to show in word and deed such a firm commitment to the society's rules that the child could not think of disobeying them. Piaget says that this situation is, unfortunately, rather common. Young children are overwhelmingly impressed by their teachers and would never learn to reason on their own about moral matters through this unilateral relationship. It is on the playground or in other dealings with their peers, who respect one another as equals, that children learn to arrive at satisfactory rules on their own.

However, evidence does not entirely support the claim that peer group socialization produces more ethical children than authoritative teaching by adults. Not all peer groups are alike, and the ones that are most effective are probably indirectly guided by adults.

FREUD ON REPRESSION

Though they favor very different ways of teaching children moral values, Piaget and Durkheim agree on one important point: Neither views the socialization process as stressful. Neither sees the child's nature as resisting society's demands. Piaget describes the child's mental skills as developing smoothly and naturally as the child is socialized through a process that can be more play than work. Durkheim believes that adult authority is necessary, but not necessarily unpleasant or coercive. After all, a blank piece of paper does not resist the pencil.

But to Freud, the child was not a blank page at all. And Freud, the father of psychoanalysis, has left his mark on modern sociology as well as all the other social sciences. It is to him that we owe the idea of repression—the view that certain impulses within the personality can be restrained (repressed) only with great effort.

The psychoanalyst's view of personality has sometimes been jokingly called a "hydraulic model" in that it sees each person as containing a fixed quantity of emotional energy. This energy can be channeled from one aspect of the personality to another, but when one tries to suppress it, it is only displaced, like water in a closed system of pipes. Such repression causes harmful changes in other aspects of the personality.

Freud was interested in the origins of this supply of energy and in how it is channeled. He concluded that its sources are the impulse to love, and the impulse to be aggressive and destructive. As he saw it, civilization opposes direct expression of both of these impulses. In *Civilization and Its Discontents*,[18] he wrote that people cannot ever expect to attain happiness. Civilization brings material well-being, security, justice, and social order, but only at the cost of requiring us to restrain our impulses at every turn. Beauty, cleanliness, and order all require self-restraint.

It is easy to understand why civilization requires the repression of aggressive impulses, but it may not be so obvious that the love impulse and civilization are in conflict. Freud pointed out, however, that two lovers feel wholly fulfilled when they are able to express their love to one another directly. They do not need the rest of society. But civilization requires that the lovers give other people some of their attention and affection. Thus society makes claims on one's emotional energy that interfere with the expression of love. The individual is asked to inhibit love by channeling some of his or her feelings into "brotherly love," or friendliness and good will toward other members of the society.

Sublimation

Society also requires creative, expressive work—art, gardening, scientific research, and the like. Such work uses energy that is channeled away from sexual concerns and into more refined, civilized concerns through a process that Freud called sublimation. Freud believed that sublimation was the most desirable response to society's claims on the individual. Still, he recognized that the pleasure of creating art, solving scientific problems, or gardening is mild "as compared with that derived from the sating of crude and primary instinctual impulses; it does not convulse our physical being."[19] Not everybody could get through life comfortably by sublimating basic impulses. Each person must develop his or her own way of coping, depending on the strength of his or her particular set of needs. Some people will cope by emphasizing emotional relationships with others. Some will get their satisfaction mainly from their own mental processes. Others, needing action, will continue to challenge society by sublimating as little as possible.[20]

Freud was the most pessimistic of the writers we have discussed. To him, socialization was a process by which people are taught to give up their greatest pleasures for the sake of the group. Freud did not expect this situation to improve. On the contrary, civilization can progress only through ever greater repression and sublimation. It is ironic that Freud is so often misunderstood on this point. It is commonly believed that psychoanalysis offers happiness by encouraging people to act impulsively, to follow their feelings. Actually, Freud never expected much happiness either for himself or for his patients, because the requirements of society would not be changed by psychoanalysis. All the psychoanalyst can do is help the patient use rational judgments about reality in trying to achieve happiness. Freud thought that most of his patients were unnecessarily miserable because they were *overly* repressed. Their guilt feelings overwhelmed them and kept them from seeking even pleasures that might have been perfectly all right.

Surplus repression

Though Freud was by no means opposed to socialism, he did not believe it would increase human happiness. In *Civilization and Its Discontents*, he presented his opinion of Marxism. Marx had claimed that most human misery was caused by the fact that there are not enough material goods to go around, so that people need to work. This situation is made worse by exploitation of the working classes by the idle ruling classes. Marx believed that over time the workers would unite and rebel against the ruling class, and that this would make it possible for all to share equally in a life of abundance, leisure, and pleasure.

Freud believed that such a revolution would not really make much difference. He claimed that human unhappiness is caused not by the lack of material goods but by the repression by people of their basic impulses. It seemed to Freud that upper-class people, who had more material goods, were more repressed and unhappy than working-class people. (We now know that he was wrong on this point. People with money generally say they are happier than poor people.)

A modern writer, Herbert Marcuse, also entered this dispute. Marcuse, who was both a Freudian and a Marxist, simply took a middle position. He agreed with Freud that a lot of repression will always be necessary even in a classless society. However, he agreed with Marx that exploitation is the cause of a great deal of repression.[21] Some repression is the price that people must pay if they are going to live together in a civilized way, he argued. But we repress more than we need to, and it makes us unhappier than we need to be. This situation Marcuse called surplus repression, and he thought that it resulted from the domination of one class by another. We work harder than we need to work in order to produce more than we need, and we wastefully consume things that we don't need and that don't make us happy. We suppress joy and sexual pleasure. Surplus repression can be overcome by political and social liberation, but basic repression cannot be overcome entirely.

Marcuse's main point seems reasonable: Probably some repression is avoidable (at least in principle) and some is unavoidable.

But I question whether his political proposals are the best way to eliminate surplus repression. He would have liked a communist revolution. Personally, however, I doubt that people experience less surplus repression in present day socialist societies than in capitalist societies. In actual practice, the socialist state can be as coercive as a group of stockholders, if not more so.

I have mentioned several points of view concerning the way in which an individual becomes a part of civilized society. All of these views are familiar to large numbers of people in Western society. Durkheim's position prob-

ably comes closest to that of most sociologists, for it assumes that society's goals are stamped on the child's character without any resistance from the child. Piaget's view is a more developmental one. He sees commitment to society's values as a mental skill that develops much like any other mental ability. Neither Piaget nor Durkheim view socialization as stressful, however, for they do not believe that the individual has any desire to resist social influence. Freud, by contrast, views socialization as highly stressful, for each individual is forced to act contrary to his or her biological needs.

SOCIAL RESEARCH:
Sociologists at Work

THE SOCIALIZATION OF WOMEN FOR SEXUALITY

So far, we have portrayed the process of socialization as almost a passive experience. I want to counter that impression, however, by discussing some research that points out how people actively select and shape their own values, and worry about the choices they must make. Consider, for example, how views of sexual behavior change over time. Norms are relaxing a bit in Western societies about the kinds of sexual activity that young women may properly experience, but we are still far from a moral code that tells girls that "anything goes." Nevertheless, about 70 percent of today's young Canadian women disregard what they learned about sexual morality when they were children and engage in some premarital sex. How do they change their views and make the transition from virgins to sexually experienced women? Do they usually feel much guilt about their behavior? If so, how do they manage these feelings? To answer these questions, Sherryl Kleinman conducted several in-depth, open-ended, three-hour interviews with nine Montreal college women, aged 19 to 23. She then described the typical "moral career" that they, and

presumably many other young women, have experienced.[22]

By "moral career", Kleinman means the regular sequence of changes undergone by a woman as she alters the framework by which she judges the behavior of herself and others. To some extent, a woman who engages in premarital sexual activity has decided to become "deviant", to violate the conventional moral code. This decision usually involves her in considerable doubt, conflict, and ambivalence. Kleinman claims that this pattern develops according to the following stages: (1) commitment to virginity; (2) tension between remaining a virgin and desiring to gain experience; (3) definition of a situation as appropriate to losing one's virginity; (4) commitment to premarital sex; (5) disillusionment with the sex-with-love perspective and acceptance of sex for pleasure; (6) a return to sex for love.

1 *Commitment to virginity.* All nine of the women in the sample had once been committed to maintaining their virginity until marriage, and three were still virgins. Even these three women, however, were no longer committed to the *idea* of remaining virgins until their weddings. Through her discussions with all nine women, Kleinman concluded that Ira Reiss was correct in describing the typical path of sexual development as involving: ". . . initial feelings of guilt at the first kiss and then a reduction in guilt as kissing behavior (continues) through time. Then movement into a more advanced form of sexual intimacy such as breast or genital petting, and then guilt reactions

which in turn are eliminated by repeated behavior, and so on until one either gets married or reaches the maximum level of permissiveness."[23]

2 *Tension between remaining a virgin and desiring to gain sexual experience*. During their teens, girls come to realize that many of their friends are engaging in premarital sex, and indeed they often imagine that such activities are far more common than is actually the case. They may come to think they are a bit "backward" if they are still virgins, and may even imagine that other people can tell at a glance that they are sexually inexperienced and naive. Virginity can become, in a way, as embarrassing a condition as being regarded as sexually "loose." Thus, one respondent told the interviewer:

R. . . . now I say, 'Oh, God, I'm so old.' It makes me nervous just to think about the subject.

I. What do you mean?

R. It's really the embarrassment of virginity at this age. I think that it's come to the point that if I were in a situation where it could come to that (intercourse), I'd be embarrassed enough about my virginity to retain it.

I. When did you first feel this way?

R. Somewhere between the ages of 18 and 19. I

just thought that one should lose one's virginity by then. It's a little funny. I sometimes feel that I'm the oldest virgin in Montreal.

I. How old are you?

R. Twenty-one-and-a-half.

3 *Definition of the situation as appropriate to losing virginity*. At this phase, young women are generally ambivalent; they are ready to engage in premarital sex, but not able to justify their actions in terms of the values they have held all their lives. They need some rationale to justify proceeding with the sexual relationship. Love is the perfect justification. A young woman may not like to ask herself, "Am I the sort of girl who will engage in premarital intercourse?" However, she can rephrase the question so it becomes much more acceptable to her: "Am I the kind of person who will be intimate with the man I love?"

4 *Commitment to premarital sex*. The young woman who has come to accept her behavior as a genuine expression of love for her partner may still have to worry about the reactions of other people. She may remember a time when she judged other girls as immoral for the very activities she now enjoys, so she may be somewhat reluctant to discuss her sexual re-

Norms that govern women's sexuality have changed a great deal in the past 70 years.

OISE/Women's Library

lationship. Over time, however, there is a shift toward the acceptance of herself as a sexually active woman, and she develops a commitment to her own actions. At this point, the woman may feel comfortable enough to let a few close friends know of her involvement in a love affair that includes sexual intimacy.

5 *Disillusionment with sex for love and pursuit of sex for pleasure.* Love does not always endure in sexual relationships. Though a woman can no longer describe her feelings as love, she may still experience sexual pleasure with her partner. This discovery may cause her to lose her commitment to the idea that sex is right and proper only if it is accompanied by love.

A woman is most likely to lose confidence in her respectability when she doubts her boyfriend's love for her. If she loses her virginity in a relationship lacking mutual love, she is likely to judge herself harshly and view her sexual activity as disreputable. She may go on to regain a respectable self-image by challenging the view that love is a necessary requirement for sexual intercourse. If so, she may accept the idea that "sex for pleasure" is respectable and needs no other justification. She may also begin to act on this point of view by entering sexual relationships with men whom she does not love. In general, however, she does not pursue these encounters with any commitment, and after a time she is likely to settle down to a relationship with one man.

6 *Return to sex with love.* When such a woman commits herself to another serious love relationship, she must find a way to justify her recent promiscuity. She has probably returned to her belief that only sex with love is satisfactory, and she needs to find some way to see her past as acceptable. Usually, this woman will claim that her promiscuity was "really" a search for a loving relationship, rather than sexual pleasure. In the long run, women seldom consider casual sex to be a viable alternative to sex with love.

Kleinman's study uses a symbolic interactionist approach; she describes sexual behavior from the point of view of the person or "actor" who is engaged in that behavior. Like other symbolic interactionist studies, this one reveals how human beings participate in their own socialization. The nine young Montreal women were not passively accepting obvious social rules when they decided to lose their virginity. On the contrary, they were struggling to maintain their self-images and establish their own principles, and it was not easy to interpret the social rules that applied to them. (It was not even clear to them whether virginity was something to protect or overcome!) This attempt to provide an inner view of a human situation is typical of symbolic interactionist research. We will discuss the approach further in Chapter 6. For now, however, I want to describe another topic of research that also examines the ambivalence that women commonly experience in Canada and other western societies.

ACHIEVEMENT AND FEMININITY

In the past thirty years, one of the most popular topics in social psychology has been "achievement motivation." J.W. Atkinson and David McClelland developed a test to determine whether or not individuals had a strong "need for achievement"—which was abbreviated as *n ach*.[24] A person with high *n ach* was one who was highly motivated to accomplish great things, and to master difficult challenges. It has been discovered that high achievement motivation is a major common characteristic of successful businessmen, especially businessmen who have used initiative and taken financial risks to build their own companies. A person with *n ach* does not normally want a routine job in a company that is already well-organized: he gets more thrill from the challenge of building a company from nothing against all the odds.

Sociologists are interested by the fact that achievement motivation is apparently a *male* trait. When social psychologists first tried to test female subjects for *n ach*, they were puzzled; the scores of the females were not correlated with any of the variables that seemed to accompany achievement motivation in males. The researchers concentrated on studying males and decided that women were simply not ambitious.

Then along came the women's movement. In a very short period of time, people became extremely interested in explaining why women have been discouraged from undertaking ambitious projects. According to many contemporary sociologists, ambition in women has been virtually impossible in a society that demands they take subordinate roles. The typically low *n-ach* of women has probably been a way of adjusting to this situation. In the past this adjustment may have been fairly satisfying for most women, but the declining birthrate has caused many women to find their traditional role unfulfilling. However, their low *n-ach* often prevents them from pursuing important careers. Most current research is aimed toward discovering the factors that make girls less interested in achievement than boys.

Childhood socialization experiences clearly form the basis of girls' motivations. It is also clear that expectations learned in childhood reduce women's levels of performance and ambition.

Matina Horner, a Harvard psychologist, has demonstrated this fact. She claims that most women *fear* success.

The assumption underlying Horner's research was that most women have powerful affiliative motivations that conflict with their achievement motivations.[25] According to Horner, because women learn throughout life that they may be considered "unfeminine" if they perform well (especially in competition against males), they acquire a need to avoid achievement. Horner assumed that talented women who have high *n-ach* are the very ones who are most troubled by this problem, so they experience internal conflict and ambivalence. Her reasoning makes sense: Most women deeply desire a close relationship with a man, but some men feel uncomfortable with ambitious women. Women who are not highly talented will probably be accepted the way they are. However, a woman who has a realistic chance of success may think twice before starting out toward her goal—especially if it means competing against men.

Horner's experiment showed that this is actu-ally the case. She gave tests similar to those used by McClelland to test for *n-ach*, but she scored them for avoidance of success. For example, she asked female subjects to complete a story that began, "After first-term finals, Anne finds herself at the top of her medical-school class." For male subjects the lead was, "After first-term finals, John finds himself at the top of his medical-school class." At first the subjects were mostly undergraduate students at a large midwestern university. The motive to avoid success was considered to be present if the subject made up a story showing conflict about success, anticipation of negative results of success, denial of responsibility for attaining success, denial of the lead statement itself, or some other inappropriate or bizarre response.

Of the 88 male subjects, fewer than 10 percent responded negatively to the cue in any way. Most of them showed confidence in John's future and a belief that this success would lead to other important goals, such as providing a good home for a wife and family.

On the other hand, of the 90 female subjects 65

Ontario Science Centre

percent were troubled by the lead statement. Most showed that they regarded Anne's success as bad news showing loss of femininity, social rejection, or some other problem:

There was a typical story, for example, in which Anne deliberately lowers her academic standing in the next terms and does all she subtly can to help Carl, whose grades come up. She soon drops out of med school, they marry, and Carl goes on in school while she raises their family.

Some girls stressed that Anne is unhappy, aggressive, unmarried, or that she is so ambitious that she uses her family, husband, and friends as tools in the advancement of her career. Others argued that Anne is a code name for a non-existent person created by a group of med students who take turns taking exams and writing papers for Anne.[26]

Horner found that people who have a high fear of success learn how to disguise their ability and drop out of the competition. To illustrate this pattern, she cites a *Peanuts* cartoon in which Sally says, "I never said I wanted to *be* someone. All I want to do when I grow up is to be a good wife and mother. So ... why should I have to go to kindergarten?"[27]

Repression of ambition is costly in psychological terms. It leads to feelings of frustration, hostility, aggression, and bitterness. For example, when asked to complete a story beginning, "Anne is sitting in a chair with a smile on her face," more than 90 percent of the women who had little fear of success produced happy stories, usually about pleasant social relationships such as dates and forthcoming marriages. Those who scored high on fear of success responded quite differently, however. Fewer than 20 percent of them completed stories in this way. Here are some of their responses:

"She is sitting in a chair smiling smugly because she has just achieved great satisfaction from the fact that she hurt somebody's feelings."

"Gun in hand she is waiting for her stepmother to return home."

"Anne is at her father's funeral. There are over 200 people there. She knows it is unseemly to smile but cannot help it. ... Her brother Ralph pokes her in fury but she is uncontrollable. ... Anne rises dramatically and leaves the room, stopping first to pluck a carnation from the blanket of flowers on the coffin.[28]

Not all women suffer from fear of success. Some override this feeling and continue their careers. Most of the fortunate female subjects have ongoing relationships with boys who have encouraged them, usually because they both recognize that the boy is the more intelligent of the two: "He's so much smarter ... competition with him would be hopeless." The greatest tension occurs between couples in which the girl is more intelligent.

During their later college years girls often find that their parents' attitudes suddenly reverse. Formerly they delighted in their daughters' achievements; now they become concerned about the girls' femininity and marriageability. They begin to suggest that the daughter stop studying so hard and find a husband instead. Is this a major cause of women's fear of failure? Apparently not. Research to date suggests that on this matter women are influenced less by their parents' attitudes than by the attitudes of their male peers.

In Chapter 2, I pointed out that after a sociological study has been completed and reported other scholars may conduct additional research that produces contrary evidence. This is one of those cases. A great many studies have followed Horner's and seem to be as likely to contradict her findings as to support them.[29] We are not yet able to conclude that women either do or do not have a tendency to avoid success. I find this issue very interesting, however, and am eager for someone to resolve what seem to be contradictory results.

SOCIAL POLICY:
Issues and Viewpoints

We cannot talk about socialization today without mentioning the women's movement's demand for changes in sex roles.

These topics are linked in several important ways. First, if we are interested in public policy, we must ask how children are affected by the increasing tendency of mothers to work outside the home. And if we are interested in the socialization of young children, we must recognize that a new pattern of sex roles is developing that may be quite different from the traditional one. We must then ask ourselves what expectations are appropriate and fair in view both of our biological needs as males and females, and the challenges of our new social structure. What expectations lead to unnecessary tension and unhappiness? Here we can touch only briefly on a few of the issues that are getting a lot of attention today.

CHILD CARE FOR WORKING MOTHERS

Imagine that you are a well-educated Canadian woman living in a suburban home with your husband and a 6-month-old baby. You have an important decision to make: Will you take a job?

It is nothing new for women to work. Even in primitive societies, women contribute as much to the household economy as men do, on the average. But they usually work in special settings with other women and with their children. They garden together, clean fish together, beat their laundry on the rocks together, and look after the children at the same time. Cross-cultural studies of mothers around the world point out how much more isolated North American women are than women in other societies. Your household is private, with its own kitchen, laundry room, car, TV, and so on. You don't even go to the village well, where you might talk with other women. You feel bored, lonely, and dependent on your husband. If you need money, you will go to work. If you don't, you may not. But the choice will not be easy, for there are costs to pay in either case. You will not want your baby to be the one who must pay those costs. Thus your personal decision, as well as the public decision on whether to provide day care services, should take into consideration the normal feelings of infants. And babies definitely tell you how they feel. John Bowlby, who has studied the mother-infant bond more than any other scholar, comments: "No form of behavior is accompanied by stronger feeling than is attachment behavior. The figures toward whom it is directed are loved and their advent is greeted with great joy. ... A threat of loss creates anxiety and actual loss sorrow; both, moreover, are likely to arouse anger."[30]

By about the sixth month of life the baby ordinarily becomes strongly attached to his or her mother and shows signs of distress when left with a stranger. Throughout the early years children are concerned mainly with their relations with members of their family; only later do they become interested in other children. Researchers who study young children are trying to find out whether various child care arrangements have any permanent effects on children's emotional development. Some psychologists[31] who believed five years ago that day care hurts children's development no longer believe this. Current research by Jerome Kagan suggests that the behavior of children who experience first-rate day care over a long period is no different from that of children brought up at home by their mothers. But "first-rate" day care is unusual. Kagan chose warm caregivers, trained them himself, and made sure that they each looked after only a few babies. Most day care institutions expect each caregiver to look after a number of children. This, plus the fact that the child may have a series of caregivers, means that day care may not usually provide the sort of social environment in which a child's attachments are respected. As some researchers have noted,

The great tragedy of hastily conceived and inadequately funded all-day programs may well be in the creation of deficiencies that might not normally occur.

Our concern for the immediate welfare of the child leads us to believe that his distress signals are important messages to which environments must respond, whether in the form of policy decisions, planning concerns, or caregiving behaviors. Although we do not know the long term consequences of separation or deprivation we do know that they can produce acute immediate distress. We maintain that these grounds alone are sufficient for the serious attention of researchers and practitioners alike.[32]

About half of all working mothers in North America leave their children in the care of relatives. This is, in fact, the most commonly preferred arrangement for very young children, probably because the children have more secure, permanent, and loving relationships with these caregivers and show less separation distress with them than they show when they are left in day nurseries. Parents of somewhat older children prefer day care arrangements to home care.[33]

My own view is that the best policy would be the one that gives mothers the greatest opportunity to make their own choices. After all, mothers know their infants' needs better than anybody else and usually care more about them than anybody else. Unfortunately, public policies do not always allow much room for choice. For example, day care institutions are sometimes set up on the basis of the belief that all welfare mothers should go to work whether or not they think their children would be happy in the day nursery. I think poor mothers should have the same right to respect their children's feelings that other parents have.

I believe women should be able to choose among several alternatives. Without implying that mothers should or should not take jobs, we might find other ways of decreasing the isolation and economic dependency of mothers who choose to stay home. Some people are saying, for example, that homemaking should be a paid job. I don't know whether this idea is practical or not, but I suggest that in judging this and other ideas the welfare of children should always be a major factor.

SUMMARY

1. *Socialization* is the process by which people acquire the motivation, knowledge, language, skills, roles, values, and norms that enable them to function as members of a particular group. This process works by channeling biological needs into more specific patterns of behavior that fit together with the behavior patterns of other members of the social system.

2. Early socialization usually takes place in the family, and researchers have found that the structure of the family has an important influence on the results. For example, children in large families and later-born children get less attention from their parents than children in small families and firstborn children. As a result the achievement, language development, and general adjustment are less satisfactory in the latter than in the former. Children form close ties with their parents, and their emotional well-being depends on this closeness. But this does not mean that children cannot be separated from their mothers for certain periods.

3. Children who are subject to influence by adults with very incompatible ideals and values usually experience much emotional stress. The children of subcultural groups are an example of this.

4. The controversy about the effects of day care centers should be viewed in the light of the evidence suggesting that collective child care can be more beneficial than unsupervised peer group experiences. However, separation from parents is known to be traumatic for a child who is not ready for it.

5. Learning to live in society is largely a matter of learning at least a little about a number of different roles. Often this involves *anticipatory socialization*—learning possible roles in advance.

6. Unlike children, adults can choose the kinds of socialization to which they are exposed. Sometimes, however, they may be forced into experiences that are designed to *resocialize* them. *Total institutions* have this as their main purpose.

7. Durkheim viewed socialization as a situation in which society teaches its ideas to the child through the authority of adults—for example, teachers. He did not see the child's readiness to learn as an issue requiring any attention. On the other hand, Piaget views socialization primarily as a process in which the child learns through exploration and interaction, especially with peers. Normal cooperative play, not heavy-handed instruction by adults, provides the setting in which moral values are acquired.

8. Freud's view of socialization, unlike that of Durkheim or Piaget, assumed that there are forces within each person that resist the socialization process. Love impulses and aggressive impulses are both strong, but both must be *repressed* for the sake of social order and the benefits of civilization. *Sublimation* is the process of channeling these impulses into creative activities. Marcuse, influenced both by Marx and by Freud, concluded that some repression is necessary but that some is not. This *surplus repression* could be decreased by eliminating economic exploitation.

KEY TERMS

anticipatory socialization trying out a role in advance because one may play that role at some time in the future.

institution a complex structure of roles organized around a central activity or social need.

internalization the process by which one makes the society's values part of one's personality.

moral realism the view that rules were laid down by God or some other authority figure and cannot be changed.

morality of cooperation the view that rules and obligations are rational agreements rather than fixed principles.

repression the effort to restrain certain impulses within the personality.

resocialization the process by which an adult whose previous socialization was inadequate is made to behave in ways that the society approves of.

role the part each person must play to create a collective activity.

role conflict the situation in which a person occupies two roles that are regulated by incompatible norms.

socialization the process of learning the rules of behavior for a given social group.

sublimation the process by which energy is channeled away from sexual or aggressive concerns and into more refined concerns.

surplus repression repression in excess of what is necessary for people to live together in a civilized way.

FOR FURTHER READING

ARCHIBALD, W. PETER. *Social Psychology as Political Economy.* Toronto: McGraw-Hill Ryerson, 1978. This is a sophisticated discussion of theoretical problems concerning the relationship of personal psychological orientations to the social context of political and economic reality. It is particularly relevant to the Canadian scene, but not exclusively so.

ARIES, PHILIPPE. *Centuries of Childhood.* New York: Knopf, 1962. Aries is a Frenchman, an amateur historian, whose research into the way children were treated in Europe in earlier periods used some imaginative research strategies. Fascinating.

BRIM, ORVILLE G. and STANTON WHEELER. *Socialization After Childhood.* New York: John Wiley, 1966. Most research on socialization looks only at childhood. Brim's special field is adult socialization, and whenever you see his name you can link it to that topic.

ENTWISLE, DORIS R. and ALEC HAYDUK. *Too Great Expectations: The Academic Outlook of Young Children.* Baltimore: Johns Hopkins University Press, 1977. This is a useful discussion of the "self-fulfilling prophecy" as applied to the achievement of children in school. The general theory behind it is called "expectation-states theory."

GOFFMAN, ERVING. *Asylums: Essays on the Situation of Mental Patients and Other Inmates.* New York: Doubleday, 1961. This is the book in which Goffman develops his concept of the total institution. He worked in a mental hospital and watched how patients coped with being confined.

ISHWAREN, K. *Childhood and Adolescence in Canada.* Toronto: McGraw-Hill Ryerson, 1979. A collection of readings about the socialization of youth, with a strong focus on the upbringing of children in ethnic families.

PAMMETT, J. H. and M. S. WHITTINGTON. *Foundations of Political Culture: Political Socialization in Canada.* Toronto: Macmillan of Canada, 1976. Political socialization means, of course, the learning that people must undergo before they can participate in the political life of a social group.

PIKE, R. M. and E. ZUREIK, eds. *Socialization and Values in Canadian Society, Vol. II., Socialization, Social Stratification and Ethnicity.* Toronto: Macmillan of Canada, 1975. You may already know a great many ways in which the socialization experiences that take place in Canada (and elsewhere too) differ from one social level to another, and from one ethnic community to another. This book treats that subject in detail.

5

SEX ROLES

Sex: the biological facts
   Prenatal factors
   Hormones
Gender
   Sex and gender identity
   Gender roles
Sources of sex role differentiation
   Sex roles and socialization
   Origins of sex role differences
Gender roles in Canada
   Gender and status
   Gender and housework
   Gender and jobs
   Women in higher education
Feminism
   Social Research: Sociologists at Work
   Social Policy: Issues and Viewpoints

Imagine that this morning when you awoke you made an amazing discovery: During the night you changed your sex! You became, in every physical way, a member of the opposite sex—your genitals, your muscles, your whiskers, everything! Nothing else changed. If you were twenty pounds overweight yesterday, you still are. If you knew how to play the saxophone yesterday, you still do. You are the same old self, only now your sex is different. Naturally you phone your doctor, who is surprised enough to make a house call and who confirms what you have discovered.

Now, pull yourself together and decide what to do about this situation. How do you feel about it? Is it your childhood dream come true or your worst nightmare? Will you have surgery to change back to your old sex or will you accept yourself as you are? In any case you will have to act differently in public, whether temporarily or permanently. Suppose you throw yourself into the experience and imagine what it would be like.

How will you dress, walk, and move? Will your gestures be expansive and energetic? Will you do many things that require strength and endurance? Will you change your own flat tires? Will being twenty pounds overweight handicap you socially and in finding jobs? Will you knit in public? Will you play your saxophone or switch to a violin?

How about showing your feelings? Will you express anger more readily? Will you cry easily? Will it be easy to say no to other people's requests in a straightforward way? Will you hint a lot or will you say what you want outright? If you have always been a bit of a clown will you have to change your act? How important will it be for you to be warm, sympathetic, and sensitive to other people? How competitive will you be in games, in work, and in bargaining for a used car? How will you behave when you are hurt? When you meet a person who attracts you sexually, will you feel free to express this fact? If so, how?

How about your interests? Will you read the sports and business pages? Will you form strong opinions about public affairs? Will you try hard to gain recognition for your work? Will you change your major in college? Will jobs open up or close for you? Will you take a job as a nursery school teacher? As an engineer? When you are on a committee, will you offer to take the minutes and brew the coffee or will you expect to chair the meeting?

Now compare the person you have just created—the self you would be if you were of the opposite sex—with the "ideal mate" whom you have always hoped to find. How do these two personalities differ? You may find that they are very far apart. Do you expect your ideal guy or girlfriend to live up to standards that you would hate to live up to yourself? Perhaps you have always wanted a gentle, quiet girlfriend who likes to cook and has no particular desire for career achievement—and perhaps you find that you would hate to be such a person yourself. Or maybe you have always wanted a competitive, responsible, assertive leader for a boyfriend, but you see that you wouldn't like the pressure of keeping up such an act yourself.

The point of this exercise is that both men and women are people—that they are all partly soft and partly hard, partly ambitious and partly dependent, partly competitive and partly sympathetic and tender. Sex roles are the source of much pleasure, for through them we find our place in the world. But sex roles can also be too harsh and rigid, limiting people in the expression of many human traits and needs. It is unkind to expect any person to be ambitious and strong all the time. It is unkind to expect any person to be tender and compliant all the time. Today we seem to be taking a new look at the claims we make on each other—at what we demand of a "real man" or a "real woman." Perhaps out of this effort will come the chance for people of both sexes to be, above all, "real human beings." Having a male or female body does not automatically make one masculine or feminine in one's social relationships.

Sex is the biological fact of being male or female. The first words you heard after coming into this world may have been those that announced your sex: "It's a girl!" or "It's a boy!"

Gender, on the other hand, is a social-psychological fact—the *awareness* of being a member of one sex or the other. Gender has two aspects, gender identity and gender role. **Gender identity** (often used interchangeably with *sexual identity*) refers to whether one considers oneself a male or a female. Ordinarily, of course, if your sex is male your gender identity will also be male. However, this is not always true, for it takes a child a couple of years to learn his or her gender identity. Moreover, there are certain unusual cases in which a male has a female gender identity or vice versa. We'll discuss these situations later.

Gender role (which for our purposes can be used interchangeably with *sex role*) consists of the culturally defined set of behaviors that are considered sex-appropriate within a given society. Gender roles, like all other roles, are specific to particular social groups. Thus in Canada it is considered appropriate for men to carry heavy loads, while in most societies gender roles specify that women should do so. A man may ride along on a donkey, followed by his wife on foot carrying a load of firewood.

The culture defines what things are appropriate for a male or a female to do, based on the assumption that some behaviors fit better than others with certain biological facts about the two sexes. In reality, those biological "facts" may only be generally accepted beliefs. For example, our idea that it is more appropriate for males than for females to carry heavy loads is part of our definition of the male gender role, based on the "fact" that men are naturally stronger than women. This fact seems obvious to us, but it is not so obvious to all social groups everywhere.

It is true, of course, that there are certain natural, biological differences between males and females, but this does not mean that one particular division of labor between males and females is more natural than all other

Vivienne/DPI

She certainly seems to know her gender identity.

possible divisions of labor. Thus, though gender roles in Canada say that it is appropriate for women to knit and for men to change flat tires, this is not because men and women are "naturally" good at these activities. Gender roles are not natural—they are cultural. That is, they are determined not by biology but by social agreement. *Sex* is natural; *gender* is social. This does not mean, of course, that gender roles can defy the laws of nature. We cannot have norms that require human beings to flap their arms and fly, nor can we have gender roles that require males to give birth. But Mother (or Father?) Nature has nothing conclusive to say about who should knit and who should change tires or carry heavy loads. Because people are often ethnocentric, they may think their customs are natural and appropriate when in fact they are simply social agreements that could easily be changed.

What, then, are the biological facts that cannot be changed?

Sex: the biological facts

We can usually tell men from women at a glance: They differ in their typical patterns of size, body weight, and hairiness, as well as in ways that are usually covered up by clothing—the genitals and breasts. (Of course there is much overlap in these traits. Many normal women have flatter chests than many normal men. Many normal men have less body hair than many normal women, and so on.) Men can usually defeat women in a physical fight, which may be one reason why males have almost always dominated women socially. In other ways, especially physical endurance, women's strength compares favorably with men's—which may be why women often carry heavy loads in other societies.

Gender roles cannot violate these physical facts. This is why, for example, the division of labor in almost all societies has assigned child care to women. Their biological traits are thought to be very suitable for this activity. We will come back to this point later. Now, however, let's consider two biological facts about the sexes—prenatal and hormonal differences.

PRENATAL FACTORS

Each of us began when a sperm crashed into an ovum, adding its 23 chromosomes to the ovum's 23 and thus creating a new cell with 46, or 23 pairs of, chromosomes. Each chromosome is a long string with hundreds of genes strung along it like beads. The genes carry a precise pattern of the physical traits of the person who will be born.

One pair of chromosomes determines the baby's sex. The ovum always contributes an X chromosome, but the sperm may contribute an X or a Y. If it is an X, the baby will be female; if it is a Y, the baby will be male. Most conceptions are XY combinations—possibly as many as 140 for every 100 XX conceptions. However, miscarriages are more numerous for XY conceptions, so that by birth the ratio is about 105 males to every 100 females. After birth, as well as before, males are more likely to be affected by disease and pain than females. As a result, by the time they reach old age, women almost everywhere outnumber men by a wide margin.

During the first six weeks after conception, male and female embryos form the tiny beginnings of identical sex organs. After the sixth week, however, the Y chromosome somehow signals these organs to develop testicles and start producing various (mostly male) hormones. If they don't receive this message, the organs will become ovaries. The amounts of various hormones in the embryo's system determine how the genitals develop from this point on. Inside the womb are female hormones from the mother, which will produce a female infant unless they are counteracted at critical times by the addition of male hormones produced by the embryo's testicles. If those male hormones are added to the mix, however, male genitals will develop, as shown in Figure 5.1. (If such hormones are artificially injected into a female embryo, it will develop male sex organs.)

Every embryo has a small organ that will enlarge to become the penis or will remain a small but highly sensitive female organ, the clitoris. In later years, the woman's orgasms will depend on the stimulation of her clitoris either through manual stroking or through friction by a penis during intercourse. Likewise, every adult male has an organ that would have become the female womb if the testicles had not produced male hormones at the right moment in his prenatal life. However, most men do not notice this organ until old age, when it may cause prostate enlargement.

FIGURE 5.1

External genital differentiation in the human fetus

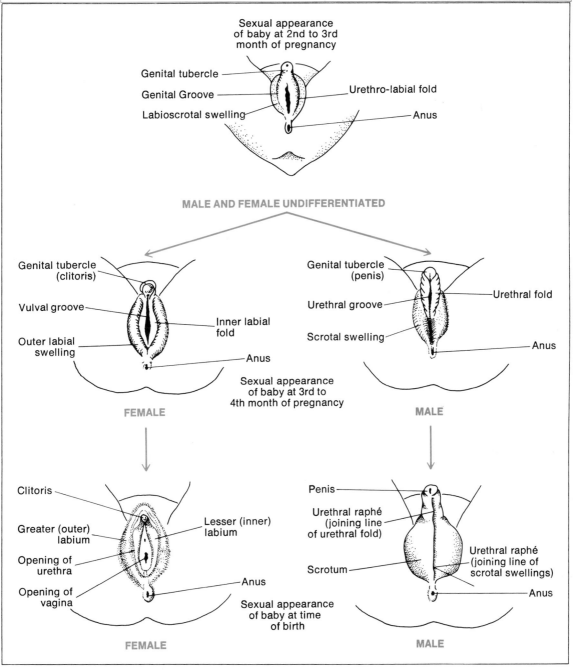

Source: Money, Hampson, and Hampson. *Bulletin of The Johns Hopkins Hospital,* 1955.

HORMONES

Hormones are "chemical messengers" produced by various glands. They circulate in the bloodstream and regulate many bodily processes. We have already mentioned the importance of female and male hormones in the prenatal molding of sex organs. Scientists have begun to discover how our feelings and behavior are influenced by these substances.

It is somewhat misleading to refer to "male" and "female" hormones, although these are common terms. In reality there are a great many different hormones that regulate all sorts of bodily processes, not just sexual ones. Moreover, both sexes produce both male and female hormones, though in different proportions. It has been found that an animal of either sex that is injected with male hormones will be sexier and more aggressive than usual. Many other abnormal behavior and growth patterns have been shown to result from prenatal hormone imbalances in animals, and some such effects may be important in human beings as well. For example, girls whose mothers took certain hormones during pregnancy may have a greater tendency toward tomboyish behavior than most other girls.[1]

The relationship between hormones and social behavior is one of mutual interaction. The hormones affect feelings and experiences, but social experiences and ideas, in turn, affect the body's output of hormones. To be sure, these biological factors do cause social and psychological experiences—but the reverse is also true. Research has not yet gone very far in linking personality to hormonal imbalance, and although this is a field that is well worth exploring further, we can hardly expect it to explain very much about gender roles.

Gender

Both gender identity and gender role are socially learned. I feel sure that I am a woman. That is my gender identity. I may also cook, care for children, arrange flowers, be devoted to a man, be sentimental and sensitive, and so on. That is the gender role of women in my society. The two things are not the same. Today many women refuse to perform many parts of the female role, though they have no doubt about their identity as women. Once acquired, gender identity almost never changes. But gender roles may change, since they are nothing more than social agreements.

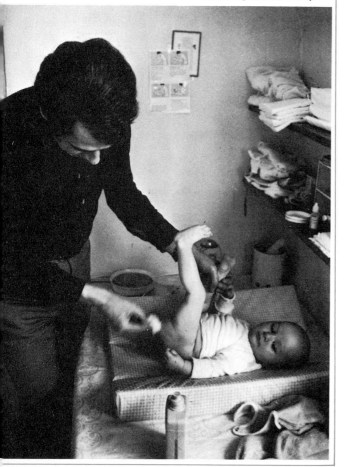

Do infants sense in the way they are handled whether their fathers and mothers are glad or disappointed in the sex of their child?

Thomas Hopker/Woodfin Camp

SEX AND GENDER IDENTITY

Sex is a fact. Gender identity is a belief. People usually learn their gender identities at about the age of 2. But it is possible for them to learn the wrong gender identity, and once it has been learned it cannot be changed. Hence, there are certain unusual cases in which sex and gender identity do not match. For example, transvestites' gender identities differ from their sex. They feel that they were accidentally born into the wrong kind of body and that they should dress and behave according to their identity, not their sex. They may expect their friends to pretend that they are the sex they feel they should be. Transsexuals have gone even further: Their sex has been changed through surgery and hormone treatment. Such medical procedures are uncommon, of course, but they are becoming less so. Doctors insist that a patient undergo a psychiatric examination before they will consent to do such an operation, and very few transsexuals regret the operation.

Once in a while a baby is born with genitals that are not quite normal, so that it is assigned to the wrong sex. Looking at the child's chromosome pattern under a microscope will reveal its true sex, but this may not be done until he or she is older. Then the doctor and parents have to decide what to do about the mistake. This decision depends mostly on whether the child is old enough to have learned the wrong gender identity. Children under 2 may not have learned their identity yet, so the parents can simply "reannounce" the child's sex by telling friends that they were mistaken, and the child will grow up with the right gender identity. Children who are 3 or 4 have probably learned their gender identity. If a child has learned the wrong one, the doctor may change his or her sex through surgery because it is easier to do this than to change gender identity, even if the identity is mistaken. In some cases children of

5 or 6 have not learned a clear gender identity because their sex was uncertain and their parents have not known what to tell them. Such children are miserably unhappy until the confusion is cleared up. The doctor may ask them to decide which sex they want to be, and this can sometimes be arranged with medical treatment.

GENDER ROLES

Culturally shared understandings about what forms of behavior suit members of the two sexes differ widely. Margaret Mead's study of sex roles in New Guinea, done between 1931 and 1933, shows how great these differences can be.[2] Within a radius of 100 miles Mead found three tribes that had very different definitions of gender roles. The first tribe, the Arapesh, were a gentle people who believed that males and females are much alike. Members of both sexes were passive, warm, and noncompetitive. They were equally likely to initiate sexual relations and equally responsible for the care of children. The Arapesh verb meaning "to bear a child" was applied as much to fathers as to mothers, for the parental role was as important to men as to women.

Not far away lived the second tribe, the Mundugumor, whose standards emphasized competitiveness and independence for both sexes. They were a violent, cannibalistic people. Members of both sexes were expected to be aggressive in their sexual encounters and equally jealous and vengeful. The women lacked any of the traits that we consider feminine. They disliked pregnancy and breast feeding and were not tender toward children, particularly their daughters.

The third tribe, the Tchambuli, defined male and female roles very differently, but their definitions were exactly opposite from ours. Tchambuli men were given the job of shopping and trading. They were nurturant toward children and they liked to gossip, play the flute, and spend a lot of time each day choosing clothes and jewelry to wear. Their wives, on the other hand, were domineering, practical, and uninterested in clothes or jewelry. They were the main economic providers for the family.

Mead concluded from her study that culture can define gender roles in endless ways. Other scholars agree, but we know today that not all possibilities are equally likely. When we compare gender roles around the world we find that the tribes Mead studied were all somewhat unusual. The most common pattern among known societies is one of **patriarchy**—male dominance over women and children. Indeed, equality between the sexes is unusual. Even when it exists, it is limited to certain areas of life, such as the running of the household or (sometimes) work situations. Although the Tchambuli women were strong and assertive, they were not matriarchs. In fact no true **matriarchy** has ever been found— that is, no society in which the women hold political power and dominate the men. Many societies have existed in which kinship is traced through the female line rather than the male line, but even in those societies men usually dominate.

Some of the most important aspects of gender roles are the norms for the division of labor between the sexes. There is no worldwide agreement as to which jobs are best for males and which are best for females; each society has its own rules. The most common pattern is for women to be assigned tasks that they can do near home or while caring for children. However, women do some sort of work in every society and often contribute as much or more to the family's economic needs as the men do. (See Table 5.1 for a summary of the division of labor by gender in various societies.)

Scholars do not agree on the reasons for the prevalence of patriarchy in human societies. Some believe that it is so common because women must, for at least part of their lives, depend on men for economic support.

Karl Marx and Friedrich Engels believed that the sexes would become socially equal as soon as women became economically self-sufficient and no longer had to care for children at home.

Not everyone agrees with this view, however. Another important explanation is based on the fact that men and women are not equally able to coerce each other when sexuality becomes a contest. We like to think of sexual intercourse as "lovemaking," but it is sometimes more a matter of physical combat than love. And in such a combat women are the losers. Men can rape women, but women cannot rape men. Moreover, men can forcibly impregnate women, thereby making them vulnerable and dependent for a longer time. Therefore the unique advantage that enables men to dominate is not their greater economic productivity so much as their power to make women into "sexual property." Knowing their own weakness, women rarely challenge men in physical confrontations but make use of psychological manipulation instead.[3]

It is not necessary to choose between these two explanations of patriarchy. Probably both are true. Thus people who are trying to create equality between the sexes usually work on both factors. They try to gain economic independence for women by opening up more jobs for them. And they also try to protect women against sexual exploitation by providing child care services, birth control information, abortion referral, and self-defense training (e.g., karate courses).

Some societies have gone further than others in creating such conditions, but in no society has patriarchy been entirely overcome. The Scandinavian nations, especially Sweden, have equalized social opportunities for the sexes to a great extent by providing many more social services at public expense than formerly. The Soviet Union has been officially committed to equalizing sex roles since the revolution. Partly because of the heavy loss of soldiers in World War II, Rus-

TABLE 5.1

The division of labor by sex: a cross-cultural comparison

NUMBER OF SOCIETIES IN WHICH ACTIVITY IS PERFORMED BY:

ACTIVITY	MEN ALWAYS	MEN USUALLY	EITHER SEX EQUALLY	WOMEN USUALLY	WOMEN ALWAYS
Pursuing sea mammals	34	1	0	0	0
Hunting	166	13	0	0	0
Trapping small animals	128	13	4	1	2
Herding	38	4	4	0	5
Fishing	98	34	19	3	4
Clearing land for agriculture	73	22	17	5	13
Dairy operations	17	4	3	1	13
Preparing and planting soil	31	23	33	20	37
Erecting and dismantling shelter	14	2	5	6	22
Tending fowl and small animals	21	4	8	1	39
Tending and harvesting crops	10	15	35	39	44
Gathering shellfish	9	4	8	7	35
Making and tending fires	18	6	25	22	62
Bearing burdens	12	6	35	20	57
Preparing drinks and narcotics	20	1	13	8	57
Gathering fruits, berries, nuts	12	3	15	13	63
Gathering fuel	22	1	10	19	89
Preserving meat and fish	8	2	10	14	74
Gathering herbs, roots, seeds	8	1	11	7	74
Cooking	5	1	9	28	158
Carry water	7	0	5	7	119
Grinding grain	2	4	5	13	114

Source: Adapted from George P. Murdock, "Comparative Data on the Division of Labor by Sex," *Social Forces* 15 (May, 1935), pp. 551–553. Copyright © The University of North Carolina Press.

sian women have been employed in a variety of jobs—ranging from construction worker to cosmonaut—that are usually held by men in the West. However, women's employment has not always brought equality; often it has simply added to their household work, which men are unwilling to share. Furthermore, it has not led to female dominance. For example, although most Russian physicians are women, their status is lower than that of doctors in the West. Physicians who are in higher positions—specialists, researchers,

and the like—are usually men. Thus patriarchy is perhaps weaker in the USSR than in the West, but it is not absent.

One of the original goals of the *kibbutzim*, or agricultural communes, of Israel was to create equality between the sexes. Men and women were expected to work together at similar tasks, and many management positions rotated so that everyone had a turn. By minimizing specialization, the communes have produced more equality than is common elsewhere. However, in recent years sex role differentiation has increased on the kibbutzim. Women do most of the kitchen jobs and schoolteaching, for example, while men drive the tractors and pick the oranges, just as in other societies. Still, gender roles are more equal on the kibbutzim than almost anywhere else.

In the light of all the evidence, we must conclude that gender roles are remarkably persistent social agreements. The societies that have tried hardest to erase the distinctions between masculine and feminine behavior patterns seem to have failed, or at least not to have succeeded. I am not proposing that we give up trying. I am suggesting, however, that the processes through which gender roles are passed from one generation to another have yet to be fully explained. We are not yet sure just how little girls learn to be feminine and little boys learn to be masculine. Even less do we know why adults hold so strongly to their ideas of what is appropriate for men and women to do. Gender roles are behavior patterns about which people have very strong feelings. What is the basis for such feelings? What are the psychological components of sex role differentiation?

Sources of sex role differentiation

In recent years social scientists have increased their efforts to find out how and why gender roles are so sharply defined. Some researchers have concentrated on explaining early childhood socialization for masculinity. Others have concentrated on finding out whether certain biological factors make male gender roles more natural to the male sex and female gender roles more natural to the female sex. I want to describe some of the explanations that have been proposed in both areas. First we'll discuss the work of Eleanor Maccoby and Carol Nagy Jacklin[4] on sex role socialization. Then I will point out

some of the biological facts that have been emphasized by Alice Rossi.

SEX ROLES AND SOCIALIZATION

Maccoby and Jacklin have undertaken the most complete review to date of all known research on early childhood socialization for gender. In their survey of research on behavioral differences between the sexes, they began by making three lists: (1) unsupported beliefs about sex differences, (2) sex differences that are supported by evidence, and (3) "open questions"—differences for which there is not yet conclusive evidence. I will present the first two lists but not the final one.

Let's begin with the unsupported beliefs. The first was most surprising to me, for I had always assumed that it was true: Girls are more "social" than boys. Research has shown that this is not the case. Boys like the company of others as much as girls do, are as motivated as girls to gain social rewards, and appear to be as sensitive to the emotional reactions of others as girls are. They are more oriented toward peer groups and tend to form large groups. Girls, on the other hand, "associate in pairs or small groups of age mates, and may be somewhat more oriented toward adults, although the evidence of this is weak."

Other beliefs that are not supported by evidence include the notion that girls are more "suggestible" than boys and are less "analytic" in their thinking than boys. Both of these assumptions have been disproved. Also, there is a false belief that girls are better at simple, repetitive tasks while boys are better when the task involves more complex reasoning. Actually, neither sex is superior at either type of task.

Maccoby and Jacklin argue against the idea that girls are more affected by heredity and boys are more affected by environment. In reality, boys and girls are equally likely to resemble their parents and equally able to learn in a wide variety of situations. Nor are

Are males more aggressive than females, or are males taught to be more aggressive? Some adult gave these children their guns. Who? And Why?

girls more sensitive to auditory stimuli and boys more sensitive to visual ones, as some people once believed. The fact is that they are equally sensitive to both kinds of stimuli.

Here is another mistaken notion: Girls have lower self-esteem than boys. Actually, males and females are equally self-confident and self-satisfied throughout childhood, adolescence, and (as far as we know) adulthood. However, girls tend to pride themselves more on their social poise while boys more often value their strength and dominance. During the college years women do have a greater tendency than men to see themselves as vic-

tims of fate rather than as able to control their own lives and to perform well. This may be because females are not expected to take the initiative in courtship while males are, so that women actually do have less control over their fate in that period. After the courtship years, women regain confidence in their ability to control their own lives.

Finally, there is a mistaken notion that little girls are not motivated to achieve. In fact, during childhood, girls' desire to achieve is generally at least as high or possibly higher than boys'. The difference is that boys are more influenced by competitive situations

129

than girls are. When boys are stimulated to compete, their interest in achievement shows a marked increase and surpasses that of girls. Girls' achievement needs are not as strongly affected by competitive situations. This research on early childhood achievement motivation should be compared with Matina Horner's research on college-age women, discussed in Chapter 4.

Let's take a look at the sex differences that Maccoby and Jacklin believe are fairly well supported by evidence. Surprisingly, they list only four:

1 True: *Girls tend to have greater verbal ability than boys.* Verbal skills are about equal until age 11, when girls begin to surpass boys. Female superiority in this area increases throughout high school and possibly later.
2 True: *Boys tend to have greater visual-spatial ability.* Males' superiority in these tasks begins in adolescence and continues throughout adulthood.
3 True: *Boys tend to have superior mathematical ability.* This superiority also begins to appear in adolescence and cannot be explained by the number of math courses taken.
4 True: *Males tend to be more aggressive.* This has been found to be true in all societies that have been studied so far. Even at age 2, most boys' play is noticeably rougher and more aggressive than that of most girls, and this continues to be the case at least through the college years, if not beyond. Males usually choose other males, not females, as their victims.

ORIGINS OF SEX ROLE DIFFERENCES

Having determined the basic facts about differences between the sexes, Maccoby and Jacklin turned to the more complex problem of finding out where those differences come from. They paid close attention to the many studies that compared the ways parents treat males and females in the very early years of childhood. We know the differences in degree of aggressiveness show up in the first two years of life, and shortly thereafter other differences, such as the preference of boys for trucks and of girls for dolls, may be seen. Children identify themselves as male or female quite early—even before they know that sex is permanent—and they have definite ideas about what males and females do. Maccoby and Jacklin conclude that these differences in identity and behavior cannot be due to the way children are treated. What they find surprising is that most mothers really do not treat little girls and little boys very differently. Certainly the greater aggressiveness of boys cannot be explained by parental encouragement. Parents dislike aggressiveness in both sexes; if anything, they discourage it in their sons more than in their daughters. They worry that boys may carry it too far.

Do biological factors account for some of the differences between the sexes? Maccoby and Jacklin point out that a sex-linked recessive gene has been shown to be at least part of the basis for the ability to do visual-spatial work. About 50 percent of all males have this gene and about 25 percent of all females have it. Other abilities may be genetically linked to sex, but this has not yet been determined. Maccoby and Jacklin conclude that it is probably easier for members of one sex to learn some things and easier for members of the other sex to learn other things. This suggests that special help is needed to make males and females equally able to perform in most areas of work—if society decides to pursue this goal.

Macoby and Jacklin do not mean to imply that all sex role differences are biologically determined. They simply point out the drawbacks of two of the theories that have been proposed to explain the process of learning sex roles: reinforcement theory and modeling theory. The idea behind reinforcement theory is that adults cause sex role differences by rewarding small children for behavior that they feel is appropriate for their sex and discouraging them from "inappropriate" behavior. But most parents don't seem to do this to any great extent—at least not enough to explain the early and definite sex differences that normally appear.

The role model theory is not satisfactory either. According to this theory, boys imitate their fathers' behavior and girls imitate that of their mothers. But they don't actually seem to do this. They seem to choose role models more at random. According to Maccoby and Jocklin, their behavior is clearly sex-typed *before* they choose same-sex role models. Besides, boys still usually prefer to play with toy trucks rather than dolls even when they see their mothers driving the family car more often than they see their fathers driving.

A better explanation of sex role differences goes like this: Society vaguely realizes that there are biological differences between males and females that make certain activities easier for members of one sex and other activities easier for members of the other sex. We develop a division of responsibilities that fits our ideas about these biological differences. These expectations then become stereotypes—exaggerated images that children learn and try to live up to. Thus a learning situation is built onto a biological tendency. The learned roles exaggerate whatever small differences may have been inherited. Children develop their own ideas of what they are supposed to do, ideas that are based on evidence from many sources. Thus one little girl insisted that men could be doctors and women could only be nurses, even though her own mother was a doctor!

Some social scientists and a great many biologists have become more interested lately in finding out just how important biological differences are in leading people toward distinctly different sex roles. The feminist sociologist Alice Rossi has made an effort to tell sociologists about biological findings that we have tended to overlook because of our strong interest in social variables.[5] Thus Rossi believes that many more of the differences between males and females can be traced to biology than we realized in the past. Not all the differences between sex roles result from

Toronto Star

Changing expectations of parents and community for their children may expose the extent to which socialization rather than biology has dictated sex roles.

socialization experiences. She points out many universal tendencies of women around the world, traits that seem not to be learned but to be more or less instinctive.

In particular, Rossi claims that the norm that assigns child rearing to the mother is based on the recognition in all societies that there is a special bond between a mother and

131

her child. While the male has a biologically based attraction only to the female, the female is attached *both* to the male and to her offspring. In no society (nor in any primate species) do males specialize in child rearing. Indeed, females often seem unwilling to leave their babies in the care of males.

Rossi points to the existence of certain unlearned responses in mother-infant interaction. Thus infant crying stimulates secretion of the hormone oxytocin in the mother so that milk is "let down" for the baby before and during nursing. Mothers, whether they are left- or right-handed, almost always cradle their babies in their left arm, where the baby can hear the mother's familiar, soothing heartbeat. Mothers approach their newborn infants for the first time with a common set of gestures and expressions. Mothers of premature babies who are allowed to handle their babies briefly show more interest in them months later than mothers who are not allowed to touch them. Some researchers report that the amount of early mother-child contact is directly related to the closeness of the bond between mother and baby throughout the baby's first year. Separating the mother from the child at birth, even for part of the day, is dangerous both to their relationship and to the health and development of the baby.

Moreover, there is a biological link between the mother's experience with her baby and her sexual experience. Oxytocin, the hormone that lets down milk for the baby, is also related to sexual pleasure. Whether the nipples are sucked by a baby or by a lover, oxytocin is secreted, causing the uterus to contract. After lovemaking these contractions may help move the sperm up the uterus to the ovum. During labor they move the baby down the birth canal. During nursing they help restore the uterus to its prepregnancy condition. And each pregnancy and childbirth contributes to the woman's later sexual pleasure by increasing her ability to experience intense orgasms. Thus the various parts of a woman's biological system are interrelated so that her

sexual attachment to the male and her nurturant attachment to her baby reinforce each other.

The child too is strongly attached to his or her mother. Jerome Kagan notes that the biological parent has a

mysterious ability to remain the preferred target of attachment, even for young children who spend a considerable amount of time with substitute caretakers outside the home. ... There is something special about the mother-infant relationship. The parent appears to be more salient than the substitute caretakers to the child. It is not clear why this is so.[6]

These recent studies, then, strongly suggest that the activities that are typical of male and female roles are related to biological tendencies that we inherit as members of our species. Many of these tendencies may have had important functions in prehistoric times—they may have been necessary for the survival of the species. This does not prove that they are still necessary now. But it does suggest that it may not be possible to achieve a dramatically different pattern of sex roles by shifting our methods of socialization.

Gender roles in Canada

Many women in our society have been entering the labor force who in earlier times might have been full-time homemakers. By 1975 almost half of all North American women of working age were holding jobs.[7] Those women find themselves at a disadvantage compared to male workers and have called public attention to the inequalities between existing gender roles. Let's look at some of the differences between the typical life situations of men and women.

GENDER AND STATUS

Traditionally, the social ranking of females depended on their ties to men. In childhood a girl's status was determined by her father's position in society, as was a boy's status. But a boy was expected to begin finding his own level in society as soon as he grew up and became independent. This was not so for women. Adulthood for a woman did not mean independence or the chance to achieve her position in society through her own efforts. Instead, it generally meant marriage, which made her dependent on her husband instead of her father. From that point on, she would hold the same position on the social ladder as he did. Much of this system remains. A married woman's own achievements may be recognized and admired, but these may still carry less weight than those of her husband.

GENDER AND HOUSEWORK

Most women work because they need the money. However, married women who have careers have a double burden. A study of Vancouver couples analyzed the time budgets of various kinds of family.[8] It was found that women spent about 34 hours per week doing housework (including shopping and repairs) while men spent about 8 hours. Naturally, families with small children had much more housework than those with no children. However, the amount of time that men spent doing household tasks did not increase: The women did almost all of the additional work themselves. Furthermore, wives who had paid jobs continued to spend about as much time on housework as other women who had no paid jobs, mostly by catching up on weekends. Their husbands, on the other hand, did not spend more time on household jobs if their wives worked. Thus the extra burdens of a two-career family are borne more by women than by men.

GENDER AND JOBS

In the work setting, women are also disadvantaged. Certain jobs are thought to be appropriate for women and others are not. Women are still segregated into a narrow range of jobs. Indeed, a Canadian study done in 1975

Toronto Star

Will women become less feminine by taking "masculine" jobs? Or will society stop considering these jobs as masculine?

showed that there has been no decrease in the sex-typing of jobs during the past thirty years.[9] Women are still found in large numbers in such jobs as nursing, typing, and teaching. Moreover, they earn less social prestige than men do for exactly the same jobs. And, worst of all, they are paid less than men, even when they do the same jobs. The average income of paid women workers in Canada was less than half that of men in 1971.

WOMEN IN HIGHER EDUCATION

Women are less successful than men in climbing the occupational ladder. When they do succeed in getting and holding high-status jobs, it is generally because they have been outstanding in their academic performance. A 1975 study of Ontario university graduates showed that women must visibly demonstrate a higher degree of ability than men to succeed, even when there is a large demand for qualified workers.[10] That particular study

133

showed that only women who had exceptional marks in a field such as science, usually chosen by males, were taken seriously by employers and allowed to perform challenging work. But that study was based on data collected when the demand for university graduates in the work world was fairly high. Since then, this demand has dropped. This means that higher education today is probably more crucial to Canadian women who want successful careers than it was a few years ago. Women have to do more to prove their ability, and a graduate degree offers that proof. The choice of a "masculine" field of training offers further proof to employers who value "masculine" work higher than traditionally female occupations.

What is a "masculine" field of study? You can probably guess. Saul Feldman's study of graduate students showed that both sexes know which fields are considered feminine and which masculine.[11] Engineering is the most masculine field, and nursing and home economics are the most feminine. The percentage of women enrolled in a particular field of study is a perfect indication of how feminine the field is supposed to be. The fields which stimulate exciting scientific and intellectual discoveries, and which offer the most promise for successful careers, are precisely the fields

People who live in coeducational dorms may come to know each other well and work out new agreements about sex roles.

Susan Meiselas/Magnum

in which the fewest women enroll. Women tend to have a low opinion of their potential. When they do enter graduate study, they usually say that they hope to teach, not do research. Moreover, they plan to teach in high schools or community colleges, not at the university level.

Clearly, many university students assume that women cannot hope to do as well as men do. At what point in their lives do they reach this conclusion? It appears that they do so quite early. In a study carried out in 1969 for the Royal Commission on the Status of Women, young boys were more convinced than young girls that females ought to work in the home and males outside the home, and that males ought to have more power in families.[12] Girls tend to lose their confidence in women a little later in life.

A 1978 study of Ottawa high school students found that girls begin high school with better marks than boys and have no particular difficulty with "masculine" courses like science and mathematics. However, as they continue high school, girls generally lose their ambition and slack off in their studies; boys, on the other hand, tend to become more involved with school work and more interested in pursuing higher education. The researcher concluded that girls this age learn the feminine role that is suggested to them, even though adults are not aware of discouraging girls from excelling. Though unaware of it, teachers pay more attention to boys in class than to girls; this attention encourages boys to speak up and participate.[13]

Feminism

Many of the facts that I have presented in this chapter are widely known today, though ten or fifteen years ago they went unnoticed. The women's movement has been responsible for drawing the public's attention to the *sexism*, or extreme sex role discrimination, that still exists in Canadian society. The following is a description of the course that feminism has taken over the past century or so. I shall draw from the accounts of Jo Freeman,[14] Lynn McDonald,[15] Lorna Marsden, and Edward B. Harvey,[16] who have each presented reasons for changing views on sex roles in Europe, the United States, and Canada.

According to Jo Freeman,[17] the modern feminist movement is supported almost entirely by white middle-class women; these are women who, on the basis of their background and education, might reasonably expect to hold jobs at a professional or executive level. Working-class women and women of various minority groups have not generally been active in the feminism that has emerged since the mid-1960s. Why only middle-class women? To answer this question we must recall a few facts about the history of female emancipation and female participation in the work force.

The first feminist movement was led by the "suffragettes" in Europe and North America. These were women who devoted their energies to gaining the right to vote and to take part in political affairs. The suffragette movement began in several different countries around the turn of the century.

In Russia and Germany, the movement was linked to particular social classes and its leaders opposed any cross-class cooperation. There were separate socialist and bourgeois (propertied class) suffrage organizations, but no organization that represented the interests of both. In Germany, women gained the right to vote in 1918. Unfortunately, the Social Democrats of that day failed to keep their promises to women; as a result, many feminists joined extremely conservative German political parties, including the Nazis.

In Russia, on the other hand, the socialists succeeded in dominating the women's movement. Many socialist women successfully gained university training in such areas as medicine, and took part in politics. By 1912 these Russian women had considerable political influence. Russian women were involved in socialist terrorist movements since the 1870s. A woman led the assassination of the Czar and several women took part as skilled soldiers in the revolution. After the revolution, women gained opportunities unequalled in any other society of that time. The feminist leader was Alexandra Kollontai, a cabinet minister and diplomat in the communist regime. To this day, Soviet women have certain rights, particularly regarding occupations, that are not offered elsewhere. However, the deaths of so many men during the war created a shortage of husbands which men have used to their advantage. Women do a greater share of the family's housework in the USSR than in the West, even if they have jobs. They probably wield about the same amount of political influence as Western women.

In France, the suffrage movement never really got underway. Although the movement was split on the same class lines as in Germany and Russia, neither the socialists nor the bourgeoisie succeeded in building a strong mass organization to support women's rights. In fact, women's groups remained small, ineffectual, elitist organizations until very recently. Women did not receive the vote until finally de Gaulle gave it to them in 1945.

In the early days, the Canadian women's movement was most influenced by movements in Britain and the United States. A number of foreign representatives of women's suffrage groups came to Canada and spoke with great effect. Lady Aberdeen, the British wife of Canada's Governor General at the time, founded the National Council of Women in 1893. The British and Canadian movements were not divided by the hostility between the bourgeoisie and socialists that occurred in continental Europe. Even the daughter of Karl Marx, an ardent socialist who was brought up in England, acknowledged the value of the work that bourgeois feminists did in Britain. The Canadian leaders of the suffrage movement were largely of middle-class origin,

though some upper-middle-class women were also involved. The reforms that these women initiated, however, were geared to the needs of working women. The concerns of the National Council of Women went beyond simply attaining suffrage. Its main objective was to protect working class women and children. By 1898, for example, it had succeeded in the appointment of women factory inspectors to female workplaces in Quebec and Ontario.

The Toronto Women's Literary Club, formed by a woman physician, was one of the early organizations influential in women's rights. It brought together a number of people who were interested in improving the status of women. Its bland title disguised its radical intention: the appreciation of literature and music provided a "cover" for their meetings. In a short while, this organization founded the Toronto Women's Suffrage Society.

Another important early Canadian organization was the WCTU—the Women's Christian Temperance Union. This group had attempted since the 1870s to fight alcoholism among the working class. It supported suffrage for women in the belief that if women could vote they would change the liquor laws. Nellie McClung, a Manitoba woman, became a feminist leader as a result of her participation in the WCTU.

The right to vote was granted to women in many countries as a result of the political crises that occurred around World War I. Women gained the right to vote between 1916 and 1922 in every Canadian province except Quebec. Quebec women did not have the right to vote in provincial elections until 1940.

After they had won suffrage, women in most countries still remained largely uninterested in careers. Nor did they enter national politics in any major way. Most reform-minded women of the 1920s played rather traditional female roles; they confined their political activity to such issues as prohibition, eliminating child labor, and cleaning up the sweatshops.

With the Depression of the 1930s came

Take a guess about the people in this picture. How do they like what they are doing? How do they like what the others are doing? The answer you give shows the ideas and attitudes you have yourself.

high unemployment levels and a widespread attitude that the few jobs that existed ought to go to men, who were supposed to be the main breadwinners. The magazines portrayed working women in an unfavorable light, suggesting that only a callous, uncaring mother would willingly choose a job over the role of full-time homemaker. Not until World War II was this trend reversed. When the men went to war, it suddenly became acceptable for married women to work. Indeed, "Rosie the Riveter" was the mythical heroine of posters and songs throughout the war years. Even middle-aged women were hired. Many of them liked working and wanted to go on working after the war ended. But they were disappointed. With peace came the closing of child care centers and training programs. Still, many women continued to work in low-level, low-paid jobs; those who were married sought a little extra income to supplement their husbands' pay cheques, usually because they wanted to buy cars, appliances, and other expensive consumer items.

The number of working women did not return to pre-war levels, and their pay scales lagged badly. At the same time, the media campaigned to undermine women's aspirations outside the home. Ads featured gentle ladies in frilly aprons baking cakes. The traditional homemaker was again the only *real* woman, and working women were portrayed as tough, unfeminine, selfish, and unconcerned with their children's welfare. Ironically, just when child rearing began to take up a shorter portion of a woman's lifetime than ever before, women were told, for the first time in history, that motherhood should be their full-time occupation.[18]

Yet many women found it financially necessary to work. The outcome was that they took jobs but claimed that they didn't really *want* to work—they'd much rather be at home. Call it role conflict. Women were damned-if-

137

they-did-work and damned-if-they-didn't. Feeling guilty about working, they didn't protest about their low pay, their inferior jobs, or their lack of promotions. It was a no-win situation.

Well-educated women were the most likely to work. And as Freeman points out, "the median income of full-time working women with college degrees is still lower than that of male high school dropouts, and this relationship has shown little indication of changing over time."[19] Thus these working middle-class women are especially subject to *relative deprivation.* It's not that their incomes or living conditions are worse than those of working-class women. It is that they are in work situations in which they can reasonably compare themselves to the men they know whose education is no better than their own. Relative to *these men* they certainly are deprived. When they compare their own salaries and opportunities to those of their husbands and the men they knew in college, the difference seems extremely unfair. No wonder it is

these women who have become the new feminists of our day.

But why now? This situation is not new. Women have been underpaid since World War II. Yet throughout the 1950s they supported the traditional homemaker ideal instead of protesting about their frustrating situation. Freeman argues that the grounds for protest existed for about twenty years before the women's movement began. What explains the delay?

You can't have a social movement without a communication network that will mobilize people who feel that they have a complaint. And no such network existed for women for many years. True, there were women's organizations such as the Business and Professional Women's Club. But they had decided not to become a vehicle for protest and women who were frustrated in their careers could not "co-opt" them—that is, they could not take them over for their own purposes.

Knowingly or not, President Kennedy created the first organization that enabled

FIGURE 5.2

Percent of married working mothers in the U.S. in 1960 compared to 1975. Note that the percentage of women in the work force has increased, particularly for women who have also been raising children.

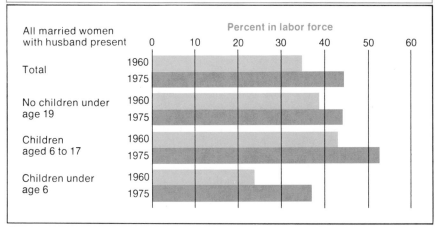

Source: Population Bulletin, *Marrying, Divorcing, and Living Together in the U.S. Today.* Population Reference Bureau Inc., Vol. 32, No. 5, October 1977. Adapted from Table #2, p. 11.

angry women to get in touch with each other and plan action. In 1961 he set up the President's Commission on the Status of Women. This organization, which was chaired by Eleanor Roosevelt, not only collected a great deal of evidence showing how women were denied important rights but also led to the establishment of fifty commissions to do similar work at the state level. Most of those commissions were made up of politically active women who were dedicated to improving the condition of women. Thus a nationwide American network devoted to the concerns of women came into existence.

Another major event happened in 1963. Betty Friedan published a highly readable best-seller, *The Feminine Mystique*, that led many women to see their own upbringing and acceptance of the traditional female role as ideological brainwashing. Some women who had previously blamed themselves for feeling unhappy with their situation now blamed the social system. The lady in the frilly apron was no longer seen as the model woman but as a chump.

In Canada, two communication networks emerged to support the rights of women. The first consisted of established women's organizations that cut across various socio-economic levels and political groupings. Among this network were found such groups as the IODE, the National Council of Women, the Fédération des Femmes de Québec, the Women's Institutes, and the Canadian Federation of University Women. This set of organizations brought renewed attention to social reforms affecting women's welfare.[20]

The second communication network consisted of relatively younger women who had been influenced by the civil rights movement in Canada and parallel movements in the United States and Europe. These women took up "consciousness-raising" activities to inspire one another. Many of the women in this network had participated in New Left organizations; they were usually radical university students, as compared to the older, mostly

middle-class women in the more established network.

The established groups of women were inclined to use the existing political system to attain their purposes. They formed an organization called the Committee for Equality of Women in Canada, which called for the creation of a Royal Commission on the Status of Women. Prime Minister Pearson authorized such a commission in 1967; that inquiry generated additional communication among

In the past decade, women have come to demand, instead of ask for, equal rights in Canadian society.

Jim Anderson/Woodfin Camp

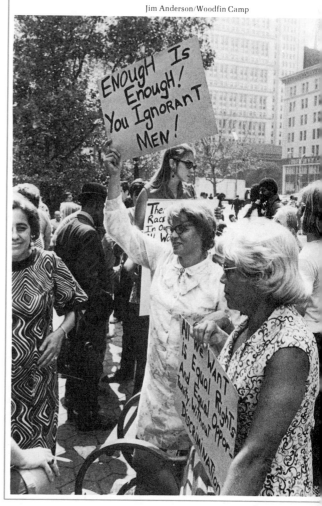

potential feminists. The report of its findings in 1970 led to a number of important legal reforms.

Since 1970, the most important women's organization in Canada has been the National Action Committee on the Status of Women. It includes many different women's groups and maintains a communication network that draws them all together. Its president, sociologist Lynn McDonald, has urged the development of a theoretical perspective that will help reduce the divisions among Canadian feminists. According to McDonald, the women's movement is primarily divided between those who stress economic issues and those more concerned with other issues, such as violence against women. McDonald claims that this division is unnecessary; the same woman who is raped on her way home from work is the one who faces discrimination and low pay on the job. All of these problems equally require urgent attention.

SOCIAL RESEARCH:
Sociologists at Work

SECRETARIES AND BOSSES

Rosabeth Moss Kanter's book, *Men and Women of the Corporation*,[21] describes the office life of one of America's largest companies, which she calls by the fictitious name Indsco. I think her best chapter is about secretaries and their bosses. Almost all secretaries are women, and their bosses are almost all men. Kanter has served as a consultant to businesses that are trying to create new, high-ranking job opportunities for women. She is able to tell us from first-hand experience why this is harder to do than she would like.

The most obvious fact about the relationship between an executive and his secretary is that it is personal, even within a huge bureaucratic organization. Secretarial work is not a set routine that follows an orderly plan. The boss may buzz his secretary every few minutes and ask for some personal service. There is no clear line between an official, legitimate request and an unofficial or even illegitimate one. Hence, a secretary may wind up (either resentfully or willingly) mailing back her employer's wife's mail-order shoes or dog sitting while he is on vacation. Bosses are free to set their own standards for judging their secretaries' performance.

The executives' behavior and office decoration is neutral and bland. The secretaries, by contrast, go in for big, funny posters and cartoons, celebrate birthdays, and show concern for the comfort and welfare of guests. A secretary becomes devoted to a particular boss, and when he rises in status he takes her with him and provides her with an office with drapes, a fancy ashtray, and steel file trays—though he doesn't necessarily give her a much better salary or more challenging work. She can stop worrying about improving her skills and concentrate on her relationship with the boss—for his status will determine hers. A secretary may be liked if her boss is liked and disliked if he is disliked. Much as a sultan used to "own" his personal servants, the boss sees his secretary as "my girl."

The secretary is expected to get her main symbolic and emotional rewards from this relationship, not from other business contacts. Indeed, she is expected to identify with his interests rather than resent his power or (perish the thought!) compete with him for promotion. After all, by working closely with him she learns his secrets and might use them as deadly weapons if they were to compete. Hence, bosses tend to insist that the career ladder of secretaries should be entirely separate from theirs. They usually choose as their secretaries women who have been socialized in ways that are thought appropriate—parochial or secretarial schooling that trains them not to see themselves as potential bosses and not to resent their low position in the company hierarchy. The boss can judge the secretary, but her opinion of him has no impact on his fate. If she showed any threat of being able to retaliate in the future, he would be uncomfortable about giving orders. Nowadays some companies are trying to reform by promoting secretaries to managerial jobs, but on the rare occasions when this happens the switch may be pure hell for the woman involved.

In short, tradition has idealized the secretary who is loyal and devoted to her boss and prefers symbolic rewards over career opportunities. The woman's "attitude" is considered more important than her ability, since most secretarial tasks are not difficult. Moreover, white-collar workers, especially women, can often be manipulated by means of prestige symbols.[22] Secretaries get praise, and they tend to become addicted to it. The constant flow of compliments and thanks is considered more important than money. Kanter even mentions cases in which a boss did not name his secretary for a higher-level job opening because he thought she might feel "rejected" at the suggestion that she move on. One secretary who was offered a promotion in another department reports that her boss said, "We love you. We want you to stay," but didn't

offer more pay. This woman seems to be an exception to the rule, for her thought was, "I get the love from my husband. I work for other reasons."

Most secretaries actually depend on the appreciation and warmth they receive. Kanter found the Indsco secretaries much more reluctant than other employees to enter jobs that would involve "both praise and criticism" or "having to show confidence." The secretaries, who were used to being praised for taking orders, did not want to stick their necks out or risk criticism.

Because their job security depends on their personal relationships, secretaries neither have nor want much power. Hence, to protect themselves they are likely to resort to gossip and emotional manipulation. This, in turn, reinforces the stereotype of women as unsuitable for executive positions that require an unsentimental, businesslike attitude.

Thus, the qualities for which a secretary is rewarded are the very ones that make her unsuitable for promotion in a bureaucratic organization. She

Not typical. Most secretaries would not carry this poster.

Elizabeth Hamlin/Stock, Boston

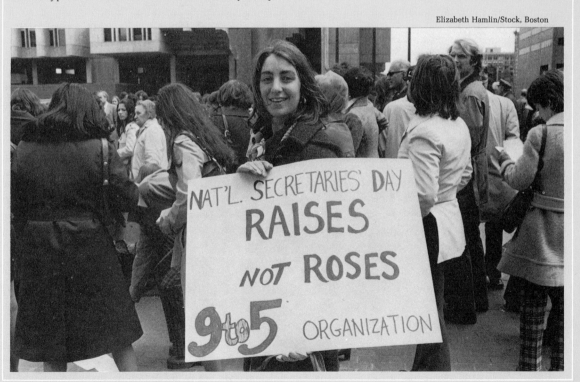

becomes timid, addicted to praise, dependent on her personal relationship with her boss, and unable to take initiative or risk criticism.

Do you find this situation discouraging? Kanter obviously does. She wanted to find out how organizations could help women in their careers, and she watched closely when Indsco undertook some major reforms to enable secretaries to move into managerial positions. The company set up a task force to work on the issue. It suggested an important change: Separate a secretary's status from that of her boss. If he moves ahead, he can't take her along. Every secretary will have the opportunity to change jobs inside the organization. As soon as secretaries see that their personal ties are less vital than before, they will begin to look for different ways of getting ahead. Maybe they'll stop being so timid and allow themselves to develop some ambition and take some risks for the sake of their careers. That was the plan.

No such luck. The company was unable to put its plan into effect because some people benefited from the old system—or thought they did. The bosses and the executive secretaries simply refused to cooperate. Worse yet, some members of the task force itself did not support the proposed reforms. The change threatened certain values—warmth and personal relationships—that many people consider important sources of relief in the impersonal and rational setting of a modern corporation.

Kanter concludes that it may be hard to open up new careers for women, but not because corporations are staffed by men who hate women and want to oppress them. The reason is more complex—it is a conflict in the hearts of good people, including women themselves. The view that personal warmth and loyalty are important values, however praiseworthy it may be, is the very attitude that helps keep women in secretarial jobs instead of executive jobs.

SOCIAL POLICY:
Issues and Viewpoints

One of the high political dramas of our day is the battle for equal rights for men and women. Most people, male or female, have strong feelings about this matter, usually involving a certain amount of resentment. It is easy for a discussion of this kind to focus exclusively on the issues of fairness and unfairness, which have to be settled by confrontation and struggle. I don't think conflict can be avoided altogether, for it is part of every relationship. However, it would be just as mistaken to treat sex role relationships as if they amounted to nothing more than conflicting claims and duties. Mutual enjoyment and caring also exist—and indeed are quite common within contexts of inequality and unfairness. For all I know, the peasant riding his donkey cares deeply about the wife who is walking behind him and carrying the

firewood. To ask him to consider helping her is not to deny that their relationship may be richly rewarding in other ways.

Still, at this moment in history the claims and demands of women are more noticeable than before. Middle-class women tend to want a different life style, and many men are glad to change their own roles as well. The outcome of these changes cannot be predicted, but we can see how women's demands are linked to other changes going on in Western culture. The main change is in the importance of achievement as a value. For a few hundred years it was valued very highly—at least for men. Now our attitude toward achievement is less clear. We are faced with high unemployment in an affluent society. This new situation tends to favor a value system that emphasizes consumption, leisure, recreation, and pleasure instead of hard work and achievement. On the other hand, at the same time that many men are getting out of the "rat race" and seeking a less competitive life style, many women are moving *toward* achievement and competition. The life of the passive consumer no longer satisfies them, and they find the kitchen boring. In the workplace, then, male and female roles are becoming more similar and more equal in terms of both opportunities and rewards—though these changes are certainly not happening as fast as they could.

However, even if opportunities do become equal, women may not take advantage of them. I have mentioned several reasons why sex role differences may not be eliminated, though they may be reduced. The main reason is that women will not change greatly if men do not want them to. Unless men approve of their wives' and lovers' achievements, women may continue to avoid success. Unless men encourage their secretaries to move into executive roles, they may stay on, typing and serving coffee, simply out of personal friendship and loyalty.

A different issue is the question of whether male and female behaviors are shaped at all by biological factors. This is a matter for further research. Certainly men and women do have different tendencies and abilities, in limited areas at least. It is unlikely that these inborn differences account for many of the social roles that they specialize in as adults. We have to go ahead and make personal and public decisions even though our knowledge is limited on this subject. And the decisions we make depend on how highly we value equality. Even if gender role differences are strongly shaped by biological sex differences (which is highly unlikely), they could perhaps be offset by special socialization programs. For example, though boys are relatively better at mathematics and girls are relatively better at verbal skills, if we thought equality was important we could set up special language and math programs to equalize the performance of boys and girls in those areas. Thus public policy is based on opinions about what is worthwhile. Whether we create more equality in our society depends on how much we want it relative to other goals. This is a judgment in which you too will take part.

SUMMARY

1. Sex is the biological fact of being male or female; *gender* is a social-psychological fact. *Gender identity* is the experience of considering oneself male or female. Once it has been learned, an individual's gender identity rarely changes. *Gender roles* are the culturally defined sets of behaviors that are considered sex-appropriate in a given society. They are established by social agreement, though these agreements may be related to natural differences between the sexes.

2. The natural differences between the sexes are biological traits, many of which are now being investigated. The sperm that brings a Y chromosome instead of an X chromosome to the ovum stimulates the embryo to produce testicles, which produce male hormones and offset the uterine environment of female hormones. This leads to the development of male genitals and other traits that would otherwise stay female during later phases of prenatal development.

3. Hormones affect people's feelings and behavior throughout life. It is possible that some sex-typed behavior patterns are shaped by the secretions of glands as well as by social agreements.

4. Sex and gender identity sometimes don't match. Children below the age of 2 may not have developed a gender identity, so that if their sex is changed they can acquire either gender identity that is suggested to them. A few adults are troubled by mismatched sex and gender identity. This is true of transsexuals and transvestites.

5. Margaret Mead's study of three New Guinea tribes shows that gender roles can be defined in very different ways by different cultures. Most societies, however, specify that women's work should involve child care and house work and that women should work near home if possible, while men may go farther away (e.g., to hunt or fish). *Patriarchy* is male dominance of women and children. It is a common pattern in many societies. *Matriarchy*, or female dominance, has not been found in any known society. Even equality between the sexes is fairly rare.

6. Scholars disagree about the sources of patriarchy. Some think it is a result of differences in the ability to produce economic goods and the dependence of women on male providers, at least for part of their lives. Others believe it is a result of the ability of the male to dominate the female through sexual coercion. Perhaps both factors are important causes.

7. Some societies are more patriarchal than others, but none of the societies that have tried to eliminate patriarchy (such as the USSR, Sweden, and the Israeli kibbutzim) have succeeded fully.

8. Research suggests that, in general, (a) girls have greater verbal ability than boys; (b) boys have greater visual-spatial ability; (c) boys have superior mathematical ability; and (d) males are more aggressive than females. Some of these differences may be influenced by biological factors.

9. Maccoby and Jacklin argue that adults' treatment of little girls and little boys is generally fairly similar and that it cannot explain the differences in behavior patterns between the two sexes. Probably society develops certain expectations about sex role differences and children learn these expectations and try to live up to them. The learned roles exaggerate whatever small differences may be inherited as tendencies.

10. Maternal behavior and attachment to infants seem to be influenced by hormonal factors. However, behavior and hormones influence each other. It is no more true that biological factors determine social ones than that social factors determine biological ones.

11. Gender roles in Canada are still marked by inequality: Working women are disadvantaged in career opportunities and payment and in doing a greater share of housework than men. Higher education is also affected by sex roles. Married women do less well in graduate school than divorced women.

12. The feminist gains of the 1920s were not maintained because the Depression took job opportunities away from women. The present women's movement is dominated by middle-class women because they feel deprived relative to the men they know.

KEY TERMS

gender   the awareness of being a member of one sex or the other.

gender identity (sexual identity)   the sex of which one considers oneself to be a member.

gender role (sex role)   the culturally defined set of behaviors that is considered sex-appropriate within a given society.

matriarchy   a system in which women are dominant over men.

patriarchy   a system in which men are dominant over women.

sex   the biological fact of being male or female.

sexism   an ideology that justifies a rigid assignment of roles on the basis of sex.

transsexual   a person whose sex has been changed through surgery and hormone treatment.

transvestite   a person whose gender identity differs from his or her sex and who may dress according to the gender identity.

FOR FURTHER READING

AMBERT, ANNE-MARIE. *Sex Structure*, 2nd ed. Toronto: Longman, 1975. This is one of the better Canadian books on the subject, written by a York University sociologist.

ARMSTRONG, PAT and HUGH ARMSTRONG. *The Double Ghetto.* Toronto: McClelland and Stewart, 1978. The authors bring together a great deal of hard factual evidence to describe the situation of women in the Canadian labor market.

CLEVERDON, CATHERINE. *The Woman Suffrage Movement in Canada: The Start of Liberation 1900-1920*, 2nd ed. Toronto: University of Toronto Press, 1974. A useful, carefully researched source of information about the earlier phases of the women's movement.

GRIFFITHS, N.E.S. *Penelope's Web: Some Perceptions of Women in European and Canadian Society.* Toronto: Oxford University Press, 1976. This is history, of interest chiefly to people focusing on a special topic. It begins with the seventeenth century and has a moderate viewpoint.

KOMAROVSKY, MIRRA. *Dilemmas of Masculinity: A Study of College Youth.* New York: Norton, 1976. This study involves both a survey and some indepth interviews with young men in a prestigious college. It investigates their problems, their goals, and especially their attitudes toward sex roles and family life. They sounded stuffier and more traditional than the men I teach. I kept wondering whether Komarovsky liked them or not. (She doesn't say.)

LAMBERT, R. D. *Sex Role Imagery in Children.* Royal Commission on the Status of Women, Study no. 6. Ottawa: Information Canada, 1971. This is one of a number of excellent studies that appeared as a result of the initiative the government took in establishing a Royal Commission several years ago.

LEVINSON, DANIEL J. *The Seasons of a Man's Life.* New York: Knopf, 1978. Levinson describes how young men have big dreams and what they go through in turning their dreams into reality, if they do. He looks at the vital relationships that emerge along the way—with women, and with older men who are mentors.

LOPATA, HELENA ZNANIECKI. *Occupation: Housewife.* New York: Oxford University Press, 1971. This is probably the best description of the life situations facing the majority of women at some point in their lives, if not indeed for most of their lives.

STEPHENSON, MARYLEE, ed. *Women in Canada.* Toronto: New Press, 1973. This collection of papers is one of the most significant works on Canadian women published during this period.

6

SOCIAL GROUPS

The need for togetherness
    Social deprivation
    Primates and people
    Personal space and expressive
        behavior
Types of groups
    Primary groups and secondary
        groups
    Encounter groups and communes
    Peer groups
    Reference groups
    Large, complex groups
Social groups and the social self
    The individual and the group
    The looking-glass self
    Ethics, the self, and the primary
        group
    Communication and the self
    The act
    How symbolic interactionists work
Group interaction
    Group boundaries
    Interaction across group boundaries
    The sense of community
Social Research: Sociologists at Work
Social Policy: Issues and Viewpoints

Let me give you a koan. Perhaps you know that in Zen Buddhism a *koan* is a puzzle that has no logical answer. It's meant to boggle your mind until something inside sort of snaps. Zen Buddhists sit for hours concentrating on the koan that their teacher has given them. One favorite koan for beginners is this: What was your face before your mother and father were born?

That particular koan doesn't hold my attention very well, but over the years I have found myself wondering about a question that is very much like a koan. There is no logical answer to my koan and I can't promise you enlightenment if you concentrate on it, but I am happy to share it with you. It goes like this: What would you be like if you hadn't ever been part of a social group? I've never solved this one, but I want to discuss in this chapter how it is that social experience is necessary for us to become fully human. You need a group in order to become yourself, just as you need parents before you can have your own face.

The need for togetherness

SOCIAL DEPRIVATION

Imagine a person who has never been influenced by a social group in any way—a person who has been completely free to act on impulse throughout his or her life, a person who has never known another human being. It is unlikely that such a person could survive to adulthood, but if this were possible, that person's behavior would be more animal-like than human.

The human infant, who depends on adults for a longer part of his or her life than the infant of any other species, needs many years of care. In a few cases, however, children have had no contact with other humans throughout most of their childhood. The personality de-

velopment of such children gives us an idea of what human nature is like without social interaction.

Unlike Romulus and Remus, the legendary founders of Rome who were supposedly reared by wolves, children who have been isolated from other human beings (*feral children*) behave in a subhuman way. They are unable to learn to relate to human beings.[1] In some cases, wild children about 8 or 10 years old have been found in the woods, where they seem to have survived alone for several years. It is rarely possible to find out whether such children were normal at birth or whether they were abandoned *because* they seemed abnormal. In any case they have become more animal-like than human—they bite and howl, for example, as if they had been reared by a mother wolf. Even after much patient mothering they never become entirely normal.

The Wild Child, a French film made in the late 1960s, is a true story based on a journal kept by Dr. Jean Marc Itard, who tried to educate a feral child who had been found by peasants near Aveyron in 1799.[2] The boy, who was about 10 years old when he was found, had evidently lived since early childhood by scrounging for food in the woods. He walked on all fours. When he met human beings he fled from them in terror, and he fought fiercely when they captured him. It was even necessary to teach the boy, whom Dr. Itard named Victor, how to walk in a human fashion. Although Dr. Itard taught Victor a few words, the boy's education was unsuccessful. According to Itard's actual record, Victor never became a normal human being.

Like feral children, many mentally disturbed children may have become abnormal because of inadequate mothering.[3] Research has shown that experiences such as crooning, cuddling, pat-a-cake, and peekaboo are very important to children's development. Those who are deprived of such interaction are backward in their physical and verbal development.[4]

PRIMATES AND PEOPLE

The need of infants for physical contact is not found only in human beings. Biologists have raised monkeys in isolation in order to see how isolation affects their behavior as adults. These experiments show the infant's need for loving contact. In one widely known experiment, baby monkeys were taken from their mothers and placed alone in a cage with two "surrogate mothers"—one of them a wire frame and the other a soft cloth dummy. The babies could nurse from bottles attached to one of the "mothers." None of the monkeys became attached to the wire mother, but all of them clung to the cloth mother most of the time, whether it was equipped with a milk bottle or not. This clinging was especially likely to occur when the baby monkeys were frightened by new experiences.

No infant monkey reared in this isolated way became a normal adult. These monkeys seemed not to understand how to mate. The few females who did mate were likely to mistreat or neglect their babies.

Researchers have found that it is possible to rear infant monkeys without their mothers and still produce normal adults if the infants are allowed to play together in a group. They cuddle together in close physical contact and through their interactions make up for their lack of mothering.[5]

These monkey experiments show that the human need for social contact is shared by other species. Still, there is a wide difference between the social life of humankind and that of other primates. Some years ago, a family tried to raise two infants as if they were twins. One of the infants was a female chimpanzee, the other their own son.[6] At first their son's development was slower than that of his "sister." The chimp could walk right away and quickly learned to use complicated toys. But by the age of 2 the boy began to catch up with the chimp, and soon there was no longer a contest. The chimp couldn't begin to master language, and for this reason she could never participate in complex human activities.

Later experiments have been somewhat more successful in teaching chimpanzees to communicate in symbol systems. Some researchers have taught a chimp to make simple sentences using hand signals,[7] and another researcher has used colored plastic shapes to communicate with his chimp.[8] At the Yerkes Primate Research Center a chimpanzee named Lana has been taught to communicate using an electric keyboard. Each key is marked with a symbol that represents an English word. As Lana presses the keys the symbols appear on a display panel and a teletypewriter prints the message in English. If Lana types "?Please, machine, give milk," a vending machine attached to the keyboard pours out a cup of milk. Lana's teacher, Timothy V. Gill, reports that she now uses the names of unfamiliar objects and invents plausible new names as well. For example, one day Gill entered Lana's room holding an orange. She had eaten an orange before, but she did not know its name. However, she did know the names of six colors and several objects, including apples. She therefore asked for the fruit in Gill's hand by typing, "?Tim give apple which-is orange."[9] Although scientists are pleased with the ability of chimps to learn to communicate, they agree that trained primates cannot match the problem-solving ability of normal human beings who have been brought up with other human beings.

PERSONAL SPACE AND EXPRESSIVE BEHAVIOR

All social scientists agree that most human behavior is *learned* and that it varies from one group to another. But they disagree over details. Clearly *some* behaviors are genetic characteristics of the human species. For example, breathing, sneezing, and muscle reflexes are certainly inborn tendencies, while harpsichord playing certainly is not. However, we cannot be so sure about all behavior patterns, and some scholars have suggested that we have failed to recognize a number of human tendencies as biologically based. They point out how our behavior resembles that of apes.

Some of these theories cannot be proved or disproved by research, but they are fascinating nonetheless. Desmond Morris' *The Naked Ape*,[10] for example, describes the human being as an odd, almost hairless primate that was forced by environmental conditions to give up bananas and berries for a carnivorous diet. This new diet required long hunting expeditions, and so the human species developed sexual bonding as a way of making sure the females would still be around when the males came home. Out of this came a number of other important social developments that gave our species a dominant place in the animal kingdom. Another book on this subject is Lionel Tiger's *Men in Groups*,[11] which suggests that males of our species have an inborn tendency to form special bonds that cannot include females.

Both of these books argue that human social patterns are at least comparable to animal traits, but neither can actually prove that there is *more* than an analogy involved. In other words, neither book proves that the human pattern of behavior is based on the fact that *Homo sapiens* is a primate species. Their arguments have stimulated interest and sometimes anger, but not much empirical research. The argument about *territoriality*, however, may turn out to be fruitful in helping us understand human social patterns.

Territoriality

It is well known that many animal species distribute their populations over a region by limiting the number of animals that may live in any given territory or zone. In some cases these zones are assigned by contests. The winner keeps the territory while the losers slink away to find another piece of land that they can call their own. The dominant animals chase away any animal that invades their territory. Territoriality is the establishment of a certain zone or space that may not be occupied by any other person or animal. In applying the idea of territoriality to human society, we should ask the following questions:

1 Do dominant people claim more space than their subordinates?
2 Do human beings, as a species, have any orderly way of assigning space to individuals?
3 Do human beings need to have a private space for themselves?

The answer to all three questions is yes.

Dominant people spread out more. This can be seen in the way people seat themselves at a crowded seminar table. The instructor will usually take a chair at the head of the table and spread out her belongings—an open briefcase on one side, perhaps a handbag on the other side, and lecture notes fanned out in front. During the lecture she may use expansive gestures while the students are squeezed together around the table, some with no room to write, all keeping their elbows out of other students' space.

Meekness can always be spotted in public by the conspicuous effort the meek person makes to fold himself or herself up into a tiny, inoffensive space. But even the meekest person maintains a claim to a certain amount of personal space surrounding his or her body. This invisible shell varies in size for different people and in different societies, but its existence can be tested by a simple experiment. Strike up a conversation with a stranger and station yourself about a foot away from him. He will probably feel that you are too close and will back away. Whenever he moves away, follow him. But be careful. Social experimentation can be just as explosive as chemical experimentation, and you may end up with a black eye.

Personal space has been described by Erving Goffman, a daring modern sociologist. Many of Goffman's brilliant insights developed out of experiments like the one just mentioned.[12] Goffman tells us that personal space is an elongated sphere that extends outward in front of the body and not as far out on either side or in back. People who interact usually stay outside of each other's sphere, though intimates may be welcomed within it. On a crowded subway more general intrusion may be permitted, but only temporarily. The size of the average sphere differs from one culture to another. Latin Americans feel a certain coldness in North Americans, who require a greater distance between bodies in ordinary conversation. North Americans back away whenever their Latin American companions move close enough to feel comfortable. In pedestrian traffic a person becomes a sort of vehicle, shuttling between the other bodies and avoiding collisions by signaling intended movements by means of glances and gestures.[13]

The human species has developed a system of etiquette for assigning space to individuals. By settling yourself in a particular spot you can stake out a claim to a large or small space, and that claim will usually be recognized by others. Robert Sommer has studied the process by which people claim space. He asked the following question: Suppose you enter a library and choose a seat at an empty table. If you want to remain alone at this table as long as possible, which chair will you choose? Sommer found that people who want to discourage others from taking a seat at that table will choose a seat in the middle.[14]

It is possible to maintain a claim to a particular space without being present in person. This is done by leaving *markers*, or personal belongings, to signal that one intends to return to the vacant space. Thus at a racetrack a folded strip of newspaper is woven between the slats of a bench to show that a seat is taken. Sommer has studied the limits on the use of markers. He found, for example, that you can hold a seat in a crowded study hall for over two hours by using a textbook and a sport jacket as markers, while a heap of magazines will work for about 30 minutes.[15]

Neither Sommer nor Goffman claim that the use of markers is a biological instinct; indeed, they would probably agree that it is not. But they both study the use of personal space in an ethological way, much as an ethologist would study the territoriality of apes or antelopes. It is likely that territoriality serves many of the same functions for all species, including our own.[16] One of those functions may be to reduce conflict. It has been noted that the street gangs of large cities have a strong claim on their "turf," often a particular street that members of other gangs dare not enter. Some people see this as an

Personal space.

Joanne Leonard/Woodfin Camp

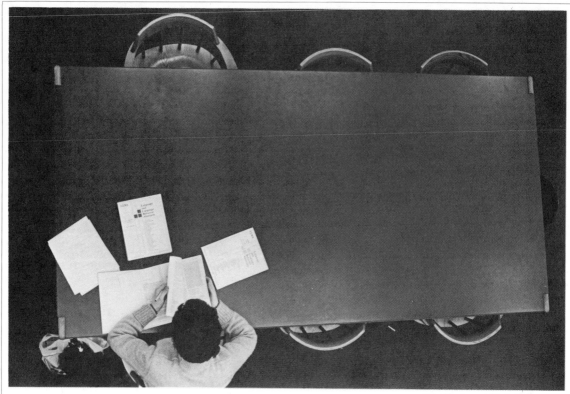

Peter Vandermark/Stock, Boston

Does he want the entire table for himself? Why don't you think so?

example of territoriality, evidence that the human social system faces many of the same problems that animal societies face.

Interaction rituals

Sociologists and ethnologists share an interest in another important aspect of animal behavior—interaction rituals. Most, if not all, primates have regular ways of signaling their relationships to one another through gesture, touch, and voice, especially when they meet or part. Some greeting and leave-taking rituals are similar across species. The following is Jane van Lawick-Goodall's description of the wild chimpanzees that she has studied:

Chimpanzees, like people, exchange greetings when they meet after being apart for any length of time. When this occurs, an observer can usually determine the relationship of one chimp to the other. They may meet as two friends and show pleasure in their reunion, or one may make submissive gestures, acknowledging the other's higher rank.

When Mike arrives in any group the other chimps invariably hurry to pay their respects, touching him with outstretched hands or bowing, just as courtiers once bowed before their king. And, just as the king chose either to acknowledge a courtier or to ignore him, so Mike may take notice of his inferiors, touching them briefly, or he may do nothing. Depending on his mood, he may even threaten or strike those who hasten to greet him.

Many of the apes' forms of greeting startlingly resemble our own. They often kiss. Rodolf in particular frequently touches the face of a subordinate with his lips, or presses his open mouth onto the neck or shoulder of another adult male. Pepe and Figan, to mention but two, often press their mouths to the lips of other individuals. Handholding, as a gesture of greeting, is not common in the chimpanzee community at the reserve, but it does occur. Melissa for one, when first arriving in a

152

group, occasionally holds her hand toward a dominant male until he reaches out and reassures her with a touch.

One of the most memorable reunions took place between old Mr. Worzle and timid Olly. As she approached him, panting nervously, he raised both arms as though pronouncing a blessing. Encouraged, Olly crept closer, crouching and holding her hand toward him. Mr. Worzle took her hand in his and drew her close, placing his other hand gently on her head. Then each flung both arms around the other and exchanged kisses on the neck. Finally, to complete the picture, Olly's daughter Gilka ran up, and Mr. Worzle reached out and drew her into his embrace.[17]

Goffman calls greetings and farewells *access rituals*. He has analyzed the rules governing such rituals among human beings. Most human greetings are less expansive than those of Olly and Mr. Worzle, though a good deal depends on how long the people involved have been separated. Moreover, humans follow an "attenuation rule":

Nowhere can this be seen more prettily than in the conduct of long-separated, closely related friends who newly come together during a social occasion. On first contact, an expansive greeting will occur. A moment later when the next proximity occurs, a reduced version of the initial display will be provided. Each succeeding contact will be managed with an increasingly attenuated greeting until after a time the two will exhibit the standard minimal middle-class social recognition—only a rapid grimace involving little change in eye expression, the two ends of the mouth stretching a little in a cheek flick. (After this point has been reached, the two may cooperate, of course, in seeing to it that one of them can act as though his eyes have not fallen on the other, thereby obviating all display, even the most attenuated.)[18]

Facial expressions and emotion

Facial expressions are somewhat different from interpersonal rituals. Some scholars argue that facial expressions are learned through social interaction and that different societies have different conventions for expressing various emotions. Ray Birdwhistell, a specialist in nonverbal communication (*kinesics*), claims that humans have no universal gestures or expressions. He believes

that all gestures and expressions are specific to particular cultures.[19] This is still a subject of much debate, but the research seems to be going against Birdwhistell's position. For one thing, it is clear that people who are born blind express emotions with the same facial movements that sighted people do, yet they can hardly have learned those gestures by imitation.

Probably the most important research on facial expressions has been done by Paul Ekman and his associates. These researchers believe that although a smile or a frown may provide evidence of pleasure or displeasure, it is not necessarily *intended* to show one's feelings. In fact facial expressions may even show feelings that a person does not want to show. Grief, anger, disgust, fear, and happiness seem to produce the same muscular reactions in all normal people, but these reactions may be held back when one does not want one's feelings to be known. To use Mead's terms (see page 168), the "I" may feel like weeping, but the "me" may force a smile for the sake of appearances. Moreover, each society may specify the emotions that may be shown in particular social situations, and those expressions may "overlay" the natural feelings of the people involved. For example, in some parts of Indonesia funerals are supposed to be occasions of joy and merrymaking, but anthropologists report that the laughter at these ceremonies has a tense quality that betrays the underlying presence of darker feelings.

In order to find out whether facial expressions of emotion are universal, Ekman photographed members of a variety of cultures. He was especially interested in photographing people who had never seen a white person and could never have learned to "read" a white person's face.[20] Their expressions of sadness, anger, or disgust looked just like the white person's expressions of the same emotions. Moreover, people in one society are also quite accurate in identifying the emotions of members of other societies as recorded in photo-

Courtesy of Paul Ekman and Wallace V. Friesen. *Unmasking the Face.* Englewood Cliffs, NJ: Prentice-Hall, Inc., 1975.

Look at the three faces. The arrows on the face to the left indicate elements of the expression which reveal disgust. (1) The raised upper lip caused a change in the appearance of the tip of the nose. (2) Wrinkling along the sides and bridge of the nose. (4) The lower lip is lowered and slightly forward. (5) The cheeks are raised, and this produces a change in the appearance of the lower eyelid, narrowing the opening of the eye and producing many lines and folds below the eye. Now look at the other two faces. Can you tell which elements of the expression convey the particular emotion expressed? What emotions do we see in the middle and righthand faces?

graphs. Apparently emotions are hard to hide. One of Ekman's most important discoveries is what he calls "leakage"—momentary lapses when one's face reveals an underlying mood.[21] Movies capture such fleeting lapses very clearly, but in ordinary interaction people don't notice them, probably because we are all taught to be tactful toward one another. When a person fails to control her face properly, her companions will normally glance away until she has recovered, though they may not even be aware of the lapse. (The same courtesy applies in other, similar lapses, as when one is caught scratching or picking one's nose.) Interaction can continue smoothly because everyone is careful to ignore such behavior. However, in some situations it is useful to be able to recognize emotional "leakage." For example, a clinician may need to decide whether a depressed mental patient is really feeling well enough to be released or whether the patient is faking happiness in order to get out.

Types of groups

Human behavior is far more varied than that of other species. These variations are caused largely by the fact that human social interactions vary so greatly. Sometimes insects are described as "social" because they live together in large colonies and interact in complex ways. However, the social activities of insects are fixed by instinct, while those of human beings are much more flexible. This is because the patterns of human behavior are passed from one generation to the next through culture, not through genes. Among animals, similar situations lead

154

to similar responses. A swarm of bees will build a hive that looks much like all the other hives bees have been building for millions of years. A human city, however, is never like any other human city. Smash a beehive and it will be replaced by a duplicate of the old one. Destroy a human city and it will be rebuilt on a new design. The social activity of human beings is invented, not determined by biological factors. The activities of humans depend on the past experience built up by the group. Therefore it is necessary to discuss the various types of groups that are important to human beings and to study their effects on human life.

Two of the most important words used in sociology books cannot be defined precisely because they are not really technical terms. These words are *group* and *collectivity*, and sociologists use them as loosely as anyone else does. Often they are used interchangeably. One can usually tell from the context which of several possible definitions the writer has in mind. The first meaning is simply *any collection of people who are together in the same place.* (We could also call this a *physical aggregation.*) Thus the words *group* and *collectivity* might be used to refer to all the people in an elevator or all the window shoppers walking past a department store.

The second meaning is *any number of people who have some characteristic in common.* (We could also call this a *category.*) Thus the words *group* and *collectivity* might be used to refer to all the people whose names in the Montreal phone directory begin with the letter D. Or they might be used to refer to all the black shopowners in Vancouver. Or to all left-handed optometrists over the age of 90. The people in a category may not think of themselves as belonging together. The category is simply a pigeonhole into which people may be classified.

Finally, a third definition of group and, less often, of collectivity is *a social system with a name and an identity to which people are seen as belonging.* Examples are the nation

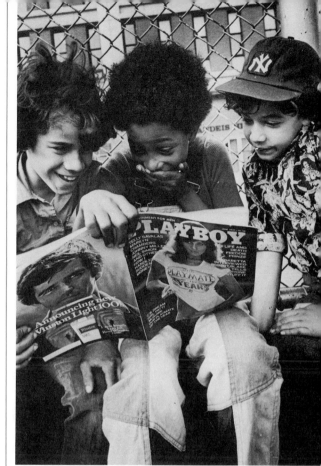

Joe Gordon/DPI

A peer group.

of China, the National Geographic Society, and the Hamilton Tiger Cats. This definition implies that the people involved have some form of ongoing interaction among themselves. All the readers of this book do not qualify as a group in this narrow sense. You cannot all meet one another, nor do you feel even the slightest bond with one another.

Sometimes *group* is used in contrast to *collectivity*. For example, we may say that the passengers of a jet plane were merely a collectivity until the plane crashed in a jungle, and then the survivors became a true group. In this narrow sense all groups are collectivities but not all collectivities are groups. They become groups if they interact and if they think of themselves as groups.

The largest collectivity with which sociology is concerned is the *society*. To be termed a

155

society a group must meet the following standards:

1. It must be able to exist longer than the life span of the individuals in it.
2. It must gain new members at least partly by means of sexual reproduction.
3. It must share certain values and standards.
4. It must be self-sufficient.

According to this definition, the ordinary North American township, despite its high standard of living and complex organization, is not a society. It is not self-sufficient because it can't supply all its own needs and must rely on others for such things as food, water, power, medical services, and defense. A monastery is not a society because it does not gain new members through sexual reproduction. One way to decide whether a collectivity is a society is to imagine what would happen if all other groups suddenly disappeared. If there is a good chance that the remaining group could survive, then it is a society. Most primitive tribes and almost all nation-states meet this standard.

PRIMARY GROUPS AND SECONDARY GROUPS

In this chapter we will discuss not only the *structure* of various sorts of groups but, even more important, the *quality* of those groups. In terms of quality sociologists distinguish between two types of groups: (1) primary groups, whose members interact in a personal, intimate, and emotional way, and (2) secondary groups, whose members interact in a more impersonal, unsentimental, and businesslike way.

A primary group is an intimate group whose members have a sense of "we-ness"—a family, for example, or a group of close friends. Members of such groups respond to each other as whole, unique personalities, not merely on the basis of the particular role that each performs. Primary groups are always small and usually involve face-to-face inter-

action. The members mean a lot to one another—so much so that a major change in their relationship requires an emotional readjustment. The members of such a group are not interchangeable. If your brother leaves home, for example, you can't rent his room to a boarder and expect him to play the role of your brother. Families are primary groups, though sometimes members of the same family become so estranged from each other that their relationship is no longer altogether "primary."

Sometimes even actual primary groups are not characterized by happy feelings. Two bitter enemies who have agreed that neither will speak to the other have, in that understanding, an intensely intimate personal relationship. To hate someone is, after all, to care about that person in a special way, and this makes it a primary relationship. This is not true of people who are indifferent to one another. The primary group is often a scene of mixed feelings, for the people we hate the most are often the people we also love the most.

There are many different kinds of primary groups, and each person needs to participate in several kinds. We need our original family in a unique way: It is the place where socialization begins and where we first experience deep emotions and serious personal commitments. Shallow primary relationships among family members make it harder for a person to develop warm relationships later on.

Friendship groups are, to varying degrees, primary groups. They differ from one another, of course, and are not the same as families. Suppose you play basketball with the same friends every Saturday for years and always have a beer together afterwards, along with a lot of horseplay and joking. This may be a rewarding primary group, but it will mean something different from the other primary experiences in your life—such as your summer love affair or your heart-to-heart conversations with your best friend.

We can understand the primary group best by comparing it with the secondary group, which is more impersonal. The relations between, say, a hotel guest and the porter are usually secondary, not primary. Guests do not care which porter takes them to their rooms and do not expect to participate in long discussions of either the porter's or their own private affairs. Each member of a secondary group is involved with only a part of the others' lives—and sometimes that part is very small. Thus, to the motorist, the toll booth attendant is hardly more than a hand that reaches out to take a coin. Any hand will do, for the members of a secondary group are interchangeable. Their relations are unsentimental and limited.

I do not want to imply that primary groups are good and secondary groups are bad. Actually, we need many different kinds of relationships, and not all of them can be intimate and personal. Businesslike relationships have their place, and very little business would get done without them. Indeed, primary groups that form within business organizations sometimes reduce the effectiveness of the larger group. For instance, some offices get little work done because all the employees are great friends and talk all the time. Moreover, loyalty to a primary group can conflict with a loyalty to a larger group. For example, a small group of friends may promote one another to high positions in a business organization even though better-qualified people are available. Attachment to a primary group is particularistic and may be contrary to the interests of the larger group.

Many city dwellers complain that too many of their relationships are secondary. Whether or not this is really true, it shows that many people believe that traditional village life was full of intimacy and emotional interaction. They believe that modern life is made

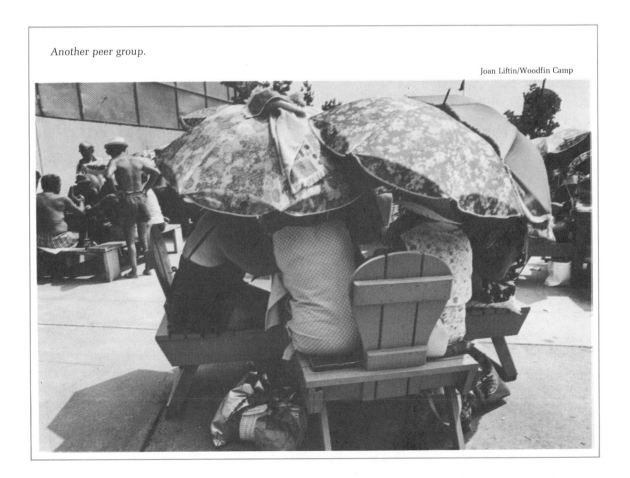

Another peer group.

Joan Liftin/Woodfin Camp

up mostly of impersonal meetings between strangers who use each other only as a means to an end, not as individuals to be appreciated for their own sake. This complaint, which reflects a sense of isolation and estrangement, has become widespread and has given rise to a number of new social groups designed to counteract this situation.

ENCOUNTER GROUPS AND COMMUNES

The workaday world of Europe and North America calls for a universalistic, emotionally neutral attitude toward others that leaves little room for mutual caring. Without quite knowing how it happened, some people find that their sensitivity even to other members of their family has become blunted. If you want to overcome this lack of closeness and reach out to others, it is not clear how you can do so safely. There are norms that limit how much you can reveal about yourself or find out about your coworkers. Not everyone has a family, and not all families want to encourage closeness. Sometimes they function only by "agreeing to disagree" and not discussing controversial topics. As a result many people have turned to strangers to share their emotions.

The *encounter group*, an idea not much more than ten years old, is a type of group that is formed to act as an "instant" primary group. It may be set up in a church, a YMCA, or some other private organization. The members may agree to meet every week for several months with a leader who may have had some training in psychotherapy. Other groups may go away together for "marathon" weekend sessions. The members are usually strangers when the group forms, but they agree to listen to each other, to speak honestly about things they feel deeply about, and to show their emotional reactions to each other. And those reactions are often intense. Encounter groups encourage a kind of closeness that would rarely develop in an office or factory. This

experience is often exciting and can lead to personal growth and change. On the other hand, it is also a risky adventure. Direct emotional interactions can shatter a personality that is going through a period of crisis. To be sure, even skilled psychotherapists sometimes make mistakes and hurt their patients, but they are less likely to do so than a group of strangers. Still, the popularity of encounter groups indicates that they may be filling a need for intimacy that is not being filled in any other way. Critics rightly point out the dangers of encounter groups, but they do not suggest other places where people might find primary groups that encourage the sharing of personal feelings.

Communes, like encounter groups, are set up for people who are looking for genuine caring relationships. Encounter groups are brief, isolated experiences. In contrast, the member of communes live and often work together. They may pool their income and share their expenses. Often, but not always, they live in a rural area and try to simplify their life style, avoiding waste and frills. They are trying to develop a permanent, stable primary group that is more natural than the encounter group. However, communes have problems and disadvantages too. For one thing, they often attract people who dislike rules of any kind and want to work in an environment that is free of planning or coercion. This hope rarely comes true, and many communes have been forced to make strict demands on their members to avoid falling apart.

PEER GROUPS

Groups of people of similar status are called peer groups. Examples are classmates or teammates. Most close friendships are formed between members of peer groups because they have much in common and can share experiences as equals. Think about the last five people you invited to your home for dinner. What was your relationship with them? In

Bob Nadler/DPI

Encounter groups offer instant intimacy.

most cases you will notice that most of those five people have a social status that is not too different from your own and that they are about your age. This is because we usually find dinner conversations easier, more enjoyable, and more relaxed when we are with peers. For the same reason, friendships most often develop between children in the same class at school or between workers of the same rank at the office or factory. Not all peer groups are primary groups, of course, but many of our most important primary groups are made up of our peers. This is because groups often form on the basis of similarities between people and also because they come together by participating in similar activities. Often peers meet and see each other regularly because they are in the same class at school or the same scouting group, or because they live on the same block, or because they work side by side on the assembly line.

REFERENCE GROUPS

A group to which we compare ourselves when we judge our own status is called a **reference group**. Often, but not necessarily, the reference group is our peer group. A parent may ask a teacher whether little Freddy is doing as well as the other kids in his class. In this case the class is both a peer group and a reference group. When someone is undergoing anticipatory socialization, the reference group may be a group to which he or she wants to belong. For example, a high school girl may have friends who go to an expensive boarding school. She may follow their styles of clothing and speech instead of those of her own school. She may think of herself as poor compared to members of her reference group, though her classmates do not think of her as poor.

The people we envy usually belong to a reference group that is just a little ahead of us. We do not envy people who are much richer or more successful than we are, but we tend to envy those who might be in our position if things had worked out a little differently. A young sociologist does not envy the president of the American Sociological Association, but he may envy a classmate who finished his Ph.D. very quickly, has published several articles in the *American Sociological Review*, and is under contract for a book or two. You probably do not envy Prince Charles, but you may envy your brother-in-law, who at age 28 owns a speedboat and a ski chalet.

LARGE, COMPLEX GROUPS

Every person belongs not only to some small groups that may be either primary or secondary but also to large groups that are almost always secondary. If a group is made up of hundreds, or even millions, of members, those members cannot all know one another on a personal, intimate basis. In order for large groups to function well there must be some specialization of roles and responsibilities.

Members of such groups may form small primary groups with those whom they get to know within their special roles, but the organization as a whole is likely to be impersonal in nature. Also, for the decisions and actions of the large group to fit together, there must be a system of authority and rank in which each member has authority over a particular area of responsibility.

Large groups of many kinds play a part in all our lives. Even primitive societies form large groups, which we call *tribes* or *clans*. Clans are kinship groupings—people who are related to one another—and several clans together make up a tribe. In later chapters we will deal with many different kinds of large, complex social groups. Chapter 8 deals with formal organizations. Chapter 9 focuses on *social classes*, large categories of people in similar economic positions who may or may not think of themselves as a group. In Chapter 10 we will discuss *ethnic groups*, loose categories of people who share cultural patterns and (usually) some physical traits. In Chapter 11 we will study *crowds*, large groups of people who gather in one place without any organized system of roles or authority. A crowd may become excited and act in a spontaneous way. It may hang someone in effigy or carry a football hero on their shoulders. In other chapters we will discuss large groups such as churches, universities, multinational corporations, cities, and the nation-state. All of these groups are important, but in this chapter we will deal mostly with the small, primary group.

Social groups and the social self

Interpersonal relationships within primary groups have been the main focus of an important school of sociologists—the *symbolic interactionists*. These scholars have written a great deal about the process of socialization. They are interested in showing how an individual's personality and thinking habits develop through social interaction. The originator of this line of inquiry was the American sociologist Charles Horton Cooley (1864-1929). One of his most fruitful contributions to sociology was his description of the development of the social self within the primary group.[22] Further work on this topic was done by George Herbert Mead and his followers, as we will see later in the chapter.

THE INDIVIDUAL AND THE GROUP

It seemed clear to Cooley that the distinction between the person and the group is often overstated. He argued that it is a mistake to see the individual as limited by the demands and rules of his or her social community, as if a person could be entirely free if it were not for the "oppressive" force of society. His own view of the person and the group emphasized their interdependence: Each is an aspect of the other. Cooley believed that society is a whole made up of many individual parts. A group may be said to have a "mind" in a sense. Individuals contribute to this public mind by communicating their own ideas. Moreover, individuals gain from this process, for it is through communication that they build up their own minds. Even when there is conflict between individuals, the conflict arises only because they share a particular concern. By dealing with others each member of society both expands his or her inner experience and contributes to the whole. For example, a novelist cannot create a novel alone, uninfluenced by other literature. Novels are shaped by, and become part of, a literary tradition. Similarly, each person's mind is shaped by, and becomes part of, the intellectual tradition of his or her community.

Cooley saw each human being as a product of two distinct historical streams: (1) his or her unique biological inheritance, which is passed on to his or her offspring, and (2) his or her cultural inheritance, which is also passed to future generations. Each person is, in a sense, a fresh organization of life in which these two streams meet.

THE LOOKING-GLASS SELF

Though Cooley described the person as a channel through which life passes, he was quite aware that each person feels unique. In fact Cooley was very interested in the phenomenon of *self-regard*—how it develops and its effects on group life. Many of his theories were stimulated by watching the psychological and linguistic growth of his own children. It seemed to him that a sense of self is first experienced in pride of ownership. A little girl feels a special regard for the things that she can call her own and control—the things that she calls "mine." Her blanket is not interchangeable with any other blanket, for example, and her toys, her shoes, and her spoon may be loved for the same reason.

From this sense of ownership, other important attitudes arise. Thus the child can take possession of the *reactions of others* just as she takes possession of a blanket or a toy, and she can feel pride in those reactions, a sense that they are "hers." If a babysitter shows delight at the little girl's mastery of the tricycle, the youngster may feel proud of herself. In effect, the child sees herself through the eyes of people whose opinions are important to her (i.e., **significant others** such as family members) and whose approval she desires. She takes pride in the image of herself that she sees through their eyes. This self-image is "hers," something that she "owns" and seeks to control. If the babysitter tells her she is naughty, she feels shame—a stinging loss of pride in her "self." The self-image that you acquire in this way remains the core of your personal identity throughout life. Your body may change, but the sense of being "you" will remain stable and continuous even in old age. Cooley called this identity the **looking-glass self**, the self-image that a person acquires as if reflected from the eyes of others. You acquire your social self by seeing yourself as others see you. This capacity to take the

Ontario Science Centre

The looking-glass self.

perspective of others is the phenomenon that Mead later recognized as the process that makes human society possible. He called it "taking the role of the other."

ETHICS, THE SELF, AND THE PRIMARY GROUP

Pride in oneself is often discouraged, as if love of self made it impossible to love others. Cooley realized that some forms of pride could be selfish, but he did not think this was true all the time. Pride in itself is not evil; rather, it is

161

necessary. It does not stop you from wanting to help others; in fact it is necessary if you are going to serve others. For example, the idea of "my duty" may be full of self-importance, although it clearly involves helping others. One can take pride in one's duties and responsibilities. Moreover, we make moral commitments on the basis of self-pride. For example, Cooley suggested that maternal commitment grows largely out of a proud sense of ownership: The baby is special to the mother because it is her own.

Pride in oneself (or self-feeling) may extend to include other people or groups. It then becomes "we-feeling." Each of us, especially in childhood, needs to spend a lot of time in intimate groups whose members have a strong sense of "we-ness"—in other words, primary groups.

Rich emotional experiences occur in primary groups, and Cooley claimed that a person's highest moral capacities are always developed through primary interactions. He emphasized the importance of the play group

as a context for learning to care for others and to follow rules of fair play. This view was expanded by Mead and Piaget (see Chapter 4). But Cooley first convinced social scientists that moral behavior is learned mainly through mutual relations with peers, not as a result of moral instruction by adults.

According to Cooley, there is no sharp difference between thinking about moral problems and thinking about other problems. Cooley held that being moral is being rational. Moral behavior develops out of the capacity for *sympathetic imagination*. This is the ability to create images that are inspiring. To pray, for example, is to confront our moral problems and questions with the highest "personal ideal we can form."[23] To develop this ability we need privacy from influences that are not morally instructive, Cooley suggested, and communion with those that are. Our active imagination "enables us to live with the best our lives have afforded and maintain higher suggestions to compete with the baser ones that assail us."[24]

A primary group

Tatarsky/DPI

Cooley's writings show a generosity and humanity of spirit that strike today's reader as refreshing, if somewhat quaint. His influence on American sociology is still felt, especially within the tradition of *symbolic interactionism.*

COMMUNICATION AND THE SELF

At the turn of the century, the University of Chicago was an important center of sociological study. A number of creative social theorists, including George Herbert Mead, taught and wrote there. John Dewey was there too, directing his Laboratory School and writing about education.[25] The two men shared many ideas, and both made important contributions to sociology. Mead was known more for his teaching than for his writing. After his death, however, his students published the notes they had taken in his lectures.[26] One of those students, Herbert Blumer, conveyed his teacher's ideas to a whole generation of sociologists and coined the term *symbolic interactionism* to refer to Mead's theories and to the theories of like-minded sociologists.[27] Symbolic interactionists believe that social relationships and personality develop out of social interaction at the *symbolic* level of language and gestures.

Mead suggested that people do not respond directly and instinctively to events themselves but respond in terms of their *interpretation* of events. Among lower animals, specific behavior is an automatic response to specific stimuli and is guided entirely by instincts. Human beings, however, can perform much more complex acts, and their behavior is guided by their mental images of the world. These images include abstract ideas and can extend forward and backward in time and space. Each of us carries with us a mental map of the universe, and we orient ourselves by that map. For example, we may imagine that we are sitting on a speck of dust and circling around a dot of light on the edge of a galaxy that hovers in a black and sparkling cosmos. We can imagine our planet as it may have appeared a billion years ago or as it may be a billion years in the future. Moreover, we can conjure up images that we will never experience directly—the beauty of Cleopatra, Snow White's trance, the X-ray vision of Superman, the madness of Nero, or the rage of Thor as he throws his hammer across the sky, splitting the clouds with lightning.

We act according to our imaginative interpretation of events. Columbus' crew came close to mutiny because they believed that they were sailing toward the edge of a flat world and were in danger of falling off. Their interpretation of the situation differed from Columbus'. But the fish swimming around their ships had no interpretation of the situation at all; fish have no ideas, no symbols. They simply react to internal and external stimuli. Fish do not pray to gods, nor do they make political commitments or discover mathematical laws or scold themselves for having eaten a fellow creature or wonder where the ocean came from. Adult human beings may do all of these things, however, for our world is not only a world of objective stimuli but also a subjective world of meaningful objects. For us, the nature of the objects that surround us depends on the conceptual framework within which we perceive them. Even our perceptions are based on social experience. What a North American would perceive as a baseball bat might not be perceived in the same way by other people: Australian aborigines might perceive it as a valuable piece of firewood; New Guinean tribesmen might perceive it as an excellent weapon. A baseball bat is simply not among the objects that exist for these tribesmen. Here we must emphasize Mead's distinction between mere "stimuli" and what he called "objects." The nature of an "object" is determined subjectively according to the *concept* that one applies to it, and that concept is based on social experience.

Humans begin life as empty of concepts as animals do. The newborn child has no concept of baseball bats or firewood or weapons or worlds, whether flat or round. Mead was interested in describing how a child acquires the set of *meaningful objects* that make up his or her world as an adult. Objects are perceived in terms of their meanings, and those meanings are acquired through social relationships. The baseball bat is not a meaningful concept to an infant because the infant does not know how to act toward it and has no idea what kind of experiences he or she could have with it. Other people have to define it by acting toward it in a characteristic way. The infant sees people swing bats at balls a few times, and then he or she knows a little about the meaning of bats. Much of the work involved in caring for children takes the form of defining objects for the child. ("A chair is to sit in, not to scoot around the floor, Jimmy." "We don't chew on tea bags, Lynn, we soak them in hot water.") The "meaning" of chairs and tea bags is found in the experiences one can have with them, and this is learned by seeing how other people act toward them.

Our perceptions are guided by our concepts. We don't just "see" things at random; we organize our perceptions of them as they occur. We "carve out of experience" the objects that we perceive. The objects that exist for us are organized as such by the future experiences that we could have with them. Thus the future is telescoped into the present in our perceptions. For example, if we "see" a baseball bat as smooth and hard, what we are "seeing" is really our expectation that if, in the future, we run our hands over it we will not get splinters in our fingers, and if we poke it or hit it, it will not crumble into tiny fragments or bend like a garden hose. Our perception of it as smooth and hard is really an expectation of future experience based on past experience. Likewise, our recognition of the bat as equipment for a baseball game is an expectation of future possibilities based on past experience. The bat *could* be used in the kitchen (e.g., as a rolling pin), but we do not recognize this

possibility in it when we see it as a baseball bat.

Now that you understand something about Mead's basic ideas, we can take a closer look at the nature of the interaction through which we acquire a set of concepts. In doing so, we will see why Blumer called Mead's theories *symbolic* interactionism. Social interaction may be symbolic or nonsymbolic. A dog fight, for example, is non-symbolic interaction that occurs when one dog threatens another, the other responds by growling, and so on. No complex interpretation goes on; it is simply a matter of direct stimulus and response. Human beings can also interact on a nonsymbolic level, automatically, without thinking. For example, ballroom dancing is largely nonsymbolic—the dancers coordinate their movements through muscular cues. Reflex action is certainly nonsymbolic. Screams of pain are nonsymbolic communications. Boxers and wrestlers maul each other in rounds of non-symbolic interaction. Two people who pass each other on a sidewalk avoid a collision by interacting in primarily nonsymbolic ways, that is, by automatically moving out of each other's path. Nonsymbolic communication is the simplest sort of communication; action and reaction take place at almost the same time, and there is no need to interpret the other person's behavior.

Symbolic interaction is far more complex, but Mead wanted to show how it develops out of nonsymbolic interaction. He suggested that the beginning of an act could come to be understood as a symbol standing for the whole act. Suppose a foreigner who does not know your language feels angry and wants to warn you that he is thinking of punching you. He may make a jabbing gesture but not complete the punch. This movement is symbolic. It is meant to represent a future event that both you and he can interpret in the same way. If you do not recognize what future event the jabbing gesture stands for, you do not share the symbol. You may fail to understand the warning and change your behavior accordingly.

Mead argued that the lower species are able to understand symbols only in the simplest sense, if at all. My dog becomes very excited when he hears the words *outside* or *leash*, for they come at the beginning of a trip outside. But the dog's vocabulary of symbols is tiny compared to that of human beings. The human infant quickly learns that the word *hot* can be the first phase of an impending burn, that the word *car* can be the first phase of an impending trip, and so forth. The symbols (words) stand for the events that will occur in the future; when we learn the symbols, we acquire some control over our future experience. Thus a person who understands the word *hot* can be warned in time to avoid being burned. A child who can use the word *car* can wheedle her parents into taking her for a ride. The meaning of an action, a gesture, or a word is what it stands for in terms of future action. When two people recognize it as standing for the same future, they share a significant symbol. By sharing significant symbols, human beings can communicate in ways that would otherwise be impossible.

Role taking

Perhaps the most remarkable contribution of the symbolic interactionists to our understanding of human nature is their analy-

People learn to guide their actions according to the anticipated reactions of others. To make music, a musician must know how his fellow musicians will play in response.

Tourism British Columbia

sis of role taking, the ability of a person to imagine the role of another person with whom he or she interacts. In order to interact with another person one must be able to anticipate the other's future actions. When one person starts to do anything, the other must imagine the rest of the act, anticipate future phases, and shape his or her own acts accordingly. If the two participants do not anticipate later phases of acts in the same way, one does not understand what the other is doing, and the two may fail to fit their actions together.

People guide their own acts according to the anticipated reactions of others. Take two tennis players, for example. Each player decides where to place a shot by deciding whether or not the other player can reach it. Or take the shopper buying meat in a supermarket. He may pick up a package of liver but, anticipating the groans of his children at the dinner table, may put it down and choose hamburger instead. In both of these examples the present action is guided by the expected future actions of others.

When you want to understand another person you take that person's role. Social life depends on role taking—each person must try to see the world through the other fellow's eyes. A person who is unable to do this cannot be a full member of human society.

Through role taking, the individual acquires a set of meaningful concepts. We learn that a flag is not an ordinary piece of colored cloth, for instance, by watching how others act toward flags. We learn that the school principal has more authority than the teachers by watching how the teachers act toward the principal. In this way the child learns the meanings of the concepts shared by his or her social group—be they flags, principals, or baseball bats.

Among the many concepts that the child acquires through social interaction, the most important of all is the *self*. Mead took Cooley's notion of the looking-glass self further by suggesting that just as you define such concepts as flags, principals, and baseball bats by the way other people act toward them, so also you define your *self* as a particular kind of person by the way they act toward you. As a child you were limited to the perspectives of the people you knew. You learned the concepts that made up their world, however limited that set of concepts may have been. You were also limited to the self that you saw through the eyes of others. Thus, if the group had viewed you as a slave, you would have grown up viewing yourself as a slave. If your group had viewed you as a prince, you would have grown up viewing yourself as a prince. In both cases you would have behaved according to your view of yourself. The self is a social product, defined at the beginning by the actions of others.

Self-reflexive behavior

The possession of a self as an object makes it possible for a human being to interact with himself or herself much as he or she interacts with other human beings. This interaction with the self is called self-reflexive behavior. You can look at yourself from the viewpoint of another person. For example, a child may see herself from the viewpoint of a parent. She may warn or scold herself in a gruff voice for doing something that her father disapproves of, or she may praise herself for building a fine castle in the sandbox. This sort of interaction does not end with adulthood. On the contrary, each of us continues to be an *object of our own activity*. Your self is an object in the world just as much as your car or house is an object in the world—and it needs as much attention as a car or a house. You may stand in front of a mirror and admire yourself. You may become angry with yourself and pound on your own head. The self is an object of great concern in your world, and as Mead showed, it is an image that you acquire through role taking.

The play and game stages

Mead was curious about the process through which a child develops the ability to step outside of himself or herself and into other points of view. All children go through a stage of make-believe play during which they step outside of their own roles and become someone else. The **play stage** is a stage when a child is learning to take the roles of people he or she knows. Children play cowboy and Indian, nurse and doctor, Martian and astronaut. Mead believed that this sort of play is an important aspect of normal growth, for through it the child gains skill in role taking, in taking other viewpoints beside his or her own. A little boy steps inside an imaginary phone booth, strips off his imaginary Clark Kent clothing, and creates an adventure in the role of Superman, using all the powers available to that talented gentleman. He thus extends his knowledge of role behavior by acting out roles that he may never perform in real life. But if the opportunity arises, he will have practiced his role; he will be ready.

The activities of children who play together in this way are not usually very well organized. The *play stage* occurs while children are fairly young, perhaps 5 or 6. There is some interaction between the players—the young nurse will hand a spoon to the young surgeon when a scalpel is needed, and the patient (often a younger brother or sister) will amiably expose his or her navel to the spoon. But the players do not fit their activities together in any very complex way. For the most part, they play their separate roles side by side, not yet being skilled enough to perform actions that are truly interdependent.

However, by the **game stage**, the stage at which a child can understand a set of roles as a system, new kinds of behavior become possible and the interaction of children takes new forms. It is not possible to teach most 5-year-olds how to play baseball. They can learn to pitch, to bat, to catch, and to run, but they can't understand the game as a system. Baseball players must constantly interact with one another in terms of a whole set of roles that all of the players understand. For example, all the players know that a runner will try to steal a base if he can. Therefore all the basemen must

F. Leinwand/Monkmeyer

Role playing is a major activity during the "play stage."

be ready to catch a fast ball if he tries to do this, and all the players know what all the other players will do when this happens. Thus each player must take the roles of all the other players at the same time. Young children cannot take so many roles at a time, and therefore they cannot understand the game, but a 10-year-old is in the game stage of development and is likely to be very interested in it.

The roles of baseball players can be described in terms of rules that are agreed upon by everyone who knows baseball. A little leaguer who plays first base does not have to pretend to be a particular famous ballplayer. "Playing" baseball is not like "playing" Superman; it is not make-believe. The point of the game is to follow the rules as closely as possible. In a game, a participant does not take the role of *one* person, as in play, but takes the role of the **generalized other**. This is an abstract role that stands for a whole set of particular roles. The generalized other is a person's understanding of what the whole group has agreed upon. An individual can therefore take the viewpoint of the whole community in judging his or her performance and guiding his or her behavior. It is a sort of reference group built up by the individual through his or her relationships with people who share certain views. Thus the whole community of baseball players and fans agree about the rules and share expectations about performance. A player will take the views of this community and be guided by them.

Games are ways in which the 10- or 11-year-old practices taking the role of the generalized other, judging his or her own behavior in terms of the understandings of a large group of people. No longer guiding himself or herself from the viewpoint of one particular person at a time, the child takes the role of a whole group and guides his or her behavior by their anticipated reactions.

When the child is able to take the role of the generalized other, he or she is mature enough to go beyond the particular situation and behave in a stable way in a variety of different situations. In early childhood he or she saw the world first through one role and then through another and was unable to cope with contradictions between those roles. After the game stage, however, the child may become interested in reconciling different interpretations of reality. He or she will try to arrive at the most general interpretation—that which best explains the views of all the individuals he or she knows. The child is now able to decide that so-and-so's reaction to his or her actions is odd and need not be taken seriously. He or she is able to form a stable self-image and maintain it in the face of contradictory reactions.

Among the highest forms of human activity, according to Mead, is the work of building a generalized other. For example, intellectuals use different points of view as material for their work—different views of society, politics, poetry, or even God. A physicist may spend a lifetime trying to reconcile two contradictory interpretations—such as whether light is a wave or a particle. This abstract work with symbols can be done only by people who have experienced all the earlier stages of role taking.

All normal adults have within them a miniature society. Each person continually makes indications to himself or herself about the immediate situation. He or she may have long internal conversations in which conflicting interpretations are discussed and perhaps reconciled. Mental activity is *internal symbolic interaction*.

I and me

Mead distinguishes between two aspects of the self, which he terms the *I* and the *me*. The "I" consists of the impulses and feelings of the present moment—it is the spontaneous aspect of the person. But normal people do not act on all their impulses; they control themselves. One behaves in a consistent way in terms of a stable self-image. The "me," the ability to control one's impulses so as to organize one's behavior rationally, is developed through social experience. The "me" brings past experience to bear on the present. Still, in the next moment new impulses arise in the "I" phase, for both "I" and "me" are endless.

THE ACT

Symbolic interactionists claim that human conduct is purposeful, goal-directed, problem-solving, adjustive activity and not simply a collection of responses "released" by stimuli. The basic unit of human conduct is the **act**, which the person develops in the course of interacting with self and others. Almost everything important that one does is part of an act, whether it takes a split second or fifty years to complete. Acts nestle inside acts, like the little sets of wooden dolls you buy in Chinatown. Picking up a pencil is an act. It may also be part of a larger act, such as writing a term paper, which, in turn, may be part of the larger act of earning a college degree, and so forth.

The act begins with a feeling of restlessness in the person, which is based on an impulse or desire. This is the "I." You may feel thirsty, for example. In order to organize an act, however, you must first identify the impulse by making an indication to yourself that you are thirsty. If you don't, you will feel restless but will be unable to carry out any complex adjustive behavior. Suppose that you do say to yourself that you are thirsty and need a drink. The act that may follow has two phases—covert and overt. During the **covert phase** you are preparing to act but have not yet begun to do so. Many acts never move beyond the covert stage, for the "me" aspect of the self may simply decide not to act on the desire. For example, if you are thirsty and find yourself in a lifeboat with twenty other people and only a quart of drinking water, you may decide to limit the amount you drink or even offer your share to someone else. The feeling of thirst does not automatically lead to the act of drinking. During the covert phase one

interacts with oneself and organizes future phases of the act. You may tell yourself which beverages are available, warn yourself to avoid caffeine or high-calorie drinks, or remind yourself that your companion is a teetotaler. Having taken such factors into account, you may think of a way to satisfy your desire and then take action (the **overt phase**) to reach your goal. This may require a series of subordinate acts such as finding a glass and turning on the faucet. Throughout all the phases of the act you will continue to adjust your plans by making indications to yourself about your situation—your glass is cracked, perhaps, and must be thrown out; the water is too warm; and so on.

Thus it is that human acts are built up. A person may undertake a very complex act that may take many years to perform and involve interactions with thousands of other people in highly changeable situations. Human beings are able to fit their acts together only because (1) they can define for themselves the nature of their situation and (2) they can build up shared ways of interpreting reality through symbolic communication. Mental activity is primarily linguistic—we are constantly talking either to ourselves or to others.

HOW SYMBOLIC INTERACTIONISTS WORK

Mead died in 1931, but his influence on sociology has never faded. Symbolic interactionism is not the dominant approach to the study of society, but it is an important approach. Most sociologists, including most of those whose work is described in this book, like to show causal relationships—patterns of association between independent and dependent variables. To explain a given behavior pattern, they look for social experiences that happened to the actor before the act was performed and therefore "caused" him or her to behave in that way. Symbolic interactionists do not attempt to answer questions about the "cause" of behavior; rather, they try to find the "meaning" of behavior. That is, they want to know how the actor interprets the situation and what he or she has in mind when responding to the situation. One comparison will illustrate this approach. Sheldon and Eleanor Glueck, two Harvard researchers, looked for the causes of juvenile delinquency by comparing 500 delinquents with 500 nondelinquents living in the same district. Both groups were of comparable age, intelligence, and ethnic origin. They found that delinquent boys were much more likely to come from families that often moved or in which there was only one parent, the father had bad work habits, alcoholism was present, and so on through a host of disadvantages. In other words, they isolated a number of important independent variables that were related to delinquency.[28]

Contrast this to the symbolic interactionist approach taken by Gresham M. Sykes and David Matza in a similar study. They did not ask what *made* a boy delinquent; rather, they asked how such boys managed to offset their own guilt by rationalizing their actions. They show that much delinquency is based on various reasons for deviance that "are seen as valid by the delinquent but not by the legal system or society at large." For example, a young mugger may deny that his victim is a victim by asserting that the victim "started it" or "asked for it." The mugger makes himself into a Robin Hood. Notice that Sykes and Matza's approach does not "explain behavior but only outlines the meaning that it has for the actor."[29]

Symbolic interactionists claim that the only way to determine how people interpret situations is to get inside their world by communicating with them directly. Thus they prefer to collect evidence by means of participant observation instead of using such methods as questionnaires. They argue that a questionnaire presents the respondent with a fixed set of answers to choose from, while none of the answers may fit his or her own interpretation. The researcher should listen to explanations instead of trying to get them to fit a predetermined list of replies.

Group interaction

Having discussed the importance of social groups in the formation of personality and the self, let's look at some of the processes that go on within groups. We want to focus on the boundedness of groups, the interaction across group boundaries, and the sense of "we-ness" that draws members of some, but not all, groups together.

GROUP BOUNDARIES

The University of California at Berkeley is a very informal place. I never realized this until, having done my graduate work there, I went to work at Harvard for two years. At about the same time a friend of mine moved from Harvard to Berkeley and found it almost as hard to adjust to Berkeley as I found it to adjust to Harvard. We used to phone each other and complain. Her complaint was that Berkeley people were "rude." When she joined a group, most people would stay sprawled on the floor; nobody shook hands with her or welcomed her. They treated her as if she had been part of the group all along. She could talk or not talk, whichever she preferred, and when she left nobody seemed to notice. She could drift in, talk, and drift out again without forming any relationships at all. Everyone seemed to have the same informal relationships with everyone else. Whatever happened, happened in public; anybody could take part.

My problem was the opposite. I was shocked to find that Harvard was a set of tight, private cliques. When I sat down at a cafeteria table and overheard an interesting conversation, I joined in, the way I would have in Berkeley, but people often reacted as if I was being "rude." We had not been introduced; we had not shaken hands! What became clear to both my friend and me was that Harvard groups had boundaries while Berkeley groups did not. When a group is described as cold and formal by outsiders and as warm and cohesive

These kibbutz children, unlike the adult members of their community, have very strong group boundaries.

by insiders, it probably has a strong *group boundary*—a clearly defined standard for distinguishing between members and nonmembers. Such a standard allows members of the group to develop closer relationships than they could maintain otherwise, but it keeps out outsiders so that they see it as cold and unfriendly. By the same token, you may find it easier to enter a group with weak boundaries, but once inside it you may not have as strong a sense of belonging.

For some purposes, clear boundaries are important. Friends of mine who belong to an Israeli kibbutz say that their group's worst problem is its guests. Kibbutzim are communes that are devoted to building up cohesiveness (we-feeling) and mutual concern among members. However, each kibbutz accepts a number of outsiders who come to work there for several months, living much the way

members do. The kibbutzim benefit financially from the presence of these visitors, but so many guests (sometimes one guest for every four members) tend to decrease the cohesiveness of the permanent community. The boundaries are weak, with strangers entering and leaving all the time. Some members try to ignore the guests, but they feel bad about doing so. No one has found a solution to this problem.

One way to maintain boundaries is to have a sense of territoriality. This is the idea that all the people who live in a given area are an in-group while others are an out-group, to be excluded from full participation and perhaps even chased away. As mentioned earlier, street gangs often show a sense of territoriality, and it may also be seen in nationalism and other forms of regional loyalty. It has both advantages and disadvantages: It allows the

171

in-group to build up a strong "we-feeling," but at the same time it fosters unfriendly behavior toward members of the out-group.

INTERACTION ACROSS GROUP BOUNDARIES

The "network" approach to sociology is a new way of looking at social groups. This approach, stimulated primarily by the work of Harrison White at Harvard, describes the structure of groups as a series of ties linking different individuals. These networks can be "loose-knit" or "close-knit," depending on whether the people in them all know one another. If you and I know each other and both of us know Tom, Dick, and Harry, and if Tom knows Dick and Harry and Dick knows Harry, our five-person network is completely closed. (See Figure 6.1.) But if I know you, Tom, Dick, and Harry but none of you knows each other, my five-person network is completely open. (See Figure 6.2.) However, this is not likely to happen unless I have a strange sort of secret life. If you and I have a close personal relationship (a strong tie), you are likely to meet my other close friends (Tom, Dick, and Harry) sometime when we are together, and you will probably form at least a weak tie with them. That is, you may not become close friends but you will probably become acquaintances. Your relationship with them may not be primary, but it will be at least secondary. Thus Figure 6.1 is a more common pattern than Figure 6.2.

A person can maintain only a limited number of strong ties; we have only so much time and energy. My network could hardly include more than 20 or 30 strong ties at any given time. Again, that network could be relatively close-knit or relatively loose-knit, depending on how my friends feel about each other.

Mark Granovetter has suggested that we could diagram a large group (such as a city) as a number of clusters of networks, either close-knit or loose-knit and either separate or linked

together.[30] If the city were made up mostly of separate, close-knit networks with few ties linking them together, it could be described as cohesive from one point of view but as fragmented from another point of view. Such a city is cohesive because any person who lives there would have a close, cohesive network of friends who spend all their free time together; they would rarely spend time with outsiders. However, as a whole the city would be fragmented because each network would have strong boundaries and nobody in one network would know anybody in other networks.

Granovetter claims that the ties linking separate networks together and permitting information to flow from one to another are almost always weak ties—acquaintanceships rather than friendships. He also believes that these weak ties are more important than sociologists used to think. They give members of a network access to information that they would otherwise miss. For example, if you are looking for a job, you usually ask people for leads. However, if you are in a very closed network your information will be limited.

FIGURE 6.1

Close-knit network

FIGURE 6.2
Loose-knit network

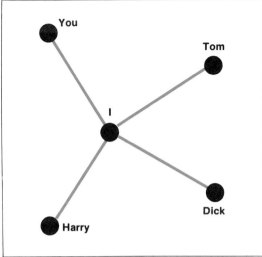

Among members of your closed network, one person is unlikely to know anything the others don't know. Information travels around inside that network, but no new information comes in from a different network. You have to branch out and talk to acquaintances who have "connections" that you don't have. In doing so, you use your weak ties, your bridges or links to other social networks. Indeed, most people find jobs through their acquaintances, not through close friends.

Another reason weak ties are important is that they tie the networks together so that they are not a set of separate islands but form a large, integrated system. In doing so these "bridge" relationships build a larger sense of community. Indeed, Granovetter suggests, though he admits he cannot prove, that some communities are able to muster resistance to a threat (such as a plan for urban renewal) only because their networks are tied together by a large number of weak relationships. Without those links, members of different networks would not trust each other enough to organize on a community-wide basis.

A number of Canadian studies have employed network analysis, chiefly because the University of Toronto is a leading center of network sociology. One researcher, Barry Wellman, has spent twelve years examining "intimate networks" in East York, a borough of Toronto.[31] Wellman and his co-workers began their survey in 1968, asking a number of respondents to name and describe their relationships with up to six intimates ("the persons outside your home that you feel closest to."). We may suppose that their answers are not unlike the responses that would be obtained in a great many other Canadian communities.

Perhaps the most encouraging finding was that almost all of the respondents (98 percent) reported at least one intimate relationship; each person felt close to at least *someone*. The majority reported having five or more such relationships. About half of these relationships were with kin and half with unrelated individuals, mostly friends who were neither neighbors nor co-workers. The respondents generally ranked their kin as closer to them than their non-kin intimates. Three quarters of the East Yorkers' intimates lived in Metropolitan Toronto, but only 13 percent lived in the same neighborhood as the respondent. As a result, most close ties were maintained by phone and by regular visits; if the intimate person lived a great distance away, and phone calls were too expensive, the relationship was put "on hold" to be resumed when the occasion arose.

The great majority of East Yorkers (81 percent) reported that help in an emergency situation could be found somewhere in their intimate network. A smaller majority (60 percent) said that help was available in their intimate network for everyday matters. However, many people turned to "weak ties" for assistance with such ordinary routine problems as borrowing a monkeywrench or arranging for newspaper pick-up when they were away on holidays. These favors were generally performed by neighbors.

Are intimate networks usually mutual or asymmetrical? Think about your own network. Make a mental list of the six people outside your home that you feel closest to. Now imagine that someone asked each of them to name the six people whom *they* felt closest to. How many of their lists would your name be on? The researchers actually tracked down the intimates named by a sub-sample of the East Yorkers and asked them that very question.[32] Only 36 percent named the person who had originally named them. Clearly, intimate relationships are often asymmetrical. They mean different things to the two people involved.

THE SENSE OF COMMUNITY

In the early days of sociology, the favorite indoor sport of evolutionary theorists was comparing traditional societies to modern ones. In general, they believed that although modern societies had advanced in many ways they had gone downhill in other ways. One such theorist was Ferdinand Tönnies (1855-1936), who was concerned about the break-down of primary social relationships. In the old days, he said, society had been held together by a set of inflexible bonds that created stability and security. Such a social environment was a real community, and sociologists still use Tönnies' German term for community—gemeinschaft. With the modernization of many societies, however, relationships have become more impersonal; as the division of labor into different roles has increased, there has been a decline in the importance of kinship and of tradition as a way of life. This pattern of social life may be called associational or, to use Tönnies' term, gesellschaft.

This view was shared by Durkheim, among others, who believed that the changes were caused by the spread of new technologies that called for increasing division of labor and a kind of solidarity based on the differences between people rather than on their similarities. Many present-day sociologists agree that modernization brings with it a loss of community. We will discuss this question again in Chapter 18, which deals with urban life.

SOCIAL RESEARCH:
Sociologists at Work

OBEDIENCE TO AUTHORITY

Society is a collaborative system that would not function if many of its members balked. We routinely place our lives in the control of strangers, trusting in their good will and their ability, such as when we cross a street on a green light in the path of a dump truck. We follow instructions that make no sense at all to us, as long as they are issued by an expert. Compliance is necessary, and yet it can also be the source of irresponsible acts, as the social psychologist Stanley Milgram has shown in a grim experiment.[33]

COMPLIANCE WITH EXPERT AUTHORITY

Milgram investigated the assumption that societies differ in the degree of compliance expected of their members. In some countries repression is extreme and subordinates obey without question, while other societies are characterized by a generally critical population. Milgram hoped to study the sources of submissiveness in authoritarian societies, but first he needed a way to test its limits, to see how far people would go in obeying an authoritative command. He and an accomplice arranged a way to test large numbers of subjects in the United States so that this sample could be used as a baseline against which to compare levels of compliance in more authoritarian societies.

The test is simple. A subject presents himself to Milgram's laboratory for a memory experiment, with the accomplice posing as another subject. Both subjects are shown the equipment, and the accomplice, seemingly by chance, draws the assignment of memorizing a list of word pairs and undergoing a "slight punishment" whenever his memory fails. He is then hooked up to a machine in another room while the subject is taught his part in the experiment. The subject is told to give electric shocks to the other "subject" whenever the latter cannot recall the right words, according to the list. The subject is shown an impressive electrical device that can be adjusted for voltages ranging from 15 to 450 volts. The device bears labels describing the severity of the shock, ranging from "Slight shock" to "Danger: severe shock." The subject is given a sample of the "slight" shock, which in fact hurts quite a lot and convinces him that the severe shocks must be terrible. (Actually, the accomplice gets no shock at all.) Then the experiment begins. The accomplice fails more and more often as time goes by, and the subject is told to increase the voltage. The subject thinks he is giving real shocks and the accomplice acts his part well. He complains, pleads, shouts, bangs on the walls seeking release, and finally falls silent when the voltage is supposedly very high. If the subject protests against his cruel task, the experimenter merely tells him that the test must continue and that he, the experimenter, will be responsible for whatever happens.

What percentage of ordinary American citizens are willing to increase the voltage to the most severe level? Milgram expected that perhaps 1 or 2 percent would do so, but he was amazed to find that *over half* of his subjects gave what they thought were the most severe electric shocks. However, most of the subjects did not enjoy the task and became more anxious and unhappy as they gave greater shocks. They would beg to be freed from role of torturer (nothing kept them from quitting if they decided to), but most of them went on as long as the experimenter told them to continue.

This experiment has been repeated in various forms many times since Milgram's first attempt. It is true that authoritarian compliance varies somewhat in different countries and in different settings. For example, an experimenter who wears dirty overalls and conducts his research in an abandoned warehouse will gain compliance from fewer subjects than a professor in a university laboratory. Well-educated subjects are somewhat less compliant than less well-educated ones. Still, the important discovery is that even among a sophisticated and humane sample, about 40 percent will give the most extreme shock. People will do almost anything when they are told that it is an experiment, presumably because of their willingness to comply with expert authority.

An important aspect of the experiment is the willingness of the experimenter to take responsibility for the outcome. Other research has shown the same effect: When people can assure themselves that they are following orders and therefore are not responsible for their actions, they may do great evil.

GROUP PRESSURE

A person tends to lose his or her sense of personal responsibility in situations that call for compliance with authority. The same thing seems to happen in situations that call for conformity to a group. Many people will agree with almost any ridiculous claim if they have heard a number of other people in the group agree with it. This was shown in some famous experiments conducted by Solomon Asch.

In 1951 Asch arranged for groups of five people to take part in a study of "visual perception."[34] Each subject was given two cards. On the first card a single line had been drawn; the other card contained three parallel lines of different lengths, one of which was exactly as long as the line on the first card. The subject was asked to decide which of the three parallel lines was most similar in length to the one on the first card. These three lines differed so much in length that it was perfectly obvious which one matched the line on the other card. However, of the five people in each group only one was a true subject; all four of the other "judges" were trained stooges. The participants announced their judgments aloud, one after another, with the true subject's turn coming last. Asch had instructed the stooges to give a wrong answer, and they did so in a matter-of-fact way. Asch found that in about 35 percent of the tests the subjects' answers conformed to those of the group instead of to their own perceptions. Later they said that they had not *believed* that the group was correct but had given the wrong answer anyway for the sake of conforming. The results of this experiment have been confirmed in repeated tests by other researchers under varying conditions.

It has been shown that the group must be *unanimous* to have such power over the individual. Hans Christian Anderson was correct: If a single little boy announces that the Emperor has no clothes (or that a 6-inch line is obviously shorter than an 8-inch line), others will regain confidence in their own perceptions and will no longer be swayed by the rest of the group. The fact that disagreement is possible leaves room for the individual to doubt the majority and resist its pressure.

It seems that group influence is effective mainly because most people don't want to be considered deviant.[35] Individuals are highly affected by group pressure if they have doubts about being accepted by a group to which they very much wish to belong. They are also more affected if they have to respond publicly to the other group members than if they can respond in private or anonymously.

I have described group pressure in a negative light, and it is true that many studies show that such pressure decreases personal responsibility and causes people to deny both their perceptions and their moral judgment. We must not forget, however, that group pressure can be useful to society. Such pressure helps establish and maintain social norms and makes group cohesiveness possible. When we see a group doing or saying something we don't understand, most of us assume that the group members know something we don't, so we tend to follow along. Individuals could not participate in group life if they believed most of the other members were stooges who were purposely misleading them. It is normal to trust one's fellow group members and to be impressed by their opinions. It is unfortunate that this normal trust can sometimes lead to personal irresponsibility.

SOCIAL POLICY:
Issues and Viewpoints

Satisfying, emotionally enriching personal relationships are probably the most important aspect of human experience, yet they are the hardest to control by means of social policy. The quality of our relationships with others depends on two factors—our personalities and the structural opportunities we have for spending time together and getting closer. Neither factor is open to much control at the level of public policy. Our personalities are a result of our personal histories. Whether we are warm or cold, kind or suspicious, talkative or secretive depends on old emotions left over from earlier relationships that went well or badly. These color our present and future relationships, and nothing short of intense psychotherapy is likely to change these attitudes in any deep sense. As for our opportunities for getting close to others, the kind of society we live in requires many of us to give most of our attention to a large number of secondary relationships. Moreover, our networks tend to be increasingly open rather than closed. Your fellow workers will not know your fellow squash club members or your school friends, and, even within those separate settings, most of the participants you meet probably don't know each other. There are too many people—and besides, few middle-class people stay in the same neighborhood for long. A few years ago, for example, I realized that although for the past eight years I had given a Thanksgiving dinner party for six or eight of my close friends, none of those friends had come twice. Each had left town by the following year. Primary groups are almost impossible to maintain in such a situation.

The growth of encounter groups is probably due to the desire to fill a need for intimate relationships. Many people today feel the lack of such relationships, and there aren't many institutions that meet their needs in a satisfactory way. Every modern trend seems to break up neighborhoods, scatter individuals over wide areas, move people from one job to another, and so on. These trends are hard on primary group relationships. On the other hand, a stable, closed society with permanent primary relationships provides only the *opportunity* to develop intimacy and emotional warmth. If the personalities are not able to interact in a fulfilling way, a primary group may become not warm and satisfying but vicious and spiteful. In that case, moving away becomes, like some divorces, a move toward liberation.

I want to mention again a topic that is related both to social science and to ethics. This is the issue of group pressure and personal responsibility. Social science is discovering how human beings manipulate each other. Already we can give practical advice to advertisers, political campaign managers, brainwashers, army generals, and directors of concentration camps. But we can also advise those who want to do positive work with groups—camp counselors, group therapists in prisons, planners of library reading rooms and rock festivals, and so on. What are the ethical limits of studying such manipulation? Should social scientists refuse to do research that may be used to manipulate human beings? This is not as simple a question as it may seem. In principle we oppose any policy that would deprive individuals of free choice. But we all try to "manipulate" others at times, though we call it "influence." Parents try to influence their children to behave properly. Psychiatrists try to influence their patients to behave sanely. These efforts, like all efforts at social control, are, in a sense, manipulative.

We know from Stanley Milgram's work that it is possible to get at least half of the people in the world to torture other people. Milgram's subjects believed that they were torturing their partners, yet they followed orders without punishment or reward.

Should Milgram have done this experiment? Is it good for people to know how to manipulate others? What effect did Milgram's experiment have on the subjects who agreed to give the maximum shock? Milgram reports that many of them broke down emotionally but thanked him afterwards for showing them their own weaknesses. Often they claimed to have learned from the experience and vowed never to follow orders blindly again. Milgram's experiment is so upsetting that few social scientists could have done it, yet if it had not been done we would never have found out how many people are ready to obey like robots.

Personal irresponsibility is a major social problem. However, it is rarely called a *social* problem because we do not know what to do about it collectively. Public policy cannot easily change human character, for character is formed in private socialization through loving relatedness and through the experience of compassion.

Still, social science has a message to tell: Most of the evil in this world is done not by brutes and madmen but by Everyman. Adolf Eichmann was not mentally ill; he was an ordinary Nazi bureaucrat who followed orders to the letter.[36] Ordinary citizens are often afraid to take responsibility, even when they might prevent a violent crime. This attitude is a serious social problem—one that social scientists hope to understand better in the future in order to "manipulate" the situations that give rise to it. Social phenomena that are understood may perhaps be controlled.

Irresponsibility is not a new problem. In Shakespeare's *Henry V*, two soldiers discuss the morality of doing battle. One of them says, "We know enough if we know we are the king's subjects: If his cause be wrong, our obedience to the king wipes the crime of it out of us."[37] The reasoning is always the same: Evil is no evil if it is conformity.

SUMMARY

1. A human being's need for social interaction has biological bases that are also found in other species. Territoriality is one trait that is shared by humans and nonhumans. Interaction rituals are also found in primates as well as human beings.

2. Human behavior is variable because it is guided not by instincts but by group relationships. A *primary group* is an intimate group bound together by a sense of "we-ness." The members of such a group relate to each other as individuals. Families and close friendship groups are primary groups. Impersonal ties based on role relationships characterize *secondary groups*.

3. *Peer groups* are made up of people of similar status. A *reference group* is the group to which we compare ourselves. Large, complex groups include tribes and clans, social classes, ethnic groups, crowds, churches, universities, and nation-states.

4. *Symbolic interactionists* such as Cooley and Mead emphasize the importance of the group for the development of our perceptions of ourselves and the world. Cooley's major contributions were the notions of the primary group and the looking-glass self. Mead distinguished between symbolic and nonsymbolic interaction, though he recognized that they are related in complex ways. People communicate mostly by sharing significant symbols and through the process of *role taking*.

5. Through role taking we learn the meaning of the objects, including our selves, that exist for the other person. With a self-concept one can interact with oneself. This is mental activity. It involves taking the role of the *generalized other*, an abstract role that stands for a set of particular roles with which we have become familiar. The generalized other is not formed until the *game stage* of childhood.

6. The "I" is the spontaneous aspect of the self, while the "me" is the aspect that limits the impulses of the "I."

7. Human behavior is goal directed. It involves building up *acts*, each of which has a *covert* (internal) *phase* and an *overt* (external) *phase*.

8. The strength of the boundaries around groups varies. One way in which such boundaries are maintained is *territoriality*, which distinguishes in-group members from out-group members on the basis of where they live.

9. Networks can be close-knit or loose-knit. They can also be separate or linked together by a number of weak ties. A large group made up of a series of close-knit networks is cohesive from the individual's point of view but is fragmented as a larger community. Weak ties are important because they act as bridges between networks.

10. *Gemeinschaft* refers to a sense of community that is believed to characterize traditional, stable, preindustrial life. *Gesellschaft* refers to the associational type of life that is characteristic of modern societies.

KEY TERMS

act   the basic unit of human conduct.

covert phase   the phase during which one is preparing to act but has not yet begun to do so.

game stage   the stage at which a child can understand a set of roles as a system.

gemeinschaft   a society held together by a set of stable, secure bonds; a community.

generalized other   an abstract role that stands for a set of particular roles.

gesellschaft   a social system in which relationships are impersonal or associational.

looking-glass self   the self-image that a person acquires from the opinions of others.

overt phase   the phase during which an act is actually performed.

peer group   a group of people of similar status.

play stage   the stage at which a child is learning to take the roles of people he or she knows.

primary group   a group whose members interact in a personal, intimate, and emotional way.

reference group   the group to which one compares oneself when judging one's own status.

role taking   the ability of a person to imagine the role of another person with whom he or she interacts.

secondary group   a group whose members interact in an impersonal, unsentimental, and businesslike way.

self-reflexive behavior   interaction with self.

significant other   a person whose opinions are important to one; often a family member.

territoriality   the establishment of a certain zone or space that may not be occupied by any other person or animal.

FOR FURTHER READING

BLUMER, HERBERT. *Symbolic Interactionism.* Englewood Cliffs, N.J.: Prentice-Hall, 1969. Blumer was one of my favorite teachers and everything I know about symbolic interactionism and George Herbert Mead I learned from him. Several thousand other former students can say the same thing. This is his own collection of essays—mostly theoretical, but clear, plain writing.

BROWN, ROGER. *Social Psychology.* New York: Free Press, 1965. This textbook is sophisticated, but the style is marvelously personal. Brown takes various topics in social psychology and tells the history of each idea as it was developed by one researcher after another. He even manages to inject a little suspense as you wait to see how each new study turns out. Sometimes he makes little side comments, such as "Whoops! It works out wrong!"

DIMOND, STUART J. *The Social Behavior of Animals.* New York: Harper & Row, 1970. Those of you who are interested in species other than your own may find this a rewarding source of material.

EKMAN, PAUL and WALLACE V. FRIESEN. *Unmasking the Face.* Englewood Cliffs, N.J.: Prentice-Hall, 1975. These are the results of their work on the expressions that reveal human emotions. I find this research intriguing.

HAAS, JACK and WILLIAM SHAFFIR. *Shaping Identity in Canadian Society.* Scarborough, Ont.: Prentice-Hall, 1980. This book takes a symbolic interactionalist approach to the question of Canadian identity.

HARE, A. PAUL, EDGAR F. BORGATTA, and ROBERT FREED BALES, eds. *Small Groups: Studies in Social Interaction.* 3rd ed. New York: Knopf, 1962. For years this has been one of the basic texts on small group research.

LOFLAND, LYN H. *A World of Strangers: Order and Action in Urban Public Space.* New York: Basic Books, 1973. This is a book on social interactions in public.

LUCAS, REX. *Minetown, Milltown, Railtown.* Toronto: University of Toronto Press, 1971. This is a descriptive account of life in Canadian towns that are organized around a single industry.

MEAD, GEORGE HERBERT. *On Social Psychology: Selected Papers.* Rev. ed. Edited by Anselm Strauss. Chicago: University of Chicago Press, 1964. I have never found Mead's writing easy to follow, and I never managed to get through *Mind, Self, and Society,* which was compiled posthumously by his students from his lecture notes. This collection of his papers is somewhat easier to read.

SCHOECK, HELMUT. *Envy.* London: Secker and Warburg, 1969. Some contemporary sociologists do research on human emotions and sentiments as they relate to social interaction. This is the only such book I have seen that deals with envy, an emotion that is particularly important in understanding social stratification.

SOMMER, ROBERT. *Personal Space.* Englewood Cliffs, N.J.: Prentice-Hall, 1969. A treat to read, Sommer's book is the definitive work on such topics as how people arrange their chairs when they want to talk or when they want to maintain privacy, and so on.

7

DEVIANCE AND CONTROL

Types of deviance
    Deviant behavior
    Deviant habits
    Other types of deviance
The social construction of deviance
    Making the rules
    Enforcing the rules
    Labeling the deviant
Controlling deviance
    Socialization
    Informal group pressure
    Social sanctions
The consequences of deviance
    Deviance and disorganization
    Positive functions of deviance
    The normality of deviance
The relativity of deviance
    Norms govern roles
    Role conflict
Theories of deviance
    Kinds-of-people theories
    Situation theories
Social Research: Sociologists at Work
Social Policy: Issues and Viewpoints

The subject of this chapter is knavery, skulduggery, cheating, unfairness, crime, sneakiness, malingering, cutting corners, immorality, dishonesty, betrayal, graft, corruption, wickedness, and sin—in short, deviance. When we say that someone is deviant we do not simply mean that he or she is "odd" or "different." We mean that he or she is *guilty of violating a norm*. Deviance is everywhere, for all societies have rules, and where there are rules there is deviance. It may be a matter of cheating on your income tax or on your wife, of disrespect to the flag, or of not taking out the trash when it's your turn.

Why do so many people insist on violating rules? Or, to turn the question around, why, despite the obvious convenience of violating rules, do so many people insist on complying with them? Most of us do not just "go along with morality" but, as Durkheim pointed out, "find charm in the accomplishment of a moral act prescribed by a rule that has no other justification than that it is a rule. We feel a . . . pleasure in performing our duty simply because it is our duty."[1]

The satisfaction of doing right has something to do with the fact that it *is* right, even if it is difficult, dangerous, or costly. Sometimes we seek out, so to speak, moral mountains to climb and exult in the strenuous task. It makes as much sense to ask, "Why should we do wrong, despite our sense of duty?" as to ask, "Why should we do right?" These are two ways of asking the same question, because if we can explain why human beings behave properly we will at the same time explain why human beings sometimes misbehave. Thus a theory of deviant behavior is also a theory of conformity.

Whatever people want—food, shelter, sex, or contract bridge—they must get through organized social patterns in which the actions of many people fit together. There must be some understandings about who is supposed to do what and in what situations. Though we can debate whether any *particular* rule is necessary or useful, we must agree on the need

for *some* rules, however arbitrary they may be. For example, if traffic is to move along the highways, it is less important whether the rule says that people must drive on the right or the left than that there be a rule.

However, you can't take it for granted that if you play by the rules things will go your way. You may get bored. The costs may not be worth the possible rewards. You may find that you can get what you want more quickly and easily by not following the rules. There are always temptations to cut corners or otherwise violate the norm. Every rule, then, creates the possibility of deviance.

Let's define **deviance** as any form of behavior that violates the norms of a social group or of society. You will remember that norms cover a wide range—from, say, the norm requiring us to eat fried chicken with a knife and fork in a fancy restaurant to the rule forbidding murder. Not all deviance consists of breaking laws. If you spend every dollar you own and every minute of your time playing pinball machines, you will not be a criminal but you will be deviant. If you are drunk by ten o'clock every morning, you may not be violating a law but you will be violating a strong social norm (and you won't feel very good either!). As long as any rule (or norm) is recognized as valid, however informally, then breaking that rule is an act of deviance. However, the norms that people believe in most firmly are usually backed up by laws. For this reason, the study of deviance is largely a study of serious social problems, especially crime.

Types of deviance

It is convenient to classify deviant behavior into four main categories: (1) deviant behavior, (2) deviant habits, (3) deviant psychologies, and (4) deviant cultures. In the rest of the chapter we will deal primarily with the first two categories.

DEVIANT BEHAVIOR

Crime as deviance

The deviant acts that generally cause us the most concern are aggressive crimes such as murder, rape, and robbery. The frequency of such acts increased throughout North America for twenty years or so, though not at the same rate in every region or city. Over the past few years, crimes have probably leveled off in frequency because the bulk of such acts

are carried out by adolescent boys; because the birth rates declined in the early 1960s, fewer adolescent boys are around these days to get into trouble.

I say that the crime rate has *probably* leveled off because it is very hard to estimate how much crime actually occurs in society. Official police statistics may record as few as one out of every twenty-three crimes.[2] A constable who catches a teenage boy committing a crime may decide to simply warn him and not record the crime. Throughout North

FIGURE 7.1

Juvenile delinquents classified by type of delinquency and percentage distribution, 1973

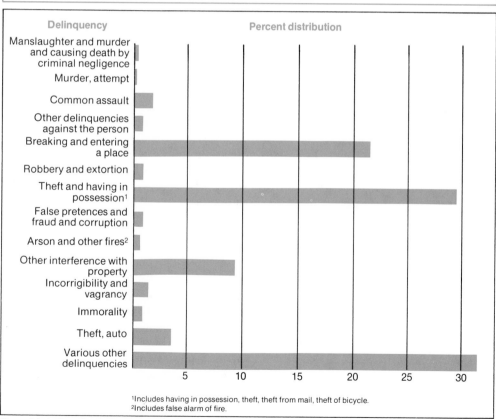

¹Includes having in possession, theft, theft from mail, theft of bicycle.
²Includes false alarm of fire.

Source: Adapted from Canada Year Book, 1928, p. 59.

America, the police can use wide discretion in deciding what to consider a crime. Canada's Juvenile Delinquent Act defines delinquency extremely vaguely, and frequently allows the police officer to judge whether an offence has been committed. In 1970, the Metropolitan Toronto Police Youth Bureau interviewed about 24,000 juveniles for possible violations, but only referred 21 percent of those to juvenile court. The rest were cautioned and released to their parents; occasionally they were referred to social agencies.[3]

Some crimes are more likely to be detected than others. Public outrage pressures the police to concentrate their actions on finding those who commit such crimes as armed robbery or sexual assaults on children.[4] The public is less concerned, however, about illegal gambling or false advertising. Moreover, a vast number of crimes are not reported. Crimes without victims are generally not detected because they are "invisible." For example, the people involved in crimes such as drug use, prostitution, and gambling are willing participants and therefore do not report the crime.[5] Women usually do not report rape because they will be questioned about their personal lives[6] and, as lawyer Maureen McTeer has shown, they may have to produce color photographs later in court to prove that they have been physically injured.[7]

Obviously, then, police records do not reflect the true patterns of deviance in a population. We can correct for the bias in crime statistics to some extent, but we are always left with some doubt about the actual rate and pattern of crime in a given population. The best estimates of crime rates are based on three kinds of information: (1) police statistics; (2) surveys asking people how many crimes they have experienced as victims; and (3) surveys asking people how many criminal acts they have participated in. Surveys are expensive, and the ones that are conducted usually try to obtain estimates of the number of victims, not the number of offenders in a population. One of the most

thorough of the Canadian surveys regarding crime was conducted in Toronto by M. C. Courtis in 1970.[8] It showed that about five times as many crimes were experienced as were reported to police.

Despite their shortcomings, crime rate estimates have to be used by government officials and by social scientists all the time. How can better estimates be obtained? P. J. Giffen has proposed that census takers should routinely ask all Canadians whether they have been victimized by crime; results should be included in Canadian census data. Giffen maintains that standardized reporting will lend greater reliability to the statistics produced by the Ministry of the Solicitor General. This improvement could then be followed by the development of more consistent methods of counting and classifying crimes at the level of the police department, the court, and the correctional institution.[9]

Who commits deviant acts?

Canada's crime rates are neither among the lowest nor the highest of contemporary societies. A comparison of Canadian and American rates in 1973 is presented in Table 7.1. The only category in which the Canadian crime rate exceeded the American rate was theft. On the other hand, the comparison with British rates found in Table 7.2 is less favorable to Canada; though the Canadian homicide rate averaged lower than that of the U.S., it was substantially higher than that of Britain. Of course, all of these conclusions have been determined by official crime rates that we have already admitted are poor estimates of the true rate of crime.

A number of studies have shown that more criminal offences are committed by males than females. In 1973, Canadian statistics showed that boys committed 17 times as many crimes against property with violence as girls did. For crimes against property *without* violence, the disparity, though not as great, was still quite marked; boys committed 4 times as many such crimes as girls did. Since

1973, the gap between boys' and girls' crime rates seems to be steadily decreasing.[10]

Offenders, or people who commit deviant acts, are not a sinister minority. Even if we limit our discussion to people who, at one time or another, violate criminal law, most of us are offenders. In a survey conducted in the New York area, 99 percent of the respondents admitted having committed one or more technically criminal offenses. In their adult lives, men had committed an average of 18 offenses, and women an average of 11. Probably very few of the crimes came to the attention of the police.[11]

TABLE 7.1

Comparison crime index rates per 100,000 population in Canada and the United States, 1973

CANADA	RATE	UNITED STATES	RATE
Murder and manslaughter	2.4	Murder and non-negligent manslaughter	9.3
Rape	7.2	Forcible rape	24.3
Robbery	59.6	Robbery	182.4
Wounding and attempted murder	10.7	Aggravated assault	198.4
Breaking and entry	896.3	Burglary	1210.8
Theft	2163.3	Larceny and theft	2051.2
Theft—motor vehicles	324.0	Auto theft	440.1
Total crime index	3463.5	Total crime index	4116.4

Source: P.J. Giffen, "Official Rates of Crime and Delinquency," in *Crime and Its Treatment in Canada,* ed. by W.T. McGrath (Toronto: Macmillan, 1976), p. 108.

TABLE 7.2

Average rates[1] of reported offences for rape, robbery, and wounding in Canada, England and Wales, and the United States, 1963-67

NATION	RAPE	ROBBERY	WOUNDING[2]
Canada	4	37	6
England and Wales	2	9	56
United States	12	77	110

[1]Rates per 100,000 population.
[2]Termed aggravated assault in the United States.

Source: Donald J. Mulvihill and Melvin M. Tumin (co-directors), *Crimes of Violence, Vol. 11, Staff Report Submitted to the National Commission on the Causes and Prevention of Violence* (Washington D.C.: United States Government Printing Office, 1969), p. 124.

TABLE 7.3

Self-reported delinquent behavior of middle-class adolescents by age group

TYPE OF OFFENSE[a]	PERCENT ADMITTING OFFENSE		PERCENT ADMITTING OFFENSE MORE THAN ONCE OR TWICE	
	AGE 13-14	AGE 15-19	AGE 13-14	AGE 15-19
Driven a car without a driver's license	28.6	62.3	9.1	27.9
Taken little things that did not belong to you	61.0	67.2	10.4	16.7
Skipped school without a legitimate excuse	13.6	40.8	3.9	13.6
Driven beyond the speed limit	5.8	51.2	1.3	39.7
Participated in drag-races along the highway with your friends	6.5	31.1	2.0	16.3
Engaged in a fist fight with another boy	45.8	56.0	7.1	8.7
Been feeling "high" from drinking beer, wine, or liquor	11.7	39.0	2.6	17.9
Gambled for money at cards, dice, or some other game	42.2	66.0	16.9	37.4
Remained out all night without parents' permission	19.5	25.8	5.2	9.5
Taken a car without owner's knowledge	5.2	12.5	0.7	3.1
Been placed on school probation or expelled from school	0.7	5.6	0.0	1.2
Destroyed or damaged public or private property of any kind	44.8	52.0	11.7	14.8
Taken little things of value (between $2 and $50) which did not belong to you	9.7	16.0	0.7	3.5
Tried to be intimate with a member of the opposite sex	18.2	37.8	7.8	17.6
Broken into or tried to break and enter a building with the intention of stealing	5.2	7.5	0.7	1.0
Sold, used, or tried to use drugs of some kind	1.3	1.0	0.0	0.3
Bought or tried to buy beer, wine, or liquor from a store or adult	3.3	24.8	0.7	11.7
Taken money of any amount which did not belong to you from someone or someplace	30.5	32.7	7.1	6.9
Taken a glass of beer, wine, or liquor at a party or elsewhere with your friends	32.5	64.8	8.4	35.2

[a]Two items are omitted because they were used solely to check reliability.

Source: Edmund W. Vaz, "Delinquency among Middle-class Boys," *Canadian Review of Sociology and Anthropology,* 2 (1965), 514–515.

The violator of the law, then, is Everyman. In Edmund Vaz's study of middle-class Canadian high school boys, about two-thirds of the boys aged 15 to 19 admitted that they had taken little things that did not belong to them, gambled for money, driven without a license, or drunk alcoholic beverages with friends. Over half of the boys admitted that they had driven faster than the speed limit, gotten into fistfights, or destroyed property. These boys were rarely labeled delinquent, however. These kinds of misbehavior usually cause little damage to property or harm to other people, so police overlook them and concentrate on the more aggressive acts of lower-class boys.[12]

Many similar studies have focused on "hidden offenses."[13] It does not follow that there are no differences between "hidden" and "official" offenders. On the contrary, those who find their way into court are, *on the average*, likely to have committed a greater variety of offenses, more serious offenses, and the same offenses more often.[14] We are all offenders, but we differ in our patterns of offending.

Organized Crime

There is a large and rich organization that supplies a variety of illegal goods and services—especially gambling, narcotics, and high-interest loans. It is also involved in legitimate businesses, in labor unions, and even in the corruption of public officials. This enormous secret organization or "mob" is so powerful that its victims do not dare complain about its activities or testify against its members. Witnesses who help government investigators may have to change their names afterward and leave the country for their own safety.

The major illegal business of the mob is gambling, whether through numbers lotteries, sports, off-track betting, or hidden casinos. Canada probably loses from $100 to $200 million per year in illegal gambling, 10 percent of which goes to the Mafia. Gambling opera-

tions are linked to organizations in other cities and other countries. The telephone records of known Montreal gambling houses have revealed long-distance charges which amount to thousands of dollars per month, spent for calls to Toronto, Chicago, Miami, New York, Hamilton, Sarnia, Guelph, and other cities.[15]

Loan sharking is another profitable business. Gamblers borrow to pay for their losses, heroin addicts borrow to pay for their habits, and some businessmen borrow if they are desperate and cannot get loans through legitimate channels. Interest rates on such loans range from 1 percent to 150 percent a week, and loan sharks use violence to collect payments or to prevent borrowers from reporting them to the authorities.

Organized crime is increasingly penetrating legitimate business. Some mobs own real estate. Some influence labor unions. (The Montreal waterfront has long been troubled by the strong-arm tactics of mobsters.) The most profitable rackets in large cities are often controlled by La Cosa Nostra, sometimes known as the Mafia. The code of La Cosa Nostra demands loyalty and absolute obedience of its members. If necessary, lower-level members are expected to go to prison quietly in order to protect their bosses. The boss may order the killing of any member for any reason. Because the code is so effective, it is very hard for law enforcement officials to penetrate the organization with spies, and so it largely operates beyond the control of the law.

There are a number of different organizations within La Cosa Nostra, all referred to as "families." One of these families generally won't interfere in an area controlled by a different family; otherwise gang warfare may break out between the two groups. The center of the entire system is New York City.

In Canada, two different families are suspected to be operating, one in Toronto and the other in Montreal. Toronto crime is apparently less organized than crime in Montreal. The Montreal family is rivalled by a French

Canadian mob run by eight brothers; however, they seem to have an agreement to share control of the city, for no war has so far taken place between the two gangs. La Cosa Nostra is evidently not established in Canada west of Ontario. There is a gambling operation of some size in Winnipeg, but its ties seem to lead to California, not to any Mafia organization. Vancouver, the largest drug market in Canada, has supported a number of competing narcotics syndicates that have different sources of supply. The control of distribution in Canada shifts according to the success of various groups in importing the drugs.[16]

Other deviant behaviors

SEXUAL DEVIANCE   Several forms of sexual behavior are considered deviant. Among them are homosexuality, prostitution, and incest. Laws on these matters vary from place to place, but sexual relations between siblings and between parent and child are forbidden everywhere. Prostitution, even where it is illegal, is not usually considered a very serious offense.

Most Canadians view homosexuality as deviant, but this opinion has not been shared everywhere and at all times. Indeed, a study that compared the attitudes of 76 known societies found that homosexuality was considered normal in 64 percent of those societies.[17] Furthermore, homosexual activity occurs between males and occasionally between females in animal species in the wild.[18] Studies of North Americans suggest that over one-third of white males and a somewhat smaller percentage of females have engaged in a homosexual act at some time, and that between 1 and 4 percent of the population is exclusively homosexual.[19] Any sexual act is now legal in Canada if it is performed in private by two consenting adults. When one of the partners is under the age of 18, the older person can be charged, regardless of whether he or she initiated the sexual action.

SUICIDE   Some societies have viewed suicide as noble, but in Canada it is generally seen as a sign of moral failure. Suicide is a major cause of death among males. In 1976, for example, over 2000 males and over 800 females committed suicide in Canada. Each year, some 18 percent of male deaths and 7 percent of female deaths are officially recognized as acts of self-destruction.[20] Emile Durkheim's book *Suicide* is an early and important work on this subject.[21]

DEVIANT HABITS

Sometimes deviant behavior becomes a habitual way of life; deviant habits include alcoholism, drug addiction, and compulsive gambling. Acts that are acceptable when performed only occasionally may become social problems when they dominate a person's life. Thus a minister may sponsor bingo games to raise money for the church, yet become very concerned about a church member who cashes his insurance policies to raise money to bet on horses.

The most familiar example of a deviant habit is problem drinking. In 1960 it was estimated that there were at least 228,000 alcoholics in Canada. Only about ten percent of these had been treated and no one could say how effective any treatment had been.[22] Researchers have compared the effects of alcohol and other drugs that are popular in Canada, such as marijuana, LSD, or even heroin. They insist that alcohol causes more misery, more death, more property damage, and more legal complications than any other drug, and possibly more than all the other drugs together.[23] In most murders, the killer, the victim, or both have been drinking; this is especially true of homicides involving a domestic or social relationship.[24] Alcohol is a factor in most divorces. It is also a major factor in traffic accidents; in about half of all fatal collisions in Canada, the drivers have been drinking. The current legal limit to the alcohol percentage in a driver's blood stream is .08, yet research shows that driving skills are impaired at about half that level.[25]

Who are the heavy drinkers and why do

they drink? Heavy drinking is most common among middle-aged people. Younger people tend to drink large amounts now and then, while older people drink smaller amounts more often. Single, divorced, or separated people are more likely to drink heavily than married or widowed people. Males drink more heavily than females. People of higher socioeconomic status are more likely to drink but less likely to be heavy drinkers than people of lower socioeconomic status. City dwellers are more likely to drink than country people. Whites and nonwhites drink about the same amount, except that black women are especially likely to either not drink at all or drink heavily.[26]

There are a great many theories and a lot of empirical evidence on the causes of problem drinking. Most studies of this problem have focused on personality as the cause. A popular

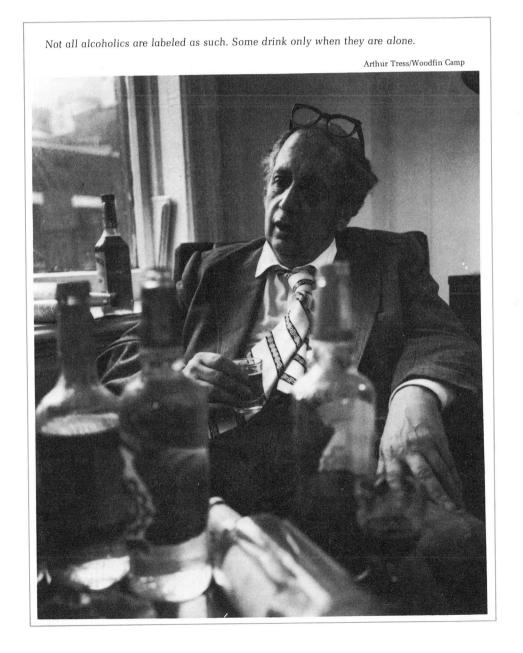

Not all alcoholics are labeled as such. Some drink only when they are alone.

Arthur Tress/Woodfin Camp

theory claims that alcoholism is an attempt to make up for a lack of oral satisfactions, such as sucking, biting, and kissing, during infancy. Unfortunately for this theory, empirical results do not support these claims. For one thing, drinking does not relieve the alcoholic from anxiety or depression. Indeed, these negative feelings seem to be greater during a drinking spree, and more so for problem drinkers than for others. Moreover, although a few studies have found problem drinkers to be especially dependent, most have not. On the contrary, what is more striking is that—at least for males—people who drink too much have tended since childhood to be aggressive, masculine, hyperactive, and seemingly self-confident.[27] Some researchers have assumed that this is only a mask covering feelings of anxiety and insecurity, but more recently the explanation has turned in another direction.

David McClelland and his associates have studied males who drink too much and have concluded that they drink primarily in order to feel stronger.[28] Heavy drinkers are especially concerned about personal power and for various reasons choose drinking as an outlet rather than, say, wearing flashy clothes, gambling, or showing off in aggressive ways. Of course drinking can bring on other attempts to show personal power, such as fights, car accidents, and sexual exploitation. But some men who can afford to do so may do things like collecting motorcycles instead of going on a drinking spree. It is a question of channeling the need for personal power in one direction or another. Men who turn to drinking tend to spend all their money this way, so it becomes even harder for them to express their need for power in other ways.

Personality is not the whole explanation for problem drinking, of course. There is plenty of evidence that both biological and cultural factors play a part in this behavior— possibly even a larger part than personality. The biological aspect is supported by the fact that identical twins have the same degree of addiction to alcohol more often than fraternal twins (whose genes are as different as those of nontwin siblings).[29] Also, animal researchers have produced a strain of inbred mice that prefer alcohol.[30]

The importance of the cultural factor was shown by Don Cahalan's American survey, which tried to find out which of several factors most influences drinking habits. Cahalan concluded that personality tests were much less effective than cultural attitudes in identifying heavy drinkers. That is, problem drinkers are not noticeably maladjusted, but they are located in groups that have a very permissive attitude toward heavy drinking. They began drinking at an earlier age than other people and seem to have learned to expect at that age that alcohol would do great things for them—that it would make them feel good, improve their social life, and so on. Groups that encourage such ideas encourage problem drinking.

OTHER TYPES OF DEVIANCE

Deviant psychologies

About one out of twelve North Americans will spend some part of his or her life in a mental hospital.[31] A far greater percentage will become so upset by an emotional crisis that they must take time out from their usual roles, whether they admit to being "neurotic" or not. Mental and emotional disorders are forms of deviance when they interrupt routine social life. Sociologists are reluctant to use terms such as *psychosis* and *neurosis* the way doctors use the terms *pneumonia* or *appendicitis*. Even well-trained psychiatric workers do not always agree in their diagnoses of mental illnesses, which are actually matters of degree and do not fall into clear-cut categories. Indeed, a few researchers believe that being classified as mentally ill often gives a person a "role" to live up to. For this reason, a person who is thought to be mentally ill is more likely to act in odd ways than he or she would be if

Beckwith Studios

It is hard to diagnose many cases of mental illness—but not catatonia. If someone raises the patient's arm, she will leave it up for a long time.

earlier odd behaviors had been overlooked or defined as ordinary quirks.[32]

The researchers who take this view claim that "mental illness" is not really a medical problem, by and large. They acknowledge that sometimes a patient's brain is damaged by alcohol, syphilis, or other physical problems, and for such a patient, behavioral problems do have a medical origin. However, such cases may be a small fraction of all the conditions that are labeled "mental illness." According to these researchers, the majority of psychiatric patients should not be considered as "ill" but

as suffering from problems in living. The best-known spokesperson for this point of view is Thomas Szasz, who wrote a book entitled *The Myth of Mental Illness*. Szasz is quite aware that some people behave in odd ways, but he wants them put in jail, rather than in mental hospitals, if they break the law.

Not many sociologists would take such an extreme position.[33] Many would agree, however, that most forms of mental illness should be examined with more skepticism. Just because someone is judged insane and kept in a hospital, we should not assume that there is a

191

precise, scientific diagnosis behind this label. For one thing, the other members of the patient's family may be quite disturbed themselves and may be "scapegoating" the weakest member of the family, whose madness can be best understood as a response to a crazy situation. This does happen.

Most psychiatric examinations are brief, and in some provinces (such as Prince Edward Island and New Brunswick) only one physician's examination is needed to commit a person to a mental institution. Once committed, the patient loses all ordinary rights to choose the medical treatment that will be administered. In the Maritimes, many mental hospital inmates are forcibly detained and committed to institutions against their will. All that is needed to keep a patient locked up for a lifetime is the physician's belief that the patient (1) suffers from mental disorder; (2) needs to be kept in hospital for his own safety or that of others; and (3) is not suitable for "voluntary" admission to the hospital.[34] Not surprisingly, Canadians concerned about civil liberties have protested that this situation endangers our most basic human rights. Most people have periods of stress when they fail, at least temporarily, to act "like themselves." Once they find themselves in hospital, however, they may find that it's not so easy to get out again.

A study of Canadian rates of hospital treatment for mental illness has shown that, per 100,000 population, the number of patients in hospitals at any given time has been quite constant over the past 40 years. However, a greater number of individuals today are admitted to mental institutions, and a greater number are discharged from them. The greater discharge rate is the result of the use of tranquilizers. More patients are treated with drugs and treated on an outpatient basis than before. We do not know, however, why so many more patients are admitted to hospital than before. Are there more disturbed people in today's society than forty years ago? Or are people being admitted to mental hospi-

tals today on the basis of less severe symptoms? This is not clear.[35]

Deviant cultures

Many groups within a society develop patterns of thought and behavior that set them apart from the larger group. These groups are to varying degrees deviant in the eyes of the members of "straight" society. The most obvious examples of "deviant" cultures are *countercultures*. Kenneth Westhues, who has studied countercultures ranging from the early Christian gnostics to the flower children of the 1960s, believes that countercultures are characterized by rejection of rationality and pursuit of "transcendence," or heightened consciousness. Westhues lists seven behavioral characteristics of countercultures:

1 Relationships among members of the counterculture tend to be communistic in that they share the ownership of property.
2 Sexual relationships among members of the counterculture deviate from the nuclear family and monogamous marriage. They may practice group marriage, complete abstinence from sex, or anything in between these extremes.
3 The counterculture claims superiority over the dominant society, but it does not try to impose its way of life on others. It sees itself primarily as a spiritual elite.
4 Members look to spiritual leaders who claim to have had transcendental experiences.
5 The counterculture is not political in its orientation, except when the parent culture opposes it. When this happens, the counterculture must fight for survival as a group.
6 The members reject many of the status symbols of the larger society. They are rarely concerned about the beauty of their material possessions.
7 Because of the preceding factors, the counterculture exists in social isolation from the main culture and builds up a system of norms all its own.[36]

Besides countercultures, there are a number of other types of subculture that are deviant to varying degrees. Street gangs, organized crime, and certain religious sects have norms and beliefs that are quite different from those of the larger community.

The social construction of deviance

Deviance results not only from the actions of the offender but also from the actions of conforming members of society. It is the conformists who (1) make the rules, (2) enforce them, and (3) call the offenders deviants.

MAKING THE RULES

Deviance is possible only because there are rules to break. But rules do not just come into existence whenever they are "needed" or "wanted." This is particularly true of laws, as opposed to informal social norms. Howard Becker has shown that someone must have a strong enough interest in getting a law on the books to push for its passage. He calls such people "moral entrepreneurs." They make it their business to sew another patch onto the moral fabric of society.

One kind of work that the moral entrepreneur does is to persuade others that the proposed law will protect a recognized social value. Values are general statements about what is good or desirable, but their implications for conduct in specific situations are not always obvious. Someone must search for a general value that will justify the new rule. In addition, the moral entrepreneur must defend the new rule against its opponents, who may invoke a different value in support of their position. The work includes publicity—the arousal of a sense of urgency about the proposed law. It also includes neutralization of the objections of others whose interests will be adversely affected by the law.

Becker illustrates this process by showing how the Marijuana Tax Act of 1937 was enacted. The U.S. Bureau of Narcotics was the moral entrepreneur in this case. Before 1937 marijuana was not regarded as a serious social problem, and state laws banning it were not enforced. Then the Bureau of Narcotics began to promote the idea that marijuana was a major threat to the general welfare. As a result, a federal law outlawing the use of marijuana was quickly passed. The Bureau's motivation for this action is obscure, though it was probably linked to the fact that the Bureau had acquired a lot of prestige as a bulwark against the evils of opiate drugs, which, unlike marijuana, are addictive. Enlargement of the Bureau's operations and enhancement of its reputation required the identification of new public enemies.[37]

Shirley Small has found that Becker's analysis of marijuana laws in the United States provides an interesting parallel to the history of narcotics legislation in Canada. In Canada, Mackenzie King performed the most prominent role as "moral entrepreneur" in this area, but he was backed by a number of other groups that had reasons of their own for demanding harsher laws. The main lobbyists were in Vancouver, and their real motivation was to attack the Chinese immigrants, who were coming to Vancouver in some numbers before the turn of this century. King arranged for the speedy passage of the Opium Act of 1908 that outlawed trafficking in narcotics. Because it is very hard to catch someone actually selling a drug, the Vancouver police force asked the federal government to also ban possession and smoking of opium.

A great publicity campaign was mounted to turn public opinion against opium. There were pictures of sinister-looking Asians corrupting young Canadian women in opium dens. Debates in Commons featured passionate speeches by members from Vancouver, where anti-Chinese prejudice was running high. Predictably, in 1911 narcotics possession was outlawed. Enforcement of the law was turned over to the RCMP. In the early 1920s, the RCMP was not particularly popular; it is possible that only its zealous narcotics work kept it from being disbanded.

A considerable number of addicts were not Chinese at all, nor were they connected with the criminal underworld. Physicians of the day dispensed opium-based medicines very freely, and many people became addicted as a result of this medical treatment. However, neither these physicians nor their addicted patients were treated as criminals. Criminal sanctions were reserved for supposed members of the underworld, and for people whose status in Canadian society was already low and insecure.[38]

ENFORCING THE RULES

Deviance exists partly because laws exist, whether or not the laws are of genuine social value. Deviance also exists partly because laws are *enforced*, and, again, that enforcement may or may not be socially valuable. Indeed, a few sociologists argue that the police actually *cause* crime. This may be true in two different ways.

First, when one looks for crime, one tends to find it; the more that police look for crime in any one area, the more crime they will find there. If the police believe that crime is to be expected in a particular region, they may turn all their attention to that area and away from other regions that they believe are basically law-abiding. This can create a "self-fulfilling prophecy." It is well known that during a riot or parade, the crime rate in other parts of the city usually drops. This is because the police are so busy at the scene of the excitement that they cannot detect the usual number of crimes elsewhere. Several sociologists have pointed out that many crime statistics in Canadian communities can be explained largely as the result of "over-policing" in those areas, and not as the result of genuinely high numbers of illegal actions.[39] The police describe the areas that they patrol lightly as "old established parts of town", but refer to the areas that they patrol carefully as "row housing, high in new immigrants," "high rises and townhouses with lots of neighbor complaints," and "a recent mix of immigrants."[40]

Second, the police may themselves commit criminal actions. Police work involves a certain amount of strain. The combination of personal danger and authority tempts police officers to use their authority in ways that are contrary to the rule of law. Sometimes police have lost patience and have rioted, attacking members of a quiet crowd with their weapons. This can, of course, provoke a violent reaction from an otherwise peaceful assembly of people. Police have attacked pickets in strike situations, demonstrators in protests against nuclear power plants, and similar orderly groups. However, over a period of several generations, police forces have become more restrained and disciplined,[41] by and large, so that such incidents are fortunately rather uncommon. Under most circumstances, police officers manage to move through trying situations with courtesy and self-control.

LABELING THE DEVIANT

It is one thing to commit a deviant act—lying, stealing, homosexual intercourse, or heavy drinking—but it is quite another thing to be **labeled** deviant, to be socially defined as a liar, a thief, a homosexual, or a drunk. Such labels suggest that one is habitually given to a particular kind of deviance and may be *expected* to behave in a deviant way. Fortunately, however, most people who commit deviant acts do not have the unpleasant experience of being labeled deviant. Indeed, we are all "hidden offenders," having at least technically violated some law or other, but few of us are labeled deviant. Our chance of being defined as deviant depends largely on whether we are caught performing deviant acts. Crimes without victims—drug abuse and prostitution, for example—are not likely to come to the attention of the police or the newspapers. Therefore people who commit such acts are less likely to be labeled deviant than someone who makes a habit of stealing a police car and tearing through town with the siren on. Millions of respected homemakers secretly drink all afternoon while watching television. They may be alcoholics for several years before their neighbors find out and begin to refer to them as "that lush."

White-collar crime

Even crimes that get onto the public record do not necessarily result in the offenders being labeled as deviant. In 1949 Edwin Sutherland published a study of what he called "white-collar crime."[42] This was an analysis of crimes committed by 70 large manufacturing, mining, and other corporations and their subsidiaries over an average of 45 years. The offenses studied included false advertising, violations of patent, trademark, and copyright laws, financial fraud, and other offenses committed by businessmen in the course of their work. Most of these offenses had been detected by independent government commissions, and the decisions Sutherland recorded were all on acts that are defined as criminal by law. A total of 980 decisions were made against the corporations studied, an average of 4 convictions each. What these offenses cost their victims in terms of money cannot be estimated, but only a handful of cases of fraud and false advertising can cost consumers many millions of dollars. However, in most of these cases the public image of the corporation involved was not damaged and its officers continued to be respected citizens of their communities, with their good names undamaged by deviant reputations.

Business practices such as these are not limited to the United States, but have been documented by Canadian researchers in this country as well.[43] According to Colin H. Goff and Charles E. Reasons, the Canadian pubic pays a huge cost for the violation of anti-combines legislation by large corporations. Anti-combines laws were designed to prevent business firms from making high profits at the consumer's expense by agreeing not to compete against one another. This legislation has

by no means been wholly successful. The violation of anti-combines laws by Canadian business leaders is not defined in the same category as robbery, or even drunk driving; no anti-combines offender has ever been sent to jail in Canada. Apparently, the public does not believe it has the right to question whether the profit margin of corporations is fair, reasonable, and legally obtained. As a result of this public apathy, 75 percent of the residential land required for building homes in the next year or two is held by the *six* major developers in each of Canada's twelve largest cities. Similar conglomerations have resulted in the food business from continual mergers among food store chains and food processors, packagers, and distributors.[44]

Stigma

Not all offenders are as lucky as the well-to-do corporation executives studied by Sutherland, Goff, and Reasons. Many have to live with ruined reputations that are in keeping with their disvalued roles. Of course not all disvalued roles are viewed as deviant. The roles of slave, hunchback, moron, and blind person are disvalued, but they are viewed differently than the roles of coward, thief, scab, or adulterer. It is assumed that no one *chooses* the former class of roles and that people who are forced to play such roles are "unfortunate" but not "reprehensible." However, the unfortunate and the reprehensible both experience **stigma**, the mark of disgrace that is attached to those in disvalued roles.

Erving Goffman has analyzed the effects of stigma on self-image and the often vain struggle of the stigmatized person to maintain self-respect and a reputable image.[45]

Redefining deviance

Certain kinds of acts may "migrate" from one deviant category to another. What was once a "sin" or a "vice," for example, may be elevated to the gravity of a "crime" or be reduced to mere "bad taste." Similarly, the

Jim Anderson/Woodfin Camp

Not everybody minds being labeled as deviant.

Controlling deviance

Social control consists of the various ways in which members of a group punish deviance and try to get others to live up to society's norms. The example that comes to mind most readily is the system of laws, police, courts, and prisons, but there are other sources of social control as well. The control of deviance is a matter of continual public concern, and we will return to this topic in the section on social policy. For now it is enough to mention three of the main sources of social control: socialization, group pressure, and social sanctions.

SOCIALIZATION

Most social control is *self*-control. As we saw in Chapter 4, we usually behave properly even if no one is looking because we have *internalized* the norms of our group. This is why many patterns of deviance—especially delinquency and other antisocial acts—result from inadequate socialization. Poor interpersonal relations in the home during childhood may have long-term effects on personality and increase the likelihood that a person will perform deviant acts. Children who are close to their parents are unlikely to misbehave, whether the parent is of high or low status. Almost all delinquents say that their upbringing was unpleasant, that their parents never understood them, and that their parents were too strict.

Inadequate socialization in childhood may be the cause of many other patterns of deviance, such as alcoholism and emotional illness. However, sociologists are still trying to find out exactly what aspect or aspects of socialization must be lacking for these tendencies to arise. Some researchers suggest that some mental illnesses may be due to peculiar patterns of communication within the family, patterns that involve contradic-

sinner may be redefined either as a "criminal" or as a "boor." Social structure and the cultural context determine the direction in which a given act will migrate. A major cultural trend of the past fifty years or so has been to reclassify as "sick" certain forms of behavior that were once viewed as vicious, depraved, or criminal; homosexuality and drug use are among those behaviors.[30] (Of course many people would rather be regarded as "bad" or "immoral" than as "mentally ill.") Homosexuals have a good chance of being redefined as neither vicious nor "sick" but simply "different," especially since 1973, when the American Psychiatric Association moved in that direction.

196

tory messages expressed in different ways. For example, a little boy's mother may talk a lot about how much she loves him, but whenever he touches her she may stiffen, move away, or look annoyed. Which "message" should he believe—the verbal one or the nonverbal one? If he calls attention to the discrepancy, his mother may get angry. This situation has been called a "double bind" and is said to be common in the families of mental patients.[46]

INFORMAL GROUP PRESSURE

For adolescents, perhaps even more than for adults, peer group approval is extremely important. This is why so many delinquent acts are committed by gangs rather than by individuals acting alone. By the same token, peer group pressure to conform can be an important means of social control. James Coleman, who compared the adolescent cultures of different high schools, argues that peer group pressure is far more influential than parents' opinions. He claims that each high school builds up a unified teenage culture that may differ greatly from that found in other high schools, even though the schools are similar in socioeconomic makeup. For example, one school may be sports oriented and another intellectually oriented. A teenager who goes to the sports-minded school is far less likely to be interested in schoolwork than one who goes to the other school, regardless of his or her parents' attitudes.[47]

SOCIAL SANCTIONS

We do not depend only on socialization and peer group pressure to maintain social order. Society also uses many different sanctions— rewards for desirable behavior and punishments for undesirable behavior. One can be sent to jail, for instance, or fined. Even though this does not happen to many people, the fact that it *can* happen encourages law-abiding be-

havior. Thus we know that by giving tickets to speeders police officers actually save lives. The more speeding tickets are written, the fewer accidents there are. The reverse is also true. The more "lenient" a police force is with speeders, the more accidents occur in that area.

Even so, punishment is not a very effective way of preventing serious offenses. There is little evidence, for example, that spending time in prison makes criminals less likely to commit new crimes than if they had not been sent to prison. The sad fact is that social scientists have no reliable suggestions as to how to induce criminals to reform.[48] In his review of treatment programs for Canadian delinquent youths, James Hackler has shown that researchers have little new to offer in shaping public policy.[49]

The consequences of deviance

Almost any group can tolerate quite a bit of deviance, and in fact most groups expect it. They make plans to cope with it and to limit its disorganizing effects. Department stores, for example, allow for a certain amount of merchandise to be lost through theft, just as they allow for breakage. They may even "insure against" theft by bonding their employees.[50]

DEVIANCE AND DISORGANIZATION

A group can manage to survive despite considerable deviance. However, certain actions are more vital than others, and failure to carry out essential functions brings disaster to the organization. This is so, for example, if the commanding officer of a military unit deserts in the midst of a battle or if a contractor fails to honor a contract and refuses to deliver essential building materials.

Idlers, fakers, chiselers, and the like undermine an organization by making other

This could be you or me if we slip up, and we know it. That's one reason we are careful not to violate important norms.

members of the group unwilling to play their parts. If the deviant shares in the rewards without sharing in the work, the virtuous members become resentful and may withdraw from the organization.

The worst effect of deviance on organizations is the erosion of *trust*—the confidence that others will play by the rules. After all, each member has made an investment in the future of the collective activity on the assumption that if he or she plays by the rules others will too. The individual's contribution, whether it is chasing a ball in a baseball game or doing a homework assignment, makes sense only if others do their part. To distrust others is to see one's own effort as pointless and the future as hazardous and uncertain.

One then feels like "pulling out of the game" and investing one's efforts elsewhere.

All organized social activity requires a certain amount of trust among the participants. This is true even of activities that are themselves deviant, such as illegal betting. A bookie, for example, cannot enforce his claims in court because his business is illegal. He must therefore be able to trust the handicappers, the wire services, and the "layoff bettors" who take large bets from minor bookies. He must also trust the honesty of the sporting events on which he is taking bets.

A study conducted several years ago showed that in New York State less than 1 percent of the money spent on illegal betting on sporting events went for boxing bets. Why?

198

According to the report, this is a "sorry indication of the low state to which that so-called sport has fallen. Even the bookmakers avoid it because the characters who control it consider a fix to be normal procedure.[51] Here we see one line of business that has suffered as a result of widespread lack of trust.

POSITIVE FUNCTIONS OF DEVIANCE

We must not assume that deviance is only harmful. There are times when it can be useful. For one thing, deviance from the rules of a destructive organization can perform a service to society. This is because there is a difference between what the rules *are* and what they *should* be. We may disagree on the desirability of a rule but agree on its *validity*. I may think that the speed laws in my city are silly, but I recognize that they are valid rules and that the authorities have a right to enforce them. Even so, deviance from valid but undesirable rules can be a valuable act of courage. Louis Riel has become a folk hero for resisting Canadian officials because they were not representing his people.

Occasionally there are other ways in which deviance may be useful. Deviance can cut red tape, act as a safety valve, clarify rules, unite a group, reinforce conformity, and act as a warning signal.

Cutting red tape

An organization's rules may usually make sense. However, in some situations conformity to the rules will defeat rather than support the organization's goals. If those goals are to be achieved, someone must break the rules. For example, an organization may have a sensible way of distributing supplies—certain forms must be filled out, certain people must sign the forms, and so on. This system permits budgeting and planning. However, if the authorized person is not around to sign the forms, someone will usually be willing to forge his or her signature. Such deviance may

actually be in the interest of the organization whose rules are being broken.

Acting as a safety valve

Some people have wants that the rules of society do not recognize as legitimate, or they may lack access to the legitimate means of satisfying their wants. If enough people are frustrated, they may attack the rules themselves and the social institutions that they support. Therefore, a certain amount of deviance, condemned but not firmly repressed, may take some of the strain off the legitimate order. For example, consider the rule that legitimates sexual relations within marriage; this norm is socially useful because it motivates people to have families. However, if a man's sexual desires are not satisfied within marriage he may turn elsewhere. If his extramarital relationship is kept impersonal, it will threaten his family much less than if they had to compete for his emotional attachment. The prostitute does not share the social status of her sexual partner the way a wife does, nor is she socially acceptable as his companion in public. It can be argued, therefore, that prostitution, a severely limited and disvalued kind of relationship, is the form of extramarital sexual behavior that is least likely to keep men from marrying, to threaten the status or security of the wife, or to create emotional ties that will compete seriously with the obligations of marriage.[52] Thus the results of this form of deviance are not wholly *dysfunctional* (against the interests of the whole social system), and laws against prostitution are not strictly enforced in most societies.

Clarifying rules

The precise meaning of a rule is not always obvious, but when you have overstepped the bounds you will discover your mistake in the raised eyebrows, chilly looks, or amused smiles of the people around you. When one is learning the rules of a new role one may experiment a bit with borderline behavior. In a way, the person who is daring enough to confront his or her group with borderline behavior does the group a service by forcing it to "make up its mind" about a fuzzy rule. Appellate courts provide the same service by reducing the ambiguity of laws. Deviance forces the clarification or reaffirmation of a rule, thus enabling other members to understand better what other people think they should or should not do.[53]

Uniting the group

Sometimes a deviant does a service to his group by pulling it together. This can happen in two different ways: The group can either oppose the deviant or try to convert him or her.

It is well known that nothing unites the members of a group like a common enemy, but this is also true of enemies within the group. Although it is not pleasant for him or her personally, the deviant may serve as a "built-in out-group," a scapegoat who contributes to the unity of the group in much the same way that witches, devils, and hostile foreign powers do.[54]

On the other hand, the deviant may unite the group through his or her very need to be "converted." Unity increases when members of a group subordinate their personal interests to some common goal. The goal could be to protect or reclaim a deviant or to show the group's patience and kindness in the face of repeated provocation by the deviant member.[55] Some groups seem to thrive on taking care of erring members.

Highlighting conformity

The good deed, said Shakespeare, shines brightest in a naughty world. Most of us can remember feeling exhilaration in talking to members of a group about the blemishes and failings of some third party. In the process of criticizing another person's deviance we reward one another for our superior merit and enhance the sense of community among the conforming members of the group.[56]

Acting as a warning signal

Truants from school, deserters from the army, runaways from prisons, and the like may force people to take a closer look at how they are running such institutions and may lead to greater efficiency and morale. Thus the deviant, by sticking his or her neck out, is acting to the benefit of conformers who suffer in law-abiding silence. Acts of civil disobedience may, in fact, be organized and planned with the goal of using deviance as a warning signal. Here is an example:

Several years ago the Indiana University faculty had a high rate of violation of campus parking regulations, in part because of the disjunction between the demand for parking spaces and the supply. The virtuous left early for work and hunted wearily for legitimate parking spaces. The contemptuous parked anywhere and sneered at tickets. One response to this situation was to create new parking lots and to expand old ones. Since the new parking spaces were available to all, and not only to the former violators, this provides a clear instance where the virtuous—or perhaps the timid—as well as the deviants themselves are the beneficiaries of deviance.[57]

**THE NORMALITY OF
DEVIANCE**

For all of the reasons I have listed, some sociologists have concluded that, even though conformity is the usual response of human beings, a certain amount of deviance is useful in any social system. Therefore deviance is tolerated, and even encouraged, within limits. Durkheim claimed that deviance is normal and that if a society runs short of it, it will always create more by making major issues out of minor offenses. He wrote,

Imagine a society of saints, a perfect cloister of exemplary individuals. Crimes, properly so called, will there be unknown; but faults which appear venial to the layman will create there the same scandal that the ordinary offense does in ordinary consciousness. If then this society has the power to judge and punish, it will define these acts as criminal and will treat them as such.[58]

Kai Erikson has taken Durkheim's theory seriously and has attempted to test it. He searched history for a "society of saints" to find out whether deviance occurred at a relatively constant rate in that society, as Durkheim suggested. He chose the New England Puritans, who at least called themselves a community of saints, and he found that to the Puritans minor acts of religious nonconformity were crimes punishable by death. The number of deviants who were alive and active in this society remained about the same over several decades, as measured by the number of offenders brought to trial. When the supply of "real" deviants began to run low, the New Englanders discovered witches in their midst. Erikson concludes that "deviance is not a property *inherent* in any particular kind of behavior; it is a property *conferred upon* that behavior by the people who come into contact with it."[59]

The relativity of deviance

The study of deviance, then, is not simply the study of drunkenness, drug use, extramarital sexual relations, prostitution, and so forth *as such*, for each of these behaviors is socially acceptable in some society and in some situations. What makes an act deviant?

NORMS GOVERN ROLES

Behavior is deviant only *if the person who performs the act is subject to the norms that his or her behavior violates.* A person is deviant only in terms of his or her role as a member of a particular collectivity. Part of the meaning of a role in a collectivity is to be subject to the norms of that collectivity. Even people who do not belong to the collectivity

and do not approve of its rules may still take its norms into account when judging its members. Thus, for example, non-Catholics may recognize the difference between a "good" Catholic and a "bad" Catholic. They may even admire the "good" Catholic for his or her faithful adherence to patterns of conduct for which they would criticize members of their own religious collectivity.

There are interesting borderline positions, such as that of the "guest," whether in a household or in a foreign country. Only in a limited sense are guests "members" of the collectivity they are visiting. Their roles are governed by a special set of understandings

To be or not to be? That is a social question. One's life belongs to oneself, but also to other people.

Allen Green/Palmer Photo

that may include special duties and special privileges. Guests may be deviant, but only in terms of this special set of rules. For example, it would ordinarily be deviant for a guest to reorganize your kitchen cabinets or to join in a squabble over the family budget.

ROLE CONFLICT

Sometimes a person may have two different roles with contradictory norms so that it may be difficult or impossible to conform to them all. Conformity to one role may require deviance from another. This situation is called **role conflict**. For example, the role of examination proctor and the role of friend may make quite different demands on a person; however, the system may be organized in such a way that no individual is likely to play those two roles at the same time.[60] Role conflict is a source of deviance that is built into the structure and rules of the system itself; it is a *structural* source of deviance.

We have said that deviance is specific to the norms of a collectivity. Sometimes, however, people may not know exactly what those norms are. As agreement on the rules declines, the idea of deviance becomes less meaningful and less useful, and we may have to figure out *whose* version of the rules matters at any given moment. Deviance may be created or ended by changes in the rules themselves or by changes in the interpretation of the rules.

Theories of deviance

The theories that we will mention here all seek to answer the question, How do people happen to violate norms? Two approaches can be taken in answering this question. The first assumes that offenders are different from nonoffenders and tries to show in what way they are different and how they become different. We call this the *kinds-of-people* approach because it accounts for deviance by explaining "what kind of person" would do a particular thing. Psychologists often take this approach.

The second approach assumes that a deviant may be just like anyone else and not a different "kind of person." We call this approach *situational* because it tries to explain deviance in terms of situations that lead ordinary people to violate norms. Most sociologists take a situational approach to the question of deviance.

KINDS-OF-PEOPLE THEORIES

Theories that attribute deviant behaviors to particular kinds of people may account for the behavior in terms of either biological characteristics or psychological characteristics. Here we will discuss both biological and psychodynamic theories of criminal or delinquent behavior.

Biological theories

LOMBROSIAN POSITIVISM In the 1870s an Italian physician, Cesare Lombroso, founded the "positive school of criminology"—a theory that explained criminal behavior as caused by a genetic defect. According to this theory, a deviant person inherited a body structure and personality that were characteristic of a more primitive stage of evolution.[61] Lombroso's followers believed that they could identify "born criminals" with calipers, scales, and cameras, for all such deviants were supposed to be marked by the physical "stigmata of degeneracy." Early in this century this theory was destroyed by the research of Charles Goring, an English prison officer who compared his prisoners to a control group of noncriminals and found no evidence of a distinct physical type among criminals.[62]

SHELDON'S CONSTITUTIONAL TYPOLOGY Another effort to link physiology and criminology was made by William H. Sheldon, an American psychologist and physician.[63] After examining 200 wayward boys Sheldon concluded that boys with hard, rectangular ("mesomorphic") body structures were more likely to become delinquent than boys whose physiques were either soft and round or lean and fragile. Later research by Sheldon Glueck and Eleanor Glueck supported William Sheldon's findings, though 40 percent of the Gluecks' delinquent subjects were *not* primarily mesomorphic.[64] We still don't know why mesomorphs are any more likely to become delinquent than skinny boys or roly-poly ones. Perhaps the most satisfactory explanation is that people have a tendency to do the things for which they are best equipped. Delinquent street life rewards strength and physical toughness, which are characteristic of the athletic mesomorph.

XYY CHROMOSOMES Some researchers are exploring the question of whether criminality is connected with abnormal chromosome patterns. Chromosomes are threads of living matter that contain the genes that determine our inherited characteristics—eye color, hair color, and so on. There are normally 23 pairs of chromosomes in every human cell (46 chromosomes in all). The twenty-third pair is the one that determines sex. In females, the last pair consists of two identical chromosomes called X chromosomes. In males this pair consists of two different chromosomes, an X chromosome and a Y chromosome. But some males have an extra Y chromosome, and some researchers think that criminality occurs more often in such men than in men whose chromosomes are normal. This condition seems to be present at birth but not inherited. But even if there is a connection between XYY chromosomes and criminality, only a small percentage of crimes can possibly be due to this physical anomaly.[65] As of now, therefore, all biological theories of deviance are inconclusive, though there is good reason for continued research.

Psychodynamic theories

Most kinds-of-people theories stress, not biological, but psychological characteristics. These theories try to account for deviance in terms of events in the life history of the deviant. Perhaps the deviant acquired weird motives at some point or else failed to learn the internal controls that conformists learn. Such theories are usually based on Freudian psychoanalysis, which points to defects in the superego and the ego as well as to the frustration of needs as a source of deviant conduct.

SUPEREGO STRENGTH A person's conscience is supposed to develop out of early loving relationships with moral adults. According to Freudians, failure to develop a strong conscience, or *superego*, results in a *psychopathic personality*—a character with no guilt feelings, pity, or respect for others.[66] It is sometimes claimed that most of the prisoners in penitentiaries are psychopaths. However, some psychologists believe that the psychopathic personality is a rare condition, and still others deny that it exists at all.

EGO STRENGTH In recent years psychoanalysts have paid increasing attention to ego defects. A weak ego is not a lack of conscience but an inability to organize one's activities in the real world. It can involve, for example, inability to control impulses, to postpone pleasure, and to follow plans.

FRUSTRATION-AGGRESSION A theory based on Freud's thought but best explained by John Dollars is called the *frustration-aggression* theory.[67] It holds that frustration produces aggression, which, in turn, produces deviant behavior. If the aggression is directed outward, the person may attack the source of his or her frustration or some substitute target. If the person's controls are very strong, the aggressive energy may be made harmless by sublimation. In this case the energy is used up in some socially acceptable or constructive way—by smashing a squash ball around, perhaps, or by writing a critical letter to the editor of a local newspaper.

This theory has been used by Andrew F. Henry and James F. Short to account for variations in suicide rates (aggression against the self) and homicide rates (aggression against another).[68] They suggest that low-status people can easily blame others, rather than themselves, for their frustration and that they will feel justified in turning their aggression outward, commiting homicide rather than suicide. Higher-status people, on the other hand, will be more likely to commit suicide under stress. Available data are consistent with this theory, though there are other theories supported by equally strong evidence.[69]

DEFENSE MECHANISMS Psychoanalysis is the source of yet another theory. Unlike the others, which suggest that the offender loses control of his or her deviant impulse, this theory suggests that the deviant act is a device contrived by the personality to *protect itself against anxiety or guilt*. It works by concealing from the actor his or her unacceptable impulse, and only skilled analysis will bring its "true meaning" to light. Theories of this sort interpret deviant acts as *mechanisms of defense*.

In *Delinquent Boys*,[70] Albert Cohen tries to use such a theory to explain why lower-class youths tend to be delinquent in ways that have no utility but show a spirit of pure meanness and negativism. Cohen argued that American children of all social classes and ethnic origins must compete against one another for approval and status under the same standards. They are rewarded for verbal ability, polished manners, achievement, and sustained effort toward long-term goals. Lower-class children are the losers in this competition because their socialization experiences in childhood differ from those of middle-class children. To cope with the feeling of being a loser, lower-class children withdraw from the game, reject the middle-class rules, and set up a new game using rules under which they can perform satisfactorily.

But the dominant value system is also in some sense *their* value system. They have, to a certain extent, internalized its rules as well as their own. They can tell themselves that they don't really care what people think of them, but their internalized values, though repressed, threaten to break through and reduce their satisfaction with the path they have chosen. To protect this choice from "the enemy within, as well as the enemy without," they fall back on reaction formation, which is, in Freudian theory, a mechanism for denying an unacceptable element of the personality through behavior that seems to *overprotest, overdeny*. They not only reject the dominant value system but do so with a vengeance. They engage in malicious, spiteful, ornery behavior of all sorts to show, not only to others but to themselves as well, their contempt for the game they have rejected. For example, a teenager may "prove" that he does not like or want a sports car by slashing the tires of all the sports cars he sees.

Problems with kinds-of-people theories

All kinds-of-people theories claim that the deviant act is caused by a weakness in the character of the individual. However, this model suggests that such weak people are *consistently* deviant, that is, that they always commit the same deviant act in a given situation. But this is not the case. Most people who commit deviant acts are not consistently deviant. Most students who cheat do so only sometimes and behave "normally" most of the time. To explain why *this* person commits *this* deviant act at *this* time, it is necessary to borrow explanations from other theories. Besides, most deviant acts are committed by people who are basically normal and do not have marked psychological disorders. Recall Sutherland's work on white-collar crime, for example. These acts were carried out by pillars of society, people with well-organized personalities who do not have obvious psychological problems.

SITUATION THEORIES

In this section I will describe several theories that explain deviant behavior as arising out of the properties of social systems. The first is anomie theory as developed first by Durkheim and later by Merton. The second is cultural-transmission theory, especially as developed by Sutherland. The third is role-self theory, or symbolic interactionism.

Anomie theory

DURKHEIM Durkheim believed that new problems—mainly class conflict and the decline in social solidarity—had resulted from increasing division of labor. The jobs of individual workers had become so specialized that the workers could no longer operate according to shared rules and understandings.[71] Therefore people doing different jobs worked at cross-purposes, and this led to confusion, inefficiency, and even social disintegration. There were no common rules for regulating the social system. Durkheim called this situation anomie, meaning normlessness or deregulation. Any period of upheaval or economic uncertainty, such as a depression, is a period of high anomie.

In his book, *Suicide*, Durkheim suggested that periods of rapid change—especially economic booms and depressions—make it impossible for people to expect specific rewards for conforming to society's norms. When society and the economy are unstable, the benefits of conforming or deviating are not predictible enough to count on. People may work hard and save money for their old age, only to have their savings wiped out in a stock market crash or bankruptcy. A telephone quiz or jingle contest may, by a fluke, turn a drifter into a rich man without his making any contribution to his society. If such events occur often, they weaken a social group's ability to back up its norms with systematic rewards and punishments.

In his discussion of "anomic suicide" Durkheim noted that suicides increase both in times of depression and in times of rapidly increasing prosperity. He believed that this is due to changing ideas about how rewards should be distributed among the members of a society. It is understandable that hard times might make life seem no longer worth living.

But why should prosperity produce similar results?

According to Durkheim, human wants are endlessly expandable. There is no "natural" limit to what people might crave and, therefore, to what might satisfy them. What, then, keeps us from being constantly dissatisfied? Our norms tell us how high to aim. Social rules, not biology, define what each social class is entitled to. People regulate their wants accordingly, and this creates the possibility of feeling satisfied. But a period of fast-growing prosperity upsets the usual definitions of the goals that a person may have. There is no limit on aspirations, and thus nothing produces satisfaction. Durkheim felt that the desire to live is weakened under such conditions. Suicide is caused by this state of anomie.

MERTON Four decades after the publication of Durkheim's *Suicide*, Robert Merton published a short paper entitled "Social Structure and Anomie," that developed Durkheim's theory further.[72]

Merton described anomie as a gap between effort and reward that makes it impossible for people to have realistic goals or to plan legitimate ways of achieving their goals. He listed three different factors: (1) culture goals, the wants and ambitions that people are taught by their society; (2) norms, which prescribe legitimate means of pursuing these goals; and (3) institutionalized means, the actual resources available to the individual.

Merton claimed that North American society expects all of its members to have the same *goal* (success and high income) and the same *norms* (hard work, thrift, and the like). However, society offers different social groups quite different *institutionalized means*—unequal opportunities for education, challenging jobs, business loans, and so forth. This situation puts a strain on the lower-status groups because the means available to them don't help them achieve prescribed goals.

Frustration, hopelessness, and anger result, not from any single one of these factors—

goals, norms, or means—but from the relationship among them. If a group has modest goals, follows the society's norms, and has the means to achieve its goals legitimately, there is no problem. Strain results when there is a gap between goals and institutionalized means. A person's response may be to weaken his or her commitment either to the prescribed goals, to the prescribed means of achieving the goals, or both. Merton believed that there are five possible responses to this gap. (See Figure 7.2.)

The first of these responses is *conformity*; the others are all varieties of deviant behavior. *Innovators* (e.g., professional thieves, white-collar criminals, cheaters) believe in the goals but reject the prescribed means. *Ritualists* (e.g., bureaucrats who rigidly follow the rules without thinking about why the rules are there) make a virtue of overconformity to the prescribed means at the price of underconformity to the prescribed goals. *Retreatists* (e.g., tramps, drunkards, hippies, drug addicts) withdraw from the "rat race" by abandoning both the goals and the means. *Rebels*

(e.g., members of revolutionary movements) respond in a fifth way—like retreatists, they reject both the prescribed goals and the prescribed means, but they put other goals and means in their place. They withdraw their support from a social system that they believe is unjust and seek to rebuild the society with new goals and new means of achieving them.

Notice that this approach to deviance focuses not on the characteristics of individuals but on the positions that individuals occupy within the social system. It is therefore a sociological, not a psychological, theory, but it is a limited one. Merton did not try to explain why some people choose one response while others choose another. Nor did he face the question of why some people who are under great strain continue to conform, as many do.

Cultural-transmission theory

We turn now to a different kind of theory, sometimes called *subculture* theory and sometimes *cultural-transmission* theory. This approach comes from the Chicago school of sociology and has been used most fully by Edwin H. Sutherland.

All of the cultural-transmission theories should be distinguished from anomie theory. The latter views deviance primarily as the individual's way of adapting to a situation in which no means are available for achieving prescribed goals; therefore he or she must innovate by inventing illegitimate means instead. Cultural-transmission theory does not picture deviant *individuals* as innovating at all. They don't think up their crimes independently. Rather, they are simply following norms that are prescribed by a limited subculture—a social group that exists within the larger society but has beliefs and norms that deviate from the point of view of the larger society. The deviant is seen as *conforming to a deviant subculture*. For example, a child brought up by thieves is not deviant, in their opinion, for stealing. He or she is simply living up to different standards from yours or mine.

FIGURE 7.2

A typology of modes of individual adaptation illustrating Merton's theory of anomie

	Commitment to prescribed means	No commitment to prescribed means
Commitment to prescribed goals	**Conformity**	**Innovation**
No commitment to prescribed goals	**Ritualism**	**Retreatism**

Cultural-transmission theory should also be distinguished from most kinds-of-people theories, which see the deviant as abnormal and warped. According to cultural-transmission theory, deviants learn their behavior patterns the same way anyone else does—their personalities are shaped by the knowledge, attitudes, and beliefs of the people with whom they interact. They may wind up as different "kinds of people" (e.g., pick-pockets or prostitutes), but they acquire such habits in the same way that we become pinball wizards or sociologists—usually by spending a lot of time with people who play pinball machines, pick pockets, study sociology, or hustle, as the case may be.

SHAW AND MCKAY In a series of important books[73] based mostly on research done in the city of Chicago, Clifford Shaw and Henry McKay tried to explain the delinquency rates in American cities. They noted that the high-rate areas in 1900-1906 were also the high-rate areas in 1917-1923, though the ethnic makeup of these areas had changed. As an ethnic group moved into these areas, the group's delinquency rate rose; as it moved out, its delinquency rate fell. Shaw and McKay concluded that crime had become a traditional way of life in these areas and that this tradition was passed along through personal and group contacts.[74] A deviant tradition is sometimes called a *delinquent subculture.* It is passed along mainly by the play group and the gang. An individual becomes deviant not by planning to commit a deviant act on his or her own but by behaving the way the group behaves. Such a person is not an innovator but a special kind of conformist.

SUTHERLAND Sutherland tried to develop a general theory of criminal behavior based on cultural transmission. He called it the theory of *differential association.* According to this theory, criminal behavior is learned; it is not inherited or invented by the criminal. It is learned through communication with other people, mostly in small, intimate groups. Our

companions define the law favorably or unfavorably, and we take over those definitions. A person becomes criminal or delinquent because the definitions to which he or she is exposed favor violation of the law. Everyone has some contact with both kinds of defini-

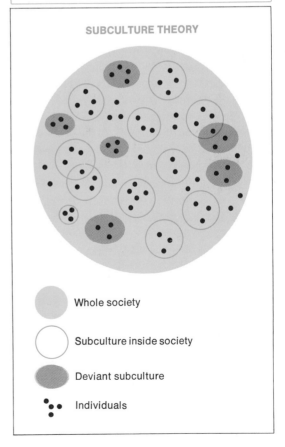

FIGURE 7.3

In any modern society, such as the one represented below, there are many subcultures. Some of them are not deviant (e.g., antique collectors and rock music fans), while other subcultures are deviant (e.g., pot smokers and prostitutes). Any person's likelihood of becoming deviant is explained (in subculture theory) in terms of whether he or she is in contact with members of a deviant subculture.

SUBCULTURE THEORY

Whole society

Subculture inside society

Deviant subculture

Individuals

tions; what is important is the ratio of one to the other. Note that Sutherland does not emphasize contact with criminals or noncriminals; rather, he focuses on exposure to *definitions* that are favorable or unfavorable to crime. A person may have very few contacts with criminals but may have a great deal of exposure to procriminal attitudes. By the same token, however, many kinds of criminal behavior may be defined unfavorably even by criminals. The professional pickpocket may disapprove of rape, drug addiction, or murder as much as any conforming citizen. On the other hand, procriminal attitudes toward matters such as tax evasion may be learned from people who are basically conforming and respectable. Contacts with people are not all of equal weight; some have more impact than others. This impact varies with *frequency, duration, priority, and intensity.* If we could measure these factors, we would have a formula that would allow us to make precise predictions in any particular case.[75]

Sutherland's theory implies that the larger culture is not homogeneous but contains contradictory definitions of the same behavior, one of which is backed by the people who make the laws. Rates and prevalence of each kind of criminal behavior depend on the extent to which social arrangements foster or prevent exposure to procriminal and anticriminal attitudes. For example, the mobility, diversity, and anonymity of urban life create more opportunities for procriminal contacts than the more controlled interaction patterns of rural society. Likewise, people who live in one part of town may be exposed to more criminal definitions than people who live in another area, and so the crime rates will differ between the two areas.

Role-self theory

Role-self theory is the view that deviant behavior sometimes results when a person tries to justify his or her claims to a particular role. This theory is based on the symbolic interactionist view described in Chapter 6. You will recall that George Herbert Mead and

his students emphasized the fact that we have to identify, define, and classify the objects we encounter, for we live in a world of socially meaningful objects. We have to decide what sort of objects we are dealing with. Once we identify them—an "antique," a "Picasso," a "mongrel," a "poker game"—some set of attitudes and expectations is called to mind, and this largely determines what we will do with the object. These socially defined objects include people. By living in a social group we learn the categories into which we classify people. We learn the system of roles; we have ideas about what different people are like, expectations about how they should behave, and standards for judging their behavior.

As we learn roles, we acquire our own identity, for the self is also a social object. We must *learn* how to see, label, classify, and judge ourselves. Until we do so, we have no "self-consciousness," and indeed, no "self." Prime Minister and bartender, citizen and alien, old person and teenager, hip person and square are part of the culturally defined set of roles in Canadian society. Some of these roles are assigned to us whether we like them or not; others are matters of choice.

The self, then, is developed in the process of interacting with others. We discover the categories to which we have been assigned and to some extent we decide what we will be. We claim to be a certain sort of person, and we must make the claim stick. To do so we must meet the cultural standards of the role. We know that we have done this when others show that they accept us as valid examples of that role. To lay a claim is to say, in effect, "I am a such-and-such sort of person. I invite you to deal with me on this basis. You may expect certain things of me." If we are accepted, we thereby confirm our view of ourselves. We cannot really tell whether we are "leaders," "glamour girls," "pool sharks," or "brains" without venturing into the icy waters of social interaction, trying out the role and seeing how others respond.

Not all of our roles are actively sought and cultivated. Some, like those of alcoholic and ex-convict, we may actively resist and deny. Some, like that of mental patient, we may accept but not enjoy. Some, like that of prostitute, we may accept for practical reasons, looking forward to a time when we may exchange it for some other, less stigmatized but equally profitable occupation. When we cannot escape being assigned to deviant roles, we still try to avoid identifying with the role and claim that it does not express our "real selves."[76]

Our behavior may be designed to confirm our role claims. Thus, to justify one's claim to being a philanthropist, one must sooner or later "put up or shut up." We take on some roles, not because they are directly important to the self, but because they make it easier to perform other roles. For example, although both boys and girls steal, boys steal all sorts of things, often things that are of no earthly use to them. Girls tend to steal only things that they can use—clothing, cosmetics, jewelry, and the like. Stealing *as such* may be *role expressive*—a way of showing that one is "all boy." Girls' stealing, on the other hand, is *role supportive*; stealing as such does not express the feminine role, but the objects that girls steal help them be pretty and charming. Thus stealing *supports* the feminine role while it *expresses* the masculine role.[77]

A great deal of deviance that seems irrational makes some sense when it is seen as an effort to proclaim or test a certain kind of self. Much sexual activity, for example, is motivated less by glandular secretions than by role anxiety.[78] The novice smoking his or her first marijuana cigarette before an audience of peers is not necessarily looking for "kicks." The teenager tearing down the highway at ninety miles an hour is not necessarily going anywhere. It is clear that such behavior does not fit Merton's anomie theory because it is not a *means* to a goal. It is better understood as *evidence* that is being produced to support a claimed role.

Role-self theory is the basis of another explanation of deviance. According to this explanation, called *labeling theory*, a deviant

Jean Boughton/Stock, Boston

Cultural transmission theories explain deviance in terms of "hanging out with the wrong crowd."

identity may be *forced upon* a person through the very process of law enforcement. The person is "labeled" a deviant. A youth who is caught in a delinquent activity may not have seen himself as a "delinquent." However, the process of being arrested, brought to trial, and put in jail is an official "degradation ceremony" by which the deviant role is forced upon him. It is sometimes argued that this experience may be the turning point by which a youth begins to see himself as a criminal and to organize his future behavior around that interpretation of himself. This means that the act of labeling someone as deviant may be the most important cause of later deviance.

Problems with situation theories

We have already mentioned the limitations of cultural-transmission theory and anomie theory. Cultural-transmission theory does not explain how or why deviant subcultures come into existence. To do that, we must use some other approach.

Anomie theory, on the other hand, does not try to explain why some people endure

209

strain without turning toward deviance, nor why others turn toward one deviant response rather than another. This theory is admirable for its logical simplicity but is still far from adequate.

Besides, as pointed out in the discussion of role-self theory, much deviant behavior cannot reasonably be interpreted as means (legitimate or illegitimate) of achieving any goal but only as role-expressive behavior. Tire slashing is not a way of getting something—it is merely a defiant gesture.

Role theory contributes most in combination with anomie theory because cultural goals and normative rules are closely connected to roles and to the self. Businessmen are *supposed* to make money, professors are *supposed* to write books, and ballplayers are *supposed* to win games. By pursuing those goals we try to express and justify ourselves as genuine businessmen, professors, or ballplayers. When the means and goals do not fit together nicely, businessmen may gyp their customers, professors may plagiarize, and ballplayers may cheat. However, they may also respond to the strain by *abandoning the role for another role* that they can play without violating the rules. I once chided a used-car salesman for selling me a bad car; the conscience-stricken man changed jobs as a result, explaining that business was so bad that he could no longer be a good Mormon and still make a living selling cars. Abandoning roles is one of the most common ways of avoiding the strain that Merton talked about, but it does not seem to fit into any of Merton's categories of responses.

I am not suggesting that role-self theory can replace cultural-transmission and anomie theory. Each seems to shed light on some aspect of deviant behavior. But deviance theorists still face the job of fitting the contributions of each of these theories into a single, more powerful theory, without giving up the logical unity that is characteristic of the work of Sutherland and Merton.[79]

SOCIAL RESEARCH:
Sociologists at work

OFFICIAL DEVIANCE: THE CASE OF THE RCMP

Deviance is often created by official labeling. Usually, a recognized authority "pronounces" someone a criminal, a madman, or a security risk, and establishes this claim with an authorized investigation and an official report. There is another kind of deviance, however, called "official deviance." In cases of official deviance, the same official agency that is empowered to investigate deviance turns out to be violating rules itself. Recently, in the United States, the scandalous Watergate episode showed that the nation's highest authorities were corrupt. Without implying that any agency of the Canadian government can be compared to the Nixon administration, I want to review some of the findings and suggestions of a controversial book, *RCMP Vs. The People*,[80] by two Canadian sociologists, Edward Mann and John Alan Lee.

Mann and Lee begin their book by paying their respects to the fine, dedicated group of Mounties that have rightfully been honored throughout Canadian history. The questions that Mann and Lee raise about the RCMP are limited to one small branch of the organization, the Security Service; they are not concerned with the group that conducts criminal investigations and serves as the police force in eight provinces. The Security Service is supposed to be concerned with the protection of national security. Its duties involve the collection of intelligence about Canadians and about foreign agents; it carries out the work that would be done by the CIA and FBI in the United States, or by the KGB in the Soviet Union. Mann and Lee examine the role of the Security Service as a "secret police force" that poses a threat to the rights of Canadians. They do not examine this issue as calm and impartial social scientists, but as outraged journalists exposing what they believe to be misdeeds.

According to Mann and Lee, the RCMP, as it is presently organized, has far too much power, and sometimes acts as though it were a secret police force. The public has no way of learning about violations of civil liberties or the performance of "dirty tricks" by the Mounties, and therefore has no way to bring them under control. Because the force maintains a very high degree of internal discipline, a Mountie who disapproves of his orders cannot "go public" with his information; therefore, an outsider can rarely learn what events occur inside the Security branch. Because the public has recently learned of possible law violations on the part of the RCMP, various commissions have been empowered to investigate them. Mann and Lee have not waited for a report from the Royal Commission; in the hope of preserving civil liberties, they have instead published their own muckraking account of deeds that they consider contrary to the public interest.

Traditionally, Canadian government has not attempted to guarantee rights of information to its citizens. Any citizen seeking information, supposedly a right guaranteed by the Freedom of Information Act, must prove that he or she has a right to that information. The government, however, does not have to prove its right to keep the information secret.[81] The Official Secrets Act of Canada imposes fourteen years imprisonment upon any Canadian or British citizen who reveals secret government documents. Unlike a regular defendant, anyone accused under this act is considered guilty until proven innocent. The trial can be conducted in secret and the accused person can be found guilty on the basis of alleged motives, without having committed any actual deed. There is no available public information stating which officials are allowed to stamp government documents as secret. Nevertheless, these officials have the power to label anyone who reveals the contents of the documents as a criminal.[82]

The Canadian government can also claim secrecy on other grounds besides the Official Secrets Act. It has the option of claiming a "Crown Privilege," which allows it to withhold documentary evidence in court even when the government is one of the parties to litigation. In effect, the government can legally keep secret almost anything that it wishes to.[83] It is natural to wonder how often such legal strategies are misused to cover up secrets that do not involve national security. No clear answer is possible, but Mann and Lee have reviewed two cases in which the Official Secrets Act was invoked

'It's safe to talk. The RCMP have checked the phone for bugs!'

Ben Wicks/Toronto Sun

to suppress information that apparently did not concern national security. The Act was used to prosecute Peter Treu, a scientist and businessman, and Peter Worthington, the editor of the *Toronto Sun*, who published information about Soviet-Canadian relations that apparently had no security value.[84]

In the past few years, the public has learned of several occasions on which the RCMP apparently used illegal tactics. One of these events took place shortly after the FLQ crisis in October 1970. The separatists, who were not considered a legitimate political group, were kept under close observation by the RCMP. In collaboration with the municipal and provincial police, the RCMP participated in a break-in; without a search warrant, they entered the premises of a left-wing separatist organization in Montreal, and removed the files. On another occasion in 1973, several Mounties "borrowed" computer tapes containing the membership list of the Parti Québécois, copied these tapes, and then returned them to the filing cabinets of the computer center where they were stored.[85] On yet a third occasion, the RCMP burned the barn belonging to the family of certain FLQ members; leftists and separatists had frequently met at this farm.[86]

These events certainly give separatists reason to worry about their privacy. But what about other Canadians, ordinary citizens who are not separatists but loyal to the unity of Canada? Does the average Canadian have anything to worry about? Mann and Lee think so. They point out that government intelligence agencies collect files insatiably. They write,

It is hardly necessary to tell a modern citizen the extent to which government operates on the basis of documents. Nothing exists, nothing has really happened, until it is recorded on paper, or more recently, on computer tape. But most civilians do not realize the life taken on by the files themselves. Once created, a file is not an inert thing, but a positive force which may be as destructive as a bullet. Anyone who has attempted to correct an error in a government file knows this. After much struggle with officialdom it may be possible to include a correction in the file, but often the error will remain there too. The error retains its own unique reality.[87]

Why would *you* have a record in a police file? Have you taken part in a political demonstration? Have you been on strike with a union? Have you been a militant feminist? A religious evangelist? These are only some of the grounds that might be used for collecting information on you for a police file. Such files can last indefinitely, and they can become part of a network that stretches around the world. Information collected by police in Vancouver can be transmitted by computer to Ottawa and even to the FBI in Washington. The information that the RCMP collects may be available to Interpol, the international agency that provides information for 125 national forces around the world. Although Parliament has never approved Canada's involvement with Interpol, the RCMP does participate in it. Some degree of international exchange of information is, no doubt, essential. The control of terrorism, drug traffic, organized crime, and financial swindlers requires exchange of information among the world's police forces. Nevertheless, the existence of these files is a basis for real concern. The Solicitor General of Canada reports that Interpol has files on 6000 Canadians who, though under observation, have never been charged with any offense.[88] Documents that have been collected for good purposes can be put to terrible uses by a totalitarian regime. The possibility of a future police state is one reason not to allow too much information about Canadian citizens to be centralized. The accumulation of too much information poses a real possibility for repression under certain circumstances.

Too much technology for the gathering of information may already be in use. For example, electronic bugging is commonly used by Canadian police, though of course only with a judge's approval. Mann and Lee claim that Canadian police are seven times more likely to use electronic surveillance than police in the 24 American states which authorize secret bugging.[89]

Mann and Lee are not only worried about the

RCMP's secret tactics, but also about its considerable rate of growth. They point out that between 1971 and 1977 the RCMP had a growth rate of 41 percent, which was more than 6 times the growth rate of the population.[90] They claim that the RCMP Security Service, which now has about 2000 men, is overstaffed. The expansion of police organizations is not unique to Canada, however. The British Secret Services and the American CIA and FBI have increased enormously since World War II. American police have average growth rates of between 5 and 6 percent a year, while the U.S. population grows at about 2.5 percent a year.[91] In Canada, however, the RCMP growth rate may shortly be curbed. The MacDonald Royal Commission, responsible for investigating the activities of the RCMP, has not yet reported its conclusions. When it does so, perhaps new safeguards will be introduced to protect the civil liberties of Canadians.

Mann and Lee have their own recommendations to offer. They believe that the RCMP's intelligence operations should not be linked to any police unit. Though security service may be necessary, it should not proceed in secrecy, but should publicize its findings whenever possible. According to Mann and Lee, any organization that collects information about people should be prepared to expose its findings. It should also be committed to a set of professional ethics; like reporters and sociologists, police should attempt, for example, to use deception as little as possible. No organization should use its power in secret either against individual citizens or to hide embarrassing facts from the public.

Two years before *RCMP Vs. The People* was published, another sociologist, Richard Henshel, attacked the RCMP's "disruptive tactics." Henshel listed several occasions when the Security Service "planted" evidence to discredit a disliked individual or group. Henshel could not prove how often this kind of trick was used, but he considered two theories. The "few bad apples" theory holds that there are a few wrongdoers in every large police force, and that RCMP misdeeds are actually rare. Henshel himself supports the "tip of the iceburg" theory, which claims that there are many more misdeeds than the scandals have revealed. According to Henshel, an officer who violates laws for personal gain is penalized, while an officer who breaks laws for the purposes of the force can be promoted. This self-righteous law violation makes a police force especially dangerous to a democratic society.[92]

SOCIAL POLICY:
Issues and Viewpoints

In this section we will discuss the problem of how to turn bad guys into good guys. And we must hurry: There is not a moment to lose! Let's look at the major theoretical approaches already mentioned and see if they can offer any specific recommendations for public policy.

POLICY AND KINDS-OF-PEOPLE THEORIES

Psychodynamic approaches to deviance recommend that *all children should experience stable affection, consistent discipline, and security*, especially in their early relationships with their parents. Thousands of studies show the effects of unhappy family life on subsequent behavior.

However, the family is the most private area of social interaction. Only in totalitarian societies does the public have the authority to tell people how to bring up their children. If Canadian children are abused, they may be protected from their parents; in other family matters the state is not allowed to interfere. Hence, public policy in matters of socialization is almost useless. Therapy and support should be available to anyone who needs help in family matters, but it does not look as if this will greatly reduce adult alcoholism or other forms of deviance. Fortunately, however, there are other approaches.

POLICY AND SITUATION THEORIES

All three forms of situation theory—anomie, cultural-transmission, and role-self—make important recommendations. As with all important policy issues, these recommendations are subjects of much debate, and we expect many readers to disagree with them.

Policies derived from anomie theory

Merton's basic idea is that when people do not have a chance to pursue culturally approved goals through legitimate activities, they are likely to turn to illegitimate activities. There are two ways of avoiding this problem. One is to persuade people to be satisfied with less. In earlier times this approach actually worked; peasants never hoped to wear velvet and eat roasted peacock, as the lord of the manor did, because they were taught to be content with their "station in life." However, those days are over. It is useless to tell working-class Canadians to be content with poverty.

The alternative, then, is to provide more *legitimate opportunities*. People often turn to crime when they cannot get what they want in any other way. This is why crime rates are often higher among underprivileged groups. Opening up new legitimate opportunities would fight crime more successfully than punishment does.

Policies based on cultural transmission theory

Cultural-transmission theory holds that individuals learn deviant behavior by participating in deviant subcultures. Therefore we should get the individual out of a procriminal subculture if possible. The state should carry out any policy that will undercut the procriminal subcultures and turn their members toward other social groups. This, paradoxically, may be done by legalizing certain activities that are now illegal. Deviant subcultures often attract members by offering things that people want but cannot get legally—homosexual contacts, crap games, abortions, marijuana, or pornographic movies, for example. The reasons for participating in an underground community disappear if the illegal things are made legal. Thus, during Prohibition, people who wanted liquor had to deal with the underworld. Their contacts with this subculture led to greater tolerance for other kinds of illegal activity, and the gangsters got richer. Ending Prohibition automatically removed the ordinary wine drinker from a deviant subculture and put most bootleggers out of business.

Making an undesirable activity illegal often leads to more serious problems. Outlawing abortion does not prevent abortions; instead, it creates abortion rackets and causes many women to go through unnecessarily dangerous operations. Outlawing homosexuality does not change people into heterosexuals; instead, it makes it impossible for them to lead normal lives and enables blackmailers to exploit them. Outlawing drug use does not prevent pot smokers from turning on or junkies from shooting heroin, but it does pull them into the underworld subculture, where they learn positive attitudes toward the violation of laws. This is where marijuana users learn to become heroin users. It also enables organized crime to profit from illegal drugs and forces the addict to turn to crime to pay for drugs that would be cheaper if they were sold legally. Legalizing the use of these drugs under certain conditions would take business away from criminal outfits and, by making it unnecessary for users to have contacts with other users, eliminate the deviant subculture.

Policies based on role-self theory

Role-self theory has attracted a lot of attention recently, especially because of its emphasis on labeling—the view that a deviant career generally begins when the offender is officially labeled "deviant." Who is a "juvenile delinquent"? It is a youth who has been caught violating a law. Many of us have *qualified* for the same role, since we have broken many laws, but we have not acquired that identity because we were not caught. Who is a "skid row alcoholic"? It is the drunk who is taken to jail instead of home. Only the official action thrusts the stigmatized role upon the offender. Once the label has been assigned, however, the offender continues to play the part of the delinquent or the drunk, as the case may be. Role-self theory suggests that we should avoid stigmatizing people or labeling them as deviant. Do not make them into outsiders or endanger their relationships in normal society; instead, protect the dignity of their self-image and

preserve their roles as normal, reputable human beings.

Sometimes efforts to help people backfire because this point is ignored. For example, the government has provided aid to the poor through welfare payments and housing projects. But the poor can claim these benefits only by playing a stigmatized role—that of "welfare recipient." Likewise, probation officers want to identify delinquents as early as possible so that they can be "treated" before their character is firmly established. In many cases this may be the wrong approach: The "treatment" itself gives the child a delinquent identity. When in doubt it might be better to treat children as if they were expected to behave normally rather than as if they were expected to get into trouble.

It usually causes fewer problems to let people have what they want legally (even if it is not good for them) than to try to stop them from getting what they want illegally. Thus the best way to stop organized crime might be to legalize gambling and provide free medical maintenance for narcotics addicts. The best way to keep marijuana users from switching to harder drugs might be to legalize pot. And so on.

Unfortunately, this policy is not a cure-all. Legalizing people's vices may not get rid of them, and in some cases it may even encourage them. Ending Prohibition did not end alcoholism. Thus we have not solved the problem of evil in this chapter, but we have used up our space and must leave the remaining problems for you to work on.

SUMMARY

1. *Deviance* is any form of behavior that violates the norms of a social group or of society. It includes deviant behavior (e.g., crimes, sexual deviance, and suicide), deviant habits (e.g., alcoholism, drug addiction, and compulsive gambling), deviant psychologies

(mental and emotional disorders), and deviant cultures (e.g., the counter-culture). Deviant behavior is not uncommon. A number of studies have shown that most people have violated the law. Deviant habits are a major problem too. Heavy drinking, for example, not only has a harmful chemical effect on the body but also tends to damage social relationships.

2. Deviance is an interactional process that is created as much by conformist behavior as by deviant behavior. The conformers make the rules, enforce them, and label those who break them "deviant."

3. *Social control* consists of the methods by which members of a group try to get others to follow the prescribed norms. Among these methods are socialization, informal group pressure, and the use of social sanctions—rewards and punishments.

4. The worst effect of deviance on social organizations is its erosion of members' trust in the organization. However, deviance may also have effects that support social organization. These effects include (1) cutting red tape, (2) acting as a safety valve, (3) clarifying rules, (4) uniting the group, (5) highlighting conformity, and (6) acting as a warning signal.

5. Durkheim believed that a certain amount of deviance is required by society, and, in testing this theory, Kai Erikson found that deviance occurred among the New England Puritans at a fairly constant rate.

6. Behavior is deviant only if the actor has to answer to the group whose rules his or her behavior violates. *Role conflict* happens when one has two or more different roles that make contradictory demands.

7. Theories of deviance may be classified into two basic types—*kinds-of-people* theories and *situation* theories. Kinds-of-people theories can, in turn, be classified as biological or psychological. The biological explanations include Lombroso's positivism, Sheldon's constitutional typology of body forms, and the chromosomal explanation. The psychodynamic explanations are based on Freudian psychoanalysis. They claim that deviance is caused by a weak superego, a weak ego, aggression caused by frustration, or defense mechanisms such as reaction formation. All of the kinds-of-people theories have one weakness: They don't explain why a certain "kind of person" commits a deviant act once in a while but not always. To explain that, one must turn to situation theories, (e.g., anomie theory).

8. According to Durkheim, *anomie* is a condition of social instability in which people cannot organize their behavior rationally in relation to a predictable system of rewards and punishments. This is especially true in periods of prosperity or depression, and suicides increase at such times. Durkheim believed that this happens because people's goals can't remain stable under such conditions.

9. Merton extended the idea of anomie as a gap between culturally approved goals and institutionalized means. He listed five types of response to this situation—conformity, retreatism, ritualism, innovation, and rebellion. This theory does not explain why some people choose one type of deviant response and others choose another type, nor does it tell us why some people continue to conform even when they are suffering from anomie.

10. Cultural-transmission theory is another situation theory. It holds that the deviant is merely conforming to a subculture that is, from the point of view of the larger society, deviant. Sutherland's version of this approach (called *differential association theory*) holds that a person becomes criminal because he or she is exposed to a larger number of definitions that are favorable to violation of the law than definitions that are unfavorable to violation of the law.

11. Role-self theory, a symbolic-interactionist approach, is based on the assumption that a person's identity is built up and maintained by social interaction. An individual claims to be a certain kind of person and must behave in ways that support that claim. However, a deviant identity is sometimes forced on people against their will. *Labeling theory*, a version of role-self theory, holds that being arrested or committed to a mental hospital are events that label a person as delinquent or criminal or mentally ill. Cultural-transmission theories do not explain how or why deviant subcultures come into existence. Role-self theory contributes most in combination with anomie theory.

KEY TERMS

anomie normlessness or deregulation; confusion about what one may hope for or expect to accomplish.

culture goals the wants and ambitions that people are taught by their society.

deviance any form of behavior that violates the norms of a social group.

institutionalized means the resources available to the individual and considered appropriate to use in pursuing his or her goals.

labeling the social definition of a person as deviant.

norms rules that prescribe the legitimate means of pursuing one's goals.

reaction formation a mechanism for denying an unacceptable element of the personality.

role conflict the situation in which conformity to one role requires deviance from another.

sanction a reward for desirable behavior or a punishment for undesirable behavior.

social control the ways in which members of a group punish deviance and try to get others to live up to society's norms.

stigma the mark of disgrace that is attached to people in disvalued roles.

FOR FURTHER READING

COOPERSTOCK, RUTH, ed. *Social Aspects of the Medical Use of Psychotropic Drugs*. Toronto: Addiction Research Foundation, 1974. For a good discussion of drugs, this collection of sociological papers is a sound choice.

DURKHEIM, EMILE. *Suicide*. Translated by George Simpson. New York: Free Press, 1951. First published in French by Alcan, 1897. One of the classic books in sociology, this is nevertheless not very hard to read. I assign it every year to students in Introductory Sociology, firmly believing it will do them good. Some of them agree.

GROSMAN, BRIAN A. *Police Command*. Toronto: Macmillan of Canada, 1975. There are lots of good criminology books using Canadian materials. This discusses how police forces function.

HACKLER, JAMES C. *The Prevention of Youthful Crime: The Great Stumble Forward*. Toronto: Methuen, 1978. Addressed to policy-makers and researchers on delinquency, this book deals with the difficulty of evaluating treatment programs in Canada.

HAGAN, JOHN. *The Disreputable Pleasures*. Toronto: McGraw-Hill Ryerson, 1976. This is a fine sociological analysis of deviant behavior that employs quantitative data when appropriate and discusses its application. Most of the disreputable behavior that Hagan discusses would not seem pleasurable to many of us though. A good Canadian source of information.

MCDONALD, LYNN. *The Sociology of Law and Order*. London: Faber and Faber, 1976. This is a "conflict" approach to the issue of crime control. McDonald argues that the emphasis on crime as a social problem is drummed up to deflect public attention from such issues as war and starvation. As part of her argument, she tackles the methodological problems of estimating crime rates.

SIMON, RITA JAMES. *Women and Crime*. Lexington, Mass.: D.C. Heath, 1978. I have my own sexist stereotypes: When I refer to a criminal, I automatically say "he," not "she." This book, however, shows how male and female offenders are punished for similar crimes. It also discusses the future of women in crime.

TURK, AUSTIN T. *Criminality and Legal Order*. Chicago: Rand McNally, 1969. Future criminologists or lawyers would do well to begin with this book—future policepersons, too.

VAZ, E. W. *Aspects of Deviance*. Scarborough, Ont.: Prentice-Hall, 1976. This is a theoretical book but, like many such books in the field of deviance, quite readable. Insofar as it employs data at all, the sources are largely Canadian; it is, however, quite general in its applicability.

TWO

social interaction

8

ORGANIZATIONS

How many organizations have you had dealings with today? The phone company? The post office? The subway system? Your college? Your church? The public library? That's only a beginning. Think of the products you have used that are made by corporations—Ford, IBM, Esso, Borden's, and so on. Go on. There's more. The Weather Bureau? NBC television? The garbage collectors? Termite control? The fact is, you're in it. You're part of the system. There is no way you can avoid it!

Organizations are not modern inventions. Through organizations the pharaohs built pyramids, the emperors of China built irrigation systems, and the first popes built a universal church. But it is fair to say that modern society is an *organizational society*.[1] Not only are there more organizations now than ever before, but modern life depends on them.

By fitting together a large number of human activities, the organization becomes a powerful social tool. It combines its members and its resources, bringing together leaders, experts, workers, machines, and raw materials. At the same time, it is constantly judging how well it is performing and trying to adjust itself in order to achieve its goals. As we will see, this allows the organization to serve the various needs of society and its citizens more efficiently than they could be served by smaller and more natural human groupings, such as families, friendship groups, and communities.

In this chapter we will discuss all sorts of organizations, ranging from voluntary associations, such as the sisterhood of a synagogue or the Bruce Trail Association, to huge multinational corporations, such as ITT or General Motors. Most of our attention will center on complex, formal organizations called bureaucracies. These organizations greatly increase the effectiveness of human labor, but at the same time they demand obedience from members and ignore their unique personal needs.

Characteristics of organizations

Organizations are social units (or human groups) that are deliberately constructed and reconstructed to pursue specific goals.[2] Corporations, armies, schools, hospitals, churches, public utilities, and prisons are examples of organizations, while tribes, classes, ethnic groups, friendship groups and families are not. Three characteristics of organizations set them apart from other types of social groups: (1) division of labor, power, and communication; (2) power centers; and (3) substitution of personnel.

DIVISION OF LABOR, POWER, AND COMMUNICATION

The organization plans how to divide up the responsibilities of its members in order to achieve its goals most efficiently. Not only is the work divided into different jobs for different people, but the division of power is carefully planned. In addition, a system is set up for providing particular kinds of information to appropriate members of the organization. None of these matters is determined by tradition or chance, as they might be in a family or a friendship group. Instead, organizations make these arrangements quite deliberately.

POWER CENTERS

Organizations have one or more power centers that control the workings of the organization and direct it toward its goals. These power centers review the organization's performance and adjust it, where necessary, in order to increase its efficiency.

SUBSTITUTION OF PERSONNEL

An organization can assign its members to particular roles and jobs as needed to achieve its purposes. It can remove unsatisfactory people or demote them. It can transfer members or promote them.

Other groups have some of these characteristics too, of course. Organizations are not the only groups that plan. (For example, your family may keep a budget.) Nor are organizations the only groups that have power centers (tribes have chiefs) or replaceable membership (married people can divorce and remarry). However, organizations do much more purposeful planning and have more frequent member turnover than other social groups. They are more in control of their characteristics and goals than any other social group.

Kinds of organizations

Organizations differ in the types of goals they pursue and in the complexity of their roles. Almost all organizations have a recognized system for setting goals and changing them. Stockholders or trustees may do this by voting, for example. Organizations differ in their degree of formality—they range from the local Boy Scout troop to a complex modern hospital with research, therapy, and teaching responsibilities. Thus voluntary organizations are the least formal and bureaucracies the most formal. Let's start with voluntary groups.

VOLUNTARY ASSOCIATIONS

You may have mixed feelings about large organizations such as insurance companies, the army, or the tax bureau. I do. We are forced to deal with such organizations in order to get along in our society. However, you are probably more favorable toward certain other organizations. I am thinking, for example, of such groups as the YMCA, the Lions Club, the Ontario Historical Society, fan clubs, and amateur symphony orchestras. These are **voluntary associations**—groups that people join

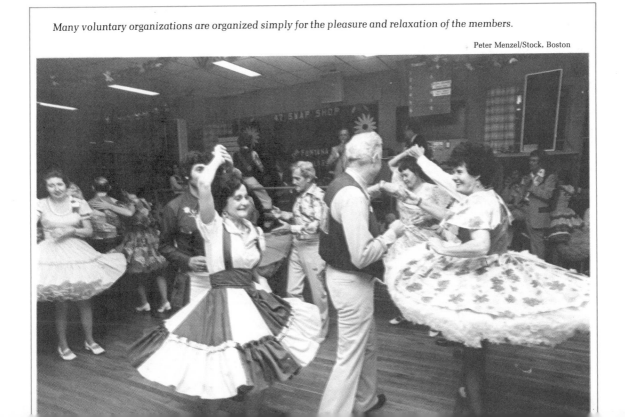

Many voluntary organizations are organized simply for the pleasure and relaxation of the members.

Peter Menzel/Stock, Boston

because they support the organization's goals and values. You join such groups knowing that you will probably participate in them only in your spare time and that you can quit whenever you choose. As a result, the members are usually committed to the group and feel that it is responsive to them.

Sociologists have made many studies of voluntary organizations, and we know a lot about the people who join them. Middle-aged people are more likely to join than younger or older people. The higher your social class, your education, and your income, the more likely you are to join. Married people join more than single people. English Canadians (especially women) are more likely to join than French Canadians. Finally, men are generally more likely to join than women. However, this factor differs quite a bit from one country to another.[3]

Do citizens of different countries differ much? Yes. James Curtis compared patterns of joining in the United States, Canada, Great Britain, Germany, Italy, and Mexico.[4] I'll present his results, leaving out the figures on people who belong to labor unions. After all, it's not clear whether a union is a "voluntary association" or a kind of bureaucracy. Curtis finds that Canada and the United States are about equally "nations of joiners." The other four countries are less so. In every country, education is the most powerful factor in the rate of joining (See Table 8.1.) In most countries, men are far more likely to join groups than women—but this is not so in Canada and the United States. Here the sexes are about equal in this respect. (See Table 8.2.)

If you haven't already looked at the tables, try to guess what percentage of North Americans are members of some group (other than a union). The answer: about half. Among the Italians and Mexicans only about one-quarter are members of groups. Males don't differ much when compared cross-nationally. It's the women who differ. Much of the strength of voluntary associations in North America is due to the exceptionally active participation of women. This is an important contribution to the integration of democratic society—one that has not been fully recognized. Let's hear it for the altar guild and the Girl Guides!

BUREAUCRACIES

Bureaucracies are organizations with a hierarchy of offices set up to do work; the army

---

TABLE 8.1

Voluntary association membership (nonunion) by education, six countries

COUNTRY (YEAR OF SURVEY)	PERCENTAGE OF RESPONDENTS BELONGING TO ASSOCIATIONS		
	ELEMENTARY EDUCATION	SECONDARY EDUCATION	POSTSECONDARY EDUCATION
Canada (1968)	42	60	79
United States (1960)	36	48	79
West Germany (1959)	29	61	53
Great Britain (1959)	26	43	70
Italy (1959)	22	31	46
Mexico (1959)	12	29	67

Source: James Curtis, "Voluntary Associations Joining: A Cross-National Comparative Note," *American Sociological Review*, 36 (October 1971), p. 874.

TABLE 8.2
Voluntary association membership (nonunion) by sex, six countries

COUNTRY (YEAR OF SURVEY)	PERCENTAGE OF RESPONDENTS BELONGING TO ASSOCIATIONS		
	MALE	FEMALE	TOTAL
Canada (1968)	51	51	51
United States (1960)	55	46	50
West Germany (1959)	47	22	34
Great Britain (1959)	41	27	33
Italy (1959)	36	17	25
Mexico (1959)	21	12	15

Source: James Curtis, "Voluntary Associations Joining: A Cross-National Comparative Note," *American Sociological Review,* 36 (October 1971), p. 874.

and the government are examples. Generally, bureaucracies are much more formal than voluntary associations; they have detailed rules and norms. A hierarchy is a chain of command in which each person has authority over several other people, who may in turn have authority over lower-ranking members, and so on. You might call it a pecking order. The hierarchy of ranks in the army is a familiar example.

I always think of a tangle of red tape when I think of a bureaucracy. In fact, however, bureaucracies are very efficient in their handling of routine matters. They may not always be personal, but they *are* rational. Unfortunately, efficiency and human happiness do not always support each other. Instead of being society's obedient servant, the organization sometimes becomes its master. Not all work can be profitable and satisfying, and not all regulations are acceptable to everyone. Thus the problem of modern organizations is how to build efficient human groups that offer the maximum satisfaction to all of their members.

The organizational revolution

An important aspect of modernization is the development of many large organizations. Nearly half of the corporate wealth in the United States, for example, is held by 200 large corporations. Modernization means building factories, schools, universities, political parties, and, of course, the modern state, itself a huge bureaucracy. It is true that some forms of bureaucracy existed in preindustrial society (e.g., medieval universities, commercial organizations in the Italian city-states, and state bureaucracies in ancient Egypt, China, and Byzantium). However, these groups were few in number, had relatively few members, and differed in a number of ways from modern bureaucracies. It is only in industrial societies that organizations have become important. For example, today about half of the American labor force works for giant organizations.[5]

Max Weber on bureaucracy

Most of our understanding of bureaucracy is based on a model that was first proposed by Max Weber. Let us begin by sketching his model of bureaucracy.[6] This is an imaginary bureaucracy that represents the principles and tendencies of real bureaucracies with which Weber was familiar. No single business or government office would show all these traits all the time. Weber's model simply outlines the traits of a perfectly rational social machine. He personally had mixed feelings about bureaucracy, for he saw that all organizations have to limit human freedom in order to be efficient. The organization has to get all its members to obey it, and this results in the loss of individual freedom to make decisions. A person becomes a "cog" in the machine. Thus an organization has two somewhat contradictory requirements: (1) to make people do what it wants them to do and (2) to make them happy with this arrangement.

As Weber saw, an organization has power—the ability to get its way despite opposition. It can use punishments and rewards to get people to meet its demands. But this may be a self-defeating process. People who are *forced* to obey tend to become alienated. They show no initiative, and in periods of crisis they may successfully disobey the rules.

Weber showed, however, that there is another way of getting people to obey. If a person sees the rules as conforming to his or her own values, he or she will consider them legitimate and find it much less uncomfortable to obey them. This is called legitimation. It does not necessarily make the rule pleasant for the person to obey, but it fulfills the person's need to follow rules that match rather than conflict with his or her own values.

Weber emphasized that there is a big difference between the need served by legitimation and other human needs. Legitimation does not change anyone's material interests. It does not make taking orders either more or less satisfying. An order may be recognized as legitimate and still be quite unpleasant, but this is not always the case.

Thus Weber used power to refer to the ability to get people to take orders and the term legitimation to refer to people's acceptance of the use of power because it is in line with their values. He used a third term, authority, to refer to the combination of the first two. A leader is said to have authority if he or she has power that is regarded as legitimate. As you will see in our discussion of politics in Chapter 15, these terms apply equally well to leadership in private organizations and in public office. A corporation president and a prime minister have much in common, and so did medieval popes and kings. All of them have the authority to make and issue binding orders.

Weber's typology of authority

Weber described three different types of authority with three different bases of legitimation. In traditional authority, the orders of superiors are seen as legitimate because that is how things are "always done." Tradition itself justifies the existing use of power. The authority of parents over their children is traditional, even if the parents have radical values. Another example of traditional authority was that of the lord of the manor during the Middle Ages.

The second type of authority is charismatic authority. The orders of a charismatic leader are viewed as legitimate because the leader has a magnetic, compelling personal style. This type of authority is often seen in periods of social change, when old rules are pushed aside by the force of a social movement, as when a revolution or a new religion arises to challenge established authority. Russia after 1917 and Nazi Germany after 1933 are examples of societies with charismatic leaders.

But it is the third type of authority—bureaucratic authority—that interests us most. The members of an organization see a ruling as legitimate if it is consistent with a set of abstract rules with which they all agree and from which the ruling is derived. In this sense it is "rational," and Weber sometimes called bureaucratic authority "rational-legal authority." The Roman courts developed this type of authority: They gave legitimacy to specific rules derived from more general principles.

Weber suggested that modern organizations require a bureaucratic pattern of authority. Neither traditional nor charismatic authority is as effective as rational-legal authority in keeping a production line or a subway system running smoothly. But bureaucratic authority is hard to maintain; it requires impersonality, self-denial, and narrowness—traits that people may find oppressive. Thus bureaucratic organizations often break down and are replaced by either traditional or charismatic relations.

Characteristics of bureaucracies

Weber described bureaucracies as having seven typical characteristics:

1 A bureaucracy is a "continuous organization of official functions *bound by* rules." Rules save effort by eliminating the need to derive new solutions for each case as it comes up. They standardize the treatment of many cases. These advantages are impossible if each person is treated as a unique case, that is, as an individual.

2 Each member of bureaucracy has a specific *scope of competence.* Division of labor, rights, and power is necessary in a rational organization. Each member must know his or her job and have a set of duties. Each person must have the resources needed to do the job, including the authority to command others, and each position must have defined limits, rights, and power.

3 "The organization of offices follows the principle of *hierarchy*; that is, each lower office is under the control and supervision of a higher one."

4 "The rules which regulate the conduct of an office may be *technical* rules or norms. In both cases, if their application is to be fully rational, specialized training is necessary." The bureaucrat's knowledge and technical skill is the basis of his or her claim to legitimacy.

5 Organizational affairs are kept separate. The property of the organization is completely separate from the private property of its members. The bureaucrat's personal residence is

Charismatic leaders are followed because of their magnetic, compelling personal styles.

AP Photo

separate from the organization. This keeps the person's status as a bureaucrat from becoming tangled with his or her status in other groups.

6 The official does not "own" his or her office. On the contrary, a bureaucracy's resources have to be *free to be redistributed* according to the needs of the organization.

7 Administrative acts, decisions, and rules are *recorded in writing.* When carried to an extreme, this procedure is often referred to as "red tape," but Weber considered it important. He argued that it is impossible to interpret norms and enforce rules in a consistent way without written records.

Weber pointed out that bureaucracies have nonbureaucratic leaders. Bureaucrats follow rules, but the person at the top decides the goals that the rules are designed to serve. Although bureaucrats are appointed, their leader is often elected or inherits his or her position. It is helpful if the leader provides a warm, visible image with which the members can identify. Historically, some bureaucracies have developed out of charismatic movements—for example, the organized church developed out of the early Christian movement and the Soviet Union developed out of the communist movement. The successors of charismatic leaders may have little charisma of their own, but keep the support of the lower-level members by using the charisma of the position they occupy. Thus the pope is viewed as representing Jesus and for this reason has inherited some of his charisma. These secondary leaders, according to Weber, never have as much charisma as the founder of the movement. On the contrary, they gradually use up the charisma of their position, until finally it is gone and they lose their legitimacy. Weber's theory of history thus suggests that an organization falls apart when a new charismatic leader overthrows the old regime and replaces it with a new one.

Because low-ranking bureaucrats have to obey orders from those above them, it does not much matter who occupies these lower positions. When a lower officer is replaced, obedience continues without interruption. This is true all the way up through the hierarchy,

except at the very top. The nonbureaucratic leader of the organization is the one person to whom commitment is personal rather than bureaucratic. His or her departure or death may bring on a major organizational crisis— the crisis of succession.

Actually, needed changes are often made during this period. It may or may not be a dangerous moment in the life of an organization. For example, often a university suffers a decline after the death of its founder, only to recover when another charismatic leader takes office. Thus Weber's description of bureaucracies should not be viewed as valid in every case, even though it is the working model used by almost all later analysts.

The structure of organizations

FORMAL STRUCTURE

All organizations are planned. This planning involves setting up a formal structure of definite rights, duties, privileges, hierarchies of authority and power, and routines that the group is supposed to follow in carrying out its collective work. This *formal* structure can be called the "blueprint" for the organization. In the case of a large, complex organization it can be illustrated by an organization chart, a pyramid of little squares that each represent an agency or position. (See Figure 8.1.) A written constitution may also set forth rules about authority and its limits, who is to perform what jobs, what sanctions will be used to reward or punish good and bad performance, and so on. A small voluntary organization, such as a babysitting pool, may not need to write down all of its rules, but all members must understand them. For example, decisions must be made on questions such as who will keep records, how many points should be given per hour of nighttime sitting and how many per hour of daytime sitting, and the like.

INFORMAL STRUCTURE

The formal structure is vital and cannot be ignored, but everybody who participates in a large organization soon realizes that it does not fully describe the way that an organization really works. Many informal structures develop in addition to the formal ones. These are the unwritten rules and other understandings that members must keep in mind in order to get through the day. Thus, on paper, the vice president in charge of marketing may be responsible for contract negotiations. However, her subordinates may realize that she is absentminded and that they can get a contract approved more quickly if they go to her secretary, who knows everything and influences everything she does. Formally, the vice president has the power; informally, the secretary does. The informal structure that develops in an organization depends largely on the personal relationships among the various members. Thus, if the vice president's secretary resigns and is replaced by a dimwit, the informal system cannot work the way it did before and some new system will develop. As we will see shortly, the human-relations approach to the study of organizations is especially concerned with informal structures.

Figure 8.1
Typical organization chart of a small corporation

A prison is one example of the coercive power used by governmental organizations to see that the members of a society follow the rules.

Organizational control and leadership

Here's the part we don't like: Every organization has to control the actions of its members. Not every action, of course, but some of them. Little control is necessary when the needs of the members fit the needs of the organization. In this happy situation, people will do what is best for the organization because it also satisfies their own needs. And the organization, by serving its own needs, will serve those of its members. Unfortunately, such a delightful fit between individual and organizational needs is rare. Usually organizations have to reward those who conform to its rules and punish those who do not. Organizations are artificial, planned social groups. Unlike natural social groups such as the family and the ethnic group, they cannot rely on informal social control to get their members to do their jobs. They require additional incentives. An organization gets its members to do what it wants in several ways. Let's look at some of those ways.

Organizations may use three types of social control: physical, material, and symbolic.[7] Physical means of control include devices such as guns, whips, or locks. This is **coercive power**. Material means of control consist of rewards such as goods, services, or money. If you use material means of control, you are using what we will call **utilitarian power**. Finally, symbolic means of control are such rewards as respect, prestige, love, and acceptance. When you use symbolic means, we will say that you are using **normative power**. For example, a successful pep talk requires normative power.

Different kinds of organizations use different kinds of power. For example, prisons are basically coercive, factories basically utilitarian, and churches basically normative. Prisoners are locked up; factory workers are paid; and church members are thanked and prayed for. We may thus classify organizations as coercive, utilitarian, or normative.

The more commitment a kind of power stimulates, the less alienating its effect is on the members of the group. Normative power stimulates more commitment than utilitarian power, and utilitarian power more than coercive power. Alienation follows the opposite pattern. Prisoners will be most alienated and least committed, factory workers somewhere in between, and church members least alienated and most committed.

The more coercive an organization is, the less its officials can rely on *personal* power to control its members. Thus prison wardens are obeyed not because of their personal qualities but because of their coercive resources. The informal inmate leaders are the true leaders in a prison, and this is due to their personal qualities. At the other extreme, officials of normative organizations such as churches use personal power as a major resource. Parish priests may be chosen on the basis of their persuasiveness and may get further training in persuasiveness. Priests without personal power may be transferred to positions that exercise little control—to scholarly work, for example.

Hospitals are also normative organizations. Doctors must persuade patients to follow orders voluntarily. A doctor's bedside manner, or persuasive power, is extremely important because he or she has no coercive power and because patients have no way of determining whether doctors are competent or not. The instructions of the most intelligent physician may not be followed if they are given in a wavering voice.

Organizations that are basically normative are usually successful in maintaining the authority of their formal leaders. In contrast, coercive organizations often find social control slipping into the hands of informal leaders, with whom the officials have to make some accommodation. Utilitarian organizations often distribute control among organizational officials and informal leaders of employees. In industries where workers are alienated and feel coerced, informal leaders usually control all of the expressive activities and many of the instrumental ones. (Expressive activities are those that involve emotional and interpersonal relationships, such as a party or a bowling team. Instrumental activities are those done for some practical purpose, such as the work done on the job.)

In organizations where workers are less alienated, formal leaders have more control, particularly over instrumental activities but even over some expressive activities. For example, the Christmas party is typical, not of the alienated factory, but of the less alienated business office, where white-collar workers feel at ease socializing with one another and with their bosses under the influence of company liquor. It is assumed that factory workers probably would not enjoy such a party.

Alternatives to control

We can think of these three forms of control—coercive, utilitarian, and normative—as ways of coordinating the activities of members of an organization so that the organization can achieve its goals. However, none of these forms of control is indispensable. There are other ways of making sure that members cooperate according to plan. One alternative to control is *selectivity*; another is *socialization*.

An organization that can be selective in choosing members can spend less time and effort on control. Coercive organizations usually cannot reject anyone who is sent to them, and they therefore have to pay a lot of attention to the problem of control. However, some coercive institutions operate selectively and can use less control. Open wards in mental hospitals and unguarded prison farms are more effective than locked wards and fenced-in prisons, but this is probably because inmates who are chosen already show promise of responding well to such programs.[8]

Utilitarian and normative organizations differ in how selective they are. For example, most democratic political parties in the West are highly unselective; the Soviet Communist Party, by contrast, is highly selective. Private schools are far more selective than public schools. Highly selective organizations usually are more effective and get more commitment from their members than unselective organizations. However, this is only partly because of their selectivity; for the most part it is because such organizations are generally richer and have more resources available to them.

The second alternative to control is socialization. The more effective the socialization, the less the need for control.[9] However, socialization is itself affected by the means of control used. For example, coercive organizations cannot effectively socialize their members, simply because they *are* coercive. (Remember, in Chapter 4 I said that socialization consists largely of learning to *want* to do what you *must* do—learning to want to play the roles that will be available for you to play, for example. Socialization works best when it works *with* your will instead of against it. If you force people to do something it is likely that they will hate doing it.)

Utilitarian organizations expect other organizations, such as schools and universities, to do their socialization for them. They can then select as their members people who are already socialized. Medical schools, for example, tend to choose students who are relatives of physicians. Why? Because they are already partially socialized, and this makes the medical school's job easier. Such students

have already been exposed to professional attitudes and norms. Finally, organizations that rely heavily on normative power are the most successful in their socialization of members.

Theoretical approaches to organizations

In sociology, as in all other fields, a point of view becomes fashionable, attracts criticism, and finally is replaced by other points of view. I want to tell you about three approaches to organizations that have been popular. The first of these goes by several names. I will call it the *classical approach*, but it is also known as the *formal* or *scientific-management* approach. The second approach is called the *human-relations* approach. The third may be called the *structuralist* approach; it is the dominant view today, so we'll pay more attention to it than to the others. But let's discuss these three points of view in the order in which they developed.

THE CLASSICAL APPROACH

This approach was especially concerned with establishing principles that might help a manager run a productive enterprise such as a factory. Hence the term *scientific management*. The main idea was that if a job was broken up into smaller, more specialized activities, workers would become more efficient and output would increase. Those who favored this idea supposed that workers were motivated only by material rewards.

The classical school always thought of an organization in terms of its formal structure. This was the "blueprint" that defined responsibilities and authority in a rational way. The organization was supposed to be very specific about its division of labor and to have highly specialized members and a clear hierarchy of authority. A forerunner of the classical school was Adam Smith, an economist who, in *The Wealth of Nations* (1776), described how a rational division of labor increased pin production in a factory several hundred times over.

There is no question that the classical approach has influenced the way organizations function in modern society. Ordinary people think of an organization in terms of a pyramid of little boxes. I imagine you sitting in yours and me sitting in mine, with arrows connecting us. We also think in terms of incentives to get the work done better and ways of dividing up a job to get it done faster. The person who first dreamed up such plans was Frederick W. Taylor, the father of the time-and-motion study.[10] Taylor seems to have seen human beings as the parts of a machine. Many factory managers took to "Taylorism" with great enthusiasm. Charlie Chaplin made fun of Taylor's approach in a 1936 movie called *Modern Times*. See it if you ever have a chance. Chaplin plays a little man on the assembly line trying to keep up with his machine under pressure from exploitive managers. They speed up the conveyor belt, feed him on the job with an automatic feeding machine that misfires its spoon, and so on.

Taylor suggested that if material rewards are closely linked to work output the worker will respond with maximum performance. Taylor's students, the "human engineers," wanted to determine which physical motions were the least tiring so that the human body could do more work with less fatigue in a given amount of time. Taylor believed that workers should be paid piecework wages, for in that way their pay would be directly determined by the amount of actual work they did. Although some engineers still do time-and-motion studies, few social scientists today accept Taylor's idea that people are driven by economic motives—the fear of hunger and the search for profit. There's more to it than that.

The classical theorists tried to improve the division of labor in organizations.[11] They assumed that the more a particular job can be divided up, the more specialized and skilled a worker can become at his or her part of the job. And the more skilled each worker becomes, the more efficient the whole system will be. As the division of labor increases, the whole system has to be coordinated and supervised according to a central plan of action. Workers need supervisors, who in turn must be supervised by someone else. Nobody should control more than five to ten subordinates. Hence the pyramid of control, with the executive leader at the top.

So far, so good. What the classical writers disagreed about, however, was the way in which the labor should be divided. There were four different principles of specialization, and no one knew for sure which one was most efficient:

1 Specialization by *goal*. For example, the army specializes in land defense, the navy in sea defense, and the air force in air defense.
2 Specialization by *process*, so that workers whose work is similar are grouped together. For example, everyone who gathers military information has similar proedures to follow, whether the information is to be used by the air force, the navy, or the army. Accordingly, they all work together as a single unit.
3 Specialization by *type of clientele*. For example, teachers of the very young work in different schools from teachers of adolescents.
4 Specialization by *geographical area*. This principle proposes that jobs be grouped together if they are in the same geographical area. For example, all American military units in Southeast Asia—whether army, navy, or air force—are under one command.

Although many classical writers have tried to apply these four principles of organization, the results have not been very useful either for analyzing existing organizations or for planning new ones. It is hard to test these principles to find out which is the most efficient. Besides, managers rarely have to decide what sort of structure to set up. Most organizations simply grow up like a jungle, as a result of many separate decisions, instead of like a building, which is planned at one time.

So the classical approach has changed over time. Nowadays people aren't trying so hard to find the "right" organizational structure. But there is more interest in comparing certain *types* of structure. For example, classical writers today are discussing whether centralized or decentralized decision making is more efficient. There is no "right" answer; there are advantages and disadvantages to both approaches. It seems that centralized organizations can often provide facilities more easily than independent local organizations. However, this advantage may be offset by the fact that they may become too rigid to meet special local needs.

THE HUMAN-RELATIONS APPROACH

The human-relations school began when various researchers made several discoveries that contradicted the assumptions of the classical approach:

1 They noticed that the amount of work done is not determined by a worker's physical capacity (as Taylor had suggested) but by his or her "social capacity," that is, relations with co-workers.
2 They saw that noneconomic rewards play a central role in the motivation and happiness of the worker.

A cog in the machine.

Culver Pictures

3 They found that specialization is not always the most efficient form of division of labor.

4 Finally, they found that workers react to the norms and rewards of management not as individuals but as members of groups.

On the basis of these observations, the human-relations school focused on the roles of communication, participation, and leadership in motivating workers.

The Hawthorne studies

Many of these conclusions were reached as a result of research done by Elton Mayo and a group of researchers at the Western Electric Company's Hawthorne plant in Chicago between 1927 and 1932. The results of these Hawthorne studies were so surprising that they seemed to call for a closer look at the assumptions behind the classical approach.[12]

The Hawthorne studies began as an effort to test the claim of the classical school that there is a simple, direct relationship between physical working conditions and rate of production. In their experiments, they set out to vary "physical" factors such as the amount of lighting and the length of the workers' rest periods, but it soon became apparent that whether they increased these factors or decreased them the production rates rose and continued to rise! The researchers discontinued the rest breaks altogether and dimmed the lights, and still the production rate was high. The puzzled researchers were forced to conclude that the increasing production rate resulted from a "social" factor—the satisfaction the workers felt because they were put into the experimental room and given attention. This was to become the major finding of the Hawthorne studies.

The breakthrough in the Hawthorne research came with the famous bank-wiring-room experiment involving a group of fourteen workers whose job was to wire sets of switchboards (called "banks"). This experiment called into question almost all the assumptions of the classical approach. Many additional, more complicated studies verified the findings of the bank-wiring-room study. When this experiment was set up, the researchers already knew that the workers were producing far less than they could if they worked at full capacity. The investigators were simply interested in observing the workers and finding out what factors influenced their rate of production. They found the workers were following a social norm, enforced by their coworkers, that defined the proper amount of production. They did so despite the fact that they were paid the way Taylor had suggested: individual hourly rates based on individual average output, plus a bonus determined by average group output.

The workers in the wiring room set a norm for a "day's work." This norm called for each man to wire two complete sets of switchboards each day. Workers who produced more than two sets were ridiculed as "speed kings" or "rate busters." Those who produced less than two sets were called "chiselers." The actual production averages were, day in and day out, surprisingly close to the group's norms. The workers believed that if they produced a great deal more their pay rate would be reduced or some of them would lose their jobs (the study took place during the Great Depression). They also felt that if they produced much less it would be unfair to management and they would get into trouble. Neither belief had any basis in reality.

The Hawthorne experiments concluded that the level of production is set by social norms, not by the physical abilities of the workers. Noneconomic rewards and sanctions affect the behavior of the workers and limit the effectiveness of economic incentives. Members who produced more or less than the socially determined norm lost the friendship and respect of their coworkers. This affection seemed to be more important to them than money. Workers act as members of groups, not as individuals. The lesson for management was that workers should not be treated as if they were separate units because they are clearly influenced by the group. Finally, an important finding of the bank-wiring-room study was that there are two kinds of leaders in the work force—the *formal* leaders chosen by management and given authority and the *informal* leaders, who are the best-liked workers in the group. In the bank-wiring room the informal leader was admired the most; his advice was sought the most; and he spoke for the group in dealings with other factory employees. The supervisor did not have much influence on the group but was himself under pressure to conform to its rules. Later studies have shown that a foreman is more likely to be accepted if he or she uses informal leadership instead of trying to use authority to control the workers.

The human-relations approach, then, developed as a reaction against the classical tendency to view the organization wholly in rational economic terms. By contrast, the human-relations school emphasized the informal, interpersonal aspect of organizations. It stressed the importance of communication between levels of authority, of explaining to lower-level workers why a particular action is necessary, and of involving them in decision making, especially in matters that affect them directly. In general, the human-relations approach called for democratic, noncoercive leadership that is concerned with the problems of workers. Canadian management has been greatly influenced by the human-relations approach, and thousands of executives and supervisors have participated in human-relations workshops.

The human-relations approach has been widely applied for a whole generation. However, a recent criticism of the approach is devastating in its implications. Sociologists were first alerted to the weaknesses of the human-relations approach in 1967 when Alex Carey launched an attack on the original Hawthorne studies.[13] Carey argued that the original researchers had distorted their evidence to support their claim that the informal structure influenced productivity more than such economic factors as wages. Indeed, much

of the evidence reported in 1939 seems to have been too skimpy to support the researchers' conclusions. For example, one of the Hawthorne experiments involved only 5 female workers, too small a sample to bother reporting. Carey suggested that the poor research procedures used in the original study may have led scholars astray.

In 1978, Richard Herbert Franke and James D. Kaul followed up this criticism by conducting a thorough statistical analysis of the evidence collected by Hawthorne researchers. Such an analysis was not made by the Hawthorne researchers, in part because statistical techniques were not sufficiently advanced in the 1930s. Franke and Kaul concluded from their analysis that the Hawthorne researchers were quite mistaken in their findings. Human-relations factors proved to be relatively unimportant in comparison to the ordinary factors that scientific-management experts had relied upon all along. Group morale, for example, did not determine workers' output as much as pay scale, rest breaks, and good supervision on the job. Franke and Kaul concluded that the importance of good human relations must be justified on grounds other than their effect upon workers' productivity.[14]

The concept of harmonious interests

In most ways the classical approach and the human-relations approach were exactly opposite, but they did share one assumption. Neither school saw any conflict between organizational goals and individual human needs. The classical approach assumed that the most efficient organization would also be the most satisfying one, since it would maximize both productivity and the worker's pay. It assumed that the worker wanted to maximize his or her income but was satisfied with his or her share of the organization's income. It followed from these assumptions that what is best for the organization is best for the workers, and vice versa.

The human-relations approach also concluded that the most satisfying organization would be the most efficient one. It did not suppose, however, that workers could be happy in a cold, formal, "rational" organization that satisfied only their economic needs. On the contrary, management should recognize the workers' needs for communication and informal social relationships on the job. If management encourages communication and democratic leadership, then life on the job will be happy. If the workers are happy, they will be more willing to cooperate, and thus the efficiency of the organization will increase. Many writers of the human-relations school describe factories in almost lyrical passages. They portray the worker as anxious not to miss a day at the factory or to be late because he wants to spend time with his friends on the job. The worker is careful not to disappoint the foreman, who is compared to a warm and understanding parent. The work team itself is often called a "family." While the classical school saw a natural balance between the organization's goals and the workers' needs, the human-relations school believed that such a balance could be achieved only after social scientists had straightened out old-fashioned managers and taught them about informal groups.

THE STRUCTURALIST APPROACH

Although the human-relations and classical approaches are important, not all theories of organization belong to one of these schools. Marx and Weber both had important things to say about organizations, but neither could be called a classical theorist or a human-relations theorist. Moreover, many important modern sociologists strongly oppose both approaches, particularly the human-relations approach, arguing that social science should not help either workers or management manipulate the other side.

A new approach to organization theory seems to be developing, one that combines the first two. The classical idea of *formal structure* has been kept. It refers to the organizational pattern designed by management, or the blueprint of how labor is to be divided, who is to have authority over whom, the rules about wages, fines, quality control, and the like. In addition, although most current writers on this subject are opposed to the manipulative aspects of the human-relations approach, they are very interested in *informal organization*, that is, the social relations that develop among workers. Thus modern organization theorists are discussing such matters as the relationship between the formal organization and the informal organization of a work group.

Organizational conflict

Structuralist writers generally disagree with the assumption that the interests of management and workers are harmonious. The structuralists argue that there is a built-in conflict between organizational needs and personal needs, between rationality and non-rationality, between formal and informal relations, and between management and workers. This conflict will always exist, so that management cannot get workers to work without eventually alienating them.

According to Marx, the factory worker sees his or her job as meaningless, monotonous, and uncreative. The worker has no control over the pace or the location of his or her work because workers own neither the means of production nor the product of their labor. To Marx, and also to Weber, this alienation is a major problem in the industrial world. Workers, unable to control how their labor is used, are frustrated and unhappy. Such frustration can hardly be eliminated, despite beliefs of human-relations theorists. Workers spend much of their time thinking about what they are going to do after work.

Human-relations writers too often tended to see workers' dissatisfaction as a result of poor communication and not as a real conflict of interests. They emphasized the effectiveness of social rewards rather than material rewards. Their ideas were sometimes put to use by management, which tried to encourage workers by giving them inexpensive symbols of prestige and friendship such as fancy ashtrays and a more impressive job title, instead of an increase in wages.[15] In general, these human-relations writers believed that conflict between workers and management was undesirable.

Current writers (mostly structuralists) are more likely to base their ideas on a conflict model of society. They see value in open conflict and argue that if conflict is ignored rather than brought out into the open, it will damage both the worker and the organization.

Structuralists are well aware that human-relations techniques have been used to help higher-level employees to manipulate those at lower levels. This happens, for example, when management invites lower-level employees to

participate in "democratic" decision making; usually, the decisions have already been made and the real purpose of the discussion is to get the employees to accept them. Another human-relations idea is to set up suggestion boxes and "gripe sessions." Sometimes management has used such techniques to reduce the workers' alienation without actually improving their situation.

Human-relations theorists defend themselves by arguing that workers and management are always manipulating each other in some way and that the study of manipulation did not create that situation. Besides, many organizations that have human-relations programs also have the highest pay, the best working conditions, and the most respected unions. Using the human-relations approach may improve the worker's social situation without sacrificing his or her economic interests.

Japanese society is highly organized.

Wide World

Structuralism today

The human-relations approach is not a thing of the past. And there are some writers who still take the classical approach to the study of organizations. In general, however, the structuralists have broadened and combined the other two approaches in the following ways:

1 They study both formal and informal aspects of organizations.
2 They do not make too much of informal groups, as the human-relations writers did. For example, in his study of 1200 industrial workers, Robert Dubin found that only 9 percent of his sample enjoyed the informal group life on the job.[16] Another study of 179 assembly line workers showed that there were almost no social groups on the job.[17]
3 They emphasize both material and social rewards. Workers care about both. One study showed that many steelworkers were willing to exchange their relatively nonrepetitive,

skilled jobs for assembly line jobs that were more repetitive but paid about 30 percent more.[18]
4 They study both work and nonwork organizations. While the classical and human-relations theorists studied factories, banks, insurance companies, and the like, the structuralist writers often study a variety of organizations—the Communist party, the Catholic Church, or even a maximum-security prison.
5 They do not try to determine the "best kind of structure," as if one single blueprint would do for all sorts of organizations, as the classical school assumed. Instead, they recognize that different kinds of organizations are required to meet the goals of different groups. Thus, instead of saying that each supervisor should have, say, five subordinates, the structuralists recognize that the ideal number may be three subordinates in one organization and fifteen in another, depending on the work they do.[19]
6 Above all, they concentrate on the *structure of the situation*, confronting various organizations, focusing on such factors as the technology that must be used and the kinds of raw material to be processed.[20]

SOCIAL RESEARCH:
Sociologists at Work

WORKING IN CANADIAN ORGANIZATIONS

Canadian sociologists often study organizations in order to understand other aspects of Canadian society. In this section I want to show how the internal practices of large organizations are vitally linked to various important issues in Canada.

It may not be clear to you that the study of organizations is a good way to understand Canadian society. After all, you may say, big organizations are the same everywhere, and can shed little light on the distinctive aspects of Canadian life. Very well, then. Let us discuss two distinctive developments in Canada: (a) the competition between French and English Canadians, and (b) the heavy involvement of the Canadian population in extractive labor, chiefly mining and lumbering, in areas far from big

cities. Both of these are regarded as crucial to any grasp of Canadian society as a whole, and both of them require a study of the impact of organizations.

In a mid-1960s study of the Canadian Public Service, Christopher Beattie established that anglophone public servants fared better than francophones despite government guarantees of equal rights.[21] Francophones were paid lower salaries and denied good jobs. His report also indicated that no improvement had taken place by the 1970s. According to Beattie, the problems of francophone civil servants resulted from inequalities in the opportunity structure of Canadian society. (This study took place before the changes initiated by the Parti Québécois in Quebec. We do not yet know how the new policies have affected Québécois civil servants.)

Beattie distinguished between two groups of francophone public employees: the Québécois and the Franco-Ontarians. He found that each of the groups faced a different set of problems.

The two groups differed in the extent to which they could speak and receive schooling in their own language. In Ontario, francophones lack political

Ontario Ministry of Industry and Tourism

The impact of organizations is not limited to cities. In a remote, single-industry town, the company's influence can be all-pervasive.

anglophones. They did not. Indeed, precisely this younger group of men were the most disadvantaged in salary levels.[22] If career discrimination has declined in the public service, it has done so only among the older civil servants.

This study, then, of a major Canadian organization provides at least a partial explanation of the strength of separatist support among the young, middle-class, educated members of the francophone community. What began as research on an organization ended by shedding light on the political conflict between Canada's two major language groups.

In a similar manner, Rex Lucas's study, *Minetown, Milltown, Railtown*,[23] caused him to examine the impact of major organizations on the everyday lives of the people who live in single-industry towns. Because Canada's economy depends, to a greater extent than most, on the "extractive" industries of mining and logging, a large number of its towns have grown up around mines and paper mills. Other towns have been built to maintain the railroads that unite Canada's economy. Practically all the people in these single-industry towns are employed by "the company". Moreover, the industry provides the setting for the social life of the entire community.

Towns built around mines, mills, or railways usually have fewer than 30,000 people and are located in isolated regions of both French and English Canada. Lucas observed a prevailing sense of fatalism and isolation in single-industry towns. The isolation felt by townspeople was not merely the result of being geographically situated "100 miles from noplace." The townspeople also felt isolated because they believed that their way of life was dictated almost entirely by the organization, and that they had very little real power over their lives. Despite the remoteness of these people from the urban centers of organizational life, they were more strongly affected by large organizations than if they were urban dwellers.

There are many single-industry towns in the USSR, South America, Africa, Australia, India, and other countries that rely heavily upon natural resources. Canada, however, has more than its share of such towns. Lucas believed that, to understand Canada well, one must understand the distinctive culture of single-industry towns. The people of these towns share a tendency to "put up with things", to forego the attainment of legitimate desires, and to accept limitations in the system.[24]

People who live in isolated rural areas, then,

power and have to adjust to an educational system geared to English. They learn fewer professional skills for advanced careers than do the Québécois. In Beattie's survey, the Québécois tended to desire careers that were intrinsically interesting, while the Franco-Ontarians tended to choose more routine jobs that were secure and well paid. It is likely that the Franco-Ontarians were forced to place job security and job benefits ahead of creative job potential because their actual prospects were so limited.

Beattie also found, however, that those workers who chose routine jobs were better able to keep up their ethnic-religious roots. The "creative" jobs, held most often by Québécois men, demanded more contact with anglophones. Assimilationist pressures resulted in a loss of cultural identity for those francophones who moved up the job ladder.

In a postscript, Beattie added that, since the Quiet Revolution of the 1960s, the education of Québécois men has been about level with the education of Quebec anglophones. One might expect, then, that the young francophones in the Public Service would earn as much as the young

238

cannot escape the dominance of organizational society. Half of Canada's population lives in communities of less than 30,000, and many of these communities are single-industry towns. There is no reason to expect the number of such communities to decrease, and they may even increase. Nor is there any reason to expect the impact of "the company" to decrease in such towns. Organizational society is here to stay. To study other aspects of it, we must start by recognizing how embedded our daily activities are in the organizations to which we belong.

Oswald Hall is the Canadian sociologist who has perhaps done most to draw attention to the pivotal role of organizations in our society. According to Hall, sociologists have too often described job roles without taking into account their organizational backgrounds.[25] In order to describe, for instance, the role of a nurse, a sociologist must consider whether he or she is employed by a physician in a private office, as a ward nurse in a children's hospital, or as a public health nurse in the Arctic. A job's title means little until we know something about the kind of organization that surrounds it.

Hall also pointed out an especially strong link between the organizational structure of a society and the ethnic relations that develop in it. Ethnic groups tend to be drawn disproportionately into particular job categories, and those jobs are determined by the needs of particular economic organizations. For example, Hall refers to a study of the Montreal construction industry, which is divided into four components that are ethnically divided. Large industrial engineering equipment is controlled and operated by Anglo-Saxon Canadians. Construction is financed by Anglo-Saxons and by the Jewish community. French Canadians do most of the small

scale contracting, and they hire Italians in large numbers. Finally, the organization of Montreal real estate is mostly in Jewish hands.[26] Obviously, the relations among members of these ethnic groups is affected by their positions in this structure of production and distribution. To understand the rivalry among various ethnic groups in Montreal one must know about such factors as the organization of the building industry.

Hall further points out that the occupational needs of Canadian organizations determine patterns of immigration. In the past, immigration was encouraged because the demand for workers exceeded the supply. Candidates for immigration are still chosen largely on the basis of the skills they offer potential employers. Ultimately, this affects the ethnic mix of Canadian organizations. People of a given nationality may be admitted simply because that group is believed to be especially qualified for the available jobs. In professional and technical fields, as many as 80 percent of the jobs have sometimes been filled by new immigrants.[27]

Every corporation develops certain specialized occupations within it; there are a certain number of supervisors, a certain number of laborers, and so on. The people who work in these jobs generally find that their entire lives are affected by their work experience; their jobs affect their friendships, their choice of residential neighborhoods, their "exposure" to particular ideas and political opinions, and so on. Clearly, then, the organization has a vast influence upon the structure of Canadian society. It produces a certain mix of occupations with very unequal salaries and unequal amounts of power and prestige. As a result, many of the political issues and social problems of our day are a direct result of the organizations in which we work.

SOCIAL POLICY:
Issues and Viewpoints

How do you like the system you are part of? Would you like to change it, drop out of it, go along with it? In what ways? Let's discuss some possible ways of viewing the situation.

You may think you understand it well enough to give it up. You may be a guitar-playing commune member and raise vegetables and marijuana in your back yard. If so, your view of organizational society is probably different from that of your brother, who is a stockbroker and yachtsman. During the 1960s there were plenty of young people who felt so disgusted with the impersonal rigidity of modern society that the hippie movement was born. At least, some writers think this is what it was all about. Theodore Roszak[28] and Charles Reich[29] both described the counterculture as a rebellion against the life style required by "the system." Rather than becoming managers and "paper pushers," members of corporations or government agencies, most members of the counterculture chose to live a frugal life of spontaneous expressiveness. They did not want to be programed to work from nine to five.

Reich argued that to avoid wastefulness, pollution, and endless consumerism, we must conquer the large corporations. It will be necessary, he says, to change a culture that prescribes impersonality and competitiveness into one that allows for affection and openness. He may be right. But the youth movement of the 1960s and early 1970s is a thing of the past, while corporations and other large organizations are still with us. They may still be wasteful, impersonal, and so on, but more people are coming to terms with them and fewer are dropping out.

Besides, who can really drop out anyway? Unless you become a living Robinson Crusoe, completely isolated from human contact, you will depend on the technology of modern organizations. It may be pleasant to drop out of the system and raise potatoes in British Columbia. But potato growers use pickup trucks, at least. And this brings them into a distant but very important relationship with Ford, Exxon, and all the other villains they want to escape from. So who is kidding whom?

So what are the problems and how serious are they? It depends on your point of view. It seems certain that complex organizations are increasing in number and also in power. What effect do they have on their members? In *The Organization Man*, William H. Whyte, Jr. has suggested that the man or woman at the upper levels of an organizational hierarchy experiences an invasion of privacy. The social life of the family, for example, is affected by the organization.[30] The bureaucrat's personality is also affected, if only because he or she must be able to tolerate a lot of frustration and must be able to postpone rewards. (No impulsiveness is allowed. Look at the rule book before doing anything.) The worker must also be able to ignore his or her personal preferences and relationships, treat clients as "cases," and follow rules consistently. He or she must have the drive to get ahead.

The organization consists of a hierarchy of positions through which an employee may move, and promotion rewards both performance and conformity. Does the worker pay a high emotional price for this? Drive! Strive! Conform! Workers dress alike—neatly and conservatively. What are the personal costs of sacrificing one's individuality and impulses to the beige-carpeted world of the corporation? We have assumed that the costs are high. Robert Merton's work, for example, has suggested that bureaucracy's system of rewards (e.g., the seniority basis of promotion) leads to timidity and conservatism and discourages initiative and adventurousness.[31]

But recently another view has appeared, that of Melvin Kohn. Kohn's research has shown that instead of being unusually rigid and conforming, bureaucrats tend to be more flexible, more open to new experience, and more self-directed than people who work in nonbureaucratic settings.[32] Kohn believes that this is because bureaucrats feel secure—the organization protects them from the arbitrary power of their superiors. Instead of being in an "iron cage," as Weber thought, the bureaucrat is freer than most people. The rule book is there, of course, but it can be used as protection against the whims of the bosses. There are no sultans or dictators around IBM, General Foods, or the civil service, or so Kohn seems to believe. But it seems to me that working in a big organization does lead people to forget that they are responsible for making their own decisions. There is a real danger of becoming too obedient to the rule book, even when it conflicts with one's own moral beliefs and human feelings of pity or concern.

I have to believe that it is bad for the human soul to be always following orders. It is true that people in many other social situations manage to pass the buck and avoid responsibility when they want to. Bureaucrats have no monopoly on cowardice. But I wonder: Are they more *tempted* to be irresponsible than the rest of us? Is it harder for a bureaucrat to say, "No, I won't!"?

Agreed, there are cowards in every social system and every occupation. But I'll be more willing to take my chances with officials in a democracy. There's a chance to control them there. The problem is that bureaucracy is not democratic. Sometimes bureaucracy even poses a threat to a democracy. If you're in a bureaucracy, authority runs from the top downward—never upward. Democracy runs in the other direction. These two principles don't fit together very well.

CP Photo/Mitchell

These leaders have their power supported by an enormous bureaucracy.

Here's how it is supposed to work: Elected government officials are supposed to set policy and then pass their orders down through the civil-service bureaucracy so that laws and decisions are put into effect. But one problem is that the civil servants and the government agencies often have enough power so that they can ignore orders that they don't like. Elected officials are dependent on their staff members, and this may make it impossible to supervise or control them. So democracy may actually be the victim, not the master, of its own bureaucracy. Suppose the top bureaucrats, who are not elected officials, get too much power. Suppose they are able to pass orders all the way down through the hierarchy. Suppose their orders are obeyed. This happens.

You may be concerned about other issues that have to do with bureaucracy—such as whether you can live a fairly independent life in an organization or whether you have to become some sort of robot. If this is what troubles you, there is reason to hope. Modern society may be moving past bureaucracy as described in this chapter. It seems to be moving toward professional colleagueship. For example, I work in a university and have more freedom than you can imagine. Bureaucracy is for the typists and lab technicians, not the faculty. It's the same for physicians and lawyers and engineers. Once you are a professional, the rules of bureaucracy don't apply to you in the ordinary way. Professionals don't boss each other around. They ask each other for advice, but if they decide to ignore the advice that's their own business. They have to cooperate to some extent, but they do it as equals, not as supervisors and subordinates. The chairman of my department would never come into my class to tell me how to teach. Nor would a surgeon barge into another surgeon's operating room to criticize the performance.

In modern society, more and more work relationships are becoming "collegial"—not bureaucratic. As we move toward a highly educated, highly professional organizational structure, there is a possibility that more jobs will be done by task forces than through the bureaucratic "system." *Task forces* are independent units within a large organization staffed by professionals whose relations to one another are more collegial than hierarchical. They encourage initiative, independence, and authority based on skill. Professional, not bureaucratic, social relationships may well become the typical pattern in the future.

241

SUMMARY

1. *Organizations* are planned social units with specific goals. They have a planned division of labor, one or more power centers, and can substitute personnel in various roles and tasks.

2. *Bureaucracies* are structured hierarchies that coordinate the activities of their members through the use of *authority*. Weber suggested that authority is power plus legitimacy and that there are three types of authority—traditional, charismatic, and rational-legal.

3. According to Weber, bureaucracies have the following characteristics: (1) They are organized on the basis of rules; (2) each member has a specific area of activity; (3) each lower position is under the control and supervision of a higher one; (4) the bureaucrat's legitimacy is based on knowledge and technical skill; (5) organizational affairs are kept separate from the bureaucrat's personal affairs; (6) the official does not "own" his or her office; and (7) administrative acts are recorded in writing.

4. Organizations have both a formal structure and an informal one. The formal structure is planned, but the informal structure results from the personal relationships of individuals.

5. Organizations differ in the means of control they use. Some use physical (coercive) power, others utilitarian power, and still others normative power. The more coercive an organization is, the less committed and more alienated its members will be.

6. There are three theoretical approaches to organizations: classical, human relations, and structuralist. The classical theorists were interested in improving the division of labor in organizations. The human-relations approach grew out of the Hawthorne studies, which found that productivity was affected less by the formal structure of an organization than by the informal structure—the personal relationships and feelings of the workers. Thus the human-relations school emphasized informal matters such as communication between ranks and nonauthoritarian leadership.

Neither the classical nor the human-relations approach saw any conflict between the organization's desire for rationality and the members' human needs. The structuralists, however, see a major conflict between these goals. Structuralists look at both the formal blueprint of an organization and its informal structure. They do not overemphasize informal groups because most industrial workers do not have close personal ties to their coworkers.

KEY TERMS

alienation the frustration and unhappiness of workers who have no control over how their labor is used; the loss of commitment of members for the goals of their groups.

authority power that is regarded as legitimate by the members of the group.

bureaucracy an organization with a hierarchy of offices set up to do work.

bureaucratic authority authority that is seen as legitimate if its rulings are consistent with a set of abstract rules with which the members of the group agree; also called rational-legal authority by Weber.

charismatic authority authority that is seen as legitimate because of the leader's magnetic personality.

coercive power power based on physical means of control, such as guns or locks.

hierarchy a chain of command in which each person has authority over several other people.

legitimation acceptance of the use of power by the leaders of a group because it is in line with the values of the members of the group.

normative power power based on symbolic means of control.

organization a social unit deliberately constructed and reconstructed to pursue specific goals.

power the ability to get people to take orders.

traditional authority authority that is seen as legitimate because it has existed for a long time.

utilitarian power power based on material means of control.

voluntary association a group that people join because they support its goals and values.

FOR FURTHER READING

BEATTIE, CHRISTOPHER. *Minority Men in a Majority Setting: Middle Level Francophones in the Canadian Public Service.* Toronto: McClelland and Stewart, 1975. This chapter discusses Beattie's book briefly. Many of the factors considered by Beattie probably are as applicable today as when his data was collected.

BROCK, M. *Social Work in the Hospital Organization.* Toronto: University of Toronto Press, 1969. Many students who enroll in sociology courses do so with the goal of a career in social work. This is a useful discussion of the role of social work in the hospital context.

ETZIONI, AMITAI. *Modern Organizations.* Englewood Cliffs, N.J.: Prentice-Hall, 1964. Part of this chapter was drawn from Etzioni's book. For a really thorough introduction to the field, have a look at the original book, which has enjoyed great popularity.

HOROWITZ, GAD. *Canadian Labour in Politics.* Toronto: University of Toronto Press, 1968. We will discuss the labor movement in other chapters, but this is a good introduction to the organizational side of it.

RINEHART, J. W. *The Tyranny of Work.* Don Mills, Ont.: Longman, 1975. In a later chapter we will discuss "alienation," which in most contexts can be translated as "hating your job." Work certainly can be tyrannical when it is hated.

WHITE, HARRISON C. *Chains of Opportunity: System Models of Mobility in Organizations.* Cambridge, Mass.: Harvard University Press, 1970. There is a sort of cult within sociology composed of former students of Harrison White at Harvard. They find his work masterly and exciting. It does not have that effect on me, but admittedly I have not given it a fair trial. It may do wonders for you, especially if you have a flair for mathematics. Start with this book.

WHYTE, WILLIAM H., JR. *The Organization Man.* New York: Simon & Schuster, 1956. This was an immensely popular book when it first appeared. It describes, humorously but pretty accurately, the life style of executives in large organizations. If you are planning such a career, read this first. Then go ahead and read Kanter's book too.

VOLLMER, HOWARD M. and DONALD L. MILLS, eds. *Professionalization.* Englewood Cliffs, N.J.: Prentice-Hall, 1966. One topic that is often studied as part of the field of organizations is the way in which professionals organize their work using a different system of authority and accountability from bureaucrats. This collection of papers discusses that topic.

SOCIAL STRATIFICATION

Social class and social status
    What is a social class?
    Social status
    Components of class and status
Social inequality
    Characteristics of social stratification
    Income inequality
    Who is poor?
    Inequality and unfairness
The results of stratification
    Class and family
    Class and health
    Class and life style
    Class and voluntary-association
        membership
    Class and religion
    Class and politics
    Class and personal adjustment
Social mobility
    Mobility in North America
    Who gets ahead?
    Some effects of mobility
Three approaches to stratification
    Marx
    Weber
    The functionalist view
Social Research: Sociologists at Work
Social Policy: Issues and Viewpoints

Every year I begin a lecture on social stratification by asking my students this question: Why do some people have more wealth, privilege, and influence than others? I jot down their answers on the blackboard, and then we discuss them.

I find that the students tend to divide into two groups and that before the class hour is over the two groups are at war with each other. The first group (whom I call "functionalists") gives answers like these: "The rich have earned it!" "Because they contribute more to society and are rewarded more for their efforts than other people." The other group ("conflict theorists") gives answers like these: "Because the rich take advantage of the poor." "Because they have the power to take what they want, whether it is fair or not." "Because they can afford to educate their children better than poor people can."

The issue the two groups are arguing about is whether social stratification results from open, fair competition or whether it results from unfair use of power by the dominant groups in society. The functionalists believe that our society is open and fair and that competition is a good thing. The conflict theorists believe that our society is neither open nor fair. They also believe that the masses would be quite justified in starting a revolution.

A third point of view is possible; if I were teaching in a different society I might hear it often, but I never hear it in Canada. It consists of answers like these: "It's fate." "The rich are powerful because it is God's will." Such answers reflect a belief that social stratification is permanent, that one cannot change one's position, and that one *should not try* to do so, either through competition and hard work or through revolution. Such answers support an unchanging, castelike society in which social status is inherited.

In this chapter we will discuss these points of view and take a look at the inequality that exists in our society.

Social class and social status

WHAT IS A SOCIAL CLASS?

Obviously, not all people have the same amount of money, prestige, or social influence. These things are desired by almost everyone but are unequally distributed in any population. It is possible to rank the people in a society in terms of their income, prestige, education, or power. A person's rank, based on these standards, is his or her socio-economic status. When we speak of "status," we usually mean socioeconomic status.

More often, however, we classify people much more loosely on the basis of only one or two standards—usually income alone—and usually into only a few categories such as "upper class," "middle class," and "lower class." We may define a social class as a set of people of similar socioeconomic status. Most of the time, the terms *socioeconomic status* and *social class* are interchangeable.

The most influential social classification system was proposed by Karl Marx. His system was based on only one standard: ownership of the means of production. The ruling class owned the means of production. The working class did not. Marx recognized that many different social classes had existed at different times according to the technology used in any particular period. For example, the aristocracy, who owned the land, were the ruling class in preindustrial Europe, while the peasants, who tilled it, were the workers. However, he regarded two classes alone as the forces that shaped history during the industrial period. These were (1) the *bourgeoisie* or capitalists, who owned the factories and other means of industrial production, and (2) the *proletariat*, or workers, who had to work to earn a living. The members of a class might become aware that they had common interests; Marx called this awareness "class conscious-

What is your socioeconomic status?

Sociologists commonly rate respondents' socioeconomic status (SES) by means of a composite index, using data of various kinds. The following index is an example of the sort of classification scheme that is commonly used.

	CATEGORY	POINTS
EDUCATION	College graduate	5
	Some college	4
	High school graduate	3
	Some high school	2
	Grade school only (or none)	1
FAMILY INCOME (ANNUAL)	$50,000 and over	5
	$25,000 to $49,999	4
	$15,000 to $24,999	3
	$ 9,000 to $14,999	2
	Under $9,000	1
OCCUPATION OF CHIEF BREADWINNER OF YOUR FAMILY	Professional or managerial in large firm, proprietors	5
	Semi-professional or managerial in small firms	4
	Clerical and sales	3
	Skilled and semi-skilled labour	2
	Agriculture and unskilled labour	1

To calculate your own socioeconomic status, add the number of points you score for all three items.

IF YOUR SCORE IS	YOUR SES LEVEL IS
15 points	Upper
12 to 14 points	Upper-middle
9 to 11 points points	Middle
6 to 8 points	Lower middle
3 to 5 points	Lower

ness." If they did not have this awareness, he believed that they had "false consciousness."

Most people, whether they are sociologists or not, do not refer to the ownership of the means of production when they distinguish among social classes. They may refer to income, life style, education, occupation, or perhaps some other standard of classification. This is why Marxists and non-Marxists classify people in somewhat different ways. For example, you and I might say that a man who lives on an income of $500 per month from his part ownership of a lumberyard is lower-middle-class and that a surgeon who earns $100,000 a year doing face lifts is upper-class. A Marxist, on the other hand, might call the lumberyard owner bourgeois because he does not have to work but derives his income from the profits of the work of others, while the surgeon can be seen as working-class because she makes a living from her own labor. If each person lost the use of his or her hands, the surgeon might soon be poor, but the lumberyard owner's income would not be affected.

How many social classes are there? There is no single answer to this question. Sociologists usually use between three and six categories. For years many surveys referred only to "upper," "middle," and "lower" classes, and most North Americans would claim to be "middle class," even though they did manual labor and therefore should be called "lower class." However, it finally became clear that people knew when they were "lower class" but did not like to describe themselves in those words. When the term *working class* was added to the list of choices, most respondents chose it instead of middle class or lower class.

When six categories are used to describe a stratification system, the upper, middle, and lower classes are divided into upper and lower levels. Thus the upper upper class consists of "old money"—people whose families have been rich for generations. Members of the lower upper class may be just as rich, but they have become rich more recently and have not yet learned the upper-class subculture. Their clothes are more likely to be flashy and their vocabulary not as plain as that of the upper upper class. In Toronto's Forest Hill Village, lower-upper-class drivers may be seen in shiny new Mercedes Benz cars, while the upper-upper-class drivers are content with old, weathered Rolls Royces.

The upper middle class consists mostly of business and professional people who live comfortably in attractive surroundings. Members of the lower middle class are not as well off; they work as shopkeepers, in clerical jobs, and the like.

An upper-lower-class person may earn as much as any middle-class worker, but he or she does manual work—as a machinist, a plumber, or an assembly-line worker, for example. Finally, the lower lower class consists of welfare recipients, the unemployable, and people who do unskilled work when they do any.

SOCIAL STATUS

Ascribed and achieved status

Chickens in a barnyard, I understand, establish a "pecking order." The top chicken can peck all the others. The next chicken can peck all the others except the top one, and so on down the hierarchy. The bottom chicken, poor dear, can be pecked by all the others but can peck no one else at all.

People work out such arrangements too. If you are invited to dinner at an embassy, the seat you will be given at the table depends on how you rank in comparison to the other guests. You will quickly find out whether to defer to a given person or to expect that person to defer to you. Your rank is your social status.

What determines whether you will rank high or low, whether you will be seated near the host or far away, whether you will take orders or give orders more often, whether you will bow and scrape to other people or they will bow and scrape to you? What determines your social status? Your status is determined by the roles that you occupy. Some roles rank higher than others and are assigned more privileges and assets than others.

In principle, it is possible for a group to assign roles and status to its members on the basis of any agreed-upon standard—the color of their eyes, how far they can throw a javelin, whether they are left-handed or right-handed, or anything else. Sociologists are often interested in whether roles are assigned on the basis of standards over which a person has some control (**achieved status**) or over which he or she has no control (**ascribed status**). When status is ascribed, people are assigned to high or low positions on the basis of their characteristics—such as skin color or royal birth or sex. When status is achieved, people are assigned to high or low positions on the basis of how well they have shown their ability to perform various roles. The high rank of a physician is achieved status; she has to show certain abilities before she is allowed to practice medicine. The high rank of a princess is ascribed; she is assigned to that role simply by being born to her particular parents instead of to the plumber and his wife, the waitress.

All societies assign status on the basis of both kinds of standards. In general, however, preindustrial societies are more likely to use ascribed status and industrial societies are more likely to use achieved status. It sometimes offends us to see people given special privileges that they have not earned. Yet our lives are influenced by ascribed status in ways

that we sometimes fail to notice. Physical beauty, for example, influences life chances, especially for women. Attractive women generally marry men of somewhat higher status than less attractive women do.[1] Men are affected in similar ways: Tall men earn somewhat more money than short men and are more likely to be promoted to high rank.[2]

Age is another characteristic that is hardly "achieved," and yet it is a basis for social discrimination. A person is granted certain rights upon reaching a given age, regardless of his or her maturity and ability; the same person is stripped of certain rights upon reaching "retirement" age, again regardless of his or her ability.

A final example is sex. Males have almost always been chosen as leaders and females expected to be followers, regardless of their other characteristics. The aged, the unattractive, women, short men, and teenagers are all

Ascribed status. (She never had to audition for the role.)

UPI

discriminated against in one way or another on the basis of ascribed status.

However, industrial societies tend to move away from ascribed status and toward achieved status. As mentioned in the preceding chapter, industrial work requires division of labor. We break up the work into more and more specialized jobs and assign each of these to people who are able to do them. If all jobs were equally difficult and all human beings equally talented, it would not matter how we decided who should do what job. But that is not the case in today's technological society, so it really matters to us that the person who pilots the airplane we fly in or performs open-heart surgery on us is the best person for the job. This is why we insist that roles be based on *what people can do*, not on the basis of *who they are*.

In preindustrial societies, on the other hand, most status is ascribed. The division of labor is not very extensive, and most jobs are simple enough for almost anyone in the society to perform satisfactorily. No competition is necessary. In primitive societies kinship determines status. In feudal society, too, a serf's son was a serf and a noble's son a noble, with rare exceptions. The system of stratification was ascribed and closed; no movement up or down the hierarchy was possible.

ASCRIPTION BY CASTE Probably no society has ever been totally closed. However, the caste system of India until the past few decades was the most closed stratification system we know of. It was justified by the Hindu religion, which holds that (1) every soul is reborn over and over again into new bodies, human or nonhuman; (2) a person's sins or virtues follow him or her from life to life and determine his or her life chances; and (3) one has a duty to perform well in the role to which one was assigned at birth. A person is born to be a potter, a prostitute, or a priest because this is the status he or she has earned in former lives. One must try to be good at potting, prostitution, or priesthood, as the case may be.

It would do the potter no good to try to perform the role of the priest; it is not that person's duty. A low position or any other misfortune in this life was earned by past misdeeds. Thus striving for a higher social position is fighting against the law of the universe.

Every Hindu belongs to one and only one *jat*, or caste. There are some 3000 such groups in India, and membership in each is permanent and hereditary. Marriages are legitimate only between a man and a woman of the same jat. (The government recognizes intercaste marriages, but powerful traditional authorities do not.) Originally all male members of any one jat had the same occupation, and it was their duty to provide services for other castes. Nowadays Indians often take jobs other than those traditionally performed by members of their caste, but in the villages it is not unheard of for members of a local jat to be beaten by their neighbors for failing to perform their customary duties. The traditional Hindu's occupation is predetermined, and he or she is not permitted to carry out the duties of other jats. A high-caste Hindu may not sweep, for example, and is therefore dependent on the very low-ranking sweeper group for clean floors.

There is some upward social movement in India, but it is generally the entire jat, not the individual, that moves up. For example, the leaders of a jat may make up a story that the jat was originally of high rank but was not recognized as such. At the same time, the caste members may adopt upper-caste customs such as banning meat, alcohol, and the remarriage of widows. After a generation or two, they may succeed in being reclassified at a higher rank.

CASTE WITHOUT HINDUISM The anthropologist Gerald Berreman holds that caste in India is not very different from the two-caste system (black and white) of the United States.[3] He defines caste as a hierarchy of social groups in which membership is hereditary and permanent and in which marriage between people who belong to different groups is forbidden. In both societies the dominant caste maintains its position by means of economic and physical sanctions and uses the lower castes as a supply of cheap labor. Men of the dominant caste have sexual access to both high- and low-caste women, while low-caste men have access only to low-caste women. Members of different castes avoid each other in both societies; members of the upper caste believe that they would be contaminated by contact with members of the lower caste.

The main difference is that in India there are many castes, and each one gets certain satisfactions from being above others and certain dissatisfactions from being below others. Most people claim that their group deserves to be ranked higher than it is, but few oppose the whole caste system the way the black American usually does.

The Canadian situation is somewhat different. Most black Canadians are recent immigrants from the West Indies. Although they do encounter discrimination, their status in Canadian society is similar to that of many other recently arrived ethnic groups who have yet to establish themselves in middle- or high-status jobs.

Status inconsistency

The various standards of social status are never perfectly correlated. Many people rank higher by one standard than by another, and this results in status inconsistency. Some people are well educated but earn very little, like the Ph.D. who drives a cab. Some earn a lot of money through activities that bring them little or no prestige, like rich gangsters or rich junk dealers. Some people have power even though they are poor, like a welfare recipient on a grand jury.

Gerhard Lenski has observed that such status inconsistencies may be a source of psychological stress.[4] His theory is based on the assumption that people try to maximize their satisfaction even at the expense of other people. This means that people with incon-

sistent statuses tend to think of themselves in terms of their highest status or rank and to expect others to do the same. Meanwhile, those who come into contact with them tend to treat them in terms of their lowest status or rank.

You can see how this works by imagining the interaction between a poor novelist and a rich bricklayer in a situation in which neither writing nor bricklaying is relevant. The writer will try to base their relationship on occupation, while the bricklayer will try to base it on income. Because each believes his own point of view is right and proper, and because neither is likely to view the problem objectively, one or both are likely to be frustrated, and probably angered, by the interaction.

"One-upmanship," as this pattern has been called, is so common in everyday life that most of us give it hardly any thought. One result, however, is feelings of stress for many people with inconsistent statuses. Lenski believes that the psychological stress of status inconsistency leads such people to demand social changes.

Lenski's argument is sometimes applied to explain the zeal of particular reformist groups. For example, it has been suggested that the First World War led many Canadian women to become feminists. They were put into positions that had always been held by men, and yet they did not have the same political rights as men did.[5] This status inconsistency led them to demand the right to vote. S. D. Clark has pointed out how a similar kind of inconsistency may have explained the student movement of the 1960s. Large numbers of young people were able to acquire as much knowledge and experience as established adults generally have, but were still in a position of economic dependency, without the political rights that go with adulthood. It was this inconsistency that prompted many of them, says Clark, to push for more recognition and rewards.[6]

It has not been definitely proven that status inconsistency prompts demand for social reform. Recent studies seem to show that the effect is often too small to be important. No doubt new studies will shed light on this question.[7]

COMPONENTS OF CLASS AND STATUS

The term **social stratification** refers to a hierarchy of layers, or *strata* (singular: *stratum*) of people who are unequal in terms of property, power, and prestige. In short, stratification means social inequality.

You can't buy a Nobel prize.

UPI

Property may be defined as rights or control over goods and services. It can be converted into money, and so for most purposes wealth and property are the same thing. However, as Thorstein Veblen has pointed out, one gains a certain amount of prestige by showing off one's wealth, and to do that one must display it in the form of property.[8] This was more true a generation or two ago than it is today, but even today if you have a million dollars in the bank but live like a pauper you will miss out on a lot of the social deference that comes to those who consume property wastefully and showily.

In Marx's view, on the other hand, the crucial standard determining one's social class is not rights over consumer goods or income but ownership of a special *kind* of property—the means of production.

Power refers to the ability to achieve one's goals even in the face of opposition. The amount of power we have depends mostly on the roles we occupy. Certain jobs carry with them responsibilities and the right to give orders to others. Thus a police officer must have such powers as the right to reroute traffic at the scene of an accident, the right to stop and question a stranger in a dark alley and so on. Roles that carry especially heavy responsibilities usually carry considerable power as well. Often, though not necessarily, power and property go together. He who pays the piper calls the tune. Money can buy power to a certain extent, and power can help one get the chance to accumulate money. Moreover, both high income and power usually come with the same jobs.

Some kinds of social honor are distributed unequally, so that some groups and some roles enjoy great respect and deference, while others do not. This kind of social honor is called **prestige**. It is usually attached to roles that also have property and power. Yet prestige and wealth are not interchangeable. For example, no matter how rich you are you cannot buy a Nobel prize or influence the judges to award it to the person of your choice. The prize is awarded in recognition of remarkable achievements, and its prestige value would be lowered if it could be won on some other basis.

Not all kinds of social honor are stratified. Thus we sometimes distinguish between prestige and esteem, the kind of appreciation we feel for each other regardless of rank. For example, in hard times my grandmother picked cotton to help support her family, pushing her two children along in a baby carriage between the rows of cotton plants. One feels high esteem for such a courageous approach to life. Later on, as the wife of her town's only physician, she received not only esteem but also the prestige that is generally given to doctors and their families. Esteem is the respect we hold for a person who does her best to meet a situation well, whether she is in a high position or a low one. Prestige is respect that we have for a high position simply because it is high. Esteem is not necessarily limited, but prestige is. Thus you may have high esteem for all your classmates and enjoy each one's company. However, only those of your classmates who are ranked above average can have high prestige.

Fortunately, not everything that is worthwhile about human beings is either scarce or arranged in a hierarchy of values. For example, we may esteem others because they are playful, helpful, honest, kind, or creative, so that every member of a group may have some special traits that win esteem. This is not so in the case of prestige. My son claims that he enjoys prestige among his high school classmates because he uses notebooks marked with a university coat of arms. If all the students possessed such notebooks, nobody would derive prestige from them. Prestige is unequal social recognition.

The kind of prestige that is most important in society is based not on such trivial symbols as the kind of notebooks one uses but, rather, on one's occupation. Your job determines not only how much property and power you have, but also how much respect you are likely to get from others. Although esteem and prestige

need not go together, they often do. Thus most Nobel prize winners have both prestige and esteem.

When sociologists want to compare the prestige levels of different occupations, they must use a common scale. Common scales can be derived by asking a large number of ordinary people to give their impressions of the relative rank of a number of occupations, and then averaging their responses. Table 9.1 is a list of occupations ranked according to a scale derived by Bernard Blishen and his associates from a large sample of Canadians. The highest prestige was assigned to administrators, who were allotted a rank of 1.

If occupation largely determines one's social status, education in turn largely determines one's occupation. This is why educational achievements are so important in modern society. But education affects your social status not only by determining your occupation but also more directly. People recognize each other's level of prestige right away. Go to a party and see how quickly people recognize a high-ranking guest and show their admiration. It takes only a few questions; a person's education shows up in the accent, vocabulary, and content of his or her answers. More than any other factor, one's level of education is a clue to one's life style, and prestige depends on the respect people have for one another's life style.

Social inequality

CHARACTERISTICS OF SOCIAL STRATIFICATION

Stratification is social

We have said that biological, inherited characteristics such as differences in strength, intelligence, age, sex, height, and looks may be the standards for assigning status. However, what makes such traits important is the judgment of a society's members. Height would not make any difference unless people

TABLE 9.1

*The Blishen Scale. Prestige ranking of selected occupations in Canada.
Larger numbers indicate decreasing prestige levels.*

OCCUPATION	RATING	OCCUPATION	RATING
Administrators, teaching and related fields	1	Electronic installers, repair	87
Nuclear engineers	2	Air transport support staff	91
Dentists	3	Radio and TV announcers	97
Optometrists	5	Insurance salesmen	102
Physicians and surgeons	6	Advertising salesmen	105
Veterinarians	7	Chemical processing foremen	108
Meteorologists	8	Electronic assembly foremen	118
Lawyers and notaries	9	Physiotherapists	137
University teachers	10	Product and interior designers	141
Pharmacists	11	Telephone operators	158
Metallurgical engineers	16	Actors	176
Osteopaths and chiropractors	17	Athletes	177
Post secondary teachers	24	Advertising artists	185
Physicists	27	Railway conductors	194
Computer programmers	28	Office clerks	208
Commissioned officers, armed forces	34	Chefs and cooks	214
Accountants	37	Textile foremen	226
Government inspectors	39	Musicians	240
Producers and directors, performing arts	40	Construction foremen	247
Mathematicians, statisticians	41	Mail carriers	252
Chemists	46	Hotel managers	287
Writers	47	Dancers	302
Elementary school teachers	49	Nursing assistants	318
Biologists	50	Insulating construction	335
Foremen, electrical equipment	52	Metal assembly	343
Dieticians and nutritionists	59	Motor vehicle mechanics	358
Supervisors, library filing	61	Longshoremen, freight handlers	365
Psychologists	67	Messengers	391
Social workers	74	Recreation attendants	394
Bookkeeping supervisors	76	Captain fishing vessels	398
Sociologists, anthropologists	83	Concrete finishers	408
Physical science technicians	84	Babysitters	420
Policemen, detectives	85	Carpenters	422
		Barbers and hairdressers	449
		Elevator operators	479
		Farmers	480
		Fish canners	499

Source: Bernard R. Blishen and Hugh A. McRoberts, "A Revised Socioeconomic Index for Occupations in Canada," *Canadian Review of Sociology and Anthropology*, 13 (1), 1976, pp. 71-79.

decided that it was important, and the same goes for sex, age, color, and many other traits. In some societies, for example, fat women are considered gorgeous; in others thin ones are; and in still others a woman's shape is not important. This example shows that stratification on the basis of physical characteristics is still determined by social judgments. No biological trait is a standard for social classification until it becomes part of the beliefs, attitudes, and values of the members of the society.

Stratification is found everywhere

No society (not even a socialist society) can be found in which there is no stratification at all. Even among the Kung Bushmen, who hunt and gather food and live in self-governing bands of 50 to 100 people, some stratification is found. There are socially determined inequalities between men and women and between adults and children. Thus inequality of power, property, and prestige is universal.

Stratification varies in form and degree

Though some inequality is universal, the amount and nature of the inequality varies greatly from one society to another. Traditional India was perhaps the most highly stratified of all societies, and the kibbutzim of Israel approach total equality.

Stratification is important

If you ask a number of sociologists to choose the factor that most often predicts differences in social life, almost all of them will choose social class. Different social strata have different life styles. This means that they have different patterns of eating and dressing, of cultural and recreational activities, of relationships between parents and children, and so on. We'll come back to some of these differences later.

More important, different strata also have very different life chances. That is, patterns of infant mortality, physical and mental illness,

childlessness, marital conflict, separation, divorce, and the like vary from one social class to another. The chance of getting a good job varies by class. The chance of going to jail varies by class. The chance to travel abroad varies by class, and so on. Our opportunities are opened or shut for us by the social class we belong to. We will return to this subject later, too.

INCOME INEQUALITY

Although stratification exists everywhere, it differs in extent from one time and place to another. Those who are most seriously affected by it are the poor. Although we will be discussing poverty in Canada, we must remember that the widest gaps between standards of living in the world today aren't between individuals but between whole societies. Societies such as Canada and the United States are far richer than societies such as India, Bangladesh, or Haiti, where millions of people live on the sidewalks or in cardboard packing crates, eating garbage or whatever scraps they can find, wearing rags, suffering from sores and toothaches, feeling too weak to work even if they could find jobs. Poverty in our own society is mild compared to the misery of people in less developed nations. Moreover, the gap between the rich nations and the poor ones is not decreasing—quite the contrary. And *within* the poor nations there is even greater inequality of income than in advanced societies.[9] That is, the gap between the income of the poor and the income of the well-to-do is greater than in North America. We will return to these problems in a later chapter. For now, however, let's stick to the situation in Canada.

Leo Johnson has shown that, although the income per capita has increased greatly since the end of World War II, and living standards have generally improved, not all sections of Canadian society have gained proportionately from this period of economic growth.[10] Though the well-to-do have become vastly more affluent, the poor have felt much less improvement in their living conditions. To determine the distribution of wealth in Canada, Johnson sorted the earning population into 10 equal categories according to their relative income level; he then calculated the average income for each group in 1974. In other words, Johnson compared the average income of the poorest 10 percent of the Canadian population ($633.00) to the average income of the richest 10 percent of the population ($23,575.00). He found that the poorest group earned less than 3 percent of the amount earned by the richest

FIGURE 9.1

Average income of income earners by decile in current dollars: 1946 and 1974

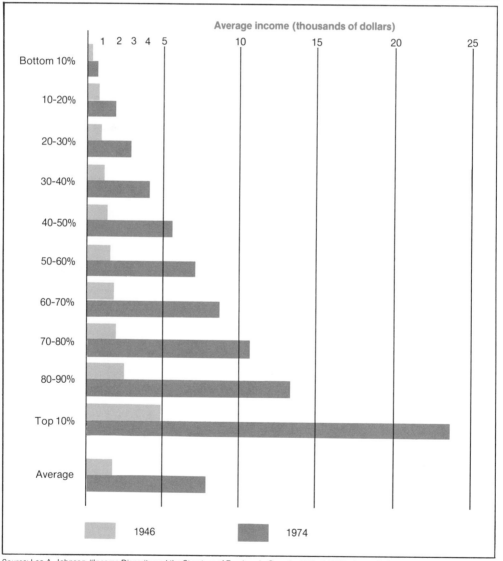

Source: Leo A. Johnson, "Income Disparity and the Structure of Earnings in Canada, 1946-1947," in James E. Curtis and William G. Scott, eds., *Social Stratification in Canada,* 2nd ed. (Scarborough, Ont.: Prentice-Hall, 1979), p. 143.

group in 1974. Half of all earners received $6625 or less. These data are summarized in Figure 9-1. Johnson also provided similar income figures for 1946, and adjusted them to reflect the buying power of 1974 dollars. In 1946, the poorest 10 percent of the Canadian population earned the equivalent of $247 in current dollars, while the richest 10 percent earned $4995. In 1946, then, the poorest group earned about 5 percent of the income of the richest group, while in 1974, that figure was down to less than 3 percent. Johnson showed that economic inequality is much greater than most Canadians imagine, and that *it is increasing, not decreasing, over time.*[11]

The data in Figure 9-1 are misleading in some respects. The table seems to suggest that 10 percent of the Canadian population is trying to survive on $633 per year. In reality, a good many of the people in that lowest category are probably employed part-time and are also being supported by some family member. For example, university students often live at home but work during their Christmas vacation. Thus sociologists commonly try to gauge income levels per *family*, not per earner. Different sociologists favor different methods for the accurate measurement of income. Whatever methods are employed, however, the results tend to be the same: According to various estimates, between 15 and 25 percent of the population is poor, and cannot afford a reasonably comfortable standard of living. The average Canadian spends about half of his or her total income on basic necessities like food, clothing, and shelter. But the quarter of the population living below the poverty line spends over 70 percent of its income on such staples.[12] There is little money left for them to spend for optional goods or services.

WHO IS POOR?

Poor people come in all shapes and sizes, all colors, ages, sexes, and personalities. No generalization applies to all individuals, rich or poor. It's bad enough for people to have to suffer poverty without being stigmatized as

well. Many people think it's disreputable to be poor. They believe that any decent person who works hard will not be poor, or at least won't stay poor very long. There is also an opposing view, which claims that all poor people are helpless victims of the social system or of fate, and that they are unable to escape from an impossible situation. The truth, of course, is that the poor include both drifters and hard-working people who have had bad luck, as well as all sorts of people between these two extremes.

However, although all sorts of people may be poor, there are a number of circumstances that increase the probability of poverty. Living in a rural area is one such circumstance. Although only one Canadian in five lives in a rural area, almost half of all *poor* Canadians are rural dwellers.[13] Living in the Maritimes makes poverty more likely. Single persons are more likely to be poor than married persons, and francophones are more likely than anglophones. Old-age pensioners have a high likelihood of poverty, especially in a period of inflation. But the major factors of poverty are employment, education, sex, region, and ethnic membership.

Employment

Most poor people do work. Many more would like to. Over half of the poor earn most of their income from wages.[14] However, because they often have trouble finding regular work, they take temporary and part-time jobs and usually find themselves unemployed for part of the year.[15] About one-third of the working poor are under age 25.[16] Unemployment rates are very high for young workers, especially in Quebec and the Atlantic Provinces.[17]

Education

One factor that is closely related to poverty and unemployment is lack of education. Young people who have skills and a basic education have better luck finding good jobs than dropouts. The average family income in 1973 of Canadian families whose heads had a university degree was about two and a half times that of families whose heads had four years of schooling or less.[18]

Canadian provinces do not offer equal educational opportunities. A young person in Ontario, Alberta, or British Columbia is considerably more likely to attend university than one who lives in New Brunswick or Newfoundland.

Even a high school diploma is of some help in finding a job, especially in the Maritimes and Quebec. However, the general level of education among job-seekers increased by 15 percent between 1960 and 1970.[19] As a result, many employers require some post-secondary education, even for very ordinary jobs. People with lower levels of education are finding job-hunting increasingly difficult.

Sex

Income is by no means equally available to the two sexes. Nowadays almost half of all women have paid jobs, but they are not paid at the same rates as men, nor do they have the same chance of getting better jobs. Although laws have been passed requiring greater equality, the results of these laws cannot be seen in the actual earnings of the two sexes.

Women are still largely segregated in the lower-paid jobs and they tend to rely on short-term jobs more often than men. Even if this were not true, women still receive lower pay, even for the same jobs, than male workers.[20] Moreover, there is some evidence that in Canada this income gap is increasing.[21] Part of the gap can be attributed to the lower ambitions of women that result from lifelong socialization for a dependent role, but part of it can be attributed to the continuing discrimination against women in hiring and promotions.

Region

Wealth is far from equally distributed among the various regions of Canada, primarily because economic circumstances vary greatly according to geographical conditions.

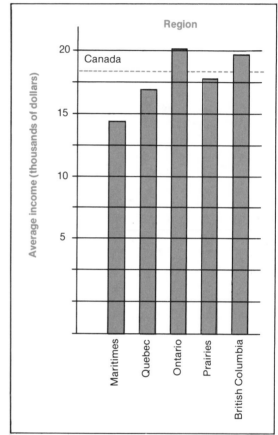

FIGURE 9.2

Average family income in current dollars by region, 1975

Source: Canada Year Book, 1978, p. 247.

Poverty is much more common in the maritimes, in Manitoba, and Saskatchewan than in the three richest provinces, Ontario, Alberta, and British Columbia. Quebec is between these two extremes.

The maritimes have declined in agriculture and have also failed to industrialize their economies, chiefly because of their remoteness from the rest of Canada. However, vast oil resources in Newfoundland, if and when they are exploited, may improve economic conditions generally throughout the area.

Poverty in the prairies is chiefly among

farmers, whose incomes have fallen far behind those of other occupations. Every year, many farmers must quit farming and move to the cities. Saskatchewan, in particular, has lost a good part of its population for this reason. Alberta has fared much better, since its cattle ranches, meatpacking plants, and particularly its oil fields have expanded enough to absorb most of the farmers who would otherwise have moved away. Indeed, Alberta has recently drawn many Canadians from all over the country.

British Columbia's high average income derives almost entirely from its natural resources, especially its forest and mineral reserves. Ontario's wealth, on the other hand, is obtained through manufacturing, though its northern regions depend on logging and mining. Recently, these northern regions have not fared well; northern Ontario has severe unemployment problems.

Ethnicity

Poverty is not distributed equally among all the ethnic groups of Canada. By far the most disadvantaged are the Indians, Inuit, and Metis. Francophones earn less, on the average, than anglophones, but this income gap is probably narrowing.[22]

Even if we allow for differences in educational levels, age, region of residence, occupation, and type of industry, the various ethnic groups still have markedly different incomes. One study in Montreal found that even when all these factors were taken into account, English-Scottish, Irish, Northern European,

A family of 10 shares this one-room log cabin on an Indian reserve in northwestern Alberta.

Edmonton Journal/McNichol

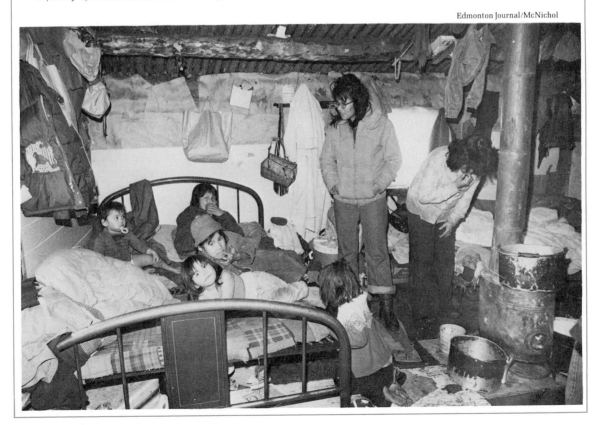

Jewish, and German groups still had above-average incomes, while French, Italian, and Eastern European groups had below-average incomes.[23]

INEQUALITY AND UNFAIRNESS

I have mentioned the stigma on poor people—the fact that they are often blamed for their misfortune. Now I want to point out a few of the ways in which the societies we live in are unfair to poor people. You may not be aware of how middle-class Canadians get opportunities and advantages that they do not "deserve."

For example, rich people pay less for goods and services than poor people do. Why? Because poor people can't pay cash. They turn to merchants who will let them buy television sets, washing machines, and other appliances on credit. Middle-class people are in a better position to shop around and find bargains. Not only do goods cost more when they are bought from "credit" merchants, but by buying on the installment plan the poor pay far more in the long run because of the very high interest rates on what are actually loans. Sometimes the payments are not made, and then the merchant repossesses the furniture or appliance, something that rarely happens to middle-class families. And it is not only expensive appliances that cost more. Poor people spend more even for groceries and clothing.[24]

You have probably heard a lot of grumbling about the welfare system and the people who benefit from it. However, there is a system of disguised welfare that you may be unaware of, and it pays out far more benefits than the one you know about. Its benefits go more to the rich than to the poor. This disguised welfare system is income tax. Its "disguise" is the odd way it operates—it "pays" without sending checks to anyone. The benefits consist of the money the government allows people to keep. Moreover, unlike welfare recipients, who are stigmatized for being on welfare, the well-to-do who receive their disguised welfare benefits are admired for their cleverness.

How does it work? Tax rates are supposedly based on the principle that those who can afford to should pay at a higher rate. Very poor people shouldn't be taxed at all, and they are not. We operate with a set of "tax brackets" that resembles a staircase. Suppose that you are climbing a stairway of "brackets" each year. The first few thousand dollars you earn are all in the lowest bracket and you will be taxed at a very low rate—maybe 25 percent or so—on that income. But if you earn a few thousand more and move into the next-higher bracket, this additional amount will be taxed at a higher rate. If you are lucky enough to earn a lot more than the average person, the top few dollars you earn may be taxed at a rate of 50 percent or even more. Not your *whole* income, of course. Just the part of it that is in the topmost bracket.

This is fair enough. But the catch is in the deductions. It seems reasonable that we should be allowed to deduct whatever expenses we pay out as a necessary cost of earning our income. And we are. But the deductions are subtracted from the topmost bracket. Suppose you and I each paid $500 last year for necessary travel expenses. We each deduct it from our taxable income, as we are permitted to do. But suppose my income was so great that my top dollars are taxed at 50 percent while you earn much less, so that your top dollar is taxed at 25 percent. This means that I can subtract 50 percent of my $500, but you can subtract only 25 percent of your $500. I am richer than you are, and though our travel expenses were equal, the government in effect sends me a welfare cheque for $250 and sends you one for only $125.

As it happens, there are many more ways for a rich person to subtract from his or her taxable income. As a result, well-to-do people are given subsidies that amount to far more than what the government spends annually on direct assistance to the poor. These figures are published by the U.S. government and are open to congressional control. In Canada, however, these subsidies are not matters of public record or discussion.[25]

The results of stratification

It is obvious that poor people have a hard time getting ahead. We don't really have a system of equal opportunities; it is not nearly as equal as we sometimes like to think.

What are the results of stratification? So far we have limited ourselves to economic issues, and indeed these are serious problems. To be lower class means, above all, to be poor—to have to watch every penny you spend. But it also means to be uneducated. And it means to be looked down upon—not invited to certain parties, not considered a suitable date, not called "Mr. Brown" but only "Jim." Such experiences take their toll, especially since they happen day after day in many different sorts of situations. To be middle-class is to experience the world in a very different way from upper- or lower-class people in the same society. Let's look at just a few of the effects of class—on family life, health, life style, participation in groups, religion, politics, and the problems of life.

CLASS AND FAMILY

First of all, your class has a lot to do with the mate you choose. There is a good chance that you will marry somebody with about as much education as you have. And if you have a lot of education, your marriage is likely to be more stable than if you (and your spouse) have less education. That is, you are less likely to divorce and remarry if you are well educated. However, this stability is only partly a result of education itself. It depends partly on the age of the bride and groom. Couples who marry young have higher divorce rates than couples who marry when they are more mature.[26] And well-educated couples are, of course, somewhat older, on the average, than less-educated couples.

Life chances depend on differences in social class.

CP Photo/Montreal Star

John McQueen

Fertility

Fertility is the rate at which children are born into a population. Middle-class families in Western societies tend to limit the size of their families more than either working-class or upper-class families. In Canada, education has more relationship to fertility than income does. Highly educated couples are much less likely to have large families than less-educated couples.[27]

Child rearing

Patterns of child care have changed a good deal since World War II. Between 1930 and 1945, working-class mothers were more permissive than middle-class mothers. Middle-class mothers followed a rigid feeding schedule, while working-class children ate whenever they were hungry. After World War II, baby-care manuals began to offer more permissive advice; as a result, middle-class mothers have become more easygoing, and often allow their children more freedom than working-class mothers do. However, although they are more indulgent, middle-class mothers also expect more of their children than working-class mothers do.

When disciplining their children, working-class parents are more likely to slap or spank, while middle-class parents are more likely to reason with them, send them to their room, or try to get them to feel guilty. "Love withdrawal" techniques are also used by middle-class parents; they simply let children know how disappointing their behavior is. Sociologists who have described the socialization practices current in working-class Toronto neighborhoods have contrasted it strongly to the "talking" approach of the middle-class. Working-class fathers, especially, depend on physical force.[28] This approach may partly explain why working-class people in Canada and elsewhere are generally seen as more strict, intolerant, and authoritarian than middle-class people.[29]

CLASS AND HEALTH

High-status people have a greater chance of staying alive than low-status people, though the difference in death rates has decreased sharply during this century.[30] In Canada, a positive step has been taken to alleviate this problem through the introduction of guaranteed health care. Nevertheless, the provision of medical insurance and other services cannot, by itself, erase the disadvantages of poverty. There are still discrepancies for people of varying social classes in, for example, nutrition, transportation, and access to dentists. There is also a very uneven distribution of medical facilities across the regions of Canada. Health care workers do not always locate their practices where they are needed; they may prefer to live in Vancouver, Winnipeg, or Quebec City, where there are already enough medical practitioners. In British Columbia and Ontario, there are far more physicians and dentists relative to population than in the far north, the Maritimes, or rural Saskatchewan.[31]

CLASS AND LIFE STYLE

Max Weber was particularly interested in the life styles—patterns of taste, speech, and manners—of different status groups, and sociologists continue to compare life styles as clues to social status. When you meet someone at a party, how long does it take you to estimate his or her social class? How long does it take in a phone conversation? The clues you use are aspects of life style.

A life style may develop as a result of other inequalities. For example, in order to enjoy literature, one needs education, leisure, and the company of others who like to talk about books. But these opportunities are distributed unequally. On the other hand, a life style is sometimes used as a tool for gaining higher status: Thus a person may change his or her place of residence or join a different church to move to a new social level.

CLASS AND VOLUNTARY-ASSOCIATION MEMBERSHIP

Several studies have shown that social class is related to participation in voluntary associations. For example, Melvin Tumin and Arnold Feldman found that, in Puerto Rico, higher levels of education were linked with membership in organizations.[32] James Curtis found the same relationship in Canada, Great Britain, Germany, Italy, Mexico, and the United States.[33]

CLASS AND RELIGION

There are several ways in which social class and religion are connected. People of different strata tend to belong to different denominations or to different parishes of the same denomination. John Porter showed that there tends to be a high concentration of Anglicans among Canadian upper-class business leaders.[34] United Church members,[35] Jews, and Presbyterians are also above average in social status. On the other hand, Catholics, Lutherans, Greek Orthodox, and members of such fundamentalist groups as the Jehovah's Witnesses are, on the average, working-class. Church attendance also varies from one class to another. Churches tend to be middle-class institutions. The very rich and the very poor are not usually active in their churches.[36]

CLASS AND POLITICS

As you might expect, social classes often differ on political issues. People know "which side their bread is buttered on;" the bread of the upper class is not buttered on the same side as the bread of the working class. Not only do their interests conflict, but their life styles, educational levels, and access to information differ; all of these factors may lead to political differences.

In Europe, party support tends to be divided very much according to class lines. In North America, working-class voters are somewhat more attracted to left-wing politics than are middle-class voters, but the differences in party support are not great. In the United States, working-class voters normally support the Democratic Party and middle-class voters are more often Republicans. However, in Canada the Liberals and Conservatives are both supported by middle-class voters, while working-class voters often support either the NDP or the Social Credit Party.[37] Nonetheless, classes do not differ as much in party affiliation in Canada as in many other nations.

CLASS AND PERSONAL ADJUSTMENT

Because classes have different subcultures, they also have somewhat different personality patterns. Families in different classes orient their members along different lines. Thus the upper class works to maintain its social position; the middle class concentrates on achievement and mobility; and the lower class is concerned with problems of income, illness, and unemployment. One review of research on stratification and personal adjustment came up with the following conclusions:

1 Lower-class women show less imagination, are more impulsive, have greater fear of the unknown, and are more likely to fear that they will not succeed.
2 Lower-class women participate more in basic household decisions.
3 Lower-class families are less willing to postpone rewards than other families.
4 Lower-class men and women are more direct and unrestrained in their expression of emotions.
5 Lower-class parent-child relationships are more hierarchical and rigid.
6 Middle-class people are more strongly oriented toward achievement, and this is reflected in their personalities.
7 There is a higher percentage of authoritarians in the lower class than in either the middle class or the upper class.

TABLE 9.2

Marital life style and social class

	HIGHBROW	UPPER MIDDLEBROW
How Girl Meets Boy	He was an usher at her best friend's wedding	At college, in the psycholo[g] lab
The Proposal	In his room during the Harvard-Princeton game	In the back seat of a Vol[ks]wagen
The Wedding	In her living room, by a federal judge	College chapel (nondenor[mi]national)
The Honeymoon	Mediterranean	Bahamas
Marriage Manual	*Kama Sutra*	*Sexual Efficiency in Ma[r]riage,* volumes I and II
Sleeping Arrangements	Double bed	King-size bed or twin be[ds] with one headboard
Sleeping Attire	He: nothing. She: nothing	He: red turtleneck nightsh[irt] She: gown with matchi[ng] peignoir
Background Music	Ravi Shankar or the Beatles	Wagner
Turn-Ons	Pot	Champagne and oysters
The Schedule	Spontaneously, on an average of 2.5 weekly (that means 2 times one week and 3 times another)	Twice a week and when t[he] kids go to the Sunday ma[t]inee
Number of Children	1 each by a previous marriage, or as many as God provides	2.4
Anniversary Celebrations	A weekend in Dublin	He gives her a new dis[h]washer. She gives him [a] power lawn mower
Quarrels	"I don't care what your analyst says"	"I don't care if he is yo[ur] brother"
If the Marriage Needs Help	He consults her analyst. She consults his	They go (a) to a marria[ge] counselor; (b) to the minist[er]
The Affair	"But I assumed you knew"	"It was basically a proble[m] in communication"
Sex Education	"Ask Doctor Grauber, dear, when you see him tomorrow"	"Well, you see, Daddy ha[s] something called a . . . et[c.] And Daddy and Mommy lo[ve] each other very much"
Vacations	Europe in May. She takes the children to the Cape. He commutes	Europe in July. Family cam[p]ing in Yosemite
Financial Arrangements	Separate trust funds	Joint checking account
Who Raises the Children	English nanny, boarding school, and Dr. Grauber	Mommy and Daddy, C[ub] Scouts, and Dr. Freud

From William Simon and John Gagnon, "How Fashionable Is Your Sex Life?," *McCall's* (October 1969), pp. 58–59.

264

LOWER MIDDLEBROW	LOWBROW
In the office, by the water cooler	On the block
After three drinks in an apartment he borrowed	In her home one night when Mom and Dad were at the movies
City Hall	Neighborhood church
Any Hilton hotel	Disneyland
Van de Velde	None
Twin beds with matching night tables	Double bed
He: pajamas. She: pajamas	He: underwear. She: nightgown
Sound track of *Dr. Zhivago*	Jackie Gleason and the Silver Strings
Manhattans and whisky sours	Beer
Twice a week and when the kids go to Sunday school	Twice on Saturday night
3	As many as God provides
Corsage and dinner out	Whitman Sampler and dinner at Howard Johnson's
"What do you think I'm made of?"	"Drop dead!"
He: to his successful brother. She: to her best friend	He: to the bartender. She: to her mother
"It was bigger than both of us"	"Some things no woman should have to put up with"
"Well, you see, Daddy puts the seed in Mommy's tummy, etc., etc."	"We got you at the hospital"
He hunts or fishes. She visits Mother with the children	They visit Brother Charlie in Des Moines
She budgets	He gets weekly allowance
Mom and Dad, the Little League, and Dr. Spock	Mom, the gang, Ann Landers, and good luck

265

8 There is a greater sense of helplessness, powerlessness, and distrust among members of the lower class, who are more likely to see the world as hostile.

Not all of these generalizations have been proven, but enough of them are supported by evidence to suggest that considerable emotional stress accompanies lower-class status. To experience life as a lower-class citizen is to undergo stress every day. This stress weakens one's trust and ability to cope. Self-esteem is the most important ingredient of emotional well-being. And it is hard to have high self-esteem as a member of the lower class in a society that expects people to compete for status and judges their worth in terms of their rank.

A relationship has been demonstrated between social class and hospitalization for mental illness. Working-class persons are far more likely to be admitted for psychiatric treatment than persons with higher status. This is especially true for those psychiatric problems that are clearly linked to physical disorders. As a result, some researchers are looking for medical treatments rather than social cures to alleviate the problem.[38]

Social mobility

Social systems differ greatly in their openness, that is, in the degree of opportunity their members have to move from one job or status level to another. The study of such movement is the study of **social mobility**. Movement toward higher status is called *upward* mobility; movement toward lower status is called *downward* mobility; and movement either upward or downward is called **vertical mobility**. The opportunity to change jobs without gaining or losing status is called **horizontal mobility**; for example, if a file clerk becomes a phone operator, this is horizontal mobility.

In this section, we will concentrate on *intergenerational* vertical mobility—that is,

the occupational status of a person relative to the occupational status of his or her father. If the son of a Supreme Court justice ends up as a street sweeper, he has shown a dramatic degree of downward mobility; if a street sweeper's son becomes a Supreme Court justice, he is an example of upward mobility. Few people move so far up or down the stratification ladder, however.

In a perfectly open society, one's chance to occupy a given position is limited only by one's preferences and ability. At the opposite extreme is the totally closed society, in which mobility is impossible; once a person has been assigned to a given position it cannot be changed. Both of these types of societies are imaginary and all real societies fall somewhere between these two extremes. (Even traditional India was not totally closed.)

For two reasons, industrial societies all have higher rates of social mobility than agrarian societies. First, industrial societies tend to assign status on the basis of achievement rather than ascribed characteristics. Second, the percentage of upper- and middle-class jobs increases as a society industrializes. This means that upward mobility is more common than downward mobility in industrial societies, while the reverse is true of agrarian societies.

MOBILITY IN NORTH AMERICA

Mobility rates have remained fairly stable in North America for many years. Between 1962 and 1970, there was a trend toward managerial, professional, and skilled work and away from less-skilled manual work. Though this change was more rapid during the 1960s than the 1950s, it was slower than during the period from 1942 to 1952.[39]

There is evidence that these rates are not, on the whole, higher in the United States than in other Western countries, contrary to popular belief.[40] In *Social Mobility in Industrial Society*, Seymour Martin Lipset and Reinhard

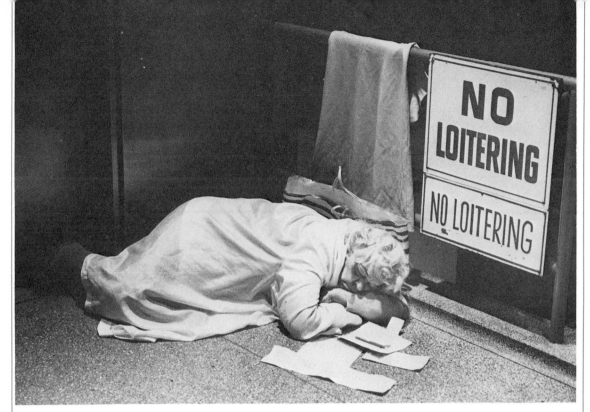

Toronto Star/Lennon

A "shopping-bag lady." There are shelters for down-and-out men, but very few for women like this one.

Bendix present evidence that the general pattern of social mobility is much the same in all the Western industrial societies.[41] Other researchers, however, have found that although the United States does not differ from other countries in *total* upward mobility, it is more open for *low-status males* than other countries. That is, while middle-class American males do not have a very high chance of moving up, lower-class males do.

The percentage of working-class American men who move into high-ranking jobs may indeed be higher than in any other society.[42] However, very few international comparisons of mobility have been proven conclusively. Though researchers have occasionally tried to compare American and Canadian rates of mobility, they have generally been unable to find much difference between them.[43]

Canadians probably are, to some extent, kept out of the highest management jobs in international corporations. These corporations tend to be controlled from other countries, especially the United States. Too few jobs are in this category to affect the rates of mobility in general. However, as we shall discuss elsewhere, there are other important reasons for concern about this trend in the Canadian economy.

Lipset and Bendix argue that mobility patterns in Western industrial societies depend far more upon occupational opportunities than on attitudes or values. They claim that "the desire to rise in status is intrinsic in all persons of lower status . . . Individuals and groups will attempt to improve their status (and self-evaluation) whenever they have any chance to do so."[44] According to Lipset and Bendix, upward mobility results whenever changing technology opens up a lot of jobs for skilled, educated workers; this mobility is not the result of ambition and dedication on the part of the workers, but of the mere presence of jobs for them. Lipset and Bendix explain mobility as a function of events in the economy and not of the personal qualities of individual workers.

If mobility is dependent upon occupational opportunities, then the rate of mobility is greatly influenced by the age structure of the population. As Lorne Tepperman has explained,

If we are running water into a sink and want the water never to rise above or fall below a certain level, the rate at which the water enters must come to be identical to the rate at which water leaves the sink ... The factor limiting mobility, in a working population or in an organization, is not the rate of entry but the rate of departure ... The question then becomes how to achieve a high rate of departure from the top positions of an organization or society in order to maximize upward mobility.[45]

One way, then, to maximize upward mobility would be to demote people in top positions to make room for people from the bottom; this rarely happens, probably because the people at the top are in control. Another possible solution is mandatory early retirement. Still another is the filling of top positions with people who are likely to leave early: sick people who may have to quit for health reasons; women, who may quit when their babies are born; or old people, who are likely to die.

When top positions are filled with young, healthy people who like their jobs and plan to keep them, mobility is very low. New jobs may open at the top because of changing economic conditions, but they, too, are soon filled by healthy, young, and enthusiastic workers; for each successful applicant, there are many other healthy young people who have to settle for jobs with much lower status. This is the situation today in Canada and in many other societies that experienced a "baby boom" twenty or thirty years ago. The career prospects for those many young people born in the 1950s are not very promising. The top jobs are already filled by people who are unlikely to

retire, die, or be demoted for a long time. And economists do not anticipate a period of great expansion in business or industry, so very few new jobs are being created. The rate of upward mobility is expected to remain low for some years to come.

WHO GETS AHEAD?

We have discussed factors that affect the *amount* of mobility. There is also a body of research that seeks to explain *who* is likely to experience upward mobility. (Not many studies concentrate on explaining *downward* mobility.) The most important recent study of upward mobility was done by Christopher Jencks and 11 other researchers at Harvard; it dealt with the mobility of American men.[46] Who, then, gets the prestigious, well-paid jobs?

The Jencks study established that a number of factors that are determined early in a person's life largely decide that person's later success. The most important early factor is whether or not one is born into a high-status family. A good deal of ascription still exists in all industrial societies. A male child born to a family in the top-fifth income group of the population is likely to earn nearly twice the national average income. Another important factor is early success in school. In the Jencks study, boys who did well in their academic tests in grade 6 were very likely to continue their success throughout school; this led them to finish university, and greatly enhanced their career mobility. Boys who were bright in school but did not go to university later acquired much less money and prestige than those who graduated. Leadership traits that showed up in high school also proved to be a financial asset; boys who were leaders but not particularly good students did well in later careers, especially if they finished college. Boys who were very sociable in high school, and spent their time dating instead of studying, did not get the plum jobs later on, but often were paid well compared to other low-status workers. ("You're a swell guy, Ron, and we'd

Ira Kirschenbaum/Stock, Boston

The people who live under systems of closed stratification have very little chance for vertical mobility. India's traditional caste system was the most closed society known.

like to promote you, but you don't have the qualifications. So you're getting a nice raise instead.")

The main finding of Jencks and his colleagues was the importance of finishing university. Finishing high school had little effect on a man's salary, unless he also went to college. His choice of college, his marks, and his course of study also made little difference. The really essential thing was that he *finished*. A college degree opened doors to a large variety of jobs that paid well and commanded prestige and power. Evidently, a college degree was the most important credential a man could have for occupational upward mobility.

Probably the best Canadian study of occupational mobility was reported by John Goyder and James E. Curtis. Unlike the Jencks study, this one compared the occupations of a sample of Canadian men to those of their fathers and grandfathers to see how much ascription was operating. Goyder and Curtis concluded that Canadian society is clearly marked by considerable mobility, both upward and downward. Grandsons did not necessarily hold the same status that their grandfathers held. Moreover, like Jencks' results, the findings of the study underlined the importance of education. A grandfather's status had less effect on that of his grandson than the level of education attained by the grandson. Because the white-collar sector consistently placed the most value on education, it was the group most likely to maintain the same status over at least three generations.[47]

SOME EFFECTS OF MOBILITY

What are the effects of mobility on a person's values and attitudes? We're not sure. Early studies suggested that the political and social outlook of downwardly mobile people is similar in all countries. They appeared to vote more conservatively than the other members of the class into which they had fallen. Mostly they held to a conservative view of stratification itself, a view that would have been appropriate to their original status but not to the lower one to which they had fallen. It was as if they were trying not to identify with the working class and hoped that by thinking of themselves as middle- or upper-class they could regain the status they had lost. "Skidders," as they are called, continued to believe that they lived in an open-class society and to hope for middle-class positions for themselves and for their children.[48]

Later studies have not always supported the findings of the earlier studies, and today some sociologists doubt that socially mobile people differ in any consistent way from other people. It is pretty clear, however, that a change in status causes psychological strain, whether the movement is upward or downward. There is some evidence that downwardly mobile people tend to hold onto their self-esteem by showing scorn for others. Other researchers have also found a slight tendency for upwardly mobile people to have liberal political attitudes.[49]

Upwardly mobile people have their own problems, however. It has been shown there is a relationship between emotional tension and upward mobility.[50] Moreover, upwardly mobile people are likely to judge their own occupational group favorably if they are accepted by its members, and in this way they reduce the strain of mobility. But if they are not accepted by the members of their occupational group they are likely to react by disliking that group.[51]

Three approaches to stratification

There are three main approaches to social stratification: (1) Marxism, (2) the ideas of Max Weber, and (3) the functionalist view, best represented by Kingsley Davis and Wilbert Moore.

MARX

"The history of all hitherto existing societies," Marx declared in his famous *Communist Manifesto*, "is the history of class struggle." And struggle is the most important concept in Marxist sociology. Marx pointed out that classes develop on the basis of the different positions that exist in a given system of production. In an agrarian society, the main classes are landowners versus tenants. In an industrial economy, the main classes are the capitalist owners of the factories versus the workers.

Marx referred to industrial workers as the *proletariat* and to capitalists as the *bourgeoisie*. The bourgeoisie should be distinguished from the *petty bourgeoisie*, or class of independent, small-business owners who do not employ workers. Barbers, shoe repairmen, and women with their own bakeshops are petty bourgeois. Other classes also exist in every society, though they may be less central to the dramatic class struggle of their times.

In the industrial society, for example, Marx recognized the existence of the *intelligentsia* and the *lumpen proletariat* classes. The intelligentsia consists of such workers as writers and sociology professors who produce the ideologies that bolster the claims of particular classes in conflict with one another. (If he were alive today, Marx would include TV newscasters and movie directors.) The lumpen proletariat consists of the lowliest class of people—beggars, bums, and other groups who do not contribute their labor to society. According to Marx, these people play a pivotal position in the class struggle at certain times. The capitalist system depends on keeping a "reserve army" of industrial labor for the bourgeoisie to use as strikebreakers in its struggle against the proletariat. The lumpen proletariat provides this labor reserve.

According to Marx, different classes have opposing interests. The bourgeoisie always keeps whatever profit it can squeeze out of the workers. And the workers cannot afford to complain much because the bourgeoisie is in control. Besides, the workers may not understand their situation very well. They may not even know that they are a social class. Marx referred to a group that is a class but is not aware of this fact as a class "*in* itself." Its members are in the same economic boat.

Marx was confident that in time workers would develop "class consciousness" and thereby become a class "*for* itself"; that is, they would recognize that they had common interests and develop a sense of solidarity. The final stage of class consciousness would be reached when the working class came to believe that only by overthrowing the capitalist owners could they take what was rightfully theirs. Then they would join together to take over the means of production—the factories, the tools, and all the rest.

Marx's theory of social classes cannot be separated from his theory of economics. We shall discuss his ideas in other chapters, but we must briefly mention them here as well. Marx defined social classes with reference to their access to the means of production. Products of all sorts—potatoes, violins, canoes—are made from natural resources, but they vary in value. Why is a violin more valuable than a block of wood, some strings, and some varnish? Only because of the labor required to make it from these ingredients.

To Marx, there is a world of difference between the situations of the factory owner and the worker. The owner can hire workers to make products that he can sell for profit, but the worker, lacking any equipment, can make nothing to sell by himself and must therefore sell his labor. The owner has the worker "over a barrel." To be sure, he must pay the worker enough to survive on, but *only* that much and no more. If the owner can get the worker to produce more than it costs to support him, the owner can keep all the surplus. This surplus is the source of capitalist profit. *All* profit is extracted from workers who are in no position to keep the proceeds of their own labor. Class consciousness, said Marx, would arise as workers came to recognize their common plight. They would then organize a resistance against their oppressors, the bourgeoisie.

WEBER

Max Weber is sometimes seen as holding opposite views to those of Marx. This is a mistake; Weber agreed with many elements of Marxist thought. In particular, he also saw the economy as the main cause of stratification. For both Marx and Weber, control over property is a basic factor in the life chances of an individual or class. However, Weber added to the economic dimension of stratification two other dimensions: *power* and *prestige*. Weber saw property, power, and prestige as three separate, though interacting, factors. Property differences produce *classes*; prestige differences produce *status groupings* or *strata*; and power differences produce what he termed *parties* (meaning factions or political blocs).

So far we have used the terms *status* and *class* as if they were interchangeable. In most sociological writings they do mean about the same thing. But to Weber they did not. Classes were based on property, status groups on prestige.

While Marx assumed that the members of any economic class would develop class consciousness and recognize their common interests, Weber did not expect this to happen all the time. In fact, Weber said that economic classes do not normally form communities while status groups do. Status groups are based on shared prestige or honor, and economic factors alone do not determine honor or prestige. Many people who have suddenly become rich have found that their new fortune will buy a mansion but will not get them invited into the homes of the old-rich families who live next door.

Usually, Weber says, members of a high-status group feel united in trying to "put down" people who think money entitles them to prestige. Indeed, the high-status group usually tries to make its status independent of property. Its members may lose their money, but they continue to emphasize the superiority of their life style, family connections, and so forth. This limits movement into or out of the high-status group.

According to Weber, property differences have important effects on life chances but status differences lead to differences in life style—tastes and manners. Whether you spend an evening at the opera or at the bowling alley may say nothing about your financial condition but say quite a bit about the status group to which you belong. Differences in life styles are an important element in the exclusiveness of various status groups. To feel comfortable in a high-status group one must be able to use the proper accent and the right fork; such elements of life style can be acquired only through experience, often expensive experience. Thus, along with Marx, Weber recognized the importance of property differences *in the long run* in forming status groups and in hardening the lines between them. Over many generations money will produce status group-

How much can you guess about the life styles of these men off the job?

CP Photo

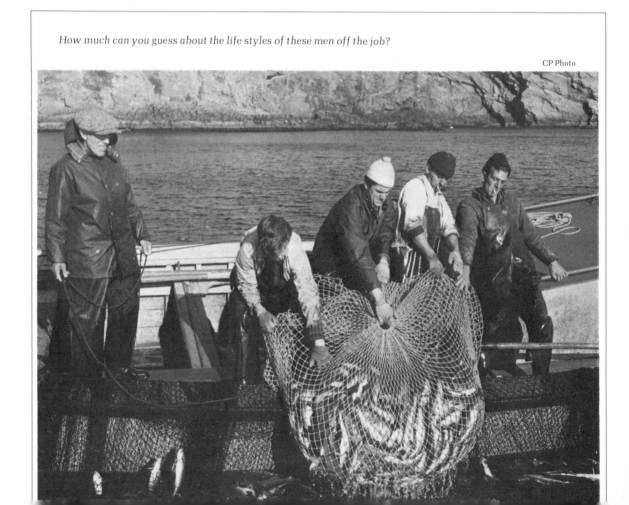

ings, but only if it is used to "buy" a life style. Newly rich people may not be invited to dinner, but if the children go to private schools and learn "proper" manners they will eventually gain prestige and honor.

Weber differed from Marx in that he emphasized the importance of status groups and believed that it was unlikely that the working class would develop class consciousness. Also, he was very interested in the social changes that result from the interaction between status and class. Marx's theory simply does not lead us to look at the psychological strain involved in having status inconsistency (conflicting status and class), but Weber's theory is well suited to this question.

The third type of stratification listed by Weber is the *party*. Although according to Weber the basis of classes is property and that of status groups is honor, "'parties' live in a house of 'power.'" Parties are possible only within communities that have rules of order and a "staff or persons who are ready to enforce [them]. For parties aim precisely at influencing this staff, and seek, if possible, to recruit it from party followers."[52] Again, we must remember that the term *party* is used here to refer to any group that is formed for the purpose of dominating an organized group. It refers as much to a group seeking power within a social club as to a political party. Weber believed that parties may form on the basis of similar "class" interests or similar "status" interests or both, "but they need be neither purely 'class' nor purely 'status' parties, and frequently they are neither."[53]

To sum up, Weber's approach suggests that society is made up of three kinds of social groups. These groups differ in unity and in the kind of social resources with which they are concerned. Classes are based on economic resources, status groups on prestige or honor, and parties on power. These groups often have overlapping memberships, and sometimes an economic class is practically identical with a status group and a political party. But this is only one of many possibilities.

Suppose a sociologist agrees with Weber on the matter of stratification. How does this approach differ from the Marxist approach in practice? The answer is that the Weberian will probably classify people into different social strata according to subjective rather than objective standards. The objective Marxist would use property ownership or levels of income. The Weberian would use more subtle indicators of social status than the Marxist. In fact, most Weberians rely on techniques developed in 1930 by W. Lloyd Warner in the study of a community that he called "Yankee City."[54] Warner's approach asks how the people within a given population see themselves and one another, regardless of the objective differences in their incomes or occupations. Warner would seek information on the following questions:

1 What are the standards by which the members of a society judge each other to be equal or unequal?
2 How much importance do they give to each of these standards?
3 How many groups or strata do they see in their community?
4 How do they rate themselves?
5 How are they rated by others?
6 Who associates with whom in various social contexts?

Once a population has been divided into strata, a sociologist of the Warner school studies other factors, such as patterns of career ambitions or rates of mental illness, to see the extent to which these factors (or "dependent variables") differ for members of the different social strata. The Warner approach assumes that life chances and life styles are determined not only by place of residence, occupation, and the like but also by the importance given to these various factors by the population being studied.

THE FUNCTIONALIST VIEW

Although Marx strongly emphasized social inequality, he did not think it was a permanent condition of human society and certainly did not believe it was either useful or necessary. To Marx, stratification represented injustice and exploitation, nothing more. But many social theorists both before and since Marx's time have disagreed, and none have been as convincing as the modern functionalists. More than thirty years ago, Kingsley Davis and Wilbert Moore proposed a theory that has been debated ever since.[55] Today the Davis-Moore theory is challenged by more sociologists than ever before because it is the kind of conservative, functionalist doctrine that is maddening to reformists.

Davis and Moore argued that there are limits to the possibility of creating social equality, that social stratification is not only universal but functionally necessary for any society. (By *stratification* they mean unequal distribution of prestige and material rewards.) The reason stratification is necessary is very simple: Society uses prestige and material rewards to get people to occupy positions that are socially important and difficult to perform, jobs that require special training and uncommon ability. It is a matter of getting the best-qualified people to fill the most demanding and key positions in society. They wrote:

Some positions require innate talents of such a high degree that the persons who fill them are bound to be rare. In many cases, however, talent is fairly abundant in the population but the training process is so long, costly, and elaborate that relatively few can qualify. Modern medicine, for example, is within the mental capacity of most individuals, but a medical education is so burdensome and expensive that virtually none would undertake it if the position of the M.D. did not carry a reward commensurate with the sacrifice. ... The position, if functionally important, must have an attractive power that will draw the necessary skills in competition with other positions. This means, in effect, that the position must be high in the social scale—must command great prestige, high salary, ample leisure, and the like.[56]

Davis and Moore saw social stratification as a sort of market system, with scarce skills selling for high prices (prestige, power, and high salaries). They claimed that every society has to be stratified in order to motivate people to take on heavy responsibilities.

But you may have already noticed some problems with this explanation. For one thing, no society shows a strict one-to-one relationship between rewards and performance in important, socially useful positions. Swindlers sometimes become rich without performing any useful service to humanity. Some people inherit property and never have to work. Movie stars are paid astonishing salaries, but are their roles more "important" or do they need more training than truck drivers? It is possible to accept the functionalist argument and still think that there is a great deal more inequality in any given social system than is needed to fill important roles. Thus even if Davis and Moore have correctly described how societies use social rewards to attract qualified people to fill important roles, it does not follow from this theory that any particular society has the best possible distribution of rewards.

Worse yet, one must assume that even if there is a good distribution at first, any system of rewards will tend to drift toward inequality because power is one of the rewards attached to key positions. Once people gain power, they are likely to use it to maintain their privileges even if they fail to perform socially useful services. They are also likely to use it for their relatives and friends. In short, power corrupts, and therefore no system of social rewards is free from the possibility of injustice. Thus even a person who accepts Davis's and Moore's basic theory still has to worry about social justice.

We must go further, however, and question whether the basic theory is worth accepting at all. Davis and Moore argued that if key positions were not highly rewarded qualified people might not be attracted to them. This is not necessarily so. No one argues that varying rewards keep an *ascriptive* society going. In India, as we have seen, people traditionally performed whatever role they were assigned by birth, regardless of how unattractive it was.

Only an achievement-oriented society can be said to depend on a hierarchy of rewards, and even in such a society there are many exceptions to this rule. In the family, for example, role performance does not depend on rewards for good behavior. We do not think up "incentive plans" to get women to be good mothers. If the role is not its own reward, no system of rewards will do any good.

But what makes certain jobs more attractive than others, if not the pay and prestige that go with them? Possibly the authority they carry.[57] Authority is so important that it may make other rewards unnecessary. A key position is one that is *necessarily* authoritative. In that sense does the executive play a

"key" role while his or her secretary does not? The answer is this: The secretary's activities are organized around the executive, not vice versa. We can imagine a company in which a secretary's salary is higher than that of the president, but we can hardly imagine a company in which the president must dictate only the kinds of letters that the secretary enjoys typing. The role of the executive involves authority, not because it is a "reward" but because it is an essential part of the role. Because most people enjoy having authority, the "key" positions in society carry with them a major reward; the pleasure of using authority may render other rewards of a material nature unnecessary.

SOCIAL RESEARCH:
Sociologists at Work

SOCIALIZATION FOR INEQUALITY

At what age do children learn that upper-class people supposedly look and act differently than working-class people? How do they identify people of different social statuses? What qualities do they believe that people of different social classes have? Do working-class children learn the same attitudes to social class as middle- or upper-class children? Or do they have different expectations of rich and poor people? Bernd Baldus and Verna Tribe, two Toronto sociologists, have tried to answer these questions in their paper "The Development of Perceptions and Evaluations of Social Inequality among Public School Children."[58]

Baldus and Tribe interviewed 108 children in Toronto-area public schools. They talked to 36 children in each of three economically disparate schools; within each school, 12 children were selected from grade one, 12 from grade three, and 12 from grade six. The interviews were taped and transcribed. The researchers presented each child with several sets of photographs. We have repro-

duced the photos here, except that, to protect the privacy of individuals, we have made substitutions for pictures of people. Set One shows two men; "Mr. Gordon" is dressed in expensive, neat clothes, while "Mr. Ellis" is dressed in worn, casual clothes. Set Two contains pictures of two houses, one in the high-income Rosedale area, and the other in a working-class district of Toronto. Set Three portrays two living rooms, one in Rosedale and the other in a rented apartment with worn furniture. Set Four shows two automobiles, a small old car and a sleek Lincoln Continental. Set Five shows two more men, again dressed in clothes of very different quality.

The experiment consisted of having the children match the photos. The children were presented with the pictures of Mr. Ellis and Mr. Gordon, and were asked to compare them and mention any differences that they noticed. The children were asked which house, car, and living room belonged to Mr. Gordon and which to Mr. Ellis; they were also asked to explain their answers. They were then told that both men were planning to give parties. From the two pictures of men in Set Five, they were told to choose which would be invited to Mr. Ellis's party and which to Mr. Gordon's.

For this first phase of the study, the results

were clear. Even by the first grade, most children concluded that the expensive belongings were Mr. Gordon's and the poorer things were Mr. Ellis's. This was especially true of the cars; only 9 children matched the cars incorrectly in grade one, while 27 matched them correctly. However, the grade one children did not necessarily know which house or living room was working-class; they made wrong guesses about housing almost as often as right ones. Finally, the grade one children were generally correct in their matching of "party guests," selecting the appropriate man to be invited to each party.

When the responses of various school grades were compared, it was found that older children made progressively fewer "mis-matches." By grade six, about 90 percent of the matches were "correct," that is, consistent with apparent similarities in social class. The explanations of the logic of their matches included statements like: "Mr. Gordon looks kind of rich. I don't know why. But he slicks up his hair. Mr. Ellis looks like he is tough, maybe a big mouth. These houses are close together. Mr. Gordon's house looks really like a mansion." Or, "Mr. Gordon looks like a salesman, with a suit and a tie. Mr. Ellis looks like an ordinary guy who lives in an apartment, a pop-corn salesman with enough pennies."

The researchers then proceeded to the second phase of the study. They read a series of short stories aloud, each one about a child who was either successful and popular or who was having a problem of some sort, such as an inability to read well, a tendency to start unprovoked fights, or habitual lying. The young respondents were asked to guess whether each story was about Mr. Gordon's child or Mr. Ellis's child. Most students guessed that the happy, successful children belonged to Mr. Gordon, while the children who misbehaved or had poor competitive skills belonged to Mr. Ellis. Again, the older students were more likely to hold these views than the grade one children. This time, they explained their choices with statements such as: "(It is) Mr. Ellis's son, because people who don't have jobs seem to lie about their work and say that they have done what they have not done. Mr. Gordon probably taught his son that lying doesn't pay, and that you get into a lot of trouble just by starting with one lie." Or, "Mr. Ellis looks like a man who would lie a lot. His face looks like a man who would lie a lot, while Mr.

Gordon looks like a cheerful man, a good-minded man. Mr. Ellis's son is more likely to pick up such ideas at home." Or, "(It is) Mr. Ellis's son because poor people usually lie."

It seemed natural to the children that someone with a big house, a fancy car, and an expensively furnished house would be admirable in most other respects, and that someone without these high-status symbols would be less worthy. To some extent, the children also regarded these worthy and unworthy traits as hereditary, or, at least, as capable of transmission from parent to child.

Baldus and Tribe found, rather disturbingly, that these opinions were not affected by the social position of the children's own parents. All the children, whether working-class or middle-class, seemed to recognize the symbols of social status in their environment at about the same age. By the first grade, children could identify cheap and expensive cars and express fixed ideas about the sort of people likely to drive them. The ability to differentiate between cheap and expensive cars, clothes, houses, and furnishings is not in itself surprising; children overhear their parents' conversations and receive additional information from television. What is surprising, however, is the widespread conclusion that rich people are probably good and that poor people are probably bad. Mr. Ellis was described as "tough," "rough," "lazy," prone to swearing, stealing, and drinking, and as apathetic to the concerns of himself and his family. Why?

Baldus and Tribe suggest that by about age eight or nine, children acquire the outline of an ideology that legitimates inequality and makes it seem natural. This ideology, shared by most members of this society, portrays high-status positions as rewarding and desirable and low-status positions as disreputable and unpleasant. The children quickly learn to *want* to be upper-class. In the early phases of this process, children often have a very limited understanding of the ideology. Nevertheless, they are internalizing a set of standards for measuring social respectability and social accomplishments.

And what of the working-class children? What of the children whose fathers look and dress like Mr. Ellis? According to Baldus and Tribe, they too learn this ideology, and internalize feelings of inadequacy, self-doubt, and insecurity as they compare themselves and their families to standards of "success" that they can probably never achieve.

Who and what belongs to whom? Mr. Gordon is wearing a suit, while Mr. Ellis is dressed more casually.

Baldus and Tribe

SOCIAL POLICY:
Issues and Viewpoints

I am going to ask you some questions. Take your time to answer—they're hard. You may need the rest of your life to think about them.

1. *What kind of stratification system do you want?* You get three choices: (1) an ascribed, highly stratified society; (2) a stratified but open society in which rank is assigned on the basis of merit; and (3) an unstratified society in which rewards are distributed equally to all members who meet certain standards of behavior.

We needn't bother to talk about the first choice, because I doubt that you want such a society. Hardly anybody, these days, desires a caste system. With the second and third choices, however, we run into some real issues. These are expressed in the following questions.

2. *To industrialize, does a poor society have to choose between inequality and totalitarianism?* Our period of history is one in which many societies are trying to make the leap from an agrarian to an industrial economy. But how can they get the cash to pay for factories, dams, schools, and the like? There is simply not enough money to build all these institutions, but somehow it has to be scraped together. Later we'll talk about how this was done in the West when our own industrialization was taking place. But what is happening today in very poor nations?

If a country's wealth were distributed equally, and if people were allowed to spend their share, they would certainly do so. They would buy bread, shoes, refrigerators, bikes, and other things. But a developing country has to get people to go barefoot and invest the money in power plants, steel mills, and so on, until these industries are established. In most underdeveloped countries, land and wealth are held primarily by a small elite, a group that consumes scandalously more than its fair share. But there is *some* surplus for investment—probably a lot more than there would be if wealth were distributed equally.

It has been argued that if material inequality is to be corrected in a poor nation it must be replaced by a coercive political system that will repress the masses just as harshly as private ownership. Capital formation requires squeezing the peasants. The question is, Who will do it? The rich owners or the government? Neither choice is pleasant, but poor nations have to choose one or the other if they are to catch up. Or so it is generally argued. I'm not sure. But obviously this is an important issue that must be considered before we can answer the first question. We'll discuss it again in later chapters. We can look for factors that seem to affect economic development, but the issue is too complex for this book to settle. We may not know the answer to this question for a generation or two.

3. *In an open, stratified system, would the children of upper-status people still tend to win upper-status positions?* Suppose we provide all children with equal socialization experiences, equal education, the same vitamins every morning, piano lessons, trips to Europe, and equal opportunities to get good jobs. After that they would be promoted strictly on the basis of merit. What would happen? Would the children of professionals and business executives continue to take the lion's share of the professional and executive jobs? Or would the children of plumbers and bus drivers move into these high positions in great numbers, while the children of the middle and upper classes have no more career success than any other group?

We don't know. A few sociologists think that ability is largely passed on through genes. I mentioned this possibility in the chapter on socialization. If, unlikely as it seems, children succeed or fail mostly on the basis of the genes they acquire from their parents, then more equal opportunity would not lead to more social mobility. Most working-class youth would become working-class adults, as they do now. Would that seem unfair to you? If so, the only remaining way to reduce unfairness would be to reduce stratification itself. That is, we could deliberately equalize incomes and status (e.g., by changing the tax laws). Your point of view on this issue will affect your answer to the first question.

4. *Would equal rewards undermine economic growth?* Economic conservatives think so. They think people work simply to get ahead. If it were not possible to get ahead because equality was guaranteed to all, people might stop working hard. The economy would come to a screeching halt.

There is some historical evidence to support

this view. Early experiments in equalizing rewards in the Soviet Union had to be given up because the economy actually did not work very well. Yet in other places much greater equality has been achieved—communist China is one example.

Some say that people could be socialized to work regardless of whether they were rewarded with money or prestige. In the family, for example, we do our share of the work because we feel love or a sense of duty, not a need for rewards. Could society be organized in such a way that people would do their jobs in the same unselfish way?

5. *Could we enforce a policy of equality?* Suppose we passed a law that everyone must be paid the same wages. We know that some secretaries, for example, are better at their jobs than others. I think an employer would find a way to outbid other employers seeking to hire the best secretary. "Come to work for me, and I'll give you an office with a carpet, two afternoons a week off, and all the postage stamps you can use." How long would equality of rewards hold up?

We could probably maintain a lot more equality than we do, but never total equality.

6. *Could a society do without authority?* I think this is where equality is most likely to break down. Things don't run well if no one is in charge. Someone must make decisions. In a very simple organization, we could rotate authority so that you would be chairperson this week and I'd take over next week, and Judy and Sam would have their turns too. But in a complex system, specialization is necessary. I don't want flight attendants and baggage handlers to take turns piloting the airplane I fly in or running the air traffic control system. And you don't have time to learn all you would need to know to be prime minister for a week. Besides, by the time you have learned how to be a good prime minister you may want to keep the job, and you may have enough power to do so. The chance to use power appeals to many people. Those who like power often manage to keep it. Thus it is hard to equalize power or even to rotate it.

Now go back and think about our first question again. Take your time!

SUMMARY

1. A *social class* is a set of people with similar socioeconomic status—similar amounts of property, prestige, and power.

2. *Ascribed status* is assigned on the basis of characteristics that one cannot control, such as race, sex, height, or age. *Achieved status* is assigned on the basis of performance. Both achieved status and ascribed status are found in all societies, but industrial societies use achievement as a standard more than preindustrial societies do. Caste is the most obvious example of ascribed status. Social classes are more open to mobility than castes are.

3. The term *social stratification* refers to a hierarchy of positions that are unequal in property, power, and prestige, the three bases

of status. *Property* may be defined as rights over goods and services. *Power* refers to the ability to achieve one's goals even in the face of opposition. *Prestige* is social honor given to a person on the basis of the roles he or she occupies.

4. *Status inconsistency* results when a person has high status by one standard but low status by another—for example, high power and low prestige.

5. Life chances and life style are affected by social status. Compared with upper- and middle-class people, lower-class people have less chance of a successful marriage, have more children, are less permissive in their child rearing, and are somewhat less likely to have a long life. They are less likely to belong to a church, less likely to support conservative economic policies or liberal policies on matters of civil liberties and civil rights, and are more likely to be hospitalized for mental illness.

6. *Social mobility* refers to movement from one level of a social system to another or from one job to another. *Vertical mobility* refers to upward movement (gaining status) or downward movement (losing status). Changing jobs without gaining or losing status is called *horizontal mobility*.

7. Marx's views of social classes are based on the assumption that there is a conflict between the owners of the means of production (e.g., factories) and the workers, who must sell their labor to survive. He assumed that the workers would develop class consciousness and would seize the means of production.

8. Weber's interpretation was not entirely opposed to Marx's, but he viewed status as consisting of three different, though interacting, hierarchies—classes, status groups, and parties (or factions). The three groups are based on differences in property, prestige, and power, respectively. Weber believed that class consciousness is rather uncommon but that status-group consciousness is usual. A high-status group usually tries to make its status independent of property. In the long run, money *does* produce status groupings, but only by "buying" a special life style for the well-to-do.

9. W. Lloyd Warner used a subjective method of classifying populations into strata. His approach is still used by researchers who hold to Weber's interpretation of status groups as different from social classes.

10. Functionalism views social stratification as necessary and universal. According to this approach, society uses prestige and material rewards to get people to perform roles that are socially important and difficult.

Critics of functionalism argue that no society has an entirely logical distribution of rewards. Besides, we have no way of finding out how much inequality is necessary. Clearly, however, authority cannot be equalized even if prestige and material rewards can.

KEY TERMS

achieved status   status assigned on the basis of standards over which a person has some control.

ascribed status   status assigned on the basis of standards over which a person has no control.

caste system   a closed stratification system.

esteem   appreciation of a person regardless of his or her rank.

horizontal mobility   social mobility that does not involve a gain or loss of status.

life chances   patterns of infant mortality, physical and mental illness, childlessness, marital conflict, separation, divorce, etc.; the opportunity for well-being.

life style   patterns of eating and dressing, cultural and recreational activities, relationships between parents and children, etc.; the way people express their personal taste.

power   the ability to achieve one's goals even in the face of opposition.

prestige   social honor attached to particular roles.

property   rights or control over goods and services.

social class   a set of people of similar socio-economic status.

social mobility   movement from one status or occupation to another.

social stratification   a hierarchy of layers or strata that are unequal in terms of property, power, and prestige.

status   a person's rank based on income, prestige, education, or power.

status inconsistency   the situation in which a person ranks higher by one standard than by another.

vertical mobility   social mobility that involves movement toward higher or lower status.

FOR FURTHER READING

AMES, HERBERT BROWN. *The City Below the Hill.* Toronto: University of Toronto Press, 1972. This is a contribution to the social history of Canada. It discusses a working-class area of Montreal in 1897, and shows how unemployment affects the life of a slum.

BOTTOMORE, THOMAS B. *Marxist Sociology.* London: Macmillan, 1975. You may notice that I have not listed any work by Karl Marx as suggested reading. You might like to start your Marxist education with *The Communist Manifesto* or something brief, but don't start with *Capital,* Marx's most famous book, as it is difficult. Bottomore is a contemporary sociologist who discusses Marxism fairly clearly, though his book is quite sophisticated too.

CLEMENT, WALLACE. *The Canadian Corporate Elite: An Analysis of Economic Power.* Toronto: McClelland and Stewart, 1975. Clement leapt to fame in Canadian sociology on the basis of his Ph.D. dissertation, which picked up where John Porter left off. He also wrote *Continental Corporate Power: Economic Linkages Between Canada and the United States.* Toronto: McClelland and Stewart, 1977. Clement's two books will be mentioned in several places in this book; Canadian social scientists make extended use of them today.

COPP, TERRY. *The Anatomy of Poverty: The Condition of the Working Class in Montreal, 1897-1929.* Toronto: McClelland and Stewart, 1974. Copp has added to the work that Ames began on the Montreal poor. This is sad reading.

CURTIS, JAMES and WILLIAM SCOTT, eds. *Social Stratification in Canada.* 2nd ed. Scarborough, Ont.: Prentice-Hall, 1980. An excellent collection of articles on the nature and sources of social inequality in Canada.

FORCESE, DENNIS. *The Canadian Class Structure.* Toronto: McGraw-Hill Ryerson, 1975. This is an excellent brief overview of the whole area of stratification in Canada.

FRY, JOHN ALLAN, ed. *Economy, Class and Social Reality.* Toronto: Butterworth, 1979. A collection of articles on class, unemployment, and related issues in Canadian society, from a critical perspective. (Here, as usual, "critical" mostly means "Marxist.")

GRAYSON, J. PAUL. *Class, State, Ideology, and Change.* Toronto: Holt, Rinehart, and Winston, 1980. This is another collection of critical essays, which includes a more historical approach than that of the Fry book.

JOHNSON, LEO. *Poverty in Wealth: The Capitalist Labour Market and Income Distribution in Canada.* Toronto: New Hogtown Press, 1974. Johnson's Marxist views are elaborated by his presentation of hard evidence about the declining position of the bottom social class in Canada. Not everyone agrees with him, however.

NEWMAN, PETER C. *The Canadian Establishment. Vol. 1.* Toronto: McClelland and Stewart, 1975. You may have already read this book: It was a bestseller. Newman is himself part of the "media" establishment, and he was able to conduct interviews with the executives who control Canadian corporations. Fascinating.

PHILLIPS, PAUL. *Regional Disparities.* Toronto: Lorimer, 1978. This book offers the best analysis available today of the reasons for the gross income inequalities that exist in various provinces. It locates the causes of regional disparity in the day-to-day workings of the Canadian economy.

PORTER, JOHN. *The Vertical Mosaic: An Analysis of Social Class and Power in Canada.* Toronto: University of Toronto Press, 1965. This is probably the Canadian sociology book that has been most influential so far. Because it was so influential, many of the facts that it reports are outdated. By calling attention to problems, the book helped cure some of them. John Porter died in 1979.

TEPPERMAN, LORNE. *Social Mobility in Canada.* Toronto: McGraw-Hill Ryerson, 1975. This focuses on one particular aspect of social stratification—the movement that people experience up or down the social ladder. It points to subgroups in Canadian society, such as women and ethnic minorities, that face special problems.

10

RACIAL AND ETHNIC GROUPS

Toronto, where I live, is a city of immigrants from many nations. Every Friday at sundown one of the elevators in my apartment building observes the Sabbath. It starts going up and down, stopping at every floor automatically, so that Orthodox Jews can enter or leave their apartments; pressing the button is considered work and must not be done on the Sabbath. Most of the names beside the door buzzers downstairs are non-Anglo-Saxon. When I enter clothing stores nearby the salespeople speak to me in Portuguese or Italian. In one area the street signs are in Chinese as well as English. Children go to special classes after school or on Saturdays, usually in church basements, to learn how to read and write in their native language—Ukrainian, Greek, or one of the dozens of other tongues I hear spoken on the streets.

Ethnicity means different things to different people. I enjoy restaurants and movies, newspapers and grocery stores that cater to West Indians, Israelis, Poles, and so on. But a Pakistani friend is sometimes insulted by teenagers on the subway. And a student from India, who drives a cab at night to pay his way through college, says that a passenger makes a rude remark to him about once a night. Nobody calls me insulting names, but I can remember what it was like when my family moved from Oklahoma to California and, as a girl of 13, I blushed with shame and anger at being called an "Okie."

Okies were white Oklahomans who had long been American citizens, yet we were discriminated against as an ethnic group. We were recognized by our accents, but other aspects of our life style were different too. Okies came to California in search of jobs, and they had to take jobs at lower wages than local workers, who naturally hated them and wanted to keep them out.

My experience has been shared by members of many minority groups—ethnic groups that are discriminated against. I wish discrimination and interethnic conflict were things of the past. But they are not—just look at your morning paper. You will read about Arab refugees in the Middle East, about American Indians who are jobless, about Jews in the Soviet Union, or about the demands of some linguistic group for political separation from another linguistic group—the Tamils in India, the Québécois in Canada, the Basques in Spain.

Ours is an era of ethnicity. At the end of World War II, we thought this would not be the case. We had seen in Nazi Germany what nationalism and racism could lead to, and we thought the world had learned its lesson. We hoped that the boundaries between nationalities, races, religious groups, and linguistic communities would soon be erased and that we would become "one world." Unfortunately, this did not happen. There are more new movements led by ethnic groups, nationalities, and religious groups now than there were then. Contrary to Marx's prediction, the history of our period is not one of *class* conflict but one of conflict between ethnic groups, including religious communities, linguistic groups, tribes, racial groups, nationalities, colonized native peoples—any big group that is held together by ascribed, not achieved, bonds.

Clearly there are two ways of looking at ethnicity. It produces variety, but it also produces conflict and discrimination. As you read this chapter you may find that your feelings are mixed. Pay attention to your feelings as you read about these matters. Feelings of resentment and scorn always accompany our beliefs and attitudes about justice and injustice, about dignity, equality, and our place in the ethnic hierarchy. It is likely that you will be more indignant about discrimination against "your people" than you would be about discrimination against your social class. By "your people" I mean your ascribed community. Whom do you have in mind when you say, "My people, the ..."? Is it "We, the Arabs"? "We, the Inuit"? "We, the Quebec anglophones"? You probably don't ever mean "We, the middle class"; rather, you mean your ethnic group.

Ethnic groups, minorities, and racial groups

ETHNIC GROUPS

An **ethnic group** is a large collectivity in which membership is generally inherited. Its members share a feeling of identification with the group. Examples are Polish Canadians, Irish Catholics, Palestinian refugees, and the Parsis of India. The terms *ethnic group, ascribed community*, and a *people* are interchangeable. An ethnic group has the following characteristics:

1 It is largely biologically self-perpetuating.
2 It shares basic cultural values that are expressed in unified cultural forms.
3 Its members communicate and interact with one another.
4 Its members form a category that can be distinguished from other, similar social categories.[1]

The term *ethnic group* is sometimes used to refer to people of a particular national origin, such as Polish Canadians. Our definition includes nationality, but it also includes tribes, linguistic groups (such as anglophones and francophones), racial groups (such as blacks and whites), and ascribed religious groups (such as Catholics and Protestants). Our definition is not limited to the small subgroups within a society but may include the dominant group as well, such as the WASP (White Anglo-Saxon Protestant) group in North America. Jews are an ethnic group because they feel a strong sense of "peoplehood" and meet the other standards of our definition, but it is not clear whether they should be understood as a nationality or as a religious community.

Ethnic groups always have **boundaries** — codes and customs that define a person as a member or nonmember. One knows whether or not one belongs to the group because belonging means accepting the group's norms.

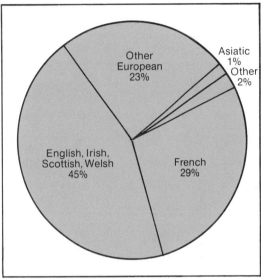

FIGURE 10.1

Percentage distribution of the Canadian population by ethnic group, 1971

Source: Statistics Canada, 1971 Census of Canada, Bulletin 1.3-2 (Ottawa: Information Canada, 1973), Table 2.

Indeed, it is highly unusual, and can even be dramatic, to cross group boundaries. It would be strange, for example, for a French Canadian to refuse to reply in French to a question asked by a fellow francophone, or for a Jew to take communion in an Anglican church.

It's hard to change ethnic groups. Membership in the group is supposed to be once and for all. To see other people as fellow members is to recognize that they are "playing the same game." They have the same social codes that you do. You know that outsiders have different ways of looking at things, and you limit your relationships with outsiders.

Of course you are bound to meet members of other ethnic groups. Indeed, interaction between members of different groups can go on in many situations without any trouble. But such interaction is regulated by specific norms. Interethnic contact is not permitted in areas where there is any threat to group traditions, otherwise called *boundary norms*.

Some topics are kept private as a matter of etiquette, and this helps keep the groups' identities separate. Ethnic identity is *imperative*: You are not allowed to switch around and be, say, an Arab this week and a Jew next week. Many ethnic groups discourage close friendships with outsiders and frown on participation in their ceremonies. In addition, most ethnic groups' boundary norms include strong norms of *endogamy*—the rule that members must marry within the group. Some groups disown members who violate this rule.

Strong boundaries keep ethnic groups separate, and therefore very few people are marginal. A **marginal person** is one who belongs to two or more separate groups that are supposedly mutually exclusive. An example would be a child whose mother is Christian and whose father is Muslim.

A society usually has certain rules for determining the identity of marginal people so that they can be defined as members of only one community. In societies that trace kinship through the father's side of the family, the child is usually assigned to his father's community. Children of Protestant-Catholic marriages are assigned to the Catholic community. In the case of black-white unions in North America the child is defined as black. Other societies have different ways of defining marginal black-white people, however. In some Latin American societies, a child of a black-white marriage will be defined as black if his or her parents are poor but as white if they are rich. Indeed, if a poor black child becomes a rich adult, the boundary norm will permit him or her to cross over from the black group to the white group! In South Africa, the community of black Africans is defined as completely separate from the other three ascribed communities—the whites, the Asians, and the "coloreds," or mulattoes (mixed black and white). It is important to realize that these boundary norms are *social* definitions. They are not biological facts about a person but social rules that differ from one society to another. A mulatto, for example, would probably be considered black in the United States,

"colored" and *not* black in South Africa, and perhaps white in Latin America.

The boundaries between some groups are much weaker than those between other groups. When boundaries are weak, the number of marginal people may increase over time; people may stop paying much attention to which group they belong to, and the communities may gradually merge. Eventually the original groups no longer have separate identities. This is rare, however. Usually it is hard for a person to change his or her ethnic identity, either because the new group does not accept him or her or because changing is considered disloyal. Loyalty to an ascribed group can be a powerful social bond. One may view oneself as a traitor for "passing" as white if one was born black or becoming Christian if one was born Jewish. One may not feel guilty if one moves out of one's parents' social class, but ethnic membership is supposed to be permanent.

It is sometimes useful to distinguish between *ethnic groups* and *ethnic categories*. A group has boundaries and a sense of cohesion. A category may not. For example, your parents may be Armenian, but you may have very little contact with other Armenians. Indeed, you may rarely think of yourself as anything but an ordinary "Canadian." If a census form listed you as a member of your parents' ethnic community, it would be partly inaccurate. It would be more correct to classify you as a member of their ethnic category. Whenever a community blends into the surrounding population, it gradually stops being an ethnic *group* and becomes an ethnic *category*. Even when an ethnic community hardly exists as a group anymore, its members can still be classified together as a category. We'll discuss this process further in various places throughout this chapter.

MINORITY GROUPS

In some societies, there are many ethnic groups that are about equal in prestige and privileges. In other societies, some groups are dominant and others subordinate. We call the subordinate ethnic groups **minority groups**, although in many cases their members actually outnumber those of the dominant groups. Examples are Catholics in Northern Ireland, and Indians and Inuit in Canada. A minority group suffers from discrimination regardless of whether it is large or small in proportion to the dominant community.

Boundaries are often used to control intergroup interactions. In certain cases, however, members of minority groups accept their low status and feel shame (stigma) because of it. In such cases, boundaries still exist in that members can recognize one another, but they may try to "pass" as members of another community.

For example, the Norwegian social anthropologist Harald Eidheim reported that the Lapps of northern Norway try to conceal their ethnic identity, which they treat as a shameful secret.[2] In previous generations, Lapps were all nonliterate nomads, whose living standards were far below those of most Europeans. During the early stages of his study, Eidheim was unable to determine who was and who was not Lappish, except that some people spoke a slightly broken Norwegian. He did notice, however, that many villagers made an effort to show off their Norwegianness by, for

The worst thing about ethnicity is that members of minority groups may even feel ashamed of their identity. Many Lapps in Norway hide the fact that they are Lappish.

Dirk Ketting/Stock, Boston

instance, pretending to know a lot about other parts of the country. He also found that many homemakers took pride in their kitchens and talked for hours about their cleanliness and good housekeeping habits. (Among Norwegians, Lapps are considered dirty.)

Eidheim avoided any mention of ethnic differences until he had shown that he was unbiased and that he knew a great deal about the Lappish population. Gradually the villagers told Eidheim that they spoke Lappish in private; Eidheim then told them that he could speak Lappish too. This led some villagers to admit that they had identity problems. They confessed that they were, after all, a kind of Lapp. Their parents had lived in turf huts and had worn Lappish costumes. They even revealed that they were worried that their low standard of living might be due to their being members of an inferior and stupid race.

The Lapps' poor self-image reflected the poor opinion Norwegians had of them. Eidheim noted that the Lapps were afraid to reveal their identity in relationships with Norwegians, who even consider the use of the Lappish language in their presence as highly improper. Thus two or three Lapps may speak Lappish quietly in a public hallway or staircase, but when a Norwegian approaches they shift languages temporarily. This norm, maintained by both groups, is part of the boundary governing the interaction between the two peoples. The Lapps know perfectly well who is a member of their community. However, because they want to be full members of Norwegian society, they reserve their ethnic identity for life "backstage."

RACIAL GROUPS

Physical anthropologists are scientists who classify the human species into various groups based on certain physical characteristics. These groups are commonly called *races*. (Not all physical characteristics are used to define races. For example, all people with red hair do not make up a race.) Some anthropologists claim that there are several hundred different races, whereas others recognize only a few. In fact, many physical anthropologists do not use the term *race* at all.

People who have certain racial traits in common may or may not constitute an ethnic group sharing a sense of "peoplehood." If they do, we define that community as a **racial group**.

Belonging to a race is a matter of biological heredity, but belonging to a racial group is a matter of social experience. Thus a racial group is merely an ethnic group with a special type of boundary norm; it defines membership on the basis of biological characteristics.

Still, people may be members of a racial group without having inherited the racial traits that are supposed to define membership in the group. Many "black" people are blue-eyed blonds with hardly any Negroid traits, but if their social background is the black community they are full members of the black racial group.

Prejudice and ideology

PREJUDICE

Prejudice means "prejudging." In inter-ethnic relationships it means prejudging *against* individuals on the basis of characteristics believed to be shared by members of the entire ethnic group. Moreover, this prejudging tends to be intense. A prejudiced person looks upon members of the out-group (usually a minority group) with such disfavor that no amount of evidence can persuade him or her to accept them.

Every normal person acquires the basis for certain prejudices against members of other ethnic groups in the course of growing up. It is impossible not to pick up such notions, for they are part of the culture. Through social interaction one learns the normative boundaries that define one's group and how to identify "our people" and "them." At the same time, one learns the relative ranks of "our people" and "them." One learns not only one's

Owen Franken/Stock, Boston

Human rights has become an international concern, particularly for groups who have members throughout the world.

group's position but also the group's views on how it should be ranked.[3] A person does not develop this view independently on the basis of personal experience. Instead, it is the product of the group. A person's own experiences with the out-group may have been delightful. Still, if his or her group defines the out-group as a threat, a loyal member will be expected to maintain a guarded attitude toward out-group members. Prejudice is created and maintained by the group; it is an ideological system that looks down upon the cultural and psychological traits of a rival group.

Prejudice involves making up a **stereotype**—a sort of mental cartoon—that exaggerates the traits of the typical member of the rival group. Perceptions of real members of that group tend to be distorted by the expectation that each person will resemble the stereotype. Thus blacks used to be stereotyped as

unintelligent and irresponsible, with a strong sense of rhythm. The individual may never be given a chance to show his or her unique qualities; instead, he or she is judged entirely on the basis of his or her group membership. Prejudice is based on stereotyping, assuming too much on the basis of too little information. It is unreasonable to assign all the statistical facts about a collectivity—even if they are accurate facts—to each individual member of that collectivity. If a man's ethnic group has a mean income of $10,000 per year, a mean of 2.3 children, and a mean IQ of 102, this hardly proves that *he* has an income of $10,000 per year, 2.3 children, and an IQ of 102. Members of all ethnic groups vary in endless ways.

We all learn prejudice simply because we all learn popular culture. However, some people go on to learn a more sophisticated culture, usually through advanced education.[4]

289

This second, more sophisticated culture offers a far more complex way of viewing human beings and members of other groups. It encourages a more tolerant outlook. People who reach this level of culture set aside simplistic prejudices they learned from popular culture. These stereotypes are never really "lost," however, for even a well-educated person remembers many childish descriptions of minority groups just as he or she remembers the myths that Scots are stingy and that redheads have hot tempers. But he or she does not take such myths seriously or base his or her actions on them. The prejudiced (often uneducated) person, on the other hand, continues to believe them.

RACISM

One of the most influential ideologies of the past few centuries is racism. It arose and was passed along through the popular culture because many people did not know the difference between "races" and "racial groups." Racism can be defined as the belief that ethnic and racial groups are based on genetic similarities rather than on social agreements between people. That is, according to this theory the members of a racial group are bound together biologically rather than by choice.

Boundaries between peoples have existed for thousands of years, but the theory of racism has existed for only about 200 years. It began in northern Europe, and some of the people who developed it were liberal, humane scholars who appreciated the variety of human communities. They never sugested that one national community was better than any other. During this period the peoples of eastern Europe, especially Germany, were entering a period of ethnic awakening. The romantic movement made much of their growing nationalism, portraying humanity as made up of a number of ethnic groups, or "folk," each of which had its own collective "Geist," or spirit. The folk dances, art, history, mythology, and other national traditions were all expressions

of this Geist, which should be enjoyed and preserved. Each Geist was spiritually attached to its soil, its homeland. Its members were bound together by common ancestry, or "blood." One could find one's own identity only by fully participating in one's ancestral community. Each folk Geist was a single collective mind emerging into consciousness—a real, living being.

This racist theory confused a number of different ideas. It mixed together "race," "culture," "language," "homeland," and "group spirit." The implication was that one's membership in a particular group was determined by one's genetic makeup, not by the socialization process. The theory romanticized group membership as mystical and wonderful. Still, the theory was not necessarily harmful, for it did not imply that one folk was better than another or that one group should dominate another.

The transformation of racist theory into belief in the natural superiority of the German people came later, and with it came the conflicts leading up to World War II. The anti-Semitic composer Richard Wagner glorified the folk myths of the "Nordic race" in his operas, which inspired nationalists to believe that the Germanic "folk" were genetically equipped for dominance. Writers like Houston S. Chamberlain and Madison Grant urged that the "great" race not be mixed with inferior races—people who were fit only to be slaves.[5] Such ideas were very attractive to colonialists who wanted to justify aggression against "inferior races." As Ashley Montagu has noted in the title of one of his books, racist theory may be one of man's most dangerous myths.[6]

Let us repeat: A *race* is an objective classification based on skull measurements, blood types, endocrine secretions, hair texture, and the like. A *group*, on the other hand, has boundaries. Members can identify each other and have a sense of belonging together. However, groups *may* use a variety of different standards to define their boundaries—for example, religious affiliation, native language, or even physical traits such as shape of the head, hair texture, and skin color. Though a race does not always constitute a group, a group may form on the basis of easily seen racial similarities. Social boundaries may be defined on any basis people choose, and the boundaries will be as real as people decide they are. If people decide that the basis for full membership in their group should be vegetarianism or baptism or circumcision or even Nordic ancestry, then any of those standards can become the boundary norm.

However, racists held that social boundaries were natural, not merely social. Something deep in the genetic system tied people together as a "folk" and gave them a spiritual attachment to their native land and a feeling for a certain language and culture. One could not escape one's racial-social identity. Indeed, one could find personal identity only through the culture to which one was biologically tied. Perhaps some people enjoyed a warm sense of belonging when they turned this idea over in their minds. But others had reason to feel otherwise, for the theory implied that psychological qualities are necessarily linked with physical traits and that they can never change. The "inferior" ethnic group must remain inferior forever.

Racist theory is far less widely accepted today than in the past. However, intergroup conflicts did not begin with racism and will not end with it. Groups can hate each other for all sorts of reasons that do not refer to hereditary qualities. You and I may agree that our enemies, the Xrplmrqvtsp community, have bad manners, false gods, an unpronounceable language, clumsy art, animal-like sexual behavior, and halitosis without attributing any of these qualities to their genes. We may be uncharitable, but we are not racist for feeling this way. Only if we explain their behavior in terms of *hereditary qualities common to their breeding population* are we racists.

Although few Canadians today would admit to racist ideas, there is evidence that such ideas still play a part in Canadian society. Ronald D. Lambert and James E. Curtis have recently compared the responses of Québécois and English-Canadian communities in a survey on multicultural attitudes.[7] They found that the Québécois respondents tended to select hypothetical immigrants on the basis of cultural heritage; presumably, they preferred immigrants whose traditions were compatible with French-Canadian culture. English-Canadian respondents, on the other hand, more frequently selected immigrants according to color of skin; the groups that they most often excluded were all non-white.

NATIONALISM

Social scientists agree that social boundaries are arbitrary conventions. But this does not answer the question of why group feeling runs high in some historical periods. For example, nationality simply was not important in the Middle Ages or in the Roman Empire, but it became important in Europe in modern times. Will tribalism, religious conflict, and nationalism become unimportant in the near future? If so, why?

Any answer to these questions requires a theory that will account for variations in the importance of ethnic-group membership. Karl Deutsch has proposed such a theory. He argues that modernization almost always increases ethnic consciousness (nationalism) and leads to demands for national autonomy. He uses the term *mobilization* to refer to periods of rapid modernization.[8]

Mobilization consists of increased communication. In a peasant community, most interaction is limited to contacts between lifelong friends. Because peasants are not mobile, their social network is small and is composed of people they know well. They may worry about drought, bugs, and disease, but they do not have to worry about their relationships with other human beings. Modernization breaks up this social network and makes it necessary to interact with strangers. Peasants

When nationalism leads to fights for control of a particular homeland, some group is usually left homeless. This camp is the only home remaining for Arab Palestinian refugees, who have still not been resettled since Israel was founded as a Jewish state in 1948.

go to sell their crops in the market and must bargain with people who may be untrustworthy. They learn to read newspapers written by people with strange and perhaps dangerous ideas. They move to town and see shop windows full of objects whose value they don't know. They register to vote and must choose which stranger to vote for.

These are all aspects of modernization. They move a person into a larger social network in which he or she must make fateful decisions in a context of uncertainty. The peasant does not know whom to trust, for it is necessary to communicate with strangers, both face to face and through mass media.

Gone are the days when his or her dealings were only with people he or she knew.

Deutsch suggests that it is in just this situation that people try to reconstruct their familiar world. If they do not know whom to trust, they tend to choose people who are most similar to themselves. They seek out and magnify all the things they have in common, telling themselves that they have found new people who resemble those whom they have always known. Similar dialect, similar cooking, similar religion, similar folklore become the basis for solidarity. An ersatz community is built up out of desperation in an alien world. People may seek to live and work with others of their own ethnic group; they may vote for members of their "own people"; and they may demand political autonomy for their group. This is nationalism, or ethnic-group patriotism. The nationalistic fights of the Balkan region are the classic examples of this pattern. The separatist movements within India, Belgium, Canada, and Nigeria also fit this pattern, and so does black nationalism in the United States. Whenever a group's we-feeling is built up, as happens in nationalism, conflicts with other groups become more likely.

It is obvious that more people will be uprooted in the future and that even the most remote village will be reached by communications from the outside world. All this mobilization will be unsettling and will lead to greater emphasis on ethnicity and nationality. On the other hand, other forces will tend to *integrate* groups into their wider social environment. These forces of integration sometimes have a stronger effect than mobilization itself. People may find it possible to gain some control over their social situation through the political process and other forms of association such as trade unions and schools. Thus they may set up business and social connections beyond the limits of their ethnic community, so that any nationalistic appeal may strike them as chauvinistic. Such developments lead toward assimilation and reduce the importance of ethnic affiliations. In most countries, however, mobilization will probably occur more rapidly than integration. In the future, nationalism will probably flare up more and more often, causing many nations to split into smaller regional units.

A criticism of Deutsch

Before leaving our discussion of nationalism, we should note that it is possible to agree with Deutsch's prediction of future nationalistic upheavals while disagreeing with his explanation of them. Indeed, many Canadian sociologists take issue with Deutsch's account of nationalism, as it applies both to Quebec's "Quiet Revolution" and subsequent separa-

tism, and to the sporadic upsurges of nationalism in English Canada. These sociologists claim that Deutsch fails to take into account the role played in the growth of nationalism by economic and political exploitation. A group may become nationalistic and enter into conflict with another group for other reasons besides increased "mobilization." Usually, a nationalistic group occupies a lower position than seems fair in the ethnic, religious, or linguistic stratification system. According to this view, nationalistic movements have their origin in oppression, and end only when justice is attained.

Patterns of group interaction

In this section I am going to introduce a classification system of *typology*. My typology of ethnic relations consists of three outcomes that might result when two or more ethnic groups come into contact with each other. They are (1) ethnic stratification, in which the groups form a hierarchy of dominance, as in the caste societies and colonial regimes (e.g., South Africa); (2) ethnic pluralism in which the groups become equal and live together on good terms, neither dominating the other (e.g., Switzerland); and (3) integration, in which equality is achieved by reducing the separation between the groups and encouraging them to participate in the same activities (e.g., Mexico). Let's discuss each of these possible outcomes in turn.

ETHNIC STRATIFICATION

Ethnic stratification exists when two or more ethnic communities in an area have regular relationships of dominance and subordination that all members understand. The groups may depend on each other in some ways. The dominant group fares better in these transactions than the subordinate group. Two familiar examples are colonialism and segregation.

Colonialism

For several hundred years, European nations have dominated the rest of the world. This began when Columbus planted the Spanish flag on the soil of the New World, claiming the land for Spain. Before long almost every patch of territory around the globe had been "claimed" by one European monarch or another. Traders, settlers, and colonial administrators went to every corner of the world to bring "civilization" to the natives. Only in recent years have native peoples begun to win back the right to manage their own affairs. But until they won their independence and founded the many new nations of the world, they were treated as subordinates by the colonizers from Europe.

Colonialism was the most widespread system of ethnic stratification. As we have seen, the Europeans justified their exploitation of nonwhite natives in terms of racism. The colonizers considered themselves superior because of their biological traits and therefore felt no guilt about controlling and oppressing countless brown or black "subjects" in Africa, Asia, or America. The effect was to destroy the way of life of the colonized groups. Most tribes of Canadian Indians and Inuits are no longer societies, for example, but colonized minorities without much social organization of their own.

Segregation and discrimination

Colonialism is not the only form of ethnic stratification. Far more common is a pattern in which two or more ethnic groups live in the same area but have unequal status. Certain groups have minority status while others are in dominant positions. Indeed, in heterogeneous societies this pattern is more common than equality. The dominant group maintains its advantage through segregation and discrimination.

Segregation is the practice of forcing minority group members to work or live in separate areas whenever possible and to use facilities separate from those used by the dominant group. Whites in the United States used segregation as a way of maintaining distance between themselves and blacks, though the courts have ruled it illegal. Segregation in South Africa, called *apartheid*, is still an official policy. Peter Carstens has pointed out parallels between the South African pattern of segregation and the Canadian system which provides "reserves" for Indians to live on. Segregation can result from the exclusiveness of one or more ethnic groups. Usually the dominant group enforces segregation, either through laws or through informal agreements. Discrimination is the process by which the dominant group informally deprives the minority group of equal access to privileges and opportunities—good jobs, seating in restaurants, membership in clubs and the like.

Sometimes the minority group prefers a policy of self-segregation. Its members choose to live and work in a certain area simply because other members of the same ethnic community live and work there. Such areas in cities may be considered "ghettos" if people live there out of economic or political necessity and "neighborhoods" if people live there voluntarily. The Hutterites voluntarily live on rural communes in the prairies, segregated from the other Canadians around them.

When segregation is carried to an extreme, the result is partition, in which various ethnic groups live in separate areas that are no longer parts of the same country. When nationalism divides various ethnic communities in a single nation, some members of one or all of the groups often propose partition as a solution. This does not necessarily end the conflict between the groups, however. For example, the partition of Palestine led to the creation of the state of Israel but did not end the tension between Israel and its Arab neighbors. The partition of Ireland into Protestant and Catholic regions did not end the religious conflict in Ulster. The partition of Canada into two separate states would have created an independent Quebec, with results that are, even now, debatable.

When partition occurs, the ethnic-group

members who are located in the area claimed by the other group may find themselves in an unfavorable position. For example, the Arabs living in what became Israel do not have the same status as Jewish Israeli citizens. Similarly, Catholics living in Northern Ireland are at a disadvantage compared to Protestants. Their militant members, the Irish Republican Army, turned to terrorism in an attempt to change this situation. Though English Canadians in Quebec have not been particularly threatened by the separatist movement, many of them have left Quebec because they did not like the changes they saw.

Expulsion is often used by new regimes to put down dissent. The minority group members are simply sent to another country. Many Chinese people were more or less expelled by the Vietnamese; they became known as the "boat people" when most of them were refused entry by Malaysia. Idi Amin expelled all Asians from Uganda.

Expulsion is a severe way of treating minorities, but a far worse policy of annihilation has sometimes been pursued. **Annihilation** occurs when one ethnic community simply attacks another and destroys its entire population. Many American Indians were annihilated during the opening of the West. Over four million Jews were annihilated by Germany during World War II. It is sad to realize that *genocide*, or the planned annihilation of whole peoples, is not a rare outcome of ethnic stratification.

ETHNIC PLURALISM

The second category of our typology is ethnic pluralism. This is the situation that exists when two or more ethnic groups live side by side with neither group trying to dominate the other. Each community is politically, economically, and culturally distinct from the other. The groups do not interact to any great extent. The boundary norms are well understood and discourage group relations in most matters. Members of the different groups do not try very hard to communicate across the gap

between them but are satisfied to consider each other strangers. You can think of a plural society as two or more quite separate communication networks in the same region.

Societies that are characterized by ethnic pluralism are attractive in many ways. After all, ethnic pluralism is the basis of cultural diversity. Each ethnic community keeps its own traditions, and these special ways of life enrich the lives of their members. Those who

Ethnic pluralism can greatly enrich a society.

Ontario Ministry of Industry and Tourism.

belong to a community with its own folklore and rituals are in possession of symbols that enhance experience. Who would want to blend all these traditions into a single, unified culture? Not I. Exploring a foreign country is exciting simply because it is foreign. Diversity is enriching.

Canada is, or at least tries to be, a plural society—a "mosaic." Canadians often say that they want their society to be not a "melting pot" but a "salad bowl." This has not always been the Canadian ideal. Until a decade or two ago, there was widespread pressure on all ethnic groups to adopt Anglo-Canadian ways. French-Canadians, of course, did not want that to happen. The Canadian government today supports a policy of *multiculturalism*; it encourages diversity whenever possible, helping groups to maintain their own identities and traditions.

Switzerland and India, in their own ways, are also plural societies, though their situations are quite different from Canada's. The best historical examples of pluralism occurred in Far Eastern societies before colonial rule. Wolfram Eberhard has described the Orient in general, and medieval China in particular, as a series of "layers" of peoples. These groups lived in the same area but had separate cultures.[9] Sometimes several groups were unable to speak to one another because of language differences, yet they lived in the same towns for generations. Each community had its own norms and its own legal system. Though all the Chinese were subjects of the emperor, the only authorities that most people knew about were the leaders of their separate communities.

These communities were sometimes spread over a large area. For example, a trading group may have had members living in separate communities in every large town throughout the Far East. They would visit one another to find brides and keep in touch, even though they were living among aliens. Every person's social world was centered in his or her "layer,"

which was usually an ascriptive community. The Chinese peasants did not know that they were part of the Chinese empire. They did know that they were part of their layer—their "people." The layers were not integrated into a nation. They were so separate that members of one layer would be quite unfamiliar with the jokes, songs, or even languages of their neighbors.

If a country is interested in pursuing a policy of ethnic pluralism (and Canada says it is), it will support the various groups' efforts to keep up their own institutions and traditions. It will provide schooling in ethnic languages instead of just in one or two national languages. It will support ethnic newspapers, churches, businesses, and festivals. It will give

Toronto's Caravan is one of the many multicultural events in contemporary Canada. Latvian-Canadians perform on an ancient instrument, the "kokle".

Ontario Science Centre

people time off from work to celebrate their group's special holidays, while taking care not to favor one ethnic group more than the others. It will encourage each group's development of institutional completeness.

Institutional completeness

In a plural society, not all ethnic groups maintain their identity. Raymond Breton has pointed out that whether a group maintains its boundaries depends mostly on the extent of its **institutional completeness**.[10] Some ethnic groups have a complete set of special institutions that serve their own members. They have their own banks, radio stations, newspapers, real estate offices, travel agencies, shops, clinics, resort hotels, and so on. Such groups are "institutionally complete." Their members can get along quite nicely dealing almost exclusively with one another. They may not have to understand any language but their own to meet all their ordinary daily needs.

Clearly, a community that is relatively complete institutionally is more likely to endure than one that is not. In Canada, for example, the Ukrainian community is generally far more institutionally complete than the German community. Instead of going to a German church and reading German newspapers, most newcomers from Austria or Germany have quickly switched to English or, less often, to French. They have not made any special attempt to group together or to preserve their traditions. There are actually a great many Canadians of German origin; their presence is not very obvious because they have generally merged quickly into the dominant culture.

As we shall discuss later, it is not at all clear whether most ethnic groups gain more than they lose from institutional completeness. The advantage of working in their own communities and speaking their own languages may be offset by a lack of education and job opportunities. The careers that offer the most wealth and prestige are found in the institu-

tions that serve the *wider* Canadian society, such as corporations, universities, major law firms, and hospitals.

This dilemma points to a built-in, or structural, problem with ethnic pluralism. With true ethnic pluralism, the various ethnic communities in a region are *equal*. When they are *unequal*, the region does not have ethnic pluralism, but ethnic stratification. Yet clearly, different ethnic communities cannot all maintain completely separate and equal economic structures when the best jobs are in international corporations, government agencies, and other huge organizations. A young, talented Chinese person will probably prefer a career in one of these organizations to selling groceries or insurance policies in Chinatown. But once he or she joins a large institution, structural integration has begun and other changes will soon follow. Canada's policy of multiculturalism may be unrealistic in its goal of equality for different ethnic groups. Canadian society may have to choose between ethnic stratification on the one hand and integration on the other.

INTEGRATION

Integration is the opposite of ethnic pluralism. In an integrated society, different ethnic groups participate fully in the same activities. Instead of maintaining institutional completeness, they all take part in the same institutions on an equal basis. Instead of separate rules for each community, a single set of rules applies to all. Rather than clear-cut memberships, the groups have weak boundaries, with many marginal members and many chances for members to associate with people in other groups. Instead of segregating itself from other groups and discriminating in favor of its own members, each group shares its culture with anyone who wants to participate. Each group may adopt aspects of other cultural traditions in turn.

The process by which a group integrates

into the dominant culture is called assimilation. Just as there is a price to be paid for cultural pluralism, assimilation can be costly. When a group assimilates, it gives up its distinctive life style, adopts the culture of the larger society, and eventually loses its identity as a separate community. It might contribute some aspects of its own culture to the larger culture; such traditions as the Ukrainian custom of painting Easter eggs have been adopted by other Canadians. However, such contributions are small consolations to a group in comparison to the traditions it is likely to lose by assimilating. The choice between integration and cultural pluralism is a difficult one. However, in theory, one could hope for integration of ethnic groups into the same economic structures, while avoiding the assimilation of their cultures.

Integration has two different aspects: structural and cultural. *Structural integration* refers to the full participation of various groups in the dominant set of institutions, such as schools, banks, and churches. *Cultural integration* refers to the adoption by various groups of the dominant ideas, traditions, languages, life styles, values, and religions. It is cultural integration that most ethnic group members would prefer to avoid. Many would favor structural integration if it were not accompanied, as it generally is, by cultural integration. Usually, of course, the minority groups adopt the culture of the dominant group. However, cultural integration can travel, to a limited extent, in both directions: Many Canadians regularly enjoy Italian pizza or Middle-Eastern fallafels for their lunch.

In a society that has been integrated for a very long time, enough inter-marriage has taken place to produce a great deal of physical similarity among members of the whole society. This blending of racial types through long interbreeding is called amalgamation. Amalgamation has taken place to some extent in Hawaii, where whites, Hawaiians, and Asians have intermarried for a long time. Many Hawaiian people have some physical traits that are characteristic of all three original populations.

Reactions of minority groups to dominance

People who are mistreated may react in many different ways, depending on the situation and on their beliefs, values, and ideologies. In general, the reactions of minority groups can be classified into three patterns: (1) passivity and withdrawal, (2) nonviolent resistance, and (3) violent resistance.

PASSIVITY AND WITHDRAWAL

When a dominant group is far more powerful than, and is oppressive toward, a minority, the minority group must hide any tendency of resistance and must seem to accept whatever the oppressor says or does. As we saw earlier, the Lapps of Norway were unable to openly express their anger toward the Norwegians. Many other native peoples have had to conceal their hostility toward their European rulers, particularly during the colonial period before nationalistic movements began. At such times, the minority group turns to its own members in privacy for mutual support. Members avoid the dominant group whenever possible. In accordance with fixed social rules, they appear humble before the dominant group.

Such humility is hard on the self-esteem of minority group members. They may lose confidence in themselves because of their low status and their inward-directed anger. Passivity, dull acceptance, and withdrawal are not healthy responses, but they may be the only responses possible. Withdrawal can take many forms, including alcoholism, lack of ambition, and a variety of other behaviors. Many of Canada's native peoples still find few alternatives to a passive acceptance of the dominant white group. This view is unfortunately not unrealistic; even today, few opportunities exist for Indian and Inuit organizations to influence the lives of their people.

NONVIOLENT RESISTANCE

When a minority group resists its oppressor, the resistance sometimes takes the form of a peaceful appeal to the oppressor's conscience. This type of demonstration was the great innovation of Mahatma Gandhi, the barefoot leader who used non-violent protest to free India from the British. In the United States, Martin Luther King adopted the same methods for the black civil rights movement.

Non-violent resistance requires great self-discipline. Participants may have to steel themselves to accept blows without fighting back. Non-violent protesters demonstrate that they do not hate their oppressors and will not fight them, but that they will no longer cooperate in their own oppression. They may sit down passively and wait to be jailed. Often such quiet action makes the oppressors ashamed of their violence.

VIOLENT RESISTANCE

Finally, minority groups sometimes react to their oppressors with violence. This violence may take the form of collective riots and armed rebellion or individual antisocial behavior such as crime.

Frantz Fanon, a black psychiatrist, worked with his Algerian countrymen to win independence from France. He believed that the

Ireland has been the scene of an ongoing violent conflict that has proven very difficult to end because of the overlapping religious and nationalistic conflicts.

Jim Anderson/Woodfin Camp

personalities of oppressed peoples were so damaged by the treatment they had received that only through violence could they regain any psychological strength. Psychologists who are familiar with other minority groups have noted that many forms of mental illness and personality disorders are direct results of longtime discrimination. The need to cope with anger and channel it in a healthy way is one of the daily emotional problems that minority people have to face. Not all have to become aggressive, fortunately, but when aggression does occur it is usually due to the smoldering resentment created by deprivation and discrimination. The victims of this anger are not always members of the dominant group but are often whoever happens to be nearby at the moment—even other members of the minority group.

Fortunately for Canada, violent resistance has seldom featured in relations between various ethnic communities. There have, of course, been exceptions to this: Louis Riel led two Métis rebellions; there are occasional violent outbreaks by the Sons of Freedom, a sect of the Doukhobors; and there have been incidents of terrorism in Quebec, most prominently in 1970. Normally, however, protests in Canada are carried out through orderly, political means. Let us turn, then, to a consideration of the ethnic composition of Canada's population and to the relations among Canada's ethnic communities.

Ethnic groups in Canada

We can group the Canadian population into three broad categories: (1) the native people, Indians and Inuit, who were here when the first Europeans arrived; (2) the two "charter groups," French and British, whose relations came to be organized politically under the British North America Act; and (3) the other immigrant groups that have entered Canada from all parts of the globe.

NATIVE PEOPLES

When Columbus arrived, there were probably between one and three million native people living in North America. Perhaps 200,000 of them lived in the area that is now Canada. As a result of European settlement, these Indians were crowded out of their land, exposed to diseases for which they had no immunity, and were often involved in violent confrontations with the whites. Eventually, the Indian population declined so greatly that 50 years ago their numbers were fewer than before the arrival of the white man.[11] However, since the 1930s, their population has gradually increased. In 1971, the census reported over 300,000 Canadian Indians and Inuit, constituting a little more than 1 percent of the Canadian population.[12] Of these, about one-third live on reserves and belong to one of the 550 native bands that are recognized by the government. In eastern Canada, each band lives on a separate reserve, while in western Canada several bands may share a reserve. Each band is administered by an agency and is "registered", or acknowledged to have certain land rights as a result of treaty.

About half of the Indians in Canada are registered and half are non-registered. There is also a large but undetermined population of Métis in Canada. The Métis are of partly Indian ancestry; their white ancestors were usually French. They do not ordinarily live on reserves, nor do they have any land rights recognized by treaty.

About 25 percent of Canada's Indian population lives in Ontario, about 20 percent in British Columbia, and the rest are distributed throughout the country. Actually, statistics concerning Indians are not very accurate. Some Indians, especially those in cities, try to pass as non-Indians. Also, some Indian families move six or eight times a year. Because Indians, unlike other ethnic groups, seldom occupy particular regions of a city, their numbers are hard to determine and they are usually inconspicuous as a group.[13]

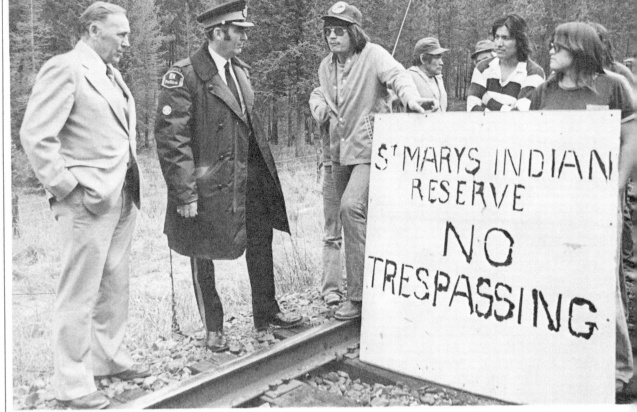

As Indians become more aware of their collective identity, they are likely to make more demands on Canadian society.

By almost any standard, the native people of Canada are more disadvantaged than any other ethnic minority. Partly because schools are regarded as a means of white assimilation, Indian parents often do not encourage their children to become educated. This helps to perpetuate a number of other economic and social problems. Far more than half of the Indian population lives in poverty.[14] Unemployment rates are sometimes three times greater for Indians than for the total Canadian labor force.[15] Over 80 percent of Indian homes are overcrowded; that is, the number of people in the house exceeds the number of rooms. All of these factors have detrimental effects upon physical health and social life. Until the age of 35, Indians have much higher death rates than the general population.[16] The crime rate among Indians is also extremely high. In part, the high crime rate may be due to a number of social problems that affect Indians. A high rate of alcoholism is a large factor in the Indian crime rate; as many as one Indian in five may be an alcoholic.[17]

The serious social problems facing Indians today can only be understood in a historical context. The cultural autonomy of Indian societies was continually blocked by government policies since the earliest days of European settlement. Indians were not even allowed to vote in Canada until 1960, and still have little chance to administer their own affairs. The laws regulating their society were imposed upon them by outsiders. Confused government policies have pursued both assimilation and Indian cultural autonomy; the result has been a sorry record of administrative bungling, and the frequent development of passivity and dependence by Canadian Indians.

In the past few years, a new political movement has arisen to unite Indian leadership and propose reforms. New leaders are urging the government to turn over the Bureau of Indian Affairs to Indian control. They want to make Indians responsible for their own trust funds, to seat Indians on a claims commission to clear up unsettled land claims, and to develop reserve lands by promoting native industries.[18]

The Inuit are defined as a tribe of Indians and are controlled under the Indian Act. Their standard of living has increased in recent years, but relative to that of the Kabloonas (whites) it is still very low. Before the fur trade period, the Inuit were nomadic, hunting animals wherever they roamed. After trading posts were established, the Inuit frequently settled near them in small communities of between 300 and 500 people.[19]

The social life of the Arctic has been greatly affected by the presence of the military and of the government, which has made the native people its wards. Housing standards have improved, though they are still far below those of Canada as a whole. Famine is no longer likely, and the death rate has been reduced; as a result the population of Canadian Inuit, which numbered 8000 in 1948, has almost doubled since then. The region is overpopulated now relative to the wildlife, so it is no longer possible for the Inuit to return to their former way of life.

Today only a minority of Inuit are full-time hunters and trappers. The others work for wages, sell handicrafts, or live on public support. Less than one-quarter of Canadian Inuit are fully employed; most of these are government laborers. They generally live in permanent settlements of pre-fab housing, using electricity and oil heating.

Several organizations, such as the Canadian Welfare Council, are trying to find young Inuit with leadership ability who can encourage political participation and autonomy. There is no tradition of strong leadership among the Inuit, however, and this is a real problem today.

FRENCH CANADIANS

The successful European colonization of Canada began with the exploration and settlement of New France. Because it was a French colony, its system of land distribution and its social structure were similar to those of France. Land was held by an aristocratic class of seigneurs, or lords, while agriculture was the responsibility of tenant-farmers. While most settlers earned their living by agriculture, the French were also extensively involved in fur trapping, trading, and fishing.

In the seventeenth century, France's North American empire extended from Hudson's Bay through the Ohio valley and the Louisiana territory to New Orleans. The boundaries of this large, unwieldy area were in a constant state of flux as French outposts clashed with Indian nations and the expanding British and Spanish colonies. The land in New France was not as arable as originally hoped and its importance was rapidly surpassed by the ascendency of the fur trade. Furs were the basis of New France's wealth and reinforced the power of the merchants, government officials, seigneurs, and of the clergy which allowed these groups to dominate the colonial society.

Territorial disputes between New France and the more heavily populated English colonies continued throughout the seventeenth and eighteenth centuries. They resulted in a series of wars which culminated in 1759 at the Battle of the Plains of Abraham where Wolfe's victory secured New France for the British crown. The British were then faced with the prospect of integrating a large French population with a well established English society and culture within their North American empire.

Britain's initial response to the Canadiens was to emphasize a policy of assimilation as embodied in the Proclamation of 1763.[20] Assimilation, however, threatened the interests and power of the Canadien elite, namely the clergy and seigneurs. As relations between

UPI

In 1976, English Canadians were stunned by the victory of the Parti Québécois in Quebec, led by René Levesque.

Britain and her American colonies became more strained, the importance of not alienating the Canadiens and their leaders also increased. The British government recognized this fact and passed the Quebec Act of 1774. This Act reversed the Proclamation of 1763 and committed the British to support the seigneural system of land ownership, the French civil law, and the claims of the Roman Catholic Church.[21]

Britain's decision to maintain the social system of the old French regime through the Quebec Act reinforced traditional French-Canadian society and militated against social reforms well into the 19th century. For example, while the seigneural system diminished in its effectiveness, it still did not end until 1850.

Through the Quebec Act, the British chose to support the traditional claims of the Cath-olic Church in French Canada. The Church in French Canada was particularly conservative; even in France, the Catholic Church was feeling the impact of the Age of Enlightenment and the French Revolution. The Church in French Canada was given the power to administrate all francophone education in Quebec, a situation that continued until the Quiet Revolution of the 1960s.

A few British settlers, mostly entrepreneurs from New England, moved to Quebec in the wake of the Conquest. However, it was not until the American Revolution that thousands of United Empire Loyalists immigrated to Quebec. At this point, the rivalry for numerical dominance between the French- and English-speaking populations intensified. The Loyalists formed the basis of the anglophone Canadian population, one that steadily increased with subsequent immigration.

303

The French Canadians maintained their numbers through an extremely high birthrate which was motivated by the need of a primarily rural population for large families. However, the French Canadians were subject to a high rate of emigration; up to one-quarter of the young people of Quebec moved away.[22] Most moved to the United States, especially New England, where they quickly assimilated into American society and never returned to Quebec.

If those French Canadians had instead moved westward, they might have been able to secure the Canadian west as francophone provinces. This, however, did not occur, and in the 1860s only 10 percent of the population in what became Manitoba was French-speaking. These were the Métis who, led by Louis Riel, fought for the recognition and protection of their language and culture in the Red River Rebellion (1869-1870) and the North-West Rebellion (1885). The Métis were defeated and within a generation the western francophones were denied the kind of schooling they sought for their children. It became clear that western Canada was to be dominated by anglophones.

Thus for much of its history Canada has been bicultural—French and British. Almost the whole of its population has belonged to one or the other of these categories, and political conflicts have frequently resulted from tensions between them. The British influence was strongest in Ontario and the other territories that became western provinces after Confederation. Many of the British settlers in Ontario were Orangemen—fiercely anti-Catholic Protestants, whose parades and rhetoric stirred up inter-group tensions. Nevertheless, the sensitive equilibrium between the two groups was maintained for a relatively long time, and this prevented any dramatic political changes from taking place.

In the past several decades, however, a number of factors have disrupted that equilibrium. Francophones have increasingly come to view their language and culture as endangered. For one thing, the birthrate of French Cana-

dians dropped markedly, so they could no longer hope to hold their own through the "revenge of the cradle." Moreover, the many immigrants from other language groups who came to Canada almost always adopted English as their working language, even in Quebec. Francophones in other provinces became scattered and greatly outnumbered, increasingly unable to prevent their children from being assimilated by English Canada. Many more French than English Canadians became bilingual; as a result, the francophones became even more vulnerable to assimilationist influences. The decline in the proportion of francophones in the Canadian population began to accelerate and upset the balance that had been maintained between the two groups over several generations.

At the same time, anglophones were migrating into Quebec to fill new jobs that required specialized skills. Until recently, francophones could only receive inferior educations. Even when their educational levels became equal, however, francophones were discriminated against in the world of business. Statistics reveal that francophones have been paid inferior incomes and denied good jobs, regardless of educational level.[23]

For a number of years, the Quebec government was under the leadership of Maurice Duplessis's *Union Nationale*, a conservative party that appealed to rural francophone voters and advocated provincial rights. However, this party was also indicted by its opponents for its use of physical coercion to maintain its influence. After Duplessis's death in 1959, reformist groups became more vocal and persistent. A Liberal government, led by Jean Lesage, was elected in 1960 on a platform promising educational reforms and more government jobs for francophones. The Quiet Revolution, using the slogan *maîtres chez nous* (masters in our own house), began with Lesage's election.

The constitutional changes sought by Lesage failed to meet the more radical demands of those Québécois who advocated an independent Quebec. The separatist movement gained increasing credibility and support during the 1960s. In 1968 the numerous separatist parties and associations merged to form the *Parti Québécois* which was an important political force from its inception. It promised to protect French language and culture and to work towards a negotiated independence.

The *Front de Libération du Québec* (FLQ) was an active terrorist organization, impatient with the conventional political process. It initiated a series of violent actions in the early 1960s that culminated with the October crisis of 1970. The federal government responded to the October crisis with repressive actions that violated the civil liberties of many Québécois. Most of English Canada supported the government's reaction, and this attitude alienated the francophones even more.

In 1974, Quebec passed the controversial Bill 22, which regulates the education of children in Quebec whose native language is not English. About 90 percent of new immigrants to Quebec had previously chosen to educate their children in English-language schools. Bill 22 forced children to switch to French schools unless they could speak English well by the age of six. Many anglophone Montrealers were outraged by this law, which will certainly reverse the trend of anglophone assimilation in Quebec.

Surprising as it was, Bill 22 was only the beginning of social change in Quebec. The 1976 provincial election was won by René Levesque's Parti Québécois, which immediately introduced legislation to require English businesses to use French as their working language. Levesque promised Quebec's voters a referendum to determine whether to commence negotiations that would ultimately lead to separation from Canada. The referendum was held in 1980. Though the results were very close, the proposal was rejected. There is now a danger that the population of Quebec is dramatically split in two. Clearly, Quebec's position within Canada is far from settled.

The effect of Quebec's Quiet Revolution

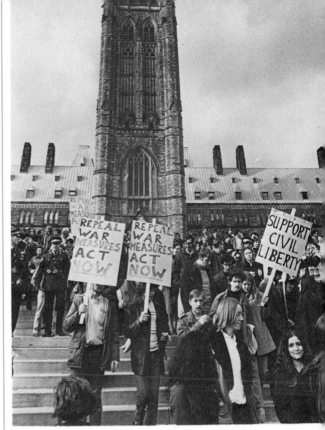

CP Photo

Many French Canadians became bitter when the Canadian government invoked the War Measures Act during the October crisis of 1970.

has been to increase the cohesiveness of Quebec's francophone population and, at the same time, to increase the alienation of French Canadians outside of Quebec. French-Canadian language and culture may well prove unable to survive outside of Quebec; assimilation is likely to continue or even increase, so that eventually English will be used exclusively throughout the rest of Canada.[24] Francophones outside of Quebec have come to see their own cultural needs as separate from those of the Québécois. Local francophone groups have formed to press for political rights within their own provinces; for example, the "Franco-Ontarians" have begun to view themselves as a politically distinct population.[25]

Whether they act as one group or as many in relation to the anglophone community,

French Canadians all face a new political reality in Canada: the growth of multiculturalism. Canada used to possess a dual society, but it is now composed of many cultural groups, all with different traditions and languages. The two "charter" groups have always assumed the predominance of their ways of life. No other community has had sufficient numbers to claim equal rights for its language and culture. But if large-scale immigration continues and the francophone population declines, Canada, at some distant point in the future, may come to regard French as simply one of many minority languages spoken in Canada, deserving no special consideration. Let us look then at some of the other ethnic groups that compose Canadian society.

OTHER ETHNIC GROUPS IN CANADA

In 1971, the Canadian census reported that over 15 percent of the population had been born in other countries. Although this reflects considerable recent immigration, 1971 was by no means a peak period of growth. In 1931, the foreign-born and their children constituted 46 percent, or almost half, of the population.[26] From Confederation until 1895, immigration was open to all; during this period a great many people came to Canada, especially from Eastern Europe. Selective immigration began in 1896 and continued until World War I. Between the wars, fewer people entered Canada, but after World War II a new upsurge in immigration took place.

Most ethnic groups immigrated to Canada in "waves." Each group generally entered Canada during a particular period of history when, for a variety of reasons, a large segment of its population was pressured to leave its native country. A great wave of Jewish immigration began in the 1870s. During this decade, the Jewish population of Canada more than doubled, as Russian Jews fled from the pogroms. Because they had lived in isolated villages in Eastern Europe, this group main-

tained a strongly orthodox culture quite different from that of sophisticated Western European Jews.

The Jews from Eastern Europe took jobs as unskilled tradesmen or small businessmen, threatening the status of previously settled North American workers. As a result, these Jews became early victims of anti-Semitism in North America. During the 1920s and 1930s, anti-Semitism was at its peak. Jews were either entirely excluded from important public institutions or admitted under a quota system. Since World War II, anti-Semitism has greatly declined, no doubt as a response to the holocaust of Nazi persecution and genocide. Jews are readily accepted as members by most institutions. Their general level of education and income is considerably above the Canadian average.

While the Jews mostly settled in cities like Montreal and Toronto, the Ukrainians mostly settled on farms in the prairies. As the Canadian Pacific Railway was built, the newly opened west began to require workers; blocs of free land, confiscated from the Indians and Métis, were given to European immigrants as an inducement to settle the west. This was not easy to do. Although Clifton Sifton, then Minister of the Interior, made extravagant promises to them, many immigrants, such as the Russian Doukhobors, found that local Canadian governments were inhospitable to their religious beliefs.

Many immigrants were poorly prepared to cope with the harsh climate and rugged landscape of the west; as a result, many of them left Canada. Among the more successful groups were the Poles and Ukrainians, some 170,000 of whom immigrated from Eastern European villages to prairie settlements in the 1890s. They developed a high level of institutional completeness, and organized a variety of voluntary associations around their churches.[27]

The Asians were first admitted to Canada to work on the construction of the Canadian Pacific Railway. The Chinese were brought in

The Vietnamese "Boat People" are one of the most recent refugee groups to arrive in Canada.

first, and many of them left work on the railroad to settle in a scattered pattern throughout Canada. After the railroad construction was completed, Chinese immigration was effectively stopped. British Columbia imposed a "head tax" of 50 dollars on each new Chinese immigrant. The tax was increased regularly until 1923, when the Chinese Immigration Act was passed to exclude further Chinese entry.

Japanese immigrants began arriving in Canada in large numbers after Chinese immigration tapered off. The Japanese mostly worked as railroad, cannery, and logging camp laborers, but gradually moved into agriculture, in which they were highly successful. In 1942, shocked by Pearl Harbor, Canadians expected a Japanese invasion. Japanese Canadians were forced to sell their farms quickly at large losses, and they were sent to spend the war

years in relocation centers. After the war, restrictions were placed on where these Japanese-Canadians could resettle.

In 1962, a change in immigration laws reopened Chinese immigration and, in the 1970s, a new group of Asian immigrants began to arrive in Canada. These included Chinese from Hong Kong, Singapore, and Malaysia, as well as Koreans, South Asians from India, Pakistan, and Bangladesh, and a number of refugees from Africa and Southeast Asia.

There have always been many refugees among the immigrants to Canada. United Empire Loyalists sought refuge after the American Revolution. American blacks escaped slavery through the "underground railroad." Jews fled, first from Russian pogroms and later from Nazism. Various Russian and Baltic peoples sought refuge from Siberian labor camps. Czechs and Hungarians fled

307

TABLE 10.1

*Occupational status of Canadians by ethnic group, 1971 (in percentages)[1].
Class I offers the most prestige, and Class VII the least.*

OCCUPATIONAL[2] CLASS	ETHNIC GROUP								
	ENG-LISH	FRENCH	GER-MAN	NATIVE INDIAN	ITAL-IAN	JEW-ISH	SCANDI-NAVIAN	UKRAIN-IAN	CANADIAN AVERAGE
Class I, II	13	10	10	1	8	39	10	6	12
Class III, IV, V	53	40	49	14	38	38	50	48	48
Class VI, VII	34	50	41	85	54	24	10	46	41
Total	100	100	100	100	100	100	100	100	100

[1] Figures have been rounded and don't necessarily total 100.
[2] Adapted from Blishen (1958). Class I represents jobs with the most occupational prestige; Class VII, those with the least.

Source: Lyle E. Larson, *The Canadian Family in Comparative Perspective* (Scarborough, Ont.: Prentice-Hall, 1976), p. 56.

Soviet-controlled regimes. Greeks and Chileans fled right-wing military juntas.

Not all immigrants, however, have come to Canada to escape political oppression. Many have been "pulled" here, rather than "pushed." Large numbers of Portuguese, Italians, and West Indians have arrived in the past 10 or 15 years who have been attracted by a higher standard of living than they could attain in their home countries.

For many of these immigrants the actual economic results of their move have fallen short of their expectations. Up to 20 percent of some groups have returned to their native countries. British and American immigrants do well, but others tend to do much less well. John Porter's book, *The Vertical Mosaic*,[28] written in 1965, established that minority ethnic groups generally have to settle for very low-status jobs for the first years of their stay in Canada. As they gradually move up, their low positions are taken by the next immigrant wave, but they cannot expect ever to enter the top levels of Canadian society. The highest social strata are strictly the preserve of what

Porter termed the "Charter Groups", especially the French- and the English-speaking Canadians. Some immigrants have caught up with French Canadians, but anglophones are still unrivaled. Subsequent research by Anthony Richmond confirms that prejudice operates in Canada to exclude immigrants from many social opportunities.[29] Employers commonly refuse to hire immigrants because they lack "Canadian experience," even though their qualifications in their home countries may have been outstanding.

Social status for members of ethnic communities is determined much as for everyone else, by their educational and occupational levels. And tension between ethnic groups is usually based on resentment and rivalry over the jobs open to the members of various groups. In most modern societies, ethnic conflict is hard to distinguish from class conflict, for both kinds of struggle are founded upon the frustrated desire for material gain. Indeed cohesion within ethnic groups is often a result of the necessity for economic support, as the following study shows.

SOCIAL RESEARCH:
Sociologists at Work

ETHNIC COHESION IN
CANADIAN CITIES

In his book, *The Survival of Ethnic Groups*,[30] Jeffrey Reitz attempts to determine the reasons for the persistence of ethnic groups in a modern industrial country. Is it because they share certain economic interests in relation to the predominantly Anglo-Saxon society? Or are the reasons related to a need for cultural continuity, ancestral roots, and the sense of belonging to a community? Why are some groups more cohesive than others?

For his study, Reitz chose ethnic group cohesion as his dependent variable. Ethnic group cohesion is the degree to which ethnic persons act and identify themselves as a group distinct from the dominant society. Ethnic group cohesion is not the opposite of assimilation. The two can vary independently; members of a highly cohesive group may have assimilated in many ways into the mainstream society. Reitz measured cohesion according to respondents' ethnic identification and the extent of their interactions with members of their own ethnic group as compared to "outsiders". He then attempted to discover the extent to which ethnic group cohesion is related to economic factors.

The study was based on historical records and interviews with 2,433 respondents in Montreal, Toronto, Winnipeg, Edmonton, and Vancouver. These interviews were conducted during a policy-oriented study that Reitz was involved in, along with K.G. O'Bryan and O.M. Kerplowska, in 1973.[31] The researchers interviewed members of ethnic groups that originated in the following areas of the world: Northern Europe (Germany, Holland, and Scandinavia); Eastern Europe (the Ukraine, Poland, and Hungary); Southern Europe (Italy, Greece, and Portugal); and China (Hong Kong, Taiwan, and the mainland of China).

In Canadian society today, these four categories of ethnic group occupy quite different positions. The circumstances of their arrival differed significantly. About 10 percent of the Canadian population is composed of Northern Europeans. Most of them arrived a long time ago and settled in cohesive groups chiefly on farms in southern Ontario or the prairies. Today, however, the Northern Europeans are the least cohesive category in the entire multicultural spectrum.

Eastern Europeans are also quite numerous, and account for about 5 percent of the Canadian population. Many of them faced discrimination when they came to Canada; for example, they were frequently offered extremely poor land that forced them to take extra jobs in such areas as railroad construction to earn a living. But not all Eastern European ethnic groups experienced the same difficulties. Unlike the Poles and Ukrainians, most Hungarians arrived in 1957 in one single immigration wave, fleeing Soviet oppression. Because they arrived so recently, they have encountered less discrimination than other Eastern Europeans. However, Eastern European ethnic groups are all intermediate in level of cohesion.

Southern Europeans arrived in several different waves and settled in cities. They have a strong economic basis for group solidarity. They often work together in construction jobs and, even after they join the middle class, they frequently depend on one another for support in finding jobs.

The Chinese that Reitz surveyed were mostly from Hong Kong and were much better educated than the earliest group of Chinese immigrants. The Hong Kong immigrants had generally finished their schooling in English before coming to Canada. Their outstanding educational backgrounds often led to high-status jobs. In their level of residential segregation, the Chinese were second only to the Southern Europeans.

The Chinese and the Southern Europeans were the most cohesive of the immigrant groups studied. There were, however, certain variations in ethnic group behavior that offset this generalization. For example, because the East Europeans were very active politically, they appeared to be far more cohesive than they actually were.

What accounts for differences in cohesion? Why are the Chinese and the Greeks more likely to think of themselves as Chinese and Greek than as "Canadian"? Why do they tend to associate so closely with other Greeks or Chinese, while the Dutch and the Swedes show much less in-group identification? Reitz tried to decide how to weigh the various factors that account for these differences. He used various statistical calculations and found that many of the differences in ethnic cohesion could be explained by certain economic variables.

Before studying the economic bases for ethnic cohesion, Reitz first determined how recently each ethnic group had immigrated. He found that there was a distinct connection between recency of immigration and ethnic cohesion. Northern Europeans had been in Canada longest, and they had the lowest cohesion. Southern Europeans and Chinese came most recently and had the greatest cohesion. Reitz found that about half of the differences in cohesion among the different ethnic communities could be explained by the length of time they had been in Canada.

Reitz concludes from this that the United States and Canada may not be as different for immigrants as they are generally believed to be. The United States has always promoted the ideal of the "melting pot," the assimilation of immigrants so they become plain "Americans" soon after their arrival. Canada's ideal has become one of cultural pluralism to produce a "mosaic" instead of a melting pot. And it is true that many ethnic groups seem to have much more cohesion in Canada than in the United States. However, Reitz points out that the peak of immigration in the United States was a generation or two ago. The fact that most ethnic groups in Canada have immigrated more recently may account for their higher degree of cohesion. After a while, they too may be absorbed by a melting pot. According to Reitz, the durability of their cohesion will depend greatly upon how long their economic interests remain distinctive.

The first economic factor that Reitz considered was the occupational position of the four categories of ethnic group in relation to the dominant Anglo-Saxon group. How unequal were they in job status and income? Is ethnic cohesion partly the result of a need to "stick together" in the face of economic adversity?

Reitz measured occupation status according to the Blishen scale of occupational prestige (see the preceding chapter). Reitz found that the Chinese had attained the highest status, higher in fact than the average job status of Anglo-Saxon Canadians. The Eastern and Northern Europeans held about the same job status as Anglo-Saxon Canadians. The Southern Europeans, however, were at the bottom of the ladder, considerably

below the others in the prestige of their jobs. For the Southern Europeans, at any rate, low occupational status played a clear role in encouraging cohesion. There was also evidence that the high status of the Chinese tended to discourage cohesion; without prestige jobs, they would probably have been more cohesive than the Southern Europeans.

Income, however, did not play a role. Although the Southern Europeans held jobs with very little prestige, their incomes were often higher than those of the other groups. Many of the Southern Europeans, particularly Italians, held highly-paid jobs in the construction industry. When assessing the role of occupational position in ethnic cohesion, then, Reitz concluded that a group's occupational status was far more significant than its income level.

Reitz next considered the role of social mobility in the ethnic cohesion of the four groups. Researchers have frequently tried to determine whether an ethnic group tends to maintain the status that it first holds upon entering Canada, or whether the children of immigrants have a good chance of moving up the social ladder. John Porter held that a group's "entrance" status tends to be kept for a long time. Reitz, to the contrary, found that groups apparently gain considerable upward mobility. He compared members of ethnic groups who had been raised in Canada with those who had immigrated to Canada as adults, and found that, by and large, those who were raised in Canada did have jobs with higher status. However, although the children of immigrants did gain more prestige than their parents, their income levels were not much higher. Adult immigrants often earned quite good incomes in low-status jobs. Their children gained in dignity, but not much in dollars.

Reitz found that social mobility played almost no part in determining ethnic cohesion. Group members who attained a significantly higher education level than the group average did tend to dissociate themselves somewhat from group ties. However, those members who maintained average educational levels but who attained significantly higher income and job status levels continued to maintain group ties.

Finally, Reitz asked whether the cohesiveness of ethnic groups was affected by job segregation. He found that it definitely was. The Southern

Prentice-Hall Canada Inc.

Ethnic groups often stick together in the face of adversity. In Canada, Italians are concentrated in low-status jobs in the construction industry.

Europeans and Chinese were more segregated in their work than the other groups; the Italians were concentrated in the construction industry and the Chinese in small businesses. The Eastern Europeans were moderately segregated in their jobs and the Northern Europeans least so. When a particular kind of work was dominated by a particular ethnic group, the workers had many more reasons to associate with each other and to maintain group loyalty; this was especially true when their jobs had low status, which is often the case in ethnically segregated work.

Neither ethnic segregation nor low occupational status tell the whole story however. These factors explain most variations in cohesion, but not all of them. Even discounting economic differences, some groups still are more cohesive than others. According to Reitz, this is partly because

whenever the groups have faced ethnic segregation and social inequality, they have responded by creating institutions to help them get along in Canada. Once created, however, these institutions often become important in their own right. Even after they no longer serve an economic purpose, some ethnic organizations continue to attract members.

Reitz also speculates that a further non-economic reason for ethnic cohesion may be the distinctiveness of the ethnic culture. The more a group varies from the dominant Anglo-Saxon Canadian culture, the more it will try to maintain strong group ties. According to this view, Chinese and Italians are more cohesive than, say, Germans or Dutch because they have less in common with Anglo-Saxon culture.

Reitz summarizes his findings by stating that

311

ethnic cohesion generally does decline over time, and it is most likely to decline when a group becomes economically integrated into Canadian society and becomes desegregated in the work force. Group cohesion is clearly a response to the group's economic circumstances. When people stick together, it is often because they cannot afford to drift apart. Nevertheless, there are differences in cohesion that are apparently unrelated to current economic factors, though these may result from a past history of economic disadvantage.

Reitz concludes his study with an examination of the whole ideal of multiculturalism. He suggests that we should ask ourselves whether the Canadian emphasis on multiculturalism is a smokescreen used to hide social inequality and prevent the equalization of opportunities. If ethnic cohesion results from discrimination, it is not anything for Canada to be proud of. A multicultural policy should not be pursued without adequate protections to guarantee social and economic equality for all.

SOCIAL POLICY:
Issues and Viewpoints

I pointed out earlier that one can have mixed feelings about ethnicity. I like diversity, but I hate discrimination. The trouble is, we usually don't get one without the other. I also suggested that you pay attention to your feelings as you read the chapter. Ethnic relations is an emotionally loaded topic. We have strong feelings of loyalty to "our people." And we also have strong feelings about fairness, equality, and openness. This produces a dilemma: the need to choose between two opposite principles—universalism and particularism.

First, before going on, decide which of the three types of ethnic relations you would prefer for your own society—(1) ethnic stratification, (2) ethnic pluralism, or (3) integration. I will assume that you would not choose ethnic stratification. Unfortunately, we often get it anyway when we really want one of the other two systems. Both ethnic pluralism and integration are unstable and tend to break down, so that we end up with ethnic stratification whether we want it or not.

What would be required to maintain a strictly pluralistic system? A strictly integrated system? In the following pages we will look at the types of problems that must be expected if we try to pursue either of these two policies.

SUSTAINING A PLURALIST SOCIETY

Ethnic pluralism allows for group traditions and supports a rich variety of cultures—folklore, languages, styles of cooking, holiday parades, and so on. But the trick is to keep these groups from becoming stratified, with one of them holding all the advantages and keeping others in subordinate positions. We don't want domination or undue competition between the ethnic groups of our pluralist society. So in order to keep it truly pluralist—characterized by both variety and equality, we'll need to encourage (1) tolerance, (2) economic autonomy, (3) legal autonomy, (4) unambiguous group membership, and (5) some discrimination.

Tolerance

If pluralism is to succeed, people must tolerate diversity even when they find it disagreeable. Foreign travel is fun because there is charm in diversity. But diverse groups that must live together may not find each other charming. Sociology assumes that a society can hold together because it shares common values and beliefs. Agreement is the basis of harmony, but diversity is the opposite of agreement. If one group is not to impose on another, its members must ignore what it views as the errors of other groups, but this is sometimes intolerable. It is almost intolerable for Hindus to live near Muslims, who kill and eat cows. Mormon polygamy was intolerable to most Americans a century ago. It is almost intolerable for many Westerners to see

Christian Scientists and Jehovah's Witnesses refuse blood transfusions for their sick children. Cultural diversity is not as easy to maintain in a real society as in the imagination.

Economic autonomy

Each community must have control over its own resources; it must have its own productive arrangements, and consume the products of its labor. Still, any integration between groups must involve cooperative activity toward some shared goal. In real life, however, most economic interaction involves competition as well, and this usually results in more advantages for one side than for the other. For example, whenever one ethnic community is the traditional landlord group and another community is traditionally the tenant group, there is usually tension between the groups. It would be better if the two communities had their own separate economies. It is not easy to apply this policy in modern societies, however. This would require that each ethnic community own and run its own businesses and maintain its own markets, factories, farms, banks, and so forth. A good deal of integration may be necessary for an industrial economy. If an ethnic community gains control over the small businesses within its area, it may achieve considerable economic autonomy (Chinatowns are an example). However, this will not make it economically equal to an ethnic group that controls large corporations and industries. Thus the requirements of a modern economy tend to shift a society away from pluralism toward either economic integration or ethnic stratification.

Legal autonomy

For an ethnic group to maintain its own identity it must have social control over its members' lives. In addition, it must be able to make and enforce its own rules. This conflicts with the principle of having a *single* rule of law. Legal autonomy would severely limit the activities of the state.

In India, for example, the laws governing marriage, divorce, inheritance of family property, and the like are different for Hindus and Muslims. It is important to distinguish between **universalism** and **particularism**. Any rule that is followed in dealing with all people in the society is universalistic. The practice of making special rules to fit special people or groups is particularism. In India, instead of a single universalistic code of family laws there

are particularistic legal systems that apply separately to Hindus and Muslims. This permits each group to maintain and enforce its own customs with the backing of the state. In North America, some religious and ethnic communities also have rules that they try to enforce. The Catholic Church, for example, has its own legal system. But such a group can impose its own rules only on members who obey willingly. If a Catholic rejects the authority of the church, no legal power can force him or her to obey it.

We agree that the *real* law is the set of laws passed by the government. Our law is universalistic—it applies across the board to all citizens. Ethnic communities have their own particularistic norms, but they don't have the force of law. Maybe your ethnic group forbids you to marry an outsider or to drink liquor or to get a divorce. You may think twice before doing these things, but the group cannot legally prevent you from doing them. In the end such rules fade away because members won't obey them when they don't want to. Thus a universalistic legal system gradually weakens the legal systems of the ethnic groups within the society. It strips them of the power to punish members who violate their norms.

Unambiguous group membership

In a pluralistic society, everyone must belong to some ethnic community, willingly or not. And if various ethnic groups have separate economic institutions, then everyone must belong to one of those groups in order to find a job. Group membership cannot be "voluntary." The boundaries must be firm and clear-cut. Marginal people would be rare, and a person would be unable to move from one group to another. I wouldn't like to be locked into an involuntary, ascribed system—but ethnic groups *are* involuntary and ascribed. The price of admission is life-long loyalty.

Discrimination

Ethnic loyalty amounts to discrimination. Boundaries are actually patterns of discrimination. You treat fellow group members in a special way. This may or may not be harmless. When it's just a matter of sharing an in-joke or singing some old songs together or borrowing a recipe for Easter bread, then outsiders are not "excluded." No harm is done.

But all ascribed communities tend to go beyond that. They not only pass their folksongs, recipes, and jokes along to other members; they also pass along their material goods. You might feel safer buying a used car from a member of your own group. Some of the ethnic restaurants near me have two menus—one in English and one in the "other" language—Portuguese or Russian, say—and the English menu charges more than the other one. This is normal, but it's also discrimination. We could call it petty particularism.

On a large scale, discrimination in favor of one ethnic group means cutting other groups out of some important advantages. And when one group begins to have more than another, passing the advantage from one generation to another may increase the inequality. This takes us right back down the road to ethnic stratification.

AN INTEGRATED SOCIETY

We have seen how hard it would be to maintain a pluralist society, but integration is probably even harder to achieve. Integration is based on a commitment to universalism. The principle is to apply general rules equally to everyone. Never discriminate in favor of your friends, your kin, or members of your own ethnic community.

Try living by that rule for one day. You will quickly find that we hold to another rule too, one that requires us to treat our "own people" in a special way. One sociologist gave his class the assignment of acting like guests in their own homes for one day.[32] For example, a male student was to rise when his mother was standing and sit only when she sat, ask permission before getting a snack from the refrigerator, shake hands with his father upon his arrival home, and the like. In almost every case, students reported that their behavior caused major emotional upsets. Not knowing what was going on, their families tearfully or angrily accused them of coldness. One does not treat everyone according to the same set of rules.

Each person is subject to two different norms, the principle of universalism and the principle of particularism. There are rules to determine when each principle applies. There is tension between the two principles, but neither ever wins out entirely. An integrated society supports universalism more than a pluralistic society does, but one is still expected to treat one's "own people" in a special

way. You can do things for your own child that you would not do for all the children in the neighborhood. You can send party invitations only to your friends. You can donate money to charities that only serve the poor of your own ethnic community. All of these cases of particularism can be tolerated in an integrated society that is basically universalistic. Still, it is necessary to limit particularism, for it weakens equality by allowing groups to limit certain privileges and opportunities to their "own people." It is usually considered proper to be particularistic in private activities but not in public affairs. Thus you may invite only your friends to a private party, but you may not favor them when you are hiring public employees, awarding scholarships, or seating customers in a restaurant. Controlling particularism is always difficult in a society that is committed to universalism and integration.

It seems that private discrimination is all right, while public discrimination is not. This formula appears reasonable, but it may not be enough to prevent ethnic stratification. Private social relationships include families, churches, clubs, and friendship networks. Many advantages are reserved for in-group members through participation in such private groups. These are real advantages—the kind that make a person better able to compete in public life, where universalistic rules apply.

For example, suppose private relationships are segregated and your ethnic group is the underdog. You may be shut out forever. Why? Because the skills and knowledge necessary for success are passed along through family ties and other private relationships to a much greater extent than through schools, libraries, television, and other *public* institutions.

Do you see the problem? No one wants the government to meddle in private associations. But there may be no other way to achieve real equality and ethnic integration.

I asked you to choose between ethnic pluralism and integration, and I warned you that this is a loaded and complex issue. I have never been able to choose one or the other wholeheartedly. As a result I have no general principles to use in deciding what is fair or unfair in matters of ethnic relations. Or rather, I have contradictory principles. It's easy to choose between right and wrong. What is harder is having to choose between two opposing *rights*—universalism and particularism.

SUMMARY

1. *Ethnic groups* (ascribed communities) may be based on similar religion, nationality, language, culture, tribe, race, or some other standard. Such groups have *boundary norms* that define who is a member and who is not; these norms also govern relations between members and nonmembers. Relations with nonmembers are always more limited than relations with members.

2. Boundary norms are used to define a *marginal person* as a full member of one and only one such group. Ethnicity is supposed to be a secure, permanent aspect of one's identity.

3. *Minority groups* are ethnic groups that have a subordinate or oppressed status compared to one or more dominant ethnic groups. A minority group may actually have more members than the dominant group, but it is still called a minority if it is subordinate.

4. *Racial groups* are ethnic groups whose members share certain physical characteristics; these characteristics are inherited. People who have similar physical traits may or may not feel that they belong to a group with a shared identity. Thus while everyone can be classified into a particular "race," not everyone is a member of a racial group. Race is biologically determined; racial groups are socially determined.

5. *Prejudice* consists of prejudging a person by overgeneralizing. Each person in a particular group is seen as having traits that are believed (rightly or wrongly) to be typical of members of that group. Prejudice involves making up a *stereotype* that exaggerates the traits of the "typical" member of that group. Everyone acquires stereotypes and prejudices about out-group members as part of the popular culture learned during childhood. Some people, however, also acquire a more sophisti-

cated culture that is more accurate and fair in its view of minorities.

6. *Racism* is a theory that has been very influential and has had disastrous results. According to racist theory, racial groups are not *socially* defined but are biologically determined. Members of such groups are supposedly held together by biological ties, some inherited tendency to behave in a particular way, to prefer a particular language, culture, and homeland, and so on. Racist theory was used by white Europeans to justify oppression of "inferior races" around the world. It was also used to justify the Nazis' annihilation of minorities, such as Gypsies, blacks, and particularly Jews, all of whom were considered genetically inferior.

7. *Nationalism* (or ethnic consciousness) develops, according to Deutsch, when increased communication breaks down the secure social world of traditional society and forces people into insecure relationships with strangers. In an attempt to regain their former sense of community, people emphasize their ethnic similarities. When nationalism is widely accepted there is a great danger that a group will become violently hostile toward out-groups. Other theorists place more weight on actual oppression as a source of nationalism than Deutsch does.

8. Three patterns of group interaction are possible in ethnically heterogeneous societies: (1) *ethnic stratification* (in which one or more groups dominate other groups), (2) *ethnic pluralism* (in which various ascribed communities live together as equals but without much contact between them), and (3) *integration* (in which groups interact in a wide variety of settings and tend to assimilate gradually into a single group with a shared life style).

9. Minority group members may react to oppression in several different ways. They may avoid interacting with the dominant group whenever possible but show passive acceptance of the dominant group's actions when they do interact. They may resist non-violently and build up self-respect within the minority group. Or they may resist violently or even turn their aggression against their own people in antisocial behavior.

10. Multiculturalism in Canada aims to provide ethnic pluralism so groups can keep their identities yet be equal. It is not clear that this goal can be attained. As it is, the policy may be keeping various ethnic groups at an economic disadvantage.

KEY TERMS

amalgamation the blending of racial types through long interbreeding.

annihilation destruction of the entire population of one ethnic community by another.

assimilation the process by which a group integrates itself into the culture around it.

boundaries the codes and customs that define a person as a member or nonmember of a particular group.

discrimination the process by which a dominant group informally deprives a minority group of equal access to privileges and opportunities.

ethnic group a large collectivity in which membership is generally inherited and whose members share a feeling of identification with the group.

ethnic group cohesion the degree to which members act and identify themselves as a group distinct from the mainstream culture.

ethnic pluralism the situation in which ethnic groups are equal and live together on good terms.

ethnic stratification the situation in which ethnic groups form a hierarchy of dominance.

expulsion the sending of minority group members to another country.

institutional completeness the maintenance by an ethnic group of a complete set of special institutions to meet the everyday needs of its members.

integration the situation in which equality is achieved by reducing the separation between ethnic groups and encouraging them to participate in the same activities.

marginal person a person who belongs to two or more groups that are supposedly mutually exclusive.

minority group an ethnic group that is subordinate to another group.

nationalism ethnic-group chauvinism.

particularism bending rules or making special ones to fit special persons or groups.

prejudice prejudging against individuals on the basis of characteristics believed to be shared by all members of their ethnic group.

racial group an ethnic group to which members are assigned on the basis of inherited biological traits.

racism the belief that ethnic and racial groups are based on genetic similarities rather than on social agreements.

segregation forcing minority group members to work or live in separate areas whenever possible and to use facilities separate from those used by the dominant group.

stereotype a mental cartoon that exaggerates the traits of the typical member of a particular group.

universalism adhering to the same rules in dealing with all people.

FOR FURTHER READING

BELL, DAVID and LORNE TEPPERMAN. *The Roots of Disunity: A Look at Canadian Political Culture.* Toronto: McClelland and Stewart, 1979. A review of Canadians' values and beliefs about their society and its subgroups.

CLAIRMONT, DONALD H. and DENNIS W. MAGILL. *Africville.* Toronto: McClelland and Stewart, 1974. This is a chatty description of a black community that was moved to Halifax, Nova Scotia and destroyed by the move. Interesting and sound.

DAVIS, MORRIS and JOSEPH F. KRAUTER. *The Other Canadians: Profiles of Six Minorities.* Toronto: Methuen, 1971. A handy little paperback that provides a nice description of the situation of several ethnic groups in Canada.

DRIEDGER, LEO, ed. *The Canadian Ethnic Mosaic.* Toronto: McClelland and Stewart, 1978. Driedger's book documents the current shift of Canada from a bicultural to a multicultural society. It includes articles on such diverse groups as Mennonites, Inuit, Hutterites, and American immigrants.

ELLIOTT, JEAN L., ed. *Minority Canadians, Vol. 2.* Scarborough, Ont.: Prentice-Hall, 1971. The immigrant groups are treated in one volume and native peoples in another. These are articles written by a variety of sociologists; most are quite illuminating but many are perhaps a little out of date.

FRIDERES, J., ed. *Canada's Indians: Contemporary Conflicts.* Scarborough, Ont.: Prentice-Hall, 1974. This is a useful source of information concerning the situation of Canada's native peoples.

GLOCK, CHARLES Y., ROBERT WUTHNOW, JANE PILIAVIN, and METTA SPENCER. *Adolescent Prejudice.* New York: Harper & Row, 1975. A survey analysis of relations between Christian and Jewish teenagers in three towns not far from New York City. Some unexpected sources of anti-Semitism are explored.

HENRY, FRANCES. *Forgotten Canadians: The Blacks of Nova Scotia.* Don Mills, Ont.: Longman's, 1973. Many of Canada's oldest black families are settled in Maritime towns, especially in Nova Scotia. Their situation is quite different from that of new immigrants from the Caribbean.

ISAJIW, WSEVOLOD. *Ethnic Group Relations in Canada.* Toronto: McGraw-Hill Ryerson, 1976. A survey of literature on ethnic group relations, particularly with reference to the Canadian scene.

JOY, RICHARD J. *Languages in Conflict.* Toronto: McClelland and Stewart, 1972. Joy was interested in predicting whether the French language would lose ground in particular regions of Canada. As it turns out, Joy was reading the handwriting on the wall.

LIEBERSON, STANLEY. *Language and Ethnic Relations in Canada.* New York: Wiley, 1970. Lieberson is another sociologist who has contributed to our understanding of the dynamics of ethnic relations when they are affected by language concerns.

MAXWELL, THOMAS R. *The Invisible French: The French in Metropolitan Toronto.* Toronto: Wilfrid Laurier, 1976. You can live a long time in Toronto and hardly ever hear any French spoken. Though there are many francophones around, they apparently all speak English or never go outdoors. This small book is about the Toronto French community and the organizations that it has tried to keep alive.

O'BRYAN, K. G., J. G. REITZ, and O. M. KUPLOWSKA. *Non-official Languages: A Study in Canadian Multiculturalism.* Ottawa: Supplies and Services Canada, 1976. This is a good source of factual information about the immigrant populations of Canada who speak some language other than French or English at home.

WINKS, ROBIN W. *The Blacks in Canada.* New Haven, Conn.: Yale University Press, 1971. Winks is a historian and his large book is an excellent treatment of established black communities in Canada. However, Winks does not provide an adequate discussion of the West Indians who have immigrated to Canada during the past ten or fifteen years.

SENIOR POWER

COLLECTIVE BEHAVIOR AND SOCIAL MOVEMENTS

A punk-rock guitarist, chains and safety pins dangling from his cheeks, spits on his pogoing audience. A nightclub burns to the ground, its occupants piled up just inside the exit, trapped by their own stampede. The survivors of an earthquake emerge from the wreckage and organize teams to rescue their neighbors. A million Christmas shoppers pay good money for "pet rocks." A furious mob runs through a business district, smashing store windows.

What do these scenes have in common? They are all cases of collective behavior—passing events during which groups of people improvise new ways of behaving.

While ordinary activities are organized according to fairly stable norms, in collective behavior a group of people depart, without much planning, from ordinary patterns of behavior. This usually occurs in situations of stress. Collective behavior, such as panics, riots, political demonstrations, and protest rallies, is most likely to take place under stressful conditions. However, in this chapter we will also be concerned with certain other forms of behavior that are not necessarily caused by stress. Emotional religious revivals, fads and fashions, and public celebrations are examples. Such behavior may occur when people are simply bored and want a change of pace.

Indeed, when we define **collective behavior** as spontaneous, transitory, noninstitutionalized group action, we do not intend to set it off as wholly different from all institutionalized group action. Group behaviors take a wide variety of forms. They range from extreme forms of collective behavior, such as a lynching or a rout on the battlefield, to extreme forms of institutionalized, formal behavior, such as the Japanese tea ceremony or the coronation of a king. Most forms of group behavior fall between these extremes. Also, many events are institutionalized in some ways and in other ways open to collective behavior—examples are public festivities such as the Quebec Winter Carnival or the Calgary Stampede.

Even an orgy can be planned in advance. Nothing could be more institutionalized than a performance of the Metropolitan Opera in New York, yet after Joan Sutherland has sung a difficult aria the whole audience leaps to its feet, shouting "Brava!" Such a moment contains an element of collective behavior.

Actors speak of having "good" and "bad" audiences. By this they mean that one performance may win delighted laughter and applause while the next may win hardly a giggle. The difference is in the audience, not in the players. If you happen to go to a comedy on an evening when the audience is responsive, you will probably laugh louder and enjoy the play more than you would if the audience were more subdued. Some writers call this audience effect collective behavior, while others use the term only for collective outbursts that are wholly noninstitutionalized efforts by a group to cope with a stressful social situation.

In this chapter we will deal both with extreme, unmistakable cases of collective behavior (such as riots, crazes, and panics) and with certain other phenomena involving group communication. The latter include the development of public opinion as well as social movements such as the civil-rights, environmental-protection, and anti-abortion movements. We will try to explain the conditions in which these phenomena take place, the phases they go through, and some of their effects on society.

Conditions in which collective behavior occurs

The most widely used sociological model of collective behavior was developed by Neil J. Smelser.[1] This model is limited to true cases of collective behavior in which people try to arrive at quick solutions to problems arising out of strain. It does not include institutionalized events governed by social norms (such as football rallies, patriotic mass assemblies, and shouting "Bravo" at the opera) or propaganda and individual acts of deviance.

In Chapter 2, I mentioned that sociologists predict behavior in terms of "if ... then" statements. Smelser's approach is of this type, but his model has six "ifs," and they must all come true in a particular order before the model will predict that "then" a given form of collective behavior will occur. These six "ifs" are very general conditions. In each historical case the particular events that correspond to these conditions are unique; yet if all six conditions are met, they will determine the outcome. This will become clear to you as we discuss the six "ifs."

1 *Structural conduciveness* is the first "if." It is the most general condition for collective behavior. This simply means that certain situations must exist for collective behavior to be possible. For example, there can be no panic buying or selling on the stock market and no runs on banks in a society where there is no stock market and there are no banks. Similarly, race riots can happen only where there are two or more races in the same community. There would have been no My Lai massacre if the American troops had been engaged in a mock battle in the Arctic instead of stalking Viet Cong in an Asian village. All of these conditions are obvious. They refer to the kind of situation that makes collective behavior *possible* but by no means *necessary*.

2 *Structural strain* is the second condition for collective behavior. It refers to a problem in the social environment, such as a conflict, a lack, an ambiguity, or a gap between expectations and reality. Any kind of strain may lead to any kind of collective behavior. What kind of behavior, if any, occurs will depend on the subsequent conditions in this list. Thus unemployment is a structural strain that might produce a march on Parliament, support for a religious revival, an attack on a minority group, or none of these behaviors, depending on other factors.

3 A *generalized belief* is the third basic condition that can lead to collective behavior. People must be able to identify the problem and diagnose their situation before they can take action to correct the source of structural strain. For example, if unemployed workers come to believe that their misfortune is due to the mistakes of politicians, they may march on Parliament. If they come to believe that God is punishing them for their sins, they may join a religious revival. If they believe that their jobs are being taken away from them by an ethnic minority, they may start a race riot or demand that immigration be stopped. The generalized belief is a kind of shared ideology, a system of meaning that calls for certain kinds of responses. However, this condition and the first two are not enough to cause collective behavior. Other "ifs" also must be met before this outcome is predictable.

4 *Precipitating factors* are the fourth condition for collective behavior. These dramatic events may or may not happen, but if they do they may trigger a collective response. For example, a racial situation may be very tense for a long time without any open violence. However, when one fistfight or act of police harassment occurs, this event may spark a race riot. The precipitating factor is usually unpredictable, and it may be avoided. However, when it happens after the other three conditions have come into existence, collective behavior is far more likely than before.

5 *Mobilization for action* is the fifth condition that must be met. Once the precipitating factor has occurred, participants have to be persuaded to join in the action. This is the moment when leaders may come forth and start shouting suggestions or urging people to take part. If they are successful at this point, collective behavior actually begins.

6 *Social control* is the sixth and final factor determining the outcome of the event. Before or during the action of the crowd, the police, the news media, the governor, or other influential people may take action to prevent or stop the collective action. If the social control is not effective, the collective behavior will run its course.

Thus Smelser's model says that *if* structural conduciveness exists and *if* structural strain exists and *if* an appropriate generalized belief exists and *if* precipitating factors occur and *if* the participants can be mobilized for action and *if* social control fails to stop the event, *then* collective behavior will occur. In a sense these six "ifs" are a checklist that allows sociologists to look back at an event of collective behavior and see what made it happen—what generalized beliefs were involved, what situation of strain existed, and so on. However, such a list does not predict future events of collective behavior very well. The six conditions are not sure to occur; if any one of them is lacking, collective behavior may not develop.

Crowds

A **crowd** is a large, temporary group of people who have some common goal or interest. A Santa Claus parade and a lynching mob are examples. Not all collective behavior happens in crowds (streaking, for example, was practiced by many individuals but rarely by large groups), but the crowd has always been of great interest to the student of collective behavior. There is something frightening about the intense involvement that is sometimes seen in a large crowd. If you have ever seen a film showing Hitler's mass audiences, you will understand what I mean. A sea of adoring faces would turn his way, and hundreds of thousands of people would lift their arms in unison and call out "Sieg Heil!" Imagine how hard it would be to be the only person in that crowd not shouting "Sieg Heil!" The power of a mob is overwhelming.

Scholars who have written about collective behavior have been especially concerned with the harmful aspects of crowds—their fickleness, their excitability, and their ability to make people do things that they would never do alone. To be sure, all of this is true, and we will discuss these aspects of crowds. However, it is important to realize that not all crowds are destructive mobs. Groups behave in different ways, depending on the situation. For example, the behavior of a crowd at the scene of a disaster is remarkably different from a panic.

DISASTERS

Sudden disasters, such as floods, forest fires, explosions, earthquakes, and tornadoes, do not usually lead to disorganized and irresponsible behavior. In fact the opposite often happens.

Before the event actually occurs it is often hard to persuade people that a disaster is likely and that they should be prepared. If the police drive through a neighborhood and warn residents to leave because a high dam may break, many people will shrug off the warning. They think the police are overly cautious. People rarely panic at such times. When the air-raid sirens accidentally went off across a wide section of the United States, supposedly signaling an atomic attack, nobody panicked. In fact hardly anyone even turned on the radio to find out whether the alarm was real or not. Many people looked out their windows, saw that no one else was panicking, and chose to ignore the warning. Only when they hear bombers overhead or see a wall of water rushing toward them will some people believe that the danger is real.

Ordinarily the behavior that occurs after a disaster is orderly. People pick themselves up, perhaps dazed, injured, and disorganized, and check on the safety of their loved ones. Then they start helping others. The usual social organization of the community may be destroyed by the disaster, and so people step outside their usual roles. They may direct traffic or join together to fight a fire. People who hold high-status jobs in everyday life may follow orders issued by a laundry worker who seems to know how to cope with the emergency. Neighbors who have not even nodded to each other for years suddenly come to each other's aid, sometimes taking big risks. There is often a strong sense of solidarity within the community for a time after the disaster.

PANIC

Panic seems to arise only in very specific kinds of situations, and people behave far differently in those situations than they do after a disaster. When a person is in a dangerous situation (e.g., a burning building or a battlefield), a great deal of self-control is necessary to keep from running away. Often in such situations, each person's chances for survival are better if

Disasters usually bring out, not the worst, but the best traits in people. When 300,000 people had to leave Mississauga in a hurry, the evacuation was amazingly orderly.

others are willing to restrain themselves. Thus it is bad enough to be under enemy fire, but if one's comrades run away the situation is even more hopeless. If anyone is going to run away, it is safer to be among the first than among the last. This being the case, if one person runs away, all the others are likely to run too. The same is true in the case of a burning building, especially if there are not enough exits. *More people will escape if people leave in an orderly fashion than if they stampede.*

Panics take place when people believe that there are not enough escape routes. If *no* escape routes are open, there will be no panic because there is nothing to compete for. In the mine explosion reported in Chapter 2, the miners did not panic because there was no possibility of escape for anyone.

Other situations are similar to panics in certain ways. One is the stock market collapse or bank run. If a private bank is believed to have plenty of money to cover all withdrawals, there will be no panic. However, if the money is limited it is far better to be among the first to sell stocks or withdraw savings. The race to reach the teller's window is similar to the race to reach the exit from a burning building. Both show the human character at its most selfish.

THE ACTING CROWD

Herbert Blumer, a longtime student of collective behavior, uses the term acting crowd to refer to potentially violent mobs that choose a course of action on the spot, as occurs, for example, in a riot. He uses the term expressive crowd to describe groups that may simply show especially strong feelings, by, for example, dancing in the streets on Bastille Day. It is only the acting crowd that Blumer, like other

323

writers on the subject, fears. The acting crowd can become an angry mob and can be persuaded to set fires, loot, overturn cars, or attack others.

There are at least four different ways of explaining the acting crowd: contagion theories, convergence theory, emergent-norm theory, and game theory.

Contagion theories

LE BON: THE IRRATIONAL MOB The French sociologist Gustave Le Bon was the author of *The Crowd*, perhaps the most influential book on collective behavior ever written.[2] Although

Drawing of Freud by David Levine. Reprinted with permission from *The New York Review of Books*. Copyright © 1975 NY Rev. Inc.

Le Bon wrote during a fairly stable period at the turn of the twentieth century, the crowds he described were those of the French Revolution. These crowds had made some unsettling and fateful decisions. Le Bon was not alone in seeing the revolutionary mob as a frighteningly unpredictable, fickle, and even irrational phenomenon. His description makes for breathless reading whether it is accurate or not.

Le Bon believed that a certain process operates within a crowd that makes normal people lose their rational abilities and act at a primitive mental level. The reason for this loss of rationality is contagion. The members of a crowd are open to control by a leader, who "hypnotizes" them, and they are likely to imitate each other as well. As a result the crowd becomes unified. All its members perform similar kinds of actions, and all are under the influence of a single, unified group mind that is unstable and irrational. He called this phenomenon the "law of mental unity of crowds." The decisions made by such a mob are likely to be different from those that the average member would have arrived at alone. Le Bon believed that the influence of crowds on human history was almost always tragic rather than beneficial.

FREUD: THE ROLE OF THE LEADER Later writers have expanded the theory of crowd contagion, mostly by trying to explain how it operates. By far the best known of these later theorists is Sigmund Freud, who emphasized the influence of the leader on a crowd of followers.[3] Freud was not satisfied with Le Bon's explanation of how crowd behavior becomes irrational. However he did accept Le Bon's claim that people in crowds do lose their rationality and self-control. As we will see shortly, this assumption is not shared by all sociologists today.

Freud believed that feelings left over from a person's early childhood are an important factor in his or her behavior as an adult. He believed that people could be caught up in a

Wide World

Freud emphasized the influence of the leader on a crowd. He had to flee from Austria to escape the crowd that followed this leader.

crowd because of two wishes of which they might not be aware.

The first wish was to go back to being taken care of by a parent. The leader in a crowd gives the impression that he or she is like a strong parent looking after children. Freud thought people wanted a hero to worship because this satisfied their desire to be childish and dependent.

The other wish in Freud's theory of collective behavior was the wish to *identify* with other people. Identification is a psychological way of sharing someone else's experience, almost as if one *were* that other person. By

identifying with the leader, the person in a crowd imagines that he or she shares the leader's special power. By identifying with each other, the people in a crowd feel a stronger sense of togetherness and solidarity. This feeling is similar to the feeling brothers and sisters have for each other because they share the same parents.

The most serious weakness of Freud's theory is its emphasis on the influence of a leader. It is simply not true that all crowd phenomena take place under the direction of one or more leaders. Many, perhaps most, acting crowds don't have definite leaders.

325

BLUMER: EMOTIONAL REACTION In contrast to Freud's explanation for crowd behavior, Herbert Blumer's theory is based on the symbolic interactionist viewpoint described in Chapter 6. He too accepted Le Bon's view that acting crowds are irrational, but he suggested his own explanation for the contagion that supposedly occurs in such crowds.

In normal situations a person generally interprets the communications of others before responding to them. However, in the crowd situation, according to Blumer, a sort of chain reaction sets in and rationality is no longer possible. He calls this process *circular reaction* and compares it to the excitement that sometimes builds up within a herd of cattle. That is, one animal may become excited and the others, seeing its rapid breathing, bellowing, and wild body movements, will become agitated themselves and behave in a similar way. This excitement eventually *circles* back to the animal that started the whole process. In this way an acute fear builds up and may result in a stampede. People, like animals, may become excited or frightened by the behavior of others. They may then respond to this excitement *directly*, without thinking about it, and their responses may build up into a general state of hysteria.

Such circular reactions take place when some precipitating event has drawn people together and stirred up their emotions. A "milling" process then begins, in which people are influenced by each other's strong feelings and build up a state of collective excitement. At this point they may set out to achieve a common goal such as racing for an exit, attacking their enemies, or overturning cars.[4]

Blumer's work on collective behavior has been criticized in recent years for several reasons. For one thing, it is clear that acting crowds are not nearly as unified as his theory suggests. If such a "circular reaction" were going on, all the participants in a crowd would act pretty much alike, but this is not the case. In a riot, for example, different people do different things. One may smash auto windshields; another may put up a barricade or collect trash to set fires; others may throw stones at enemies; and still others may concentrate on taking home stolen TV sets. Indeed, many people may just stand around watching; some may even try to persuade the rioters to stop. There is a kind of division of labor in a riot that is not necessarily irrational.

The whole concept of the "circular reaction" is open to question. Clearly, some emotional actions may excite other people. If you stand on a street corner and scream, you will at least give passers-by a few goose pimples; they may stop what they are doing, but they may not join you in screaming. However nervous you make them, it is doubtful that they will lose their reason and respond directly, like stampeding cattle. Therefore some modern writers on this subject hold that the thinking of crowd members is not very different from ordinary thinking. If this is so, then Blumer must have exaggerated the difference between ordinary behavior and collective behavior by treating the "circular reaction" as a crowd phenomenon different from ordinary communication.

The arguments against Blumer's theory are also criticisms of the other contagion theories. If the critics are right, crowds are not irrational groups with uncontrollable and homogeneous impulses.[5] The issue is not settled, however.

Convergence theory

A basic assumption of contagion theories is that a person caught up in a crowd may be influenced to do things that are entirely out of character. Convergence theory rejects this assumption. Instead, it holds that a crowd may give people a chance to do what they have secretly wanted to do all along but have been kept from doing. According to this theory, a mob is a group of people with the same hidden impulses who suddenly let loose those impulses. Convergence theorists agree that "a crowd is a device for indulging ourselves in a kind of temporary insanity by all going crazy together."[6] In other words, crowd behavior is not something that is suddenly "caught" through contagion. If enough people with the same hidden wish gather together and one person begins to act out that wish, the others may do likewise. As Floyd Allport wrote, criticizing Le Bon's description of contagion in the French Revolution, "Nothing new or different was added by the crowd situation except an intensification of the feeling already present, and the possibility of concerted action. The individual in the crowd behaves just as he would behave alone, *only more so.*"[7]

There is some evidence for this point of view in studies of the ghetto riots of the 1960s. The behavior of rioters was not random, as the contagion theory would predict, but selective. Black-owned shops were not looted. The rioters did not forget who were their friends and who were their enemies.

It is possible to take a position somewhere between the contagion and convergence theories. That is, although it may be generally true that the participants in collective behavior act according to hidden wishes, contagion may influence people who lack such wishes. Furthermore, we each have within us not one but many hidden tendencies. What determines which one we will act out? Perhaps it is contagion that makes us choose one tendency rather than another in a particular situation.[8]

Emergent-norm theory

Collective behavior is often defined as group activity that is *not normatively regulated.* This definition does not entirely suit our purposes, however, because one theory holds that collective behavior *is* normatively regulated—but that the norm is a new one invented on the spot. This theory is called the emergent-norm theory.

According to this theory, collective behavior occurs in situations that are not covered by existing rules of conduct. Members of the crowd have to make the rules themselves. They usually begin by wondering how to

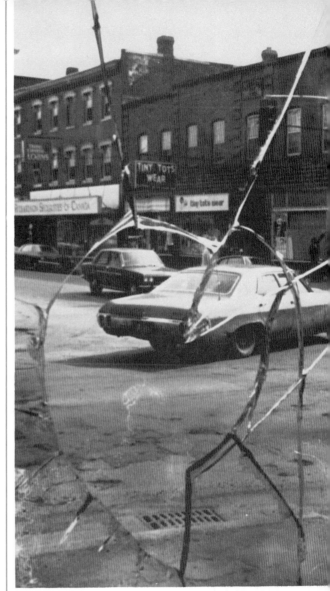

CP Photo/Gleaner

Members of a mob may do things that they would not do on their own. When Fredericton police went on strike, many of the town's young people went on a rampage.

define the situation and what to do about it as a group. Not all the members of the crowd may have the same opinion, but some members make their opinions known more than others do. If a person believes that his or her opinion is very much in the minority (whether this is actually so or not), he or she is likely to keep silent.

327

One sociologist illustrated this group experience to his class by walking out of the classroom in the middle of his lecture without any explanation. Half an hour later, students were still milling around in the classroom and the hall, trying to arrive at some shared interpretation of the situation and some norm for reacting to it.[9]

The emergent-norm theory holds that most crowd reactions can be understood in terms of the tendency to conform. Just as a person gives up his or her own opinion about which of two lines is longer when faced with the unanimous opinion of a small group, people also tend to agree with what seems to be the shared opinion of a large crowd. Crowd phenomena thus illustrate the power of social control in creating and enforcing a new, emergent norm. Unlike contagion and convergence theories, which assume that the members of a crowd become uniform in their conduct, emergent-norm theory recognizes that many different opinions may exist, even though they may not be expressed openly. The silence of those who disagree looks like passive support and adds to the illusion of uniformity.[10]

Collective behavior often happens when ordinary procedures don't work. For example, thousands of people had to hike miles across dry hills to reach the site of the Altamont Rolling Stones concert. There they found that there were not enough toilets for such a large number of people. Strangers formed small groups to discuss the situation. The norms of "straight" society were rejected, as no longer applicable. People began to relieve themselves in public. This deviance made other deviations more likely. Many people were shocked by the open sexuality and use of drugs that resulted, but they felt alone in their disapproval. There was an illusion of agreement on the emerging normative system. Besides, too few police officers were present to enforce the rules of "straight" society. A motorcycle gang undertook to "police" the crowd, and its methods resulted in injuries and one death. After the event many people looked back on their be-

havior with some shame, realizing how cowardly it had been to give in to social pressure.

Game theory

The final approach we will discuss is the newest way of looking at collective behavior. It is not inconsistent with emergent-norm or convergence theory, but it is quite different from contagion theory. Instead of assuming that some sort of emotional contagion sweeps through a crowd, turning its members into irrational beings with no self-control, game theory assumes that the members make rational decisions. Game theorists simply say that there are some special characteristics of situations in which collective behavior occurs.[11]

Game theory begins with the assumption that every person makes his or her own decisions at all times, even in an acting crowd. There is no such thing as a "group mind." It is true that individuals may have goals that many others disapprove of (such as looting a store, storming the Bastille, lynching a suspected rapist, or wiping out all the inhabitants of the village of My Lai), but they decide whether to do these things the same way that they make other decisions. They weigh the probable rewards and the probable costs of various courses of action and then try to choose the act that maximizes the rewards and minimizes the costs. Looting a store may be a "reward" and getting arrested may be the "cost" that one may have to pay for looting. This is too high a cost for most people. Standing up in church and showing intense emotion may be a "reward," but getting laughed at may be the "cost" of such an action. The "payoff" is the net reward for a given course of action—the reward minus the cost. If it seems that the payoff will be high, a rational person will undertake the act; otherwise he or she will decide against it.

According to game theory, every participant wants to maximize payoff, and each realizes that the other participants are doing the same thing. It often happens that the payoff for various possible acts depends on how other people will act. Thus a person may be unwilling to smash and loot a store alone because he or she is likely to have to pay the cost of being arrested. However, if the members of a large crowd decide to smash and loot together, the chance of any one member's being arrested may be much lower. Likewise, if several members of a congregation weep, clap, and shout for joy, the likelihood that anyone will have to pay the cost of being laughed at is lower. This is why people may be willing to do some things in a crowd that they would not be willing to do alone. As Richard Berk has pointed out, they have not "lost their reason"; rather, they see that the chance of a good payoff has been improved by the responses of other crowd members.

Because most collective behavior involves violation of conventional norms, the person who starts the action takes a high risk. The others may not follow suit, and he or she may be punished. On the other hand, by taking the risk the leader may encourage others to act because they see that he or she is getting away with it. The person who acts first is usually someone who is especially likely to violate conventional norms—perhaps a child, a drunk, or a criminal. The leaders of collective behavior are usually of low status, while those of institutionalized groups are usually of high status.

In most forms of crowd behavior, the action takes place because many members all want the same things and, by acting together, can increase the payoff for each member. This is a *collaborative* situation. However, panic is one form of collective behavior that takes place only when the situation is *competitive*. Suppose your "reward" is escape from a burning building with few exits in which there are many people who also want to escape. The "cost" may be to get trampled. If everyone pursues the same goal at once, the chances of a favorable payoff for each one are not increased but decreased. In any competitive situation each person who looks out for his or her own

interests makes it harder for the others, who are looking out for theirs. That is, by acting together they increase the costs, not the payoff, for each other.

It is likely that further study will lead to a combination of game theory and emergent-norm theory, while convergence theory and contagion theories drop out of favor. Convergence theory simply does not explain everything that needs to be explained, such as rapid shifts within a crowd from one plan of action to another. Contagion theories seem to be downright misleading. They suggest that some psychological disease sweeps the members of a crowd into actions that they would oppose if they were in their right minds.

Communication processes in large groups

All human activities involve communication, but not all group communication processes are alike. Here I will define several of them. These communication processes differ in the degree of control, manipulation, and planning involved. Rumor is the most unplanned, noninstitutionalized kind of communication, while propaganda is the opposite—the most purposeful and manipulative kind of communication.

RUMOR

A **rumor** is a piece of information that is passed from one person to another throughout a group without being checked out, such as gossip about famous politicians or secret military weapons. Rumors can arise in any social setting, but they are most likely to arise in situations of social stress, such as wartime. Rumors arise as a result of two factors: (1) the amount of *interest* people have in the subject matter; and (2) the amount of *ambiguity* in the situation.[12] Ambiguity refers to the difficulty of checking the accuracy of a story because of incomplete information. For example, during

When word gets around that a private bank is short of funds, a bank run can result. In the Depression, bank runs severely damaged an already ailing economy.

World War II many Japanese living in Hawaii believed that Japan had won the war and that the U.S. government didn't want to tell the American people that they had lost. It is reasonable to suppose that this rumor was accepted because the Japanese wanted it to be so and because there was no way of proving that it was not so.

Not surprisingly, rumors are very common in situations in which collective behavior is taking shape. During the "milling" phase, people trade stories and judge the validity of each one while deciding what they should do about the situation.

It is not possible to say whether in general a rumor tends to gain or lose in accuracy as it passes from one person to another. Most laboratory studies of rumor have been set up to pass a complex story from person A to person B to person C to person D to person E

and so on, without allowing any discussion among the subjects. A real rumor does not usually spread in this way. Rather, it is passed along within a social *network*, so that each person may hear a version from several different sources and can judge which one, if any, to believe. People differ in their ability to judge the accuracy of a rumor. Critical discussion usually makes the rumor more accurate. If the rumor goes through many interactions, so that each person hears it several times from different sources, it will probably become more accurate if the hearers are critical but may become less so if they are not critical.[13]

PUBLIC OPINION

Rumors are irregular and infrequent, but people exchange news, information, and opinions almost all the time. A public may be

330

defined as a scattered group of people who are interested in, have various opinions about, and are involved in a discussion of, an issue. The discussion is designed to produce a collective opinion that will influence the action of some group or individual.[14] Here we are talking not about *the* public but about a variety of publics, each concerned with a particular topic. For example, one public is concerned with the issue of abortion and includes both those in favor and those opposed. Another public is interested in the role of the military. It includes people who want more missiles, people who want to disband NATO, total pacifists, and others, including some who read a good deal on the subject but have no definite opinion. There are many publics in modern societies because of the large number of new issues and problems. We take it for granted that it is all right to be either for or against abortion or for or against the military. Differences of opinion are acceptable, and as information is exchanged and arguments take place public opinion may change. This is why polls "take the pulse" of the public; they want to see what shifts are taking place in the opinions of a population. On many issues people who belong to the same groups and the same social class tend to hold similar opinions, though some groups have more influence on their members' opinions than others.

Not all the members of a public have an equal impact on the opinions of others. As one might expect, high-status people carry more weight than others. In fact their advice is often sought, especially if they are well known and responsible. These individuals, called *opinion leaders*, are usually better informed than other people. They read more, discuss more, and get more information before they form their own opinions. This process has been called the "two-step flow of communication." That is, the mass media influence opinion leaders in the first step, and in the second step those individuals pass on what they read and hear to other people for whom they are influential.[15]

THE INFLUENCE OF THE MASS MEDIA

In a crowd situation large numbers of people are in face-to-face contact with each other. In a mass communication situation, on the other hand, thousands or millions of people, scattered over a large area, receive the same message from a distant source. These people have little opportunity to "talk back" to the information source or to discuss the message with one another. A million people read the same news at their individual breakfast tables. Twenty million people watch the same news on television. These media unquestionably affect public opinion and suggest certain kinds of actions to people in the audience. The effects of these media are very important, if only because they get so much attention from the average person in modern society. (Between the ages of 3 and 16 the average North American child spends one-sixth of his or her waking hours watching TV—more time than he or she spends on any other activity except sleep and play.[16]) What are the effects of the media on the public?

I have already mentioned that many people form opinions about issues through the two-step flow of communication. However, many other opinions seem to be formed through one-step processes. Some of these processes—including suggestion and propaganda—have a strong influence on collective behavior.

Suggestion

The following example shows the power of suggestion. Several years ago the mass media reported that a peculiar thing was happening to car windshields in a particular area. For some unknown reason, pitting marks seemed to appear on windshields and then to increase in size. Upon reading about this phenomenon, hundreds of people phoned the police to report pitting in their windshields. Others covered their windshields with blankets or newspapers. There was much debate as to whether the epidemic of pitting was caused by vandalism, atomic fallout, or some other factor. Finally a team of scientists announced that there was no "epidemic" at all. The number of windshields that were pitted was no higher than usual. All that had happened was that people had heard the false report in the news and had looked *at* their windshields for once, instead of *through* them. As a result they had found pits that they would never have noticed otherwise.

This is an interesting example of suggestion but a harmless one. Far more serious are the effects of the mass media on patterns of violence. As mentioned in Chapter 3, studies suggest that many people who watch violence on television are more likely to behave aggressively afterwards than people who do not watch violence.[17] Moreover, a recent study of suicide has revealed the existence of a "Werther effect." Two hundred years ago, when the famous German writer Goethe published a novel about a young man named Werther who committed suicide, many people followed Werther's example and shot themselves. In several areas the book had to be banned to protect the public from its influence. Using American and British statistics, sociologists have shown that the number of suicides increases after a suicide has been widely reported in the newspapers.[18] For example, suicides increased in number just after the death of Marilyn Monroe. Newspapers in some cities, such as Toronto, do not report suicides in which people jump in front of subway trains. This policy was adopted after reports showed that such stories tend to stimulate more suicides.

How many other, similar problems result from suggestions influencing the audiences of the mass media? We have no way of answering this question, but it is likely that the number is high. No airplane had ever been hijacked until a few years ago. The publicity given to the first hijacking seemed to stimulate more hijackings, and today every airport

is constantly on guard to prevent them. Kidnappings and embassy hostage-takings, like streaking, goldfish swallowing, and other fads, have become commonplace after they have been given wide publicity. Lately it has become a routine event for protesters to slash art in museums and even blow up famous palaces like Versailles. It seems reasonable to assume that many protest demonstrations and even riots have been stimulated, at least in part, by reports of such events in the mass media. The effects of the media have not been studied enough, but they are probably a very important factor in modern life.

Propaganda

Propaganda is the planned use of mass media to influence the beliefs and opinions of a population. Advertising is the most obvious example of propaganda, but governments have also used it in wartime to improve morale among their own troops and to lower it among the enemy. Thus during World War II the Germans broadcast radio messages from "Axis Sally" and the Japanese had a program by "Tokyo Rose," both with the goal of persuading American soldiers not to fight. The Allies, not to be outdone, dropped leaflets behind German lines. The most effective of these asked the reader to accept only a few points. The best one flattered the reader by claiming that German infantrymen were excellent soldiers who were not being outfought man for man but were being crushed by the superior weapons of the Allies. It did not use political arguments or make being captured sound attractive or even urge the reader to desert. It simply left the decision up to the reader and provided the basic facts about how to surrender. Many German soldiers were carrying this leaflet when they turned themselves over to the Allies.[19] In contrast, most of the German leaflets dropped behind Allied lines attacked so many of the soldiers' beliefs that they seemed ridiculous and persuaded no one.

Fads, fashions, and crazes

People who are exposed to the mass media become familiar with the same new things at the same time. As a result fads and fashions are more common in modern society than in earlier societies. A **fad** is a culture trait that suddenly becomes popular and then just as suddenly disappears. Goldfish-swallowing contests became a fad that swept college campuses some years ago, but today no one swallows goldfish (I think!). More recently, smiling faces on buttons, shirts, and many other objects were "in." In France, the fad a couple of summers ago was sweat shirts with names of American universities on them. At first I was fooled and started a conversation with a young man wearing one from my alma mater, but I soon discovered that he spoke no English.

Fashion consists of culture traits that are popular for a short time and then are gradually replaced. Styles of household decoration and dress come in and out of fashion—skirt lengths are a familiar example. Fashions do not change quite as fast as fads, probably because most people cannot throw away their furniture or clothes and buy new ones every year. Fashions are usually started by high-status people and then copied by people of lower status. This is not always the case, however. Blue jeans, for example, were originally a working-class fashion, but they gradually became accepted by higher strata.

What is remarkable about fashions is the speed with which they catch on throughout the world as a result of the influence of the mass media. As I write this, lots of women are wearing cowboy boots. But shoes wear out quickly, so shoe fashions change almost as quickly as fads. Perhaps as you read this book you will be wearing Grecian sandals or

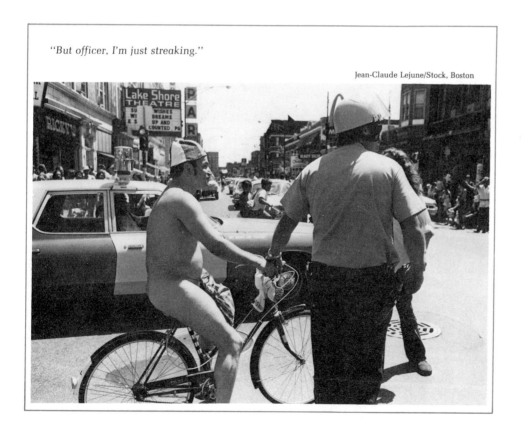

"But officer, I'm just streaking."

Jean-Claude Lejune/Stock, Boston

glass slippers, your cowboy boots having long ago been dumped into the trash can. At one time your clothing style would have been determined by your social status, and you would not have been allowed to copy higher-status men or women. You might have worn the same type of shoes all your life.

Most fads and fashions require only a small amount of attention or emotional involvement. The blue-jeans wearer does not lie awake at night thinking about his or her jeans. But a craze is different. A craze is a fad or fashion that becomes so important to people that they may spend a great deal of money and emotion on it. Land speculation booms have been a common type of craze. In the 1920s, everyone wanted to buy land in Florida, and property values there became unrealistically high. During the seventeenth century, the Dutch went through a tulip craze. People paid higher and higher prices for rare tulip bulbs until the majority of the Dutch people were buying and selling tulips. A rare bulb might sell for as much as a house. Then people realized that the craze would not continue forever and began to sell their bulbs; a panic and a financial crisis resulted.

MASS HYSTERIA

One form of collective behavior that happens rarely is *mass hysteria*. This usually takes the form of a frightening misunderstanding that is shared by a large number of people and causes a lot of anxiety. For example, in the 1930s Orson Welles produced a radio program based on H. G. Wells' story *The War of the Worlds*. Its script sounded much like a regular newscast, reporting the invasion of the East Coast by Martians, and a great many listeners believed the story and became very frightened. Some got into their cars and fled.[20]

Another example was the "Phantom Gasser" reported in sensational stories by newspapers in Illinois. This person was supposed to have sprayed gas on sleeping women through their bedroom windows. After the first incident was reported, many other women claimed to have been gassed and to have been temporarily paralyzed by the fumes. One researcher interviewed everyone who knew anything about these incidents and concluded that the gasser was imaginary. The "Phantom" was a product of psychological anxiety made more intense by frightening newspaper reports.[21]

Social movements

Not long ago the graduate students, secretaries, and faculty of my sociology department sent out for Chinese food and had a party. After everyone had finished eating, some of us began clearing away the plates and wine glasses while others made merry or got involved in conversations about ongoing research. Suddenly a lively, popular woman professor stopped and bellowed, "Just take a look around this room! Just look at what is going on!" We all laughed because we "saw" right away what she was pointing out: Every woman in the room was collecting and scraping dishes, while every man was sitting and talking.

Fifteen years ago our party might have been about the same, except that no one would have told us to look at what was going on. If anyone had done so, we would not have known what to "look for." No one would have laughed, because we would not have seen anything noteworthy. Moreover, any woman who called attention to the situation would have been considered hostile and "bitchy" and would have been disliked for complaining.

What happened during the 1970s that made such a difference? The women's movement. What has it achieved? It has improved opportunities for women on the job and in other settings, and, as my story illustrates, has changed the way people look at things. Modern Western societies—or at least most social strata within those societies—have been forced to accept a new value that was not part of the culture before: equality of the sexes. Today most men do not feel quite "right" about having their dishes cleared by female co-workers, even though it still happens now and then because of habit. Fifteen years ago both sexes felt "right" about it, so much so that only an especially aggressive woman would have complained that she was being treated unfairly.

A social movement is a collective effort to bring about a new order of life.[22] Examples include the civil-rights movement, the women's movement, the anti-abortion movement, and the gay-rights movement. A social movement is different from a public in that it supports a single point of view; a public includes all the opposing views on a given issue. It is different from a crowd because it is a long-term collectivity rather than a quick, unplanned grouping. Crowds may appear in connection with a social movement, however, as in the case of the peace marches of the antiwar movement.

Practically every other chapter of this or any other sociology book will explain that social patterns are organized in terms of the shared values of a given society. We do not often ask where those values come from. Alain Touraine does ask this question, however, and his answer is that social movements are the source of new values.[23] I think he is correct. It seems to me that a new value was shared by everyone at the sociology department's party and that it clearly was a product of the women's movement, "a collective effort to bring about a new order of life." However, not all social movements favor new values. Some urge a return to the old order and to old values rather than the creation of a new order.

Social movements are familiar to us all. We are constantly being asked to demand a new order of life that would be more favorable to various groups. Anticolonialist movements around the world involve many millions of people. The civil-rights movement, the

ecology movement, the Indian movement, the Quebec Separatist movement, and the Gay Liberation movement are familiar to Canadians. Each of these movements makes some new moral claim on the conscience of the wider society in the name of a new value. This new value may be social equality and dignity for a previously stigmatized or degraded minority, political independence for a particular group, or conservation instead of wasteful consumption.

Primitive societies and ancient civilizations knew nothing of social movements. Peasant societies had them only occasionally, in the form of revolts. During the Middle Ages, a variety of "millenarian" movements arose in Europe, usually in places where a class of uprooted poor people were living without any settled occupation or community ties.[24] These movements were often based on a belief in a messiah king with supernatural powers who was about to save the people from their misery. Often they expected this king to reign for 1000 years; hence the term *millenarian*.

Only in modern society have social movements been numerous. Industrial societies are far more complex than traditional societies; they include a great variety of competing groups, each demanding something for itself. Although all industrial societies give rise to social movements, totalitarian states try to suppress them. Totalitarian regimes often come to power as a result of such a movement and are therefore anxious to keep other movements from replacing them. The most common strategy used in such a case is to suppress dissenting movements. Sometimes this strategy is successful for a long time, as in Russia and Nazi Germany.

FUNCTIONS OF SOCIAL MOVEMENTS

Touraine has suggested that social movements have three functions: mediation, pressure, and clarification of the collective consciousness.[25] By *mediation* he means that social movements are mechanisms for involving the individual with the larger society. They give each person a chance to participate, to make his or her ideas known, and to have some impact on the social order.

By *pressure* Touraine means that social movements almost always give rise to organized groups that try to get their policies put into operation. They lobby, hand out leaflets, organize demonstrations, and the like.

Clarification of the collective consciousness is the most important function of social movements. This is a matter of developing the ideas that are used in discussions throughout a society. Marx's term *class consciousness* refers to this process. He held that shortly before a revolutionary struggle begins, the members of a social class become more aware that they have common interests. They interpret social relationships more clearly and begin to notice facts that they would have overlooked before. The women's movement is another example. It has "raised the consciousness" of a great many people, including men. People are now more sensitive to such issues as referring to a mature woman as a "girl" or hiring women on the basis of beauty instead of ability. All social movements perform a similar "consciousness-raising" function. Since the civil-rights movement, black men react with anger when they are called "boy."

Each social movement tries to make the whole society understand its own point of view, and this is what "raises" the consciousness of the society. To see how much progress has been made in our collective consciousness, look through any old pre-World War II magazine or novel. Many statements that seemed reasonable and even obvious at that time will seem outrageous today. They appear chauvinistic, racist, or snobbish. In most cases such statements embarrass us today because our collective consciousness has been clarified through the efforts of some social movement.

Thus we must recognize social movements as very important historical factors. They are a major source of social change. The participants in a social movement are not living by old, established values but trying to introduce new values. Sometimes they succeed, sometimes not. For example, the Winnipeg General Strike of 1919 was a dramatic labor protest that stopped all major services in the city for about a month and led to violence. Despite its popular support, it did not succeed in changing basic values in Canada at all.

THE LIFE CYCLE OF A SOCIAL MOVEMENT

Carl A. Dawson and Warner E. Gettys, writing in 1929 about collective behavior and social movements, outlined what they believed were the typical stages through which such movements pass.[26] The first stage is a period of social unrest. (This is somewhat like Blumer's "milling" stage.) Both leaders and followers become tense and excited.

If the tension is not resolved, the movement may pass into the second stage, "the popular stage of collective excitement and unrest." "Milling" continues, and the movement gains some focus, wider support, and the beginnings of a myth or ideal to guide it.

The third stage is the "formal stage of the formulation of publics." Policies and goals begin to emerge at this point through discussions within publics.

Finally, if the movement is successful, it will enter stage four, the "institutional stage of legalization and societal organization." That is, the aims of the movement become accepted in the laws of the society. Thus the social movement changes from an out-group to the in-group. At this point one can no longer call it a social movement, for it has achieved its goals and no longer has to fight for them.

TYPES OF SOCIAL MOVEMENT

Social movements are always based on popular discontent. They can be classified by the types of goal they pursue.

Perhaps the most dramatic type is the *revolutionary movement* that seeks to overthrow the established authority, using violence if necessary. A revolutionary movement need not be large in order to have an impact. For example, at least at the beginning, the Irish Republican Army was a fairly small group, but through terrorist activities it managed to cause a great deal of confusion.

Movements may differ greatly in the direction of their policies. A *reform movement* always looks toward new goals that its supporters think will correct existing problems. The civil-rights and women's movements are examples. A *reactionary movement*, however, wants to turn the clock back, so to speak, and bring back an old way of life that is considered better than the present order of things. The Edmund Burke Society is a reactionary movement that tries to limit the extent of government involvement in social life. A *conservative movement* may simply try to keep some values the way they are. For example, one type of conservative movement tries to preserve old buildings and slow the rate of growth and change in big cities.

Some movements have far-reaching goals that would change the life of everyone in the society. Sometimes this type of movement is called a *utopian movement*, which means that it hopes to create a whole new type of society unlike any that now exists. Groups that form communes and organize a detailed life style for their members are utopian. The Oneida Community and the Shakers were nineteenth-century utopian communities. One group of this type had such strict rules that it even spelled out exactly how its members must get out of bed each morning—where to place each foot, and so on.

Religious movements have religious goals. Many people in Europe and North America have recently become interested in Eastern religious movements. A number of Indian mystics have large followings. Near my university I often encounter pale young men with shaven heads, wearing yellow monks' robes. They greet me with the chant "Hari Krishna!"

CP Photo/Bregg

Social movements generally give rise to organized groups that put pressure on the government.

and I reply politely, "Hari Hari!"

The most important type of movement that is producing social change around the world today is the *ethnic* or *nationalistic movement*. As suggested in the preceding chapter, our time is one in which ascribed communities are developing a strong awareness of themselves as "peoples."

337

SOCIAL RESEARCH:
Sociologists at Work

CANADIAN SOCIAL
REFORMS IN THE EARLY
TWENTIETH CENTURY

Canada is not a society much given to collective behavior. Rash outbursts, panics, and faddish enthusiasms rarely occur in Canada, which tends to be rather staid. Social movements, however, are another matter. Canadian history contains many accounts of movements that have demanded social improvement; usually these movements have taken a political form and they have often produced lasting social changes. Paul and Linda Grayson and Samuel Clark, when editing their book about Canadian social movements, *Prophecy and Protest*,[27] collected analyses of three movements that took place around the turn of this century, mostly in the western provinces. These were (1) the religious movement called "the social gospel," (2) the temperance movement, and (3) the women's suffrage movement. Some of the changes caused by these three interrelated movements lasted only briefly, while others have become permanent fixtures of Canadian society.

In their introductory remarks, the editors offer a few statistics to illustrate Canada's fast rate of development at the turn of the century. For example, between 1890 and 1910, the population of Canada increased by 32 percent; this was mostly due to widespread immigration, especially to the prairies. Industrialization reached unprecedented levels and rural Canadians moved into cities in great numbers. Between 1900 and 1910, the urban population of Canada increased by 62 percent. Montreal and Toronto doubled in population, while Calgary and Regina multiplied tenfold.

Dynamic periods of growth often create considerable social stress and disorder; this was certainly true of Canada during this period. The new working-class urban dwellers lacked the strong social ties and traditions that make social stability possible. They spent more time in saloons than was good for them. Their traditional cultures became fragmented. Unfortunately, prosperous Canadians were generally indifferent to the problems of the poor, for they held to a philosophy of economic individualism and did not think it proper

or necessary to provide social welfare measures. This neglect took a high social toll. According to accounts of the period, excessive drinking resulted in widespread family problems and criminal activity among the poor. Against this social setting, the social gospel, the temperance movement, and the suffrage movement developed.

The social gospel was primarily a Protestant movement that emphasized a new kind of theology. Rather than saving only their own souls, social gospel Christians were obliged to save all of human society. According to the social gospel, as long as exploitation, injustice, bad working conditions, and other social ills existed, Christians had not fulfilled their obligation to the Lord. They claimed that Christian work should concentrate on service to the poor and the victims of social disorganization. Legislative reform was viewed as a religious responsibility. Zeal for the social gospel swept through many Christian churches and inspired many revivalistic preachers, though Catholics remained generally unaffected.

In a way, the social gospel was a conservative social movement. Rather than trying to introduce new values and norms, it tried to persuade society to live up to ideals that most Canadians already possessed. The temperance and the suffrage movements had their roots in the same Christian conservatism; their goals nicely complemented those of the social gospel. The temperance and suffrage movements attempted to remake society through legal reforms, and overcome the evils created by drink and the oppression of women.

For all their Christian conservatism, social gospel proponents often appeared radical. They pressed for a variety of social reforms. In some places, their achievements included the introduction of workmen's compensation and old age pensions, the regulation of working conditions in factories, and the limitation of child labor. Their radicalism is best demonstrated by their partial support in 1919 of the Winnipeg General Strike.

The social reform movement was generally much stronger in the west than elsewhere in Canada. Though their policies were later adapted by political parties, notably by the Progressive Conservatives, most reformers in that early period did not have any particular party affiliations.[28]

Ironically, World War I quickened the pace of social reform. Even former pacifists favored the war because they believed that it forced Canada to try harder to live up to its nobler ideals. Social

These little old ladies look mild enough here, but in their day they were fierce suffragettes. From left to right, they are Alice Holling, Nellie McClung, and Elma Kennedy.

reformers believed that Canada, previously materialistic and indifferent to injustice, was now fighting the Kaiser to combat these evils. They also thought that, after the war, Canada would be forced to clean its own house; post-war Canada would enlarge and develop its government and act vigorously to support positive human goals.

The temperance movement also gained through the war effort. Prohibitionists argued that the traffic in liquor made soldiers less effective in combating the Kaiser and his brutal hordes. One writer stated that "If a westerner would despise the Kaiser for dropping bombs on defenseless people and shooting down innocent people, he should also despise the liquor traffic, since it has waged war on women and children all down the centuries."[29] The Kaiser and the liquor trade were

made to appear as equal, allied enemies. Prohibitionists believed that in order to rescue "clean-minded, innocent young boys" from contamination overseas, liquor had to be banned from soldiers' canteens. They claimed that, whenever liquor was sold, venereal disease would inevitably result. It is not clear even today, however, whether most soldiers would have supported prohibition had they been asked.[30]

As a result of prohibitionist efforts, temperance and patriotism came to be regarded as synonymous. When the prohibition referenda for 1914-1916 were put before the electorate, they were commonly regarded as an opportunity to support the war effort. In Manitoba, a newspaper warned that "Anyone who will vote in favor of liquor might as well enlist under the Kaiser, as far as patriotism goes."[31] Though many of Saskatchewan's European immigrants did not traditionally regard liquor as dangerous, they saw the referenda as a means to prove their loyalty and patriotism for their new country. French Canadians in western Canada, however, were not moved by prohibition arguments. Because they had lived in North America for many generations, they felt no need to prove their loyalty. They also objected to the totalitarian techniques of the prohibitionists. Francophones rejected prohibition in the referenda of every province.

For a while after prohibition was enacted in the west, those who had supported it claimed that drunkenness had been reduced by 90 percent. Very soon after the war, however, it was clear that prohibition had not eradicated crime. Indeed, through the resulting bootlegging industry, crime actually increased and law enforcement agents were faced with insurmountable problems. By 1924 the western provinces had reinstated government-owned liquor stores and had abandoned prohibition.

The suffrage movement enjoyed much more long-term success. Although suffrage had been linked to pacifism before World War I, Canadian women supported the war effort wholeheartedly.[32] The idealistic arguments for the war were also arguments for women's rights. Suffragettes claimed that if Canadian women were prepared to sacrifice their sons to protect democracy, they should have democratic rights. According to the suffragettes, Canadian women, armed with the vote, would never allow Canada to return to its prewar materialism. Moreover, the war allowed women to show their competence in work. They rolled bandages and knit socks. Posters of the day pictured noble women quietly bearing their burden while men fought on the battlefield; this portrait did not do the suffrage movement any harm.[33] In 1916, the western provinces gave women the right to vote in provincial elections, and in 1919, two months after the war ended, women were allowed to vote in federal elections.

Clearly, then, the women's movement was a success. Equally clearly, the prohibitionists ultimately failed. In the case of the social gospel movement, however, success was more ambiguous. Though it ultimately failed as a revivalist religious movement, the social gospel was successfully transformed into a secular political movement, and had great influence in subsequent political struggles in the west.

SOCIAL POLICY:
Issues and Viewpoints

We have discussed the effects of the media in other chapters, but then we were concerned with their effects on culture and on individual violence. Here we will turn our attention to the relationship between the media and collective behavior.

It is not possible to find out how many riots, terrorist attacks, murders, hijackings, kidnappings, suicides, political assassinations, and so on are stimulated by reports in the mass media. One way to find out would be to ban any reports of such events in the media of, say, five or six areas for a period of several years. Then we could compare the murder rate, the number of riots, and the like before and during the censorship period. Such an experiment could never be done, of course, so we may never know the answers. In the absence of good research, your guess is as good as mine. I would guess that much of the violence of modern life results directly from ideas picked up from the mass media. For example, when a group of boys threw gasoline on a girl and set her on fire they were imitating a scene they had watched on television that week. The media suggest possible actions. Emotionally unstable people and children may be especially likely to be influenced by those suggestions.

It is reasonable to suppose that simply reporting riots, hijackings, crime, bomb scares, and the like costs human lives by stimulating people to imitate such actions. It is also reasonable to suppose that films and television help maintain our culture's emphasis on violence. These are assump-

tions, not proved facts, but they are very likely accurate.

On the other hand, citizens have a right to be kept informed. It is hard to downplay riots, kidnappings, and other acts of violence. As one newscaster has remarked, television can't "hide" a story by printing it on the back page. Should the media be forbidden to report certain facts? This could lead to other, equally serious problems. Freedom of the press is an important tool for preventing tyranny. I certainly don't want the government to control the content of television programs or newspaper articles. Government officials could protect their own interests by hiding certain facts. The Watergate scandal, for example, would never have come to the attention of the public if the media hadn't been allowed to publish the facts. Only dictators want to censor news.

But obviously we do have a certain amount of censorship. Diplomats have to negotiate in secret. Some military matters must be kept secret. Gruesome pictures of accident or murder victims are not shown on television; the body is decently covered with a blanket. Newscasters don't show pornography on their programs. Newspapers can't print stories that they can't prove about a person. So we have a free press, but not without limits. Other values have to be respected as well—the right to privacy, national security, the need to protect people from seeing brutality, obscenity, and the like. The problem is the conflict between these values. As mentioned earlier, it is easy to choose between a right and a wrong. What is hard is to choose between two conflicting rights. The conflict here is between the right to be informed and the right to be protected against violence that might result from the reporting of violent acts by the mass media.

SUMMARY

1. *Collective behavior* consists of actions by a number of people that deviate from the institutionalized patterns of everyday life. According to Smelser, it will occur only if six conditions are met: (1) structural conduciveness, (2) structural strain, (3) a generalized belief, (4) precipitating factors, (5) mobilization for action, and (6) ineffective social control.

2. Behavior after disasters is rarely disorderly. Routine, institutionalized procedures usually don't work, but people invent new ways of doing things, usually in a spirit of mutual concern and solidarity. Panics, on the other hand, arise in competitive situations where people believe there are not enough escape routes. Panic behavior is a scramble to protect oneself without concern for others.

3. The *acting crowd* is the form of collective behavior that is most often troublesome. It chooses a course of action on the spot, and can become violent. There are several theories that try to explain crowd behavior: (1) contagion theories, (2) convergence theory, (3) emergent-norm theory, and (4) game theory.

4. Contagion theories (Le Bon, Freud, Blumer) assume that the crowd is irrational and that normal people caught up in it will become irrational. People follow the crowd as a result of some sort of emotional communication. Le Bon explained this process as imitation, hypnosis, and suggestion. Freud thought it was largely a matter of identifying with the leader. Blumer believed it was caused by a "circular reaction" that goes on during the "milling stage"—a direct, unthinking reaction of people to each other's emotions.

5. Convergence theory assumes that people who happen to have similar hidden wishes and happen to gather in a crowd may, if someone starts the action, ignore their usual inhibitions and take part in mob violence. Their behavior is not acquired through "contagion" but stems from impulses that each participant already has within himself or herself.

6. Emergent-norm theory holds that in unusual situations a crowd may find ordinary norms inadequate. There may be no uniform opinion as to how to behave, but some people express their opinions and others do not. If the expressed opinions *appear* to represent those of all the members of the crowd, they become a new norm that others will follow out of their desire to conform.

7. Game theory sees collective behavior not as irrational but as the outcome of special situations in which participation in a crowd changes the payoff for some courses of action. Acting within a crowd may become rational, while doing the same thing alone would be too risky.

8. *Rumors* often arise during periods of stress, because they depend on ambiguity and on the intensity of interest in the subject matter.

9. Different *publics* exist within society, each one concerned with a particular issue. Some individuals ("opinion leaders") have more influence than others on people's opinions.

10. The mass media affect ordinary people in a "two-step flow of communication." The media first influence the opinion leaders, and they, in turn, influence others. *Propaganda* is the planned use of media to influence the opinions of others.

11. A *social movement* is a collective effort to bring about a new order of life. It is often the source of a new value. It may clarify the collective consciousness by trying to get the whole society to understand its own point of view.

KEY TERMS

acting crowd a potentially violent mob that chooses a course of action on the spot.

collective behavior spontaneous, transitory, non-institutionalized group action.

craze a fad or fashion that becomes so important to people that they spend a great deal of money and emotion on it.

crowd a large, temporary group of people who have some common goal or interest.

expressive crowd a group that shows especially strong feelings.

fad a culture trait that suddenly becomes popular and then disappears.

fashion a culture trait that is popular for a short time and is gradually replaced.

propaganda the planned use of mass media to influence the beliefs and opinions of a population.

public a scattered group of people who have different opinions about an issue and are involved in a discussion of that issue.

rumor a piece of information that is passed from one person to another throughout a group without being checked for accuracy.

social movement a collective effort to bring about a new order of life.

FOR FURTHER READING

ALLPORT, GORDON W. and LEO POSTMAN. *The Psychology of Rumor.* New York: Holt, Rinehart & Winston, 1947. A classic study which reveals how stories get transformed in the repeated telling.

BADGLEY, ROBIN and S. WOLFE. *Doctor's Strike: Medical Care and Conflict in Saskatchewan.* Toronto: Macmillan, 1967. Strikes can be part of a social movement, or they can be a routinized aspect of social life. Most social events in the prairies seem to be based on some sort of movement. See Samuel Clark's book for evidence of that assertion.

BERK, RICHARD A. *Collective Behavior.* Dubuque, Iowa: William C. Brown, 1974. A small paperback that criticizes older theories about collective behavior and argues that the phenomenon can be understood as rational behavior. Highly readable.

CLARK, SAMUEL D., J. PAUL GRAYSON, and LINDA M. GRAYSON, eds. *Prophesy and Protest: Social Movements in Twentieth-Century Canada.* Toronto: Gage, 1975. This is a collection of papers about various social movements, three of them described in this chapter. Unlike Europe with its history of violence, Canada traditionally supports a variety of radical social movements that are not really revolutionary.

CLARK, S. D. *Movements of Political Protest in Canada. 1640-1840.* Toronto: University of Toronto Press, 1969. S. D. Clark is one of Canada's most prolific sociologists. This is an important contribution to social history.

KLAPP, ORRIN. *Currents of Unrest: An Introduction to Collective Behavior.* New York: Irvington, 1972. This text is especially useful as a treatment of the communication processes that lead to unpredictable group behavior.

PINARD, MAURICE. *The Rise of a Third Party: A Study in Crisis Politics.* Englewood Cliffs, N.J.: Prentice-Hall, 1971. This is a fine analysis of the Social Credit movement in Quebec.

TRUDEAU, PIERRE ELLIOTT, ed. *The Asbestos Strike.* Toronto: James, Lewis, and Samuel, 1974. Like the Winnipeg General Strike, the Quebec asbestos strike will be recounted in Canadian history for a long time to come.

ZAKUTA, LEO. *A Protest Movement Becalmed.* Toronto: University of Toronto Press, 1964. Zakuta's book deals with the rise of the C.C.F., the precursor in Saskatchewan of the New Democratic Party. Zakuta was concerned about its transition to the national level of politics.

THREE

social institutions

12

THE FAMILY

Family organization and kinship patterns
  Rules of marriage
  Systems of descent
  Systems of residence
Functions of the family
  Regulation of sexual behavior and
    reproduction
  Socialization
  Protection
  Affection
Variations in family structure
  Illegitimate children
  Divorce
The universality of the family
  Societies without families
  Can societies survive without families?
Perspectives on social change and the
    family
  The conservative view
  The radical view
  The liberal view: functionalism
Social Research: Sociologists at Work
Social Policy: Issues and Viewpoints

Does a spirit live in your fireplace? In the days when Zeus and Apollo and the other gods lived on Mt. Olympus, every household had at least one live-in god that supposedly dwelled in the hearth and looked after the family's welfare. I imagine it chose the hearth because that was a cozy spot where the family gathered for intimacy. I don't even have a fireplace, but I think our household spirit lives in the coffee table instead.

Of course, household spirits were not awe-inspiring or majestic. If they had been, nobody could have endured having them around. Dignified spirits are for dignified places, but a home is the place for all the undignified activities that people don't like to perform in public. At home you can cut your toenails, belch out loud, and watch TV wearing only underwear.

The family is important because it comprises the people in whose company you feel free to do all of these graceless things and more. We often claim that the great thing about families is the love their members have for each other, but that is only part of the truth. The most beautiful, treasured moments of your life may be with your family but some of the worst moments will also be with them, and those times are just as important. Whoever has seen you at your worst and still cares is important to you.

In this chapter I want to discuss a little about sociologists' studies of family life. But first let me caution you not to expect too much. Because they care so much about family life, students often look to sociology for practical advice on how to live together happily. You may hope this chapter will do that for you. It won't. Sociologists who study families have no happier homes than anybody else. Human experience is complex. The deepest problems of human behavior cannot be solved with pat formulas or sociological explanations. So, without expecting too much, let's consider what sociology does have to say about the family.

Family organization and kinship patterns

Although all societies recognize special bonds between kin (people who are related either by birth or by marriage, such as husbands and wives, brothers and sisters, aunts and nieces), kinship patterns differ widely. The patterns that seem familiar and natural to North Americans would seem strange to members of most of the world's societies. Here I will simply mention some of the terms social scientists use in describing the most common patterns of kinship.

The core unit of kinship is a group that we all know well—the nuclear family (a husband, his wife, and their unmarried children). This unit is the "atom" from which larger kinship groupings are built. (It is sometimes called the *conjugal family* because it is based on marriage.) In about half of all societies, however, a nuclear family is not usually independent. Instead, it is a unit within the extended family, a household that is made up of the nuclear family plus various other relatives such as grandparents. (The extended family is sometimes called the *consanguine* family because the members are tied together by "blood"—that is, birth.)

The extended family usually consists of a husband, his wife, and their sons, plus the sons' wives and children. In some cases, however, the daughters bring husbands home and the husbands become part of the extended family. One type of extended family, called the joint family, is traditional in Hindu India, where brothers continue to share property even after their parents' death. The oldest male is the head of the family, but he cannot dispose of the family's property. Nowadays females are also entitled to a share of the property. The joint family does not always live together as a single household, however.

A composite family is formed when nuclear families live together in a single household. Besides the extended family, another important type of composite family exists in about one-fourth of the world's societies—the polygamous family, in which there are several wives or husbands. A polygamous family may be either polygynous or polyandrous. Polygyny means "several women" and refers to the marriage of a man to more than one wife. Often the various wives are sisters. Polygyny is widespread. Anthropologists have found that in 193 out of 234 societies the ideal is for a man to have two or more wives.[1] Of course it is rarely possible for the majority of the men in a society to have more than one wife. This is because the ratio of males to females is nearly equal in all human popula-

This polygymous family consists of a man, his 156 wives, and their children.

Marc & Evelyne Bernheim/Woodfin Camp

tions and remains so unless it is changed by extreme events such as war or female infanticide (the killing of female babies). In order to give men an opportunity to have more than one wife, polygynous societies often match young women with older husbands. When the man dies, his young wife can marry into another polygynous household.[2]

Polyandry (which means "several men") refers to the marriage of a woman to more than one husband. This form of family is extremely rare. Its most common form is the sharing of a woman by two or more brothers. The Todas of southern India and the lowest class of Tibetans have practiced this fraternal type of polyandry, and the Marquesan islanders have practiced nonfraternal polyandry. However, other forms of marriage are also practiced in all three of these societies. Polyandry is usually permitted as the last resort in very poor societies in which female infanticide is institutionalized.

RULES OF MARRIAGE

All societies have certain rules of endogamy and exogamy, which define for the individual the people who are eligible mates. Endogamy requires a person to marry someone within his or her own group. Pressure to marry "within the faith" is an endogamous rule found in many religious communities. Likewise, many ethnic groups require a person to marry a member of the same ethnic community. This rule may be so strictly enforced that anyone who breaks it will be shunned. (Quite apart from the rules of endogamy, people have a strong tendency to prefer mates who are similar to themselves in certain important ways. This is called homogamy, meaning the tendency for like to marry like. For example, you are likely to choose as your spouse someone from a similar social class to yours, with similar religious beliefs and similar intelligence, though there are no social norms that require you to do so.)

Exogamy requires a person to choose a mate from a different group. The taboo against incest is the most obvious example of an exogamous rule. It forbids one to mate with one's parents or siblings (and often aunts, cousins, and other kin). Many societies define marriage with any member of one's own lineage as incestuous.

SYSTEMS OF DESCENT

Western societies reckon descent from both the mother's side and the father's side, a system called **bilateral descent**. It makes no difference whether an aunt or uncle, a cousin or a grandparent is related to us through our father or our mother. Both lines are equally important. We take our father's surname, but in all other respects we are tied by kinship to our mother's family as much as to our father's.

Our bilateral system is an uncommon form of kinship; only 30 percent of all known societies use it. Much more common are **unilinear systems**—systems that consider the male blood line or the female blood line, but not both, as kin. A unilinear system may be either matrilineal or patrilineal. In a **patrilineal descent system** each person, male or female, belongs to the father's line. This includes the father's father as well as his brothers and his brothers' children. Only the descendants of males are included, however, for daughters marry men of different lines and give birth to children who belong to those other lines.

Matrilineal descent systems are the "mirror image" of patrilineal systems. In such a system a person belongs to the mother's line, which includes the mother, her sisters, and her sisters' children. When a man marries he remains part of his mother's line, but his children become part of his wife's line, not his own. The anthropologist Bronislaw Malinowski studied a number of matrilineal societies, including the Trobriand Islanders. He tells us that a male Trobriander usually has a warm relationship with his son, much like the relationship between uncles and nephews in our own society. However, a father does not have any real authority over his son. He does have authority over his sister's children and in fact is required to support them, for he belongs to their line and not to his own children's line. Some 15 percent of all the world's societies are matrilineal. The patterns of matrilineal and patrilineal descent are shown in Figure 12.1.

Matrilineal kinship systems should not be confused with *matriarchy*. The fact that the "family tree" is traced through the female line does not mean that women have authority over men. In fact, true matriarchy is unknown among all the societies in the world.

SYSTEMS OF RESIDENCE

In Western society a bride and groom are usually expected to set up housekeeping on their own. This norm is called the rule of **neolocal residence**—the new conjugal family lives in a "new locale." Societies with extended families, on the other hand, require either **patrilocal** or **matrilocal** residence, depending on whether the newly married couple moves in with the husband's parents or the wife's. A few societies have *bilocal* rules that permit the couple to live with either the husband's family or the wife's. Systems of residence do not necessarily coincide with rules of descent; a patrilineal society, for example, does not always require patrilocal or even neolocal residence.[3]

Functions of the family

In primitive societies, family and kinship ties are almost the only institutions that exist. All the functions of society—religious, political, economic, as well as emotional and protective—are carried out through these ties. In modern societies, many of these functions have been taken over by

FIGURE 12.1
Unilineal descent

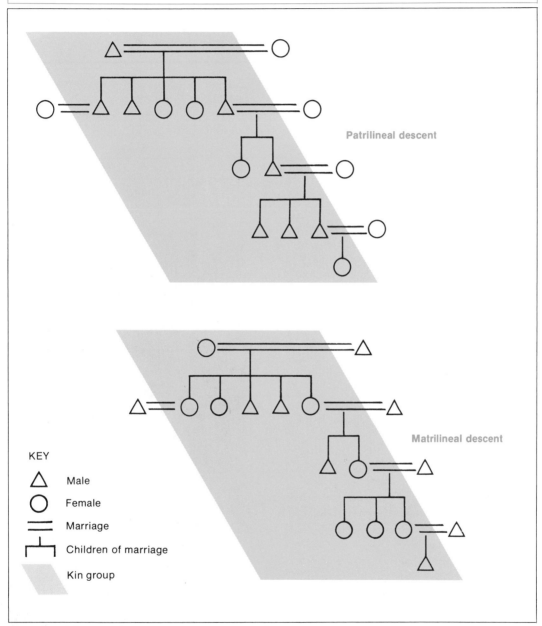

Patrilineal descent

Matrilineal descent

KEY

△ Male

○ Female

═ Marriage

┓┏ Children of marriage

Kin group

Source: David A. Schulz, The Changing Family, 2nd ed. (Englewood Cliffs, N.J.: Prentice-Hall, 1976), p. 67.

specialized institutions such as schools, factories, churches, and government agencies. Still, the functions of the modern family are numerous and vital. For example, the family assigns a social status to children until they are old enough to determine their own. Several other functions are even more important. We will discuss four of these: (1) regulation of sexual behavior and reproduction, (2) socialization, (3) protection, and (4) affection.

REGULATION OF SEXUAL BEHAVIOR AND REPRODUCTION

A marriage ceremony formally establishes a family. It has traditionally been assumed that marriage will be followed by the birth of children. Within the family, stable sexual relationships can be maintained, both for the personal pleasure of the men and women involved and for the sake of society, which needs new members. The family's basic purpose is to create offspring who will become useful members of the society in adulthood, carrying the human species forward.

Few societies today have trouble maintaining their populations. Most have the opposite problem—their populations are growing too quickly. Today we are less likely to believe that a couple has a duty to produce children. Yet most people prefer to marry rather than live alone, even if they do not plan to have children. Often these are people who feel dissatisfied with the instability of a series of temporary sexual relationships. Such a life style takes a good deal of emotional energy. Marriage offers a steady sexual relationship in the context of fairly secure interpersonal relationships. Even so, nonmarital and homosexual relationships are common in a large part of the population. We should consider them here before moving on.

Nonmarital sexual behavior

Almost all other societies have more liberal attitudes toward nonmarital intercourse

than Western society. Most societies are concerned with preventing births outside of marriage but not necessarily with preventing sexual relations outside of marriage. In fact the majority of societies permit premarital sex. One study reported that less than one-third of all societies entirely disapproved of both premarital and extramarital relations. Husbands are more often permitted more sexual freedom than wives.

There is, of course, a good deal of evidence that the rules of sexual behavior are becoming

Fredrik D. Bodin/Stock, Boston

much more permissive in most Western societies. However, the most rapid increase in permissiveness occurred not in the present generation but in the years just following World War I. A study published in 1938, for example, showed that 14 percent of the women born before 1890 admitted to having premarital sexual intercourse, as compared to 68 percent of those born after 1909.[4] After the 1920s the frequency of sexual relations among unmarried youth seems to have remained fairly stable until the 1960s, when another large increase began.[5] This increase was greater for females than for males.

In the ten years from 1965 to 1975 there were marked changes in attitudes toward sex. One study of college women found that the view of premarital sex as immoral declined steadily from a high of 70 percent in 1965 to 34 percent in 1970 and 20 percent in 1975. Moreover, in the early 1970s there was a shift from the "double standard" to a single standard of behavior for males and females. Thus promiscuity is now considered about equally unacceptable in both males and females.[6]

A study of university and trade school students in Alberta, Quebec, and Ontario showed that though some young people felt painful pangs of guilt after their first experiences of sexual intercourse, the majority did not seem to be troubled by guilt.[7] French Canadian students were more conservative than English Canadians, female students more conservative than males, and trade school students more than university students.

Comparative research on the frequency of sexual intercourse among the youth of various countries suggests that North Americans may be somewhat more conservative than Europeans. Within North America, Canadians seem to be somewhat more conservative than Americans. The researchers do not pretend to know why this may be so.[8]

What often appears as a conflict between the morals of young people and those of their parents is in fact a conflict between their roles and their parents' roles. Any parent is likely to be more opposed to premarital sexual relations than he or she was before becoming a parent. Parents also tend to be less liberal in their attitudes toward sex than nonparents of the same age. This is because parents feel responsible for the consequences of their children's behavior, and this creates anxiety. One study illustrated this point by asking parents about their own premarital behavior and also asking them whether they approved of such behavior on the part of their children. Of the mothers, some 30 percent had had sex before marriage, but only 3 percent would approve of it for their daughters and only 9 percent for their sons. Of the fathers, 51 percent had had premarital sexual relations but only 10 percent approved of it for their daughters and 18 percent for their sons.[9]

Parental disapproval does not necessarily stop children, however. Kinsey showed that the majority of boys have engaged in some sex play before adolescence and that about one-quarter of the girls have.[10] Most of this sex play is homosexual in nature for both sexes. For white youths, but not black, religious devoutness strongly limits premarital sexual behavior.[11]

Some of the studies done during the past decade by feminists and sex-therapy researchers have uncovered some surprising facts about female sexuality. Shere Hite's study of American women reported that only a minority regularly experience orgasm during heterosexual intercourse, but almost all women are able to produce intense and multiple orgasms for themselves through masturbation. Obviously, the emotional experience of masturbation is very different from that of coitus, but Hite suggests that women might improve the sexual dimension of their lives by overcoming the shame that so commonly accompanies masturbation.[12] Indeed, sex therapists nowadays often teach women to masturbate to orgasm as one phase in developing more satisfying sexual relationships with partners.

Homosexual relationships

About 37 percent of adult American males and 13 percent of adult females have had at least one homosexual experience to the point of orgasm. About 4 percent of the males and 2 to 3 percent of the females are exclusively homosexual throughout their lives.[13] Yet homosexuality is still viewed with great disapproval by most people. Thus a 1977 survey of the Canadian population showed that 55 percent considered homosexual sex between people who are in love "absolutely wrong." (The same survey showed that only 15 percent of the sample felt that sex between single adults who are in love was absolutely wrong.)[14]

In the past few years the rise of the gay-liberation movement and its "backlash" have made these opinions political in nature. The gay movement has had some success in gaining acceptance for homosexuals, but it has not been very successful in gaining actual legal rights such as recognition of gay marriages as binding contracts.

There is no clear evidence that homosexuals are more likely to have psychological problems than other people. The psychologist Evelyn Hooker gave psychological tests to 30 male homosexuals and 30 otherwise similar heterosexual men. Her coworkers were unable to tell which of these tests had been given to homosexuals.[15] However, there is no doubt that the kind of life that many homosexuals are forced to live in order to keep their homosexuality secret is quite stressful.

A study of male homosexuals in New York, San Francisco, the Netherlands, and Denmark concludes that a man's living arrangements have an important impact on his personal adjustment. This study compared homosexuals in four different living arrangements—living with a homosexual mate, living alone, living with parents, and living with a wife. Those who lived with homosexual mates had the highest levels of self-accept-ance and the lowest levels of depression, loneliness, and guilt. In addition, this group was less likely to want psychiatric treatment for homosexuality.[16] It seems that this arrangement protects the couple from the negative attitudes of heterosexuals and from much psychological stress.

SOCIALIZATION

The main beneficiary of the family is the child. One can argue that the family might not exist if children did not have to be produced and raised. Many adults get along fairly well without permanent partners, but a child without a family is at a serious disadvantage. Children need to be in close, permanent contact with a few adults so that they can be prepared to play their roles in society when they themselves become adults. No fully satisfactory substitute for the family has yet been discovered.

Parents and siblings provide emotional support and act as role models. By performing the routine acts of daily living in the presence of young children, they teach them the roles of the group. Values are taught by example and discussion. This process—socialization—occurs in an unplanned, off-hand way. For example, children overhear adult discussions while riding around in the back seat of the family car as their parents do grown-up errands. However pleasant it is for small children to spend time together in nursery schools, collective child rearing cannot take the place of family living. Socialization of children is one of the most important functions of the family.

PROTECTION

The family performs another necessary service for children—protection. No other species has young that remain dependent on their parents as long as the human child does. Someone has to provide food, clothing, shelter, and other material benefits such as trips to the orthodontist, help in crossing busy streets, and money to buy subway tokens. The family performs these functions until the child is mature enough to perform them himself or herself. However, many studies show that grown-up children often continue to receive money and other kinds of help from their parents even after they have started their own households and are parents themselves.

AFFECTION

In addition to money, presents, and other material forms of help, the family also provides emotional support for its members. This is as important as any other function of the family. As a setting for warm, intimate relationships the family is unmatched by any other type of social group. Indeed, a person who does not have close ties with a family can suffer severe deprivation. One of the great problems facing modern society is that of helping people find substitutes for the intimate family group when they lack such a satisfying relationship.

The importance of the family is not limited to emotional well-being. The family also affects health and life span. You have been told that cigarette smoking is a major cause

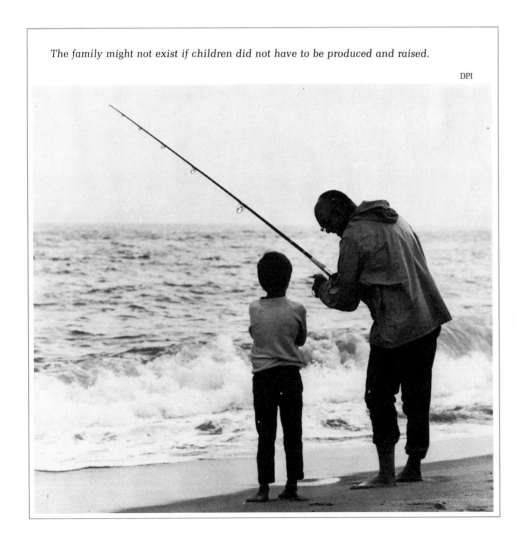

The family might not exist if children did not have to be produced and raised.

DPI

of death. But you may not know that being divorced or separated is about as harmful to your health as smoking. Loneliness kills. A recent book has revealed that heartbreak is a physical state as well as a psychological one. It shows, for example, that white adult males are about twice as likely to die of heart disease if they are single than if they are married. Among females, widows were much more likely to die of heart disease than married women. Many other diseases show similar patterns. Single, widowed, and divorced people usually die before they reach the age of 64—which is well below the average life expectancy of North American men and women.

The breakup of a family affects not only the adults' lives but the health of their children. A study of college students showed that they were more likely to die of coronary heart disease in later years if they were only children or if they had lost one or both parents before entering college.[17]

A Soviet study of life spans points to similar conclusions. It shows that people with long lives are generally those with warm family relationships, and that closeness to friends and members of the community also contributes to longevity.

Traditionally, women have found their greatest satisfaction in family relationships because they have been less involved in other matters than men. Studies have shown that women's marital satisfaction varies much more than that of males, usually declining during the first ten years of marriage. Contrary to widespread belief, having children does not contribute to marital happiness. On the contrary, the satisfaction of parents (especially mothers) in their marriage decreases during child rearing and rapidly recovers as the children grow up and leave home.[18] On the other hand, children may sometimes offer other satisfactions to the parents that compensate for unhappy marital relationships. Thus one study found that people who were dissatisfied with their marriage were more likely to say that their children were their only satisfaction.[19]

In later years parents find that good relationships with their children are a major source of satisfaction. Though most parents do not live with their children during this period, these relationships are usually close. In North America the extended family does not live under the same roof, but family members stay close enough together to make frequent visits possible. Only about 16 per-

---

TABLE 12.1

According to this Toronto survey, married women are more likely than their husbands to keep in close touch with their parents. However, the majority of both sexes call their parents at least weekly.

FREQUENCY OF TELEPHONE CALLS TO PARENTS (IN PERCENTAGES)

	DAILY	MORE THAN ONCE A WEEK	WEEKLY	MONTHLY	SEVERAL TIMES A YEAR	NEVER	
Husbands (54)	4	26	24	13	24	9	100
Wives (54)	43	20	9	22	4	2	100

Source: Howard H. Irving, *The Family Myth: A Study of the Relationship between Married Couples and their Parents* (Toronto: Copp Clark, 1972), pp. 41-61.

cent of all elderly Americans live more than an hour's ride away from their nearest child. A similar pattern is found in other Western societies.[20] Professional and managerial workers are more likely to move far enough away from their kin to weaken family relationships; among the working classes the generations keep in closer contact. One study of a British working-class neighborhood showed that the strongest tie is between the married daughter and her "mum."[21] This pattern is not found among all working classes everywhere, however. A study of workers' families in Hamilton, Ontario found that couples visited more often with the husband's parents than with the wife's.[22]

For a long time sociologists believed that the closeness of the kinship group had become weakened in industrial society. However, there is evidence that most families are *not* isolated from their relatives. In the United States, close ties between relatives are far more common than was thought only a few years ago,[23] and in the Canadian family these bonds are probably even closer.[24] A study of French Canadians in Montreal showed that a typical worker is able to recognize over 200 living relatives and that he meets an average of more than 40 relatives each month.[25]

Variations in family structure

ILLEGITIMATE CHILDREN

The anthropologist Bronislaw Malinowski discovered a universal norm that he called the *principle of legitimacy*: Every child born should be assigned to some male (whether or not he is the biological father), who will serve as the child's guardian, protector, and link to society. Malinowski claimed that in every known society a child who lacked such a "father" was deprived of some respect. Research done since Malinowski's day has supported this generalization. All societies distinguish between legitimate and illegitimate children, and all societies in some way recognize **illegitimacy**, or the birth of a child to an unmarried woman.

In almost every society a child who is conceived before marriage but born after marriage is considered legitimate. In fact in many societies pregnancy is a prerequisite for marriage. Kingsley Davis has called attention to the fact that illegitimacy is a result of the very rule that legitimates families. Because all societies require parents to be responsible for their legitimate offspring, they need rules for defining which children are entitled to such protection and which ones are not. Whatever the ritual by which a father takes on the responsibilities of parenthood, it follows that children who are not covered by the ritual are not entitled to its benefits. If the claims of legitimate children are to be protected, the claims of illegitimate children cannot have the same weight. The illegitimate child cannot claim descent in the same way as the legitimate child, does not have the same inheritance rights, and generally receives little support from the father. The child has to be provided for in some way, but at the same time, providing for that child challenges the rights that society wants to reserve for legitimate children.

Notice that this functionalist explanation of illegitimacy does not suggest that illegitimacy is functionally necessary. It claims only that the rules defining *legitimacy* are necessary and that these rules logically imply the existence of illegitimacy. However, this theory is similar to other functionalist theories in that it holds that the present rules are necessary and should not be changed.

Although illegitimate children have low esteem in all societies, illegitimacy continues to occur. The rates of illegitimacy vary greatly, however. This variation is usually thought to be due to varying degrees of social control. For example, the highest illegitimacy rates are found in the Caribbean.[26] To find out why, Judith Blake did a study of illegitimacy in

Jamaica, where some 65 percent of all births are illegitimate.[27] She discovered that there are social sanctions against illegitimacy but that other values are sometimes more important than legitimacy. For this reason the sanctions against illegitimacy are rather weak. Mothers commonly put off the marriages of their daughters so as to lengthen the time during which the daughters can help their own families. This means that a young woman often enters a sexual relationship secretly, becomes pregnant, and has an illegitimate child. One result is that the woman's bargaining power in the marriage market is reduced and she has even less chance of marrying. Nevertheless in Jamaica most people eventually do marry.

North American illegitimacy rates are not exceptionally high compared to those of certain other societies. However, illegitimacy is increasing in Canada. One might have expected that as contraception became more available and acceptable, the rate would decline, but precisely the contrary has taken place. Between 1961 and 1971, illegitimacy actually doubled, increasing from 4.5 percent of all live births to 9.0 percent.[28] The rates are lowest in Quebec and Ontario, and highest in the Yukon where one birth in four is illegitimate.[29] Evidently the stigma connected to unwed motherhood has declined. For some women, unwed motherhood is deliberately chosen as an alternative to marriage, even though the problems of single parenthood are obvious from the outset.

DIVORCE

Although no society encourages divorce, almost all societies make some allowance for it, or at least for legal separation. The United States has the highest divorce rate among Western nations (see Figure 12.2), but other societies have had far higher rates. Some 60 percent of all primitive societies seem to have higher divorce rates than the present U.S. rate.[30] In Arab countries, divorce has tradi-

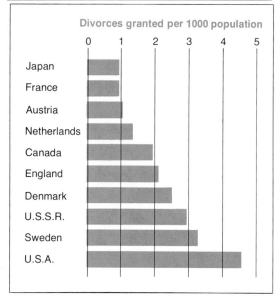

FIGURE 12.2

Crude divorce rate for selected countries, 1974

Divorces granted per 1000 population

Source: Data from U. N. Demographic Yearbook, 1975., Table 19.

tionally been a simple matter: A man could divorce his wife by saying three times, "I divorce thee."

The divorce rate has increased dramatically in Canada since the Divorce Act was passed in 1968. In 1961, the rate was 36 per 100,000 population; by 1974 it had risen to 200 per 100,000 population. Before 1968, the only legal grounds for divorce in Canada were adultery and insanity, but the law now recognizes other matrimonial problems, such as alcoholism, drug abuse, and physical and mental cruelty, as reasonable grounds for ending a marriage. "Marital breakdown" has also become grounds for divorce. A marriage is considered legally broken down if the partners have been officially separated for 3 years; about half of all Canadian divorces are now awarded simply on the basis of non-cohabitation.[31] The provision for "marital breakdown" has allowed couples to divorce without the public loss of dignity that occurred when they had to charge one another with disreputable behavior. While this reform has made divorce less shameful and more humane, it has also made it more acceptable and widespread.

Who gets divorced? One major factor in divorce is early marriage, especially teenage marriage. In 1971, women who had married as teenagers were three times more likely than others to be divorced.[32] The relationship between teenage marriage and divorce may be partly due to the fact that young brides were frequently pregnant at the time of their weddings.

Another factor influencing divorce rates is urban residence. Rural people may still attach a social stigma to divorce, or they may anticipate more difficulty in meeting new potential mates; whatever the reason, rural couples are less likely to divorce than urban couples.[33] Region also affects the divorce rate (see Figure 12.3).

Income is also related to marital breakdown.[34] Financial difficulties increase the likelihood of divorce. Not only the amount of money, but who earns it, is a factor; when the wife earns a large part of the family income, divorce is somewhat more likely than when the husband is sole breadwinner.[35]

Differences between spouses in social class, religion, or educational achievement often lead to divorce. Also, people who have been previously divorced are more susceptible

FIGURE 12.3

Divorce rate per 100,000 population by province

Source: Adapted from Lyle E. Larson, *The Canadian Family in Comparative Perspective* (Scarborough, Ont.: Prentice-Hall, 1976), p. 92.

to marriage breakdown than those who are married for the first time.

In any group of divorced Canadians, females will usually be found to outnumber males. Divorced males are more likely to remarry than divorced females, and are also likely to die sooner than their ex-wives.[36]

Robert Whitehurst, with various co-workers, has carried out several studies of Canadian divorces to determine the emotional factors that lead to marital breakdown. Not surprisingly, he reports that both husbands and wives felt that their feelings had been neglected prior to the separation. Women saw their husbands as excessively demanding, somewhat abusive, and unwilling to discuss problems. Men, on the other hand, commonly complained of too little physical affection and sexual participation from their wives. They also often objected to their wives taking outside jobs and expecting the housework to be a shared responsibility.

In almost half the cases, the presence of children made parents reluctant to separate or divorce. However, even in these cases, professional help and deliberate efforts to improve communication rarely worked out successfully.

Separated individuals generally experienced considerable loneliness and social isolation. Women, more than men, reported that economic problems resulted from their separations. Interestingly, separated women who had felt themselves subservient to extremely dominant husbands seemed to have fewer problems than other separated women.[37]

Possibly Canadians expect a greater degree of emotional support and communication between spouses than do members of many other societies. Whitehurst's comparative study of divorce among Canadians and Israelis suggests that these expectations do vary, at least between Canada and Israel. According to Whitehurst's study, Israeli women tend to be less assertive than Canadian women, and seldom question their husbands' directions. Israeli women most often

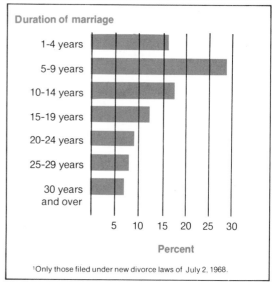

FIGURE 12.4

Divorces[1] in Canada by duration of marriage, 1975

Duration of marriage

1-4 years
5-9 years
10-14 years
15-19 years
20-24 years
25-29 years
30 years and over

5 10 15 20 25 30

Percent

[1]Only those filed under new divorce laws of July 2, 1968.

Source: Canada Year Book, 1978-79, p. 185.

cited adultery as the chief cause of divorce, while Canadian women more frequently cited "husband's low sex drive." Canadian wives claimed that a successful marriage depended on the husband's willingness to discuss problems openly and to be considerate. Canadian husbands saw sexual communication as the key to successful marriage; lack of sexual desire was frequently cited as a wife's chief shortcoming.[38]

What about the children of divorce? Studies of university students whose parents were divorced suggest that few children remember the trauma. Most of the students surveyed claimed that, in unhappy homes, divorce was best for everyone concerned.[39]

To some extent, family breakup seems to result in delinquency. However, it is not clear what causes this relationship. Both divorce and delinquency tend to occur in low-income families more than in higher-income families, so maybe it is really poverty rather than divorce that is responsible for delinquency. Several studies have shown that divorce is no more harmful for children than unhappy families that stay together.[40]

The universality of the family

The family may be the only institution that is found in all human societies. Its apparent universality suggests that no society could survive without it. It seems clear that without families, a society would have trouble meeting certain important human needs. Who would look after the children and socialize them? The family has many other important functions besides caring for children—such as emotional support and regulation of sexual relations.

Is the family universal? G. P. Murdock studied 250 societies and found that each had small social units consisting of a husband, wife, and children, that is, a nuclear family. He defines the family as a social group with the following characteristics: (1) Sexual access is permitted; (2) reproduction occurs legitimately; (3) the group is responsible to society for the care and upbringing of children; and (4) the group is an economic unit—at least in terms of consumption.[41]

SOCIETIES WITHOUT FAMILIES

A few social scientists challenge Murdock's claim that the family is universal. They admit that reproduction, socialization, and consumption are always managed by a kinship unit of some sort. But they argue that this unit is not necessarily a nuclear family. In some cases, the nuclear family's roles do not fit together to form a unit, separate from other units, that performs the four functions named by Murdock. For example, the Nayars of southern India and the present-day Israeli kibbutzim lack families of the sort described by Murdock, and the Russians practically abolished the family after the Revolution.

The Nayars

Nayar households were once composed of a brother and a sister and the sister's children. Women did not ordinarily have husbands. Instead, they had a number of regular lovers. When a girl reached puberty her relatives chose a "husband" for her, whom she married in only a formal sense, and from whom she was divorced within a few days. After her divorce a woman was permitted to take lovers. The lovers might give her presents but were not expected to provide for her. If a child was born, one of the lovers paid a fee to legitimate the child. This lover was recognized as the *legal* father even though he may not have been the child's *biological* father. He lived not with his child but with his sister and her children. If he did not have a sister he might live with some other woman of the same lineage, have authority over her household, and be called her "brother." Thus the Nayar nuclear family did not live together, and the actual social unit was not the nuclear family but the brother-sister household.[42]

Kibbutzim

On the Israeli kibbutz, the basic economic unit is the entire community rather than the family. People do not own private property—even personal supplies are owned by the kibbutz. When a man and a woman marry they are assigned a room to share, and when a child is born it lives in the children's house under the care of a nurse. The children visit their parents for a few hours each day, but they spend most of their time with their nurse and the other children in their group. The entire community is a primary group, and it socializes the children. Marriage rarely occurs between people who grew up together in the same children's house, since they feel like brothers and sisters.[43]

There is some debate as to whether the kibbutz is an exception to the generalization

Marvin E. Newman/Woodfin Camp

The Israeli kibbutz is like one large extended family.

that every society has nuclear families. The kibbutz is not a society but a segment of Israeli society. It is not clear that an entire society based on the kibbutz pattern could survive.

The USSR after the revolution

Perhaps the largest experiment in changing family responsibilities was carried out in the Soviet Union. After the revolution, the Bolsheviks decided that the family was a counterrevolutionary institution. They made major changes in family law that had important effects on sexual, marital, and parental relationships. Marriage and divorce became simple matters of registration. The distinction between legitimate and illegitimate children was blurred in two ways. First, parents were no longer responsible for the behavior of their

children; nor were they always expected to support their children, whether they were legitimate or not. Second, mature children, legitimate or illegitimate, were not responsible for their aging parents' financial welfare. It was official policy for children to be placed in child care centers so that their mothers could work. Ideally, children would be brought up in boarding schools away from the influence of their families. The Soviet Union remains officially committed to this program, but the boarding schools proved to be too expensive and there is still a shortage of child care centers.

Thus the Soviet ideal of collective child socialization has never been achieved. A 1926 Soviet law held that any man and woman who lived together (whether or not they registered the fact) were legitimately married in

360

terms of property rights and the rights of the spouse and children. A religious marriage had no legal effect in itself, but if it was followed by sexual relations it became a legal marriage. It was expected that as socialism progressed the family would disappear completely: "The family, creating a series of rights and duties between the spouses, the parents and children, will certainly disappear in the course of time and will be replaced by governmental organization of public education and social security."[44]

The goals of these laws were liberal, but their effects were questionable. For example, bigamy became legal, and parents were unable to control their children. By 1935 Soviet law had shifted back toward the family, mostly because the society could not cope with the strain of raising children outside of family settings. Parents became responsible for the behavior of their children and could be fined by the authorities if their children misbehaved. By 1936 *Pravda* was saying that free love was "bourgeois" and contrary to socialist principles. Since 1944 only a registered marriage has been legal in the USSR, and divorces are more difficult to get than in many capitalist countries. Moreover, children born outside of the father's registered marriage cannot claim his property or his name. This policy has created a status of illegitimacy similar to that found in other societies. In the late 1960s Soviet family law was again becoming more liberal, though not as liberal as in 1926. Yet today family life is stronger in the USSR than in the United States. The main function—socializing children—is performed by the family whenever possible.

CAN SOCIETIES SURVIVE WITHOUT FAMILIES?

Of the three cases discussed here, the Nayar society is the most convincing case of a workable and stable alternative to the nuclear family. It was successful in assigning the upbringing of children to adults in a house-

hold that included a responsible male, even though the sexual needs of adults were not fulfilled by members of their own household. This arrangement, however, is not among those suggested by people who object to the traditional roles of the Western conjugal family.

Sociologists cannot agree as to whether the nuclear family is a necessary part of every society; perhaps some new social experiment will fulfill the functions of the family more

Despite wide-scale experimentation with state-controlled child rearing, family influence remains strong in the USSR.

Constantine Manos/Magnum

successfully. But for the present it is probably correct to consider the family universal. The kibbutzim do not constitute a whole society, nor did the Nayars. Each of these groups was only part of a larger society. One can find groups *within* almost every society that do not conform to Murdock's generalizations (communities of monks, for example), but these are not whole societies. It has yet to be shown that a society that lacks nuclear families can be a whole, independent, self-supporting system.

Perspectives on social change and the family

If you are like most people, you have strong opinions about what families should be like. Here we will discuss the views of several important writers, past and present, on this question. For the sake of simplicity, we may call these views conservatism, radicalism, and liberalism.

THE CONSERVATIVE VIEW

Conservatism is a minority viewpoint among sociologists today. A true, old-fashioned conservative is hard to find. He or she would oppose individualism and rationalism as means of improving the human condition and would depend on tradition instead. The conservative views rapid social change as dangerous because it threatens tradition. Consider, for example, the conservative views of Le Play.

LePlay

Pierre Guillaume Frederick LePlay (1806-1882) wrote *The European Working Class* (1885) in an attempt to explain why family patterns varied from one society to another. He divided family life into three categories and discussed the situations in which these types were likely to occur. The first type was the *patriarchal* family—one in which the male head has complete authority.

LePlay thought this system was suitable only for groups that didn't have enough social authority or an adequate political system outside the family—nomads, for instance.

LePlay's second type of family was the *unstable* family. This pattern is found in societies that are undergoing serious disorganization. According to LePlay, the late Roman empire, France after the revolution, and Athens after the war against Sparta were characterized by unstable families. The unstable family is individualistic. It is more like a private contract than an institutional duty. Property is not often passed down through the unstable family.

In the *stem* family, LePlay's third category, children leave home when they grow up and form "branch" families of their own. Those who remain at home inherit all of the family property, but they must be prepared to help the others when necessary. LePlay liked this system because it encourages the young to become independent but at the same time offers them some security. However, it works well only where land is plentiful. Where land is scarce, the branch families have trouble and the men have to become wage laborers instead of farmers. Private property and religion are necessary for the smooth maintenance of the stem family. This is why it is a conservative institution.

THE RADICAL VIEW

The radical does not look back to an ideal past when families were supposedly stable but looks to a future in which the family will no longer exist. This position was held both by Marx and his close associate, Friedrich Engels, who wrote more on the family than Marx did.[45]

Marx and Engels

Radicals assume that the monogamous family has been held together by the institution of private property and that it is now a tool of capitalism. The family exploits humanity, especially women. Women have always been subordinate because of their dependence on the higher economic productivity of men. And women and children alike were forced to participate in an inhumane productive system when factories were first created.[46]

Engels believed communism would free people from exploitation, and he envisioned the changes that would follow. He decided that, when the two sexes were economically equal, men would become even more monogamous than they are now. But then marriages could be ended without making people "wade through the useless mire of divorce proceedings."[47] Child labor would, of course, be abolished. He looked forward to a time when men would not "purchase a woman's surrender" with money or social power and when women would not have to give in to any man.

THE LIBERAL VIEW: FUNCTIONALISM

We have already discussed functionalism. I mentioned that it leads one to think of a group as a whole system. Sociologists who specialize in the family have been especially interested in functionalism. Here we will look at two issues that concern functionalists: the relationship between modernity and the nuclear family and the functional explanation of sex role differences.

Industrialization and the nuclear family

What is a modern society? Among other things, it is a society with an *industrial* economy and a *neolocal* residence pattern. Is there a functional reason for these two characteristics to be connected? Is industrialization encouraged when nuclear families live separately from their kin? Does industrialization lead to neolocal residence? Functionalist writers such as Talcott Parsons, Neil Smelser, and William J. Goode have argued that there is a causal link between industrialization and the neolocal residence of nuclear families.

According to Parsons, social change always involves *differentiation*.[48] One example

of differentiation is the separation of the family from the economic enterprise. Max Weber held that this separation was an essential condition for the rise of capitalism. Why? Because the success or failure of a business had to be distinguishable from the success or failure of a private household budget. The keeping of separate checkbooks for office and home is one result of differentiation.

Smelser has examined how the family became differentiated from the economy. This took place during the Industrial Revolution, and Smelser paid special attention to the textile industry in England.[49] At first families wove textiles for their own use and sometimes for sale. But as the market for textiles increased, the question of efficiency came up. The businesses that succeeded assigned particular jobs to the most skillful workers, no matter what family they belonged to. Eventually the factory came to be separate from the family. As a result, two separate institutions now carry out tasks that used to be performed by the family alone.

Parsons shows that as modernization continues, more and more functions that used to be performed by the family are taken over by new, specialized institutions. This, again, is differentiation. For example, the family used to educate children, but now the school performs this function.

Functionalists think the detached nuclear family is better for an industrial society because it opens up the labor market. Each family can move around and change jobs easily. The extended family made it harder for industrial workers to move around. William J. Goode explains the fast industrialization of Japan (as compared to China) as due to the fact that the kinship system was looser in Japan. Japanese youth were free to decide whether or not to move for the sake of a better career; Chinese youth were not.[50]

It's reasonable to believe that the detached nuclear family is especially compatible with industrialization. But several recent studies cast some doubt on this notion. For one thing, the modern nuclear family is not as isolated as Parsons and others believed. It is true that the extended kin don't live under the same roof, but they usually live nearby. To be fair to the functionalists, we might say that the Western family is more independent of its extended kin than lots of other societies; that is, it is *comparatively* isolated.

But there is an even more important point against the functionalist position.[51] Recent research has shown that the detached nuclear family is not *always* associated with industrialization and that it did not become the household pattern in Europe as a *result* of the Industrial Revolution. Most Europeans lived in detached nuclear families long before industrialization began. Nor does industry require the isolation of the family. In Yugoslavia, for example, an extended-family system has not prevented industrialization. Indeed, no country that has industrialized has developed a conjugal family pattern as a result of industrialization. We must conclude that industrialization and the nuclear family are sometimes found together but that the connection between them is not *necessary*.

Sex role differentiation

We have called the functionalist model "liberal" because it demands neither a return to traditional family patterns nor an end to the family as an institution. In fact functionalists are not as interested in supporting any particular policy as they are in explaining whatever patterns actually exist. Unfortunately, it is not always clear whether they are explaining the status quo or justifying it. For

The couple entering this marriage may not hold to traditional views of the family. How can two people decide what claims and responsibilities are right for each of them?

Joel Gordon/DPI

this reason they are sometimes viewed as reactionary—especially when they provide functional explanations of social phenomena that the critics want to change. Sex role differences within the family are an example of such an issue.

The leading functionalist theory regarding sex roles is that of Parsons and Robert Freed Bales.[52] They hold that kinship is becoming less important in modern society because we emphasize achieved status more than ascribed status. The more we emphasize the importance of, say, occupational achievement, the less we can emphasize the importance of extended-family relationships. And the status of the family is determined more and more by the achievements of the husband-father. Therefore the parents in the nuclear family specialize in different activities. This division of labor within the family leads to major differences between the roles of men and women. Dad is the instrumental leader of the family. Thus his job provides the income and determines the life style and

prestige of the family. Mom is the expressive leader of the family. Thus she specializes in such matters as the children's emotional growth, their table manners, the color of the new sofa, the planning of outings, church attendance, and sending birthday cards. Expressive activities are done for their own sake, while instrumental activities are done for some practical reason.

Although the family no longer performs many of its former functions, it is still vital in certain areas—especially the socialization of children. Parsons thinks the detached nuclear family is especially good at socializing children—far better than any other type of family. This is because the small, isolated nuclear family is emotionally involved with the needs of family members—especially the children. Within ten years of the time that Parsons and Bales published their work, however, many women made it clear that they did not find their traditional roles satisfying at all. If Parsons and Bales were writing their book today, it would probably be quite different.

SOCIAL RESEARCH:
Sociologists at Work

In this section we will discuss two different topics. The first is the situation of old people in the stage of the life cycle in which "the nest is empty." The second is a review of the evidence on present-day family trends and what they suggest about the future of the family in Western societies.

OLD AGE AND THE FAMILY

The Canadian population is getting older. By the year 2001, one Canadian in ten will be 65 or older. An increase in life span, along with a decline in the fertility rate, means that more and more

married couples can expect to spend many years together after their youngest child has left home. What do we know about this phase of "childless" old age?[53]

First, older people are not usually as isolated as one might suppose; most of them have kin living nearby. Older people generally prefer to live in their own homes rather than with their children, in institutions, or in hospitals. Usually they are able to do so. Among Canadians over 65, a large majority live with their spouses in single-detached housing. Only 8 percent live in "collective housing," such as nursing homes, rooming houses, or hospitals. However, almost 25 percent of elderly females live alone.[54]

For the first decade or more after the youngest child leaves home, most couples continue to be helpful in supporting their children, who usually live nearby. In general, the parents are middle-aged, not old, and often the woman has a career

Old people need as much variety, diversity, and sheer fun in their lives as anyone else.

when her first grandchildren are born. The parents thus can provide a constant flow of money to their children as well as services such as babysitting.

The marriages of middle-aged couples become more satisfying as the children leave, and this "upswing" seems to continue through the later years.[55] However, the nature of their relationship changes with time. Couples tend to value companionship more and romantic affection less, so that by the time they are over 65 their conversations are limited to conventional topics such as health, home repairs, and religion, and they rarely go away for an adventure together. After retirement their concerns as a couple become more expressive and less instrumental—the husband has given up his instrumental role. Sexual relations decline over the years, though this seems to result from boredom, not physical inability. The sex drive of normal women does not decline, and the decline among men sems to be a self-fulfilling prophecy. Upper-class couples keep up an interest in sex longer than working-class couples.[56]

Unfortunately, most women can expect to be widows. Because female life spans are longer than those of men, only 39 percent of Canadian females over 65 are married.[57] The first year or so after the loss of a spouse is a period of great loneliness; the death rate of surviving spouses increases, and so does the likelihood of suicide. In some ways, however, older widows are better off than younger ones. Young widows are left out of social life because their female friends are still occupied with their own husbands; older widows have the company of other old widows. Widows have less chance than widowers of remarriage, but when remarriage does occur among older people it is usually successful. The aging widow usually moves in with the family of a daughter. Widows are more likely to move in with their children than widowers are.[58]

Relationships with siblings (brothers and sisters) become more important in old age, for old people generally have more living siblings than any other relatives, including children. "Old people who have never married tend to maintain much closer relationships with their brothers and sisters than those who marry and have children. Persons without children tend to resume closer associations with siblings upon the death of a spouse, but interestingly, not as close as single persons."[59]

Most relationships with grandchildren are not very close; the grandparents are "glad to see them come and glad to see them go." Small grandchildren are gratifying, but the older ones do not usually want to bother with their grandparents.

So it is that the life of older people is often not richly satisfying, and is frequently lonely. The situation of the elderly ought to give rise to a widespread "liberation movement." People are forced into retirement at a fixed age, regardless of their wishes or ability, and are stripped of all roles that carry social power. Although few old people want to live with their offspring, about one-third have no choice. Other lifestyles would be possible if public attention were turned to improving the situation of the aging. For example, "retirement villages" are useful communities in which well-to-do aged people live together and generally enjoy life together.[60] Such villages could be provided on a wider scale for old people with average incomes. The problem of continuing involvement in public life for the elderly has not yet been given serious public attention, however.

THE FUTURE OF THE FAMILY

Is the family a dying institution? Mary Jo Bane hints at her conclusions in the title of her book,

Here To Stay.[61] According to Bane's evidence, the American family is alive and well. A similar study, compiled by Jean E. Veevers[62] from Canadian census data of 1971, offers an encouraging picture of family life in Canada. Both these studies provide useful correctives to the commonplace notion that the family is a dying institution.

Bane begins her study by examining changes in the relationship between parents and children. The steady increase in the divorce rate is, of course, upsetting; family disruption is seldom a positive experience for children. However, according to Bane, there has also been a steady decrease in the percentage of children who lose a parent through death. Moreover, many more widowed and divorced women now continue to live with their children after their marriage ends. In 1940, less than half of all mothers without husbands took charge of their own families. The rest, we must suppose, sent their children either to orphanages or to other relatives. In 1975, even though divorces were more common, only about 3 percent of all children under 14 lived with neither of their parents. This means that the *total amount* of family disruption has not increased, though the *pattern* of disruption has changed; more family breakups are now caused by divorce and fewer are caused by death.[63]

FIGURE 12.5

Marriage and divorce rates in Canada per 1,000 population

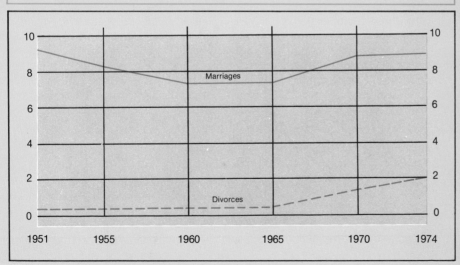

Source: Canada Year Book 1976-77, p. 172.

Veevers' study demonstrates that, despite the new acceptance of alternative living arrangements, most Canadian adults continue to live in families. Moreover, 90 percent of those families involve both a husband and a wife. The popularity of marriage did not seem to decline between 1961 and 1971; indeed, during this period, the rate actually increased, and there was a decrease in the percentage of persons over 30 years of age who had never married.[64] The vast majority of people get married at some time or other.

Recently, however, there has been a tendency for people under 30 to stay single. It is not yet clear whether this indicates an absolute rejection of marriage or merely a postponement. If young people are simply postponing marriage until later in their lives, there will probably be more marital stability in the future. As we have seen, youthful marriages are most likely to end in divorce.

Do people still want to raise children? We know that the birth rate is lower now than ever before. We also know, however, that fewer families are remaining childless. It seems that most people do want children, but they want fewer children than their parents and grandparents did.[65] Smaller families mean children receive more attention from their parents. And as we saw in the chapter on socialization, children who grow up in small families have many advantages over children who grow up in large families. Moreover, in 1971, despite recent efforts to provide day-care facilities and other systems of baby-sitting, the growth of Canadian female employment outside the home was mostly among women whose children were older, rather than among mothers of infants or pre-school children.[66]

What about teenagers? Do they continue to have close relationships with their parents, or do we find more youths leaving home at an early age? In the mid-nineteenth century it was very common

for young men, and to a lesser extent young women, to leave their families to live with other families as lodgers or as servants. Today this pattern has almost disappeared. More youths live at home and go to school. Teenagers are much more dependent on their parents for shelter and support than they were in earlier generations.

The high divorce rate is not the most extreme change in North American marriage patterns in the twentieth century. The changes in family life cycle are more dramatic. Because women are having fewer children, they spend less time in the child-rearing phase of their lives and more time doing other things. Increased life expectancy has brought an increase in the number of years a couple spends alone together after retirement. Marriages that don't end in divorce have to last longer—47 years will be the average during the next few decades.[67] Women are spending more time on their careers, and working seems to be good for them. Working wives seem to have somewhat better physical health than homemakers. However, the marriages of working wives are less stable and satisfying than those of homemakers.[68] This is at least partly due to financial problems. The women who work usually do so because they need the money. The burden of a job in addition to housework increases pressure and tension, and this may affect the marriage.

The conclusion remains, then, that marital disruption has not increased greatly but that the disruption that does occur is more often voluntary than involuntary, resulting from divorce instead of death. And this is not necessarily discouraging. Getting divorced can be like getting out of jail: a release from a wretched situation. What is happening now is that more couples are choosing to recognize a bad situation and look for a way out. Divorce is not a pleasant thing. But neither is old age—except in comparison to the alternative!

SOCIAL POLICY:
Issues and Viewpoints

There are two very different kinds of relatedness within the family—love and power. These are opposing tendencies. When love

is full, the needs of each person are as central to each family member as his or her own; when power comes into play, each person demands his own rights and pursues his own goals. To be sure, even lovers have their own needs. Often these are needs that can be met only through some sacrifice on the part of the other person, though that person may not see it as a sacrifice when love is present.

Several books about the role of power have appeared in recent years. *Sexual Politics*[69] and *The Politics of the Family*,[70] for example, are books that refer to the ways in which manipulation, exploitation, and power struggles operate in relationships where love is absent. Once an issue becomes defined as a power contest, someone must lose if anyone is to win. It is by unifying the purposes of family members that love prevents an issue from becoming a contest.

Though love is the greatest healer of social problems, it is a private experience, not a matter for public policy. It is useless to command parents to love their children or a man to love his wife. This aspect of the family is a private, not a public, one. Society stands back, giving love a space in which to work without interference. While we make rules to govern all sorts of unimportant public affairs—stand behind the white line on the bus, do not feed the pigeons, do not fold, spindle, or mutilate—within the family there are few recognized guidelines for resolving conflict. If one partner wants to make love and the other does not, who should "win"? If one wants to have a child and the other does not, who should "win"? If a young woman wants her own apartment and her parents want her to live at home, who should "win"? These are not matters for public policy, for the answers to these questions come from the heart.

Yet duty exists also—in the family perhaps more than in any other institution. One has obligations to others that one must honor even if it stops being a pleasure to do so. One's love may disappear, but the children don't. Each person is dependent on the other members of his or her family to different degrees in different stages of the life cycle—sometimes completely, sometimes hardly at all. The claims of the dependent one are real, and, when love is inadequate to support those claims, social or even legal sanctions may be required. Most laws come into play only when standards are broken.

Technology has brought about two important changes in Western society that have affected all of us and led to demands for changes in the norms of family life. First, advances in medicine, agriculture, and sanitation have increased life expectancy by many years. Where more children survive than before, populations grow more quickly, and it is no longer necessary to give birth to large numbers of children in order to produce the next generation.

Second, the development of contraceptives makes it possible to enjoy sex without reproduction. Contraceptives free people from responsibility for children but not from a responsible relationship with their sexual partners. Both of these changes raise ethical questions.

Other ethical situations are also changing. The extent of a woman's dependence on her husband changes when child rearing takes up less of her time. What are her legitimate claims in this new situation? Moreover, when one no longer has to produce large families to maintain the population, the attitudes toward homosexuality must be reconsidered.

I have called these questions "ethical" problems rather than "public policy" problems, but they have a "public" aspect. Many social movements are demanding changes in the norms that bear on these matters: the Sexual Freedom League, the women's movement, the gay liberation movement, and so forth. What their members are actually seeking is not freedom but a different set of obligations and claims in relation to other people. No one in society is ever "free" to act toward others as he or she pleases; we are all bound by norms that fit together as a system.

CHALLENGES TO TRADITIONAL SEX ROLES

The traditional role obligations and claims of the sexes in the Western nuclear family centered on the function of bringing up children. Any movement that seeks to change these norms should first recognize why they have been maintained until now.

Male and female parents have traditionally played very different roles, and until recently, the obligations and rights of each were backed by social sanctions. The female was expected to look after the young, and society protected her claim for support in this task. The male was expected to support and defend his wife and children, and society protected his claim to a job that would permit him to meet these obligations. However, sanctions are used to enforce these norms only when the family cannot solve its problems on its own. Thus if a husband and wife agree that the husband will stay home while the wife supports the family, no one tries to stop them. However, if they cannot agree and both claim the right to stay home with the children, social sanctions will be imposed on the husband. He will have to show why he should not be required to support his family.

But suppose both the husband and the wife want to work and find themselves competing in the same limited job market. The husband would be hired. The wife would have to show why she should be given an equal chance.

Thus two different norms must be seen as part of the same system: (1) Men are expected to support their families if they can do so, and (2) they have first claim to a job that allows them to do so.

If a society changes one of these norms, the other will be affected as well. The women's movement has demanded that women and men be given equal employment opportunities. This new norm must be matched by a change in the first rule: Men and women should have an equal obligation to support their families if they can do so.

If neither parent wants to work, one or the other must take a job whether he or she likes the idea or not. But if the opportunities and obligations of men and women are equal, there is no way of deciding who must go to work. Society needs a rule. It may be an arbitrary rule (such as whether to drive on the right or the left), but any rule that assigns responsibilities in a workable pattern will do. Perhaps there are reasons for thinking that men are better suited for work outside the home; perhaps not. In earlier days the fact that the female could provide milk was a good reason for her to stay near the baby, but the use of baby bottles means that this may no longer be a major issue. Still, *some* rule is better than none. If society changes the norm so that the wife must work if the husband chooses not to, then society must change the other norm and give women priority in employment opportunities so that they can support their families.

Furthermore, if a woman is to meet her obligations she must have a good deal of authority over the family. For example, if she finds it necessary to move across the country to find a job, her dependents must be willing to go with her. If she is to pay the bills, she must be able to determine the family budget. If she is to perform well on the job, her dependents must protect her mood, her rest, and her health by obeying her with good grace. These are the rights customarily enjoyed by men and now resented by many women.

In a word, the head of the household is the adult who is responsible for the economic welfare of the family. He or she must be given enough authority and privileges to carry out this obligation. If both parents find these tasks enjoyable, then the work, as well as the rights, can be shared equally. If both parents find them unpleasant, then one of them must do them anyway, and present norms define this as the obligation of the husband.

In childless families, on the other hand, there is no logical reason for either spouse to claim the right to be supported by the other. As the birth rate decreases, there are fewer children to be cared for by the average woman, and so the fairness of the traditional system may be called into question. Changes may be demanded either by men (who may feel that women are no longer making a full contribution to society) or by women (who may feel that they are denied the chance to find fulfilling alternatives to child-rearing). However, it should be recognized that (1) many women are still in an economically dependent situation while they care for children, and (2) they may be making a vital contribution to society in this role and have good reasons for preferring it to a career in the business world. Moreover, many mothers are working because they have to work. Any movement for true "liberation" will demand the right to choose among many alternatives, including both the opportunity to work and the opportunity to remain at home, depending on the situation.

ALTERNATIVES TO THE PRESENT FAMILY

The family as an institution has survived for many thousands of years. However, during this century technological changes have affected group life beyond anything earlier generations could have imagined. The population explosion has brought our species to the limits of the earth's resources, and therefore humans *must* reduce their fertility. While previous generations were taught that they had a duty to produce many children, our children may pass laws requiring couples who want to have a baby to get a license showing that they are healthy, emotionally mature, and able to support a child.

There is plenty of evidence that not everyone is happy with present family norms. What was suitable and necessary in an agrarian economy with a high death rate may be unsuitable in the modern world. Thus the family is changing and probably will continue to change, though it seems that some form of family group will remain important for the foreseeable future.

Marriage involves two kinds of commitment: (1) that of the partners to each other, through loyalty, concern, shared responsibilities, and sexual relations, and (2) that of the partners to their children in a lifelong relationship. Besides these two basic commitments, marriage also leads to a set of relationships between each person and a wider network of people, including the mate's relatives, friends, and coworkers. A single, divorced, or widowed person misses out on relationships of this sort. For some this may mean freedom from unpleasant obligations, but for many others it results in a sad state of isolation. Therefore one of society's most pressing needs is to find ways of making up for these lacks.

The basic need for a partner is not always easily filled. Large numbers of people are deprived of committed, socially approved, stable relationships. Homosexual marriages, for example, are still not approved by society. Moreover, because women mature earlier than men and outlive men by several years, there are millions of women who must get along without mates. One change that would help solve this problem would be to encourage marriages in which the bride is somewhat older than the groom. Some writers have proposed a form of polygyny as a possible solution, but this has little chance of being accepted.

The anthropologist Margaret Mead has suggested that family formation be divided into two steps—marriage and parenthood. She proposes that couples be allowed to enter into partnership quite freely and to break up just as freely. However, only after a couple have been together for several years and known each other well should they be allowed to have children. It should be understood that their partnership *as parents* should be permanent whether their marriage is permanent or not. A couple's most serious commitment is to their children, not toward each other as marital partners. Adults may be better off without each other, but children are not better off without a parent. Hence, parenthood should be permitted only for couples who can guarantee lifelong commitment to their children as well as the children's network of grandparents, friends, aunts and uncles, half-siblings, and so on.

Not only do many people lack spouses, but millions of people lack family ties of any kind. Many have been deprived of such ties by divorce or by the death of a parent or spouse. Others live far away from their extended kin or are on bad terms with them. People living without the help and emotional support of the family need something to replace it, but there is no socially accepted institution that really substitutes for the family. Communes, for instance, are rarely successful. One worthwhile suggestion is for three or four families to meet regularly, share their work and their feelings, and not hesitate to influence one another's values and attitudes.[71]

Such experiments have not been widespread, and indeed the general opposition to them proves that most people are strongly committed to traditional family norms. Perhaps this in itself is the best sign that the family is in no real danger of disappearing.

SUMMARY

1. The *nuclear (or conjugal) family* consists of a husband, his wife, and their unmarried children. The *extended family* is composed of the nuclear family plus the couple's siblings, parents, and other close relatives. *Composite families* are sets of nuclear families living in the same household. The *polygamous family* is a type of composite family. There are two basic types of polygamy: *polygyny* (several wives of the same husband) and *polyandry* (several husbands of the same wife).

2. *Endogamy* is a rule that one must marry someone within one's own group. *Exogamy* is a rule that one must choose a mate from a different group. The taboo against incest is an exogamous rule.

3. Western society reckons descent using a *bilateral system*, including the relatives of both mother and father. Most societies use *unilinear* systems of descent. These may be either *matrilineal* (descent through the mother's family) or *patrilineal* (descent through the father's family).

4. Western society is characterized by *neolocal residence*. That is, newlywed couples set up their own households. Other societies expect newlyweds to live either with the husband's parents (*patrilocal residence*) or with the wife's parents (*matrilocal residence*).

5. The main functions of the family are (1) providing for regular, stable sexual relations and reproduction; (2) socializing children; (3) protecting children; and (4) providing for affectionate interpersonal relationships. Despite the influence of the industrial way of life, most families are not isolated from their relatives.

6. Every society expects that every child born should be assigned to some male, whether he is the biological father or not. This male is to be the child's guardian, protector, and link to society. Children who have not been recognized by such protectors are considered illegitimate. *Illegitimacy* is a necessary result of rules that define legitimacy.

7. Almost all societies provide for divorce or legal separation. Studies of the effect of divorce on children suggest that it is better for them than situations in which parents stay together even though they do not get along well.

8. Some scholars believe that the nuclear family is bound in all societies. Others disagree, pointing to the Nayars of India, the kibbutzim of Israel, and the early years of the Soviet Union as cases of societies in which the nuclear family as a group has not performed all of the following functions: (1) permitting sexual relations, (2) legitimating reproduction, (3) caring for children, and (4) acting as an economic unit—at least in terms of consumption.

9. We have discussed three views of the family—conservative, radical, and liberal-functionalist. The conservative values the traditional family. This approach was taken by Frederick LePlay.

10. The radical view is seen in the writings of Friedrich Engels. He believed that when the sexes became equal economically men would become more monogamous but marriages would be ended more easily. No couple would have to stay together for economic reasons.

11. Functionalists view the modern family as having been greatly influenced by industrialization. Many scholars see a connection between industrialization and the relative isolation of the nuclear family. However, there is evidence that the family is not as isolated from its kin as the functionalists have sometimes assumed.

12. Talcott Parsons suggests that sex role differences and the relative isolation of the nuclear family are beneficial to children and contribute to the emotional well-being of all family members. This view has been challenged by the women's movement.

KEY TERMS

bilateral descent a system that reckons descent from both the mother's side and the father's side.

composite family a number of nuclear families living together in a single household.

endogamy a rule requiring a person to marry someone within his or her own group.

exogamy a rule requiring a person to choose a mate from a different group.

extended family (consanguine family) a household made up of a nuclear family plus other relatives.

homogamy the tendency to choose a spouse similar to oneself.

illegitimacy the birth of a child to an unmarried woman.

joint family a type of extended family in which brothers share property but do not always live in a single household.

kin people who are related either by birth or by marriage.

matrilineal descent system a descent system in which a person belongs to his or her mother's line of descent.

matrilocal residence a rule requiring a newly married couple to live with the wife's family.

neolocal residence a rule requiring a newly married couple to set up housekeeping on their own.

nuclear family (conjugal family) a husband, his wife, and their unmarried children.

patrilineal descent system a descent system in which a person belongs to his or her father's line of descent.

patrilocal residence a rule requiring a newly married couple to live with the husband's family.

polyandry the marriage of a woman to more than one husband.

polygamous family a family in which there are several wives or husbands.

polygyny the marriage of a man to more than one wife.

unilinear descent a system that reckons descent from either the male blood line or the female blood line.

FOR FURTHER READING

BOISSEVAIN, J. *Italians of Montreal.* Ottawa: Queen's Printer, 1970. This focuses on the family life of Montreal Italians, though other aspects of this community are explored as well.

GAMMON, MARY ALICE BEYER. *Violence in Canada.* Agincourt, Ont.: Methuen, 1978. Much of this book deals with family violence. That's where most violence takes place—within the family. The people we hate are usually the people we also love.

GOVERNMENT OF CANADA. *Perspective Canada II.* Ottawa: Supply and Services, 1977. This is an excellent factual presentation of basic information about social life in Canada, especially strong in its presentation of family trends.

GUYATT, D. *One Parent Family in Canada.* Ottawa: Vanier Institute of the Family, 1971. The number of families headed by a single parent will probably continue to grow over the next several years. This book is useful for anyone who is interested in this trend.

ISHWAREN, K. *Family, Kinship, and Community: A Study of Dutch Canadians.* Toronto: McGraw-Hill Ryerson, 1977. The literature on family life among various ethnic communities of Canada is surprisingly rich. Also see Ishwaren's other book, *The Canadian Family,* 2nd ed. Toronto: Holt, Rinehart, and Winston, 1976. This is a collection of papers, largely descriptive. It does not assume that "the Canadian family" is WASP ("white Anglo-Saxon Protestant").

LARSON, LYLE E. *The Canadian Family in Comparative Perspective.* Scarborough, Ont.: Prentice-Hall, 1976. This is another collection of articles on various aspects of the family.

LEE, JOHN ALLAN. *Colours of Love.* Don Mills, Ont.: New Press, 1976. Lee interviewed a lot of people in Britain and Canada about their experiences with love. Then he classified people in terms of the way they generally approach love. This is a stimulating and rather odd book, not a garden-variety sociological survey at all.

LIBBY, ROGER W. and ROBERT N. WHITEHURST. *Marriage & Alternatives: Exploring Intimate Relationships.* Glenview, Ill.: Scott, Foresman & Co., 1977. The authors have collected essays and arguments that support the view that intimate relationships can flourish in nonfamily settings too, and enhance life greatly.

SHORTER, EDWARD. *The Making of the Modern Family.* New York: Basic Books, 1977. A first-rate history of changes in family life in Western society. Shorter makes one glad we aren't living in the bad old days.

VAN STOLK, MARY. *The Battered Child in Canada,* 2nd ed. Toronto: McClelland and Stewart, 1978. I am including something else on family violence because so many of my students lately have wanted to write term papers on battered children.

WAKIL, S. PARVEZ, ed. *Marriage, Family and Society: Canadian Perspectives.* Toronto: Butterworth, 1975. Still a third collection of readings on the family.

13

RELIGION

Every Sunday I spend a couple of hours with about fifty of my friends. We go through a routine of activities: We sing some songs, read some verses aloud together, and listen as one of us reads a passage from an old book. A few of my friends wear special robes and sing together. Usually there are some candles burning. People shake hands or hug and kiss, and it's not uncommon for someone who feels bad to weep quietly and be comforted by someone who is sitting nearby. Near the end of the session, we gather around a table and solemnly eat small pieces of bread and sip port wine, reminding each other that we are eating the body and drinking the blood of a man who died 2000 years ago.

Does this seem weird? Of course not. My friends and I are ordinary, nice people. If we had been asked to write the script for a worship service, it is unlikely that we would have invented a mock-cannibalistic feast. Yet I feel all right about going through such a ceremony. In fact, it's one of the high points of my week. I am in touch with myself then. I feel sure that I belong on this earth—that indeed, I belong right there with those people, singing *Amazing Grace*, passing around a cup of wine, forgiving each other for our shortcomings, and looking forward to the future.

People sometimes do strange things in worship services. If you are an Orthodox Jew, you may wrap phylacteries around your arm and give thanks to God that you are not a woman. This doesn't mean that you hate women. It's just what your group has always said at a certain point in the prayer. If you lived in some other society, you might sacrifice an animal as an act of worship. The varieties of religious practices are endless. We can agree that many of these practices make no sense when looked at from a logical viewpoint. But religion is not logical. It is something else entirely.

Social scientists cannot show the validity of any particular faith, nor do they try to. **Religion** is the relationship of humankind to some ultimate reality. Sociology deals with the relationships among human beings and can say nothing about ultimate reality, which, after all, cannot be studied empirically. Yet some of the greatest sociologists—especially Durkheim and Weber—were deeply interested in religion. They showed that faith and human social life are closely linked. Religion is at the root of the loyalty and involvement that draw human beings together. Viewing it in this light, both religious and nonreligious people may find that sociology has much to say on the subject of religion.

Classification of religions

David Sopher has classified religions into three categories: ethnic, universalizing, and segmental.[1]

Ethnic religions are tied to a specific place and people. Most primitive or tribal religions are of this type, and so are some of the largest worldwide religions. Both Hinduism and Judaism must be considered ethnic religions because they are both closely tied to the land and people in which they originally developed. It is hard to say what the Chinese believe about ultimate reality today, since religion is discouraged by communism, but in the imperial period Chinese religion was clearly ethnic. It was a mixture of ancestor worship, Buddhism, and the worship of nature deities. Thus, if we include the Chinese, about one-third of the world's people are members of ethnic religions.

Universalizing religions are not tied to any particular region or ethnic group, although they may have been when they began. Members of universalizing religions consider their beliefs to be right for all humankind and feel that they have a duty to convert others to their religion, either personally or through organized missions. Each of the major universalizing religions—Buddhism, Christianity, and Islam—has at one time or another

TABLE 13.1

Estimated membership of the principal religions of the world

RELIGIONS	ESTIMATED MEMBERSHIP
Total Christian	983,620,900
Roman Catholic	566,686,800
Eastern Orthodox	72,815,000
Protestant[1]	344,119,100
Jewish	15,032,378
Muslim[2]	576,160,200
Zoroastrian	233,550
Shinto[3]	55,156,000
Taoist	31,116,100
Confucian	174,189,200
Buddhist[4]	260,685,550
Hindu[5]	517,897,450
Total world religious membership	2,614,091,328
Total world population[6]	4,123,957,000

[1]Protestant statistics usually include "full members" (adults) rather than all baptized persons and are not comparable to those of ethnic religions or churches counting all constituents.
[2]The chief base of Islam is still ethnic, although some missionary work is now carried on in Europe and America (viz. "Black Muslims"). In countries where Islam is established, minority religions are frequently persecuted and their statistics are hard to come by.
[3]A Japanese ethnic religion, Shinto has declined markedly since the Japanese emperor gave up claim to divinity (1947).
[4]Buddhism has several modern renewal movements which have gained adherents in Europe and America and other areas not formerly ethnic-Buddhist. In Asia it has also made rapid gains in recent years and shown greater staying power under persecution than Taoism or Confucianism.
[5]Hinduism's strength in India has been enhanced by nationalism. Modern Hinduism has also developed renewal movements that have reached Europe and America for converts.
[6]United Nations, Department of Economic and Social Affairs; data refer to midyear 1977.

Source: Data from *Britannica Book of the Year 1978,* William Benton Publisher.

been the dominant religion in a particular region.

Christianity has been the most successful in gaining converts and has become by far the most widespread religion in the world. However, it has so many variations that it may be misleading to call it a single religion.

Segmental religions are ethnic offshoots of universalizing religions or new systems that integrate small groups into larger communities. These religions don't usually want to universalize. Often they develop in Third World countries exposed to European culture. They usually appeal to a particular social

class and create a new sense of community among groups whose former religions were ethnic in character. The Native American (Peyote) Church, for example, unites groups of American Indians with different ethnic (tribal) backgrounds. Some new segmental religions claim to be part of a major universalizing system. Examples are the Neo-Buddhists among the lower classes of India, the Black Muslims, and the Happy, Healthy, Holy ("Sikh") organization in America. Although the segmental religions account for only a small portion of the world's population, they are important because they encourage social

FIGURE 13.1
Distribution of the world's religions

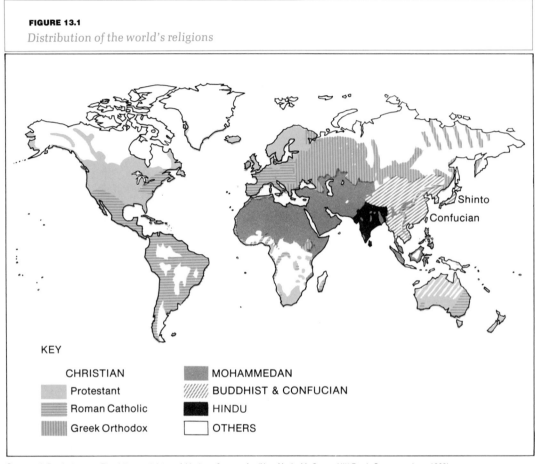

KEY

	CHRISTIAN		MOHAMMEDAN
	Protestant		BUDDHIST & CONFUCIAN
	Roman Catholic		HINDU
	Greek Orthodox		OTHERS

Shinto
Confucian

Source: J. Bartholomew, *The Advanced Atlas of Modern Geography* (New York: McGraw–Hill Book Company, Inc., 1962).

change. At least they tend to appear where major social changes are going on.

The institutionalization of religion

Suppose you have your own beliefs about ultimate reality, your own religious practices, that are not shared by anybody else. Suppose you worship privately without telling anyone else about it, and suppose you are extremely devout in this personal way. Could we say that you are religious? Most sociologists would say not. This does not mean that we think such experiences are unimportant—they can be very important—but sociologists are concerned primarily with the practices, beliefs, and experiences that people share as a group. Religion is a social institution. Any private, personal experience is religious, by this definition, only if it is linked to the *shared* orientation of a social group toward ultimate reality. Thus, the great sociological studies of religion have dealt with traditions that are passed down from one generation to another.

Much of what we know about the development of religions we owe to Max Weber. He found regular patterns in the way major world religions develop over time. Changes occur in leadership, in ritual, in beliefs, and in the way members organize. Let us look more closely at these types of change.

CHARISMATIC LEADERSHIP

Religions begin through the leadership of charismatic founders (such as Christ, Mohammed, or Buddha) and their immediate followers. *Charisma* means "gift" in Greek, and Weber thought of a charismatic leader as gifted. Such a leader seems to have supernormal, possibly divine, powers.[2] Charisma is a source of social change, for it is opposed to the traditional institutions of society. Every charismatic leader says, in effect, "It is written . . . but I say unto you . . . !" Charisma is spontaneous, creative, and it stimulates new ways of thinking.

THE ROUTINIZATION OF CHARISMA

But the charismatic phase of a religion is short and temporary. The religion can take hold only by becoming *routinized*—by becoming an institution in society. How does this happen? The crisis occurs when the founder dies. If the followers want to continue their religious experience, they have to decide how to replace the charismatic founder.[3] Generally they build up an authoritative institution to take the place of the founder. Weber called this process "the routinization of charisma." The movement is changed from an unusual, tradition-breaking phenomenon into an organized, socially accepted institution.

This process has three different aspects: (1) The patterns of worship become ritualized; (2) ideas and beliefs become more rational; and (3) the religious community becomes organized, with well-defined roles and responsibilities.

Ritual

Worship consists of ritual, liturgy, and other forms of expression that become established patterns. Ritual grows up naturally as the means by which human beings express their deepest experiences in a symbolic manner.[4] But as time goes on, ritual becomes standardized. It then *elicits* attitudes instead of spontaneously *expressing* them. Thus one may enter church preoccupied and nervous, but, by lighting a candle, kneeling, and murmuring a memorized phrase, one may call up a feeling of reverence that lasts all day. Weber believed that, as a charismatic religion becomes an institutionalized religion, the ritual tends to become more complex.

Belief

The second aspect of the institutionalization of religion is the development of beliefs. Every religion has a number of stories—such as the Biblical ones about Adam and Eve, Noah and his ark, the miracle of the loaves and fishes, and Lot's wife turning into a pillar of salt. They are myths. Myths are nonhistorical stories that are known by almost everyone in a group and symbolize great truths to the group's members. I don't mean that they are necessarily false when I call them nonhistorical. But whether they are historically true or not, people use myths to celebrate a fundamental reality in which both the narrator and the listener participate emotionally. Myth relates human beings to their environment, to their ancestors, to their descendants, and to the hereafter. Even the most primitive religions are rich in myths—stories that explain the world symbolically.

Besides myth, there is also theology, the organization of religious beliefs into a unified doctrine. Theology consists of philosophical speculation about ultimate reality. Weber suggested that, before a religion could develop a rational theology (one that people could discuss reasonably and logically), it had to have a professional priesthood.[5] Not all major reli-

Religious rituals may allow people to release deep emotional feelings in symbolic ways. This New Guinea burial involves the entire community.

gions develop a rational theology. Classical Chinese religion and ancient Buddhism were not rational; nor did they have a professional priesthood. But both a professional priesthood and a rational theology developed in the early period of Christianity.

According to Weber, there is a rational trend in all world religions, a tendency to make the intellectual aspects of their beliefs clear and consistent. This involves a general shift from myth to theology—from story telling to reasoning and arguing. This shift is especially noticeable in Western culture.

Religious organization

Weber held that the crisis of replacing the founder forces a religious movement to either adjust or fail. Usually, after the leader's death, the movement begins to organize and to create a system of roles. This creates problems of authority: The new roles have to be given certain responsibilities and powers. In the Christian Church, this was done by 100 A.D.

During the charismatic period, there is an outpouring of new teachings. But, after the crisis caused by the founder's death, the religion develops ways of determining which teachings will be considered authentic. In Christianity, the clergy decided these questions of authenticity. Thus the routinization of charisma actually amounts to a limiting of charisma. The teachings have to be acceptable to the authorities. In time, according to Weber, the religion that began as a dramatic break from tradition becomes orthodox and fits in smoothly with the other institutions of society.

ADJUSTING TO
THE SOCIAL ORDER

As a religious movement adjusts to the loss of its founder, we have seen that it changes *internally*—by developing its rituals, its belief system, and its organization, and by becoming more and more rational and routine. It also changes *externally*—by coming to terms with the outside world. While the founder lived, the new religion was very different from other groups in society. Its members left their old lives, emphasized equality with other members, and considered their former status unimportant.[6]

But, after the founder's death, the group has to decide how to relate to the rest of society. It has three choices. (1) It can reject the old social order entirely. (2) It can accept the old order entirely. (3) It can accept the old ways in practice but reject them in spirit. If it chooses the third alternative, the group can encourage equality *within* its organization without attacking the status differences in the society around it. The early Christian Church took this position. For example, Saint Paul claimed that there was "neither bond nor free" in the Church yet also advised slaves to obey their masters (Epistle to Titus 2:9). This is the process of adjusting to the social order. Most religious movements have taken the same route, according to Weber. This is the final phase in a religious movement. At this point, it is no longer a new religion but an old, established one. Indeed, another new religious movement may begin at this point and shatter the routine of the old religion.

The organization and functions of religion

The priesthood, or clergy, has two duties toward the members of its religion: to comfort them and to challenge them.[7] These duties seem contradictory. Much depends on the kind of religious organization in question. In general, comforting is the easier job, involving the soothing of grievances and the unification of the congregation. Challenge is more difficult, and involves speaking out on matters of social or moral evil and urging the congregation to live up to a higher moral standard, even if this requires some sacrifices. The priest or minister must be careful not to antagonize members in challenging them. Whether he or she can take an unpopular stand depends on the way the church is organized.

TYPES OF CHURCH
ORGANIZATION

There are three different types of church organization, though any given church may not fit exactly into any of these types. Although these organizational patterns are called by the same names as three denominations of the Protestant Church, they should not be confused with those denominations.

A **congregational religious organization** hires and fires its own leader. Each local church is governed by lay members, and there is no church hierarchy with authority over the individual congregations. Baptists, Disciples of Christ, and the Quakers are organizations of this type.

An **episcopal religious organization** is characterized by a well-defined hierarchy of authority. Clergy are assigned to their posts by officials higher in the hierarchy and are accountable to them for their performance. Both the Roman Catholic and the Anglican (or Episcopal) churches are of this type, though there are variations within both groups. In French Canada, for example, lay wardens control church funds.

In a **presbyterian religious organization**, authority is in the hands of an elected regional board of ministers and lay members from a number of different congregations. This board, or *presbytery*, assigns clergy to their posts. However, a good deal of authority remains in the hands of a committee of laymen, or *elders*, in each church. The Presbyterian Church in the United States and the United

Church in Canada are two examples. This type of organization is a representative democracy.

The relationship of the minister to his or her "flock" differs according to the organizational structure of the church. Ministers in congregational churches change posts more frequently than those in churches of the episcopal type, often in order to avoid conflict with church members.[8] Whether a congregational or episcopal type of church is more likely to stimulate social change depends on whether the proposed change is supported mostly by the membership or by the clergy. For example, the Catholic Church was able to encourage the integration of parochial schools and other religious institutions in the southern United States more effectively than congregational Protestant churches because the Catholic hierarchy supported the policy of integration.

The clergy does not always take the lead in stimulating social change. In fact, if the hierarchy of a church of the episcopal type is basically conservative, it may actually slow the process of change. For example, the hierarchy of the Roman Catholic Church has long opposed birth control, despite a growing popular movement supporting it. In this case, a parish priest is required to speak out against a particular social change because he is accountable to the bishop, not to the parishioners. Some priests refuse to speak out, of course, just as many Catholics ignore church doctrine in this case, and so the hierarchy finds it hard to maintain its authority in this area. Still, the clergy in episcopal organizations generally have greater power over their parishioners than clergy in other systems.

THE FUNCTIONS OF RELIGION

Does it really make any difference whether a group of people is religious or not? Does a group function any differently because of religion? One would have to answer these questions in different ways for different cases. At some historical times and places, religion has had a great impact on group life, while at other times and places it has had little effect. Later in this chapter we will compare some of these cases and look for differences in the effects of religion on group life. But is it possible to generalize about the effects of religion? If so, what are they? Let me suggest that religion—or the lack of it—usually does have an important influence but that any impact it has may be beneficial (*eufunctional*) at one time and harmful (*dysfunctional*) at another. I will list five functions of religion—as you will see, each of them can have both positive and negative aspects.

1 Religion provides *support, consolation, and reconciliation*. In doing so, it strengthens group morale. Human beings need emotional support when they are uncertain and disappointed, and they need reconciliation with their society when they are alienated from its goals. But this can be dysfunctional too: By reconciling those who are alienated, religion can stand in the way of useful protest and thus contribute to a buildup of resentment. This may make reform more difficult in the long run, and revolution more necessary.

2 Religion provides authoritative teaching. This is its *priestly* function. It contributes to security and order. The dysfunctional aspect of the priestly function is that it may *sacralize* (make sacred) incorrect ideas and backward attitudes. This may have a harmful effect on a society's understanding of its environment and efforts to control nature. The trial of Galileo for the "crime" of suggesting that the earth revolved around the sun is an example of this kind of effect.

3 Religion sacralizes the norms and values of society, upholding the importance of the group's goals over the wishes of individuals. This is its *social control* function. Religion also provides ways of forgiving wrongdoers and bringing them back into the social group. The dysfunction is that it can set back a society's adjustment to changing conditions. For example, the Christian Church long refused to allow its members to lend money at interest, despite the great need for this practice in a developing economy. The sacral freezing of norms is a source of many social conflicts, as is illustrated by the debate over birth control and abortion in the Catholic Church.

Religion can promote or discourage social reform. The sculpture in this Toronto church is meant to remind us that "women have been crucified in many cultures, including our own."

Toronto Star/Bull

4 Religion provides standards for judging institutionalized norms. This is its *prophetic* function; an example is the Hebrew prophets, who were troublemakers in their own society. Prophets scold their followers and urge them to reform or repent. The dysfunction is that prophetic demands may be so extreme that they prevent the working out of practical solutions to social problems. By making demands on its members in the name of God, religion may make compromise impossible.

5 Religion performs important *identity* functions. It links the individual to the past and future. It gives his or her spirit a place in the universe and makes the universe meaningful.[9] However, there is a dysfunction here too. By sacralizing the identity of the individual within his or her group, it may increase intergroup conflict. Other ideological systems, such as communism and nationalism, have the same effect: They give people an identity but at the same time tend to increase inter-group conflict.

Meaning, magic, and sorcery

MEANING AND RELIGION

Why do human beings need religion? Possibly because it gives them a framework within which to deal with experiences beyond their control. We each have to face situations of *uncertainty, powerlessness,* and *scarcity.* By uncertainty, I mean that we can never plan or control our affairs in such a way that they all work out well. Sometimes we fail. And yet, knowing that the outcomes of our plans are always subject to chance, we have to be able to function anyway; we have to cope with uncertainty. By powerlessness, I mean that we have to live with the fact that some things are impossible. We cannot do everything we want to do, and yet we have to face our powerlessness with courage. By scarcity, I mean that we have to face the fact that there may not be enough of everything to go around. What we have must be distributed in an orderly way. Thus social life may require that some people be deprived and frustrated.

Cary Wolinsky/Stock, Boston

Religion cannot be explained in practical, reasonable terms. What "practical" purpose is being served by the activities of these people?

Ira Kirschenbaum/Stock, Boston

Ann Hagen Griffiths/DPI

Ian Berry/Magnum

We all have to deal with a crisis at some point, and it is then that religion helps us adjust. Why should a loved one die young? Why must we suffer illness? Why should a person go on living when his or her love is not returned? Such questions demand meaningful answers. If they are considered meaningless, support for society's norms is weakened. How can we maintain our morale when disappointment lurks at every step—and when we know that death awaits us in the end?

Religion makes life meaningful by fitting it into the context of an existence beyond the present. It supports our commitment to society's norms when we are at the breaking point. It helps us adjust to the frustrations that are part of human life.

RELIGION AS THE SACRED

When asked to define religion, most people say that all religions involve belief in, and worship of, a supreme being. This notion is mistaken. Some religions (including some forms of Buddhism) are entirely *agnostic*. That is, they hold no opinion about the possible existence of God.

Then what is religion? As Durkheim pointed out, the quality that seems to be shared by all religions is a sense of *sacredness*. The religious experience is the experience of the *holy* or the *sacred*—a quality that calls for great respect. Here is what Durkheim said about the sacred:[10]

1 It is recognized as a power or force.
2 It is ambiguous—both physical and moral, both human and cosmic, both positive and negative, both attractive and repulsive, both helpful and dangerous.
3 It is nonutilitarian. (You cannot control it for practical purposes.)
4 It is nonempirical. (You cannot study it by observation or experimentation.)
5 It does not involve knowledge. (It goes beyond logic or reasoning or proof.)
6 It strengthens and supports the worshiper.
7 It makes moral demands on the worshiper.

Sacredness is not something that objects have by nature; rather, it is assigned to them by religious thought and tradition. For example, a cross is not something that everyone would recognize as holy. It is a symbol that is meaningful to Christians and to others who have come, through cultural experience, to attach a sacred quality to it. Religion is very different from ordinary experience. It never helps people control nature—so it is useless in any practical sense. It is not based on ordinary forms of knowledge, judgment, or sensory evidence—it is separate from the everyday world.

RELIGION AND MAGIC

I have just written that religion is not useful as a way of controlling nature. Yet most societies have traditional practices that seem religious but are actually directed toward the control of spirits or other forces beyond the reach of ordinary human powers. These practises constitute magic. Examples include rain dances, love potions, and the curing of warts with incantations. It is difficult to separate magic from religion because they may be mixed into the same ceremonies and institutions. Magic shares with religion the idea that people can make contact with forces beyond the world of the senses. But while religion offers a way of relating to supernatural forces, magic goes further. It offers techniques for *manipulating* those forces.

Bronislaw Malinowski distinguishes between religion and magic by pointing out that magic has an *end*. He contrasts a *magical* ritual (performed, say, to prevent death in childbirth) with a *religious* ritual (such as one performed to celebrate the birth of a child). While the magical rite has a practical purpose that is known to all who practise it, the religious rite has no practical purpose. Christening a child is not a means to an end but an end in itself. Its only purpose is to express the feelings of the participants[11]—to give thanks, perhaps, and to express the idea that they

and the newborn are all children of God and that they care for one another.

Malinowski argues that people use magic when they lack practical ways of controlling the environment. For example, the Trobriand Islanders were skilled fishermen who sometimes practiced magic in the belief that it

Magic is the effort to gain control over supernatural forces and use them for human purposes.

Maje Waldo/Stock, Boston

helped them catch fish. But they used these rites only in specific situations. When the Trobrianders used poison to kill fish in an inner lagoon, they made a huge catch with little risk or danger. In such cases they did not use magic. However, when they fished in the open sea, which was more dangerous and uncontrollable, they engaged in magical rituals.[12]

Both magic and religion relieve emotional stress. They help people cope with situations over which they have no practical control. Both involve mythology, taboos, and an atmosphere of wonder or awe. Magic strengthens human confidence in the face of the unknown, while religion helps human beings face and adjust to misfortune. It is quite common for people to mix the two experiences.

WITCHCRAFT AND SORCERY

A special form of magic is "black magic," or witchcraft and sorcery. These are used to call on sacred forces to bring misfortune to others. But sorcery is not necessarily bad. I can think of several points in its favor. For one thing, it's a safe outlet for nasty emotions that might disrupt society if they were expressed directly. (Better to stick a pin into a voodoo doll than to run a sword through a real person.) Moreover, believing in witchcraft gives you the satisfaction of pinning the blame for your troubles on a witch. ("Sorry the cake fell, folks. It's that darn witch again!") Probably the main advantage of black magic, however, is that it is answered by "white" magic and religious ceremonies. When people really believe that a loved one has been "hexed" or "possessed," they often call in their friends and spiritual advisers to ward off the expected evil. Thus by reinforcing social norms black magic actually performs a positive function.[13]

But sorcery certainly has bad aspects too. Obviously, the purpose of black magic is to harm others. Such rituals may release hostile

feelings, but they also *create* hostile feelings. They probably do more harm than good. I have strangled many pillows in my time, imagining that they were the people I hated at the moment. I don't regret those imaginary murders at all. But I might be very frightened and guilty if I believed that by strangling a pillow or sticking a pin in a doll I could actually kill someone or that someone could kill me that way. Some people do believe such things.

Religion and social stratification

WEBER ON THEOLOGIES AND SOCIAL STATUS

Weber is remembered mainly for studying how religion *causes* various effects. But here I want to talk about his view of religious beliefs as *effects* rather than causes.

Think of a religion as a package of beliefs, a set of assumptions about what is proper or improper, possible and impossible, and so on. It is reasonable to suppose that the religion shared by the members of a society will affect their ways of behaving. That is, religion is a *cause* of certain phenomena—an important independent variable. Weber believed this, and he showed how certain religions have functioned as important independent variables. We'll come back to this point when we discuss the Protestant ethic.

But Weber realized that religion is also a dependent variable. He wanted to know why certain groups choose particular types of religions. He thought there were structural explanations for this. According to Weber, people choose their theologies according to how well they help them cope with the problems of daily living. Different social systems have different religious systems. What attracts particular groups to particular theologies?

Weber noted that *social classes and status groups differ in their religious preferences.*

For example, groups such as craftsmen and small traders are less involved with nature than farmers and more involved in a way of life based on rational economic calculation. For them, honesty is important and even profitable. So these groups (which are mostly lower-middle-class) tend to favor a religion that preaches that hard work and devotion to duty will bring a "just reward." Thus small traders and artisans generally support an

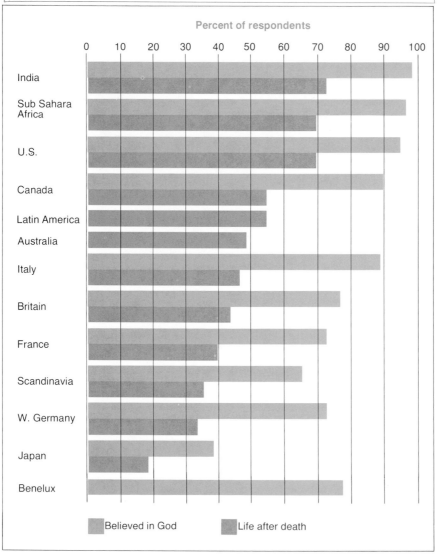

FIGURE 13.2
Beliefs of selected countries of the world, 1975

Believed in God   Life after death

Source: Data from Lee Sigelman, "Multi-Nation Surveys of Religious Beliefs," *Journal for the Scientific Study of Religion* 1977, 16(3), pp. 290, 292.

"ethic of compensation."[14] That is, they tend to think that in the long run people get what is coming to them. No more, no less.

Peasants, on the other hand, are subject to the unpredictable processes of nature. Lacking a market economy (at least in traditional societies), they have no reason for believing in rational calculation. They don't hold to the idea of a "just reward." They are very concerned about the irrational forces of nature that affect their lives. Hail, for example, seems to fall on the just and the unjust alike. So peasants usually are attracted not to a rational theology but, rather, to a system that offers magical ways of controlling nature.[15]

Weber found that rich business classes everywhere are oriented toward the here and now, not the hereafter. They are not attracted to prophetic or ethical religions. Indeed, the richer they are, the less likely they are to develop an otherworldly religion.[16]

What about militaristic societies? Weber pointed out that the warrior does not need an ethical system. He does not worry about ideas such as sin, salvation, and religious humility. He faces death, and unpredictable forces are part of his daily life. The things that are important to a warrior are honor and protection against evil magic. He prays for victory or happiness in a warrior's heaven. Neither an otherworldly religion nor a belief in ethical compensation attracts him.

As for bureaucrats, Weber thought their religious tendency was best seen in Confucianism. This Chinese religion had a strong ethical emphasis—yet it was practical, lacking any feeling for "salvation" or any otherworldly basis for ethics. Bureaucrats do not care for a personal religion with an emotional basis. Weber noted that the Chinese official performed rites for his ancestors but actually felt a "certain distance from the spirits."[17]

Finally, Weber compared the religions of upper and lower status groups and classes. The upper groups emphasize honor rather than salvation, sin, or humility. They choose religious beliefs that justify their own life patterns and their situation in the world.[18] Underprivileged groups, on the other hand, tend to choose religions of salvation, to favor an ethic of compensation, and to support greater equality between men and women in religious affairs.[19] The reason salvation is important, according to Weber, is that people who experience stress and oppression in this world may look to the next world for relief. And Weber was aware that a different version of "salvation" was growing in popularity among the working classes of Europe. This was not the hope of salvation in heaven but a secular salvation—the revolution and the justice and equality that would follow it. This hope was not based on religion in the usual sense but on a secular ideology—Marxism. It is probably fair to think of Marxism—and indeed of many other ideologies, such as nationalism—as having similar functions to those of religion. Ideologies often offer support, consolation, hope, and meaning to people in times when sacrifice and endurance are required of them.

Religious groups in Canada

Religious experience is a subjective, inner experience, hard to describe, impossible to measure. Despite their otherworldly concerns, however, religious organizations play an important social role in this world. Participation in religious organizations can be measured by censuses, church membership rolls, and public opinion polls. To a certain extent, then, we can describe the religious involvement of the Canadian population in objective, scientific, and even numerical terms. Though these terms signify little about the *quality* of religious life in Canada, they are useful in determining the rate of participation in religious organizations at various times, and in various regions, of Canada.

A Gallup Poll in 1979 showed that 37 percent of Canadians had attended a religious service within the past seven days. There were marked differences in this percentage according to age and religious affiliation. Only 22 percent of persons under 30 years of age had attended services in the past week, as compared to 46 percent of those who were 50 and over. Of Protestant Canadians, 26 percent had attended, while 53 percent of Catholics had done so.[20] All of these figures are generally lower than attendance levels of the 1950s, a period when religious participation peaked in Canada.

The population of Canada is almost equally divided between Catholics and Protestants. Only about 10 percent belong to neither group. Among Protestants, 75 percent belong to either the Anglican Church or to the United Church of Canada. (The United Church resulted from the 1925 merger of Methodist, Congregational, and most Presbyterian churches.)

Marked variations occur within Canada according to region. The Catholic church is strongest in the French-speaking areas of Quebec and New Brunswick. The Maritimes are generally limited to relatively few denominations, namely Catholic, Baptist, United, Presbyterian, and Anglican. West of Ontario, there are many more religious denominations. This is partly because the prairies were settled by people from diverse ethnic and religious backgrounds. Also, new sects have chosen to settle and expand in the west, possibly due to its higher degree of religious tolerance.[21]

There is a close relationship between linguistic groups and religious affiliation. French-speaking communities tend to be Catholic and to participate in religious practices quite regularly. One study found that in Quebec, 53 percent of the population attends church at least once or twice a month, as compared to 23 percent in Italy and 18 percent in France. Northern Ireland and Poland are the only other Christian countries with equally high rates of church attendance. Even within Quebec, there are regional differences in church attendance; in the Gaspé and the

Saguenay areas, 60 percent of the population attends church every week, while in Montreal only 29 percent attend that often.[22] In contrast, populations in long-settled English-Canadian areas, such as Ontario, tend to belong to well-established Protestant churches, and to attend services less regularly.

In general, Canada has not been a place where small new sects have easily taken root. In the United States, groups like Mormons, Seventh-Day Adventists, Jehovah's Witnesses, and Christian Scientists have expanded to a far greater degree than in Canada. This may partly be a result of the difficulty that such groups have encountered when attempting to establish accredited colleges in Canada to train religious leaders.[23]

Substantial differences are usually found between the religious practices and beliefs of middle-class and lower-class Canadians. The lower-class tends to participate much less than the middle-class in church activities. Lower-class people also tend to be more orthodox in their religious beliefs; they tend, for example, to believe in hell, the devil, and life after death.[24] In Quebec, however, people with high incomes and education levels are *less* likely than lower-class members to attend church.[25]

Different religious organizations tend to attract members from quite different social strata. Thus, Jews, Anglicans, Presbyterians, and United Church members are usually upper- and middle-class, while members of other Protestant denominations and Roman Catholics are generally lower-class.[26] Not surprisingly, then, members of different churches typically support different political parties. Protestants generally vote for the Progressive Conservative Party, while Jews and Roman Catholics more frequently vote for the Liberal Party.[27] The recent shift of Québécois voters to the Parti Québécois can be seen partly as a move away from the Church led by urban highly-educated voters. The present leader of the Liberal Party in Quebec, Claude Ryan, is a devout Catholic and federalist, and is said to have much in common with conservative rural voters; René Levesque, a divorced and remarried leftist who has no obvious commitment to the church, finds his support in urban Quebec.[28]

Like the Catholic Church in Quebec, most religious organizations in Canada have recently been faced with secularization and loss of commitment on the part of their members. Canada is by no means unique in the decline of popular participation in religious organizations. Though shortly after World War II there was an upsurge of religious involvement in several Western societies, for the past 10 or 15 years this trend has been reversed. Almost all faiths, liberal and conservative, Protestant and Catholic, have lost members. Some, of

course, have lost more than others; and generally, evangelical and fundamentalist Christian groups have fared better than more established denominations. A few new sects, particularly those derived from Asian religions, have actually gained members, but even these have proved less popular in Canada than in the United States.

North Americans have rather mixed views concerning Eastern-inspired sects, such as the "Moonies," the Children of Light, and the Krishna Consciousness groups. Since the tragedy of Jonestown, in which several hundred followers of Jim Jones committed suicide under his orders, many North Americans have become concerned about the God-like

FIGURE 13.3

Religious denominations of the Canadian population, 1971

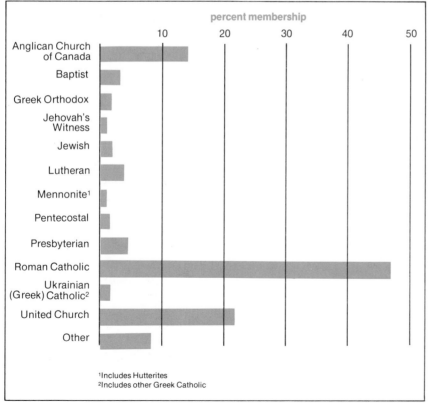

Source: Adapted from Canada Year Book, 1978-79, p. 162.

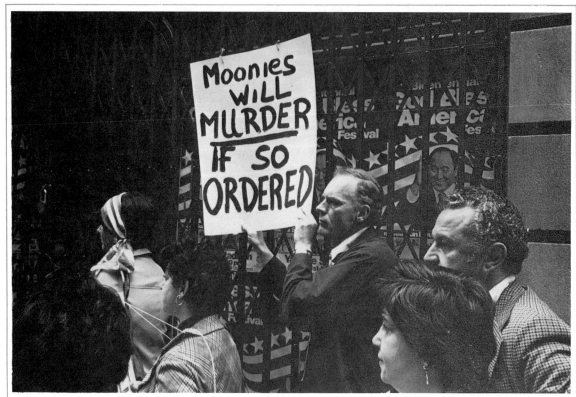

People who want to forcibly "deprogram" others justify their point of view with extreme, ideological attacks against the unusual religion.

authority wielded by cult leaders. A Canadian Gallup Poll in February, 1979 showed that half of the adult population believes that more government supervision should be imposed upon small religious groups. Legal experts and social scientists, however, are usually much more reluctant than the general population to support governmental control over religious organizations; they fear that freedom of religious expression might be endangered as well-meaning lawmakers seek to protect the public from its own gullibility.

Despite misgivings about religious sects and cults, a sizeable proportion of Canadians believe in some of the occult theories that accompany Eastern religions. For example, in the Gallup Poll of February 1979, it was established that over half of all adult Canadians believed in extra-sensory perception, or ESP. Some 44 percent believed in precognition, the ability to foretell the future through non-rational means. As many as 38 percent believed that déjà vu experiences echoed previous experiences in another life, a dream, or another state of consciousness, and 27 percent believed in the validity of astrology.[29] None of these phenomena can be explained by scientific laws, but many Canadians believe in them anyway. In general, the study showed that younger people were more open to these beliefs than older people, and well-educated people were more open to them than less educated people; only the belief in astrology was fairly constant among varying age and education levels in Canada. We shall return later to a consideration of various theories about the upsurge in popularity of Eastern-influenced religious ideas.

Theoretical approaches to religion

At the beginning of this chapter, I said that social scientists do not take positions on religious questions, for we cannot determine the truth or falsity of theological statements. And it is true that social scientists *as a group* don't take such positions. But lots of individual social scientists do. Here we will discuss the writings of four of them—Durkheim, Freud, Marx, and Weber—all of whom made strong statements about the part religion plays in social life. None of these scholars thought of himself as religious. Indeed, both Freud and Marx were highly critical of religion and actually hoped it would disappear.

EMILE DURKHEIM: RELIGION AS WORSHIP OF SOCIETY

In the years before World War I, Durkheim wrote one of his most important contributions to functionalist sociology—*Elementary Forms of Religious Life*. In it he asked two questions: (1) What is religion? (2) What are the functions of religion for human society? It struck him that religion was very much a "social thing." He felt that to understand it at all, one must focus on its collective basis.

Durkheim divided human experience into two very different areas, the *sacred* and the *profane*. The profane experience took place throughout everyday life, while the sacred experience involved anything that stimulated awe and worship. Durkheim decided that the purpose of religion was to maintain the separation of the sacred from the profane through the practice of ritual. Today many people assume that the most important feature of religion is the private, inner experience of the individual; the rituals performed in group meetings are often seen as unimportant outward displays with little bearing on one's deep experience. But Durkheim thought that the ritual itself was of central importance.

People everywhere worship a sacred object, but what they consider sacred differs greatly from one place to another. Durkheim felt that people everywhere worship the same object but symbolize it in very different ways. What is this object of worship? It is society. According to Durkheim, *God is society*. The group is made into a personalized, living entity. Religion sacralizes the traditions on which society is based. Society is a being greater than the individual. It is the source of the ideas and values that render a person's life meaningful, and makes him or her a social creature. The purpose of religion, therefore, is to preserve society. Religion expresses the value of society to humankind and makes society an object of reverence. In collective acts of worship, society reaffirms and strengthens itself.

Although he was interested mainly in the group rather than in the individual, Durkheim recognized the supportive role of religion for the believer. Religion gives the believer a feeling of comfort and dependence. "The believer who has communicated with his god . . . is a man who is stronger. He feels within him more force, either to endure the trials of existence, or to conquer them."[30]

SIGMUND FREUD: RELIGION AS ILLUSION

One of the most influential social theories of the twentieth century is Freudian psychoanalysis. While functionalists interpret religion as an invention designed to maintain the stability of *social groups*, Freud interprets it as an invention designed to maintain the stability of the *individual personality*. Both approaches stress the *usefulness* of the religion, though, according to Freud, religion serves infantile needs that should be outgrown.

Nature, says Freud, often mocks our attempts to control it. The task of culture is to

Brantford Expositor

From outlaw bike-gang member to devoted Christian. Is religion a crutch or a solution? A source of social oppression or social change?

attempt to defend us from nature, and from this effort come all the achievements of civilization. On this point, Freud agrees with the functionalists. However, he adds two new ideas: (1) that religion has done a poor job of defending us against nature, including our own human nature, and (2) that religion is an illusion because "wish fulfillment is a prominent factor in its motivations." Religion disregards reality.[31]

Religion, Freud writes, "is born of the need to make tolerable the helplessness of man." Freudian analysis has shown not only that human behavior stems from hidden motives but also that it often reenacts behavior learned in earlier situations. These earlier responses, usually of an infantile nature, are repeated in adulthood in a disguised form. Religion, to Freud, is an example of this kind of repetition. It is a reenactment of infantile behavior in the face of human limitations. With maturity, however, people should put aside childish things. Freud claims that, despite the consolations of religion, humans remain helpless. He believes that religious ideas which "should solve for us the riddles of the universe and reconcile us to the troubles of life" have "the weakest possible claim to authenticity."[32] He believes people should give up such infantile responses. Each person will then have to come to terms with himself as "no longer the center of creation. . .". For "is it not the destiny of childishness to be overcome?"[33]

KARL MARX: RELIGION AS IDEOLOGY

Not all social scientists (nor, indeed, all psychoanalysts) agree with Freud's view of religion. But his interpretation raises important questions. Many theologians have tried to develop a truly mature religious doctrine. Does maturity necessarily lead to the claim that there is "nothing else" beyond one's own life? Freud thought so, and so did Marx, who believed that religion is a delusion imposed upon one class by another in order to dupe it into obedience.

Marx's views on religion are usually discussed in connection with a controversy between his followers and Weber's over the impact of religion on society. Marx's followers believe that the only basic forces in society are economic and technological; Weber's followers see religion as also influencing social life, causing changes that would not otherwise occur. Marx tended to see religion as an *effect* of other factors; Weber saw it more as a *cause* of other factors.

Marx held that groups of people tend to choose belief systems, or ideologies, that can be used to justify their own economic advantages. Some social groups have leisure time and the chance to communicate with one another; therefore they develop convincing doctrines to support their dominance. Other groups (workers and especially peasants) may have neither leisure nor the chance to discuss their situation, and they may not be fully aware of the fact that they are exploited. Indeed, through the doctrine of the ruling group, the workers may come to believe that their rule is proper and that any rebellion against it is a sin.

According to Marx, religion is such a doctrine, an "opiate of the people" that prevents them from rebelling against their oppressors. Clearly Marx did not argue that religion has *no* effect. It has to have some effect if it is used by the ruling classes to dominate the workers. However, Marx did not expect religion to be a source of social change, and Marxist sociologists have generally ignored the study of religion.

MAX WEBER: RELIGION AS A SOURCE OF SOCIAL CHANGE

Against the background of Marxism, Weber's book, *The Protestant Ethic and the Spirit of*

Capitalism,[34] stands out sharply. Weber, like Marx, was curious about what caused industrial capitalism to develop. In other books, he discussed the organizational, technological, and economic origins of capitalism.[35] In this study, he focused on religion. He wanted to show that capitalism was a result of Protestantism, a result that early Protestants both expected and regretted.

Weber had noted that an unusually high number of European business leaders were Protestant. Remembering that the Industrial Revolution began shortly after the Protestant Reformation, Weber wondered whether the Reformation somehow caused the Industrial Revolution. He reasoned that the character traits that the Protestant value system encouraged were precisely the traits that a person would need to succeed in business. He did not claim that the early Protestant leaders meant to encourage the acquisition of material goods; they were concerned with the salvation of souls. Protestantism did not *cause* acquisitiveness, a trait as old as human nature, but it did create a system of *legitimate, rational* acquisitiveness. Several aspects of Protestantism contributed to this effect: (1) the legitimation of interest on loans, (2) the idea that secular work is a "calling" by which God may be served, and (3) the anxiety caused by the belief in *predestination*, the doctrine that each person is predestined to go either to heaven or to hell and cannot change that destiny.

The Catholic Church had forbidden Christians to lend money at interest, for this allowed a person to profit from the misfortunes and needs of others. This rule made capitalism impossible. Jews were allowed to accept interest, and during the Middle Ages their services were needed for business to be transacted on a regular basis. Some time after Calvin's day, Protestantism began to allow the taking of interest, and this freed devout Christians to invest their capital.

Protestantism also taught that one's work

in the world could be viewed as a "calling" from God. One should devote one's life to worldly tasks with the same zeal that hermits or priests have for religious matters. No longer did one turn away from worldly things to serve God. The work of the world was God's work, and it required no less sacrifice than the work of a monk. A person was to forego the pleasures of the flesh and instead work hard and prudently invest the profits of his or her labor in God's name.

Finally, Protestantism (especially Calvinism) created a terrible sense of loneliness and anxiety by emphasizing that God had already decided whether each individual was to be saved or damned. People could not earn salvation and should never allow themselves to believe that they were among the chosen. Indeed, in the minds of early Calvinists, there were no clues as to whether one belonged to the chosen or to the damned. People must live out their lives in anxiety, waiting to learn their eternal fate.

By the time Protestantism was in full swing, however, this chilling doctrine had been modified in a way that was vital for the development of capitalism. Although one still could not earn salvation, one could measure how well one was carrying out God's work on earth by how well one's work turned out. Thus a wealthy businessman who succeeded in his "calling" was apparently acceptable to God. Money became a means of reducing people's anxiety about whether or not they were saved. Poverty, on the other hand, was evidence that people were not putting enough zeal into their work and probably were not worthy of salvation. Because hardworking Protestants were not supposed to spend their money on luxuries, and because they were not supposed to interfere with and assist their poverty-stricken neighbors, they acquired wealth that they could neither spend nor give away. Fortunately, they were allowed to invest this money—and thus to become capital-

ist entrepreneurs. This ethic of worldly asceticism is the "Protestant ethic."

Early in the Protestant Reformation, some Protestant leaders foresaw the effects that Weber later described. John Wesley wrote, for example,

I fear, wherever riches have increased, the essence of religion has decreased in the same proportion. Therefore I do not see how it is possible, in the nature of things, for any revival of true religion to continue long. For religion must necessarily produce both industry and frugality, and these cannot but produce riches. But as riches increase, so will pride, anger, and love of the world in all its branches. How then is it possible that Methodism, that is, a religion of the heart, though it flourishes now as a green bay tree, should continue in this state? For the Methodists in every place grow diligent and frugal; consequently they increase in goods.[36]

Wesley's fears were justified. The Protestant ethic became less popular among the Protestants over time, and modern Methodists are not noticeably different in this respect from members of other religious communities. Weber argues, however, that the Protestant ethic played a major role in the development of industrial capitalism.

The "Weber thesis" attracted much criticism. It was pointed out, for example, that capitalism was not unknown in the Catholic world. Several pre-Reformation Catholic groups "rivaled the Puritans in their hospitality toward capitalism in general and even usury in particular.[37] Perhaps the greatest weakness in Weber's thesis is that it is still possible even today to take the Marxist position that Protestantism didn't cause capitalism—capitalism caused Protestantism.[38]

Finally, we should note that if there ever was a distinctively Protestant ethic it no longer exists. In polls and surveys about values and ethics, Catholics and Protestants give similar answers. Indeed, if any single religious group has a "Protestant" ethic today, it is the Jews.

FIGURE 13.4

Organizational Chart of Heaven

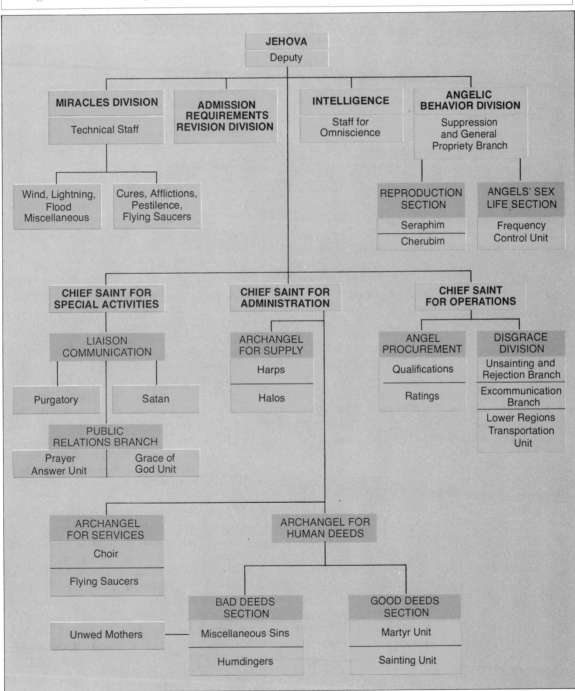

SOCIAL RESEARCH:
Sociologists at Work

In this section we will look at a variety of religious movements, most of which are not familiar to middle-class North Americans. We will begin with a look at messianic movements and then discuss the current Western interest in Eastern religions.

THE SOCIAL ORIGIN OF MESSIANIC MOVEMENTS

Under what conditions do people become attracted to charismatic religious leaders? Fortunately, it is possible to compare many different cases of charismatic inspiration, for history is filled with movements that swept through societies like wildfire, igniting the hopes of the masses for the coming of salvation on earth. Many of these phenomena pointed not to a life after death but to a transformation of society on earth under the direction of a seemingly divine ruler. Examples of such movements include the Ghost Dance cult of the Plains Indians, the cargo cults of Melanesia, the flagellant movements of thirteenth-century Germany, and the anti-Christ fantasies of the Crusaders. Such social cults are called *millenarian*—in accordance with the doctrine that Christ will return to rule for a millennium (1000 years)—or *messianic*—in accordance with the Jewish utopia, in which the Messiah is expected to rule. We will use the terms interchangeably.

Millenarian movements are very hard to explain. Why would a group of people wander around Europe in processions, beating themselves with leather scourges and iron spikes, as the flagellants did in the thirteenth century? Why would inhabitants of an idyllic South Sea island burn all their possessions and wait on the beach for ships to arrive, bringing them all the material objects of Western society, as the cargo cultists of Melanesia did? In recent years, several scholars have addressed such questions and have described the conditions in which millenarian movements arise.

First, it is well established that such movements occur mainly among the oppressed and suffering. In some cases they represent the response of a society to foreign domination. In Europe, the millenarian movements of the Middle Ages occurred especially among the peasants and those who were uprooted by being forced to become unskilled urban workers or beggars.[39] These movements often occurred after inflation, plagues, and famines had brought misery to the country.[40] In medieval Europe there was a large population living on the margin of society, without material or emotional support. They were not effectively organized in village communities, kinship groups, or guilds. There were no regular methods of voicing their grievances or pressing their claims. Instead they waited for a prophet to lead them in a movement driven by a desperate enthusiasm.[41] There is evidence that the poor were emotionally alienated from the Church, perhaps because of the showy life style of the church officials, and that they suffered as a result. What they needed was consolation in the person of a genuinely holy person. Such a person they would accept—and even adore.

In some types of messianic movements, the oppression comes from outside the society, as in the case of colonialism.[42] Such a messianic movement is often a violent struggle against the oppressor. The established political authorities may try to stifle it by force, as in the case of the Ghost Dance movement among the American Indians. Such movements arise mainly among people divided into narrow, isolated social units—villages, clans, tribes, and the like—in societies that have no overall unity or government. They have no way of acting together politically and are therefore unable to resist the oppressors. The millenarian cult is a way to overcome these divisions and to bring previously hostile and separate groups together into a new unity.[43]

Thus such religious cults are the forerunners of nationalistic movements, though they are led by religious rather than political leaders. This is because such societies are made up of fragmented parts, and any ordinary person would only identify with the special interests of his or her own subgroup. Only someone with unusual charisma can unify the tribes, clans, villages, and other interest groups in his or her society. He tells them to love one another and to forget the petty loyalties of the past. In time, especially if the religious movement is successful, political parties and other institutions replace the millenarian cult. The protest becomes rational. Thus in Melanesia cargo cults have declined as political groups have become more effective.

On the other hand, in some movements the source of the suffering is not oppression by outsiders but certain problems within the society—such as poverty and discrimination. Such movements always offer a hope of escape from the grimness of reality—usually through spiritual channels rather than through struggle against an enemy. Most of them offer a vision of material well-being on earth, though Christianity was unusual in that its hope of salvation was otherworldly.[44]

Modern Western society has seen few religious millenarian movements. However, other extremist movements have taken their place. Both Nazism and communism are similar to millenarian movements. Both have appealed to the same social groups and have offered them the prospect of carrying out a mission of stupendous importance. Some sociologists view millenarianism as the basis of the modern totalitarian party.[45]

RELIGIOUS TRENDS IN THE WEST

During the 1950s church participation in North America reached a peak. Over half the population attended weekly services, and church membership grew dramatically. Since then there has been a slow but steady decline, especially in the membership of liberal, yet conventional, churches. Fundamentalist and conservative churches have been slightly more successful in keeping up their membership. The Catholic Church seems to have lost more support than it gained by modernization.

So the basic trend of church participation is downward. At the same time, however, a huge variety of new religious organizations have recently sprung up, many of them with very unorthodox practices and beliefs. Some of these movements are within the Christian tradition and some are on its margins. Examples include the Pentecostal movement within the Catholic church—in which members "speak in tongues"—and such groups as those which have been nicknamed "Jesus Freaks," "Moonies," and "Jews for Jesus." Even more remarkable are the non-Christian groups, many of which mix religion with either the occult or psychotherapy, or both. Yoga, Zen, Transcendental Medi-

tation, Scientology, Synanon, est, Hare Krishna, and even Satanism may be included in this category.

What explains the large number of Westerners who have converted to these new religions? Are such groups likely to increase in number in the future? Three studies—one by Robert Wuthnow and his associates, one by the theologian Harvey Cox, and one by Max Heirich—try to answer these questions.

Wuthnow's study

Wuthnow's 1973 study[46] was a large-scale survey of San Francisco Bay area residents. The researchers, all University of California sociologists, interviewed 1000 randomly selected respondents age 16 and up. One purpose of the study was to find out what percentage of the population knew about or expressed interest in the new movements just mentioned. Wuthnow divided these movements into three general types: (1) *countercultural groups* (Zen Buddhism, Transcendental Meditation, yoga, Hari Krishna, Satanism); (2) *personal-growth groups* (Erhard Seminars Training (est), Scientology, Synanon); and (3) *neo-Christian groups* (Christian World Liberation Front (CWLF), Children of God, groups that speak in tongues, Jews for Jesus, Campus Crusade for Christ). He reported that

the groups show a widespread impact ... Nearly four out of every five persons claim to know a little about at least one of these movements, over half claim to know something about at least three of them, and about one person in every three claims to know something about five or more of them. More than half the population is currently attracted to at least one of them and about a third is attracted to at least two of them. Actual participation is much less common, of course; yet, one out of every five persons claims to have taken part in at least one of these groups. Eleven percent of the people interviewed also said they had taken part in other groups similar to these. Mentioned were groups such as Nichiren Shoshu, Aikido, Resurrection City, Meher Baba, and Divine Light.[47]

Table 13.2 summarizes the findings on the attractiveness of the various groups to people who have heard of them, as well as the extent to which they have participated in them. The largest number of people who have heard of these groups are attracted to est; the smallest number are attracted to Satanism.

What kinds of people are attracted to these

TABLE 13.2

Attraction to and participation in new religious and quasi-religious movements (among those who have ever heard of such movements).

	COUNTERCULTURAL					PERSONAL GROWTH			NEO-CHRISTIAN				
	TM	HARI KRISHNA	ZEN	YOGA	SATAN-ISM	SCIEN-TOLOGY	SYN-ANON	EST	CWLF	CAMPUS CRUSADE	JEWS FOR JESUS	CHILDREN OF GOD	TONGUES
Number	323	388	303	483	368	233	523	60	113	195	215	149	262
Percent attraction													
Strongly	10	1	8	9	2	3	7	17	4	9	8	13	10
Mildly	29	12	32	34	8	22	40	37	31	30	21	24	15
Turned off	12	44	11	10	66	37	13	16	19	26	24	22	40
Nothing either way	49	43	49	47	24	38	40	30	46	35	47	42	34
Ever taken part	16	4	8	16	3	5	6	24	6	15	4	6	23

Source: Robert Wuthnow, "The New Religions in Social Context" in Charles Y. Glock and Robert Bellah, eds., The New Religious Consciousness (Berkeley: University of California Press, 1976), p. 270.

In predicting the future of these movements, Wuthnow reasoned that if they appeal to categories of people who are likely to become more numerous in the future, they may be expected to increase greatly. But if they appeal to a part of the population that is decreasing in number, they may die out. So he looked at the relationship between support of these movements and a number of other movements? As you might expect, the people who like the neo-Christian movements are very different from those who are interested in the other types. Among other things, Wuthnow found that tolerance for radical political activity was highest among the countercultural and personal-growth supporters and lowest among the neo-Christian supporters.

The different types of groups attract people with different values and life styles. For example, Wuthnow asked respondents whether they approved of unmarried couples living together. He also asked whether they favored more freedom for homosexuals. He found that the countercultural and personal-growth movements appeal to people who accept unconventional life styles, while the neo-Christian movement appeals to people whose attitudes toward such matters do not differ from those of ordinary citizens.

variables, such as age and education. He found, first, that all three types of movement attract younger people more than older people. The countercultural movements tend to appeal to people in their teens, the personal-growth movements mostly to people in their twenties. (But est appeals to people between the ages of 30 and 50.) Thus we may conclude that these movements may be around for quite a while, since there is a continuous supply of young people being born and entering society. A movement that appealed only to old people might be expected to die out with them. However, if young people stay involved for life after they join, and if other young people are continually recruited, the movement could go on indefinitely.

Another fact points to the same conclusion. The new movements appeal to well-educated members of society more than to less-educated people. We know that the average level of education continues to increase. Hence, there will be a large population of well-educated individuals in the future. Any movement that appeals to poorly educated people will have a smaller base of support in the future.

But you may have thought of a different, contradictory argument. Suppose these groups do appeal to young, well-educated people. People also stop being young. Maybe the movements appeal to youth while they are in the crisis of growing up, and are at a troubled point in the life cycle. Perhaps they will eventually marry, establish careers, and generally make a place for themselves that feels more secure than their present situation. If so, maybe these movements will lose appeal for members as they grow older. In that case we could expect membership to peak in a few years and then level off or decrease as fewer young people enter the society. There is some basis for this argument. Wuthnow asked his respondents about the frustrations in their lives. He found that the countercultural groups (and to some extent the other two types as well) appeal most to people who are dissatisfied with their careers or their sex lives and are single and unemployed or working only part time. It may be that as people pass through these youth-related situations they will lose interest in the new movements. Wuthnow is therefore unable to predict how much growth will occur. However, he points out that the people who do become involved with these groups develop a life style that differs greatly from the conventional American culture.

Cox' study[48]

The nature of this lifestyle was explored by Harvey Cox in his book, *Turning East*. Cox teaches Christian religion at Harvard, which has become a center for the new Eastern (or neo-Oriental) religious groups. When the Hari Krishna devotees came to his door, shaven-headed, wearing saffron robes, and thumping on drums, Cox invited them in and listened to their views. Why, he wondered, had these three young people—a Jew, an Irish Catholic, and a Protestant—become Hindus, clanking cymbals and chanting in the street? Why had thousands of other young people like them done the same thing? Within 20 blocks of the Harvard subway station, 40 or 50 neo-Oriental religious movements thrive.

Cox decided to send his students out to study these groups and to participate in a good many himself. He reports having had a marvelous time. He and his students fanned out through Cambridge, armed with tape recorders and notebooks. They ate spicy vegetarian food at the "Golden Temple of Conscious Cookery." They twirled around with Sufi dancers (Muslims who used to be

called "whirling dervishes") in the basement of an Episcopal church. They sat on black silk cushions facing the wall with other meditators at the Zen center. They stretched and breathed deeply in yoga classes. They went to sitar concerts, Tai Chi exhibitions, Zen sword-play demonstrations, and countless introductory lectures to this and that. And the more deeply Cox became involved, the more the practices he observed influenced his own life. His description seems much richer for being drawn from personal experience instead of outside observation. He describes with vividness and passion his trip to the Mexican desert, where he ate Peyote with the Indians and then relived his prenatal life and his birth, cradled by a crooning middle-aged woman named Maria, until the morning star rose and his spirit expanded throughout the cosmos in joy. He also describes "sitting" with Tibetan Buddhists at the Naropa Institute in Colorado for a summer. It was there that he became an "East turner" himself. He says that he will continue to practice meditation for the rest of his life, combining it with his Christian faith. For despite his attraction to Eastern religions, Cox remains somewhat critical of Eastern mysticism as practiced by Americans. He believes that Christianity, with its emphasis on sacrifice, love, and interpersonal relations, continues to offer more to people who need to live and work in a meaningful world than Eastern religions do.

Cox estimates that several million Americans have been affected by some neo-Oriental practice or belief. He agrees that most of the converts are young—in their late teens, twenties, or early thirties. They are almost all white, educated, and middle-class. Men and women are about equally involved, though males take leading roles. Few come from rural areas. An especially high number are Jews or liberal Protestants.

Cox suggests that not all East turners are attracted to these movements for the same reasons. He names six motives that seemed important to the people he met during his study of neo-Oriental groups:

1 Some seemed to be looking for simple human *friendship*. The communes and ashrams offered this.
2 Some were in search of *immediacy*. They were tired of looking for God through words and abstract ideas and wanted instead to have a direct personal experience of the Holy. One East turner described his previous religion as follows: "I'd sit or kneel or stand.

I'd listen or read prayers. But it seemed lifeless. It was like reading the label instead of eating the contents. But here it happened to *me*. I experienced it myself."49

3 Some East turners were looking for *authority*—a swami or a guru with charismatic power. They needed a person who would offer them assurance and make their choices and decisions simpler.

4 Some turned East because it seemed more "*natural*." They were discouraged by the materialism and technology of the West and believed that the Asian tradition allowed more freshness, simplicity, and sensitivity to nature's rhythms.

5 A small number, mostly women, turned East *to avoid the male domination* of Western faiths. Cox notes that these people did not actually practice the neo-Oriental disciplines much—if they had done so they would have discovered that these groups have their own versions of male domination.

6 Finally, a handful of people had chosen the Oriental way because of a concern for *ecology* and *health*.

Cox says these motives are not uncommon. "When one examines this list of goals it quickly becomes evident that the East turners are not really very different from anybody else. They are looking for exactly what most people in America are looking for today. They have chosen a more visible and dramatic way of looking."50

If the turn toward the East cannot be explained by the motives of East turners, it has to be explained as a response to the problems and shortcomings of Western culture in general and Western religion in particular. In short, Christianity and Judaism may not be "working" as far as the East turners are concerned. Rightly or wrongly, they believe that Eastern approaches will work better for them and enable them to experience life in a fuller way.

If this is so, then researchers will have to explain religious conversions in a different way. Instead of searching for independent variables such as age, sex, marital status, income, or dissatisfaction with jobs or sex life, they will have to look (as Cox did) at the *content* of Christianity and of the faiths to which people are converting.

Heirich's study51

Max Heirich reached essentially the same conclusion as Cox. In his study of conversion to Catholic Pentecostalism, he began by studying the variables that sociologists usually list as sources of religious change. In this he was disappointed, for he found that conversion did not seem to result from psychological stress or from anything unique

about the convert's socialization. What, then, causes a person to switch from one religion to another? Heirich's initial answer is *social networks*. Knowing someone who was a Pentecostal was an important precondition for becoming a Pentecostal. This is not a surprising finding. People presumably develop preferences for particular religions the same way they develop tastes for pizza or ping pong or collecting dolls—by being exposed to those activities.

True, but Heirich adds a qualifying remark. Social networks don't have any impact unless people are already on a religious quest of some kind. That is, a person who is searching for a religious solution to his or her problems is open to the influence of friends. He or she may be willing to attend a service at which Catholics speak in tongues, and may even join in. But a person who is not searching for a religion is unlikely to be affected by his or her friends. What, then, leads large numbers of people to undertake a religious search? Heirich doesn't even try to answer this question conclusively—but he suggests that the answer hinges on "root realities." That is, the *content* of the present religion may no longer be adequate to cope with new ways of experiencing life. When something happens to shake up your world view, your idea of how the world functions and your proper place in it, only then will you undertake a religious search. Otherwise not. Thus when something happens to destroy one's clarity about "root reality"—one's basis for relating to the world—then the time is ripe for religious searching.

Several things may threaten a person's "root reality." Stress may play a part, in connection with other factors. (The people Wuthnow studied seemed to turn toward the new religions during the period of transition from adolescence to adulthood. This may be a stress-related source of religious conversion.) But other experiences may have a greater impact. If you have an experience that you cannot explain using the ideas you were taught as a child, it will affect your "root reality." Taking drugs might provide such an experience. An occult or ESP experience may also have this effect. Going deep into your own personality in psychotherapy or an encounter group might do it. Seeing someone levitate would *definitely* do it.

In this way, people change not only religious ideas but scientific ideas as well. The history of science shows that people develop a model that

Jim Ritscher/Stock, Boston

What is it about Eastern religions that is so appealing to Westerners today?

seems to work for most purposes—and then something happens that calls it into question.[52] This is what happened when it was discovered that the sun doesn't revolve around the earth but vice versa.

It is possible that various fairly recent events, such as the spread of psychotherapy, widespread drug use, the proven beneficial effects of acupunc-ture and yoga, and research on psychic phenom-ena, have called into question some of the "root realities" that we have always taken for granted. If some of our basic ideas about reality need to be revised, and if Eastern religious movements can help us revise them, then religious change will move in that direction. In its search for new "root realities", the whole West may "turn East."

SOCIAL POLICY:
Issues and Viewpoints

RELIGION AND THE STATE

Most modern Western societies share a common political policy toward religion, namely, to have no policy. Unlike some communist countries which use political means to oppose religion, or some other countries which use political means to en-force religion, the liberal position is to define reli-gion as a private area that should not be subject to political influence. In keeping with this general view, there is a tendency to use only secular symbols in public rituals. For example, courts have ordered some public schools to stop the practice of reciting the Lord's Prayer. This trend is part of the process of differentiation between the state and the culture. In earlier, undifferentiated times, the political system and the religious system were virtually the same thing. Indeed, when a king converted to a different religion it was understood that his subjects converted as well.

Those days are past. The process of differenti-ation is going on everywhere as an aspect of modernization, and one can predict with some confidence that it will continue. However, a number of conflicts have arisen during this process, and governments are sometimes unable to avoid mak-ing decisions that strongly affect religious groups.

The state must sometimes become involved in matters of religious practice or belief, especially when dealing with religious subcultures or with groups that hold deviant beliefs and norms. It is the proper business of the state to enforce social norms. As a result, Canadian government officials often have to deal with a number of thorny issues. Jehovah's Witnesses sometimes refuse blood transfusions for their sick children. Should they be allowed to do so if, in the opinion of physicians, a child's life is in danger? The two major religious groups in Canada, the Protestants and the Cath-olics, have the legal right to support separate schools with their tax dollars. Should all other religious communities in Canada have the same right? Should, for example, Dutch Reformed Churches and Jewish synagogues be able to pro-vide their children with tax-supported schools? The Ontario Mennonites have their own traditional ways of processing milk and are opposed to the use of new technological inventions. Should Ontario milk regulations require them to use standard modern methods when producing milk for public sale? The Catholic archdiocese of To-ronto is opposed on religious grounds to govern-ment support of birth control. It has therefore come into conflict with the United Way and other social welfare agencies that sponsor birth control. Does the Catholic Church have a right to insist that public agencies limit their support to projects that do not offend its religious principles? The Hutterite communities in the prairie provinces have become highly efficient farming communes, and they have frequently bought up large tracts of land to expand their farming operations. Their neighbors have sometimes used political strategies to restrict Hut-terite purchase of new farmland. What should the government's attitude be when faced with this economic and social competition?

In recent years, another religious issue has come before the courts: "deprograming." Some parents are troubled by the conversion of their offspring (often as adults) to various sects and movements. They claim that their children have been "brainwashed" and that equally strong methods are necessary to undo the damage. In some cases, they have arranged to have their children "deprogramed," or placed under extreme mental, emotional, and physical pressure to give up their new religious practices. In other cases they have tried to win court orders giving them the right to lock up their children for a specific time in order to keep them from practicing their devotions. Such parents have based their cases on their legal right to take custody of adult, mentally ill offspring. The assumption is that conversion to an unusual religion is evidence of mental illness, or that the conversion occurred only because the person had already become mentally ill.

Naturally, the courts are usually extremely reluctant to issue such orders. However, some have been issued, and members of groups such as the Krishna Consciousness community and the followers of Reverend Moon ("Moonies," as they are often called) have been removed against their will from their religious communities. The most aggressive "deprogramers" are no longer in business, but other clever and forceful procedures are still being used to "undo" conversions to new religious movements.

This question clearly involves the individual's civil liberties. People have every right to worship as they see fit, whether their parents approve or not. Of course if there is *other* evidence of mental illness besides conversion to an unpopular religion, the real question is how to look after the person when he or she is unable to organize his or her own life in a reasonable way. And if there is evidence that the religious group actually hyp-notized or drugged the convert or forced the conversion in some other way, the courts should interfere—at least enough to make sure that the conversion was voluntary.

RELIGIOUS MINORITIES AND VIOLENCE

We would like to believe that the era of religious wars ended several hundred years ago, but this seems not to be the case. The fights between Hindus and Muslims in India and Pakistan, between Catholics and Protestants in Northern Ireland, and between Jews and Muslims in the Middle East are evidence to the contrary. Some of the bloodiest wars in history were fought over theological points that seem trivial today. Each side usually kept up its morale by claiming that God favored its cause or even that it was fighting a Holy War in His name.

Actually, the fights between religious groups today are seldom over theological issues. Usually, neither side is interested in converting the other to its own faith. In such conflicts, the opposing sides are usually fighting because each side is an ascribed community (or ethnic group) that views itself as an in-group and the other side as an out-group. The fact that membership is based on religion is unimportant—it might just as well be based on skin color, language, caste, national origin, or any other ascribed characteristic. Hence, nonreligious Jews and nonreligious Arabs can be as hostile to each other as devout Jews and Arabs. Their hostility may actually be based on a rivalry for land, political power, prestige, or some other valued object.

SUMMARY

1. *Ethnic religions* are tied to a specific place and people. *Universalizing religions* are considered by their followers to be proper for all humankind and have been successful in converting others. *Segmental religions* in-tegrate small groups into larger communities.

2. A new religion begins with *charismatic leadership*. When the leader dies, the usual reaction is to change the movement into an organized institution, adjusting to the social order. This process has three aspects: (1) Ritual becomes more formal and elaborate; (2) the ideas and beliefs become more rational; and (3) the religious community becomes more organized.

3. There are three different "ideal types" of church organization: (1) The *congregational* type hires and fires its own leaders; (2) the *episcopal* type has a well-defined hierarchy of authority within the whole faith; (3) the *presbyterian* type has an elected regional board of ministers and lay persons from different congregations with the authority to appoint clergy.

4. Religion has five functions, all of which have both positive and negative aspects: (1) It provides support, consolation, and reconciliation; (2) it offers authority and stability; (3) it sacralizes the norms and values of society; (4) it provides standards by which to judge institutionalized norms; and (5) it gives the individual a sense of identity with the past and the future.

5. Human beings seem to need religion because it enables them to cope with the limitations of contingency, powerlessness, and scarcity that are part of their existence. The religious experience is the experience of the sacred as opposed to the profane.

6. The main difference between magic and religion is that magic attempts to control forces beyond the world of the senses in order to achieve some personal goal. Witchcraft has some good effects but probably causes more harm than good.

7. Weber showed that different social classes prefer different kinds of religious systems. Traders hold a rational world view with an ethic of "just" compensation. Peasants depend more on magic. Wealthy commercial classes prefer worldly religions; militaristic societies emphasize honor.

8. Members of the lower classes are less likely to join churches than members of the middle classes, but deprived individuals that do join tend to participate with great zeal.

9. Durkheim held that worshipers everywhere are actually worshiping society when they worship God. Ritual is the central aspect of religion.

10. Freud viewed religion as an illusion, and Marx saw it as a delusion imposed upon one class by another to lull them into submission.

11. Weber held that the rise of Protestantism enabled capitalism to develop. It encouraged an ethic of hard work and self-denial, allowed people to take interest on loans, and created a sense of anxiety about personal salvation.

12. Only about 10 percent of the Canadian population is of neither the Protestant nor Catholic faith. Different regions and social classes in Canada hold different patterns of religious commitment.

KEY TERMS

congregational organization a religious organization that hires and fires its own leader and in which there is no church hierarchy.

episcopal organization a religious organization in which there is a well-defined hierarchy of authority.

ethnic religion a religion that is tied to a specific place and people.

magic practices directed toward the control of spirits or other forces beyond the reach of ordinary human powers.

myth a nonhistorical story known by almost everyone in a group and symbolizing great truths to the group's members.

presbyterian organization a religious organization in which authority is in the hands of an elected regional board of ministers and lay members.

religion the relationship of humankind to some ultimate reality.

segmental religion a religion that is an offshoot of a universalizing religion or a new religious system that integrates small groups into larger communities.

theology the organization of religious beliefs into a unified doctrine.

universalizing religion a religion that is not tied to any particular region or ethnic group and whose members consider their beliefs to be right for all humankind.

FOR FURTHER READING

BAUM, GREGORY. *Religion and Alienation: A Theological Reading of Sociology.* New York: Paulist Press, 1975. Mixing theology with sociology is a tricky business, easily botched. But Baum makes it work beautifully.

BELLAH, ROBERT. *Beyond Belief.* New York: Harper & Row, 1970. Bellah is one of the most sensitive writers now discussing religion in terms of its contemporary meaning. He goes beyond many other sociologists in his willingness to share his own spiritual experiences and personal quest for meaning with his readers.

BURRIDGE, K.O.L. *New Heaven, New Earth.* Toronto: Copp Clark, 1969. This is about millenarianism, written by a sociologist of religion who teaches at the University of British Columbia, where there seems to be considerable interest in messianic religious movements.

CLARK, S.D. *Church and Sect in Canada.* Toronto: University of Toronto Press, 1948. One of the leading Canadian scholars in historical sociology, Clark here turns his attention to the social conditions underlying the development of various religious groups in Canadian society.

CRYSDALE, STEWART and LES WHEATCROFT, eds. *Religion in Canadian Society.* Toronto: Macmillan, 1976. This is the most generally useful collection of papers on Canadian religious life that I know of.

EPP, F. H. *Mennonites in Canada, 1786-1920: The History of a Separate People.* Toronto: Macmillan, 1974. This is a historical focus. It will refer you to several other books that are descriptive or comparative, if that is what you want.

FALLDING, H. *The Sociology of Religion.* Toronto: McGraw-Hill Ryerson, 1974. Fallding is an outstanding theorist, so his book does not so much report religious practices as the significance of religion in human life. His work is particularly important for anyone who wants to follow up Durkheim's ideas about religion.

KILBOURN, WILLIAM, ed. *Religion in Canada: The Spiritual Development of a Nation.* Toronto: McClelland and Stewart, 1968. Kilbourn is a social historian, so this collection of Canadian articles includes historical description as well as social commentary.

MOL, HANS. *Identity and the Sacred.* Toronto: Book Society of Canada, 1976. Mol is interested in how religion is involved in a group's search for meaning and collective self-definition. You may be interested in comparing his book with Baum's.

O'TOOLE, ROGER. *The Precipitous Path: Studies in Political Sects.* Toronto: Peter Martin, 1977. This book would also make appropriate reading for the chapters on collective behavior and political sociology. There is often a religious aspect of political movements, and O'Toole discusses some cases in which this occurs.

THRUPP, SYLVIA. *Millenial Dreams in Action.* Toronto: Schocken, 1970. This is another book on millenarianism.

14

EDUCATION

The functions of education
    The transmission of civilization
    Baby-sitting
    Building national spirit
    Establishing social relationships
    Job training
    Teaching values
    Certification
Trends in education
    Education in Canada
    Education in the Third World
Liberalism and conservatism—the main
      issues
    Education for stability or reform?
    The link between education and status
Social Research: Sociologists at Work
Social Policy: Issues and Viewpoints

Did I read it or dream it? I don't know. But I have in mind an image of humanity as a bunch of individuals floating around in the ocean. We have a hammer, a few nails, and a lot of driftwood, and we are trying to build a raft for ourselves. The raft represents civilization. We have nothing solid to stand on while hammering, and most of us are clumsy carpenters, so we know we may not succeed. But as we work there is one overwhelming idea in our minds and we keep reminding each other, *"Don't drop the hammer!"*

Education is the hammer.

I'm not the only person who thinks education is so important. Around the world, adults are telling young people, "Get as much education as you can. You'll depend on it later!" What they really mean is, "We'll all depend on it. Society needs you to gain knowledge and skills. Your education is for us all. Don't drop the hammer."

This, then, is a chapter about a vital institution. Education may be defined as a set of processes designed to transmit knowledge and skills and to develop mental abilities. It is crucial—in the developing societies as well as in our own, for it is through education that developing nations advance. The main difference between a modern society and a primitive one is in the nature of the symbolic, mental activity of their members. Modern societies maintain a variety of institutions that produce and transmit knowledge—research institutes, universities, publishing houses, libraries, schools, scholarly societies, opera guilds, and clubs organized around purposes such as poetry reading, paper-airplane design, coin collecting, psychotherapy, the writing of local history, and countless other activities that require special skills.

The functions of education

Education does different things for different people, but, for society as a whole, seven functions of education are especially important: (1) the transmission of civilization, (2) baby-sitting, (3) building national spirit, (4) establishing social relationships, (5) job training, (6) teaching values, and (7) certification.

THE TRANSMISSION OF CIVILIZATION

The primary function of education is sometimes forgotten because of disputes over less important functions. Civilization consists of complex ideas that can be transmitted from one generation to another only through years of interaction between students and teachers. In this activity, students develop their knowledge and their skills in critical thinking and aesthetic appreciation. Some people would like to return to a simpler way of life. They would like to allow their children to grow up as wholesome little primitives, taught by Mother Nature alone and protected from the repression and complexity of modern society. This is not a new wish; it was suggested by Jean Jacques Rousseau more than two centuries ago.[1] However, it is clear by now that Mother Nature alone is a poor teacher and that culture is too valuable to give up without a struggle. It is easy to lose and hard to maintain. The transmission of civilization is therefore education's highest function.

BABY-SITTING

The baby-sitting function of education is rarely recognized openly. Naturally, parents hope the schools do more than baby-sit, but even baby-sitting is of great value. Teachers care for such large groups of children that their services are quite cheap compared to the cost of private care for individual children. From this service parents gain the freedom to engage in personal and economic activities that they could not otherwise afford.

BUILDING NATIONAL SPIRIT

Through their schooling, many immigrant children are learning to be "New Canadians."[2]

The baby-sitting function of education is rarely recognized openly.

Schools transmit nationalistic myths and symbols, teach history, and develop patriotic loyalty probably better than any other institution. The country where one has been educated remains one's "native land" throughout life. Hubert Guindon has argued that the widespread expansion of university education in Quebec in the 1960s and early 1970s was a major factor behind the development of Quebec's strong cultural identity. Indeed, during that period, education also expanded throughout English Canada, and a strong upsurge of Canadian nationalism took place.

ESTABLISHING SOCIAL RELATIONSHIPS

Social relationships are established in educational institutions. Even if children could gain all the skills they need by reading books alone at home, they would miss some of the important benefits of schooling. A person develops social abilities through the give-and-take of peer group interactions; the playground is a school too.

Moreover, the friendships one makes in school can be an important resource for many years, particularly among upper-class members. For example, when a man needs a job he may telephone some of the "old boys" he knew in school 20 or 30 years before to ask if they know of any openings.

JOB TRAINING

Job training is another function of educational institutions. This function is often emphasized by sociologists who study economic development. Some people see their schooling as an economic *investment* through which they add to their earning power by learning well-paid skills. Others consider their schooling as an end in itself, an item of *consumption* more than an investment. Both views are correct. It would be shortsighted to consider education only in terms of its effects on the economy, but it would be equally wrong to overlook those effects.

In the mid-1960s, John Porter argued that Canadian schools did not offer sufficient training for job skills, and that this "educational deprivation" forced Canada to import skilled immigrants to fill jobs that Canadians could not perform.[3] Shortly afterwards, the level of expenditure for job-oriented education increased greatly; Porter's complaint is no longer valid today.

A more topical issue is not whether Canada offers enough education, but whether education actually improves the quality of a worker's job-performance. Certainly *some* education is necessary; basic literacy is essential to virtually every job. But does more and more education help workers to perform their jobs better and better? We shall return to this discussion shortly.

TEACHING VALUES

Talcott Parsons has suggested that the classroom is especially important as a setting in which the child learns two values that are necessary to adult roles in modern society: achievement and universalism.[4] He has pointed out that the family is based on the opposite values—ascription and particularism—and therefore cannot teach the child how to function in an impersonal social or-

ganization. Parents love their children because of who they are, not because of what they have done. Children do not have to earn their parents' admiration in a competitive market by outshining others. The relationship between parent and child is ascribed and particularistic.

Elementary school teachers are usually women who have a nurturant attitude toward children similar to the parent's. However, as children progress to higher grades, they learn that teachers measure out approval according to the pupil's performance. All pupils are judged by the same standards. This is training for new values—achievement and universalism. In order to function in most adult roles a person must be motivated to perform well

Attempts are now being made to tailor schooling to the needs of special groups. These students attend a special Inuit school in Montreal.

Montreal Gazette

according to certain universal standards, and this is not a lesson that can be learned at mother's knee.

CERTIFICATION

The certification function of educational institutions is a subject of much debate. Some say it is vital, while others argue that it is a social evil and must be eliminated.

In all technologically advanced societies, jobs are given to those who have certificates and diplomas; the better the job, the more prestigious the diploma has to be. But who gets the prestigious diplomas? There are two answers, both partly true. Answer number one is that the deserving people get the diplomas—the ones who are bright, steady, and hardworking. The others drop out or cannot keep up. Tests are given along the way to sort students into the "streams" they belong in, a process not unlike grading eggs: Extra Large Grade As go on to college and a profession; Medium Grade Bs go to trade school and a menial job.

Answer number two is that the children from the upper and middle classes get the diplomas. Modern society has no hereditary aristocracy, but its upper classes pass along their privileges to their young in indirect ways. They provide them with good schooling, which is the ticket to high status.

Because both answers are partly true, they each have to be taken seriously, though they are incompatible. One answer emphasizes the importance of quality; the other emphasizes equality. It follows from the first answer that tests, "streams," and other competitive processes are defensible because they safeguard high-quality job performance. The most able people are given the most complex jobs. Every egg to its proper carton, every student to his or her proper occupation. It follows from the second answer that all students should be treated alike throughout their schooling; no departure should be permitted from the principle of equality of op-

portunity. However, it is not clear whether the principles of equality and quality can be reconciled, and if so, how.

Several Canadian sociologists have pointed out that the upper-class people who hold the highest positions in this country are able to pass their high-ranking positions on to their offspring by buying them prestigious certifications that will be recognized as special. This is done primarily by sending their children to famous private schools, such as Lakefield School or Upper Canada College. Wallace Clement has shown that 68 percent of those members of the Canadian elite with fathers of similar status have attended private schools.[5] These private schools offer superior schooling, and, even more importantly, they offer students the opportunity to form friendships with other privileged children who can provide them with a lifelong network of influential professional contacts.

Trends in education

A world-wide "education explosion" is accompanying the "population explosion." In the past two decades, the number of students and teachers around the world has multiplied at a fantastic rate. Meeting the demand for more education is one of the greatest challenges of our time. Unlike most developing countries, Canada has enjoyed considerable success in meeting this challenge. Let us examine the Canadian educational system, so that afterwards we can compare it to that of a typical Third World country.

EDUCATION IN CANADA

One of the provisions of the British North America Act defines education as a provincial, rather than federal, concern. This provincial control produces a great deal of diversity among the education systems of the various provinces. Moreover, even within the provinces, there is considerable variety; most decisions concerning primary and secondary education are made at the local community level by elected school boards. Despite regional diversity, however, Canadian schools do face certain common problems and reflect certain common trends.

Two controversial issues have troubled Canadian education throughout its history. The first concerns the dispute over whether schools should be under secular or religious control, and the second, the dispute over whether French or English should act as the medium of instruction. These issues have usually been linked; francophones have tended to be Catholic and to want Catholic schools, while anglophones have tended to be Protestant and to want secular schools. Because education has been largely under provincial control, these disputes have been treated differently in different provinces. They have yet to be completely resolved, however. The issues of language and religion continue to pose problems for Canadian education.

Throughout Canada, dual systems of education have been developed to provide both secular and Catholic schools. The provincial government administers one of these as a "public" system, while a separate authority administers the "separate" systems with tax funds. Outside of Quebec, separate schools have usually been Catholic and public schools have been secular. In Quebec, however, the separate schools have been secular and the public schools have been Catholic.

In Quebec, public schools have generally provided instruction in French and separate schools have provided instruction in English. Elsewhere in Canada, public schools have

The issue of French-language education is an explosive one, especially in areas outside of Quebec.

Globe and Mail/Lewcun

generally held classes in English and separate schools have sometimes offered French or bilingual programs. A number of problems have resulted from this situation. English-speaking Catholic families have sometimes had difficulty finding English-language, Catholic schools for their children. Immigrant groups have sometimes desired the same right as French and English Canadians to publicly-funded education in their native languages.

The worst educational problems have developed among francophone families living outside Quebec. The children of these families have generally been offered very limited facilities and have usually been expected to be bilingual. As a result, many have been handicapped; statistics show that francophone children outside Quebec have less scholastic success and higher dropout rates than anglophone children. According to the Royal Commission of Bilingualism and Biculturalism, many Canadian bilingual schools have possessed inadequate teaching standards and have failed to encourage their students' educations.[6] Moreover, teachers have frequently perceived francophone students as less promising than anglophone students, a view that has no doubt affected the students' school work.[7]

During the past decade, French-language education, in Quebec and throughout Canada, has improved considerably. In most provinces, francophone students today can receive high school educations in their own language.[8] Quebec's recent controversial legislation, in its attempt to make French its only official language, has raised the educational standards of French schooling both in Quebec and elsewhere.

Throughout Canada, several trends in education have become evident in the past two decades. Some of these have resulted from the changing size of the school-age population, some from a fluctuating economy, and some from changing ideas in teaching methods. During the 1960s, schools at all levels were forced to expand to cope with the con-

tinuing effects of the baby boom, the influx of great numbers of immigrants, and an unprecedented demand for higher education. Between 1960 and 1970, the number of B.A.'s and similar degrees from Canadian universities more than tripled. The number of graduate degrees increased even more. New university campuses and community colleges were created to offer non-academic job-training. The government poured large sums of money into universities to produce educated Canadians to fill the new jobs created by a technologically advanced economy. Conflicts arose concerning the lack of Canadian content in curricula and the non-Canadian status of many professors in the rapidly expanding faculties.

At all levels of instruction, schools pursued the ideal of "flexibility." Students were allowed to choose their own subjects without limits. Grading standards were loosened. In the primary schools, "open plan" architecture became fashionable, so that children had more freedom to explore classroom space. Team teaching was encouraged, allowing children to choose from a variety of educational games. Alternative "free" schools were established by many school districts for children who did not take well to "structure." In the universities, students opposed to structure often participated in sit-ins and demonstrations.

In the mid-1970s, these trends began to reverse. A slower economy had neither the funds nor the job-market incentives to support higher education on such a scale. A decline in the number of school-age children left primary schools partly empty (see Figure 14.1). Teachers and parents, convinced that the "flexibility" approach had lowered standards of achievement, demanded tougher school programs. Universities tightened up marking standards and reinstituted mandatory course requirements. Budget cuts resulted from declining enrolments. Students abandoned the activism of the 1960s; instead, they applied themselves to their work to meet fierce competition for the few available jobs.

Arts programs became less popular than career-oriented programs. Like many other affluent Western countries, Canada can expect these trends to continue at least until the mid-1980s.

Although Canadian schools share several common concerns, a great many regional dif-

ferences also play a part in their operation. Many of these variations are due to economic factors. The maritimes and Quebec have the lowest levels of education in Canada. The prairies, and particularly British Columbia, have the highest. Ontario's education levels fall between these two extremes.[9] In general,

FIGURE 14.1

Estimate of full-time enrolment by institutional level in Canada,[1] 1971-72 to 1986-87

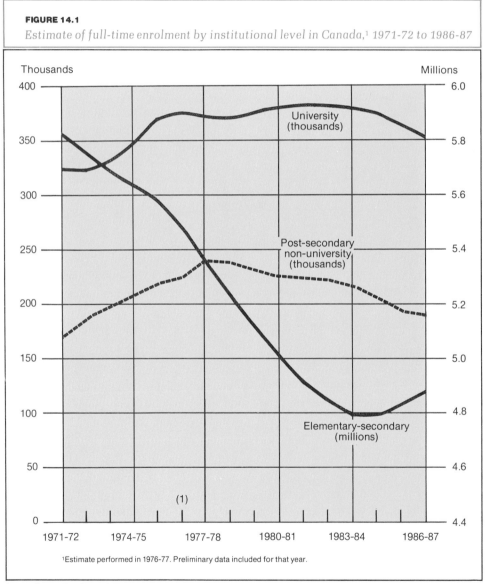

¹Estimate performed in 1976-77. Preliminary data included for that year.

Source: Canada Year Book, 1978-79, p. 292.

the provinces that offer the best educational opportunities are those with flourishing economies and low unemployment rates. The weak economies of the maritimes produce neither the funds nor the job incentives to support extensive educational opportunities.[10]

During this century, the general educational level of the Canadian population has dramatically increased. This increase has both resulted from and stimulated the overall growth of the Canadian economy. Canadians have been fortunate. Throughout most of the rest of the world, countries have found it much more difficult to attain the level of educational expansion that they so badly need.

EDUCATION IN THE THIRD WORLD

The new nations are experiencing a major crisis. Their populations are increasing fast. At the same time, their citizens are demanding that all students be given more education than their parents received. It's an impossible situation. All the new nations give very high priority to educational spending, but it is never enough. Besides, there is another problem: In order to get qualified teachers, the government must pay salaries comparable to those offered by industry. But industry becomes more productive every year and can pay its workers larger salaries because their work is more profitable. Teachers' salaries have to be raised just to keep up, but teachers don't become more productive over time. That is, an average teacher cannot teach more children or teach them any better this year than last year. Therefore, just to teach the same number of children for the same length of time, the government has to keep paying more and more. And, of course, today there are *more* children, and each one wants *more* schooling.

The developing nations are having little success in meeting the demand for education.

FIGURE 14.2

The world's secondary education enrollments 1950–1970. The absolute numbers of illiterates are increasing in the world, despite the increasing percentage of children in school. This is because of the population explosion, which has provided more pupils than any country can afford to educate.

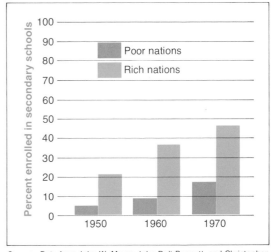

Source: Data from John W. Meyer, John Boli-Bennett, and Christopher Chase-Dunn. "Convergence and Divergence in Development". *Annual Review of Sociology*, I. Palo Alto, Calif.: Annual Reviews, 1975, p. 227.

The number of illiterate people in the world is increasing, not decreasing. This trend, unfortunately, will probably continue for some time.

Liberalism and conservatism—the main issues

In previous chapters I have asked you to decide what you think of a given issue. As we go on defining issues, pay attention to which side you are on each time. This should help you see more clearly whether you are mainly conservative or mainly liberal on most issues. Of course you can be liberal on one matter and conservative on another, but if you are like most people you will find that you are fairly consistent. Attitudes tend to cluster in a regular way. After you get a feel for these patterns of consistency, you will often find it possible to guess how strangers view most issues after you have heard their opinions on two or three topics.

When people talk about education, two issues distinguish *most* liberals from *most* conservatives. The first has to do with the relationship between education and social change. The second issue is the link between education and social status.

EDUCATION FOR STABILITY OR REFORM?

Let's start with the first question: Does education encourage social change or does it tend to keep things the way they are? The most obvious difference between liberals and conservatives is in the way they view social change. Liberals welcome it; conservatives are wary of it. They have different ideas about progress. A conservative thinks progress must be a slow, evolutionary process. A liberal is much more likely to assume that we can create progress, now, almost with a snap of the fingers. And the favorite liberal proposal for solving social problems is usually this: Educate people.

Herbert Spencer must have been one of the most conservative men of all time. He believed that human progress was slow and couldn't be rushed. Reform schemes of any kind were unrealistic dreams that could only cause trouble. Progress could occur only through evolution—the survival of the fittest and the *nonsurvival* of the *unfit*. Reformers who wanted to help the unfit survive only interfered with the process of evolution. Try-

When we read to our children, we pass along those stories that have meaning for us.

Mike Mazzaschi/Stock, Boston

ing to educate somebody with low potential was useless, Spencer thought. Thus it would be impossible to increase the potential of the working class by providing free schooling. He wanted to educate only those children whose parents could pay the fees. This view was social Darwinism—the extreme in conservative social thought.

Lester Frank Ward was a wholly different sort of fellow. I imagine him as enthusiastic and optimistic. He was from the midwestern United States and he reached a high position in the American educational system through study. To him, knowledge was the major source of social change. Through education, humankind could control its own evolution and progress beyond the law of the jungle, which Spencer believed was part of human nature.

Of course, progressives followed Ward, not Spencer. Today liberals believe education can be used to fight all kinds of social evils. Teenagers are given driver education, anti-drug education, sex education, and religious education, and are expected to become cautious, sober, chaste, and devout as a result. This doesn't always work, of course—but not for the reasons Spencer suggested. It is not because human nature is unchangeable but, rather, because driving, drug use, sexual behavior, and religious involvement are influenced by group pressure, not just by individual judgment. And it's not easy to change social norms by educating individuals. It's easy to present facts, but it's not easy to control group interaction. Education presents information. But you and I organize our lives on the basis of feelings, relationships, and the desire to win approval, as well as on information. These factors limit the ability of education to remake society.

There is another point of view besides the liberal and conservative approaches: the radical view. If Spencer was the champion of conservatives, Marx was the champion of radicals. But, in this case, Marx agreed in part with the conservative outlook. He did not

Cary Wolinsky/Stock, Boston

Should teachers always reflect the values of the community that employs them?

view education as a means to change society; this was not however because he believed in the survival of the fittest but because he viewed the educational system as a conservative institution. It is part of the "superstructure," and as such it takes its orders from the ruling class. Teachers would be fired if they tried to bring about any important social change. Besides, they could teach only what they know, and what they know depends on what they have a chance to find out. The ruling class can control what workers find out. Who owns the newspapers? The ruling class. Who controls the spread of ideas? The ruling class. The rise and fall of various social

419

classes depends on changes in technology, not on changes in the educational system.

Does education generally serve to maintain the status quo or to change society? On the whole, schools seem to be cautious in the teaching of ideas, at least at the elementary and secondary levels. Higher education is different, however. It rewards people for originality and daring—at least sometimes. Yet, conservative as they are, grade schools and high schools serve a vital function. They teach students skills that the society needs. In this sense, even a conservative institution is necessary. Besides, schooling does make a person more open to new ideas, and to this extent it leads to social change in the long run.

THE LINK BETWEEN EDUCATION AND STATUS

Now for the next question. You know that there is a strong relationship between education and social status. Well-educated people get better jobs and more prestige and authority, on the whole, than poorly educated people. Is this fair? If so, why? If not, why not?

This question is a strong test of a person's conservatism or liberalism. Most people, both conservatives and liberals, will say that this situation is fair. If you say it is unfair, you are either a very militant liberal or a radical. You object to the amount of inequality in modern

Education is used to instill the cultural values of a society.

Ruiko/DPI

society and would like to see major changes in our stratification system.

You will recall from Chapter 9 that the Davis-Moore theory of stratification[7] assumes that there are a fixed number of jobs in society and that the high rewards of some jobs are necessary in order to fill those jobs with qualified people. The skills required by those jobs are gained mostly through education. Therefore the competition for a high-quality education is intense.

I've already described the educational process as similar to an egg-sorting process in which students are sorted into different cartons to be shipped to the appropriate jobs after graduation. Employers call employment agencies and order certain grades of eggs. They want college graduates for junior-executive jobs and high school graduates for jobs in the shop. They are prepared to pay more for the college eggs. Is this fair? And is it fair to ask for a college egg for the executive job? Is it reasonable to make a college degree a requirement for certain jobs and not others? Most people assume that it is. If you ask employers why they want college graduates for certain jobs, they will probably say that the job will be done better if they hire better-educated people. What other explanation could there be?

Randall Collins has suggested another reason, however. Employers have to work with junior executives every day. They have to train them to take over their own jobs when they retire. Maybe they just like to be around college graduates because college graduates understand the jokes they tell, know enough to serve the kind of Scotch they drink, read novels by Saul Bellow and Doris Lessing, and so forth. They enjoy their company. Maybe they're only *telling* themselves that college graduates do the job better.

When we discussed Max Weber's theory of stratification, we saw that Weber believed that certain groups, called *status groups*, have a very strong sense of group consciousness. Members of a social class may or may not identify with each other as a group—usually

they don't. But members of a status group do. And money is not the key factor determining what status group you belong to. Many people have little money but have what my grandmother used to call "breeding"—taste, style, sophistication, polish.

In general, people are very aware of whether they belong to the same status group or not. It's a matter of life style; it's unmistakable. Weber noted that high-status groups hold onto high prestige by emphasizing their special life style and "high" culture. What is the main basis of membership? Education.

Here is where Collins abandons the conservative point of view—the functionalist explanation.[11] He argues that there is no *functional need* to hire educated people for the high-status jobs. The job could probably be done well enough by a person with much less education. But Weber was right: Members of a high-status group prefer to hire as their coworkers and successors other members of their own group—people with similar interests, values, background, and tastes. And the best way to be sure of hiring such people is to advertise for college graduates.

If Collins is right, then the relationship between education and social status is not fair. If it were functionally necessary, it would be fair. Do you agree with him? There is little evidence that conclusively supports either position. Both Collins and Ivar Berg[12] have done research that suggests that well-educated people are not necessarily more productive than less well-educated people—and they may even be less productive at times. But their evidence is skimpy, and the issue is far from settled.

Moreover, it won't do to carry Collins' argument to extremes. Some jobs really do require special training. If you drop out of medical school, I won't let you take out my appendix. However, it may be true that educational requirements are often exaggerated beyond the level that is functionally necessary. When this happens, hiring becomes unfair, for it discriminates against people who may be equally able to do the job.

SOCIAL RESEARCH:
Sociologists at Work

You have probably already realized that the sociology of education has many political implications. Educational research is often supported by various government agencies or school boards. Results are released not only in obscure journals, but through press conferences and television interviews. In virtually no other area of social science can the scholar expect to wield so much political influence as in the study of education. Though schools and universities are supposed to be free from overt government control, they are usually funded by public tax money. In return for its money, the public has a political voice in educational planning. Sociological research often guides public opinion and indirectly influences educational planning.

Most education sociologists are interested in the area of social stratification. Most reports by education researchers concern the relationship between education and inequalities in income, status, prestige, social power, and the like. Social inequality is the core theme of politics; no topic excites as much controversy and political action. Of course, most social scientists, like most Canadians, believe that opportunities should ideally be equal. In practice, however, the issue of equality is extremely complex. Sociologists must first find ways to assess the true nature of the relationship between education and social inequality. Then they are faced with the difficult task of determining what constitutes excessive inequality and how to correct it where it exists. Despite these problems, some sociologists have shed considerable light on the relationship in Canada between education and social inequality. They have usually begun their research by posing the question: "How much inequality is there in Canadian society?" or "How much social mobility takes place in Canadian society?"

Three sociologists have produced especially telling research on social stratification in Canada. John Porter, Wallace Clement, and James Curtis have each worked with different kinds of data but have reached similar conclusions. According to their findings, a substantial amount of inequality still exists in Canada, and the present educational system reinforces that inequality. Schools tend to perpetuate the ascription of status; they help parents in high social positions to transmit their status to their offspring. The educational system does not overcome inequality: It is structured in such a way that it supports it. Indeed, restructuring the system to avoid inequality has proved extremely difficult.

Any statement of inequality is, of course, relative. Many countries, including most developing nations, are more stratified than Canada. But several countries are also more egalitarian, as we have seen in Chapter 9. Then again, sociologists disagree about how much inequality is acceptable.

By the time a child begins the first day of school, the likely outcome of his or her education is already partly established.

Peter Vandermark/Stock, Boston

TABLE 14.1

Percentage distribution[1] of Canadian families by income group and education of head, 1975. Notice that a university degree continues to offer great earning power.

INCOME GROUP	ELEMENTARY SCHOOL ONLY, 0-8 YEARS	SOME HIGH SCHOOL AND NO POST-SECONDARY[2]	POST-SECONDARY (NON-UNIVERSITY)		UNIVERSITY DEGREE
			SOME	COMPLETED	
$ 0-$ 4,999	15	6	6	4	4
5,000- 9,999	27	16	14	12	7
10,000- 14,999	24	26	23	22	12
15,000- 24,999	26	38	43	45	37
25,000 and over	8	14	15	17	41
Total	100	100	100	100	100

[1]Figures have been rounded.
[2]Includes high school graduation.

Source: Adapted from Canada Year Book, 1978-79, p. 269.

Some claim that a certain amount of inequality serves a functional role in the economy. John Porter, for example, agreed with the functionalist approach of Davis and Moore (see chapter 9). He believed that the modern economy requires different levels of ability and training. He saw nothing wrong with wage disparity so long as Canadians had equal access to training for all jobs. Porter worked hard to upgrade occupation-oriented educational facilities. He also showed, in *The Vertical Mosaic*,[13] that exclusive schools and universities prevent Canadians of humble origins from challenging the entrenched elite. In *Does Money Matter?*,[14] written with Marion Porter and Bernard Blishen, he showed that many young Canadians are kept from higher education because of financial problems.

Wallace Clement has continued Porter's line of investigation, but has concerned himself primarily with the small economic elite that operates the Canadian branch plants of large multinational corporations. Clement shows that these Canadians are integrated with a larger business elite that spans national boundaries. Born into moneyed families, members of this elite attend the same private schools in Canada and the United States, and continue these relationships in university and in private clubs. Just as half the U.S. elite have attended either Harvard, Columbia, Yale, M.I.T., or Stanford, so half the Canadian elite have attended the University of Toronto, McGill, or Harvard.[15]

James Curtis's work is based more broadly, using survey methods to research large representative samples of the Canadian population. In his work with Carl Cuneo, Curtis compared Canadian patterns of occupational mobility with established findings in the United States.[16] Curtis and Cuneo analyzed occupational mobility patterns of male and female Canadians between the ages of 25 and 34, both francophones and anglophones, in Montreal and Toronto. They found that the respondent's education had more impact than any other variable on the status of the respondent's first job. They concluded that there was roughly the same amount of occupational mobility in Canada as in the United States, and that the same factors appeared to explain the mobility in both countries, with slight variations in the case of French Canadian men. In both countries, the status of the respondents' parents played a considerable role in the educational levels that the respondents attained. Generally, the education and occupation of the father determined this status; notably, however, the mother's education was a key factor in the educational attainments of French Canadian men.

The research of all these sociologists indicates that education is *part* of the process of social ascription. Education does not counter ascription. (Of course, hiring practices are seldom clear-cut cases of either achievement or ascription. Qualified people do not always compete freely and equally for the same job; they are more often helped by professional "contacts". People with a lot of contacts who are adept at "pulling strings" still need some qualifications for the job.

It is usually assumed that an individual's educational level and occupational status is a result of his or her own efforts to achieve. Curtis and Cuneo show, however, that the individual's family prepares the way for success or failure in schooling. Rather than measuring the student's initiative, hard work, and achievement, an educational level more often measures the parents' success in ascribing their rank to their offspring. Those who are employed on the basis of educational certification are therefore hired as much through ascription as through their own achievement. Only those students whose family backgrounds have no relationship to their success in school can claim complete responsibility for their accomplishments.

In a sense, then, it is unfair for people to get good jobs on the basis of their school performance, because that performance has largely been determined by their parents' social status. Because privileges are so often handed down from one generation to the next, we must conclude that Canadian society does not have real equality of opportunity.

There are a couple of qualifications that must be added to this conclusion. First, *education is not the whole story*. And second, *education's economic value is less than it used to be*. Neither point, in itself, guarantees more or less social inequality. However, both of these factors lessen the role that education plays in perpetuating that inequality. Let me discuss them in turn.

The basis for my statement that *education is not the whole story*, is the book, *Inequality*,[17] by Christopher Jencks and others. According to Jencks, many other factors besides education determine a person's income. Differences in education do not really account for the wide range of social inequality. Suppose, for example, that you are told that a friend has had two years of university and is now working. Can you guess her salary on this much information? Of course not. Some people with two years of university are millionaires; others are living in poverty. Obviously, education alone does not determine earnings. Although the average income of graduates with a B.A. is higher than the average income of high school graduates, all B.A.'s do not earn exactly the same amount, nor do all high school graduates. Jencks used statistics to show that if all the people in the country had the same level of education, the amount of income inequality would be reduced only slightly.

What does determine income then? According

TABLE 14.2

Education levels of various Canadian ethnic groups 1971 (in percentages[1])

EDUCATION	ETHNIC GROUP							
	ENG-LISH	FRENCH	GERMAN	NATIVE INDIAN	ITALIAN	SCANDI-NAVIAN	UKRAINIAN	CANADIAN AVERAGE
Elementary only	26	50	47	90	74	46	55	37
Secondary only	43	29	26	15	16	30	28	36
Post-secondary (non-university)	18	13	19	4	6	16	10	15
University	14	9	9	2	4	8	8	12
Total	100	100	100	100	100	100	100	100

[1]Figures have been rounded.

Source: Adapted from Lyle E. Larson, *The Canadian Family in Comparative Perspective* (Scarborough, Ont.: Prentice-Hall, 1976), p. 56.

to Jencks, luck plays a major role. Your income may depend on whether you can hit a hockey puck well enough to play professionally, whether hail destroys your crops, whether the Dow Jones average rises or falls, or whether your boss notices when you drink too much at the Christmas party. Many things besides education can affect income.

If this is the case, how can we equalize incomes? Jencks suggests that this must be done directly. If some citizens have too little money, give them more. There is no other way. Of course Jencks is aware that direct redistribution of income will meet tremendous political resistance. But he still says that there is no other realistic way to achieve greater equality.

As a matter of fact Jencks suggests that we should feel relieved by his findings, not discouraged. We have pinned too many hopes on the school. We have imagined that it could solve all of our problems. It can't. This means we can relax a bit. We don't have to have homogeneous schools, like peas in a pod. If equality of education were so important, the schools would have to be exactly alike to be fair. But we don't all agree on what they should be like. Parents have all sorts of contradictory opinions about how schools should function and what they should teach. Why not let people choose? Not all children are the same. Some flourish in a free school without competition. Others like to work on arts and crafts. Others want to play with computers all the time. Why not let them?

Jencks has suggested an "educational voucher" system. He proposes that the government pay each child's portion of the education budget to the school his or her parents choose. If the parents are disappointed by the school, they can "vote with their feet" by taking their tax money to a different school. This idea would encourage variety in education, not equality. Since we don't all agree on what is a good education and what is a poor one, we may as well allow for freedom of choice. I agree.

When discussing the notion that education perpetuates ascription, I offered two qualifying remarks. Let us turn to the second of these, the fact that *education's economic value is less than it used to be*. This is nothing to celebrate, however. It simply means that lots of educated people can't find the jobs for which they have been trained. A 1975 study by Harvey and Charner compared the occupational success of those who graduated from four Ontario universities in 1960, 1964, and 1968. By 1968, the same degree was worth much less; 1968 graduates needed more advanced degrees for jobs that had required only one degree a few years earlier.[18] Harvey and Charner do not discuss the implications of their findings for equality of opportunity. However, if education is not paying off financially, then educational advantages are bound to play a somewhat smaller role in keeping plush jobs for the offspring of the well-to-do. However, this should also be qualified. Education still pays; a person with a degree still earns more money than a person without one. But education pays less than it did 15 years ago.

SOCIAL POLICY:
Issues and Viewpoints

THE PRODUCTIVITY OF EDUCATIONAL SYSTEMS

Sociologists have pointed out a problem that educational planners will have to solve: how to get more education per dollar—or rupee, yen, or peso, as the case may be. Given present educational methods, every nation must spend an increasing portion of its national budget just to keep its educational output at the current level—and that level is not good enough. Moreover, it is very hard to establish a rational system of priorities in spending on education, and it is even more difficult to introduce new educational methods. What policies seem promising as ways of meeting the increasing demand for useful schooling?

The most important goal for new countries is to achieve literacy for all, which, according to UNESCO estimates, requires four or more years of schooling. However, in many countries, four years of schooling may not produce functional literacy, for not all educational systems are equally effective; many students repeat grades or drop out between grades. Besides the ability to write, simple arithmetic can be most useful; because farmers can become more effective in their planning if they have the ability to add, subtract, multiply, and divide, they may need more than four years.

Many community workers in developing countries have failed to teach what should be taught in the schoolroom; they give adults lessons in hygiene, agricultural technology, and the like when they should be concentrating on basic literacy.[19] After farmers can read, it will be easy to teach them other facts by passing out booklets. Literacy has a "multiplier" effect: Once a population is widely literate, additional levels of education can be reached much more efficiently.

On the other hand, modern technology may also be of great help to educators in developing countries and advanced countries alike. Some promising experiments have used television and radio for mass education. The "open university" in Britain depends heavily on correspondence and mass media instruction, and at least one Latin American country plans to use television for basic instruction throughout its elementary schools. These new ideas can greatly increase educational productivity, though of course they will not replace all of the functions of educational institutions. Considerable experience in university classrooms suggests that television is a fairly effective, but unpopular, method of learning. However, in a few years you may be able to check out a cassette-recorded television course from the library and play it at home whenever you want to—even while cooking breakfast or taking a bath. Such flexibility may make education via television far more popular than it is today.

There have been other proposals for improving educational productivity—some of them far more daring than the idea of television instruction. Consider Ivan Illich's ideas, for example.[20] Illich is a former priest who has a dramatic style of speaking and lots of offbeat ideas. He loves to challenge our assumptions about what is good about modern institutions. (For example, he argues that modern medicine does about as much harm as good.) Here I want to mention his recommendations for improving education in the developing countries.

Close the schools, says Illich. He claims that whenever schooling is set up as an official institution in a society, people get the idea that the only way to become educated is by attending classes. They come to believe that they don't know anything important unless they learned it in a class taught by a certified instructor. They believe they are unable to learn whatever they need to know by looking around and finding out for themselves. They become helpless, passive consumers of education, uncritical, unable to take charge of getting the knowledge they need or want. Unless it is organized for them and presented in a classroom, they think they can't learn.

This is nonsense, according to Illich. Just look at the things you know: how to speak English, how to knit, how to cook and keep house, how to write cheques, how to drive a car, how to use a camera, how to swim, how to fix a flat tire or a broken zipper, how to play the guitar or tie a trout fly. You may know the names of the entire Dallas Cowboy football team or the reason why Libras should or shouldn't marry Scorpios or the names and present whereabouts of all the Watergate burglars or how Catherine the Great supposedly died when a horse was dropped on her. (If you don't know that one, I can't tell you here. But you can ask someone else, which is how you found out all those other things.)

See how much you learned outside of school? Then why go to classes at all? You really go to get the diploma. Illich suggests that we should stop giving out diplomas. Then people will start finding out things just because they want to know them. Illich would like to see a number of substitutes for regular schools. One idea is to provide places full of the kinds of things people need to use, such as car engines, photographic darkrooms, and sewing machines. This would be a place to go to learn how to use equipment.

Another of Illich's ideas is the "skill exchange." This would allow all of us to list our skills and the conditions under which we would be willing to teach others what we know, along with our addresses. Then we could "earn" lessons by giving lessons, thereby contributing credits to our account. When I read Illich's book I decided to use this idea in a course I was teaching on the sociology of education. Once a week we would spend an hour exchanging lessons. On the blackboard I recorded what each student offered to teach and what each student wanted to learn. We set up contracts to last, we expected, several weeks or even months. Everyone thought it would be an interesting experiment.

It wasn't. First of all, the subjects people offered to teach were limited to trivial matters that required no preparation. No one offered to teach

calculus or French or music theory or logic, though all of the students were in at least their third year at the university and they all had advanced knowledge in some area and a fair knowledge of many complex subjects. They offered to teach crocheting, ballroom dancing, kite making, and other activities with no intellectual content. I'm not

Ottawa Citizen/Brennan

Athletic training develops fitness, team spirit, and aggression.

Arthur Grace/Stock, Boston

against crocheting. My point is that the students all underrated how much they had to contribute to other people. And so, to please the teacher (me), they signed up to learn something silly that seemed like a waste of time, given the pressure of their other courses. And then, of course, they didn't show up. In a couple of weeks it was clear that everyone was fooling around or cutting class on skill exchange day. We gave up.

Then we talked about it. I concluded that we had proved Illich wrong. If college students couldn't organize and maintain a skill exchange, if they doubted their own ability to teach so much that they offered only frivolous courses, how could anybody expect people in developing countries to do better—people who had maybe 4 or 5 years of schooling, compared to the 16 or so years that the members of my class had? But the students concluded that the experiment had proved Illich right. That is, they had been part of the educational system all their lives. They had come to believe that only a certified teacher in a class situation could teach anything worth learning. If they had been paid for their work, they would have taken the job seriously—for then they would have been real teachers and would have been expected to offer good instruction. But this was impossible for them as students. Their sixteen years in school had reduced their confidence in their ability to educate themselves or each other. Besides, they pointed out, they were enrolled in other courses that had requirements for which they would be graded. It was wise for them to put all their attention into studying for those courses. They wondered why they should learn calculus or French from each other. They would rather save the energy for the courses that counted.

I had believed that my class was the perfect group on which to experiment with Illich's scheme. They believed they were the worst possible group for such an experiment. They believed that Illich's own logic would show that they could not take responsibility for their own education—that their schooling had made them dependent and passive in learning. The only fair test of Illich's plan would have to be made on a group of people who had little or no education, people who were not also enrolled in any courses elsewhere.

If my students are right, this is a discouraging conclusion. I never thought there was any hope of educating people by closing the schools. But I did

think that the skill exchange idea might *add* to regular schooling. This seemed very promising. But it appears that regular schooling reduces the possibility of carrying out the skill exchange idea. In that case I don't think it could offer anything very useful to the people in developing countries who must find ways of increasing the productivity of their educational systems. Closing the schools is hardly the way to start improving education, despite Illich's persuasive arguments.

EDUCATION AND THE LABOR MARKET

Educators have found it nearly impossible to coordinate specialized education with the changing labor market. Such coordination is especially difficult in the case of graduate-level education, which is very expensive but often goes to waste when no suitable jobs are available for those who complete their training. There are two problems—one technical and the other organizational and political. The technical problem is the difficulty of predicting manpower requirements in various fields several years in advance. It is not possible to be very exact in predicting what kinds of jobs will be available in the future. Economists and demographers are working hard to solve this problem. Also, the predictions that are made do not always influence educational planning. It is usually the *current*, not the predicted, labor market that determines enrollment in various advanced training programs, but this method is not very efficient. For example, one less developed region found itself short of doctors. This led to a great popular demand for increased admissions to medical schools, which had already expanded according to plan. Many university buildings were converted into medical schools at great cost. The first graduates filled the shortage, and later graduates couldn't find jobs. Soon the expensive new medical schools were half empty and the entering students were competing for admission to agronomy courses, the latest field to show a labor shortage.

In effect, then, educational expansion should be planned in response to manpower predictions, not popular demand. However, in a free society popular demand is backed by political pressure that is hard for a government to ignore. The public must understand this problem before it can be solved.

VARIETY OR HOMOGENEITY?

When we plan to create equality in schooling, we need to ensure that all schools have about the same degree of excellence. But how can we do this if we don't agree on what excellence is? My idea of a good school may be very different from yours. One of us might like free schools and another might like schools that emphasize art or science or religion.

Lacking agreement, we generally solve the issue by simply making schools as much alike as possible. However, pupils probably benefit from different kinds of educational experiences. There are two approaches to providing equality. One is the "roast-beef-and-mashed-potatoes" approach. You serve everyone the same dish, choosing a menu that most people can tolerate but no one finds exciting. The other approach is the "smorgasbord" system: Give everyone the right to go back to the serving table for whatever strikes his or her fancy—even if it's five helpings of pickled herring. Since we don't know that children are any the worse for filling up in school on the equivalent of pickled herring, why not let them? This is the plan Jencks favors in his proposal for educational vouchers—different kinds of schools for people to choose among.

EDUCATION AND SOCIAL CHANGE

We have already discussed the debate between Spencer and Ward over whether education is a conservative force, teaching values and getting students to accept the status quo, or whether it is (or may be) a force for social change. Now we will take another look at this issue and try to decide which position is more nearly correct.

Sometimes education is conservative; sometimes it produces social change. As mentioned earlier, different levels of education have different kinds of effects. In the developing countries, primary school education is enabling whole populations to do things that they could never have done before. Literacy enables people to read labels on cans, find their way around a strange city by the street signs, look through the want ads for jobs or used bicycles, and read the birth control leaflets that are handed out at the village well. These events

Nicholas Sapiena/Stock, Boston

In the Thirld World, education automatically equals social change.

are social change. There can be no doubt that the lives of literate people differ greatly from the lives of illiterate people. Thus in the developing countries primary school education has the most important impact.

Yet primary school education is almost always conservative. Governments organize school systems, and the schools almost always teach views approved by the government. Schoolteachers are not revolutionary leaders. Many studies make this point. For example, polls asking opinions on racial issues show that a high school education has no impact on tolerance but a college education does.[21]

In fact there is a rather dramatic difference between the political and social values of people with a high school education and those with a college education. It seems fair to conclude that basic literacy brings a society into the modern world but that only higher education really stimulates people to question the values they are exposed to in daily life. The high school teacher is

429

not as free to criticize as the university professor. More important, high school students usually live at home and are not as free to support ideas that their parents dislike as college students are. Finally, the nature of the intellectual work done at the university level requires students to do more critical thinking than they might do at a lower level, where simple memorization often is all that is required.

Perhaps it is for these reasons that university student movements have so often been a major force demanding social change in many societies. Such movements are far less active today than in the 1960s, but college-educated people are still the most progressive group in society, whether they are quiet or outspoken in calling for social reform.

It is likely that more and more people in North America will receive a higher education—perhaps even the majority. When this happens society will have a "built-in" drive for social change.

KEY TERMS

education a set of processes designed to transmit knowledge and skills and to develop mental abilities.

SUMMARY

1. The main functions of education are (1) the transmission of civilization, (2) babysitting, (3) building national spirit, (4) establishing social relationships, (5) job training, (6) teaching values, and (7) certification.

2. The Canadian provinces administer both Catholic and Protestant schools, and are empowered to offer instruction in English or French. This has resulted in various conflicts, particularly concerning francophones outside Quebec.

3. It's hard to predict job opportunities for educated people. It seems likely that jobs will be scarce during the next ten years in most fields.

4. Less developed countries face great problems in meeting the demand for the education of rapidly expanding populations.

5. Education is partly a conservative force in that teachers must teach what the government wants them to teach. However, higher education is an important force for social change.

6. Collins has argued that the relationship between education and high status is not based on any real need to fill high-status positions with highly educated people. Rather, he believes that upper-status groups use education as a standard for judging life styles. They prefer to fill good jobs with "their own kind"—people whose tastes and values are similar to their own. Education is thus used as a way of discriminating against members of other status groups.

7. Education in Canada tends to reinforce inequalities in the social system. Solutions to this problem are difficult to find, but much research is being carried out in this field.

FOR FURTHER READING

BOWLES, SAMUEL and HERBERT GINTIS. *Schooling in Capitalist America*. New York: Basic Books, 1976. Bowles and Gintis are Marxists who view American education as set up to produce obedient workers who wil not argue with their bosses. They would include Canadian education in the same category.

BRETON, RAYMOND et al. *Social and Academic Factors in the Career Decisions of Canadian Youth*. Ottawa: Information Canada, 1972. Basically this book is directed toward explaining educational aspirations: who decides to try for a university career, who does not, and why. This is an important matter because the differential in ambition among different social groups is a large factor in maintaining social stratification.

CARLTON, RICHARD A., LOUISE A. COLLEY, and NEIL J. MACKINNON, eds. *Education, Change and Society*. Toronto: Gage, 1977. This is a good reader on education in Canada.

HARVEY, EDWARD B. *Educational Systems and the Labour Market*. Don Mills, Ont.: Longman, 1974. This is primarily about the career prospects of university graduates with different subject majors. Unfortunately, the job market changes from year to year, so it may not be the most reliable way of estimating your own prospects right now, even though it is based on Canadian statistics.

HUTCHEON, PAT DUFFY. *A Sociology of Canadian Education*. Toronto: Van Nostrand Reinhold, 1975. This text is not as Canadian as its title claims. It tends to be patchy but it provides excellent bibliographies and case studies that *are* Canadian.

HYMAN, HERBERT H., CHARLES R. WRIGHT, and JOHN SHELDON REED. *The Enduring Effects of Education*. Chicago: University of Chicago Press, 1975. The authors collected evidence from a variety of sources that prove in a dramatic way that schooling makes a tremendous difference in people's lives. Every additional year of education has effects that can be measured and that last a lifetime.

MARTIN, W. B. W. and A. J. MACDONELL. *Canadian Education: A Sociological Analysis*. Scarborough, Ont.: Prentice-Hall, 1978. This is about as thorough and accurate a review of the literature on education as any that sociologists have produced. It is not exciting, though, probably because it does not dwell on controversies.

PIKE, ROBERT M. *Who Doesn't Get to University— and Why*. Ottawa: Association of Universities and Colleges of Canada, 1970. Pike used 1961 census data to check John Porter's findings in *The Vertical Mosaic*. He found that school enrolments had improved since Porter's research (which had used 1951 data) but that many of the same relationships still held.

PRENTICE, ALISON and SUSAN HOUSTON, eds. *Family, School and Society in Nineteenth-Century Canada*. Toronto: Oxford University Press, 1975. This will be of value for readers who are interested in the historical development of schooling in Canada. It is a collection of articles, primarily done by the editors themselves.

WOLFGANG, AARON, ed. *Education of Immigrant Students*. Toronto: Ontario Institute for Studies in Education, 1975. This is probably more useful for educational planners and other professionals in the field than as a qualitative overview of the problems and prospects of immigration education in Canada.

15

POLITICS AND SOCIETY

Have you ever picketed City Hall? Signed a letter your group was sending to a Member of Parliament? Worn an NDP button? Sat in the middle of the road to prevent tractors from working on a nuclear power plant, a freeway, or an airport? Have you planted a Progressive Conservative election poster in your front lawn? Have you written a letter to your alderman about the potholes in your street? Have you stood in line to shake hands with Maureen McTeer? Have you voted?

You are a political person. Some of us are more political than others, but all of us are political. Politics is unavoidable in social life, because human beings do not always agree on their goals. When people have different goals, coordination becomes necessary. And the process of coordination is politics, which is a polite way of saying domination. When my aims differ from yours, one of us will win and the other will lose, unless some compromise is reached or one of us changes our mind. Politics concerns the ways in which a group of people with different goals establishes which ones will be pursued and which not.

Sometimes politics proceeds in an orderly and polite fashion, sometimes not. In a democratic society, the political process is generally non-violent but verbally aggressive, as seen by debates in the House of Commons. In tyrannical regimes, politics frequently results in violence, as when the state uses police force to silence opposition. Sometimes the outcome of politics is outright warfare. Hence the saying that war is simply a "continuation of politics by other means."

Political sociologists attempt to show how politics works under all these conditions. Those who study democracies may ask questions such as: How do interest groups and coalitions form and break down? What influences the extent to which citizens participate in politics? When are voters likely to support left-wing or right-wing parties? How do political parties persuade people to vote for them?

Political sociologists who study other societies are likely to ask questions such as: What determines whether a society will become democratic or totalitarian? Can we predict the results of rebellions, or when and where they will occur? What political developments can be expected in the Third World in coming years, and why?

Power, politics, and the state

WHAT IS POLITICS?

By politics I mean any action involving the collective pursuit of collective goals.[1] This definition can apply to the collective goals of any group—a family, a corporation, even a couple on a date. Thus we sometimes hear the phrase "politics of the family"[2] used to describe conflicts over issues such as where a family will spend its Christmas vacation. A seduction can be regarded as "sexual politics."[3] A factional fight within the board of directors of Stickum Glue, Incorporated can be regarded as "company politics." However, for the purposes of this chapter, I will limit our discussion of politics to conflicts over the collective goals of some unit of *government*—such as a nation, a city, or a province. Some of the concepts that political sociologists use to analyze politics can also be used in describing the internal political processes of corporations and other private, nongovernmental collectivities. This is especially true of certain terms introduced by Max Weber: legitimacy, power, and authority. Let's discuss these terms more thoroughly.

LEGITIMACY AND POWER

What is the state? That is, what characteristics define a government? What does it need in order to qualify as the real thing—*the* state, or *the* government of a particular area? Max Weber claimed that the state is the organization that has a monopoly on the legitimate

Owen Franken/Stock, Boston

Throughout history most rulers have depended on traditional authority. But the "stage-props" vary. Some rulers have crowns—some have umbrellas.

use of violence in a given territory. Only the state has the right to use force when necessary to back up its policies. If you catch a thief crawling through your window, you may hang onto him until the police arrive, but you are not supposed to punish him yourself. Only the state has the right to sentence people to prison or put them to death.

The key term in this definition is legitimacy. The state has the *right* to use force. Individuals do not. But this legitimacy comes from the people. It depends on the people's believing that the state is necessary and that its actions are lawful and valuable to society. As long as its legitimacy is unquestioned, the state will rarely need to use force. But if the legitimacy of its use of power is widely questioned, the state is in a dangerous situation. A regime is in serious trouble if the people believe that its military is illegitimate, its police brutal, and its courts unfair. It may have power—the ability to get its orders obeyed despite widespread opposition—but it does not have authority.

Authority is power plus legitimacy. It is the ability to use power because the members of the society recognize such power as legitimate. Democratic governments that lose their legitimacy do not keep their power very long. (During the Watergate scandal, for example, top government officials were stripped of their power as soon as they lost their legitimacy.) On the other hand, dictatorial governments that lose their legitimacy may remain in power even though the people do not consider them legitimate. The government of South Africa, for example, has long been viewed as illegitimate by the great majority of the population (i.e., the blacks), but that majority is powerless to rid itself of that government.

You can think of power as a naked sword and of authority as a sword in its scabbard. Power does not have to display itself as long as it is recognized as legitimate. Various "props" are displayed instead. Politicians appeal to the patriotic feelings of their audiences. Flags and military bands help make a political campaign exciting. Judges wear special robes or wigs and police officers wear special uniforms for the same reason—they are the props of legitimacy. As long as the wearer is believed to have authority, he or she actually has it. Legitimacy, like beauty, is mostly in the eye of the beholder.

CP Photo/Ball

Democratic elections are our way of choosing leaders, whose authority is rational-legal.

THREE BASES FOR LEGITIMACY

On what basis does a group back up its political leaders? Weber suggested that three different bases have been used in different times and places. Sometimes a leader is given legitimate power because custom dictates that he or she is "in line" for such status. This is traditional authority. Sometimes a leader gains power on the basis of his or her personality. This is charismatic authority. Sometimes a leader is given power because he or she has been elected or appointed under the rules of a constitution or some other legal system. This is rational-legal authority. All three forms of authority have been of great importance at one time or another.

Throughout history most rulers have de-

pended on traditional authority. Pharoahs, tribal chieftains, and landowning nobles have all been obeyed because "it has always been that way." Even today some of the most stable governments in the world are headed by constitutional monarchs. Thus British prime ministers may rise and fall, but Queen Elizabeth's status is secure, and in her lies the security of her state.

Charismatic leadership occurs when a remarkable leader steps forward to call people to a new way of life. Mao, Gandhi, and Napoleon were supposed to have had special qualities that ordinary people didn't have. Such leaders are followed because they are believed to have direct access to the truth. Their authority is based on the faith of their followers. Thus as long as Napoleon's soldiers worshiped him, disobedience would have been unthinkable and his army was almost unbeatable. However, a few errors on his part caused his downfall.

Rational-legal authority is far more common today than in the past. Our legislators, dogcatchers, health inspectors, and admirals have power that is based on a rational set of rules. In a bureaucracy each person is assigned to a particular office, each of which has a specific range of powers supported by rational-legal authority.

THE ROLE OF INTEREST GROUPS

In a constitutional democracy of the kind familiar to North Americans, politics is based on the interplay of opposing interest groups, unified groups that want to influence the state in their favor. These groups may form on the basis of economic (class) interests (e.g., labor unions, the Canadian Medical Association), though other concerns may be even more important to some people than their economic interests (e.g., gun control, gay rights). Cultural interests often lead to the formation of groups that struggle in the political arena. For example, the Quebec nationalists are more concerned with preserving their culture than with raising their standard of living. Religion is another cultural basis for interest group formation; in earlier days terrible religious wars swept through Europe because such groups demanded that everyone else accept their beliefs. Even today religious differences play an important role in political contests—for example, in fights over abortion law or state support of religious schools. Not all cultural differences are religious in nature, however. Fights over marijuana laws, the fluoridation of water, or pornography are all based on different values, each led by an active cultural-interest group.

Whenever a major interest group fails to persuade a regime to meet its demands, its members may withdraw their loyalty from that regime. If the group is powerful enough, this could plunge the regime into a **crisis of legitimacy**. When a large enough number of people question the legitimacy of the regime, a rebellion may occur. For example, in October 1970, when a terrorist group kidnapped a British official and killed a Canadian official, the government of Canada feared that a rebellion was about to occur in Quebec. It responded with drastic measures that were legally sanctioned by the War Measures Act. In reality, however, there was no crisis of legitimacy. The Quebec terrorists were a tiny minority and were not supported by the general population. But by overreacting and using unnecessary force the government increased the underlying mood of dissatisfaction. Six years later the voters chose a party that favored the separation of Quebec from Canada through nonviolent political means.[4]

Pluralism

When I was a graduate student in Berkeley during the 1960s—the time of the civil-rights movement, the ghetto riots, the War on Poverty, the assassinations, the Vietnam War, and the sit-ins and campus riots—everyone argued about politics. The political sociologists were way ahead of everyone else. They usually won the arguments. However, I finally discovered that once you understand three basic viewpoints—pluralism, elite theory, and Marxism—you can predict how most political arguments will go. And if you can anticipate the next point and say it first, very casually, you can win.

Let's consider these three viewpoints and how they have changed over the years. We begin with **pluralism**, which is the view that the best way to preserve freedom in a society is to have within it a lot of powerful groups that represent various interests. Until the 1960s most political sociologists were pluralists because pluralism seemed to offer the best answers to some of the questions that sociologists have been asking for generations.

In order to explain pluralism I should point out that it was developed at the same time that sociology was born, and for the same reason. They were both ways of answering the same question: What makes it possible for a society to hold together? People began to think about this question because their society barely *was* holding together at the time. Two hundred years ago, Western society was going through dramatic changes resulting from two "revolutions"—one political and the other economic. The economic one was the Industrial Revolution. The political one has been called the "democratic revolution."[5] It was the shift away from rule by absolute monarchs to rule by a parliament or some other elected group. The democratic revolution included the Boston Tea Party, the storming of the Bastille, and other related events. And there were other issues to be settled at the same time because the economy was shifting from an agricultural one to an industrial one.

European society in particular was giving up old, traditional relationships and developing an entirely new social structure. Tradition was the "glue" that had held society together. When it began to break apart, it was not clear whether any basis for holding society together remained.

Before the Industrial Revolution, the lives of ordinary people had been organized by their involvement in their families, their communities, and their church. Industrialization freed the serfs and turned many of them into factory workers. This "freedom" had certain negative aspects: People now worked among impersonal strangers for cash wages. They were supposed to become rational and efficient. Values that had been sacred became unimportant. Belonging to a group became less possible: People became isolated "atoms" instead of members of close-knit communities. Social life became unsettled and insecure. The "government" was no longer the local aristocrat but a mass democracy organized as a centralized bureaucratic state. People's rights became unclear; how those rights were to be enforced became even less clear.

Social theorists therefore began to search for a new set of rules, a new system by which people's lives could be more effectively organized. Harmonious and effective organization of life is what is meant by *social integration*. The main factors in social integration were described by Tocqueville and, later, Durkheim. Both emphasized the importance of secondary centers of power mediating between the individual and the state.

DE TOCQUEVILLE

A Frenchman of aristocratic background, Alexis de Tocqueville, visited the United States in 1831 because he believed that its democratic government was an image of Europe's future, in which he was deeply interested. His classic book, *Democracy in America*,[6] combines ethnographic reporting with good political theorizing. Though he thought democracy was unavoidable, Tocqueville was not very enthusiastic about it. He expected its emphasis on equality to lead to cultural mediocrity by trimming everyone down to the same size.

According to Tocqueville, democracy was a great threat to liberty because the tyranny of the majority would be more oppressive than the tyranny of aristocrats had been. The minority would have to conform, and their freedom was in danger.[7]

Tocqueville wanted to find ways of protecting democratic society from tyranny, and he found that certain aspects of American life seemed to guard minority freedom. One of these guardians was the free press. Another was the prominent role of lawyers in the state. A third guardian, most significant for pluralist theory, was the abundance of voluntary associations in the United States. Tocqueville claimed that these associations provided the individual with group support against a government that would otherwise be too powerful.

Before the French Revolution, everyone had a definite place in some established group or other. The serfs were tied to the nobility and clergy, the clergy to the church, the noblemen to other nobility and the monarchs, the artisans to their guilds, and so on. Although this system restricted the freedom of individuals, it also offered them protection. Everyone belonged to some group that dictated certain responsibilities but that would also defend individual rights if they were in danger. The elites of these groups, especially those of the clergy and the nobility, competed amongst themselves to assert their authority and limit the others' power. As a result, an ordinary person had some defense against any particular elite by appealing to a competing elite. Various powers "countervailed" against each other.

According to Tocqueville, the French Revolution endangered individual rights by creating a highly centralized state and abolishing all of the elite groups that had mediated between the top levels of power and the masses of ordinary people. The nobility was tossed out. The church lost its legal authority. Ordinary people could not communicate their grievances to those in power because there were no longer any intermediaries. Individuals were uprooted and isolated, forbidden to form groups strong enough to challenge the centralized government. Clearly, such individuals stood no chance in any conflict against the state. Only through group action can individuals gain enough power to successfully challenge the government. In modern totalitarian societies like the Soviet Union, people are not allowed to form unions, lobbies, or even artistic and literary clubs that promote ideas that the government dislikes.

Tocqueville found that Americans tended to join all sorts of free voluntary associations, such as social clubs, professional associations, and ladies' auxiliaries. These associations all had the potential to become powerful interest groups. Tocqueville saw this plurality of free, independent organizations as the best safeguard against tyranny in a democratic society.

DURKHEIM

Emile Durkheim shared many of Tocqueville's ideas and also contributed to pluralist theory. He saw that the rise of the nation-state had freed people from traditional ties and created a greater role for the individual. In earlier times people were seen not as individuals but

In a plural society, groups form to support or oppose particular points of view. Anita Bryant was the leader of one "bloc" that opposed homosexuality.

UPI

as members of families or of feudal estates; most people were under the authority of these traditional organizations. In modern society, the state regulates matters that used to be regulated by the church, the guild, the commune, or the family. Thus legal centralization meant legal individualism. By freeing the individual from the control of traditional authorities, the state itself gained control over him or her. At the same time, social controls were weakened. Social order became harder to maintain. Deviance and political crises became more common.

Durkheim's recommendation was the same as Tocqueville's: To prevent tyranny and strengthen social order in a heterogeneous population, new voluntary associations should replace defunct traditional ones.[8] By organizing into groups, like-minded individuals can attain some degree of power in a checks-and-balances arrangement. Durkheim was especially hopeful that professional associations, trade unions, and other occupational organizations might serve this purpose. Freedom in a modern society depends upon the maintenance of a plurality of competing, countervailing centers of power.

DEMOCRACY AND PATTERNS OF SOCIAL DIVISION

Since Tocqueville and Durkheim, many sociologists have continued to try to identify the conditions under which democracy is possible. Contemporary political sociologists have added to pluralist theory by suggesting that if a democracy is to be stable, the divisions within it should not *coincide* but *crisscross*.[9] Let me illustrate this point with an example.

Consider the two great nations that dominate world affairs today—Oz and Atlantis. As every schoolchild knows, Oz and Atlantis have very similar language, religion, and drinking patterns. By an odd coincidence, exactly half the population of each nation consists of teetotalers while all the others are

enthusiastic tipplers. Half the population of each nation speaks Sanskrit; all the others speak Fortran. Half the population of each nation is Zen Buddhist; all the others are Druid. The two societies are very similar indeed, except that in Oz the boundaries separating religious, linguistic, and drinking or nondrinking groups coincide, while in Atlantis they crisscross. (See Figure 15.1.) As you can see, in Oz any boundary that would separate the two religious communities would also divide the population in terms of language and drinking habits. This is not the case in Atlantis, where Druids are equally distributed among the Fortran and Sanskrit speakers and where drinking is equally common in both religious groups and in both linguistic groups.

Now you must answer this question: Which society is more likely to be torn apart by political conflicts and which is more likely to be characterized by moderate, middle-of-the-road politics and the use of compromise? Which is more likely to succeed as a stable democracy, Oz or Atlantis? Why?

If you guessed that Atlantis is more likely to succeed as a democracy, you get an A. Pluralist theory suggests that a large number of power centers can stop any would-be tyrant or even any group that becomes too powerful. This theory is correct if the lines separating the various interest groups cut across each other. However, in Oz it is clear that there are three bases for conflict—language, religion, and drinking habits. The three bases combine to create two opposite camps that disagree in every possible way. The chance of conflict is great, and there is little basis for agreement between the two groups. *Within* each group, agreement is very likely, but *between* the two groups it is unlikely. No matter which group manages to gain control of the government, it is not likely to be very concerned about the rights and wishes of the other. In Atlantis, on the other hand, most people find that their enemies in one respect are their allies in another. Therefore, they

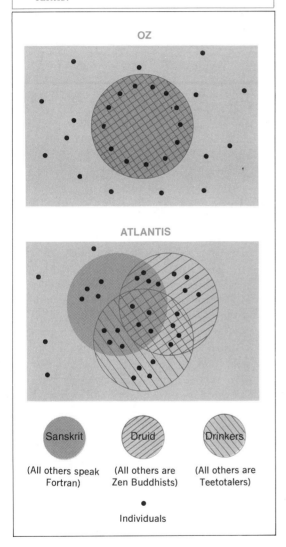

FIGURE 15.1

Population characteristics, Oz and Atlantis.

OZ

ATLANTIS

Sanskrit

(All others speak Fortran)

Druid

(All others are Zen Buddhists)

Drinkers

(All others are Teetotalers)

• Individuals

society should be composed of a variety of different interest groups, each represented freely by various competing organizations. In order to determine whether a given society is actually organized in this way, however, sociologists must gather factual, empirical evidence. Canadian sociologists are in some disagreement about whether Canada is actually a plural society. Sometimes research is carried out to determine whether various Canadian economic, political, and cultural leaders act together to constitute a unified power center, or compete with one another so that centralized power is dispersed. We have discussed this question elsewhere and will return to it again.

Other sociologists argue that danger arises when power is *too* dispersed. Those who hold this viewpoint claim that a pluralistic society is vulnerable to periods of stalemate, when little progress can be made due to the number of *veto groups*. A veto group is an interest group that can "veto" government policies; each veto group can block any action that conflicts with its values and interests, but no one group is likely to be successful with a program of its own.[10] When veto groups are too numerous and diverse in their points of view, society becomes bogged down and unable to move consistently in any direction. Pluralism, in such cases, is overdone; there is "too much of a good thing."

This view of pluralism has become increasingly unpopular in recent decades. Sociologists today are far more concerned about the possibility that Canada and other western democracies are not pluralistic societies at all. Modern sociologists are attempting to determine whether there is actually a coalition of groups in Canada and abroad that wields great power behind the scenes, shaping government policies through its involvement in international business transactions. This concern about the dominance of a unified "elite" can be better understood after we have discussed the second great tradition of political thought, namely elite theory.

have a reason for tolerating other groups. The social divisions between the plural interest groups crisscross, and this makes for political compromise.

Pluralism is a normative theory; that is, it tries to show how a society *should* be organized if democracy is to succeed. Ideally, a

Elite theory

The pluralist believes that democracy is possible; the elite theorist believes that it is a fraud. Elite theory is the belief that some group or other (an *elite*) always gets the upper hand and rules the masses. A German sociologist, Robert Michels, reached this unhappy conclusion by studying the relationship between democracy and bureaucracy in politics.

MICHELS

In 1911 Michels published his book, *Political Parties*.[11] In it he described what he called "the iron law of oligarchy," which holds that any group that organizes itself will be taken over by an oligarchy. (*Oligarchy* is rule by a

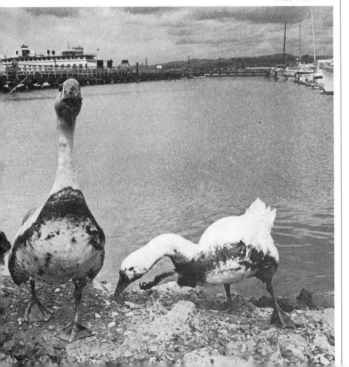

Interest groups form in a plural society to take care of such problems as protecting the environment.

Wide World

few people who can choose their own successors.) The group that Michels studied was a political party.

Michels found that the German Social Democratic party was, despite its name, an oligarchy. Although it began with the most democratic of ideals, the party was subject to the same conditions that are faced by any other organized group: The act of organizing itself endangers a group's democratic ideals. It is impossible to make decisions efficiently when too many people are involved. The only solution is to organize—to elect officers and give them the authority to make some decisions on their own.

This is a fatal move, for, once an ordinary member has tasted the joys of high office, he or she will not want to give up that position. And the chances are that this will not be necessary because, as an officer, the member will gain knowledge and skills that are beyond the reach of ordinary members who might prefer a new leader. What is good for the officer, however, is not necessarily good for the group. The officer's main concern may be to stabilize the organization and his or her own position in it, while the other members may have a more idealistic program in mind. If they find that the officer is becoming too conservative and self-serving, they may turn him or her out of office, but the job will still go to a successor that he or she has chosen. The real decisions in any organization are made behind the scenes by the elite, including those who have been voted out of office. This, said Michels, is an "iron" law: It never fails.

Elite theorists believe that democracy always loses in the end, because the people who really govern any large social group are always a very select few. A true elite theorist does not call for revolution, because it would only pass power from one elite to another and would hardly be worth the effort. Elite theorists today do not claim that rule by elites is *preferable* to participatory democracy. They simply argue that it cannot be avoided.

A PLURALIST REPLY

Elite theorists do not take seriously the pluralist argument that political freedom can be guaranteed by balancing power among a plurality of interest groups. Yet the pluralists have by no means lost the argument; in fact they may even be ahead by several points. One point for the pluralist side was scored by the book *Union Democracy*, which showed that the elite theorists' argument did not always apply to American trade unions.[12]

Michels argued that unions must have bureaucratic leadership in order to be effective, but that whoever gets into a leadership role is likely to manage to stay there. The history of trade unions shows that Michels was basically correct. Few unions are led by workers. However, the authors of *Union Democracy* were able to show that Michels was not *always* correct and that when this was the case it was for pluralist reasons. They chose a union that did not have oligarchical leadership—the International Typographical Union. This organization not only had two different "parties" among its members but sometimes even replaced its officials at election time. How was it possible for the printers to maintain democratic control of their elected leaders? Within their union, there are a number of different organizations run by members on a voluntary basis—clubs, leisure time associations, and the like—and these groups participate in political affairs within the union. Thus Tocqueville's argument defeated Michels' argument. To put it simply, a plurality of voluntary organizations within a larger organization creates bases of power that enable members to defend their own interests against the elite in power.

However, even the trade unions and other associations that are oligarchies can still help maintain liberty in a democratic society. It is better to have a plurality of strong associations such as unions, churches, lodges, and

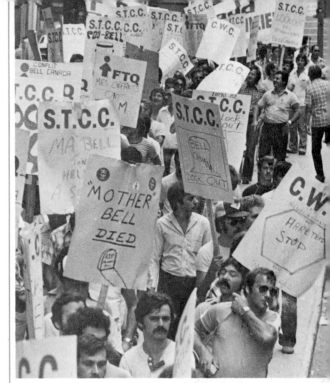

CP Photo/Stoody

In democratic societies, unions and other organizations are independent. In totalitarian societies, they are either forbidden to organize or are controlled by the state. Pluralist theory claims that independent associations help to preserve freedom.

cooperatives than for people to have to deal with the state individually. There is some protection in strong collectivities, even when those collectivities are not run according to democratic principles. But this is true only if they are independent of the state. As Tocqueville and Durkheim suggested, the associations that existed before the democratic revolution were autocratic, not democratic. Noble families and guilds, for example, did not give their members freedom, yet they were strong enough to protect their members.

It is when organizations are *not independent*—when their leaders are appointed by, and accountable to, the state—that totalitarianism is likely. In the Soviet Union, there are many organizations, but they are controlled by the state and cannot protect their members against its influence. Instead of being part of a pluralist society, such associations are tools for governmental control.

THE PLURALIST-ELITE THEORY SYNTHESIS

New ideas arise out of conflicts between old ideas. If two theories are in conflict, the theory that results from that conflict will be different from either of the original theories. Let's look at how the pluralist and elite theories have combined to create a new theory.

Vilfredo Pareto is a good example of an elite theorist. He argued that the ruling elite of any society is always very small, but that within the society a counterelite usually develops and becomes strong enough to overthrow the ruling elite. Pareto called the ruling elite "foxes" because they are clever and corrupt. The counterelite is made up of confident, idealistic young people, whom Pareto called "lions." He believed that the fate of all foxes is to be overthrown in revolutions by lions, and that the fate of all lions is to become foxes. Thus he suggests that anyone who tries to reorganize society is wasting his or her time—the revolutionary leaders themselves will become corrupt after they have come to power.[13]

How can a pluralist react to such a challenge? One solution is to become a "pluralist-elitist" like Karl Mannheim or Suzanne Keller. Pluralist-elitists accept the elite argument but change its meaning. They agree that every society has leaders and that every group within a society has leaders. They ask, What's wrong with that? It is also true that when one set of leaders is overthrown another set takes over. But this only proves that leaders are necessary.

Mannheim suggested that there are two types of power: arbitrary power and functional power. Personal power is arbitrary and, therefore, undesirable. Elites, however, usually have functional, institutional power. Indeed, Mannheim claimed that one of the main trends in modern times is toward the replacement of personal power with functional power.[14]

Keller even defines elites in a pleasant way. An elite, she says, is a minority of individuals who serve a collectivity in a socially useful way.[15] To Keller, there is nothing incompatible between saying that a society is pluralist and saying that it is elitist. A society may consist of a plurality of subgroups, each of which is led by its own elite. She suggests that as society becomes more complex and as roles within the society become more specialized, elites become more numerous and each area of social life is represented by a more or less separate elite. Thus we now have elites not only in government but in the movie industry, the arts, the clergy, and so forth.

Sometimes we admire our elites and sometimes we envy them. Social integration is easier when we admire our elites. When we envy them, social conflict is more likely—especially if the elites are snobbish and unresponsive to ordinary people.[16] Tocqueville said that the French Revolution happened mostly because the aristocracy lost its sense of duty to the ordinary peasant.

Keller believes that elites have a duty to provide not only political leadership but moral leadership as well. She reminds us of a point made by Durkheim, who claimed that integration in traditional societies was very different from integration in modern societies. The way people got along in the old days was by being alike—having similar backgrounds, similar religious practices, similar ideas about how family members should treat one another, similar ideas about morality in every area of life. There were no "oddballs" in preindustrial society, no individuality or new ideas. Everybody had to agree on everything. This was the only way people could integrate their activities harmoniously. Durkheim called this pattern mechanical solidarity. (Yes, I agree that it's an odd term.)

As the division of labor increases, the jobs and life styles of members of a single society come to differ greatly. For example, how well do you understand the problems of these farm workers?

On the other hand, the solidarity (i.e., friendly relatedness) that you and I have for each other as fellow members of modern society is **organic solidarity**. By this Durkheim meant that although we are very different, we are interdependent. As the division of labor increases, the jobs and life styles of members of a single society come to differ greatly. I may be unable to understand much about your experience, and so you and I will have different opinions and different habits. Modern society is heterogeneous. What makes integration possible is that we depend on each other. We *have* to find some way of making deals, agreements, or contracts. Our interdependence forces us to bargain with each other and offer at least a moderate amount of respect to each other.

With organic solidarity, we are much less committed to sharing values. For example, we don't say prayers in school anymore. Prayer is supposed to be private. We have a right to have individual, unusual ideas of morality. What makes it possible for us to get along when we disagree about important matters?

According to Keller, Durkheim did not realize the importance of new elites. As the leaders of the various subgroups within modern society, elites must coordinate the relationships among those groups. Keller therefore calls them "strategic elites." The special duty of strategic elites is to make sure that the people in each section of society are committed to the basic goals of the whole society. This is an important contribution. Moreover, Keller claims that it is less possible today than in the past for one strategic elite to dominate the others. This is because each represents a particular area (e.g., the arts, religion, industry) and that as a result they compete among themselves. As long as the elites are plural rather than unified, they are no threat to liberty or democracy. They cannot become too overbearing because their spheres of activity are limited and they have plenty of opposition.

Notice how we have twisted and turned and changed our minds since we began talking about elite theory. At first elites were villains; now they are heroes. Mannheim and

445

Keller have combined pluralism and elite theory, showing that they are not necessarily opposed; both theories make valid statements about modern democratic societies. But in doing so they have changed the meaning of the term *elites*. To Pareto, the word meant clever foxes and domineering lions. To Mannheim and Keller, it refers to moral pace setters and influential experts.

Still, I think the synthesis holds up. Both elite theory and pluralism began as rather conservative points of view. Elite theory suggests that it is useless to try to change the government. Pluralism suggests that the working classes in industrial societies don't need to rebel to get their interests protected. All they need is a variety of independent voluntary associations—lobbies, clubs, fraternal orders, trade unions, and so on. These enable each interest group to show its strength when necessary. And if each group is led by an "elite," why should this trouble anyone? All a democracy needs is to be sure that these groups are independent and that they are "plural"—that there are several elites representing many interests, not just one. This will do more to preserve the rights of ordinary people than anything else. If, however, the elites are not plural, a revolution might be necessary. It is this possibility that has lately drawn many pluralist-elitist theorists toward a demand for radical social change.

Without doubt, the writers who have most influenced Canadian sociology during the past 15 years are the late John Porter and Wallace Clement. Both of them were influenced in turn by C. Wright Mills, an American researcher who was largely responsible for the "critical" sociology that emerged during the Vietnam War. C. Wright Mills was a leftist social critic, one of the first to observe that a "power elite" dominated American society and that big business and big government were linked.[17] Mills's arguments were adopted by the New Left in the United States and,

through Porter and Clement, in Canada as well. The "New Left", as such, ended with the 1960s, but critical sociology is still very much alive. The main targets of critical sociologists in Canada are the powerful unified elites that dictate much of Canada's economic policy.

But Porter and Clement have worked to prove the existence of such elites. However, these two sociologists have taken very different approaches. Porter's *The Vertical Mosaic*[18] was published in 1965 and was really a pluralist argument, quite in keeping with the pluralist-elite theory synthesis proposed by Keller and others. Porter was not disturbed by the existence of elites, as long as they remained plural and confined operations to their own spheres of influence. He studied not only the financial elites but mass media elites, the leaders of various religious, ethnic, and geographical interest groups, and so on. Although he did not question their right to exist in their separate areas, Porter was troubled by the extent to which elites were closed and self-perpetuating. He showed that it was virtually impossible for people to work their way into positions of power unless they were born into the "right" families, ethnic communities, and religions, were sent to the "right" schools and so on. Porter based his work on the assumption that Canada was a plural society; he just wanted people to have equal opportunities to enter plural elites.

Clement directed his research against this assumption of pluralism;[19] his approach was closer to Marxism than Porter's. Clement demonstrated not only that the top economic elites have a far greater control of resources than most Canadians realize, but also that they are interconnected and tied into elites in other countries, especially the United States.[20] According to Clement, Canadian elites are unlikely to identify with the ordinary interests of Canadians because of their shared interests with American elites. This is not equally true in all businesses, of course. There are **indigenous elites** (people whose business ties are to Canadian-owned firms) and **comprador elites** (people whose financial ties are to a foreign-controlled base of power in Canada). Compradors are the senior executives of branch plants who follow policies issued from their foreign headquarters.

Clement was disturbed by the existence of powerful elites, especially the comprador elites. Unlike Porter, Clement not only wanted more equality of *opportunity*, but also desired more equality of *condition*. That is, like many other theorists who believe deeply in democracy, Clement argued that too much concentration of power is inherently dangerous, regardless of how many people have the opportunity to join elites. And the concentration of wealth in vast multinational corporations creates a small, unified elite whose power extends beyond national borders to the far corners of the earth.[21]

Clement's critical sociology has definitely been influenced by the work of Karl Marx. In order to understand this influence, it is necessary to discuss Marxism in its early formulations and then examine its relevance to contemporary political controversies in Canada.

Marxism

Be careful about calling people "Marxists." You never can tell, until you check, whether a person claims that title or rejects it. As a matter of fact, in his later years Marx himself declared, "I am not a Marxist." Presumably we should take his word for it and extend the same courtesy to anyone else who claims or rejects the title, because the qualifications for it are so ambiguous. Therefore, although we are about to discuss certain views that are related to Marxism, we will be using the term here in its loosest possible sense. **Marxism** here simply means any doctrine that is supposedly derived from the teachings of Karl Marx.

Marx had one thing in common with elite theorists: He believed that every society, past and present, is dominated by a ruling group. However, he differed from elite theorists by claiming that a proletarian revolution would not simply bring a new elite to power. Instead it would put an end once and for all to social classes and to the domination of one class by another. Only then would liberty be possible.

On the issue of liberty, Marx differed from pluralists by claiming that a variety of countervailing groups cannot protect individuals from a ruling elite. Freedom will come only after a revolution, and not in a capitalist democracy. Marx was not impressed with the claim that freedom and equality are guaranteed by law to citizens of democratic nations. He claimed that only *economic* equality really counts. What use is freedom of speech to someone who has nothing to eat? What use is the right to vote to someone who has no shoes? To Marx and his followers, political rights are empty, for they have never once in any country succeeded in abolishing private property and returning to the workers the profits of their own labor.

Those who have been influenced by Marx often accuse Western democratic governments of deceiving the public to protect the interests of a ruling elite. Certainly, American leftists were able to prove that Americans were duped during the Vietnam War and the corrupt Watergate period; the ruling elite during that time eventually showed that it was *irresponsible* and unresponsive to the needs of the public.[22] The American ruling elite was called the "military-industrial complex" because it was composed of high officials with ties to both the armed forces and big business. According to social critics, big business and the military "scratched each others' backs." In order to make high profits from the production of military equipment, business leaders supported politicians who would vote for big military expenditures. C. Wright Mills was the first to make this charge and discuss it in detail. His work stimulated other scholars to document the power of economic elites in other countries.

Canadian critical sociologists are also worried about powerful elites, but their concerns are different than those of Americans. Canadians are not particularly worried about the dominance of their military expenditures, which are not on a scale comparable to those of the United States. Canadians do worry, however, about the possible loss of Canada's political autonomy as its economy becomes absorbed into a single world-wide system of corporate capitalism.

MARXIST EXPLANATIONS OF HISTORICAL DEVELOPMENTS

Over the years, Marxists have found certain developments hard to explain. Things often have simply not turned out the way Marx predicted. Among these developments are the following:

1 The communist revolutions have not happened where and when Marx predicted that they would.
2 Modern corporations are owned by large numbers of stockholders who do not have any say in the management of their "capitalist" enterprises.
3 The workers in capitalist societies have become richer rather than poorer.

The communist revolutions in nonindustrial countries

There certainly have been communist revolutions. But they were not the ones Marx expected. He thought there would be uprisings of industrial workers in the most advanced capitalist societies. But the only real revolutions have taken place in countries like Vietnam, China, and Cuba—nations that are only beginning to industrialize. And instead of being led by urban workers they have been led by intellectuals with the support of peasants. In fact such revolutions are frequently

more "nationalistic" than "communistic." The real target is not local capitalists because there are very few of these. In developing countries, industrialization depends on capital controlled from abroad, and it is organized by the colonial power that dominates the society. The target, therefore, is the foreign colonial power, and the revolutionaries are people who want to modernize their society and make it independent.

Of course, the colonial power from which the developing nation wants to free itself is usually a capitalist society. And not surprisingly, the capitalist society will try to stop the revolution. For example, in the 1960s the Chileans voted a leftist regime into power using legal democratic procedures. But the new regime, led by Salvador Allende, opposed a foreign corporation, ITT, which had strong allies in the U.S. government. Allende is no more. His regime has been replaced by a right-wing government that tortures political prisoners. The people who overthrew Allende were supported by the U.S. government at the urging of ITT, whose economic interests were threatened by Allende's policies. The U.S. Government has interfered in similar ways with the rights of people around the world to choose their own form of government. This interference is strongly resented by the people of the Third World, and it is not surprising that they turn to communism.

Contrary to Marx's predictions, communism is not very attractive to workers in the advanced capitalist societies, who are comparatively well off. Most European societies have strong socialist labor parties but weak communist parties.[23] Nor have the successful communist revolutions always achieved what they set out to achieve. Elite theory has been right more often than not. The Russian revolution produced some changes, but it also brought a new elite to power. The revolutionary leaders took over the means of production and went on to exploit the workers themselves. They used totalitarian methods to rule the masses and forced rapid industrialization at a terrible price. They industrialized *after* the revolution, not before it. Their revolution was not the one Marx had expected; instead of human liberation, it produced labor camps and the repression of artists and political dissidents. Many writers call the Soviet system not communism but "state capitalism." It has the worst features of capitalism, but is run by the government instead of by business executives.

Corporate ownership

Marx did not foresee how capitalism itself

would change. Capitalism is no longer a system of family-owned firms but one of huge corporations owned by millions of people. You may own some shares yourself, but that doesn't make you a "capitalist." You don't exploit workers. You have nothing to say about the management of the company in which you own shares. You may not even know who is on the board of directors.

Then who are the "capitalists" whom Marx hated so bitterly? They might be the top executives in the corporation who actually manage the firm. But if so Marx's theory is

Marx did not expect communist revolutions in non-industrial societies. But that is where they seem to happen.

UPI

still wrong, because executives are not owners but salaried employees. Marx considered ownership the only standard for determining who is a capitalist. He thought salaried managers would not be driven to exploit workers. After all, the profits don't go directly to *them*.[24]

If neither stockholders nor top executives are the capitalist ruling class, then who is? Remember Michels and his "iron law of oligarchy"? This gives us a clue. There are too many stockholders to run the corporation themselves, so they let a tiny group of stockholders—who own maybe 5 percent of the stock—decide policy for the whole corporation. This smaller group controls the executives. Moreover, by "pyramiding" stockholdings they gain control over many other firms. A pyramid is built in the following way. The "inner circle" of stockholders owns and controls, say, 30 percent of the stock of a company. Then their company buys 20 percent of the stock of another company, thereby controlling it. That company may control yet another company, and so on. As a result, the top elite controls three or four firms (or, in the case of a Canadian pyramid like the Argus Corporation, dozens of firms) while actually owning only a small block of shares.[25] Peter Newman's popular book, *The Canadian Establishment*, shows how the leaders of these financial empires manage their subsidiary companies and merge to scoop up new ones.[26] Think about the size of large corporations. Some of them are as powerful as some nations. The decision-making elite of General Motors, Standard Oil, IBM, and ITT control as many resources as most heads of state.

Marx, then, was mostly right. Capitalism dominates the world's economy. However, he did not anticipate one thing: The ordinary stockholder today does not control the corporation. The only capitalists that Marx knew about were the "robber barons" who set up businesses and ran them by themselves. But today's capitalists, by and large, own only a small part of the company and do not control it at all. The workers, who are generally adequately paid, are not discontent enough to wage the revolution that Marx predicted. As we shall see, contemporary Marxists have been forced to develop new analyses to account for this deviation from Marx's predictions.

The increasingly affluent working class

Marx's third mistake was to predict that as industrialization progressed the situation of the working class would get worse and worse. Competition between firms would force capitalists to work their employees harder and harder. They would speed up production, lengthen the work day, force the workers' wives and children to work too, and so on. The business cycle of booms and depressions would fluctuate wildly until capitalism brought about its own downfall.

Since the Great Depression of the 1930s none of these predictions have proved correct. There have been only minor recessions, and capitalism is stronger than ever. Since World War II, capitalist economies have enjoyed the greatest wealth the world has ever known, and workers have shared in that wealth. Of course, workers don't receive the same *proportion* of wealth as the elite; indeed, as Leo Johnson has shown, the lowest-paid Canadians do not get ahead at all.[27] But with unemployment insurance and other benefits, workers in industrial nations are by no means as poor as Marx predicted they would be.

Present-day Marxists have argued that there are two reasons for the stability and success of capitalist economies since World War II. The first is the high level of military expenditure in the past forty years. The second is the exploitation of underdeveloped nations. Marx did not expect capitalism to become an international system. Contemporary critics of capitalism say that the industrial countries have acquired their great wealth by exploiting and preventing economic growth in the Third World.[28] We shall return to this argument when we consider dependency theory.

NEO-MARXISM AND CRITICAL SOCIOLOGY

For reasons that include the three historical developments just described, the Marxist view of capitalism has changed over the years and can now be labeled neo-Marxism. Neo-Marxists and other critical sociologists have agreed on certain reasons for the failure of some of Marx's predictions. Let us consider these current economic and political interpretations.

Critical sociologists have recognized that most communist revolutions today are struggles against foreign economic domination. They no longer view revolution as a struggle by workers against local capitalists; instead, they see revolution as a struggle by underdeveloped nations against capitalist nations. Rather than a direct conflict between social classes, they see revolution as a conflict between nations that *serve* different social classes.

Critical sociologists also recognize that modern capitalism is *corporate* capitalism. Power is not held by every stockholder, but by a small elite, or oligarchy, of stockholders. This ruling elite controls economic interests all over the globe and has far greater power than any capitalist of Marx's day. Finally, many critical sociologists have recognized that Marx's prediction of increasing instability and poverty in capitalist societies was incorrect. They have concluded that the success of capitalist societies depends on economic imperialism and the military domination of other nations.

Mills argued that the pluralist model applies only to the middle sector of the stratification system. In Congress, for example, one pressure group can clearly counteract another

to establish a situation of "countervailing power." Within the power elite, however, because of overlapping friendships and shared interests, there is no structure of countervailing power.

The existence of an international elite that controls the corporate economy has now been firmly established. C. Wright Mills only suspected its presence, but many subsequent researchers have documented the extent of its power and charted the linkage networks that bind it together. In the United States, William Domhoff is best known for his research.[29] In Canada, we have already mentioned the work of Porter, Clement, and Peter Newman. Neo-Marxists and other critical sociologists have made their point. Current debates between liberals and Marxist-oriented scholars do not question the presence of the elite, but examine the effect of the elite on economic development. To discuss this issue, we must introduce a relatively new approach—dependency theory.

DEPENDENCY THEORY

Just as it is risky to label people Marxists without their permission, it can also be misleading to classify certain theoretical perspectives as Marxist. Although dependency theory seems to offer a neo-Marxist perspective, it also has much in common with points of view that are definitely not Marxist. Marx would not have recognized it as his offspring. Dependency theory can best be seen as a useful approach to sociology that is especially relevant to the Canadian situation, and that is supported by many Marxists.

Canadian critical sociologists like dependency theory for two reasons: (1) Dependency theory offers an approach to Canada's development in relation to its dependence upon the United States and its original colonizing "Mother Countries," France and Britain; (2) dependency theory is consistent with the Canadian sociological emphasis on historical and economic factors, and sheds light on two popular models of Canadian development, the staples approach and the metropole-hinterland model. In fact, we should discuss both of these models before describing dependency theory.

As stated in Chapter 1, the staples approach was developed by Harold A. Innis.[30] According to the staples model, Canada's development resulted from its status as a colony that provided staple raw materials for manufacture abroad. Innis examined such staple industries as the maritime cod fisheries and the fur trade. He accounted for social and cultural change as a direct result of the economic and geographical circumstances of such industries. Innis did not focus on class conflict, the exploitation of human labor, or any other Marxian concepts of conflict and group struggle; only subsequent scholars have pinned his ideas to a Marxist framework. But Innis was extremely aware of the force exerted on events in remote parts of North America by the European market for staple products. His relating of history to the production of raw materials was the main contribution he made to sociology.

Other Canadian sociologists have focussed on the relationship between "hinterland" and "metropole" regions of Canada.[31] This approach, like the staples approach, recognizes that every major center of human settlement must depend on an outlying region for its raw materials and staple necessities. You can think of a city as a metropole and the countryside around it as its hinterland, providing food, fuel, and other staples. Or you can think of a highly developed region or province as the metropole and less developed provinces as the hinterland. Thus Southern Ontario is a metropole, carrying out much of the country's industrial manufacturing. Northern Ontario, along with more distant areas like the Yukon, forms its hinterland, supplying ore, potash, and other materials from manufacturing.

If we extend this idea further, we can see

whole nations as metropoles and other, less developed nations, as their hinterlands. The metropole nations are generally colonizing "Mother Countries", and the hinterlands are colonies. Hinterlands are always relatively underdeveloped and, although they supply the metropoles with vital goods, they have little control over their own economies. They are economically dependent on the metropoles that they supply, and are virtually powerless to change this situation. Because of Canada's role as a major exporter of staples and a relatively minor exporter of finished products, Canada can be considered a hinterland nation. Canada's metropole was formerly composed of France and Britain; it is now the United States.

Dependency theory adds one crucial idea to this analysis. According to dependency theory, it is no accident that Canada is industrializing rather slowly. Metropole nations have a definite interest in keeping hinterlands weak. *Under the capitalist system, economic development can take place in one country only by keeping another country underdeveloped.* This point of view, proposed by Andre Gunder Frank,[32] opposes the usual view that, although underdeveloped areas are a bit behind, they can "catch up" and become rich industrial nations. According to dependency theory, powerful societies have industrialized by exploiting underdeveloped societies and weakening their economies. Moreover, whenever a weak country becomes a hinterland, it becomes economically dependent and is sapped of its natural resources; therefore it cannot manufacture its own finished products and cannot adequately support itself. Dependency theorists claim that underdeveloped countries, such as those in Latin America, are consistently drained of their economic and political self-sufficiency by the corporate capitalism that is centered in the United States. Such poor countries are not "developing countries" but "underdeveloping countries." They can only escape from this predicament by freeing themselves from

Ontario Ministry of Industry and Tourism

According to dependency theory, hinterland regions such as northern Ontario (above) are used to feed the wealth of metropoles such as Toronto (below).

Ontario Ministry of Industry and Tourism

capitalism. Political and economic autonomy will go together.

Dependency theory can be criticized on a number of grounds, particularly when it is applied to Canada. For one thing, Canada cannot convincingly be described as a backward country. Although the Canadian economy depends heavily on the exporting of raw materials, it is not otherwise industrially underdeveloped to any great degree. However, critics who place a high value on national autonomy certainly have grounds for their fear that Canada may soon be completely absorbed by an international corporate world. In fact, the entire world may soon be integrated in one interdependent economy that no nation can control with laws of its own.

The major weakness of dependency theory is the way it groups countries into pairs: strong and weak; metropole and hinterland; exploiter and exploited. As Harriet Friedmann and Jack Wayne have pointed out, this is too simplistic.[33] Throughout the world, *all* nations are buying and selling in the marketplace, dominating and being dominated by, in varying degrees, every other nation. Dependency theory correctly points out that countries are often kept weak by other countries that gain from their weakness. But the market for staples like coffee, oil, and grain is worldwide. No single country can be blamed for the economic disaster befalling any other single country. The whole system of nations is involved in the economic process.

Because of its simplistic nature, dependency theory has turned into a political catch-phrase, more useful in heated arguments for calling nations "good guys" or "bad guys" than for explaining the complexities of the real world. Consequently, other theorists, such as Immanuel Wallerstein and Daniel Chirot, have turned to a more sophisticated "world system" approach. This approach classifies societies as "core" or "peripheral," with various gradations in between; core societies are world industrial leaders, such as the United States and Japan, while peripheral societies are the underdeveloped nations. There is some debate as to where Canada should be placed in this scheme. The world system model, though perhaps not as popular with Marxists as dependency theory, is still being discussed with much interest among Canadian scholars.[34]

SOCIAL RESEARCH: *Sociologists at Work*

QUEBEC AND THE FUTURE OF CANADA

Some of the most important political sociology in Canada during the past 10 or 15 years has concerned the changing relationship between Quebec and the rest of the country. Although the Parti Québécois's sovereignty referendum was rejected by the voters, we have not heard the last of the demand for more autonomy in that province. Therefore I want to review some of the research on the origins of the Quebec separatist movement and on the factors that shape the public's opinion of separatism. Two particularly significant papers originally appeared in a special edition on Quebec of the *Canadian Review of Sociology and Anthropology*, the official publication of Canadian sociologists. The first of these papers is a spirited defense of Québécois nationalism by Hubert Guindon,[35] and the second is a report of a survey by three York University researchers, Michael Ornstein, H. Michael Stevenson, and A. Paul M. Williams.[36]

Guindon does not attempt to provide "value-

OUI OUI OUI

QUÉBÉCOIS POUR LE NON

C'est NON

CP Photo/Journal de Québec

A house divided. Quebec referendum, 1980.

free" research. His commentary weaves factual evidence and political judgment so closely together that it is impossible to consider one without the other. Guindon makes it clear from the outset that he disagrees with the recommendations of the Royal Commission on Bilingualism and Biculturalism, a group that was set up to study French-English relations and to propose appropriate federal responses to the Quiet Revolution then taking place in Quebec.

Although many of the Commission's 1965 proposals were carried out, they failed to defuse the discontent that was burning in Quebec. According to Guindon, this failure was due to a serious mistake on the part of the Commission: It relied far too heavily upon bilingualism as the primary means to soothe French-English relations throughout all of Canada. The Commission members were themselves fluently bilingual, and this may have given them an unrealistic perspective on bilingualism as a policy.

With bilingualism, the Commission attempted to formulate a policy that could be applied throughout Canada and which would preserve the rights of all linguistic minorities. They did not accept the idea that special approaches should be adopted for different regions. As Guindon points out, however, the situation in Quebec is radically different from that in the rest of Canada. Quebec requires unique political solutions to its unique economic problems. Unlike the rest of Canada, Quebec possesses a dual economy that is split along

455

linguistic lines. That is, francophones and anglophones occupy opposite positions as far as jobs and other economic opportunities go. This dual economy imposes severe economic limitations upon Quebec's francophone population; it was these limitations that drove frustrated middle-class francophones to initiate the Quiet Revolution. In order to understand Quebec's dual economy, it is necessary to understand the unwritten agreement that, according to Guindon, formed a tacit basis for confederation.

Guindon claims that an unwritten agreement was made after the Conquest between the English merchant class and the French clergy in Quebec. Basically the English promised to leave the religion and language of the Québécois intact. The French Catholic clergy could therefore secure its control over most of the institutions of French Canadian society, including schools, the welfare system, and the family. In return, the English merchants were guaranteed that English would be the unchallenged language of business.

This arrangement worked for a long time because Quebec's economy depended mostly on extractive labor; jobs such as farming, trapping, mining, and logging were carried out in isolated regions of the province. Rural French Canadian communities dealt very little with outsiders, and easily maintained their language and traditions. Because of education and language limitations, rural French Canadians were discouraged from taking jobs in industry, commerce, or the professions; this suited the French Catholic clergy, who abhorred the secularism that had accompanied industrialization in Europe and elsewhere. The francophones maintained their numbers through large families while the English population was bolstered by the influx of new immigrants, who adopted English and filled urban commercial and industrial jobs.

Like the rest of Canada, Quebec's economy has developed considerably during the past generation or so. Fewer jobs are located in isolated rural settings. In the large cities, government and corporate bureaucracies have expanded. Businesses have grown, and large business communications networks have developed. However, French Canadians have not occupied a proportional number of jobs in this modern economy. In fact, except for native peoples, every ethnic community in Canada

has had a higher degree of financial success than Quebec's francophone population.

At first it was possible to blame this economic disadvantage on French Canada's substandard educational system. However, education has improved dramatically in Quebec and has developed a more secular and technical orientation. Large numbers of francophones have entered the middle-class, in their educational level if not in their jobs. Some have found government jobs, but few have become successful in big business. According to Guindon, this middle-class Québécois group provided the support base for the Quiet Revolution and provides the chief support for separatism. Middle-class Québécois believe that their careers are blocked by the use of English as the language of business in their province.

The Parti Québécois is attempting to make French the sole official language of Quebec. The separatists believe this to be necessary if francophones are to find jobs in the middle and top levels of the economy. They challenge the tacit agreement that gave Quebec's financial leadership to the English, and insist that only French be used in Quebec's public institutions, including its businesses and schools. They further insist that the children of immigrants to Quebec attend French-language schools, so that they will be prepared to use that language in their careers.

The actions of the Parti Québécois have been in conflict with federal policy. The federal government has tried, above all, to be universalistic and to operate on the same set of principles throughout Canada. Thus the government has tried to encourage all Canadians to become bilingual, and has hired and promoted bilingual civil servants whenever possible. This encouragement has, however, rarely succeeded.

The federal government has also tried to provide language services for minority groups that constitute, say, 10 percent of the population of a given area. According to Guindon, this offers no real protection to the minority language, and thoroughly annoys other people in the area. For example, a TV channel was set aside for French-language broadcasting in Toronto, whose few francophones are totally bilingual. Another channel was established for English broadcasting in a solidly francophone area. Such actions only cause the local people to resent the other language group. In the case of education, Guindon argues that French schools cannot possibly perpetuate francophone communities in anglophone areas. Graduates from these schools move away to Quebec. Few young francophones remain.

Guindon also claims that the Royal Commission failed to consider research findings in the sociology of language, that field of study that explains the circumstances under which people switch languages. Language sociologists have found that bilingualism can complicate a person's social interactions. For example, two francophones who are bilingual have to decide when to speak to each other in English. If they are around anglophones, they may use English out of politeness or out of deference. If they are speaking to their grandmother, who speaks only French, they will speak French. Other situations, however, may not be so clearcut. At what point do they stop speaking French when they are alone together and begin speaking English?

Language sociologists have also researched patterns of linguistic assimilation. For example, when the old grandmother dies, our two francophones may no longer have any reason to speak French at all. To preserve a minority language, it is necessary to preserve a "frontier," a certain number of people who speak only that language. According to Guindon, the policy of bilingualism works against the preservation of a French frontier in Canada. He claims that the actions of the Parti Québécois, on the other hand, are an effective way to protect French in Quebec and to permit the francophone middle class to participate in Quebec's modernizing economy.

The actions of the Parti Québécois are overwhelmingly popular among Quebec francophones, but are resented by many other Canadians, particularly by anglophone Quebeckers. In order to predict the results of this conflict, various research surveys have been conducted. One of the most thorough surveys was carried out by Ornstein, Stevenson, and Williams, a York University research team.

Ornstein, Stevenson, and Williams conducted a large national sample survey in 1977 to determine the positions of various social groups on the issue of Quebec's relationship to the rest of Canada. Like other surveys of that time, their findings showed little popular support in Quebec for an independence referendum. This response changed according to the wording of the referendum, but never did more than a third of the respondents support independence. Quebec voters did not consider separation to be any more likely than they had in the past. Moreover, people inside Quebec were as unlikely to predict separation as people in the rest of Canada.

The researchers wanted to determine which groups supported various positions. They asked respondents for their views on the independence of Quebec, on the rights of francophones outside of Quebec to educate their children in French, and on such political issues as social welfare payments, labor rights, and prejudice against immigrants. Their results supported Guindon's claim that separatism was primarily a middle-class movement. Supporters of independence tended to be younger, to be well-educated, to work in white-collar occupations, and to reside in Montreal or other urban centers. The researchers could not, however, predict future separatist trends; their findings represented only the first phase of a long-term investigation.

The researchers also wanted to find out the relationship between support for separatism and positions on other issues. If the separatists gain strength and eventually change Quebec's status, what sort of policies can we expect of them? What other political tendencies do separatists have? Are they narrow-minded, reactionary, and tightfisted? Would they neglect the rights of new immigrants? Would they encourage a lot of foreign investment in Canada? Would they oppose labor unions? Would they resist social welfare programs? Would they demand more efforts to combat crime? Would they oppose the legitimacy of protest activities? The answer to all these questions is no. On each issue, the views of separatists tended to lean toward socialism and equal rights. The survey revealed that separatist beliefs reflect a general concern for social equality. The separatists' efforts to re-negotiate the relationship between French and English Canada apparently represent a wider social commitment to greater equality of income and aid for disadvantaged groups. The separatists appear to be strongly committed to justice, freedom, and the rights of minority groups. Only time will reveal the extent of their commitment to the future of Canada.

SOCIAL POLICY:
Issues and Viewpoints

Two of the most controversial political problems in Canada are Quebec's future position in Canada and the loss of Canadian economic autonomy. These problems do not result from simple class conflict in the Marxian sense, for they concern questions of group identity as well as economic interests. A solution proposed for both problems is the strengthening of group identity through nationalism, and the limiting of the political influence of non-members over the group's life.

The two problems are actually based on the same principle: Quebec's separatists and Canadian nationalists both want to democratize decision-making by regaining control over their own affairs. Both groups are nationalistic and both believe in the value of political sovereignty; they both desire control and freedom from outside political interference. Quebec's francophones complain that they are not "masters of their own house" because other Canadians take part in settling disputes that they consider internal to Quebec. Similarly, Canadian nationalists worry about control of national decisions by non-Canadians who have little interest in the welfare of the Canadian people. Both groups want to solve these problems by restricting political power to those who reside within the regional boundaries.

There are, however, other ways to democratize decision-making and give people a voice in the issues that affect them. Furthermore, the maintenance of rigid national political boundaries has negative as well as positive consequences. Local voters gain more control over regional matters, but lose their ability to influence decisions made beyond their regional borders. They have no way to protect their vital interests beyond the boundaries of Quebec or of Canada, as the case may be. Will they gain more than they lose? Perhaps.

Nationalism or separatism is successful only when the society's own members can control the crucial factors affecting its fate. If Canada can successfully regain control of its economy by limiting foreign ownership of businesses, nationalism may indeed give Canadians more control over their own affairs. However, if the trend toward worldwide economic and ecological interdependence continues, a nationalistic approach may be a step backward. The nation-state may simply be unable to protect the vital interests of Canadians. At a time when economic and environmental interactions are increasing between different regions and provinces, it seems that more mutual political involvement is called for, not less.

In my view, the economic integration of the world is a historical force no nation can reverse. Canadians will probably never regain enough autonomy to make their most important decisions independently. Though the referendum failed, the Québécois will probably gain some new political arrangement inside Canada but they will never be free to influence all the events that affect them. Even had the referendum passed, it would not have offered that possibility.

No nation, no society, can regain economic sovereignty anymore. The multinational corporations are continuing to concentrate ownership of the world's wealth and are internationally organized; Canada can neither purchase nor control Exxon, IBM, Pepsi Cola, or Ford Motor Company. Moreover, the worldwide distribution of raw materials and the management of the world's natural environment can no longer be coordinated through the old arrangement of independent nations. If a nation dumps mercury into the ocean, the people of all nations bordering on that ocean are affected. Whales and dolphins may become extinct because of the fishing practices of a few nations, but the rest of us lack any political voice in the policies of those countries. Acid rain is created in one nation, but falls in another. Petroleum, water, uranium, and all the other ingredients for modern life are found in certain countries, not in others. The world's economy is becoming interdependent because the natural environment is interdependent.

It is unrealistic then to view the nation-state as the ultimate political system. When nuclear meltdowns in one nation can threaten the survival of neighboring nations, those neighbors have a right to participate in the planning of nuclear reactors. We can no longer mind our own business and allow other people's decisions to endanger our welfare. Nor can we expect people elsewhere to remain silent when we are affecting their lives. National boundaries are only as real as we believe them to be. They are created by social agreements. We don't have to erase national boundaries, but we do need to transcend them, to recognize that our interests extend beyond them. Regional governments can handle local matters. But our problems are increasingly planet-wide and we need planet-wide agreements to solve them.

Our methods for dealing with problems that affect various nations have become antiquated. Treaties and other international agreements that are organized and endorsed by nation-states can be easily broken. The SALT negotiations, aimed at the limitation of arms, may now be too delicate to withstand the breakdown in American-Soviet relations. The Law of the Sea, outlining the use of the oceans' resources, is a continual source of international dispute. The Canadian and American governments have bargained to establish auto trade

The Third World will not tolerate economic exploitation indefinitely.

Wide World Photos

agreements, the clean-up of the Great Lakes, the rights to build pipelines, and so on. But weak nations fare poorly at the bargaining table. They must have control over some vital resource to be able to significantly influence such negotiations. The Arab nations have recently learned how to use their oil resources to strengthen their political bargaining position, but not every country has oil fields.

Dependency theory, the most significant current version of Marxism, correctly states that poor nations are exploited by rich nations. When a multinational corporation converts peasant farmland to rubber, coffee, or banana plantations for the world market, local peasants can no longer grow their own food and they become economically dependent upon the international market. The peasants cannot vote against this action; indeed, no electorate anywhere votes on it. The consumers of bananas or coffee have no voice in this action, except insofar as their purchasing power is a "vote." Such decisions result from private transactions in business and agriculture, and are made by corporate elites and landowners. The people whose lives are most affected by these decisions seldom have any political means with which to influence them. Business is not "democratic." It is not controlled by elected politicians, by workers, or by consumers, but by owners and their managers.

Business executives and large landowners tend to have little interest in the welfare of mankind. They seldom look beyond the survival of the company they manage, which depends entirely on profits. Regional and national politicians also tend to view the world through a narrow perspective. They seldom look beyond the immediate interests of the voters who elect them. We need a radical shift in the way we view the world. We also need to change our economic and political institutions so that our new awareness can create a more humane, planet-wide, social system.

We live on a fragile planet, a lovely spaceship that will provide us with everything we need if we take care of it. Right now we are not taking care of the earth. We have not learned to organize mankind cooperatively, to conserve the resources we don't need and share those we do. Rather, we have organized competitively, dividing natural resources and wasting what we control. We must learn to view ourselves as integral parts of a larger world, and find ways to contribute to the welfare of everyone. Rather than grabbing whatever we can for ourselves, we must learn to conserve, share, and even add to the bounteous resources available on this precious earth.

Once we decide to govern our planet for the benefit of all humanity, we can proceed to reorganize our political, social, and economic institutions so that they become truly democratic, truly responsive to the people whose lives are affected by them. A number of methods exist for democratizing many of the institutions that we already participate in.[37] Banks and stores can include customers and employees on their boards of directors. Welfare recipients can take part in planning welfare policies. We can force large corporations to disclose their oil or mineral reserves in other countries, their pay-offs to foreign politicians, their plans for expansion, their ties to other corporations, and so on. Shareholders can follow the example of members of some churches, and ensure that their money is not used to support the economy of such oppressive regimes as the South African government. Students have already won the right to take part in planning the policies of their universities.

All private organizations affect the world politically to some degree. Although we cannot participate in every decision that affects us, we can exert some political influence at whatever level we find ourselves. As a customer or client, speak up. As the patient in the waiting room, the busboy in the kitchen, or the owner of a rusty car, speak up.

Share your opinions aloud or in letters to the editors of newspapers. Get together with others who share your problems and work collectively to find solutions. Many lawsuits today are "class actions," initiated by a group of people with a common complaint who could not afford legal costs individually. In order to make society more democratic, each individual must work to participate in the decision-making process. Look around you. There are many contributions you can make, no matter what your situation. If the policies of an organization affect your life then, no matter what your rank, it is *your* organization and it is *your* responsibility to make it work; you must come to see that. The top executives of that organization work for you. With this attitude you can help change the world.

The reorganization of our institutions is long overdue. In the next few years, we will be confronted with huge problems. Outmoded political solutions will not help us; we must invent new ones. Neither rich capitalist nor powerful socialist nations will be able to maintain economic supremacy. The poor of the world will find ways to express their outrage, possibly through the use of the nuclear weapons they are already able to build.[38] We must join with Third World members to produce more for everyone, and, at the same time, to conserve those resources that are left us. Because we in Canada have been blessed with knowledge and wealth, we have a special opportunity and obligation to see that the world functions as it should.

SUMMARY

1. *Politics* is any action involving the collective pursuit of collective goals. The *state* has a monopoly on the legitimate use of force. Its effectiveness depends in part on its *legiti-*macy (the recognition that its use of power is lawful and socially valuable). *Authority* is a combination of *power* (the ability to have one's way despite opposition) and *legitimacy*.

2. Legitimacy may be traditional, charismatic, or rational-legal. The last form is typical of modern bureaucratic states.

3. In constitutional democracies, various interest groups form on the basis of shared economic or cultural interests and try to influence the policy of the government in favor of their interests.

4. Three major theoretical views of politics are *pluralism, elite theory,* and *Marxism.* Tocqueville and Durkheim, both pluralists, held that minority rights depend on the existence of many competing groups within a society. Those groups must be independent and must be strong enough to limit the power of the centralized state. Later pluralists have added that the differences that separate those groups should not coincide but crisscross.

5. Robert Michels, an elite theorist, described the "iron law of oligarchy": Whenever a group organizes itself and chooses leaders, those leaders will gain enough power to remain in office and/or choose their successors. True elite theorists believe that democracy is a fraud and that revolution is useless because elites always rule in the end.

6. Some theorists are both pluralists and elite theorists. They recognize not only that many groups exist within society but that they always have leaders or "elites." Such writers hold that these elites are functionally necessary and are not necessarily oppressive.

7. Marx believed that all societies have been ruled by elites but that after the prole-

tarian revolution there will no longer be social classes, and hence there will be no ruling elites.

8. Neo-Marxists have had to explain why three of Marx's major predictions were incorrect. (1) The communist revolutions have not occurred in industrial societies, as Marx predicted, but in societies that were just beginning to industrialize. Workers in capitalist societies are not fond of communism. (2) Marx did not expect a capitalist system in which a large number of stockholders own most of the assets yet do not manage them. Present-day Marxists claim that the ruling class is a tiny elite that owns only 5 or 6 percent of the assets but controls much more. (3) Marx predicted that the working class would become more miserable as capitalism progressed, but this has not proved to be the case. Neo-Marxists say that this is because whole nations have become capitalists, exploiting the underdeveloped nations and sharing the benefits with the workers.

9. Dependency theory suggests that nations can be regarded as "metropoles" that extract raw materials or as "hinterlands" that supply them. Capitalist industrialization is said to necessarily result in the underdevelopment of hinterland countries.

KEY TERMS

authority power plus legitimacy.

charismatic authority power based on the personality of the leader.

comprador elites business leaders with financial ties to a foreign-controlled base of power within a given country.

crisis of legitimacy the situation in which large

numbers of people withdraw their support from a regime.

dependency theory a theory of world organization in which "metropole" regions exploit the resources of deliberately underdeveloped "hinterland" regions.

elite theory the belief that some group always gets the upper hand and rules the masses.

indigenous elites business leaders whose financial ties are to corporations controlled within a given country.

interest group a unified group that tries to influence the state in its favor.

legitimacy the right to give orders.

Marxism any doctrine that is supposedly derived from the teachings of Karl Marx.

mechanical solidarity the pattern in which people get along by being alike in their backgrounds, religious practices, ideas about morality, and so forth.

neo-Marxism the Marxist view of capitalism, updated to correspond with developments since Marx's time.

organic solidarity the pattern in which people are interdependent even though they are very different in experience, opinions, habits, and so forth.

pluralism the view that the best way to preserve freedom in a society is to have within it a number of powerful groups that represent various interests.

politics any action involving the collective pursuit of collective goals.

power the ability to get one's orders obeyed despite opposition.

rational-legal authority power based on the rules of the constitution under which the leader has been elected or appointed.

state the organization that has a monopoly on the legitimate use of force in a given territory.

traditional authority power based on the customs under which a leader gains his or her position.

veto group an interest group that can prevent any action that conflicts with its values and interests.

FOR FURTHER READING

BARNET, RICHARD J. and RONALD E. MULLER. *Global Reach: The Power of the Multinational Corporations.* New York: Simon & Schuster, 1974. Open this book at any page and you will learn something interesting, such as the fact that CBS owns Steinway Piano Company and that RCA, NBC's parent, owns Hertz car rentals, plus millions of other facts about multinationals' power.

ENGLEMANN, F. C. and MILDRED SCHWARTZ. *Canadian Political Parties: Origins, Character, Impact.* Englewood Cliffs, N.J.: Prentice-Hall, 1975. This research contains somewhat more detail than I care to read. The researchers tend to give more facts than most readers will digest and do not provide much of an overview. However, this book can be useful if you don't try to read it from cover to cover.

FOX, PAUL W. *Politics Canada*, 3rd ed. Toronto: McGraw-Hill Ryerson, 1970. This is a most enjoyable way to learn about Canadian politics, which is probably why it has so far been printed in three editions.

FRIEDENBERG, EDGAR Z. *The Disposal of Liberty and Other Industrial Wastes.* New York: Anchor Books, 1976. Friedenberg does social commentary of an imaginative, off-beat sort. I think he is more interested in stirring up questions in readers' minds than in answering them.

GLENDAY, D., H. GUINDON, and A. TUROWITZ, eds. *Modernization and the Canadian State.* New York: New York University Press, 1978. These authors are particularly interested in the situation of Quebec in Canada.

HARTZ, LOUIS, ed. *The Founding of New Societies.* New York: Harcourt, Brace, and World, 1964. Hartz has an article of his own in this book in which he discusses a theory that has become very controversial among Canadian sociologists. (They even refer to the "Hartz Thesis" as if everyone is supposed to know about it.) Hartz believes that the character of new societies depends on the nature of their "parent" societies. Hence French colonies developed along different lines from, say, Spanish colonies, which in turn took a different course than English colonies. Different "parent" countries produced cultural ingredients in the new societies, though the new societies did not duplicate them.

LIPSET, SEYMOUR MARTIN. *Agrarian Socialism.* Berkeley: University of California Press, 1971. This is Lipset's investigation into the social conditions that caused wheat farmers in the prairie provinces to found the C.C.F., the first successful socialist government in North America. The C.C.F. later became the NDP, an important national Canadian party.

MARCHAK, PATRICIA M. *Ideological Perspectives on Canada.* Toronto: McGraw-Hill Ryerson, 1975. Marchak raises questions about how Canadian sociologists filter their perceptions of society through their sets of ideological assumptions. The topic is important, but this treatment of it has not been universally appreciated by other sociologists, even those whose views generally coincide with Marchak's.

MEISEL, JOHN. *Cleavages, Parties, and Values in Canada.* Toronto: Gage, 1974. Meisel is what political sociologists call a "political behaviorist." That is, he describes political behavior objectively, recording voting patterns and survey data, without making many speculative remarks or suggestions about how things ought to be done. In this, he, Englemann, and Schwartz are all similar.

PANITCH, LEO, ed. *The Canadian State: Political Economy and Political Power.* Toronto: University of Toronto Press, 1977. Panitch's book differs considerably from Meisel's, in that it is strongly colored by a Marxist perspective. Panitch shows that Canada's political leaders share so many basic attitudes with Canadian financial leaders that they almost automatically act in the capitalists' interests. The rest of the articles are on the same theme.

16

ECONOMIC LIFE

The historical development of economic
systems
Primitive economies
Exploitation of labor
Commercial farming in England
The Industrial Revolution
Modern economic systems
Capitalism
Socialism
The development of economic thought
Mercantilism
Adam Smith
Karl Marx
The modern market system and
government regulation
Social Research: Sociologists at Work
Social Policy: Issues and Viewpoints

You are an economic theorist. That is, you have certain beliefs and assumptions about the way the economy works. Unlike professional economic theorists, however, you may take your theories for granted without knowing that you do so. I suggest that we examine some of the beliefs that many people take for granted.

The best way to discover your own beliefs is to pay attention to your feelings. They will lead you straight to a belief every time. Most of us tend to ignore feelings that are too intense to deal with. For example, when I see a picture of starving children I quickly turn the page. This time don't turn the page. Look at the picture and examine what you feel. Suppose I tell you that every minute about 28 human beings die of hunger or its effects and that three-quarters of them are children. What do you feel now? I feel hopeless, and that is why I turn the page quickly. Underneath this hopelessness there is both resentment and guilt, which are feelings that I want to avoid.

My feelings of resentment and guilt are about scarcity and waste. We can't avoid such feelings in this chapter because **economics** is the social science that deals with the production, distribution, exchange, and consumption of scarce goods and services. The key term here is *distribution*. When distribution is unequal, some people are needy and others can afford to be wasteful. When we are needy, watching someone else waste things makes us resentful. When we are rich and spending freely, seeing someone else who is in need makes us feel guilty.

Politeness involves helping each other avoid feeling guilty or resentful. Polite rich people do not have a feast in front of hungry people. Polite poor people pretend they are not hungry (even if they are) so that rich people need not feel guilty about their wonderful meals. We won't be polite here. Let's look at our resentment and guilt. This needn't lead to despair, for our feelings are a consequence of one of our economic beliefs: that *scarcity* is unavoidable.

So here is the first unexamined assumption: We can never produce enough to go around. This is certainly a common belief, but

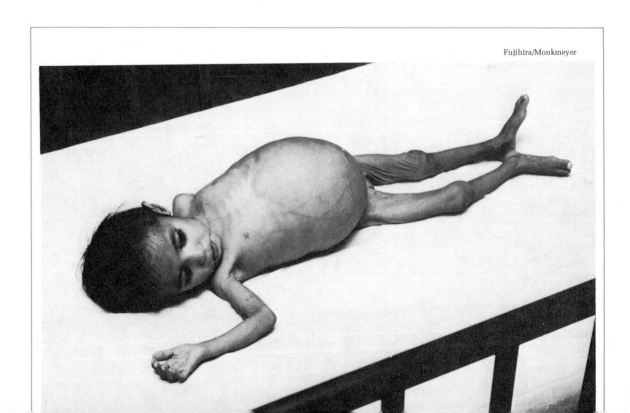

Fujihira/Monkmeyer

it is not necessarily true. I have no idea how to provide enough goods and services for all the world's needy people, but I believe it is possible. And if we start from the assumption that it is possible, we will look for ways of doing it. Nobody knows yet which solutions will work. But I suggest that we look for some. We are in this together. Those 28 deaths a minute are a part of my world, and yours.

We're not going to get all the answers here. We'll only start. The difficulty is this: You never know what information you need to solve a problem until you have the answer. We don't really know what questions to ask. We know that it is very important to find out how economies work, but we can't predict which topics will be useful as we consider the problem in the years ahead. We can prepare by developing an inquiring mind and suspending judgment until we get some good answers.

In this chapter, I will start with a quick sketch of economic history. Then we will discuss the attitudes toward the proper relationship between the free market and political regulation that have been popular at various times. After that we will devote the balance of the chapter to information about various aspects of economic life—food production, labor relations, automation, and the problems of the poor nations. Some of these findings may prove useful to you later. And I suggest that whenever you react with feeling to something you read, pay attention to those feelings and notice what beliefs they rest upon. This is how you will find out what your unexamined economic theories are. Then you can examine them.

The historical development of economic systems

PRIMITIVE ECONOMIES

Throughout most of human history, the technology of production was, by modern standards, very limited—hunting animals, fishing,

gathering nuts, grubs, or berries, and the like. Though such a life style may not appeal to many of us, it is not necessarily a life of hunger. In fact some primitive groups have more food than they need. They can afford, for example, to eat the tastiest pieces of fruit and throw away the rest. Other groups, however, are closer to the possibility of starvation. No primitive group is satisfied to limit its production to the bare minimum required for survival. Every group encourages its members to put aside something extra so that it can be offered to guests or to honored leaders or stored up for times of shortage.[1] Moreover, many primitive peoples devote a good deal of their energy to making objects that are not apparently useful. Things like feathered headdresses are not economic investments but objects that can be worn or offered to others in a system of etiquette or ritual, enabling a person to sustain his or her pride and social status. We do much the same thing when we work at our hobbies, wear fashionable clothing, or give one another bottles of cognac at Christmas time, though our leisure activities seldom have the social or religious significance that primitive peoples attribute to theirs.

Indeed, it is hard for us to understand a primitive society as an "economic" system at all, since in such societies most objects are produced and distributed as gifts, to satisfy kinship obligations, to function in rituals, and so on, and not to be owned or sold for profit. The idea of *quid pro quo* (giving something in order to get something) is at the heart of a market economy, but most primitive economies do not involve markets. In such a society people do not necessarily exchange scarce goods or labor in order to get what they need. They may give the right hind quarter of a slaughtered pig to mother's mother and half of their yams to mother's sister as a matter of tradition and without expecting to be repaid. But at the same time they may receive fish or fruit from some other relative, also as a matter of tradition, and may call upon their nephews for help in building a hut or canoe.

The French sociologist Marcel Mauss was interested in economic systems based on gift giving. He suggested that modern society is less gracious than primitive society. For us, exchanges are mostly "economic," while primitive people emphasize ceremonial exchanges. The giver is expected to give and the receiver is expected to give in return, but the timing and exact amount of the return gift are open to much variation. The gift is a symbolic binding together of a kinship unit or tribe.[2]

In 1922 Bronislaw Malinowski wrote a classic description of the *Kula* system, the ceremonial gift exchange pattern of the inhabitants of a circle of islands located hundreds of miles apart in the South Seas.[3] In the Kula system red necklaces were sent as gifts in a clockwise direction from island to island, while white bracelets were sent in a counterclockwise direction. Thus each necklace giver would eventually receive back the very necklace that he had once given. Each item would make a complete circle about once in ten years. Obviously, supply-and-demand theory cannot account for such patterns of exchange.

Economic exchanges fall into three main

In primitive economies, food is caught, trapped, or collected. Many societies still use some simple economic technologies, either as the sole or partial source of their livelihood, such as these Ecuadorian Indians do.

Jerry Frank/DPI

patterns.[4] The first pattern, reciprocity, is a two-way exchange of goods or services, as illustrated by the ritualized gift giving of families, clans, and tribes. Farmers in many societies help each other at harvest time. Goods or services are given because it is traditional to do so. The only economic calculation involved is the loose principle that the goods or services received should "balance out" in the long run.

The second pattern of exchange is redistribution. This involves bringing economic goods and services to a central source—usually governmental—and then redistributing them throughout the population. This pattern was common in ancient Asian and African civilizations. Modern examples include charity and taxation. Like reciprocity, redistribution is characterized by the absence of self-serving calculations. In this case the basic principle of calculation seems to be "justice."

The third pattern of exchange, which is more familiar in Western civilization, is market exchange. In this case goods and services are exchanged in a market context. Prices are not set by tradition but result from bargaining for economic advantage. Formal economic analysis can be applied only to this type of exchange, and we will be concerned mainly with this type in the rest of the chapter.

EXPLOITATION OF LABOR

The development of agriculture was one of the most important breakthroughs in human history, but it must have happened only under special conditions. Hunters and gatherers do not willingly take up farming because it involves more work than they are used to doing.[5] The most primitive methods of agriculture required less work than the methods to which people were driven later by the scarcity of land. In a few parts of the world this simple technology, sometimes called the "slash-and-burn" system, is still in use. The cultivator simply cuts and burns a plot of forest land, plants some seeds in the ash-fertilized soil, and waits for the harvest. The same area may be planted again the following year, but after that the soil becomes less fertile and the cultivator must burn a new area. After twenty years the first plot can be burned again more easily than a forest plot that has never been burned, so that ideally the cultivator should hold enough land so that only a small area has to be worked at any one time. This technology rarely yields a large crop per acre; on the other hand, it doesn't require much labor either. However, when land becomes scarce, cultivators have to burn a plot so often that trees cannot grow there again. As a result many large areas of the world that were covered with trees in prehistoric times are now grassland.[6]

As land grew scarce, it became necessary to increase output per acre. Agriculture began to require more labor, and, probably at about the same time, the concept of property arose. Human inequality had existed before, but now social *classes* were formed and land ownership became the basis for continuing and even increasing inequality. Those who own land can employ people who don't own land to cultivate it, paying them either with wages or with a share of the crop. Not only do the owners work less than the laborers, but they can also consume more.[7] The possibility of exploiting the labor of others occurred very early to some landowners, who used warfare to supply their manpower needs. They enslaved their captives and used the surplus created by them partly to live well and partly to maintain an army with which to capture a fresh supply of agricultural slaves. Some American Indians had slaves, and so did the Africans who were themselves caught by European and American slave dealers on the Gold Coast.[8]

The gentleman-warrior class never found it practical to keep all of the lower classes in slavery; they needed a class of freemen to keep the slaves from rebelling. The freemen were able to make a living by serving the needs of the rich. They became towns-people—artisans, traders, and the like—and sometimes built up foreign trade and a money economy. Where agriculture was very productive, quite a large class of townspeople could exist.

Still, in most parts of the world the idea of investing for the sake of profit did not develop far. Indeed, the idea of a self-regulated market economy was not accepted until about 200 years ago even in Europe.[9] Though foreign trade existed, it was held in check for a long time by the concept of a "just price," a rule that forbade taking advantage of another person's need. In other areas it was held back by rules based on status. Only in England, with its unusual historical conditions, did real capitalism develop.

COMMERCIAL FARMING IN ENGLAND

In England, as in most of medieval Europe, agriculture was carried out through a feudal organization of labor in which serfs were attached to land owned by lords. However, certain developments in England changed the nature of agriculture there and opened up the possibility of industrialization. The lords found that serf labor was inefficient and began to employ full-time workers to cultivate the best part of their land; the rest of the land was rented out.[10] The Italians and the Dutch began to manufacture woolen textiles using English wool, and many English lords enlarged their flocks of sheep. Ordinary peasants were also able to keep a few sheep, allowing them to graze on the "common," or public pasture.

By the thirteenth century the population of England had increased greatly. Suddenly the Black Death, encouraged by overcrowding, swept across Europe and reduced the population of some areas by one-third.[11] Where there had been an oversupply of labor there was now a shortage, and the peasants were put in a more favorable position. In Western (but not Eastern) Europe they gained their freedom. The population decrease also reduced the land shortage, making it possible for most families to keep sheep on open pastures and produce wool for cash.

This situation continued through the sixteenth century, when the landlords began to enclose the commons in order to prevent the peasants from pasturing their sheep there. By then farming had become a commercial activity geared to a money economy, and the enclosures made scientific agriculture even more feasible. By the eighteenth century, for example, crop rotation was widely practiced, so that land could be cultivated every year without decreasing in fertility. The enclosures were a serious loss for the peasants, however, who were freed from feudalism at the terrible price of losing their land and becoming wage laborers.[12] The development of the wool industry in England, along with the enclosure movement, led to the establishment of the cotton industry, and it was through the cotton industry that the Industrial Revolution took place.[13]

THE INDUSTRIAL REVOLUTION

As the enclosure movement was taking away the peasants' land for commercial farming and driving the peasants away, there was a new increase in population. Thus a large supply of labor became available at the time when great innovations were being made in the production of cotton textiles. This new industry absorbed many of the workers in the world's first system of factory manufacture, which was organized by merchants who were no longer content to buy from artisans. The factories were so efficient that the artisans, unable to compete with the productivity of machines, were ruined and had to become factory workers themselves. Though there was a good supply of food for this rapidly growing worker population, their situation was miserable. They worked long, hard hours for very low wages. The factory owners were constantly looking for ways to increase output per head so as to make even more profit, which could then be plowed back into the business.

Cotton textiles led the way, but industrialization spread into other industries as well. New scientific discoveries were continually being put to use in industry. Gradually the whole world was drawn into this productive system as colonial empires were built up to provide raw materials for industries in the leading industrial countries. Mining, lumbering, and other extractive industries in the colonies required the labor of native workers, who were not used to a money economy and often were not attracted by wages. In some colonies, particularly in Africa, the native populations were required to pay taxes in cash. The colonial government did not want their tax money—it just wanted to force them into the labor market which they had not been willing to enter because they had no need for cash.[14]

At home, capital developed as a source of wealth. Fortunes could be made by trading in securities—paper that entitled the owner to returns on capital investments made by others long before. Thus people might get rich without contributing either labor or money to the productive process.[15]

Modern economic systems

CAPITALISM

As we have seen, Marx failed to foresee how capitalism would develop in the twentieth century. Modern capitalism is far different from the system Marx knew. It is no longer an economy dominated by individual entrepreneurs, or "robber barons," but one dominated by giant corporations in which ownership is divided among hundreds of thousands of shareholders who formally "own" the firm but who have no control over its management.[16] Control over decisions made within

the corporation is in the hands of professional managers who may or may not own large amounts of stock themselves. In such companies the stockholders obey the management, not the other way around. Most stockholders are interested in their stocks only as investments.[17]

In general, the holders of large blocks of stock favor the payment of low dividends so that most of the profits can be plowed back into the firm. Small investors (who far outnumber the large stockholders) prefer a high rate of dividends. Although the managers are closer in outlook to the large investors, they usually compromise between the two views.[18]

In the early period of capitalism, capitalists were the masters of their own firms. Today, however, it is less obvious just who is in control. Certainly the top executives of a corporation have to pay much more attention than before to lower-level executives and experts. No one person can know enough to challenge the judgment of a committee of

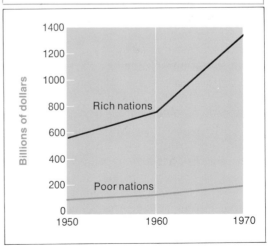

FIGURE 16.1

World Economic Development, 1950–1970, in 1964 US dollars

Source: John W. Meyer, John Boli-Bennett, and Christopher Chase-Dunn. "Convergence and Divergence in Development," *Annual Review of Sociology*, I. 1975. Palo Alto, Calif.: Annual Reviews, Table 1, p. 227.

specialists. Power to affect corporate decisions, then, is shared among a wide assortment of middle-level experts. John Kenneth Galbraith has called this new group of middle-level executives the "technostructure"; he claims that they are the real ruling class in modern capitalism.[19]

Galbraith also points out that the modern corporation is strongly connected with government, which it both influences and is influenced by. Although a decreasing number of conservatives still grumble about "government interference in the free-enterprise system," this influence is generally accepted as a fact of life by the corporation executives themselves. The government is involved in labor-management relations, workmen's compensation, commerce and business, the exploitation of natural resources, and even wage and price controls. It pays for the education and training of personnel for industry and for a lot of research that is of great value to industry. Most of all, its "defense" contracts for war matériel provide a steady demand for goods and services. Since World War II, this demand has cushioned the economic depressions that characterized early capitalism. It is small wonder that modern executives are less committed to individualism and freedom from government interference than the early capitalists, given this reciprocal relationship.

Government power over business increased in response to the public demand for coordination as the economic and social structure grew more complex. This increase in government control was a response to the difficult problem of achieving justice and equality in the face of big business. It may be true, however, that business influence over government has also increased.[20]

Corporation managers have become less hostile to government regulation partly because industry benefits so highly from a stable market. Some modern products are in the design stage 10 or 15 years before coming onto the market. Modern managers are as interested in accurate estimates of future costs and demand as they are in maximizing profits. They will do whatever they can to stabilize prices, demand for their product, and so forth, even if it means accepting government regulation or cooperating with their "competitors" in setting prices. Price-cutting competition is not characteristic of advanced capitalism.[21]

Labor relations in advanced capitalism

The history of industrialization is marked by changes in the organization of labor as well as management. One of the typical forms of labor organization before the Industrial Revolution in England was the "friendly society." These clubs of workers were interested in using political influence to affect terms of apprenticeship, wages, and the quality of goods produced, but they served a number of other functions as well. They were social and drinking clubs. They took care of workers' savings and provided insurance against death, illness, and the like. Above all, however, they showed a tendency to unite with the masters on matters affecting the welfare of industry as a whole.

With the increasing separation of workers from their capital and from the products of their labor during the Industrial Revolution, the nature of trade unionism also began to change. During the first half of the nineteenth century, more specialized unions began to develop in Britain. These unions made greater efforts to gain better wages and were definitely in conflict with the employer group. This was the type of union that fought so hard for workers' rights in Britain and throughout North America.

During the nineteenth century, labor agitation followed a roughly cyclical pattern.[22] In good times, when labor was scarce, workers could demand wage increases with more chance of success. There was also more money for union organizations and strikes. During depressions, however, strikes were less effective and workers either demanded protective legislation from the government or attempted to cooperate with industry to build a new economic structure.

In Canada, the most hostile period of relations between workers and owners took place between 1910 and the depression years of the 1930s. This was the fastest era of union growth. Eastern labor leaders tended to be moderate and were organizationally linked to unions in the United States. The prairie labor organizations, however, were much more militant, possibly because they were largely led by socialist immigrants from Europe and Britain. These western leaders unsuccessfully urged the development of "One Big Union", or OBU, to unite labor from coast to coast.

In 1919, workers in Winnipeg staged a

general strike to demand the right to bargain collectively for better working conditions and wages in whatever way they saw fit. Many Canadians interpreted the Winnipeg General Strike as the beginning of Bolshevism; therefore, they supported the government in its subsequent move to suppress the strike. The RCMP and even the army were called out against the strikers. Considerable blood was shed. Immigrant leaders were deported and the strike was decisively broken. As one result of the strike, Canadian unionism became tied to international, chiefly American organizations, thereby limiting the national autonomy of the Canadian labor movement. The Canadian labor movement was not, however, completely immobilized. Throughout the

The Winnipeg General Strike, 1919.

Manitoba Archives/Foote Collection

Depression, western radical labor leaders were able to persuade large numbers of protesters to join such events as the On to Ottawa Trek, a major cross-country march that was halted by violent police action.[23] Even today, Canada continues to have a higher rate of strikes than the United States and even Britain.

The most recent stage of labor development is "business unionism." Unions have tended to organize strikes in more rational ways, to reduce violence, and to discipline their workers. Much of the heat and emotion has disappeared from strikes, and the revolutionary overtones of strikes have clearly decreased in the mid-twentieth century. Peaceful collective bargaining has become a more common method of conflict resolution. Violence seems to be limited to the "unofficial," or "wildcat" strike, in which groups of workers not only have grievances against management but also feel that they are "getting the runaround" from big unions or big government.

Both labor and management recognize the need to maintain a demand for the company's products because both employment and profits depend on sales. This problem has promoted the need for advertising, which stimulates demand for goods often in advance of their existence. However, advertising alone could not have succeeded in keeping demand at the high levels necessary to keep modern factories humming. As mentioned earlier, the arms race has helped stabilize demand at a high level.

It is well known that the American economy is to a large extent dependent upon military expenditures. Less well known, however, is the fact that the Canadian economy is also involved with the production of armaments. For example, during the Vietnam War, the United States bought millions of dollars worth of weapons from Canada.[24] Vital minerals continue to be supplied by Canada for military stockpiling abroad, beyond the control of Canadian political leaders.

The welfare state

A number of capitalist societies have softened the edges of capitalism to give their citizens the benefits of economic stability, social justice, and peaceful international relations. Sweden is one such country. Welfare states such as Sweden cannot really be called capitalist or socialist; their policies lie somewhere between these two systems. Income is redistributed through progressive taxation; those who earn the most income pay the largest percentage of taxes, and this tax money is used to provide benefits for the entire society. Free education, including university training, is available to all citizens. Medical care costs are very low. Generous pensions are provided for the old, the handicapped, and anyone else who is unable to work. Pleasant housing is provided for the poor. Women are given paid maternity leave, and the costs of bearing a child are paid by the state.

To provide these services the Swedish government has played a strong role in the management of industrial firms and trade unions. Sometimes it has nationalized industries to control them directly. More often it has used laws and economic incentives to regulate industries and unions. Indeed, the Swedish case suggests that it is not necessarily through direct owning of business enterprises that the government can best control their exploitive practices. Rather, when the government is able to command the political support of the citizens, it is able to regulate the activities of corporations whenever necessary to protect public interests. In Sweden, corporate plans that will have a social impact must first be approved by government boards.

National control, however, does nothing to protect the wellbeing of people beyond the boundaries of the nation-state. The welfare state is still a nation-state, protecting its own citizens, but not necessarily citizens of other countries. Sweden has been remarkably generous in providing aid to less-developed nations, but there is nothing in the welfare state that guarantees a good effect upon the Third World.

The worldwide integration of capitalism

The world is becoming a single unified market for goods and services, with international trade increasing at around 5 percent every year. About 20 percent of the world's products are traded across national borders. This trade is largely organized by international corporations; socialist countries engage in far less trade than do capitalist ones. The rapid growth of international corporations is a matter that alarms many people, especially since the huge size and power of these corporations puts them beyond the political control of any government.

Some countries are more vulnerable than others to the power of corporations that they cannot control. This lack of control is especially troubling for Canada because Canada has never developed a truly independent manufacturing system. Canada originally existed to supply materials for British manufacturers. The economy was centrally organized to produce staple products such as wheat, timber, and ore, and to develop railways and waterways for export of these materials. Thus Canadian investors have made fortunes in agriculture, mining, transportation, and especially commercial trading, but very few have invested in manufacturing.

Canada's economy has slipped from British control into the control of American manufacturing firms. Today, more than ever before, Canada possesses a "branch plant economy." The power of major multinational corporations is usually centered in the United States. Foreign-owned branch plants in Canada and other countries are often managed by American personnel, while lower-level positions are filled by local people.

Entire towns often become dependent on the jobs provided by such plants. Nonethe-

less, if the branch plant proves unprofitable, the corporation executives can simply have it moved and leave their employees jobless. Canada, like most other "branch plant nations," does not have sufficient political power to protect the interests of these employees.

Wallace Clement's studies have shown that some regions of Canada are particularly subject to foreign ownership.[25] For example, Ontario is the home of about 36 percent of the Canadian population, most of whom earn their income from industrial jobs. Foreign-controlled companies pay 72 percent of Ontario's taxes from the manufacturing section. Income from manufacturing jobs produces considerable affluence in industrial centers such as Toronto. However, because the industrial centers need the hinterland areas to feed them raw materials, these hinterland areas are discouraged from developing their own industries. And discontented people in the hinterlands have little political influence with which to register their complaints, especially since Canadian workers in the foreign-owned industrial plants are generally content with things the way they are.

As Kari Levitt has shown, the money that paid for this foreign control was primarily provided from *within* Canada, from the profits on Canadian investments, and not through imported capital. As she suggests in the title of her book, *Silent Surrender*,[26] Canadians financed their own loss of economy autonomy, a circumstance that has only recently excited any worry.

It is becoming obvious that *every* nation is vulnerable to economic forces beyond its own borders. The oil-producing Arab countries exert one kind of pressure, the Japanese electronics and auto manufacturers another, and so on. Canada definitely occupies a weak position in the international capitalist system, but not uniquely so. The trend toward an increasingly integrated world economy is probably unstoppable; almost certainly the policies of any particular nation will be powerless to reverse it. There is clearly an increasing need for new international political structures to allocate the world's resources and coordinate the world's system of production—a task that is evidently beyond the capabilities of the present system of nation-states. National sovereignty is, oddly, a value idealized in Canada more than in other countries where its fulfillment is not so much in doubt. This issue will demand our further consideration later.

To appreciate Canada's vulnerability in the world market of advanced capitalism, it is necessary to understand its chief internal difficulty, namely the gross disparity between its different regions in economic development. For largely geographical reasons, some regions are far more developed than others. British Columbia is handsomely endowed with natural resources. Alberta is rich with oil and gas reserves. The prairies produce abundant wheat. Ontario is a manufacturing center. Quebec, however, has fewer assets on which to base economic expansion, while the Maritime economy is actually declining, relative to the rest of the country. Not surprisingly, each region tries to make the most of whatever advantage it possesses; however this tends to work against Canada's unity and continually creates new political crises. The precarious future of Canada as a nation stems not only from its cultural and linguistic diversity. The incompatible economic interests of its various regions are at least a factor.

SOCIALISM

Marx believed that capitalism contained "the seeds of its own destruction." The poverty of the masses would increase along with the gathering of wealth into fewer and fewer hands. The business cycle would produce wider swings between "booms" and "busts," so that in the most advanced states the means of production would at last be seized by the workers and the economy would be transformed into a centrally organized one. We have seen that capitalism has not developed according to Marx's program, but for that matter, socialism has not followed his program either.

For one thing, Marx expected the revolution to produce, fairly soon, a new social system—true communism. Under communism the state would wither away because it would be unnecessary. Goods and services would become so abundant that nobody would want to hoard anything selfishly and the very concept of private property would disappear. People would take what they needed without greed and contribute what they could, unselfishly, according to their abilities. No one would lord it over anyone else.

By now it is clear that no communist revolution has led to genuine communism. What have appeared instead are several *socialist* societies, each with its own brand of socialism. The system in the USSR differs from the Chinese approach, which differs from the Yugoslav system, and so on. But they all have one thing in common: The means of production are publicly owned, either by the nation-state or (in the case of Yugoslavia) by the workers who do the actual production in a factory. People do have private property—their own clothes, radios, jewelry, cars, and so on. But they are not supposed to own anything that earns income from the labor of anyone else. This means that no one lives on unearned income such as dividends on stocks and bonds. Making a private profit is called "profiteering" and is forbidden, though social classes still exist with some people holding privileges that others lack.

In socialist countries, the market system is not used to determine what goods should be produced or what prices they should be sold at. Instead, the state uses detailed planning to decide how much of each item should be manufactured and where it should be allocated. It is not necessary for a firm to make a profit if the government decides that its products are needed for the public welfare. Thus *in socialist societies the economy is subordinate to the political system.*

Robert W. Young/DPI

Many developing countries gain greatly in agricultural productivity when they put land redistribution plans into effect.

Let's look at three socialist societies and compare the ways in which they function.

The Soviet Union

The first communist revolution occurred in a nation only barely touched by industrialization, not in an advanced capitalist state. Therefore Marx's writings could not serve as a guide to the Bolsheviks who seized power in Russia. They had to bring about industrialization themselves. Their initial effort to make industrial decision-making more democratic was unsuccessful so they turned to political force. They attempted to force farmers to produce more for the urban population and, at the same time, to deprive the masses of consumer goods so that available resources could be used to build up heavy industry as

477

quickly as possible. Production was organized according to a plan, not according to the demands for commodities, and such planning often led to a flow of materials that was less than efficient. In recent years, the government has recognized this problem and has acted to make market forces more influential in regulating production than before.

Besides the official plan, an unofficial black market has played a major role in the Russian economy. However, consumer demand is still far less important in the Soviet Union than in capitalist countries. Consumer preferences exert little influence on the types of goods and services provided. Instead, Soviet planners now look to other countries to see what styles consumers prefer there, and then try to copy those designs. Thus a new car is likely to look like an out-of-date Ford, Volvo, or Plymouth.

The state owns almost all the means of production—mines, land, factories, and so forth. Workers earn wages and have some choice among occupations, but they are not allowed to look for work in any region or industry they please. Although the Soviet economy has made a lot of progress since the revolution, its gross national product (the total value of goods and services produced in a given year) in the 1970s was estimated at about half the U.S. gross national product.[27]

Still, the Soviet system has certain advantages over capitalism. There is no balance-of-payments problem because imports are held to the level that can be paid for by exports. Government services are paid for out of profits from business, not income taxes, and without such taxes there are fewer "loopholes" to protect special interests. There is never a problem of unemployment, for those who cannot find the jobs they want are assigned to jobs that must be done. No class of persons lives on unearned income.

The most serious problems remaining in the Soviet Union are more political than economic. One of these is the government's lack of responsiveness to the people. This is a

holdover from the period of rapid industrialization. Such unresponsiveness is not an inherent aspect of socialism, however, as the case of Yugoslavia shows.

Yugoslavia

In 1950 the Yugoslavs successfully broke away from Soviet control, though they remained committed to socialist principles. Since then, in an effort to democratize economic decision making, they have developed a kind of socialism based on workers' "self-management." An industry in Yugoslavia is owned by a Workers' Council consisting of from 20 to 100 workers. The council chooses managers and decides what to produce and how profits should be used. The councils may borrow capital or import raw materials from other countries.

The Yugoslav political system is decentralized, with the greatest power held by communes at the local level. "In the final redistribution of 'public resources,' which serve to cover the general requirements of the community (budget, social, and public services), the commune has at its disposal greater resources than the federation or republic."[28] Because of the decentralization of power, problems of coordination sometimes arise—for example, a road was built in one area but never connected to any road in the next district. Many citizens do not even think of themselves as "Yugoslavs" but view themselves as "Serbs," "Croats," and so forth. Still, the system is very effective in involving the workers in the affairs of their industry and society, and any changes made in Yugoslavia will have to conform to the democratic methods that are so highly valued there.

China

Forty years ago, the situation of China was much like the situation of India or Bangladesh today—very poor. In Shanghai, trucks drove along the streets every morning, loaded with corpses. Every block or two, a truck would stop to pick up the body of another person who had died on the street during the night. But that was before the revolution.

Unlike the Russian revolution, the Chinese revolution started in the countryside and moved to the cities. Since the revolution, social changes have been made with the cooperation of the peasants. The collectivization of land and the introduction of better agricultural methods raised productivity per person as well as per acre. Each work team owns its land, equipment, and social-welfare fund. Income is distributed to individuals on the basis of earned work points. Consumer goods are available. Unlike the situation in the early years of the USSR, peasants are never forced to sell so much of what they produce that they don't have enough left to feed themselves.[29]

Planning is more efficient in China than in the Soviet Union because the needs of consumers determine what will be produced and in what quantities. The government simply arranges contracts between industries at various points of the production process.

The Chinese are determined to destroy class divisions. Government officials must periodically work on a commune so that they will remember to serve the people. Work is praised, and people are encouraged to criticize the party and the government. The economic system is based on appealing to people's sense of moral duty, not to the desire to get ahead. It works because people *do* seem to respond

China is still an agricultural society with very little mechanization of work. The size of their population allows them to use people instead of machines in many cases. These workers are processing cotton.

Wide World

Janet Nelson/DPI

Markets have not been necessary in many preindustrial societies in the past. However, today most people in the world buy products and pay for them in cash. This is a general store in Morocco.

The development of economic thought

One of the purposes of this chapter is to make you aware of economic theories that you may have taken for granted. This is important because your theories guide your decisions and the policies you support. And these policies make life better or worse. Economic policies have a huge impact on you and me and on people on the other side of the world—and on all of our children and grandchildren.

Obviously, we cannot review the whole history of economic thought. Therefore I will use one issue—the relationship between market forces and political regulation—to show how theories have flip-flopped from one extreme to another in only 200 years.

If you have been properly socialized in a capitalist society, you probably assume (maybe with strong feelings) that the free-enterprise system is the only reasonable way of taking care of human needs. And you may also assume that any interference with the workings of the market system is unwise, to put it mildly. But markets are not a necessary ingredient of human society. Some societies distribute goods and services without using market exchange. Your parents may give tomatoes to their neighbors without expecting anything in return. The same neighbor—or perhaps another one—may send over a loaf of banana bread or offer to babysit, also without expecting to be paid. This is *reciprocity*, not exchange. We couldn't run a society as complex as ours using this kind of system alone, but many primitive societies get along quite well with simple reciprocity. On the other hand, even in our society we depend on generosity as well as exchange. Consider the system of "grants" that provides for needy people and worthy causes. You may have a

to moral appeals. The Chinese economy has not grown very fast, but it has achieved a great deal because of its commitment to equalizing the distribution of wealth in society. Unfortunately, not enough statistics are published to enable researchers to compare the effectiveness of the Chinese system with other economic systems. It is possible that our conclusions about China are mistaken because outsiders are not allowed to see the side of Chinese society that has developed more slowly.

480

scholarship, for example. Maybe your professor's research is funded by a grant from the Canada Council. Maybe you contributed to the local newspaper's fresh-air fund to send poor children to summer camp. Such grants are not given with the expectation that anything will be given in return.

However, for us the market is the primary mechanism of distribution. How does it work? Everyone is supposed to want to own things, and everyone has to sell something to earn a living. A person may sell either goods (products) or services (labor). These things are bought and sold in the market. Because so many people are buying and selling, no single individual or firm (presumably) can control the prices at which goods and services are exchanged. Price is determined by the relationship between supply and demand. When we do business, you and I, we each assume that the other is trying to get the best possible bargain and that all the other buyers and sellers are doing likewise. If I don't like your offer, I'll try to find someone who will make a better offer. You know this, so you keep the competition in mind when you make your offer.

You may take this situation for granted and feel all right about it, especially if you are used to doing business. But some people dislike the fact that in a capitalist system everyone is expected to seek the greatest possible profit instead of serving the public interest. A system of market exchange assumes that "I'm not in business for my health," that I will take advantage of every chance to make a profit. You are supposed to know this and watch out for your own interests instead of expecting me to protect your interests for you.

Of course we do set limits to competition. I'm not supposed to lie or cheat or make false claims in my advertising or run away with your rent deposit, for example. The government will punish me if I cheat you, steal from you, or break a contract that we have signed.

So we depend on the government to support the conditions that make markets able to function. This leads us to the question: To what extent should the government be involved in economic transactions? How much government regulation is desirable and how much is a nuisance? For example, if I charge an unfair price for something you need and can't get elsewhere, should the government interfere and keep me from taking advantage of you? Points of view on such questions differ greatly. Most people would agree that government should at least force people to live up to their contracts, and perhaps that it must limit monopolies or even actively fight inflation, depression, unemployment, and other economic problems. Beyond that, the government has to be involved in economic relationships with other societies. Should the government try to make its own society richer at the expense of others? May it use political and military power to force other nations to make favorable economic agreements with important companies whose interests it wants to protect? These issues have to do with the proper relationship between the government and the "natural" functioning of markets in a situation of free competition.

Not only do individuals differ on many of these issues, but the general opinion of people today differs from that of the previous generation. Public opinion on matters of economic policy is always changing, as the following paragraphs will show.

MERCANTILISM

We begin with mercantilism, the economic policy of the seventeenth and eighteenth centuries—the period when Europe was ruled by absolute monarchs. Mercantilists thought that the best way to increase national power was to increase national wealth—which meant to increase the nation's supply of gold and silver. The state encouraged this policy in every possible way. Mercantilism involved the regulation of industry and trade by centralized political power. The monarch granted monopoly power to industries that manufactured goods for export, and in return demanded a fee which was the principal source of government finance. It limited imports and set up colonies to provide gold, silver, and raw materials. Mercantilism was the dominant economic system in Europe until Adam Smith's views became popular.

ADAM SMITH

Adam Smith (1723–1790) attacked mercantilism in *The Wealth of Nations*. He began by rejecting the assumption that wealth equals money or treasure. The wealth of a nation, he argued, is its power to produce goods. Money is simply a medium of exchange. The real source of wealth is specialized labor. Why? Because the more specialized labor is, the more productive it is. And the specialization of labor depends on the size of the market for its products and the availability of capital. Thus increasing trade by enlarging the market is the key to economic growth. Smith recommended free trade instead of the protectionist policies of mercantilism. He wanted to abolish tariffs and other restrictions on international trade. Storing up gold and silver seemed unimportant to him. Wealth was not *money* but *products* being traded to meet human needs.

Smith's approach was called laissez faire, which means, roughly, "let it be." Smith held that the state should not regulate the economy but should allow it to regulate itself. If they were given the chance, businesspeople would enlarge their markets and thus enrich the nation.

You may ask, what prevents a few individuals from gaining control of the market if the government doesn't regulate them? What keeps them from fixing prices and so on? Smith believed that *in a completely free economy* businesspeople would not pool their power to control prices and output. Instead, they would put their capital into the most productive enterprises. The economy would regulate itself. And he believed that if tariffs were abolished, each country would produce whatever was most profitable, given its resources. The best possible distribution of goods would result from free international trade.

Thus Smith was opposed to government support of particular businesses. The state should not grant favors to certain economic groups but let them all compete freely in the market. The market, unregulated, would reward those who produced needed goods at the lowest prices. Both the public and the nation would benefit from free competition. The state should guarantee that contracts are honored. It should provide a setting that encourages business in general. But it should not protect particular enterprises.

KARL MARX

Although we have discussed Marx's theories at several points in this book, we haven't focused on his analysis of the relationships between economic and political forces. You will recall that Marx distinguished between the *economic structure* of a society and what he called the *superstructure*. The economic structure includes both the technology of production and the social relationships that occur when people act together to produce goods. These economic structures are basic—they determine everything else, including the superstructure. Among the social relationships that are part of the economic structure are *social classes*. Marx was especially interested in two of those classes—the bourgeoisie (the capitalists) and the proletarians (the industrial workers). It is through social classes that the economic structure gives rise to the superstructure.

The superstructure includes institutions such as laws, schools, the government, the church, and the military. In early capitalism, the superstructure serves the bourgeoisie. To put it more simply, the politicians and the armed forces help keep the workers in a subordinate position, and religious leaders feed them ideologies so that they won't rebel. Marx wasn't saying this is how the government, the church, the military, and other institutions *should* act. The capitalists ordinarily have more power than the workers. With that power they can influence the government to pass laws that are unfavorable to the workers and put down their riots, strikes, and demonstrations. Under such conditions, *the political forces in society back up the economic forces.*

But this situation does not last forever. The capitalists have to drive the workers harder and harder simply to maintain their profits. The competition between capitalists also drives them to buy more efficient machines, and this also increases productivity.

Eventually an hour of each worker's labor yields several times as many products as it did before.

Economic depressions get more severe. Workers may riot, but gradually they become more politically aware. They join unions and make demands. Finally they create a revolutionary party that destroys the capitalist system and brings in a socialist one. By then competition will have forced the capitalists to buy such efficient machinery that the workers can run it with little effort. Each person will work a few hours a day to satisfy basic needs and will be free to spend his or her spare time developing more important human qualities such as knowledge and creativity.

Thus Marx believed that as workers become more and more threatening, the political forces will no longer support the economic system. In fact it is through political force (revolution) that the workers will destroy the economic system (capitalism). In other words,

Marx expected the workers in industrial society to have an increasingly difficult life, so they would eventually rebel. This unemployed worker is unhappy, but not likely to revolt.

Wide World

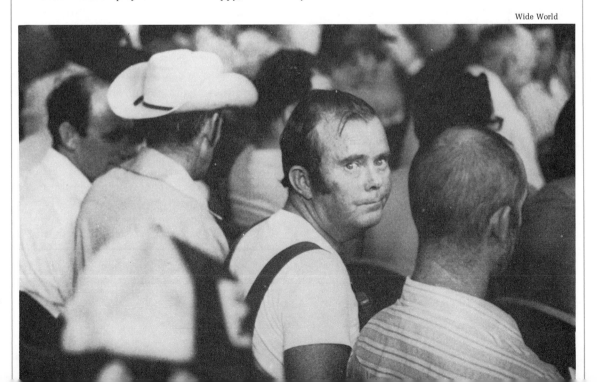

as an economic system weakens, *the economic and political forces come into conflict, and this conflict ultimately dooms the system.*

THE MODERN MARKET SYSTEM AND GOVERNMENT REGULATION

In the preceding chapter we discussed Marx's historical predictions and noted that neo-Marxists have had to revise his theory to explain historical developments. No one knows what Marx would think if he were with us today—but no one knows what Adam Smith would believe either. He certainly would not believe everything he wrote in *The Wealth of Nations.* Few people believe in free enterprise any more—at least as Smith described it. Certainly business leaders don't want the government to leave the economy to its own devices. They don't want public ownership, of course, but they like the stabilizing influence that a strong government provides. What has happened to economic theory since Smith's day?

First, Smith assumed that, if left alone, the market would be quite competitive. No firm would gain the power to control prices or output. But the trouble is obvious: The market is *not* perfectly competitive. Price and output can be manipulated more easily than Smith supposed. Suppose, for example, that you and I are two sulfur producers who control the entire supply of sulfur. We can call the tune. Since buyers cannot go elsewhere for their sulfur, we control the price. Or suppose the government builds a dam that becomes the only source of electricity for an entire region. Where is the competition in this situation? Obviously, the government will set the price for the electricity produced by the dam. Much of what we use in today's economy is produced by systems that do not set prices on the basis of competition.

During the 1920s and 1930s, economists began to realize that the model of perfect competition was unrealistic. They developed other models that assume *imperfect competition.* For example, modern economic theory recognizes that firms may set prices not on the basis of their costs but on the basis of political agreements with other firms. Businesses may behave uneconomically in the short run by cutting prices in order to drive their competitors out of business—and then raise prices as high as they please. In addition, politics may influence the price system quite directly: A firm may set its prices at a given level because the government has put pressure on it.

One of the leading economic theorists of the early twentieth century was John Maynard Keynes (1883–1946). In contrast to Smith, Keynes held that the government could and should stabilize the economy. He welcomed the partnership between business and the state because he realized that capitalist economies can develop serious imbalances that can be corrected only by government action. Not only *can* they develop imbalances—they can be *expected* to do so. Thus long periods of unemployment and depression are to be expected. In explaining depressions, Keynes suggested that the main assumption made by Adam Smith and his followers—that economic systems automatically use whatever resources are available, including capital—was wrong.

Keynes showed that you and I may save money in order to invest it in business but find that available investments are unattractive. Capital may not be needed. Businesses may not be able to obtain loans at rates that profits will cover, so there may arise both an excess of savings and a reluctance by business and consumers to spend. If enough people save their money instead of spending it or investing it, the factories lay off workers. Especially where there is no unemployment insurance, such a depression finds it hard to correct itself through the market forces. Keynes and his followers argue that the best solution is for the government to take action to correct economic instability. There are several ways of doing this. One is by buying or not buying goods. This is called fiscal policy. The government can spend like no one else. So if demand is low, the government should spend, spend, spend to bring it up. Spend on highways, hospitals, space exploration, and so on. The government can also change policies that affect the distribution of income, such as the income tax laws or the rules that determine who is eligible for welfare. These policies influence consumption, which, in turn, affects the market.

A second tool that the government can use to stabilize the economy is called monetary policy. This involves manipulating the prime lending rate or the total money supply.

In the United States, this is the main concern of the Federal Reserve Board. In Canada, the Bank of Canada determines monetary policy.

Since Keynes's day we have all become increasingly aware of how political factors influence the economy. We are deeply interested in taxation, defense, and welfare policies. We have learned that it is impossible to do what Smith recommended—to have *no* economic policy, that is, to leave the economy alone. Whatever action the government takes, it will have some impact on the economy. So when you vote, you may be voting either for the policies of Adam Smith or for those of John Maynard Keynes, though neither name will be on the ballot. Nowadays Keynes is winning far more often than Smith.

WORK

SOCIAL RESEARCH:
Sociologists at Work

Imagine that your plane has been hijacked and has landed in some unknown airport. You are put into a bus that speeds through the countryside. How long will it take you to guess where you are? Unless you see a familiar flag you may not guess what country you are in, but you will know almost immediately whether you are in a developed or less developed nation. The gap between the rich nations and the poor ones is unmistakable. We live in two worlds on the same planet—our world and the Third World. Each has its own economic problems. In actuality, the problems are interrelated. But the experiences and way of life that are characteristic of our economic system are amazingly different from those of the less developed economies.

In discussing the trends and prospects of the Western industrial societies, I want to pay particular attention to two broad topics: (1) work and (2) the shift toward a postindustrial society.

Who works? In what jobs? There are great differences in the area of employment. Age, sex, and ethnicity—to mention only three factors—affect participation in the work force. Just recently, for example, there has been a large group of youths entering the labor force—the babies of the baby boom, now maturing. Hence, there are more young people than are needed to fill the jobs that usually employ young adults. In 10 years the situation will be different; unemployment patterns will be linked to age in a different way. The best jobs are now held mostly by middle-aged men. Old people have trouble finding or holding jobs, just as youths do. Older people who have not yet reached retirement age are likely to be unemployed for a long time if they lose their jobs.

For several decades, women have been entering the work force in large numbers. Between 1961 and 1971 the participation of women in the Canadian labor force increased by more than 71 percent.[30] In 1971, women formed 35 percent of the total labor force in Canada. Slightly more than half of all single females were employed. Recently married women between the ages of 20 and 24 had an even higher rate of employment. After the age of 24, married women tended to leave work and raise children; they returned to work at about the age of 45. Nonetheless, almost 40 percent of women between the ages of 30 and 34, the most active period of childcare, were employed outside the home.[31] Younger women were more likely to work than older women, and well-educated women more than less educated women.[32] About 62 percent of women with university degrees were in the 1971 labor force.[33]

Women still perform mostly the same jobs that they have traditionally performed; they continue to work as nurses, teachers, secretaries, clerks, and so on. Jobs that were reserved for men early in this century are still reserved for men, though this pattern is changing slightly. Although few "male" jobs have opened up for women, the variety of "female" jobs has increased.

Women do have trouble combining careers with motherhood. Often one of these roles has to be eased a bit to make room for the other. Women are more likely to take up casual, temporary jobs than men. Those who continue to work often have fewer children.[34] Women who work while their children are young generally do so because they need the money; they may be single mothers or their husbands may be unemployed or poorly paid.[35] Working wives gain some authority in the household and have greater influence on the family's financial affairs. They do somewhat fewer household tasks than full-time homemakers do.

Ethnicity is also a key factor in determining occupational status. In Canada, immigrants have typically taken low-paying jobs and gradually moved up the social ladder; low-status jobs have then been filled by more recently arrived immigrants. However, various ethnic groups have increased their occupational status at different rates.

For example, in 1970 Blishen established that Italians were underrepresented in the top social classes of Ontario and Quebec, while British and American immigrants were more frequently represented than Canadian-born citizens.[36] In another study, Anthony Richmond found that the children of British white-collar immigrants in Canada have tended to achieve higher social status than their parents, while the children of European white-collar immigrants have tended to attain lower status than their parents.[37]

As John Porter has shown, Canada has often imported English and American professionals instead of training Canadians to fill professional jobs. Foreign anglophone professionals have assimilated easily and saved Canada the expense of supplying a university education to a large number of Canadians.[38] However, in recent years, this situation has changed considerably, and many more Canadians are now receiving professional training.

ALIENATION

You will spend a major part of your life on the job. What will it be like? Exciting? Dull? Exhausting? Fulfilling? Easy? Challenging? Maddening? Fun? Jobs have all of these qualities in different proportions. I remember my worst job: dipping ashtrays in glaze all day. I couldn't even stop for a drink of water. Try that job for a few months and you will understand very well the experience that we are going to discuss next—alienation.

Alienation is loss of belief and interest in the goals toward which one's activities are directed. Alienation produces a loss of commitment to one's group and a sense of powerlessness. This is particularly evident in the workplace, but also in political and other social contexts. Some signs of alienation are the rise of crime, labor unrest, and social protest. Marx was among the first to state that there was a close relationship between alienation and the system of mass production that was developing at that time. Craftsmen usually feel proud of their products because they make each item from start to finish. But industrial workers have no autonomy. Industrial work is divided into a series of repetitive acts that are assigned to different people. The pace of work is determined by the rhythms of machines, not the needs of human beings. Your arm is just one more lever to be synchronized with all the others. And the product is not yours. It belongs to the factory owner, who sells it and pays you wages. Do you feel powerless, bored by meaningless tasks, dulled in spirit and fatigued in body? That's what we mean by alienation.

Some kinds of factory work are more alienating than others. Robert Blauner has classified industrial jobs into three categories: (1) crafts, (2) assembly-line work, and (3) continuous-process manufacture. (The third category consists of processing products, such as liquid chemicals or oil, that flow continuously through tubes and are manufactured by automatic procedures.) As you might guess, assembly line work is the most alienating. Blauner found that workers who oversee continuous-process manufacture have more responsibility and that the timing of their work is fairly flexible. For example, the workers he studied kept a hot plate in their control room and could heat up a can of soup if they wanted to. They could read their meters a little earlier or a little later than required by their schedule if they wanted to eat their soup while it was hot. There are no hot plates on the assembly line. Marx was the writer who first discussed alienation. He observed the great increase in alienation in the early days of industrialization, when work was being broken into component jobs and assembly-line techniques were increasing. He couldn't foresee automation.

Blauner suggested that the growth of alienation over time could be described as an inverted U, increasing during the early and middle stages of industrialization and declining again as automation is introduced in the advanced stage—our own time.[39] Several other scholars have followed up Blauner's research with similar studies. Some of their findings support Blauner's; others don't. A study of Canadian manual workers from three industries—printing, automobile, and oil—produced results that largely agree with Blauner's. This study found work integration highest in oil, next highest in printing (a craft), and lowest in automobile manufacture.[40] Similar patterns have been discovered in a study of Detroit automobile workers, many of whom had mental-health problems or difficulty adjusting to life. The workers who performed more skilled, more varied, more responsible, and higher-paid jobs showed fewer signs of such problems. Furthermore, since prejob characteristics such as level of education did not seem to explain these differences, it seems that the job situation itself was the main cause of these personal problems.[41] On the other hand, a British study of automobile workers found that, although they were indeed alienated, many workers chose to work on the assembly line because of the high pay.[42]

Because many studies of assembly-line work have found that it alienates the worker, some industries are moving away from it whenever possible. Some automobile plants have changed to an assembly system that is quite similar to craft work in that the worker is responsible for a series of tasks. In Swedish factories, small teams of women

Jerry Frank/DPI

can be seen putting together an entire engine. They find the work far more interesting and are more committed to it than assembly-line workers. The savings resulting from higher morale partially offset the losses in productivity resulting from this shift toward handicraft assembly.

More common than team assembly work, however, is the widespread tendency of factories to mechanize even further through automation.

AUTOMATION

Strictly speaking, almost all industrial advance has meant "automation" in that tasks that require low-level skills have been taken over by automatic machines. The distinctive character of automation today, however, is that products are produced

487

continuously and are not touched by human hands. Compared with the assembly line, automated production requires less physical labor and less supervision of workers. However, the work is usually removed even further from the control of the workers than in assembly-line production. Moreover, modern automation requires higher-level skills than those needed in older factory systems. Unskilled positions are often eliminated. At the higher skill levels, new jobs requiring more knowledge and training have emerged.

The economic effects of automation are not yet fully understood. The main issue is whether automation increases unemployment among the less skilled workers, whose jobs are eliminated and who sometimes may not be able to move into higher positions. This debate has not been settled.[43]

Nor are the social and psychological effects of automation completely clear. One line of research—consistent with Blauner's findings—suggests that workers in automated settings are more satisfied with their working conditions because they have more control over their work and have to pay less attention to detail.[44] However, not all automation has these happy results. One study of automation in Pennsylvania concluded that the improved technology did not do much to reduce alienation besides raising the status of jobs.[45] Evidently the various studies produce somewhat different results because they measure alienation in different ways and focus on different aspects of the job that might affect workers' satisfaction. One study might look at the amount of physical effort required. Another might consider the degree of specialization. Another might analyze worker supervision. In any case, most workers say that they are satisfied with their jobs. When the sociologist asks more detailed questions, however, it appears that worker satisfaction is relative. For example, the worker may remark that "it's as good a job as I could probably get anyplace else. It's boring, but the pay is okay." Does this statement reveal satisfaction or alienation? I'm not sure, myself.

OCCUPATIONAL ROLES

Different types of job make different demands on the worker and therefore have different effects on the people who do them. Let's compare the problems of some of the different occupational roles, classifying them into four general categories: (1) executives, (2) professionals, (3) foremen, and (4) low-skilled workers.

The executive role

The executive is a coordinator of information. He or she makes decisions and communicates them to the departments and individuals that carry them out. The executive role is often a stressful one. People want quick decisions, yet a decision may be hard to arrive at in a situation of contradictory demands—no one can satisfy everyone. The executive must be prepared to issue unpleasant orders or to fire incompetent employees even if they are friends.[46]

The lower-level executive has problems too. Junior executives have a status that is somewhere between the top level and lower levels and is often unclear. This situation may lead to concern with the symbols of status, such as number of telephones, location of office, or size of desk.[47]

The professional role

The term *professional* implies "professing" or "believing." All professions involve commitment to standards of knowledge and excellence. Still, the professional must be paid, and therefore some tension may develop between the service and commercial aspects of the role. Freelance professionals normally charge a fee for their services. Other professionals (such as teachers and clergy) are removed from the market for their services—they do not charge their clients (e.g., students or church members) directly but receive a salary from the organization that employs them.

Many professional roles have high status, but the status of semiprofessional occupations is unclear. Engineering technicians are a good example. They may be as skilled as engineers but are usually less well paid, have less prestige, and have fewer chances for advancement. One reaction to this situation is similar to that of junior executives—concern with symbols. The technician may do a lot of job hopping and claim a lot of office space, clerical help, and other symbols of the engineer's role. People in semi-professional roles often make collective efforts to "professionalize" the role in the public eye.[48] Nurses and social workers, for example, have started movements to upgrade their status and stake out special responsibilities that only their certified members are allowed to perform.

The foreman

The foreman or forewoman in a factory is caught between conflicting expectations. The managers assume that he is their agent, and the subordinates assume he is supposed to be protecting them and representing their interests. Not surprisingly, both groups feel ambivalent toward him and he tends to identify first with management, then with workers, and then only with other foremen.[49]

The low-skilled worker

All of the occupations mentioned so far have *conflicting* role demands. Not so with the low-skilled worker. The strains in this role do not result from ambiguity. The worker knows exactly where he or she stands—at the bottom. The strains come from the facts that the pay is low, the worker may reach the end of the career line in his or her twenties, there are layoffs during recessions, and the job is unchallenging. Workers often react to these problems by focusing on outside goals such

Some professionals choose to work in areas that would otherwise be without their services rather than to earn as much money as possible. This man serves an Inuit community.

Ted Grant/DPI

as fixing up the basement or helping their children achieve greater success. Their feelings of alienation and class-consciousness may be quite strong.[50]

Let's move beyond the subject of work and consider some of the trends and prospects of modern societies. What is the general shape of our immediate future as an economic system, and what will be the cultural consequences of current trends?

POSTINDUSTRIAL SOCIETY

So many changes are taking place in the technology and life style of modern Western nations that it may be appropriate to name our era not industrial but *post*industrial.[51] One of the main changes that has taken place is in the percentages of jobs in different sectors of the economy. We generally classify jobs into three categories. (1) The *extractive* sector consists of agriculture, lumbering, fishing, mining, and so on. (2) The *industrial* sector consists of manufacturing and construction. (3) The *service* sector consists of such occupations as nursing, entertainment, transportation, the civil service, sales, and other nonmanufacturing jobs.

Over time, the relative size of these sectors has changed continuously. A few hundred years ago almost everyone in Western societies was involved in farming or other extractive jobs. Now only about 4 percent of the population of North America is actively engaged in agriculture. (In contrast, the percentage in most less-developed nations is often about 70 percent.) In general, the extractive occupations have declined in number while the industrial sector has increased markedly over the past few generations and is now accounting steadily for about one-third of the labor force.

These changes have occurred in both Canada and the United States, though Canada's extractive sector is slightly stronger and its manufacturing sector a bit weaker than in most other advanced nations. This is because Canada has been supplying minerals, lumber, and other raw materials for industries based elsewhere—a pattern that alarms some Canadian economists, who would prefer that Canada exported finished products instead of raw materials.

In all the advanced nations, the service sector is enlarging rapidly. One effect is that a smaller percentage of all workers do manual jobs and a larger percentage do white-collar jobs. Moreover,

education is becoming universal and very extensive. Most jobs require skills that are acquired in schools and universities. Thus the "knowledge industry" is itself a major part of the service sector. More people are devoting their careers to teaching or to generating and disseminating ideas and cultural products. There is a great market for books, television programs, records, magazines, films, as well as for many personal experiences, such as foreign travel, group therapy, crafts work, yoga, and so forth. Far more of your budget will go for such items than your grandparents spent for comparable products in their day. Our life style differs, therefore, as dramatically from the life style of the workers Marx observed in early factories as theirs differed from the life style of peasants and knights.

In many ways we are an incredibly materialistic society and a wasteful one. However, we may be moving into a period in which consumption will be less significant and other values will claim more of our attention. Many social scientists say that we must expect a leveling off of economic growth in our postindustrial society.[52] For one thing, supplies of the world's nonrenewable resources will become much more limited during our own lifetimes, so we will have to stop our excessive consumption. But that may be just as well. Shopping has become a pastime, and much of it is unnecessary. We often buy things out of boredom. But Toronto psychiatrist Vivian Rakoff has suggested that we are already entering a phase beyond wasteful consumerism. He argues that we will *do* more instead of *have* more. For example, the wearing of blue jeans by rich and poor alike may show that we are becoming less concerned with clothes.

Rakoff maintains that the current interest in therapy and encounter groups proves his point. We will become more concerned with human interaction and self-discovery as we give up our interest in buying and collecting belongings. For example, a generation ago, psychotherapy was a luxury that only rich people could afford and only a few well-educated people found interesting. Working-class people and most middle-class people were not interested in it. Now it is a part of popular culture. Rakoff expects members of all social classes to take up such concerns as we move into the postindustrial society. As we come to live with more material simplicity, we will develop our creativity and personal experience to find cultural enrichment.[53]

SOCIAL POLICY:
Issues and Viewpoints

The developing nations face a completely different and almost overwhelmingly difficult set of problems. Indeed, in many cases these nations are not developing at all but are going downhill. We can't be sure that they *will* develop, but we can be sure that there will be trouble for all of us in a few years if they don't.

The economic decisions and actions of nations on one side of our planet have an impact on those on the other side, sometimes in ways that may not be obvious. We all have to share the same resources, adding to or subtracting from the world's supply of raw materials, buying and selling goods that may have been produced by people in distant lands. When you eat a banana or buy a new tire, you are affecting the economic well-being of someone in another part of the world whom you will never meet and whose name you might not be able to pronounce. And that person is affecting you.

The first item on our planet's agenda is to feed hungry people. After that a lot of problems will almost solve themselves. But how can we eliminate hunger? Experts agree that this problem can be solved. There is no single solution, though, because there is no single problem. Hunger is caused by a variety of problems.

Actually, enough calories are produced on earth to feed all the world's hungry people. Why, then, do people still starve? There are many reasons, but the main one is that the food isn't where it ought to be when it is needed. There are transportation problems and storage problems (lots of grain is eaten by mice, for example). There are serious financial problems—the hungry don't have the money to pay for their supper. There is waste: Much of the world's food goes to fatten cattle or feed chickens so that you and I can eat steak and eggs instead of corn or beans.

We probably won't have to give up steak and eggs, for there is no reason why production can't be increased so as to produce a varied and protein-rich diet for everyone. Food production could double in the developing countries by the end of the century. But people have to know what to do and have to organize in new ways to get it done.

This is partly a matter of planning, but other factors are important as well. For example, education will make the job easier, since literate people can read brochures explaining new farming methods or the advantages of birth control. Health care will help too, since healthy people can produce more.

Without doubt, the most important issue related to food shortage is land tenure. In many developing countries the land is cultivated by people who do not own their own farms. Agrarian reform is badly needed in such areas—in fact many of the "communist" revolutions of recent years were actually agrarian rebellions by peasants trying to rid themselves of exploitive landlords. It is clear that agrarian reform could vastly increase agricultural productivity. There is no single "right" system of land tenure—several have been tried and have worked. Both collective farming and small family holdings can be effective. Several societies have increased their food production dramatically simply by redistributing farm land.

However, I don't want to suggest that land reform alone will solve the problem of hunger. Along with land reform must come various programs that enable the peasants to take advantage of their new situation. Credit must be made available so that the farmer can buy fertilizer, tools, and so forth. The government should send agents into the countryside to show people how to use new technologies both in the home and on the farm. In the case of collective farming systems, the government must organize and manage the plan, at least for a while.

CAPITAL ACCUMULATION
AND VICIOUS CIRCLES

A key problem in the developing countries is how to obtain capital to get the economy moving. Western societies have no problem obtaining capital. Most people have incomes that more than cover their basic living expenses; if business offers them attractive profits they will invest their surplus to pay for new factories and equipment. But economic growth is a problem in places like Chad, Tanzania, and Uruguay. There the shortage of capital makes modernization very hard to achieve. Capital is necessary to pay for the agricultural improvements that I have already mentioned—fertilizers, tools, irrigation, storage bins, transportation systems, and so on. It is also necessary for industrial growth and for social-service systems such as hospitals, schools, and family-planning centers. Even if the poor nations never produce much for export, they will need *some* industries to provide for their own needs.

Capital is scarce in the Third World because the economies of those nations are caught between two vicious circles having to do with the supply and demand of goods. One vicious circle limits the supply of capital while the other limits the demand for capital.[54]

On the *supply* side, capital is scarce because people are unable to save. They can't save because their incomes are too low, and their incomes are too low because the economy is unproductive. The economy is unproductive because it is based on obsolete, unmechanized systems of production, so that an average worker can't turn out many products per hour of work. The capital that would pay for fast, efficient machinery is not available. That's the first vicious circle.

The other vicious circle is on the *demand* side. Capital is scarce because people won't invest their savings if they don't expect to make a good profit on their investment. But businesses can't offer them high profits because they can't be sure of selling their products. There is too little demand. People certainly *need* goods, but they have such low incomes that they can't afford to pay for what they need. Thus there is not enough income to stimulate demand and not enough demand to stimulate investment. That's the second vicious circle.

Economists and politicians who study developing societies realize that if they could somehow obtain enough capital and invest it in the right places these vicious circles would become beneficial—capital would generate income, which would generate investment. Western societies obtained their initial capital for industrialization by allowing a great deal of exploitation. That's what Marx was so furious about—the long hours of work that the workers put in with so little return. The capitalist factory owners took the profits earned by the workers and invested them in more industry. It was a terrible period. Every society that has ever industrialized has oppressed workers to some extent. The Soviet Union's industrialization was achieved by oppressing the peasants—taking their food away to feed the urban workers, even if the peasants themselves starved. Thus two different models both succeeded in squeezing a surplus out of the poor in order to pay the initial costs of

industrializing. Capitalist countries (such as the United States and Britain) did it through an exploitive laissez-faire *economic* system. Some communist countries did it through an exploitive *political* regime using totalitarian methods.

After the initial capital has been invested in industry, the profits can be reinvested. Industrialization can then continue fairly steadily, and in time the system can become less oppressive. Ordinary workers can begin to share in the profits that their labor has produced. But in the early stages of development it is very hard to obtain capital. If the profits were divided up and given to the workers, they would probably consume them instead of investing in machinery and fertilizers. They are poor; they can't afford to invest. Hence, societies that are committed to fast economic growth are unlikely to be very egalitarian.

Finally, it should be noted that not all forms of investment produce equal advantages for the developing country. In many cases, foreign investment does little or no good to a country that is trying to industrialize; the profits that result from the investments are simply taken out of the country, leaving the poor nation no further ahead than before. Thus, when promoting economic growth, political leaders have to become highly sensitive to the kinds of investment that they welcome to their countries.

EQUITY VERSUS GROWTH

However, growth isn't everything. Equality is a value that must be recognized for its own sake. If it is incompatible with the goal of economic growth, then both sides must be considered fully.

The nations that are now developing give different weights to the values of growth and equity. A few societies have managed to accumulate a lot of capital without much coercion and are growing fast without oppressing their citizens. Yugoslavia is such a society. The Yugoslav self-management system has, remarkably, induced workers to reinvest an average of some 30 percent of their net income per year, without oppression.[55] China has stressed the value of equality over growth, and it is finding it very difficult to stimulate much saving for additional investment. China's economic growth rate was the lowest of any Asian nation during the period from 1957 to 1970.[56] However, it is clear that emphasis upon equity usually creates better living conditions and a

Ernest Hillen

Food supplied by international relief organizations can only be a stopgap measure in the fight against world hunger. Given a chance, these people can feed themselves.

healthier society. India, for example, has placed greater emphasis on growth than equity, but its growth rate is only slightly better than China's and most evidence suggests that its poor citizens are not nearly as well off as China's.

THE RELATIONSHIP BETWEEN RICH NATIONS AND POOR NATIONS

All the people who live on this planet are interdependent, even though we live on different continents and in different political and economic systems. You may be wondering how you can affect the people of the Third World. There are several areas in which individual decisions in the West can influence the relationship between the rich nations and the poor ones.

Think about land reform. More than once,

Western nations have supported reactionary regimes in the less developed countries, even giving them military aid to prevent land reform. Yet nothing can do more to feed hungry people than land reform. Pay attention to the government's attitudes toward reactionary regimes in the Third World.

Another issue to consider is international trade. Rich nations can exploit poor nations; they have all the power and can set the terms of trade. Rich nations, for example, can set such high tariffs that poor nations cannot sell their products abroad. Such a policy protects the rich at the expense of the poor. On the other hand, when rich nations want certain goods their demand can upset the economies of the poor nations. For example, many Third World nations produce almost entirely for export—their economies depend on coffee, cocoa, or sugar. They might do more for their people by

493

producing food for them instead of crops for export, since exports are usually controlled by giant foreign corporations rather than small family farms. Some developing nations have tried to protect themselves against the control of multi-national corporations by nationalizing industries owned by outsiders. This is risky because it angers the owners of those industries and can lead to political or military pressure.

Finally, we have to prepare ourselves for some major changes. For a long time the rich countries have been able to grow richer because they have been able to buy oil from other countries at low prices. Our technology is based on oil. Among other things, it has enabled us to produce huge quantities of grain cheaply and to sell the grain to other countries. Those countries have become dependent on the North American grain supply.

But all this is changing. Oil won't be cheap again. The countries that buy Canadian grain will have to start feeding their own populations, somehow. And they can—if we don't stop them.

SUMMARY

1. Primitive economies use principles of reciprocity and redistribution rather than market exchange. Market exchange is the principle underlying modern economic systems.

2. The earliest form of agriculture was probably the "slash-and-burn" system, which required little labor but much land. As agriculture became labor intensive, people began to enslave others in order to exploit their labor. But a free class always existed too, and these people became townspeople.

3. In England capitalism stemmed from the development of commercial farming, which was made possible by the enclosure movement that displaced peasants from the land and made their labor available for factory work. Industrialization began with the cotton factories and spread to all areas of production. The colonial governments were established to extract raw materials for the industrial nations.

4. Modern capitalism, unlike the crudely exploitive system that Marx knew, is not dominated by individual business leaders. The modern corporation is owned by thousands of stockholders and managed by a "technostructure"—a corps of experts. Modern capitalism is also more interested in plan-

ning ahead with secure control than in maximizing profits. Hence, it does not resist, but rather welcomes, government control.

5. Labor relations are less violent today than they used to be. Workers, like management, encourage advertising, which stimulates demand for products.

6. Welfare states such as Sweden are partly capitalist and partly socialist. The government owns many businesses and is involved in the management of others. Social-security benefits are very well organized, and income is equalized to a great extent.

7. Socialism has not developed as Marx predicted. There are several different versions of socialism. All of these versions use economic planning rather than the market as a system for distributing goods and services. The Soviet Union industrialized through extensive political coercion—particularly of farmers—and remains unresponsive to public opinion. The Yugoslav system depends chiefly on workers' control of industry and is highly decentralized. The Chinese system allows the consumers' rquirements to determine the distribution of supplies; the government arranges contracts between industries. The Chinese system is egalitarian, but China's industrial growth rate has not been remarkable.

8. Western views of the proper relations between the state and the market forces have undergone many changes. Under mercantilism, the system in use during the period of absolute monarchies, the government tried to regulate the economy and accumulate gold, silver, and raw materials. Adam Smith introduced the notion of *laissez faire* to economic thought, suggesting that governments should guarantee that contracts are honored but otherwise allow the market to regulate itself. Karl Marx maintained that the government, being part of the superstructure, is normally controlled by economic forces; that is, the ruling class always gives orders to the gov-

ernment. However, when class conflict leads to revolution the workers gain control of the political forces and overthrow the economic system.

9. Modern economists are aware that the market is not always perfectly competitive. Monopolies can interfere with competitive pricing. Keynes suggested that in a capitalist system government action is not only unavoidable but desirable to control the business cycle. The government can influence the market through fiscal and monetary policy.

KEY TERMS

economics the social science that deals with the production, distribution, exchange, and consumption of scarce goods and services.

fiscal policy a governmental policy of spending or not spending on goods and services.

laissez faire the belief that the state should not regulate the economy but should allow the economy to regulate itself.

market exchange a system in which goods and services are exchanged in a market context.

mercantilism the belief that the best way to increase national power is to increase national wealth (i.e., the nation's supply of gold and silver).

monetary policy a governmental policy of manipulating the prime lending rate or the total money supply.

reciprocity the two-way exchange of goods or services.

redistribution a system in which goods and services are brought to a central source and then redistributed throughout the population.

FOR FURTHER READING

ABELLA, IRVING and DAVID MILLAR, eds. *The Canadian Worker in the Twentieth Century*. Toronto: Oxford University Press, 1978. Abella is a labor historian, and this book is a social history of the Canadian working class up to about World War II.

BAUM, D.J. *The Final Plateau: The Betrayal of Our Senior Citizens*. Toronto: Burns and MacEachern, 1974. In the future, Canada's population will contain a much larger proportion of older people than in previous periods. There are serious economic consequences to be faced, and this book mentions

some of the problems that have already emerged and that must be handled.

BECKER, GARY S. *The Economic Approach to Human Behavior*. Chicago: University of Chicago Press, 1977. Becker has been proposing plain, ordinary economic models to account for complex forms of social behavior, such as crime and leisure activities. Fascinating ideas.

CRAIG, J. *An Alternative for World Development: Multinational Cooperatives*. Toronto: Western Producer, 1976. Fortunately some writers are considering ways in which the Third World can increase economic production and protect its citizens from the overwhelming power of multinational corporations. Craig's ideas, emphasizing cooperatives, deserve wide attention.

FRANK, A. GUNDER. *Latin America: Underdevelopment or Revolution.* New York: Monthly Review Press, 1969. Frank is the leader in the approach we have termed "dependency theory." You can see from the title of his book what he thinks the alternatives are.

LEVITT, KARI. *Silent Surrender: The Multinational Corporation in Canada.* Toronto: Macmillan, 1970. Levitt's book emphasizes the part that Canadians have played in helping multinationals gain their power in Canada.

ROBINSON, JOAN. *Freedom and Necessity.* New York: Random House, 1970. A charming and informative little economic history of the world. It takes hardly any time to read but is worth rereading a number of times.

THOMPSON, E. P. *The Making of the English Working Class.* London: Penguin, 1968. Several of my radical friends are extremely enthusiastic about this historical book. I include it because they would never forgive me for leaving it out.

WALLERSTEIN, IMMANUEL. *The Modern World System: Capitalist Agriculture and the Origins of the European World Economy in the Sixteenth Century.* New York: Academic Press, 1976. Wallerstein has had a major impact on analyses of the world economy and its connection to the historical development of nations. Just now there are many sociologists planning to organize their careers around the study of some aspect of this theme. Remember his name even if you don't read his book.

FOUR

changing society

17

POPULATION AND ECOLOGY

Basic demographic processes
    Fertility
    Mortality
    Migration
Population composition
    The sex ratio
    Population pyramids
    The dependency ratio
Population trends
    The population explosion
    Malthusian theory
    The demographic-transition model
    Zero population growth
The decision to have a child
    Changes in the preference system
    Changes in the price system
Ecological aspects of human survival
    Land
    Water
    Energy and minerals
Social Research: Sociologists at Work
Social Policy: Issues and Viewpoints

How many children do you expect to have? How many children did your parents have? Let me guess. I think you want two children and that your parents had three or four. I am no mind reader, but I have looked at surveys that asked large samples of respondents about desired family size. Big changes are taking place in this area. People in industrial societies are becoming highly aware of the problems facing humankind because of the population explosion.

In this chapter I want to introduce you to demography, the study of human populations. Sociologists have been interested in demography for a long time. They have been concerned with the description and explanation of the three processes that determine the size of any given population—*fertility, mortality,* and *migration,* or the rates at which people give birth, die, and move into or out of a given area. In addition, we will discuss ecology—the relationship between the physical environment and the human population that lives in that environment. Obviously, in the long run a population that uses its resources recklessly will create problems for itself and for future generations. For all of these reasons we want to take a long view in this chapter—a look at our own future as a species inhabiting a small planet. We will think about how this world can be preserved for generation after generation after generation so that our great-grandchildren can go on whirling through space, breathing our air, and walking in the forests that we have planted and saved for them. We are the gardeners of Eden, you and I.

Basic demographic processes

FERTILITY

Fertility refers to the rate at which a population gives birth. Don't confuse the terms *fertility* and *fecundity,* please. A woman's fecundity is her capacity to bear children. Female fecundity extends from about age 14 to almost 50, though adolescents and women past the age of 40 have relatively low fecundity.[1] We know little about the reproductive span of males, apart from the fact that at about age 40 the production of active sperm apparently declines.

Fertility refers to the rates of *actual* childbearing in a population. The simplest measure of fertility in a population is the crude birthrate, the number of births per year per 1000 people. In general, the poorest nations have the highest fertility rates, for reasons that we will discuss later in the chapter.

Imagine a population in which women marry at the age of 20 and bear as many children as they can. How many children do you suppose the average woman would have in such a society? You have probably seen photographs of families with 16 or 17 children lined up, like stair steps, with a beaming Ma and Pa standing in the rear. Such families would be unusual in our imaginary population. The average woman (fortunately, I think!) does not have that degree of fecundity. The most fertile population I know of is the Hutterites of Canada and the western United States. Among married Hutterite women 45 to 54 years of age, the average number of children born was 10.6 in 1953,[2] as compared to about 2.6 for a similar group of Canadian women in the general population.

Populations differ greatly in fertility. What factors determine the number of babies that will be born in a society in a given year? Kingsley Davis and Judith Blake have listed 11 different variables that determine fertility. Any other factor that you can think of will have its effect through one or more of these mechanisms. They are as follows:

1 *Age of entry into sexual unions.* Societies differ markedly in the average age of marriage. In Western societies a couple is supposed to marry only when the husband is able to support a wife and family. In many parts of Asia, on the other hand, marriages take place very early, since matches are arranged by the family and couples do not have to be self-supporting.

2 *Permanent celibacy.* Societies with a late marriage age have a high percentage of permanent celibates (unmarried people). Ireland is an extreme case: about one-quarter of all the middle-aged people there have never married.

3 *Part of reproductive life spent after or between unions.* A certain percentage of widowed and divorced people never remarry. Periods of legal and informal separation between marital unions vary in length. In some societies they may be quite long, and this reduces the number of babies born.

4 *Voluntary abstinence.* Almost all societies discourage lovemaking during late pregnancy and just after a child is born. This norm doesn't affect fertility because almost all women have low fecundity for a while after childbearing. However, use of the "rhythm method"—that is, abstinence at the time of ovulation (generally around the midpoint of the menstrual cycle) will reduce fertility rates.

5 *Involuntary abstinence.* In some societies, men's jobs require them to be away from their wives for long periods. This pattern can affect fertility rates.

6 *Frequency of intercourse.* It is possible that diet, temperature, humidity, and certain diseases may affect the average frequency of sexual intercourse in different populations. However, we don't know much about this topic.

7 *Involuntary causes of fecundity or infecundity.* Gonorrhea is an important source of infecundity throughout the world. High altitude and extreme hunger are other factors that limit fecundity.[3]

8 *Use or nonuse of contraception.* One of the most popular forms of contraception in the world is the latex condom. In North America, a pill taken orally is the most commonly used contraceptive. Contraception is the first factor that occurred to me when I thought about this list of factors. But obviously it is not the only variable affecting birthrates. Most preindustrial societies don't have the technology of contraception, yet it is unlikely that the average woman in any society reproduces to the limit of her fecundity. Various social norms have the effect of limiting births.

9 *Voluntary causes of fecundity or infecundity.* Simple operations such as salpingectomy for females and vasectomy for males provide permanent freedom from further parenthood without affecting sexual pleasure or chang-

Al Kaplan/DPI

Fertility has been declining in Western societies for several years. Raising children has become a matter of choice for both husband and wife; thus the babies that are born are usually planned for and wanted.

ing personality. Vasectomy is the simpler of the two operations, and if a reliable method can be found to reverse its effects it may become the most widely used method of birth control.

Prolonged breast feeding also limits fertility. It is estimated that the period of sterility following the birth of a child averages 13 months in a population that engages in prolonged breast feeding but only 4 months in a population with no breast feeding.[4]

10 *Fetal mortality from involuntary causes.* On the average, about 20 percent of all known pregnancies abort themselves.[5]

11 *Fetal mortality from voluntary causes.* Induced abortion is one of the most widely used means of birth control. Primitive and hazardous methods of abortion have been practiced throughout human history. Modern surgical methods make induced abortion a very safe operation when it is done early. However, abortion is illegal in many countries, so many abortions are done using unsafe methods that are very dangerous to women.

MORTALITY

Mortality refers to the rate at which a population dies. The most common measure of mortality is the **crude death rate**; this uses a midyear population estimate to determine the number of deaths per year per 1000 people. It is probably more useful, however, to compare populations according to their *life expectancy* figures. This life expectancy rate records the number of years that babies born in a given year can expect to live, on the average, assuming that current death rates continue to prevail throughout their lifetimes. This assumption seldom proves accurate, and predicted life expectancy rates are far from precise; however, they do roughly indicate a population's ability to sustain the lives of its members.

Life expectancy rates vary from country to country, and change over time as crude death rates increase or decrease. In undeveloped countries, life expectancies are very short. In several African nations, children born today can be expected to live for an average of only 35 years, while in Burma, Cambodia, and India life expectancy is about 45 years. The developed nations have much longer life expectancies. Canadian males born in 1971 could be expected to live for an average of 69.3 years, and females for 76.4 years. Even in Canada, however, infant mortality is a substantial factor in life expectancy. One-year-old babies can expect to live longer than newborn infants. A Canadian male of age 20 can expect to live 51.7 more years, and a female can expect 58.2 more years.

Life expectancy has markedly increased in all developed countries since the late eighteenth century. This has largely been due to declines in mortality among infants and youth. The diseases of older people, such as cancer and heart disease, are not yet curable; as a result, mortality rates in developed countries have stabilized somewhat since about 1955. In less-developed nations, malnutrition and inadequate medical services are large factors in high mortality rates.

Most people in industrialized societies are not very familiar with death, except among the very old. This may be the reason for the weakening of our mourning rituals. In former days, people followed strict rules of etiquette when confronted by bereavement. Today, however, neither the bereaved nor their friends know quite how to act toward one another. People commonly react to death by trying to deny its existence. The lack of mourning rituals, along with an attempt to act as if death has not occurred, may act to retard a bereaved person's emotional healing and to prolong emotional upset.[6]

MIGRATION

Migration is the movement of people into or out of an area. Canadian migration roughly equals that of the American population, which has always been regarded as exceptionally mobile. According to the 1971 census, about 47 percent of Canadians over five years of age had moved in the past five years. Those who had moved could be almost equally divided into migrants and non-migrants; that is, about 24 percent of Canadians had moved across a municipal boundary, while another 24 percent had only moved from one house to another in the same municipality. Most of the migrants were "internal migrants;" that is, they moved around inside Canada.[7] The census did not count the number of people who left Canada. "Emigrants" were presumably listed in the census data of another nation as "immigrants;" we have no way to measure how many people emigrate annually.

Within Canada, there are certain provincial differences in migration patterns. Saskatchewan's citizens have the highest rate of migration, and mobility in the other western provinces is also above the national average. Except for Newfoundland, all maritime provinces are below average in their mobility. Maritimers are more likely to move to Ontario than to any other area, although recently Alberta has been attracting many maritime migrants as well.[8]

Mobility is strongly related to one's age, marital status, education, and occupation. Movers are frequently young adults leaving home to attend school, to find a job, or to marry; the most mobile Canadians are between the ages of 20 and 34. Canadians with more education are more likely to move than, say, those with less than grade 9 schooling. Single people move more than married

Moving disrupts emotional and social life, but it has become a way of life for many Canadians.

Tana Hoban/DPI

people. Students move more than nonstudents. Those who do not belong to a labor union move more than union members. People at both ends of the occupational ladder are quite likely to move; professionals and managerial personnel often move to preferred locations, while unskilled workers frequently move to pursue seasonal employment.

There are two periods when Canada has gained substantial numbers of new immigrants; the first is between 1900 and 1930, and

FIGURE 17.1

Destinations of European emigrants, 1956-1970

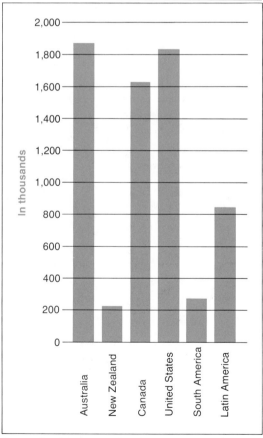

Source: Data based on statistics of receiving countries. Courtesy of the Population Reference Bureau, Inc., Washington, D.C.

the second is since World War II. Early immigrants to Canada were primarily from Britain and the United States. Later, other groups rivalled this predominance. Immediately after World War II, Italians and Germans arrived in Canada in large numbers. During the 1960s there was a large wave of immigration from Hong Kong. In the 1970s, a substantial percentage of immigrants came from Jamaica, India, the Phillipines, and Trinidad. Despite this recent trend, in the 1971 census, Asians and other non-European immigrants still constituted less than 10 percent of the total foreign-born population.

Eventually, however, Canada's ethnic composition will be significantly altered. Immigration is sure to affect Canada's French-English linguistic balance. If more immigrants continue to choose English rather than French as their working language, Quebec's francophone population will drop from 81 percent in 1971 to 70 percent by 2001.[9] In order to prevent this decline, the Quebec government has instituted strong new language laws to persuade new immigrants to become francophones.

Population composition

THE SEX RATIO

The sex ratio of a population is defined as the number of males per 100 females. Thus a sex ratio of 100 represents a population in which there are equal numbers of males and females. A ratio of more than 100 means more males, under 100, more females. The North American sex ratio is about 95, which means that there are 95 men for every 100 women. This is because of the higher death rate of males, especially older males.

A nation's sex ratio may be very unbalanced after a war. Perhaps the most unbalanced sex ratio occurred in the Soviet Union after World War II, when about one-third of the males had been killed. This means that millions of Soviet women have never married.

POPULATION PYRAMIDS

The age-sex composition of a population at a given time can be illustrated by a **population pyramid**. This diagram shows the percentages of males in each age category of the population on the left side of a vertical line, and the percentages of females in the same age cate-gories on the right side of the line. Figure 17.2 shows the age-sex pyramids of Mexico, the United States, and Sweden in 1970. The shape of the pyramid is greatly affected by fertility trends. Mexico and most other developing countries have had high fertility rates during recent years, as the wide base of the pyramid shows. Children are a large part of the Mexi-can population. Sweden, on the other hand, has had a low fertility rate for many years. The sides of its pyramid are almost vertical up

FIGURE 17.2

Population pyramids of Mexico, United States, and Sweden, 1970

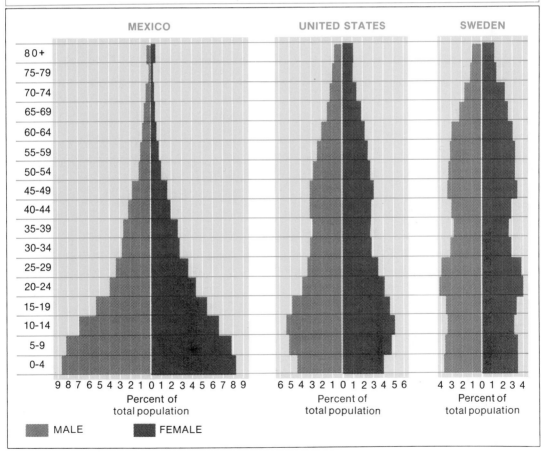

Source: From R. Freedman and B. Berelson, "The Human Population," *Scientific American*, September 1974, pp. 38-39. Copyright © 1974 by Scientific American, Inc., All rights reserved.

to the age of 60, when mortality begins to reduce the number of old people. The United States is in between these extremes. It had a somewhat higher fertility rate than Sweden for several years until the late 1960s, but its fertility never approached the high levels found in Mexico today. Look at the bulge in the U.S. pyramid below the age of 25. This represents the "baby boom" of the 1940s and 1950s, which affected the United States, Canada, Australia, and New Zealand. The nations of Western Europe had a "mini-baby boom" compared to these four nations. As the baby boom citizens grow older, and if fertility levels remain as low as they are now, the pyramids of future years will show the bulge moving higher and higher in the pyramid.

Population pyramids can be used to show how various groups differ from the general population. In Figure 17.3, for example, the wide base of the Hutterite pyramid, compared to the more vertical pyramid of the general Canadian population, shows that the Hutterites have a much higher fertility rate than the rest of the Canadian population.

THE DEPENDENCY RATIO

The dependency ratio is the ratio of people in dependent age groups (both young and old) to people in economically productive age groups (between 15 and 64). Obviously, children and very old people cannot work as hard as young and middle-aged adults—indeed, they must be supported almost entirely by others. Dependency may differ, of course, from one individual to another and from one social community to another. Farm children often contribute a good deal by looking after animals, gathering eggs, planting and weeding the garden, and so on. And, in all societies, some old people stay fit and active longer than others. I used to have my car repaired in a shop run by an 85-year-old woman in greasy overalls who poked the young mechanics with her cane if she wanted them to move faster.

The dependency ratio is related to the median age of the population, which is that age that divides any population into equal groups, half older, half younger. In 1881 the median age of the Canadian population was 20. In 1976 it was 28. Obviously, the dependency ratio was higher in 1881 than it is now. Look at Figure 17.2 again. It is clear that Mexico's wage earners have more dependents to support than Sweden's. The Mexican dependency ratio is high because of the high fertility rate in that country. This makes it hard for many Mexicans to save surplus cash to invest in industry or agriculture.

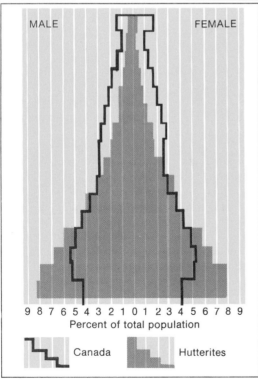

FIGURE 17.3

Age and sex composition, Canadian Hutterites and Canadians in general, 1971

Percent of total population

Canada   Hutterites

Source: Statistics Canada, 1971. Census of Canada, Bulletin 14, Vol. 4.

Population trends

THE POPULATION EXPLOSION

A million years ago there may have been 125,000 human beings on earth.[10] Today there are 4 billion. The rate of increase has grown steadily. By 8000 B.C. there were perhaps 5 million people on the earth; by 4000 B.C., maybe 85 million; by the time of Christ, perhaps 300 million;[11] by A.D. 1650, about 545 million. Then the growth rate really took off: By 1970 it was 19 per year per 1000 people. That is, if a group had 1000 members on January 1, it would have 1019 by the end of the year.

Scary? Absolutely terrifying. In 1973 the United Nations estimated that, by the year 2000, the earth's population would be 6.4 billion if that growth rate continued. This means that, at the 1973 rate, the world's population would double in 35 years. In less than 700 years there would be one square foot of earth's surface for every human being. In 1200 years the human population would outweigh the earth.[12]

But there's good news. It appears that 1970 was the peak growth year and that we may now be on the downhill side of the curve. In 1977, for the first time since data have been collected, the world's population growth rate began to decline—from 19 to 17 per 1000. But don't relax and sigh with relief yet. Compare that figure to the growth rate for the period just before the Industrial Revolution—.56 per 1000. The decline to 17 per 1000 means that, instead of doubling every 35 years, the world's population will take 41 years to double (which is a less frightening prospect but certainly nothing to celebrate).

The population explosion has not been the same everywhere. The tropical nations of Latin America have the highest rates of increase; Africa's growth has also been high. The growth rates of Canada, the United States, Japan, the Soviet Union, and Europe have all been below the world average for a number of years. The birthrates—not the growth rates—of the less developed countries averaged about 42 per 1000 in 1970. By 1977 they had dropped to 36 per 1000. The drop was greatest in South Korea, China, and Thailand. Less dramatic declines in birth rates occurred in Brazil, Egypt, India, the Philippines, and Turkey. However, some countries, including Mexico, Bangladesh, and Nigeria, showed little or no decline in their birthrates. So we may conclude that growth rates have probably peaked and are now declining because of widespread, but not universal, declines in fertility in the less developed countries.

But will the growth rate be reduced before it exceeds the rate of increase in the means of subsistence? If not, then the death rate will rise. Like the bumper sticker that reads "Cancer cures smoking," we could say, "Death cures surplus population." But we don't want to cure the population problem by starving the surplus. In fact there is a complex relationship between fertility rates and mortality rates, and we need to spend some time examining this connection. It was first discussed by Thomas R. Malthus.

MALTHUSIAN THEORY

Malthus (1766-1834), an English economist and clergyman, published his first essay on population in 1798. He developed this theory further in six revisions of the essay—the last one published posthumously in 1872. Malthus was detested by theologians and later by Marxists, but his contributions were great. Both Darwin's theory of evolution and Keynes's theory of economics were based on ideas derived from Malthus, and his influence on demography was enormous.

Many people disliked the pessimistic conclusion of Malthus's first essay. In it he suggested that it would be impossible to avoid a rise in mortality. This is how he reasoned.

Malthus noted that the means of subsistence (e.g., wheat) grows only at an *arithmetic* rate. That is, at best it increases by a fixed amount each year. A wheat farmer might, for example, produce 100 extra bushels per year every year. This could be represented on a graph by a straight line angling upward—a steady rate of growth. But populations, if unchecked, grow at a *geometric* rate, like compound interest. You add interest to your bank account and earn interest on it too, as well as on the principal. You add new babies to the population and they become parents too, adding even more children. So a population might double every generation, as is happening today. This could be represented by an upward-sloping curve. (An example is the story of the boy who is hired by a king on the following terms: On the first day he will be paid one grain of rice. Every day he will be paid twice as many grains of rice as on the day before. The king is pleased to hire such cheap labor—for a week or so. Then he realizes that the boy will soon own all the rice in the kingdom. So they talk business again and the boy gets the king's daughter instead. Moral: It pays to know about geometric growth rates.)

What Malthus was pointing out is that a geometric rate of growth will obviously tend to exceed an arithmetic rate of growth. There would always tend to be more babies produced each year than food to support them. But of course fertility can't outrun mortality for long. For a while the population may increase faster than the means of subsistence. What will happen then? There are three possibilities, all of which will raise the death rate: hunger, disease, and war. Malthus called these "positive checks." They operate to reduce the population to a level that can be supported by the available means of subsistence.

Malthus assumed that human beings are driven by sexual needs and that they will always tend to reproduce almost to the limit of their fecundity. In the early versions of his theory, he argued that human fertility would

stay high under all conditions. Only an increase in mortality could check the growth of population. People couldn't be expected to stop having babies or even to slow down! If the food supply increased, the result would simply be more babies surviving, so that food would become scarce again. There's no way to get ahead. Populations will always increase right up to the limit of their resources. This is a gloomy conclusion.

Eventually Malthus changed his mind a little. In his later writings, he expressed the hope that people could avoid hunger, disease, and war by limiting the birthrate instead. Instead of "positive checks" (factors that increase mortality) maybe populations could be limited by "preventive checks"—factors that decrease fertility. He considered birth control or any other way of limiting births within marriage to be immoral. However, he believed late marriage was the best way to reduce the birthrate.[13]

Since Malthus's day humankind has been luckier than he expected. The "positive checks" have not increased. On the contrary, death rates are lower throughout the world than they were in Malthus's time, chiefly because the means of subsistence increased far more than he could have foreseen. Agriculture has increased its efficiency many times over. A second factor, birth control, is also important. Contraception has become a common means of population control.

Then was Malthus wrong? So far, yes. But within our lifetimes he may be proved correct. The worldwide death rate will soon increase unless the means of subsistence can be increased at the same rate as the population. A rise in mortality can be avoided only through a sizable reduction in the birthrate, a large increase in the means of subsistence, or some combination of the two.

THE DEMOGRAPHIC-TRANSITION MODEL

Malthus, who lived nearly 200 years ago, was not aware of the declines in the fertility rate that were to come in this century. Modern demographers, who can look back upon these dramatic changes, have built a general model known as **demographic-transition**. This model is used to describe the process by which preindustrial societies with high rates of fertility and mortality are transformed into modern societies with low rates of fertility and mortality. Let's look at the historical developments on which the model is based.

Until about 300 years ago, the world's birth and death rates were high and usually nearly equal. Of course this is not to say that in any given year the birth and death rates would be exactly equal; death rates in particular tended to vary greatly from year to year. In years when the food supply was adequate, population growth, at least in agricultural societies, was around 5 or 10 per 1000. Death rates tended to be very high in years of scarcity. Food shortages sometimes caused death by actual starvation, but they also caused malnutrition and undernourishment, which permitted the spread of disease. One of the most famous epidemics in human history was the Black Death, which occurred in Europe between 1347 and 1352 and killed nearly one-third of the population.

The Industrial Revolution caused a large reduction in peacetime mortality throughout the world. In Europe, mortality rates decreased slowly in the eighteenth century as available food increased. During the nineteenth century, mortality decreased much more rapidly, probably because of the following factors: (1) better nutrition; (2) improvements in sanitation, especially in cities, because of improved water supply and sewage systems; (3) prevention of disease through inoculation; and (4) advances in the cure of infectious diseases, especially later, after the discovery of antibiotics. Death rates remained high in the less developed countries, however, until the end of World War II, when they dropped rapidly and thus created the huge growth in world population.

Seeing the effects of the Industrial Revolution in the West, demographers believed that economic development would lead to lower mortality and fertility rates in *any* country. This, they said, would occur in four phases. In phase 1, the preindustrial stage, birth and death rates are both high. Because the birthrate is about equal to the death rate, there is little or no growth in population. In phase 2, as industrialization begins, the death rate begins to decline much faster than the birthrate, so that the population grows rapidly. In phase 3, the birthrate declines more rapidly than the death rate and the population increases much more slowly than in the second stage. Finally, in phase 4, both birth and death rates stabilize at a low (and again about equal) level, so that population growth is small or even negative. (See Figure 17.4.)

The demographic-transition model explains why mortality declined in the West: Industrialization, economic development, and urbanization improved the standard of living. However, it does not account for the decline of fertility. Demographers more or less assumed that the birthrate would decline and that it would stay down, but they did not specify how industrialization, economic development, and urbanization would limit the birthrate.

Before World War II, when the mortality and the fertility rates of all industrialized nations had dropped and their populations were not growing at all, demographers assumed that these societies were in the fourth and final stage of demographic transition. After the war, however, demographers were astonished to find the birthrates in North America actually rising to levels that were higher than their prewar levels. Furthermore, new historical evidence from other societies has contradicted the model by showing a direct rather than an inverse relationship between economic development and fertility trends. Birthrates in England, for example, may well have increased during industrialization instead of decreasing. So the relationship between industrialization and fertility is more complex than the demographic-transition model would lead us to believe.

FIGURE 17.4
Demographic-transition model

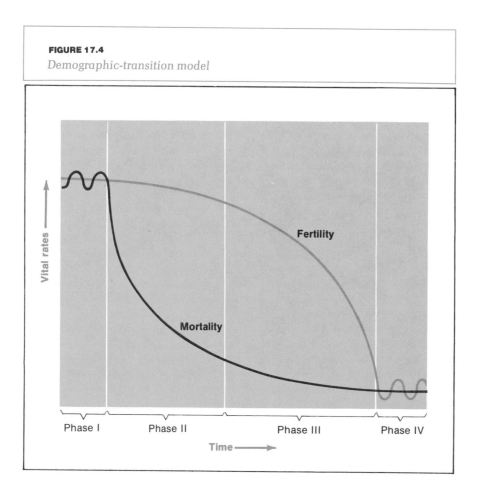

For one thing, we may need to distinguish between the immediate, direct effects of economic development and its long-term, indirect effects. These effects may contradict one another. Probably the immediate effect is to *increase* fertility. People can afford more babies, so they have them. Simple enough. But, in the long run, the effect of economic development has been to *decrease* fertility. Why? The demand for an educated labor force increases, so people have to spend more to educate each child. Hence, they can afford to educate fewer children than before. Economic development has encouraged the development of social-insurance systems (old-age pensions, unemployment and welfare payments, and so on), so people don't need to have children to look after them in their illness or old age. There are many other indirect effects of economic development that tend to decrease fertility. We'll return to them later.

In a developed economy, fertility may fluctuate widely, as the baby boom shows. Still, the demographic-transition model is probably a fairly accurate description of the long-term relationship between mortality and fertility. In the long run, after mortality declines, fertility will also drop. Unfortunately, the decrease in fertility may be delayed so long that the population expands greatly in the meantime.

FIGURE 17.5
Births, deaths, and natural increase in Canada 1951-74

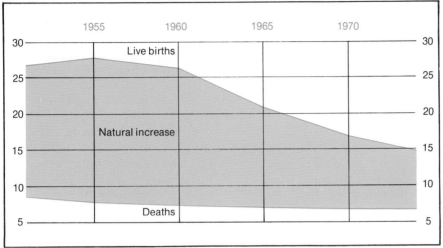

Source: Canada Year Book, 1976-77, p. 172.

ZERO POPULATION GROWTH

Throughout most of world history, the population grew very slowly. Average fertility and mortality rates remained at about the same high level. Eventually the population must again stop growing; we hope that this will happen because both fertility and mortality will be at about the same *low* level.

How can we achieve this low balance? First of all, each married woman must produce only enough children to replace herself and her husband; that is, she must give birth to an average of just over two children, depending on prevailing death rates. However, if there has been a recent baby boom, even this low fertility rate will produce an increase in population for many years. The "baby boom kids" will live for a long time after they have reproduced. During the period in which they *and* their children are both alive, the population may be approximately doubled. These "baby boom kids" must reach their sixties before death rates become as high as birth rates.

When death rates and birth rates stay equal, the population will have reached a state of stable equilibrium, in which there is no increase in population. This condition is called **zero population growth (ZPG)**. Of course, if the fertility rate were to decline *below* replacement levels, we would reach ZPG sooner; this would happen, for instance, if the average woman produced only one child, not two. The fertility rate is unlikely to drop so dramatically, however. The populations of most industrial nations will probably continue to grow for many years to come.

The decision to have a child

As mentioned earlier, the demographic-transition model is still useful as a general guide. But it has been modified to include several other factors besides economic development. Here we'll take a brief look at those factors. What factors influence the decision to have a child? Many reasons might come up, but social scientists, having tidy minds, like to organize those reasons into categories. (I can imagine a couple of married sociologists taking a checklist to bed and interviewing each other about their desire to have a baby.) Joseph Spengler's checklist is a good one.[14] Spengler believes that the decision to have a baby is a function of three variables: (1) the couple's preference system, (2) its price system, and (3) its resources.

The couple's *preference system* consists of the value it places on having the child—relative to other goals. ("Which do you prefer, a new car or another baby, honey?") The *price system* is simply the cost of the additional child—not only financial costs but time and effort as well—relative to other goals. *Resources* consist of the money, time, and energy the couple has available for all of its goals.

Spengler's theory assumes that the probability of deciding to have another child will vary *directly* with the preference system. (The more you like children, compared to other things, the more likely you are to choose to have one.) It will vary *inversely* with the predicted price. (The more expensive children are to have and maintain, the fewer children people will choose to have.) Finally, the decision will vary *directly* with the amount of available resources. (The more money, time, and energy you have, the more likely you are to have a baby, if you're at all interested in having one.)

This simple theory is very helpful in clarifying the patterns of fertility in developed countries. The resources of developed nations in terms of both money and time have increased greatly over the past few centuries. According to the theory, this should have led to an increase in their birthrates. In fact, birthrates have declined in developed nations. Changes in the price and preference systems have counteracted the effects of increased resources. There was a period when birthrates *did* increase—the baby boom of the 1940s and 1950s. Income was rising fast then, so fast that it seems to have more than offset the effects of changes in the preference and price systems.

Let's look at a few major factors that have influenced the price system and the preference system over the past century. These have all tended to reduce the desired family size in Western societies during that period. Changes in the preference system include mortality rates, child labor laws, old-age support, rewards from society, and consumption patterns. Changes in the price system result from contraception, urbanization, the value of labor, and extended education.

CHANGES IN THE PREFERENCE SYSTEM

Mortality

The most important reason for high birthrates is high mortality. People have extra babies only when they need them as insurance against the probable death of one or more of their other children. But mortality has declined in recent years, especially among infants and children. More children survive. Hence, fewer children need to be born for the parents to be reasonably sure that some will grow up.

Child labor

Farm children are economic assets—by the age of ten they can earn their own keep. During the nineteenth century, the supply of land per person declined, so that each additional child was less of an asset than before. Also, child labor was never very effective in factories. As new laws limited the employment of children in industry, the economic value of children to their parents declined. At the same time, compulsory-education laws were introduced. Since schooling is an added expense to parents, children became costly. They were no longer economic assets.

Support in old age

In Western societies, until a few years ago, the only old-age support for parents was derived from their own kin—mostly their sons. This is still true in the Third World. In most societies the poor consider children an absolute necessity. How else will they survive when they are too old or disabled to work? You and I have social security and retirement benefits. We don't need to depend on our children for support, so the value of a child is relatively lower for us than the values of other things that we may choose to spend our money on.

Rewards from society

When mortality was high, a good citizen felt that it was his or her duty to produce a large family. Otherwise, the population might decline. Both the church and government encouraged high fertility rates. Today we have the opposite problem, so that most governments and religions now discourage couples from having large families.

Conspicuous consumption

It is sometimes argued that we need status symbols more than our grandparents and great-grandparents did because our status is achieved and theirs was largely ascribed. If one's status is fixed, unchanging, limited by birth, one does not need to advertise it. It just *is*. But if our status is achieved, we are more likely to show it off. And to do this we have to buy things that we don't really need. If we want lots of status symbols (jewelry, fancy cars, and so on), we have to give up something else, namely, babies. So, at least according to this theory, fertility declines as showy display of wealth increases. (Actually, I don't believe this theory.)

CHANGES IN THE PRICE SYSTEM

Contraception

When birth control methods are crude, the decision *not* to have a child is a costly one. People have to pay a high price in terms

Family-planning clinics around the world are offering the technology of contraception. No Third World nation's birthrates have dropped without such programs.

of inconvenience, interference with sexual pleasure, and the dangers of primitive abortion methods. Thus, the introduction of cheap, effective, convenient methods of contraception raises the price of having a child and lowers the price of *not* having one. Everything else being equal, fertility will decline as a result.

Urbanization

City space is expensive. Hence, it is more expensive to raise children in the city than to raise them in the country. Urbanization therefore tends to cause a decline in fertility. On the other hand, the growth of American suburbs after World War II made living space cheaper. Freeways and subsidized mortgages made suburban living possible, and that, in turn, may have stimulated the baby boom.

The value of labor

Increasing industrial productivity means that an average man or woman can produce more things in an hour of work than before and can therefore earn more money. On the other hand, child care is no more productive than before. For example, it still takes 2 minutes to change a diaper and 20 minutes to read a fairy tale aloud. In fact, child care probably takes *more* time than it used to. This increased effort has to be weighed against a wife's increase in income if she takes a job instead of having another child. As her pay increases, the cost of giving up the job to have a child increases.

Extended education

Children need more education today than before because they will have to perform more complex jobs. This is expensive. Whether the state pays or the family pays, it is always more costly for parents if only because of the child's longer period of dependency. Hence, increasing levels of education help reduce family size.

Ecological aspects of human survival

The world is a single ecological system. DDT or mercury dumped into the Great Lakes may eventually kill birds in the South Seas or the Mediterranean. Whales killed by the fishermen of one nation are an endangered species for all of us. If the temperature rises enough to melt the polar ice caps, the penguins won't be the only ones to notice. We may exploit one another in the short run, but in the long run nobody comes out ahead. It's our own nest that we foul, our own resources that we deplete. What are those resources?

LAND

Figure 17.6 shows the distribution of the world's population. Obviously, this distribution is determined largely by the geographic characteristics of different areas—particularly the availability of land for farming. About 70 percent of the land on earth is unusable. Today crops are being produced on only 10 percent. That leaves 20 percent for further use—at most. Actually, using all of the land would create havoc because it would mean cutting down all the forests. But we could probably increase our total of farmland by about 50 percent without endangering the ecology. This would mean an increase from 1400 million hectares to about 2100 million hectares. (A hectare is about 2½ acres.) The United Nations has stated that a reasonable goal is to open up 6 or 7 million hectares of land for farming by 1985. This would certainly solve the food crisis and could be done with a small fraction of the amount of money now spend on weapons. Much of this new land would be in Africa and Latin America, but some is available in southeast Asia as well.[15]

FIGURE 17.6

World population density

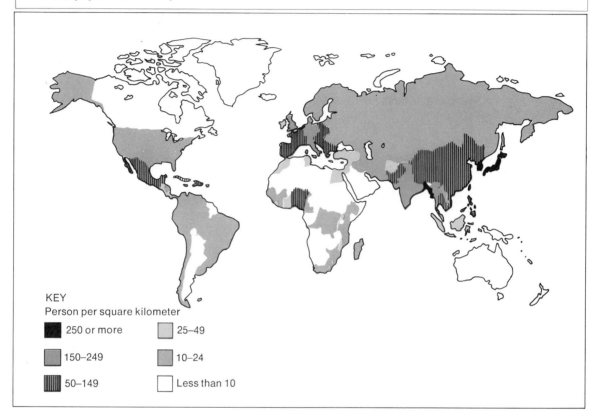

KEY
Person per square kilometer

- 250 or more
- 150–249
- 50–149
- 25–49
- 10–24
- Less than 10

WATER

Water is vital to the further development of agriculture. Many new, high-yielding varieties of wheat and rice require much more water than older varieties. In addition, an ample water supply would permit several crops a year in warm climates, rather than the single crop that is possible when the year is sharply divided into rainy and dry seasons.

Desalinization of water is done in several areas, but, because the process is costly, desalinized water is used only for drinking. Industry competes with agriculture for the use of limited water supplies. However, if pollutants could be removed, much of the water used for industrial purposes could be reused for other purposes. The most promising source of additional water may be tubewells. Only about one-sixteenth of the farm land in poor nations is irrigated properly. With additional irrigation systems and improvement of existing ones, the crop yield of much existing farm land could *double,* even without any other input such as fertilizer. This alone might solve the food problem for many years. There's enough underground water in most places to make tubewell drilling and pumping a realistic goal; this is a better solution than building enormous dams that can turn out to be failures.[16] On the other hand, large pumps may provide greater amounts of water in the short run but use up the groundwater in the long run. Providing water in dry areas will become more and more expensive as this happens.

ENERGY AND MINERALS

The demand for energy and minerals will be increased not only by population growth but also by economic development. The world's population is now doubling about every 41 years. But the world's consumption of energy is doubling about every 12 years. Use of iron ore is doubling every 11 years.[17]

We know that the supply of energy from fossil fuels is going to be used up soon, but the big question is how soon. The industrialized nations have counted too heavily upon the use of nuclear fission as a replacement for petroleum. Now that the dangers of nuclear energy are more fully appreciated, we must anticipate a grave period of fuel shortage and political crisis. Even without the danger of nuclear accidents, nuclear energy must become increasingly expensive as the world

exhausts its supply of Uranium 235. There are alternatives to nuclear energy, but organizing political support for them may be difficult. Nations have made huge investments in the future of atomic energy; Canada, for example, is eager to sell its CANDU reactor.

If governments can be persuaded to invest in them, however, such devices as the solar cell could provide infinitely renewable energy. Giant windmills could be built. Geothermal energy from the deep layers of the earth could be tapped. Power could be generated from ocean currents, such as the tides in the Bay of Fundy. Non-polluting coal systems could be produced economically. The heat differential between deep and shallow ocean waters could be used to generate power. The gas produced in sewers could be recaptured and burned.

There is no real lack of resources; the lack is in our readiness to re-organize our political and economic system to meet the challenges they pose. Human beings must learn to use energy and raw materials more efficiently. We must commit ourselves to the protection of this fragile planet and find ways to produce abundance for all without further damage to the earth.

SOCIAL RESEARCH:
Sociologists at Work

WORLD FOOD SUPPLY

In this section we will look in more detail at the problem of hunger. Our discussion will be based largely on two important books: *How the Other Half Dies,* by Susan George,[18] and *Food First: Beyond the Myth of Scarcity,* by Frances Moore Lappe and Joseph Collins.[19] We will be especially concerned with the relationship between mortality and fertility. This is the relationship that Malthus sought to explain. Unfortunately, his theory led us astray. He

believed that populations always reproduce almost up to capacity and only mortality keeps the population from expanding indefinitely. Not so. It is more nearly correct to say that *mortality determines fertility.* That is, people have extra babies when death rates from hunger are high.

This may not make sense to you. You might advise very poor people to have *fewer* children so that there will be fewer mouths to feed and more chance for their existing children to survive. The little food they do have will go further if they have smaller families. Right?

Well, look at it from a different point of view. Suppose you are a mother in Bangladesh, serving rice to your hungry children. There is not enough to satisfy them. They are sick. You know most of them will die—maybe all of them. But you *must* have a son who will survive and contribute to the family income, especially as you grow old. What will you do?

Most poor people in this situation will have another baby. These kids are dying, they say, so let's keep trying and hope that, eventually, some of them will survive. *This* is how the rate of mortality influences the rate of fertility. Malthus was wrong. It's not that fertility is unavoidably high and that only mortality (from hunger, disease, or war) keeps the population from increasing to an unmanageable size. Rather, mortality varies and people adjust their fertility in response to it.

The mother in Bangladesh faces a vicious circle. The more children she has, the greater the odds against the survival of any one of them; the greater the odds against survival, the more children are needed just to break even. But there's a good side to vicious circles: Whenever you manage to influence one variable, this indirectly affects the other variable as well. In this case we have two choices. We can try to reduce fertility so as to prevent starvation in the long run, or we can prevent people from starving, which will eventually reduce their fertility rates. Or, better still, we can work on both fronts at once, by increasing the means of subsistence and also promoting family planning programs. I vote for the dual approach.

The countries that are solving their growth problems are the ones that are eliminating hunger and, at the same time, emphasizing family planning and distributing contraceptives and birth control information as widely as possible. Almost nowhere has a nation's growth rate declined without a birth control program. On the other hand, no birth control program has been successful unless the hunger problem has also been confronted. It seems that you can't convince people to stop having babies until they see that there's plenty of food for the ones they already have. So let's focus on the hunger problem.

In estimating how well-fed a population is, we might ask: What is the average amount of food eaten per capita? But per-capita figures can be misleading. Suppose that, in one society, half the population eats 1000 calories a day and the other half 3000 calories. In another society almost everyone may eat the same amount of food—2000 calories per day. The per-capita figures for the two societies would be the same, but the deprivation and misery suffered by their populations would differ dramatically. Hence, *equality of distribution* is more important than almost any other economic factor. We are talking not simply about the *amount* of food within a society but about how fairly it is *distributed.* Both factors together determine the amount of hunger and, thus, the likely rate of population growth.

The hunger problem is largely a distribution problem. The world produces about 3000 calories of grain per person per day, not to mention fruits, vegetables, and other foodstuffs. This means that there should be more than enough for everybody. Where does it all go?

Some of it is fed to livestock to produce meat that only the rich can afford to eat. Some of that meat is also fed to pets, not people. Meat eating is a wasteful form of consumption. Think of all the grain a steer ate in order to become a filet mignon for you and a piece of leftover hamburger for your dog.

Some of it is made into expensive, nonnutritious products such as soft drinks or chocolate-flavored breakfast cereals shaped like hearts and flowers. Or baby formula. God knows how many babies in less developed countries have died because saleswomen have talked their mothers into weaning them from the breast and feeding them with powdered formula that they couldn't afford and didn't have the sanitary facilities to mix up anyway. Their own breast milk was fine.[20]

Some of the food is simply stacked up in piles, to be eaten by mice or eventually dumped because it wasn't available where and when it was needed. Poor people usually can't afford food even if it is there. The warehouses may be bulging with rice, but the hungry people outside may not have the money to buy it.

Any country on earth could feed its own population if the proper political and economic arrangements were made. So why don't the less developed countries do what is necessary to feed their people? *They can't.* They don't have control over their own economies. For example, most nations depend on the production of cash crops for export. If held by local people, their vast plantations could feed the population nicely. Instead, they produce coffee, cocoa, jute, sugar, rubber, cotton, bananas, and so forth for export. They are managed or indirectly controlled by giant multinational corporations with names that appear as famous brands on jars in your pantry.

Moreover, international food distribution is beyond the forces of supply and demand. The world's

Most of the food exported from North America goes, not to underdeveloped countries where populations are undernourished, but to rich countries.

food supply is manipulated by a group of big corporations known as *agribusiness.* These giant firms can make deals to supply whole nations with grain or beef or coffee, and those deals affect the prices you pay a month later in the supermarket. If this bothers you, imagine how a Brazilian coffee picker might feel about it. In many countries, the entire economy depends on a single export crop. The prices of that crop may be determined not merely by competition, the weather, and other such accidents of fate, but also by the policies of rich governments. The U.S. government, for example, deliberately drove up the worldwide price of food during the Nixon administration in order to fix a balance-of-payments deficit. That involved creating an artificial scarcity for a time, which any government marketing board can do without difficulty. This is not unusual. What I am pointing out is obvious to anyone who listens to the farm report once in a while on the car radio: Farm commodities are produced and traded according to government plans and regulations. Political decisions thus play an important part in the economic system that determines the production and distribution of the world's food. Our governments and our corporations have enormous influence on what gets planted around the world and by whom it gets eaten.

Scarcity is not unavoidable. It is created by people, either on purpose or as an unintended result of other decisions. Almost always, people can create more of whatever is in short supply, given different structural arrangements. Agriculture is especially flexible. Canadian officials have said, for example, that it would be possible to increase food production by 50 percent in five years if necessary.[21] But it will not happen because it is not sufficiently profitable to agribusiness.

Often agribusiness doesn't directly own the land in other countries that produces these commodities. The land is usually held by local elites. In 1960 the United Nations Food and Agriculture

518

organization found that a mere 2.5 percent of landowners with holdings of more than 100 hectares control nearly three-quarters of the earth's agricultural land. *And the top 0.23 percent control over half.* That was in 1960. We don't have up-to-date statistics, but we know that land ownership has become even *more* concentrated since then, not less.[22]

Until recently, I imagined that North America was the world's breadbasket—that our expanding agricultural productivity was the margin of safety by which millions of lives could be saved each year. There is some truth to this picture, of course. Both Canada and the United States export large amounts of food, chiefly wheat, and indeed many nations have rescued their populations in bad years by buying that food. Some of the food has been shipped as part of the foreign-aid program. However, there is another side to the story. Although a lot of food is exported from North America, most of it goes to the industrial countries, not to Third World nations. For example, in 1974 the United States exported 114.5 pounds of wheat per person to Japan but only 7.5 pounds per person to India.[23] Only a small part of food exported was in the form of aid (which involves low-interest, long-term loans to the nations receiving the aid).

Moreover, although the United States and Canada are both major food exporters, they also import large amounts of food. In 1974 the United States ranked third in food imports, and over two-thirds of those imports came from less developed countries.[24] The United States does export beef— but it also imports beef. It buys over 40 percent of all the beef in world trade. This is a large amount of food to the people who are exporting it. More meat is sent from less developed countries to industrial nations than in the other direction.[25] The United States is also the world's leading importer of seafood and is a net importer of milk products.[26]

Who, then, is sending food to whom? The hungriest people on earth may be the ones who are sending us our dinners.

I'm not suggesting that you skip dinner tonight or become a vegetarian or force your dog to become one. Individuals can't redistribute the world's food supply. We have to look for more effective answers.

What about increasing production? If there is a lot of food, then distribution may be less of a problem because even the poor will have a decent

meal if not a gourmet dinner. So how can food production be increased? Several major developments are taking place in this area—and unfortunately, many of them have negative as well as positive effects on the poor nations. The "Green Revolution" is an example.

In the past 20 years or so a number of new strains of grain—mostly wheat and rice—have been developed that can yield several times as much food as strains used in the past. These new strains are virtually miracle seeds. (They are actually called high-yielding varieties, or HYV). Naturally, the governments of the less-developed

Underdeveloped countries often have to sell crops for cash to get foreign currency to pay for their equipment. This puts farm workers out of work, and they have even less chance of buying food than before.

David Plank/DPI

countries have encouraged farmers to plant these new crops. This has made it possible for several crops to be grown in a single year where formerly only one could be produced. In many cases production has soared.

But there's a catch. These seeds don't automatically produce better crops. They also require more inputs than older strains—more water and more fertilizer. Without these added inputs, the yields may be no greater than before. And the ordinary peasant has only very limited water, fertilizer, modern farm machinery, pesticides, and so on. Moreover, little credit is available to peasants. So to pay for the new technology, it is necessary to obtain foreign currency, and in order to do that, farmers have to sell cash crops instead of using the grain to feed their own families. Hence, the Green Revolution has stepped up the rate at which food produced in the Third World is pulled into the worldwide economic market. Instead of making the local people more self-sufficient, it has actually put them more than ever at the mercy of the international economy. Who benefits? Not the poor, but agribusiness. And in the long run the crop payoffs sometimes turn out to be disappointing anyway. For example, many HYVs start out with a spectacular production record but achieve this only by using heavy pesticides. Over a few years, the pests become resistant to the chemicals. Then they can survive repeated sprayings with expensive pesticides that are injurious to other organisms. The farmer loses, and so does the world environment. The chemical manufacturers win, though.

Some less developed nations have borrowed heavily to invest in miracle seeds and in the technology that goes with them. Often this has been a serious mistake. Farm machinery increases the productivity of Western farms but is a very bad investment for most less-developed nations. Tractors and combines are efficient in terms of human labor, but they don't make efficient use of land. They cost a fortune both to buy and to operate. Worst of all is the effect on the poor farm worker whose job is taken over by the machine.

Agriculture in the less developed countries must be labor intensive. That is, output must be improved through the profitable investment of labor, not labor-saving devices. People need jobs, and there aren't enough jobs in industry for those who are displaced by tractors. Moreover, the labor is available now; the capital for tractors isn't. The

Chinese have proved that labor-intensive agriculture works: They have eliminated hunger, flooding, built backyard fertilizer plants, and equalized the distribution of food and other needs of daily life, all without importing expensive equipment. (Even the dams were built by hand.) There is work for everyone, and the population growth rate has declined.

What about foreign aid? The industrial nations have long contributed to Third World nations, both to increase their crop yields and to help them industrialize. How effective has this aid been and how much can it offer in the future?

Foreign aid is partly a myth and partly a failure. In the first place, most of the "aid" is not given outright but is in the form of low-interest loans to friendly governments.[27] The donations often consist of surplus wheat that is sent to poor nations in order to avoid a glut on the North American market. Foreign aid has helped keep Canadian and American food prices high. The friendly governments then sell the food—they don't give it away. Hence, hungry people are not necessarily any better fed because of this aid. And there have been benefits for the North American farmers. For example, sometimes wheat has been sent to areas where people had formerly eaten only rice as part of their ordinary diet. They became accustomed to wheat products, and this generated a market for wheat that has continued since that time. Only now they pay for it at commercial rates.

In the second place, despite their low interest rates, the loans made to poor nations under the aid program have become a major burden for their governments. The collective debt of 86 less-developed countries doubled in five years.[28] These nations must keep on borrowing money just to meet their interest payments. In 1973, almost 40 percent of the aid money received by less-developed countries was spent to repay the interest debt on past loans.[29] Canada and the U.S. do not mean to be loan sharks, but their relationship with many of the countries that they want to help may not be very helpful at all. To raise the money for loan payments, the countries of the Third World must export food instead of producing it for their own people. And we're back where we started from.

I'm not looking for any villains; I don't know any. I do know a lot of well-meaning people who have limited knowledge and make mistakes even though they are doing the best they can. So let's look for new solutions, not villains.

SOCIAL POLICY:
Issues and Viewpoints

How should we respond to the population explosion? I think we should break this question into three areas: fertility, mortality, and migration.

FERTILITY

Throughout history, most laws concerning fertility were designed to increase fertility, not to reduce it. For example, during the reign of Augustus Caesar, fathers were given preference in public office according to the number of children in their family, while mothers of large families had the right to wear special clothes and ornaments. More recent policies with similar goals include programs in which the government pays family allowances. Abortion and contraception have often been outlawed, and tax laws have been designed to encourage parenthood.

Laws that *restrict* fertility are much more recent. Japan was the first nation to pass such laws. After World War II, its territory was greatly reduced and its living standards were cut sharply. Abortion was legalized and the fertility rate fell dramatically.

One of the world's most sucessful contraceptive programs began in 1964 in Taiwan. Private physicians were paid for each IUD they inserted. Other contraceptives were made widely available and encouraged through the mass media. In 1963, the total fertility rate in Taiwan was 5.4, but by 1971 it had declined to 3.7.[30]

While the U.S. government has gradually come to promote family planning and to assist other nations with birth control systems,[31] the Canadian government has not taken any position on this issue. As of now, there is no official Canadian fertility policy, though family planning programs and abortion rates are increasing.

Many government policies affect fertility indirectly. For example, if the number of required years in schooling is raised, then the resulting increase in the cost of child rearing makes parenthood more expensive and lowers the birthrate. By simply informing people of the high cost of child rearing, it is possible to discourage them from

WHO Photo

giving birth: Most people underestimate how much it costs to provide for children. An increase in the jobs available to women gives them other ways of spending their time besides caring for children. An increase in urban employment will also decrease fertility; in the cities there are fewer jobs for children and more jobs for skilled workers.

Lower fertility, however, comes not from family planning alone, nor from the policies just mentioned, but from the combination of these factors with a lower death rate and an improved standard of living.

MORTALITY

Everyone is against mortality. In the past few centuries, Western technology has found effective ways of translating those feelings into action: Death rates have lowered in every country that has industrialized, except during times of war. Since World War II, death rates have dropped remarkably in most Third World countries as well. We can do many things to decrease mortality rates: Drain swamps. Purify drinking water. Install sewers. Inoculate children. Train midwives. And, most importantly, improve the amount and quality of food available to poor people.

As mentioned earlier, land reform would go a long way toward solving the problem of hunger. People will feed themselves if they are allowed to do so. The main thing you and I can do is make sure that our governments and business firms don't stop people from making needed changes. There have already been too many cases of Western interference in political struggles that might have produced real reforms in less-developed countries. If you give to a charity that claims to help a poor country, try to make sure it is controlled by the people there.

Western nations should also give some thought to their own food supplies. The poor nations can't afford to export all their crops to us and still feed themselves. On the other hand, after their own basic food needs are met, they may export a certain amount of food in return for cash payments. For example, Cuba stopped exporting sugar after Castro came to power. Once the Cuban population had enough to eat, it became possible to resume the production of sugar for export. Cuba can now afford to export part of its crop because its own basic needs have been met.

Looking to the future, algae and yeast may produce protein in large amounts. This type of protein can be produced with sixty times more energy efficiency than beef protein.[32] Moreover, technology will certainly move in the direction of using crops more efficiently. Often leaves, stalks, hulls, and roots are thrown away. These could be used to produce fertilizers, fuel, animal feed, or even food for human beings. Meat production is too wasteful to be continued, at least using present methods. Experimental farms are feeding cattle diets of wood pulp, newspapers, and even their own processed manure, and the animals seem to be thriving.[33] There are many other ways of producing more food through new technology that have yet to be applied on a large scale. Mortality can be lowered still further around the world.

Finally, I want to mention the factors that affect mortality in the advanced societies. Our problems are quite different from those of the less-developed nations. They involve changes in life style rather than medical or technological changes. Until a few years ago, I assumed that lower mortality rates in the West were due to medical advances. But not so. Mortality had already decreased greatly before penicillin and other "wonder drugs" were discovered. Diseases such as typhoid fever, whooping cough, and tuberculosis became much less frequent after industrialization had taken place, because families could provide better living conditions for their children. Indeed, if all of the doctors and hospitals in North America were to disappear today but our levels of nutrition, hygiene, and other living standards remained high, our mortality levels would not be affected very much.[34] Yet we continue to invest large amounts of money in medicine while overlooking other ways of cutting mortality rates. For example, we do nothing to improve the ambulance system, so that many people die before they can get to a hospital. When well-trained midwives deliver infants in the home, the death rates among mothers and babies are lower than when hurried obstetricians deliver them in hospitals. Changes in habits would do far more to increase life spans than any known ways of improving medical treatment. For example, people could avoid heart attacks and lung cancer to a considerable degree by getting proper nutrition and exercise and not smoking. Cirrhosis, another major killer, strikes heavy drinkers far more than other people. Breathing air in a badly polluted city is estimated to decrease life spans by an average of three years. The number of deaths caused by traffic accidents would decline if drivers used seat belts, refrained from drinking, and bought only cars designed for safety.

Governments affect mortality through legislation. Every society has policies regarding suicide, infanticide, child abuse, and homicide, as well as traffic laws, safety codes, and hundreds of other laws that directly affect one's chances of dying or staying alive. The greatest impact of government on mortality, however, is in the area of foreign policy. The worst killer of all is war.

MIGRATION

Governments also have policies that affect migration. They can control immigration, for example. However, they cannot entirely prevent illegal immigration or emigration. Some countries—especially communist countries such as the Soviet Union and the People's Republic of China—discourage emigration, but people still manage to leave those nations.

The USSR also controls migration within its borders. Even though its policies have become less severe since Stalin's death, the government, as the nation's main employer, can stimulate internal migration to certain areas (such as Siberia) through both positive inducements and coercion, and restrict internal migration to other areas by limiting the number of job openings there.

Governments are often as concerned with the type of migration as they are with the volume of migration. Many governments have tried to reduce ethnic diversity by allowing immigration only from nations that are similar in culture and racial composition. Many have also favored certain occupations. For example, the United States' 1965 immigration legislation gives preference to professional workers. As a result, the United States has been accused of draining the best-educated people from the rest of the world.

Canada's new immigration laws, passed in 1977, allow the Minister of Employment and Immigration to set annual immigration levels with the approval of the provinces, and these levels can be changed to fit changing "demographic goals." An applicant's chances of being allowed to immigrate are affected by the goals of reuniting families, helping refugees, and economic growth. The law specifically bans discrimination.[35]

The political decisions surrounding the growth and migration of human populations are a major issue. In the years ahead, professional demographers will play an increasingly important role in judging actual and proposed population policies.

SUMMARY

1. *Fecundity* is the capacity to give birth. *Fertility* is the rate of actual childbearing in a population.

2. Fertility is affected by eleven different variables: (1) age of entry into sexual unions, (2) permanent celibacy, (3) part of reproductive life spent after or between unions, (4) voluntary abstinence, (5) involuntary abstinence, (6) frequency of intercourse, (7) involuntary causes of fecundity or infecundity, (8) use or nonuse of contraception, (9) voluntary causes of fecundity or infecundity, (10) fetal mortality from involuntary causes, and (11) fetal mortality from voluntary causes.

3. The crude death rate is the number of deaths per year per 1000 people. Mortality declined between the late eighteenth century and the late nineteenth century in the industrialized nations. It has declined more slowly since then. Since World War II it has declined greatly in the less-developed nations.

4. Mourning rituals have almost vanished because of lower mortality rates. The lack of mourning rituals, combined with a denial of death's occurrence, may act to prolong a bereaved person's suffering.

5. About 20 percent of Canadians move each year. Migration is stressful and causes behavioral problems in many people. Marital breakdown and deviance are affected by mobility. On the other hand, areas with high immigration rates tend to be more tolerant and have more vitality than areas with low immigration or net out-migration.

6. Young single adults are the most likely to move. Social class is not greatly related to mobility. Well-educated Canadians, however, are more likely to move than less-educated Canadians.

7. The sex ratio is the number of males per 100 females. The North American sex ratio is now about 95. After a war, the sex ratio may be very unbalanced.

8. An age-sex population pyramid is a graph showing the composition of the population in terms of age and sex. A nation with a high fertility rate usually has a wide-based population pyramid. A nation in which fertility has been low for a long time has a pyramid with more vertical sides.

9. The dependency ratio is the ratio of people in dependent age groups (i.e., very young or old) to people in economically productive age groups. It is affected by the median age of the population, which is the age that divides any population into equal groups. The median age of Canada in 1976 was 28.

10. The peak growth year for the world's population may have been 1970, when the growth rate was 19 per 1000 people. In 1977, the rate had fallen to about 17. At that rate, the world's population will double in 41 years.

11. Malthus pointed out that the means of subsistence grow at an arithmetic rate while the population tends to grow at a geometric rate. At first he believed that the only limits on such growth would be "positive checks"—mortality caused by hunger, disease, and war. Later he concluded that human beings might use "preventive checks"—such as lowering fertility through late marriage. He was opposed to birth control. Fortunately, the means of subsistence have increased much more than he expected, and death rates have decreased. Fertility has also decreased.

12. The demographic-transition model is based on the historical experience of Western societies. Birth and death rates were high and almost equal in preindustrial times. In the nineteenth century, as a result of improvements in nutrition, sanitation, and medicine, the death rates began to drop. Fertility then began to decline too. It was expected that the two rates would level off at a low level, but the postwar baby boom occurred instead. Now we know that economic development may increase fertility in the short run while decreasing it in the long run.

13. Spengler points out that a couple's decision to have a child is based on three factors. It varies directly with the preference system, inversely with the price system, and directly with available resources. The preference system is determined by several factors—mortality, the value of child labor, the need for support in old age, and social rewards for having children. The price system is affected by the availability and convenience of contraception as well as by urbanization, the value of labor, and the extent of education.

KEY TERMS

crude birthrate   the number of births per year per 1000 people.

crude death rate   the number of deaths per year per 1000 people.

demographic-transition model   a model used to describe the process by which preindustrial societies with high rates of fertility and mortality are transformed into modern societies with low rates of fertility and mortality.

demography the study of human populations.

dependency ratio the ratio of people in dependent age groups to people in economically productive age groups.

ecology the relationship between the physical environment and the human population that lives in that environment.

fecundity a woman's capacity to bear children.

fertility the rate at which a population gives birth.

median age the age that divides any population

equally so that half are older and half are younger.

migration the movement of people into or out of an area.

mortality the rate at which a population dies.

population pyramid a diagram that shows the age-sex composition of a population at a given time.

sex ratio the number of males per 100 females in a population.

zero population growth (ZPG) the point at which there is no increase in a population.

FOR FURTHER READING

HAWKINS, FREDA. *Canada and Immigration. Public Policy and Political Concern.* Montreal: McGill-Queens University Press, 1972. Professor Hawkins is a political scientist with a particular interest in the government's immigration policy. She generally favors the admission of substantial numbers of immigrants every year.

HENRIPIN, JACQUES. *Immigration and Language Imbalance. Canadian Immigration and Population Study.* Ottawa: Information Canada, 1974. Henripin is a demographer who specializes in studying the factors that affect the composition of Quebec's population. He also has several publications in French.

HOWELL, NANCY. *Demography of the Dobe: Kung.* New York: Academic Press, 1979. This book provides an analysis of the demography of a small African Bushman tribe. It introduces new methods for studying populations that are too small for ordinary statistical procedures. It also provides valuable information on the ways in which such factors as food supply influence fertility in primitive societies.

KALBACH, WARREN E. and WAYNE MCVEY. *The Demographic Bases of Canadian Society.* 2nd ed. Toronto: McGraw-Hill Ryerson, 1979. A first-rate

overview of the factors determining the size of the Canadian population and its standards of health, housing, and so on.

KUBAT, DANIEL and D. THORNTON. *A Statistical Profile of Canadian Society.* Toronto: McGraw-Hill Ryerson, 1974. The title describes the contents exactly.

LAPPE, FRANCES MOORE and JOSEPH COLLINS. *Food First: Beyond the Myth of Scarcity.* Boston: Houghton Miffin, 1977. If I had a chance to pick one book that I could persuade everybody to read, this would be the book. No doubt the authors make some factual errors, but they are clearly right in the thrust of what they say. I think they have made an enormous contribution to the world's understanding of this subject. Reading it will shake you to your roots.

MARSDEN, LORNA. *Population Probe: Canada.* Toronto: Copp Clark, 1972. The first chapters are the most useful ones in this book, which is basically an argument for a Canadian population policy.

MITCHELL, DON. *The Politics of Food.* Toronto: Lorimer, 1975. Much of this book deals with the international food market and agribusiness, as it applies to the Canadian consumer.

STONE, LEROY O. and SUSAN FLETCHER. *Migration in Canada. 1971 Census of Canada Profile Studies.* Ottawa: Statistics Canada, 1977. Stone is a demographer who studies the migration of rural people to urban areas in Canada. This book, however, treats internal migration of all sorts.

18

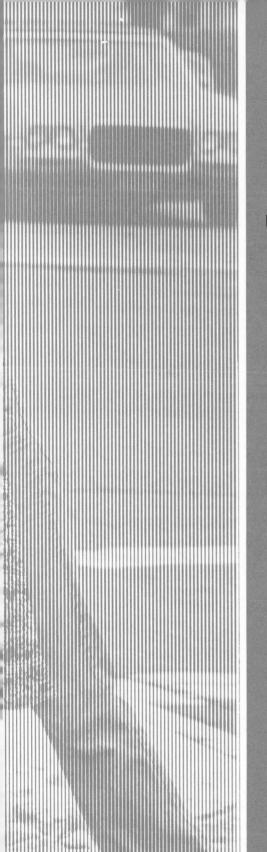

URBAN LIVING

The development of cities
    The role of agricultural surpluses
    Cities and empires
    The cities of medieval Europe
    The preindustrial city today
Urbanization
    Why urbanization?
    City growth in North America
Theoretical approaches to urbanization
    Folk and urban life styles
    Redfield: the folk-urban continuum
    Wirth: urbanism as a way of life
    The compositional theory
    The subcultural theory
Urban ecology
    Burgess: the concentric-zone model
    Hoyt: the sector model
    Harris and Ullman: the multiple-nuclei
        model
Social Research: Sociologists at Work
Social Policy: Issues and Viewpoints

Pretend that you work for a large organization that must transfer you to a different place. It promises, however, that if you make a list of three places where you would be glad to live, it will transfer you to one of those places. Here's your chance. Of all the places in the world, which three would you choose?

I'd choose a house on Telegraph Hill in San Francisco or an apartment at Place des Vosges in Paris or a house on a side canal near the Rialto bridge in Venice. All of my choices are urban. My friends tend to choose places like a chateau in the Loire Valley or a mansion on the Hudson River an hour's drive from New York City. They want a more rural place where they can play loud music without bothering the neighbors. What about you? Would you like your home to be isolated and private or close to a variety of human activities?

Gallup polls conducted in Canada and the United States in 1973 and 1974 showed that only about 15 percent of North Americans wanted to live in a city. A quarter of the population wanted to live on a farm, and the rest preferred either the suburbs or a small town.[1] Even most city dwellers apparently preferred another life style. A Toronto study found that almost 90 percent of the respondents renting apartments downtown wanted to move away from the downtown area.[2] No doubt many of them got their wish. Yet people continue to move toward urban areas from the countryside, chiefly for economic reasons. Job opportunities are better in the city.

Whether you prefer big-city or rural living depends largely on what you like to do with your time—on your tastes and life style. If you have children, you might prefer to raise them in a quiet area where you can have a big back yard. But professionals, unemployed people, and those in white-collar jobs, especially if they are unmarried, usually prefer the city. It is easier to go out for an evening. High culture is more available. The city is stimulating, alive, exciting—it's where the action is. I'd rather have a seedy apartment in a lively city than a mansion in the suburbs.

In this chapter we will talk about urban living—past, present, and future. We'll begin with a discussion of the place of cities in the history of Western civilization. Then we'll note some changes in the patterns of urbanization in North America. After that we'll turn to the old debate about the quality of life in urban and rural areas.

The development of cities

A **city** is a large, permanent, densely populated settlement. Two important points about the development of cities should be kept in mind. The first is that cities always depend on the surrounding area to supply them with food and other materials. The second is that industrial cities are very different from preindustrial ones.

THE ROLE OF AGRICULTURAL SURPLUSES

As agriculture improves, cities can grow. The two are connected. A society that is very low in economic productivity can support very few nonfarmers. But cities are large, densely populated areas in which people don't grow their own food. In a hunting and gathering society—that of the Plains Indians, say, or the Australian aboriginal tribes—one person can support only himself, occasionally his wife, and, for a few years (until they can catch their own food), his children. City dwellers, who depend on food produced by others, can exist in large numbers only when technology is advanced enough to provide a large surplus. Technology makes its greatest steps forward when some new way of using energy is developed. When horses were harnessed and put to work, more people could survive on the surplus provided as a result. The invention of electrical generators enabled even larger populations to live in cities. Future energy sources may also increase productivity, so that populations can expand

Ontario Ministry of Industry and Tourism

No surplus, no cities. Urban residents depend on farmers who produce more than they need for their own families.

still further. The more productive the food producers can be, the larger the urban population can grow.

This much is clear: No surplus, no cities. But which came first, the surplus or the cities? Scholars used to assume that agricultural development happened first and that urban development followed. A few have argued that there was no surplus—that the growth of cities created famine in rural areas. This may have been true sometimes, but most of the time there must have been a surplus—otherwise the city dwellers would have "killed the goose that laid the golden egg" by starving the farmers who supported them.

A third point of view is that city dwellers themselves created the conditions that made their growth possible. They could have done this by (1) forcing the farmers to work harder and produce more than they needed to produce and/or (2) providing technological innovations that increased productivity—for example, building large-scale irrigation projects that made agriculture more effective.[3] In other words, it is possible that cities "paid their own way" from the beginning by helping farmers increase productivity. In any case, it is clear that city dwellers have always obtained their food from the farmers and that they have often used military or political power to do so. This requires us to look at the relationship between cities and empires.

CITIES AND EMPIRES

Gideon Sjoberg has described the relationship between cities and the expansion and contraction of empires.[4] According to Sjoberg, elites have always been city people. That is, the people who have "made history"—political, intellectual, or religious—have almost always lived in cities. And powerful empires have had many great cities. The cities of the Mesopotamian river valleys supported empires that were great for their time, such as the Babylonian kingdoms. But these empires were much smaller than the ones

that came later in history as technology became more advanced—the Roman and, especially, British empires, for example. What made cities so important in the political control of large regions? Why did empires depend on the existence of cities?

Communication

The most obvious advantage cities offer is ease of communication. In the old days, cities had walls around them. Inside those walls, commercial activities could flourish. Political, educational, and religious leaders could communicate with each other, thus reinforcing their social power. Even today, bureaucratic

Many inner cities are now improving instead of decaying. Toronto's harbor area is being extensively redesigned to improve the quality of life in the city.

Ontario Ministry of Industry and Tourism

officials work best in face-to-face contact, because only through personal interaction can they spot trouble in their organization. (This is why managers are found in large numbers in downtown New York City, which has more office space than all the other large American cities combined.) The preindustrial city depended even more on oral communication, so the leaders gathered in the center of the city, where they could contact each other whenever necessary.

The capital city of the empire was the site of the royal court, which attracted travelling entertainers and merchants. These travellers often brought news from outlying areas. The lesser ruling elites were often sent to administer smaller cities scattered through the empire. Those cities were usually located on communication routes so that the administrators could keep in touch with the capital city.

Political coercion

Cities need a strong political system that can force farmers to give up their surplus to provide food for the city dwellers. The rulers usually controlled the farmers by owning the land that the farmers cultivated.

Political coercion is also necessary for commerce. Not only does it suppress bandits and pirates; it also coordinates the workers who build roads and other vital public works. All the important trading empires were great military or naval powers, and they used military force to provide the security in which trade could be carried on. Large empires often built up their cities by sending colonists to dominate outlying regions.

The decline of empires

Imperial cities usually developed by diffusion—the spread of a cultural pattern from one people to another. Often new cities began as military bases—especially on frontiers. These frontier cities socialized the natives into the culture of the dominant group. As Sjoberg points out, this was usually a fatal mistake because it led to the decline of the empire itself.

Typically, this is what would happen: The ruling group would conquer the natives and then come to depend on them, especially if their languages differed. Thus the administrators would teach the natives how to run things, for example, in the military, in the bureaucracy, or in business. Naturally, the natives would pick up certain useful skills. Eventually, when the right time came, they would be able to attack the rulers, particularly in the frontier areas. In those regions, new empires or nations might form by breaking away. Then the "mother country" would become less important and might even be invaded by its former subjects. This happened, for example, when the barbarians sacked Rome and destroyed urban civilization in the entire Roman empire. The Romans themselves had prepared the barbarians to carry out this attack. The same thing happened to the British Empire. The Indian elite who had been educated to serve as loyal bureaucrats for the British crown led the fight for independence—Mahatma Gandhi was an Indian lawyer who had been educated in England.

THE CITIES OF MEDIEVAL EUROPE

Not all cities are imperial in origin. The cities of medieval Europe were quite different from those of the rest of the world.[5] Instead of being part of an empire, the medieval city was a free enclave within the harsh world of feudalism. Some of the greatest political traditions of the West developed within city walls. The medieval city helped transform European society by protecting the middle class—a free class of people in a society that otherwise lacked any freedom at all.[6] If the medieval city had not developed the basic rights that we enjoy today, we might still think of ourselves as "subjects" instead of as "citizens."

The Roman cities disappeared by about A.D. 300. However, by about A.D. 1000, cities reappeared throughout Europe. These cities were entirely separate from the castles of the

Some of the great political traditions we cherish in the West developed in the medieval walled cities of Europe. Even the word "citizen," which implies one who may participate in one's own government, originally meant a resident of a city.

feudal lords, who didn't live in the cities and looked down upon those who did. The city was a true community—an association of people who swore to defend themselves as a group against any danger. Each city had a charter from the king that guaranteed several important rights—for example, wars had to be interrupted on market days so that people could buy and sell in peace.

The elites of the cities were not feudal lords but *patricians.* Below them were the craftsmen, who belonged to closed guilds. If an escaped serf managed to stay in the city for a year, he could keep his freedom, but this

was not very easy to do. He might be unable to gain admission to the guilds and therefore might not find a job. A number of Jews also lived in the cities. They were vital to the economy because they were allowed to lend money at interest, something Christians were not supposed to do. Besides the commercial groups, there were religious and cultural leaders as well—the artists and priests connected with the cathedrals. Universities appeared in some medieval cities and attracted students from all over Europe.

But the peculiar thing about the European city was that it was free. It made its own laws. The imperial cities everywhere else were administered by an official appointed by the emperor. But the medieval cities elected their own mayors rather than having to accept an official appointed by the state. Election of mayors is common in North America, so you may not realize what an unusual political invention it was in world history.

I'm not suggesting that the European city dwellers had no rulers. Far from it. The stratification system was as rigid there as anywhere else. The patrician elites and the guilds both had great authority. According to Max Weber, one of the main factors leading up to the Renaissance was the challenge to that authority by a powerful group of merchants and bankers—the free middle class.[6] Beginning in Venice, this movement swept through all the cities of Europe. The new group did not *displace* the old elites, but it made social mobility possible, protested against tyranny, and made major cultural contribuitons. The medieval city gradually extended the status of citizenship to more and more people.

THE PREINDUSTRIAL CITY TODAY

I began by describing imperial cities—cities in Asia and the Near East that were ruled by colonial administrators. What happened to them? They're still there, but they are not at all like the cities you and I live in. I'm not talking about the cities of Japan, say, which have become industrialized; rather, I mean imperial cities like Bombay, Dacca, Djakarta, and Calcutta. These were created to serve the empires of Europe, not the commercial needs of their own region. They were port cities in the trade network of the colonial powers. They have become much larger than they once were, but they have not yet become industrialized.

How do they differ from Western cities? For one thing, today's preindustrial city does

not separate various social classes as clearly as it separates ethnic, caste, or occupational groups.[7] The rich and the poor do not live in distinct zones. The city has no suburbs or central business district. Manufacturing is done either by independent craftsmen or by large, modern factories located at the edge of town.

Many preindustrial cities, such as those in Indonesia, are "ruralized." They look more like rural villages than cities. These cities, which may be found throughout Asia, Africa, and Latin America, have attracted migrants from the countryside in search of jobs. Since industrial jobs are still scarce, most of these migrants take menial jobs—cleaning streets, delivering packages, putting up posters, and the like—if they are able to find any jobs at all. They live in shanty towns on the outskirts of the cities, many of them keeping pigs and chickens just as they did in their home villages.

When your country cousin moves to the city, she changes her way of life. She becomes more sophisticated; she experiments with new life styles. But the migrant to a preindustrial city lives pretty much the same sort of life as before. Hence, the preindustrial city does not play a modernizing role the way Western cities do. For such modernization to occur, the city must become part of a rapidly developing national economy.

Urbanization

Urbanization can be defined as the movement of people from rural areas to cities and from small cities to larger ones. Between 1800 and 1960, the percentage of the world's population living in cities with populations of over 100,000 increased from about 2 percent to around 17 percent. In some countries, the increase was even more dramatic. Between 1950 and 1960, the rate of urbanization was double that of the preceding 50 years.

FIGURE 18.1

Percentage change of the population of Canada and selected metropolitan areas, 1971-76

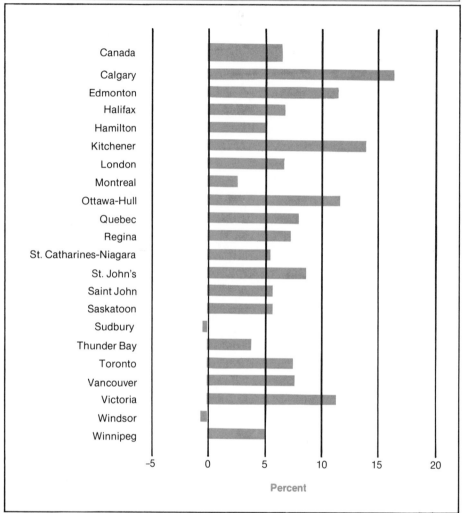

Source: Canada Year Book, 1978-79, p. 136.

However, urbanization is finite—it has a beginning and an end. The advanced nations are probably nearing the end of the urbanization process, so that the portion of the population living in cities will not increase much and in fact may decrease.

Many developing nations have only begun to urbanize. For example, only a small percentage of all Asians live in cities. However, because the population of Asia is so huge, even that small percentage accounts for a large portion of the world's city dwellers. And this growth is only in its early stages. Kingsley Davis has estimated that some cities in India will have between 36 and 66 million inhabitants in the year 2000.[8] No city in any advanced society could even approach that size by the year 2000.

WHY URBANIZATION?

What is going on? Why has the world's population tended to move into cities during the past 200 years? What is the reason behind urbanization?

There are two main reasons: (1) Urban living is more economical, and (2) food processing has become a largely urban activity.

As a nation becomes richer, its people spend less of their income on food and more on other goods and services. And those goods and services (except food) are produced more cheaply in cities than in the country. Cities have transportation and a large labor force. They are the best locations for many specialized services—wholesale trade, higher education, hospitals, banking, and insurance, for example.

The second reason for urbanization is the changing technology of food production. Before the Industrial Revolution, farmers were self-sufficient. In modern nations, they rely on artificial fertilizers, pesticides, machinery, electricity, gasoline, and a variety of other things that are produced in cities. In fact, much "farm" work is done in the cities. The food must be transported from the farm, processed, and distributed. These jobs are done by city people. Actually, for any typical food product—such as milk—the farmer today may receive less than half of the total selling price. The rest goes to city dwellers. Thus urbanization results from the economics of modern technology.

CITY GROWTH IN NORTH AMERICA

At what size does a rural community become large enough to be considered a "town?" The census officials of different countries disagree on this question. In Canada, a community of 1000 qualifies as a town, or "urban area;" in the United States a place must have at least 2500 inhabitants to be called "urban." However, despite the different census standards, statistics show that Canadians and Americans are about equally urbanized. Roughly 76 percent of Canadians now reside in urban areas.

Sometimes several towns expand until they form a continuous urban area. Even though such towns maintain separate municipal governments for statistical purposes, they are often considered a single city. Canadian officials classify a metropolitan region with a large central city surrounded by smaller, dependent cities as a **census metropolitan area (CMA)**. In 1976 there were 22 Canadian CMAs with populations of over 100,000. Montreal and Toronto each had more than 2.8 million inhabitants; Vancouver's population was over 1 million; and the populations of Ottawa-Hull, Edmonton, Hamilton, Quebec City, and Winnipeg were all over a half-million.

Suburbanization

Suburbanization may be defined as the movement of people from central cities to communities in the surrounding area. Although suburbanization is common in many industrial nations, it has been most extensive in North America. In the average North American metropolitan region, the populations in the metropolitan areas outside the city core are growing far more rapidly than the population of the inner city.

Why are people moving from the cities to the suburbs? Suburbanization has several causes:

1 *Residential use of land must compete with other land uses.* Increasingly, the land near central business districts is taken over by parking lots and commercial uses. As a result, less is available for residential use.

2 *The population is richer.* There has been an

Thomas Hopker/Woodfin Camp

CP Photo/Montreal Star

Urbanization and growth have taken many forms in North America.

Winnipeg Tribune

Tourism British Columbia

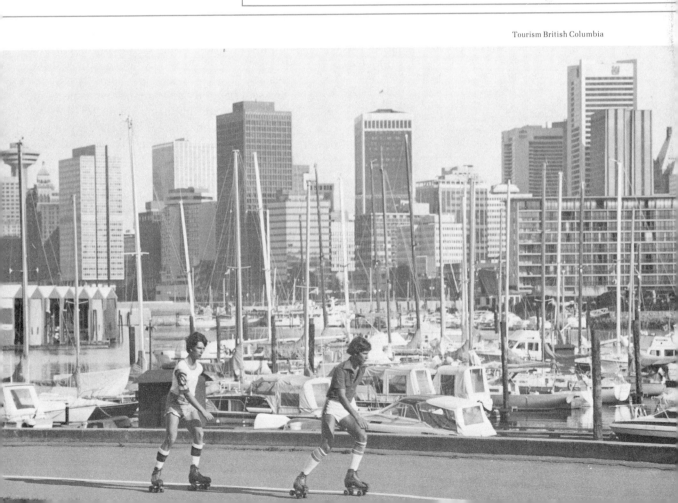

increase in average income and number of leisure hours. Almost all families now can own a car, and the federally financed highway system has enabled more workers to afford commuting by car.

3 *Transportation is more flexible.* Most shipping used to be by rail and most commuters used to travel by public transportation. Nowadays trucks ship more than trains do, and factories have been able to move farther from the central business districts and railroad terminals. The spreading out of jobs reinforces the spreading out of residences.

4 *People want larger homes.* They can afford them now. As the average income of the people in the inner city increases, their urban homes feel more crowded. Houses that were built for two families are often converted into single-family houses. Many families are willing to commute to work in order to obtain more housing room.

5 *The government has helped people afford home ownership.* This is probably the most important factor of all. The Canadian government has made it possible for the average family to afford a mortgage. You can buy a suburban tract house with a very low down payment. But it is often much harder to get loans to buy or renovate houses or apartments in the central city. In effect, the government subsidized suburbanization after World War II by making suburban housing such a good bargain. S.D. Clark has argued that people didn't really move to the suburbs by choice. They didn't much care where they lived if the housing was a good bargain. The people who stayed in the city were the ones who *did* care about where they lived and about their life style. A different mortgage policy might have encouraged further urbanization instead of suburbanization.[9]

The future of the suburbs is considerably more bleak today than when they were first built. Early suburban developers did not dream that there would ever be an energy crisis. Suburban dwellers generally own spacious houses and rely heavily on automobile transport; both heating fuel and gasoline are now becoming scarce and expensive. In the future, urban development will have to be far more oriented toward fuel efficiency than suburban development has been.

Theoretical approaches to urbanization

I have a hunch that urban sociology has been largely shaped by the fact that the University of Chicago is located in Chicago. That's where urban sociology grew up, led by such scholars as Robert Ezra Park and Louis Wirth. Robert Redfield was also a leading influence though he was not a sociologist but an anthropologist. All of these men had a very negative view of city life, and that view has persisted. We still have certain notions about the traits of city people that were inherited, either directly or indirectly, from these writers. By all accounts, Chicago was an ugly and unpleasant place in those days. My guess is that if the University of Chicago had been located in, say, Berkeley, Paris, or Toronto, these writers would have said kinder things about urban life, and urban sociology would have developed different issues.

I will begin by mentioning two aspects of urban sociology that came out of the Chicago school: (1) the question of how the way of life of city people differs from that of rural folk and (2) urban ecology.

FOLK AND URBAN LIFE STYLES

People tend to think in terms of opposites. If I say "long," you may think "short." If I say "quick," you may think "slow." Sociologists do the same thing. Hence, our traditional way of theorizing is to set up categories of opposites to describe social groups. (Max Weber called these "ideal types;" he meant that they were set up as logical concepts, and not as true observations of reality.) No real society ever quite matches these categories, but any given society will seem closer to one extreme than to the other. Thus a typology (i.e., a set of ideal types) allows us to compare a variety of societies. One such typology is the distinction between *folk* life and *urban* life, as expressed in the writings of Redfield, who spent a lot of time doing field research in the Yucatan peninsula of Mexico, and of Wirth, who was concerned mainly with urbanism as a way of life.

REDFIELD: THE FOLK-URBAN CONTINUUM

Redfield generalized from his observations of the Indian villages and towns of Yucatan.[10] As he described them, folk societies (that is, peasant societies) are small, isolated, and homogeneous, with no complex technology and no division of labor except according to

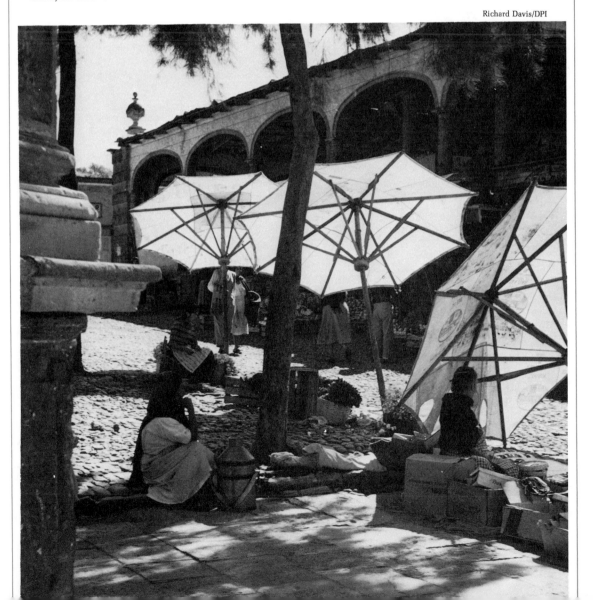

Mexican "urban" centers are still not very modern, despite Redfield's worry about how they would undermine folk culture.

Richard Davis/DPI

sex and age. Men hunt and fish and women and children gather nuts, but there is little surplus food. Such societies are non-literate. They are marked by solidarity and close relationships, by face-to-face communication between people who usually know each other well. Religion is very important, and social control is often carried out through religious institutions. Ritual is highly developed. Cultural patterns are based on feelings and tradition—not rational choice. Members of the group are uncritical and follow old folkways without questioning them. The family is the central social group. People help each other without expecting cash rewards, but only because they are bound by kinship ties in every aspect of their lives. Status is ascribed at birth.

Urban society, to Redfield, is the opposite of folk society. It is large scale, heterogeneous, and impersonal. It is too large to permit warm, close relationships. And it is too differentiated to allow any person to be socialized thoroughly into all its norms. The result is diversity. People become nonreligious, individualistic, and tolerant. They make critical judgments about the various points of view they encounter. And work becomes a means to an end, such as cash or prestige, rather than an expression of relationships with kin.

It's easy to guess which way of life Redfield preferred. Redfield worried about what was happening to folk societies. According to him, modern communication is bringing folk communities into contact with urban people and undermining the culture of the folk group. People in those groups are beginning to question their traditions. Thus urban culture destroys folk culture. This is an evolutionary view; that is, Redfield believed that the transformation of the world is a result of the spread of urban culture into backward areas. (I imagine a vacuum cleaner salesman hacking his way through the jungle with a machete to spread the word.) He had nothing good to say about city life; in his opinion

urbanization spoiled the charming rural communities that he loved.

Redfield probably exaggerated the impact of cities on the folk culture of Yucatan. Urban culture *does* tend to spread outward, but not as much in less-developed countries as in industrial societies. And Mexico was, and mostly still is, underdeveloped. I have already told you how the preindustrial city differs from the industrial ones with which you are familiar. The cities of Yucatan are basically preindustrial. They are unable to create much social change. Migrants from the countryside continue to live a rural life style in shantytowns on the outskirts of the city. The city dwellers are greatly outnumbered. Instead of threatening the folk culture that surrounds it, the preindustrial city is lucky if it can preserve urban culture.

WIRTH: URBANISM AS A WAY OF LIFE

While Redfield was developing his ideas about folk and urban societies, Wirth also became interested in the quality of city life. His description of urbanism as a way of life was consistent with Redfield's.[11] He defined the city as a "relatively large, permanent, dense settlement of socially heterogeneous individuals," and he was interested in showing the effects on social life of (1) large size, (2) density, and (3) heterogeneity. In general, he believed that it was nearly impossible to have rich interpersonal relationships in the city. Urban life destroyed the sense of community.

According to Wirth, density and size are the most important factors in city life. Heterogeneity is really an effect of these two variables, for, as Redfield also suggested, the more people who interact in a community, the wider the possible range of ideas. Furthermore, the more people interact, the less intense their interactions can be. After all, how many people can you be really close to at one time? If you have to deal with hundreds or thousands of people each week, your relations with most of them will be impersonal.

For this reason, Wirth felt that city dwellers are generally superficial in their relationships. There's only so much attention and energy to go around. If you have to divide yourself up, if you have to keep moving through many temporary relationships, you won't be a very intense person and your life may lack intimacy and depth. Families become shallow. Kinship ties weaken. Groups that might preserve a strong, rich feeling of

These French citizens in the heart of Paris are enjoying a street entertainer, just one type of action and variety that attracts people to the city.

Mark Antman/Monkmeyer

community in a rural environment lose that ability in the city. Indeed, the moral fabric of society is weakened by the temporary, fragmented nature of urban social relationships. City people live by a "spirit of competition, aggrandizement, and mutual exploitation," Wirth wrote. They are rational and unsentimental, unlike rural or small-town people, who are more personal. City dwellers lack friendly relations with neighbors and maintain a self-protective aloofness. Such a lonely, emotionally empty life destroys all natural social groups and creates a number of social problems. Crime, delinquency, corruption, mental breakdown, and suicide are all more common in large cities than in small communities.

Wirth and his many followers seem to agree that because the city is so big, so busy, so nerve-wracking, so full of activity and change, it has harmful effects on people. No stable, enriching, cohesive social community can survive in such a setting. People's lives are so pulled apart by the tension and loneliness of urban living that disorganization and mental illness must result. The health of the human personality can't escape damage in such a setting. Only a smaller, more personal, social environment allows people to nourish and support each other and maintain the order and traditions that make life worth living.

I don't think this picture is entirely accurate. The arguments concerning crime and delinquency seem to be valid. Urban areas do have more crime per person than less densely populated areas. But the argument about impersonality doesn't hold up. I find rural people at least as aloof as city people. The city people I know do not all lack friends or warm relationships. So let me also describe two somewhat different views of urban life. Borrowing from Claude S. Fischer, I will classify all three views under these headings: (1) the determinist position, which we have already examined; (2) the compositional theory; and (3) the subculture theory (Fischer's view).[12]

THE COMPOSITIONAL THEORY

People who like city living have naturally risen to Wirth's bait with numerous arguments. Among the social scientists who defend cities are Herbert Gans and Oscar Lewis. These two agree that social groups are not necessarily destroyed by big-city life. Small, intimate, intense friendship groups, kinship ties, and other communities continue to exist in many cities. Indeed, Lewis goes so far as to claim that "in modern Western cities, there may be more give and take about one's private, intimate life at a single 'sophisticated' cocktail party than would occur in years in a peasant village."[13]

The compositional view sees differences between urban and rural living, of course. But it denies that the size and density of the city has any direct effect on the psychological traits and adjustment of its inhabitants. The people who live in the city do differ from those who live in the country. They usually differ in terms of occupation, education, age, sex ratio, marital status, social class, and ethnicity—to mention only a few factors. Such factors *do* have an effect on people's experiences. Obviously, if you are a homemaker in the suburbs you will do many things that you might not do if you were a secretary in the city, and there are many things that you might do as a city dweller that you wouldn't do as a suburbanite. City and rural people differ because of the many opportunities and limitations that differ in their surroundings. But their personal qualities have nothing to do with the size or density of the city *as such.* A city environment does not affect a person's capacity for emotionally open and responsive relationships. No one is psychologically damaged by size or density. City dwellers can be as warm and generous and close to their friends as anyone else, other things being equal.

Hence, the compositional approach holds that the composition of a city's population differs from that of a small town in terms of factors such as age, social class, education, ethnicity, and marital status. But the size or density of a town does not directly influence the personal traits of its inhabitants.

Lewis, holding to the compositional approach, went to Yucatan to visit the villages and towns that Redfield had visited. He claims that Redfield was biased—that even in Yucatan the important differences were not between urban and folk cultures but between the different *social classes.* The conflict between social classes is a real conflict, whether it is in the city or the countryside, or so Lewis claims.

THE SUBCULTURAL THEORY

Fischer has recently developed what he calls the subcultural theory, which combines elements of the determinist and compositional views. On the whole, it is closer to the compositional position. It agrees that most of the factors that create differences between city and small-town people are not *direct, necessary* results of the density or size of the city or town. However, important differences do occur, and they occur regularly. There is, indeed, greater diversity in the life styles that are found in the city than those found elsewhere.

And what variety! Radicals, punk rockers, artists, and experimenters of all kinds live in cities. They experiment with life styles, science, politics, handicraft design, and almost everything else. In the past two days, for example, I have had dealings of some sort with the following people: a "school without walls" that organizes outings to factories, city council meetings, and the like; a group that is encouraging people to have babies at home; a concert pianist who stuffs his piano with newspapers and silverware and calls it a "prepared piano"; a young man selling peanuts from door to door for the Unification Church; a club that shows German horror films; a cooperative funeral society that claims to have a

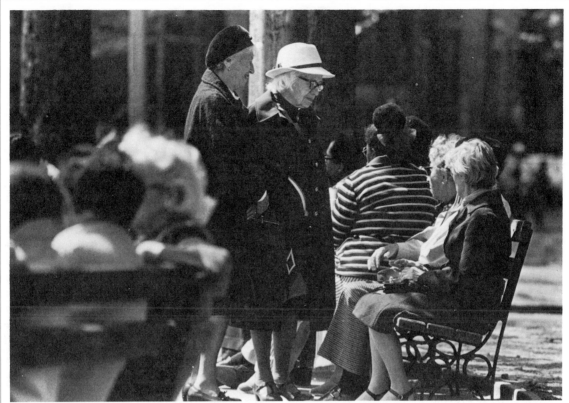

Tim Eagan/Woodfin Camp

Urban settings often attract immigrants who follow other members of their former culture. In large city parks one can see groups of people visiting together in many different languages.

cheaper way of disposing of bodies (if you don't mind being cremated); a hostel for women running away from brutal husbands (they wanted my old blankets); a sexual-information society that wants people to examine themselves and learn the proper name for each sexual part; a group that will show you how to make wine from leftovers; another group that wants to sterilize all the dogs and cats in Toronto; a group that wants to convert the old Don Jail into an art gallery; and a club that promises to teach me to survive in the woods with only a length of rope, six matches, and a hunting knife.

Who says city people are lonely? Who says they are isolated or that they don't experience close relationships? How could

anyone say such a thing! People who live in urban areas can belong to an incredible variety of different groups and can throw themselves into their activities with amazing passion and commitment. Political, religious, ethnic, and cultural groups of all kinds thrive in the city. They couldn't find members in small towns. It takes a *critical mass* to support a group. Suppose one person out of 5000 wants to learn about Japanese foot massage. In a small town that might total 4 or 5 people. In a large city, on the other hand, enough people might be interested to support a class with a paid instructor. Thus the city is *able to support a variety of subcultures*. In fact it is the density and size of the city that permits these subcultures to exist. These groups appeal to

543

certain people and not to others. Moreover, they encourage their members to become even more different from members of other groups. In a small town, people have *some* diverse tendencies and *some* varied opinions. When they become active in a particular subculture, as they can in the city, their differences become more marked. Creative, exciting subcultures can exist in the city and stimulate the intellectual growth of artists, writers, journalists, political reformers, and chess players. This is why such people often prefer to live in the city. But deviant subcultures such as criminal gangs, numbers rackets, pornography shops, and cocaine pushers can also exist more easily in cities.

Fischer argues that deviant subcultures exist more easily in the city for the same reason that other subcultures exist more easily in the city—because of the city's size and density. It follows, then, that the city encourages both deviance and creativity, and for the same reasons. If you have criminal tendencies, you'll find some friends in the city who will encourage you to commit crimes. If you have artistic tendencies, you'll find friends who will encourage you to be artistic.

As we learned in Chapter 7, anomie theory holds that people become deviant because they become less involved in the social groups that provide social control and help people live up to agreed-upon standards of behavior. This theory assumes that deviants are mostly social isolates, nonbelongers. And Wirth and Redfield, among others, seem to suggest that crime and deliquency and other forms of deviance occur more often in the city because the urban way of life fragments groups and leaves people isolated and uninvolved. Fischer disagrees. He acknowledges that a greater percentage of deviance is found in cities than in towns, but not because of isolation. On the contrary, it is because deviant subcultures can form and can support their members' deviant tendencies. Diversity is partly a result of the size and density of the

city, as the determinist approach suggests. City people *are* more heterogeneous than rural people. This is not because social groups are absent or weak, however, but because they are strong! Deviance and other forms of diversity are encouraged by subcultures. And a variety of subcultures can exist in urban environments because of the sheer number of people who live there.

Why do people often believe that urban dwellers are isolated, impersonal, and lacking in friends? Maybe it is because city people aren't very neighborly. Rural people, of course, *have* to depend on their neighbors for friendship and aid. They have no one else to turn to. But city people can, and do, choose their friends throughout the urban area, and hence are less likely to pay much attention to the people next door.[14] Not only Fischer's research but also that of other urban sociologists has shown that urban people tend to have their own "personal communities." That is, the network of personal ties will extend throughout and beyond the city. These ties may be maintained by daily telephone calls or frequent subway trips.

This does not mean that neighborhoods are unimportant, however. It is good to be able to borrow a cup of sugar from the woman next door or to offer her a geranium cutting or a ride to the drugstore. In different stages of the life cycle, the neighborhood becomes more important than at other phases. For example, young childless couples do very little neighboring, while those who have children do a great deal. Older couples whose children are grown may or may not see much of their neighbors. It depends on where they live. Older people who live in single-family homes are quite friendly with the people around them, but those who live in apartments see their neighbors rarely.[15] In any case, it is clear that, whether city dwellers are neighborly or not, they have as many social relationships as people from small towns.

Anita Sabarese/DPI

Not all of the city is overrun with people. Most cities have large parks where one can get away from day-to-day activities and have a quiet chat with a friend.

Urban ecology

Urban ecology is the study of the distribution of people and activities as it relates to the physical environment of a given city. I touched upon aspects of urban ecology when I mentioned that preindustrial cities differ from industrial cities in that they have undeveloped central business districts and poor residential areas on the outskirts of the town. Urban ecologists often study the land-use patterns of a region and observe the

way those patterns change as population density increases. Ecological studies of this sort began in Chicago in the 1920s, chiefly under the influence of Robert E. Park and Ernest W. Burgess. Burgess's description of the modern city as a series of concentric zones was used as a mental map by all urban ecologists for many years. Only gradually was the Burgess model modified by two other descriptions of the city, the sector model and the multiple-nuclei model.

BURGESS: THE CONCENTRIC-ZONE MODEL

Burgess observed that North American cities, unlike many European cities, usually grow up in an unplanned, uncontrolled way. He was interested in finding out what factors determine the growth patterns and land use of the North American city. His answer was that the *value* of land determines a city's growth pattern. As a city grows, the value of land increases, especially that of land close to the central business district that houses the big department stores and office buildings. As the value of land changes, the residential plan of the city changes too. The expensive land in the central business district is bought by commercial developers. Only a few rich families still live there, mostly in apartment buildings. Other well-to-do people move outside the city, where they can surround their big private houses with lawns, rose gardens, and swimming pools. The middle-income families of Burgess's day lived in apartments near the central business district or in detached houses with small yards farther from the center of town. (Since the 1950s, this group has generally been moving into suburban tract developments, leaving the inner city to the poor.)

Burgess diagrammed the city of Chicago according to this pattern of land use.[16] His diagram consisted of five major concentric zones, (see Figure 18.2), as follows:

FIGURE 18.2

Burgess diagram of Chicago

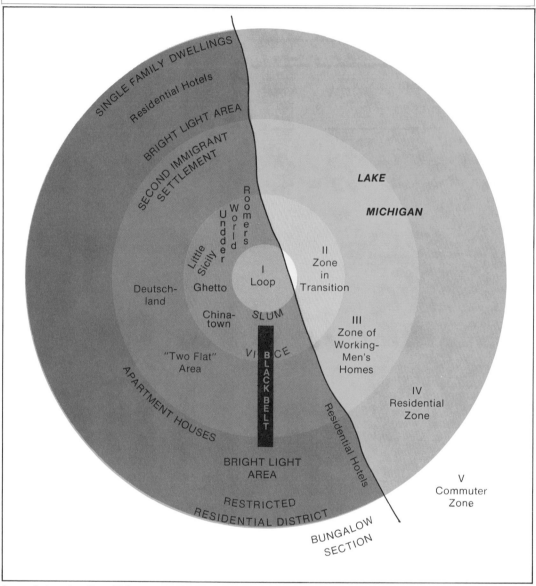

Source: Redrawn from Ernest W. Burgess, "The Growth of the City: An Introduction to a Research Project," in *Studies in Human Ecology*, ed. George A. Theodorson (Evanston, Ill.: Row, Peterson, 1961), p. 41.

Zone I: The Central Business District. This is the heart of the city and the most expensive land. At its center are found theatres, stores, elegant restaurants, investment banks, of-fices, and government buildings. A little far-ther out is the wholesale business district, with warehouses, produce markets, and the like.

Zone II: The Transition Zone. Beyond the business district is an area of seedy rooming houses, brothels, skid rows, and low-quality housing mixed with factories. In this zone, the crime rates are the highest in the city, and this is where immigrants settle when they come to Chicago.

Zone III: The Working-Class Residential Zone. In this zone are the homes of working people, often second-generation immigrants in Chicago. As these families move up the social ladder they will move farther out.

Zone IV: The Middle-Class Residential Zone. Once these areas were composed of single-family houses, but in Burgess's day many Chicago neighborhoods in this zone were built up with apartment buildings and local business districts.

Zone V: The Commuters' Zone. In this zone, the small suburban cities are located. Most of the men commute to jobs in the central business district each day, leaving this zone to their wives and children. These areas are sometimes called "dormitory suburbs" or "bedroom communities."

Burgess's model describes a nucleated, or single-center, city; Chicago and some of the older, larger, Canadian cities fit this pattern well. However, many of Canada's smaller, newer cities depart radically from Burgess's model.[17] Some of these cities have instituted strict zoning regulations to control their growth patterns and, as a result, have not expanded outward from a single center. In some cities, particularly those that have largely expanded since the 1950s, the construction of expressways has forced a pattern of development very different from that outlined by Burgess. In preindustrial cities, wealthy people more often live in the center of town than on the outskirts. Finally, the Burgess model underestimates the role of a city's terrain in determining its growth patterns. Vancouver, with its irregular shorelines and hills, does not conform to the concentric zone

FIGURE 18.3
Sector model of urban expansion

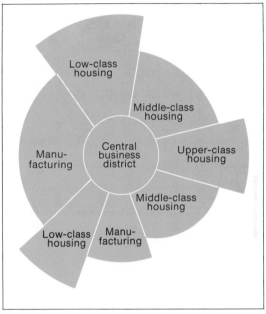

model. Unlike prairie cities, Vancouver cannot spread out equally in all directions when land values increase in its central core.

HOYT: THE SECTOR MODEL

As sociologists became aware that the Burgess model did not explain all patterns of urban change, they searched for new models. Homer Hoyt's sector model attempted to explain the changes that took place in such cities as San Francisco and Minneapolis, which appeared to be shaped mostly by the transportation routes that cut through the city.[18] Hoyt suggested that the center of the original city has various districts, such as the industrial zone, the business district, and affluent as well as modest residential areas. Each of these sectors expands like a slice of pie away from the center, usually following one of the transportation routes. (See Figure 18.3.)

FIGURE 18.4

Multiple-nuclei model of urban expansion

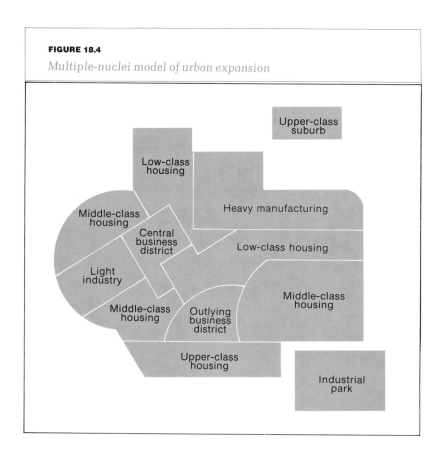

Chauncey D. Harris and Edward L. Ullman proposed a third ecological description, the multiple-nuclei model.[19] This model suggests that a city's zones are formed early in its history and that each zone expands any way it can—not necessarily in concentric circles or in a pie-slice pattern. Many separate business districts may grow up throughout the city, forming a patchwork of zones with separate nuclei. (See Figure 18.4.)

None of these three models fully explains the great variety of urban growth patterns shown by North American cities in the past few decades. "Urban sprawl" has been in-creasing so much that whole regions of the continent are becoming urbanized. We some-times refer to a number of cities as compris-ing a giant **megalopolis**, or "super city," ex-tending across a vast urbanized region. Along Lake Ontario, a single megalopolis stretches from Toronto to Hamilton. Indeed, the entire Macdonald-Cartier Expressway acts as a main artery through the urban complex that stretches from Windsor to Quebec City. Sub-urbs and new towns are filling in the gaps between the cities in such regions, and there will soon be little countryside remaining. Unfortunately, through urban sprawl we are paving over some of the richest agricultural land in Canada. The Niagara peninsula, for example, is becoming more urbanized daily.

SOCIAL RESEARCH:
Sociologists at Work

At the beginning of the chapter, I asked you to think about the kind of place you would like to live in. Would it be urban or rural? Here we will discuss some research on the trade-offs people make when choosing a place to live. Many of us have to choose between an apartment in a city and a somewhat larger place for the same price in the suburbs. In making that choice, we also make certain assumptions about what these environments are like and what we can expect from them. Some of those assumptions are correct. Some are not.

CROWDING AND APARTMENT LIVING

A common belief is that housing conditions have a strong effect on one's personality. Not so. It is good, of course, to have pleasant, clean, comfortable housing rather than a slum dwelling. However, space itself does not seem to be a factor in psychological well-being.[20]

People who avoid living in high-rise apartments usually do so for one of three reasons. (1) It is hard to keep an eye on children in apartments, so they are likely to be either underfoot or too far away to be looked after properly. (2) Crime rates are thought to be higher in highrise apartments than in single-family areas. (3) Apartment dwellers are assumed to be lonelier than other people. There is some truth to all of these points. It certainly is true that children who live in the top floors of tall buildings can't run in and out of doors and play as freely as children who live in ground-floor housing. Crime rates may be somewhat higher in apartment buildings than elsewhere. Crime does not occur, however, because the people living there mug each other. It occurs because apartment buildings contain areas such as elevators and stairwells. Criminals can usually get into such places quite easily unless there is a doorman on duty.[21]

Some parts of the city are better equipped for children than others.

Scott Mission   CIDEM/City of Montreal

I have already mentioned the argument concerning whether city dwellers are isolated and lack friends. It is true that apartment dwellers tend not to know their neighbors, but this does not mean that they are isolated. Most families that live in apartments probably wouldn't have much to do with their neighbors *wherever* they lived. For example, families in which the wife works are more likely to live in apartments than families in which the wife is at home all day. And working women do not "neighbor" much, on the whole.[22]

The general conclusion of all these studies is that, although apartment dwellers might like more privacy, more space, and so forth, they are not psychologically damaged by living in an apartment. And, as a matter of fact, urban residents are not as cramped for living space as rural people are. There are more people per room in rural areas than in urban areas.[23]

MOVING: WHY CANADIANS LIVE WHERE THEY DO

When I said that I would like to live on a canal in Venice, I was indulging in a pipe-dream. My job is in Toronto, I don't speak Italian, and I can't steer a gondola. Other people also have pipe-dreams. Polls that ask people where they want to live may not reflect their realistic plans. Realistic housing goals usually depend on a person's job, phase in the life cycle, life style and so on. Perhaps because of the exhaustive research required, only a few studies of people's housing goals have been made.

One such study was performed by William Michelson, in his book *Environmental Choice, Human Behavior, and Residential Satisfaction.*[24] In 1969, Michelson conducted a survey of people in the Toronto area to determine what types of housing they found satisfactory and how this related to their particular living conditions. Michelson defined satisfactory housing as that which suited the respondents' requirements reasonably well; he was not interested in their ultimate dream-houses.

Michelson contacted real estate agents, moving companies, and rental agents to find families who were about to rent or buy homes in the Toronto area. Of these, he chose as his respondents couples who had been married long enough to have had children, whether or not they had any. He usually interviewed them before they moved to determine their reasons for moving. After they

became established in their new homes, he interviewed them again to find out whether or not they were satisfied with their choice of residence.

Michelson was interested in finding answers to two different questions. The first question was reasonably simple and concrete. By examining respondents' pastimes, the size of their families, their housekeeping priorities, and so on, Michelson wanted to find out which living situations made particular housing choices more or less attractive. The second question was more abstract. Michelson also wanted to know whether people's behavior is shaped by their residential environments, or whether people selectively choose residential environments that suit their previously chosen behavior patterns.

Michelson knew that people with suburban, single-family homes are significantly different from people in downtown, high-rise apartments. He did not know, however, whether they differ *because* their residential environments offer them different opportunities and goals, or whether they are *already* different before they move into these different environments. Possibly people choose dissimilar types of housing because they already have dissimilar tastes. By talking to people before they moved, Michelson hoped to discover whether they chose different kinds of housing with particular goals in mind. Afterwards, he wanted to learn whether the possibilities and limitations of their new homes had caused them to change these goals.

As we might have expected, Michelson found that both happen. Certain types of people do choose certain types of housing, according to their previously developed tastes. But their new housing also forces them to adapt their life styles to some degree. Both your personality and living environment exert powerful influence on your behavior.

Michelson divided his sample into four groups, according to the type of housing they were moving into. These four groups were determined on the basis of two variables: location and type of accommodation. The location was either *downtown* in the center of Toronto or in a remote *suburb* of Toronto, such as Ajax in the east, Oakville in the west, or Thornhill in the north. Areas in between the downtown area and the remote suburbs were not studied. The type of accomodation was either a detached *single family house* or a *high-rise apartment*.

The sample was classified according to this typology with the following distribution:

high-rise downtown	109 families (14.3%)
single house downtown	94 families (12.4%)
high-rise suburban	286 families (37.6%)
single house suburban	272 families (35.8%)

Michelson found that the respondent's education level played a larger role than income level in choice of housing. Most of the respondents with university educations preferred to live downtown, while less-educated respondents tended to choose suburban residences. Downtown respondents, especially those moving into high-rise apartments, liked to read and attend downtown cultural events, such as plays. The downtown respondents tended to care more about the location than the quality of their dwellings, while suburban respondents tended to care most about quality.

The respondent's place in the life cycle influenced choice of residence even more than education level. Ordinarily, couples moving into downtown high-rises were considerably younger than those moving into other kinds of housing. They were also less likely to have children, although they often had babies soon after their move. The women in this group were by far the most likely to be employed outside the home. They cited time savings when travelling to and from work and lighter housekeeping duties as major factors in their choice of downtown apartments. (Michelson found that when a family owned only one car, the husband, not the wife, usually drove it to work; suburban working wives often spent a considerable portion of their time commuting.)

Couples who moved into downtown, single-family houses tended to be the most established in their careers and marriages. They had higher incomes than those who moved into downtown apartments, probably because their life cycles had entered a later phase. These couples generally had children. Most of the wives did not work, but did like to attend plays and other cultural events made accessible by downtown living.

The couples moving to the suburbs, especially those moving into single houses, were generally very family-oriented. Even before they moved to the suburbs, these couples expressed preference for typical suburban activities such as gardening. The suburban couples had less interest in live cultural events; the women enjoyed sewing and

knitting, while the men generally enjoyed watching spectator sports. Before they moved, the men frequently intended to spend a lot of time with their children; although they later found that they spent less time than anticipated, suburban men still tended to be oriented to family life.

Whether in the city or the suburbs, couples who moved into single houses tended to be churchgoers, to be involved in local organizations, and to enjoy such household activities as gardening and repair work. They spent far more time performing housekeeping tasks than the couples who moved to high-rise apartments; wives in houses spent two or three times as much time cooking, ironing, and cleaning house as wives in apartments. There were a number of reasons for this, some of which predated the choice of housing. Most of the women in houses had children, while most of the apartment-dwelling women were childless and employed outside the home. Husbands in downtown high-rises performed more housework than men elsewhere. Apartments are usually easier to clean than spacious houses. Finally, the women in apartments may have learned to be more efficient or may have lowered their housekeeping standards because they were less interested in household activities than the women who lived in houses.

The social lives of the downtown apartment dwellers differed significantly from those of the other groups. Downtown apartment dwellers spent less time with their neighbors than with other friends, while for house dwellers the reverse was true. This difference could be partially explained by the fact that neighbors most often become friends through their children. Unlike the other groups, the couples living in downtown apartments had few children old enough to create bonds with the neighbors. These couples tended to find friends through their work, interest groups, and so on. This does not mean that the downtown apartment dwellers were socially isolated, but simply that their friends were scattered throughout the city and beyond.

When Michelson interviewed the families after their moves, he found considerable variation in their degrees of satisfaction. The families who had moved into downtown single houses were generally the most pleased. Apartment dwellers in both the city and the suburbs had the most complaints. Apartment dwellers were powerless to solve most of their problems except by moving, while single-house residents could often remodel or take other measures to improve their situations.

Despite some inconveniences, Michelson found that few people, including the apartment dwellers, were really dissatisfied with their new homes; few people planned an immediate move to solve household problems. The respondents had evidently expected certain problems in their new homes and they took them in their stride. Michelson also found that, because most of the respondents planned to move on eventually, they did not feel unduly trapped by unforeseen difficulties, such as noisy neighbors or cramped closets. Generally, residents assumed that they would be able to afford better housing within a few years; meanwhile they

were willing to put up with a few problems. This was true even of condominium owners, half of whom planned to later buy a single house.

The selection of a dwelling, then, is generally regarded as an interim choice, not a permanent one. People gracefully accept short-term limitations because they believe they will continue to upgrade their standard of living to afford better housing as they progress through the life cycle. If they did not believe their income would increase, if they considered themselves permanently settled in a particular dwelling, they would probably become much less content with their housing. This discontent would be worst for apartment dwellers, who have the least power to remedy their housing problems.

SOCIAL POLICY:
Issues and Viewpoints

JACOBS: THE BLIGHT OF DULLNESS

Close your eyes and listen. Do you hear that jackhammer off in the distance? That's the sound of *urban renewal,* tomorrow's city under construction. Urban renewal—the demolition and rebuilding of run-down areas—is not a favorite solution just now, however. This disfavor is largely because of the criticism of Jane Jacobs, author of *The Death and Life of Great American Cities.*[25]

When she wrote her book, Jane Jacobs lived in Greenwich Village, a lively part of New York City. She has since moved to Toronto, where she has actively protested against the large development corporations that endanger the human scale of the city and against the intrusion of the Spadina Expressway into central Toronto. Jacobs's writings have been taken to heart by city planners throughout North America. Why, she asked herself in this first book, are areas like Greenwich Village such pleasant places to live while most areas in most

American cities are dull, unpleasant, and unsafe? Her book accuses city planners and urban-renewal programs of *creating* dullness and destroying the social relationships that make life bearable in some of the seedy neighborhoods in American cities. Her proposals run counter to ideas that have been assumed by city planners. For one thing, she opposes zoning laws that keep different kinds of facilities separate.

Jacobs believes that diversity is the key to vitality. Every district should have a rich variety of uses and should bring many different types of people together—rich and poor, old and young, black and white. It should mix residential buildings with industries and businesses and new buildings with old ones. She insists that people want diversity and that it encourages them to participate in the community. The main reason for the development of slums is that anyone who can afford to will leave a dull, homogeneous area. Poor people, with nowhere else to go, move in and the area decays even more. Greater diversity would keep this from happening.

Street life

Jacobs argues that vital, exciting neighborhoods have one thing in common: street life.

Ontario Ministry of Industry and Tourism

Urban vitality depends upon the quality of street life.

People like to live where the streets and sidewalks are used and where there are lots of other people to watch. Moreover, street life reduces crime rates because the people in the street and in the windows overlooking it protect each other better than police cars can.

How can designers create street life? Jacobs argues that each street should contain a variety of structures serving several different functions so that the street will be used at all hours of the day and night. The liveliest neighborhoods are those in which buildings have stores and offices on the street and apartments above them. Even a tavern down the block enlivens the neighborhood by attracting patrons throughout the evening and giving the apartment dwellers a variety of passers-by to watch from their windows. Crowds attract watchers and participants. This is why even the

parks should be small. Large open spaces let people spread out too far, and this creates dullness and attracts criminals.

Many ethnic sections of North American cities have the qualities Jacobs favors. Among them are Greenwich Village in New York, Old Montreal, Chicago's Back-of-the-Yards, and San Francisco's Telegraph Hill. In all of these areas, short blocks, wide sidewalks, and narrow streets encourage shopping and social life rather than automobile traffic. High-rent apartments are scattered among low-rent buildings that artists and small businesses can afford. Diversity causes vitality. During the past ten years, many well-to-do Canadians have shown their preference for the same formerly working-class areas that Jacobs likes. They have bought and remodeled large parts of Vancouver's Gastown and Toronto's Cabbagetown, for example.

Planning dullness

Jacobs holds that most city planners and architects create neighborhoods that are the exact opposites of those she admires. They build high-rise apartment buildings that separate the rich from the poor, the old from the young, the blacks from the whites. These buildings, which aren't very interesting, are located in residential zones. They are surrounded by large areas of useless open space where parents dare not let their children play. The residents rarely go out on the streets; instead, they drive to distant shopping centers. Because there are no small local stores, there are no friendly merchants to watch the street or to provide a place for neighbors to meet. Some of the more luxurious apartment buildings are protected by doormen, but they are still dull and impersonal. Other buildings are for the poor, and their isolation encourages crime. Jacobs blames these unattractive environments both on city planners and on the banks that refuse to grant loans for renovating old buildings in areas that are still vital. These areas are allowed to decay until they are taken over by slum-clearance programs that build new dullness to replace the dullness they tear down.

GANS: THE SOCIAL CLAUSES OF SLUMS

The most important attack on Jacobs's ideas is that by urban sociologist Herbert Gans, who has lived in, and written about, some of the neighborhoods Jacobs described.[26] His book, *The Urban Villagers,* is a delightful account of social life in a working-class Italian district in Boston, the West End, which was demolished by urban redevelopers even though its inhabitants had a rich communal life. Gans shares Jacobs's appreciation of vital city areas. However, he disagrees with many of her recommendations for city planning. He calls her ideas "the physical fallacy" in which a neighborhood's social characteristics are attributed to architectural design rather than to social, cultural, and economic factors. His own explanation of the problems of cities is based on class relations, not physical layout. He says that ethnic districts like Boston's Italian North End are actually not diverse but homogeneous. The old parts of Quebec City are good Canadian examples of this ethnic homogeneity. They are working-class areas, and this is why so much of their social life takes place outdoors. Middle-class families prefer to entertain and supervise their children's play indoors. Middle-class social life is largely invisible to passersby. Therefore, middle-class areas appear dull to the outsider, though they are not dull to the people who live there.

Gans thinks Jacobs overestimates the power of planners when she suggests that they should stimulate street life. Middle-class people *don't want* to socialize in the street, nor do they want their children to play on the sidewalks. They want the privacy and quiet of low-density neighborhoods and high-rise apartment buildings. Since their friends are scattered all over the metropolitan region, they want cars, expressways, and underground garages to make travel easy. They do not like neighborhoods where housing and businesses are mixed, even if they are more convenient than areas that are strictly residential. They prefer the supermarket, with its wide range of choices, to the small, ethnic grocery store. The places that Gans and Jacobs both enjoy are actually not holding their young people; when young residents have children of their own they move to the suburbs. Still, Gans agrees that charming working-class ethnic areas like the North End are reminders of our preautomobile past, well worth saving as low-rent districts that attract tourists and provide vital communities for people with low incomes.

Real slums

Real slums differ from ethnic neighborhoods in that few people choose to live there; most slum-dwellers simply have no other place to go. Like ethnic neighborhoods, slums consist of run-down buildings, but there is nothing quaint or charming about slum life. A neighborhood becomes a slum when the quality of neighborhood social life has clearly deteriorated. Slum housing is not merely ramshackle, but unsafe. Slums are not just densely populated, but critically overcrowded. When an Edmonton area was assessed as needing urban renewal, it was found to contain far higher than average rates of overcrowding, violence, fire, and chronic illness, and its inhabitants were less able to pay taxes than the other citizens of Edmonton.[27]

Most Canadian cities contain slums. The 1971 census found that over 9 percent of all dwellings in

Canada are overcrowded. Although this figure dropped from over 16 percent in the preceding census, it is still too high to allow Canadians to be complacent about housing. Newfoundland and the Northern Territories tend to contain the most overcrowded housing. The other Atlantic provinces have more overcrowding than Ontario, the prairies, or British Columbia.[28]

In order to clean up a slum area, more than renovation of the building is needed. Somehow, the population of the slum area must be reduced. This is difficult for a number of reasons. Absentee landlords make large profits from overcrowding and seldom want to reduce the number of their tenants. Most slum dwellers cannot easily move away because they cannot afford higher-priced housing.

A large proportion of slum inhabitants are older people who own their own homes but cannot afford to keep them in good repair.[29] Inflation makes this problem worse, because most of these old people rely upon fixed pensions and savings. As Canada's population continues to grow older, the housing problems of the aged are bound to become more severe. Even if more "senior citizens' homes" are constructed, few people who have owned their own homes want to live in them.

During the past several years, Canadian governments have wisely placed less emphasis on separate housing projects for the poor. Instead, federal and provincial governments have encouraged developers to provide low-income units in their regular new buildings. The Canada Mortgage and Housing Corporation has offered favorable mortgage breaks to builders who provide low-income housing this way. This policy subsidizes tenants with low and moderate incomes, while not isolating them as "charity cases" from the mainstream of society.

Unfortunately, however, this subsidy also encourages developers to tear down working-class neighborhoods that are not really slums and to replace older houses with high-rise apartments. As a result, few city-dwellers actually benefit from the subsidy. Since moving to Toronto, Jane Jacobs has participated in several citizens' action committees to persuade developers to build good, low-rent family housing that can be easily integrated into already existing neighborhoods. There are several alternatives to high-rise apartments for a developing city. Ideally, these should provide a higher density of people on scarce city land without producing the cramped sensations of high-rises. Some of Toronto's newer developments remind me a great deal of Paris. These developments consist of townhouses with little private gardens and six- or seven-storey apartment buildings built over shops and restaurants. Such developments are built on a human scale and allow their tenants more immediate contact with their urban environment.

As fuel for heating and transportation becomes more limited, the central city will probably attract more residents than it does now. We will have to find ways to house people in urban apartments so that they will view them as permanent homes rather than temporary residences. The apartment will become a home for a lifetime instead of a brief stop on the way to a detached single house. Well-designed, spacious, low-rise apartments, especially owner-controlled condominiums and co-ops, may supply an answer to this need.

At the end of his book,[30] William Michelson points out that there is a central paradox in the development of Canadian cities. Private corporations, who supposedly respond to the laws of supply and demand, have been building high-rise apartments at an astonishing rate even though surveys have shown that virtually everyone would prefer alternative forms of housing in the same locations. Apparently, even high-rise apartment dwellers do not like their homes; they accept them only because they cannot afford a house in a suitable place. If no one *wants* high-rises, what "demand" prompts developers to build so many? According to Michelson, developers build high-rises to offset huge increases in the value of city land; only through densely populated high-rises can builders make their expensive purchases of land pay off.

Michelson claims that this dilemma is avoidable, and arises from our habit of viewing land as a commodity to be bought and sold for profit. We *could* look upon land as a collective resource, like water or air. We could limit the rights of speculators to control land for personal gain. In Sweden, Michelson experienced the differences that such a change in attitude makes. The Swedish government halted the construction of high-rise apartments. Laws were passed that required new buildings to conform to the public's wishes; as a result, new Swedish apartments provide efficient and attractive housing. Canadians can enjoy similar housing if they work toward that goal.

SUMMARY

1. A *city* may be defined as a large, permanent, densely populated settlement. The existence of cities depends on the production of surplus food by farmers. It may be that settlements have always existed and have "paid their own way" by providing the technology that made surpluses possible. Many scholars assume, however, that cities did not exist until a fairly advanced agricultural technology had been developed.

2. Imperial cities were places surrounded by walls where the elites lived with their servants and suppliers. Since face-to-face communication was vital, the rulers of the empire stayed in the capital city where they could meet together and sent out administrators to rule the lesser cities of the empire. When an empire gained enough power to provide safety for its trading groups, it could expand over large areas. Gradually, however, the rulers came to rely on the people they had conquered, and in this way the subjects gained the skills they needed to overthrow their conquerors.

3. The cities of medieval Europe had more freedom than those of other societies. Today North American cities follow the medieval tradition by electing their own mayors. The idea of citizenship devloped out of the participation of freemen in the European city.

4. Most non-European preindustrial cities are unlike modern Western cities. Their different social classes are not separated; they have few suburbs; and the central business district is not well developed. Poor migrants from the countryside tend to live in shanty towns on the edges of the cities, maintaining a rural life style if they can.

5. *Urbanization* involves the movement of people from rural areas to cities and from small cities to larger ones. In advanced societies, this process is nearly complete. The cities of less-developed societies, especially in Asia, will become enormous in the future. Urbanization takes place because most consumer goods are produced more cheaply in the city than in the countryside.

6. In North America, more people are moving to the suburbs than to the cities. In the future, rising fuel prices will probably reverse this trend.

7. Robert Redfield and Louis Wirth took a "determinist" approach to the study of cities. They portrayed urban life as cold, large-scale, heterogeneous, impersonal, and culturally diverse. Redfield believed that urban culture was destroying folk culture around the world.

8. The "compositional" approach holds that density and size *in themselves* do not affect the psychological traits of urban or rural residents. However, urban people differ from rural and small-town people because the populations of cities and towns are composed of people with different characteristics in terms of age, marital status, social class, occupation, ethnicity, and so on. These characteristics, and not the density or size of the settlement, determine the traits of the different populations.

9. The "subcultural" view leans toward the compositional approach but admits that the size and density of a settlement determine the variety of subcultures found within it. These subcultures also have a diversifying effect on the people who belong to them. Thus city living supports more diversity—in both its deviant and its creative forms.

KEY TERMS

census metropolitan area (CMA)　a metropolitan region consisting of a large central city surrounded by smaller, dependent cities.

city　a large, permanent, densely populated settlement.

folk society　a small, isolated, homogeneous society; a peasant society.

megalopolis　a supercity in which several cities merge together to form an extended urbanized region.

suburbanization　the movement of people from central cities to smaller communities in the surrounding area.

urbanization　the movement of people from rural areas to cities and from small cities to larger ones.

urban society　a large-scale, heterogeneous society located in a city.

FOR FURTHER READING

CLARK, S.D. *The Suburban Society*. Toronto: University of Toronto Press, 1966. This is Clark's analysis of the outward spread of urban Canadian cities, as tract developers put up whole new suburbs almost overnight.

CLARK, S.D. *The New Urban Poor*. Toronto: McGraw-Hill Ryerson, 1978. A study of poor rural people who move to urban areas, where their existence is largely hidden.

GENTLER, LEN and RON CROWLEY. *Changing Canadian Cities: The Next 25 Years*. Toronto: McClelland and Stewart, 1977. This approach treats urban development as more of a technical problem for city planners than a political problem.

LITHWICK, N.H. and GILLES PAQUET. *Urban Studies: Canadian Perspective*. Toronto: Methuen, 1968. This is a valuable presentation of both general urban concerns and factual data.

MICHELSON, WILLIAM. *Man and His Urban Environment: A Sociological Approach*. Reading, Mass.: Addison-Wesley, 1970. Michelson's elegant little book will introduce you to the urban research

that examines the physical environment and its effects upon social interaction.

NADER, GEORGE A. *Cities of Canada, Vol. 2: Profiles of Fifteen Metropolitan Centres*. Toronto: Macmillan, 1976. Nader provides a strong historical coverage of the development of Saint John, Saskatoon, Victoria, St. John's, Halifax, Quebec City, Montreal, Ottawa-Hull, Toronto, Hamilton, Winnipeg, Regina, Calgary, Edmonton, and Vancouver. Rich in social statistics and factual detail about land use patterns.

SEELEY, JOHN R., R. SIM, and E. LOOSLEY. *Crestwood Heights*. Toronto: University of Toronto Press, 1956. This is one of the classics of Canadian sociology, a description of a Toronto suburb that is given the pseudonym, Crestwood Heights. The suburb is described in detail right down to the provision of a rough map. Because Crestwood Heights seems to be pretty far away from the city, my students often guess that it is Thornhill or Oakville. They are astonished to learn that is actually Forest Hill, which today is considered almost the center of Toronto.

STONE, LEROY O. *Urban Development in Canada*. 1961 Census Monograph, Dominion Bureau of Statistics. Ottawa: Queen's Printer, 1967. Stone is always thorough in whatever he writes. The data he used in this study, however, have become very antiquated due to the fast rate of urbanization in Canada since 1961.

19

SOCIAL CHANGE

Theoretical approaches to social change
    Cycle theories
    Evolutionism
    Functionalism
A functionalist theory of social evolution
Parsons: cultural breakthroughs and
    evolution
Conflict theory and social change
Social Research: Sociologists at Work
Social Policy: Issues and Viewpoints

Sociology textbooks have to be revised about every three years because life is changing so fast. Today's newspaper tells me that the United States will sell certain military equipment to China. (Imagine that!) And that a gay highschool boy has won the right to bring a male date to his school prom. And that Mr. Trudeau is going ahead with his plan to replace the BNA Act with a constitution that most people in Quebec will like better. And that the oil of a desert plant, the jojoja, substitutes well for whale oil and thus may help preserve that species from extinction. And that German Volkswagen manufacturers are investing in robots, each of which will cost $150,000 and replace 300 hand welders.

By the time you read this chapter, these stories will be old news. Canada may have a new constitution and China and the U.S. may be selling bombs to the Russians. But there will be new problems to solve. How can you prepare yourself to live in a world where the issues of today would have been utterly unpredicted a generation ago and where changes show no sign of slowing up? It won't be easy.

The rapidity of social change makes the socialization of children very chancy. Parents used to know, by and large, what attitudes and skills they should teach their children to prepare them for adult life. But today children are likely to know more about many things than their parents by the time they grow up. This fact changes our attitudes toward old people. In traditional societies, old people are respected. They know more, and their wisdom is useful. But old people in our industrial society are seldom asked for advice by younger people; old people are considered behind the times. In the past, the older generation socialized the younger generation. Now the young may socialize the old. Our culture is actually being *created* from one day to the next. The new is arising out of the old, yet it is transforming the old at the same time.

Traditional society has given way to modern society. On balance, this is a good thing, I think. People are more open to new possibilities, even though those possibilities demand more flexibility and create considerable strain. But before we talk about how modern society differs from traditional society, we need to know something about social change.

Theoretical approaches to social change

Because sociologists are concerned with the changing patterns of social life over time, they often assume that social change may be following some orderly, regular trend over long periods. It is dangerous to make such assumptions, however. When we look closely we may find that other explanations are more tenable than the one we have taken for granted. This is why we will begin this chapter with a discussion of various theoretical approaches to social change.

History may be heading in any of several possible directions. A grouch will complain that "We're going to hell in a handbasket." An optimist will cheerfully argue that we are making all kinds of progress. Another person will look for cycles, saying that there are ups and downs in everything; you win a little, you lose a little, what goes up must come down, and so on. Obviously, all three positions are whopping generalizations. Yet various scholars have tried to defend each of these positions. I won't deal with pessimism here because it is a rather limited view. But I will mention the other two approaches— cycle theories and, more important, evolutionary theories.

CYCLE THEORIES

In the days of the ancient Greeks, the cycle theory was taken for granted, even by writers like Plato. It was assumed that every natural event was repeated endlessly. In our own century, too, some social theorists have believed in historical cycles. Of these, perhaps the best known was Pitirim Sorokin, who fled from Russia after the Bolsheviks came to power and who taught at Harvard for many years. Sorokin believed that any society swings between two opposite types of culture, "sensate" and "ideational." The sensate periods are those in which a society emphasizes materialistic, pleasure-seeking values; the ideational periods are those in which it stresses ideals and spiritual concerns. While it is moving from the sensate to the ideational, or vice versa, the society is "idealistic"—a fortunate condition in which both sets of values are present.

According to Sorokin, the Gothic art of the medieval period shows that it was the most ideational period of Western history. The paintings of the time all portray Christ's suffering and the lives of the great religious figures of Christianity. By contrast, modern art shows that our time is the most sensate period of Western history. What art could be less spiritual than a giant Campbell soup can? Sorokin would have preferred to live in the Middle Ages.

Another theorist, the historian Oswald Spengler, has portrayed the life cycles of civilizations as similar to the life cycles of people. Civilizations are born, grow up, become senile, and finally die.[1] Today, however, few scholars hold to cycle theories. An opposing view has become increasingly popular —the assumption that the normal state of affairs is for societies to make progress, not to go downhill. The early sociologists took it for granted that progress was normal, and some believed it was inevitable. This view is hard to accept after the terrible wars of our century. Still, while progress is not *assumed* to be *normal,* most people think it is at least *possible.*

In many ways, human beings *have* made progress over time. The theory that is used to explain this trend is called *evolutionism.*

EVOLUTIONISM

Auguste Comte

Evolutionism is the belief that every society progresses toward perfection through stages of increasing complexity. None of the early sociologists questioned this belief. Auguste Comte and Herbert Spencer both tried to identify the various stages through which all societies must progress. Both believed that there was a single theme underlying all of human history: *It moves from the simple to the complex.* Therefore any development will always be simpler than the development that comes after it—no matter what. For example, Comte noticed that the various branches of knowledge developed at different periods in history, and he argued that this was because the later sciences were more complex than the early ones. Thus sociology, the newest science, couldn't develop until biology was in existence. And biology developed after chemistry, which developed after physics, which developed after mathematics. Obviously, then, mathematics is the least complex science!

Comte believed that human thought passes through three stages. In the first (or "theological") stage, people think inanimate objects are alive. Thus a primitive person may believe that a tree is in pain while it is being cut down. (My next-door neighbor believes the same thing. She sings to her African violets.) Natural events are thought to be caused by spirits or gods with human emotions. In the second (or "metaphysical") stage, events are explained in terms of abstract forces. The third (or "positive") stage is the scientific period, in which people explain events in terms of natural processes and do not expect total certainty.[2]

Comte suggested that not only societies but individuals and sciences pass through these three stages, though perhaps at different rates. For example, a child might believe that a vacuum cleaner is a living monster and grad-

TABLE 19.1

Time line showing important technological developments

750,000 B.C.	Controlled use of fire
10,000	Domestication of the dog
8000	Emergence of food production
7000	Domestication of the ox
4350	Domestication of the horse
3500	Use of the wheel
3500	Metal-smelting
3000	Domestication of the camel
2600	Seagoing ships
2500	Domestication of water buffalo and yak
1200	Iron technology develops
300	Invention of pulleys, levers, screw, pump, and water wheel
A.D. 650	Windmills first used in Moslem world
850	Gunpowder bombs (China)
852	Burning of coal for heating (England)
900	Widespread use of watermill for grinding grain (northern Europe)
1250	Watermill applied to making cloth, sawing wood, and extracting oil from vegetable seed
1250	Coal used by smiths as a source of energy
1386	Mechanical clock (installed in Salisbury Cathedral, England)
1448	Gutenburg Bible printed with movable metal type (Germany)
1606	Experimental steam engine (Italy)
1709	Use of coal in iron industry
1712	Commercially successful steam engine invented by Newcomen (England)
1765	Modern steam engine invented by Watt (England)
1787	Steamboat (USA)
1790	Sewing machine (England)
1800	Electric battery (Italy)
1812	Practical steam locomotive (England)
1831	Generation of electric current (England)
1852	Passenger elevator (USA)
1859	First oil well drilled (USA)
1862	Dynamite (Sweden)
1874	Chain-driven bicycle (England)
1874	Telephone (USA); four-cycle gasoline engine and carburetor (Germany)
1880	Patent of electric-light bulb (USA)
1882	Commercial use of hydroelectric power (USA)
1887	Gasoline-powered automobile (Germany)
1892	Diesel engine (Germany); gasoline-powered tractor (USA)
1900	Rigid airship (Germany)
1903	Flight of Wright brothers (USA)
1923	Bulldozer (USA)
1926	Rocket fired with liquid propellant (USA)
1926	Television (Scotland, USA)
1937	Jet engine (England)
1945	Nuclear explosion (USA)
1946	Electronic computer (USA)
1951	Hydrogen bomb (USA)
1954	Nuclear power plant put into operation (USSR)
1957	Artificial satellite (USSR)
1958	Laser (USA)
1969	Astronauts land on moon (USA)
1975	USA and USSR astronauts link in space
1976	Scheduled flights of supersonic aircraft (USSR, Britain–France)

Source: "The Conquest of Energy," from *Humankind* by Peter Farb. Copyright © 1978 by Peter Farb. Reprinted by permission of Houghton Mifflin Company.

ually give up this theory as he or she grows up. Positivism is the scientific outlook—the assumption that natural causes can explain everything. Comte believed that human beings all tend to move toward this sophisticated outlook as we mature. This tendency is the underlying force that moves history in a forward direction, rather than backward or in cycles. Everything moves onward and upward in a single line of development. This view is called unilinear evolutionism. It assumes that there is a single set of stages through which every person, every branch of knowledge, and every society must proceed.

Herbert Spencer

Spencer was Comte's best-known follower. In thinking about Comte's comparison of a society to an organism, he decided that societies that are at the same stage of growth must be similar in a number of ways.[3] And if this is so, then by comparing the accounts of travelers in foreign countries one should be able to classify societies in terms of their level of development. You may notice a problem with Spencer's approach: If societies are like organisms, they will grow old and die instead of getting better all the time. Spencer was inconsistent because he didn't follow his analogy to its conclusion.

Spencer was inconsistent on another issue as well. He seems never to have made up his mind whether he believed in unilinear evolution or not. In some places he wrote that all societies follow the same line of development. In other places he wrote that various societies follow different lines of development—a view that is called multilinear evolutionism. However, he leaned toward the unilinear theory and tried to fit the diversity of human societies into a single classification system. This effort made for bad history writing; it meant creating an imaginary series of developmental stages and then trying to make the histories of real societies fit that model. Spencer had to trim off a few awkward facts to make history fit his models. Historians call that sort of

trimming "cheating" or "fudging." Good historians "tell it like it happened," not like they imagine it was *supposed to happen,* according to some theory of development. Historians accused Spencer and other evolutionary writers of distorting historical evidence, and even sociologists became uncomfortable about the idea of unilinear evolution. And so, in the first part of this century, people began to drop evolutionism.

Diffusionism

Evolutionism views different societies as if they were so many cabbage plants in a row, all planted at the same time and growing up under slightly different conditions. These conditions affect the rate of growth, so that some societies (or cabbages) are more mature than others. By looking at the mature organisms you can predict what the more backward ones will look like a little later. Little cabbages all grow up to be big cabbages, never turning into carrots or onions. Similarly, according to unilinear evolutionary theory, less developed societies will come to look like advanced societies when they have matured further.

Of course this analogy breaks down when it is applied to human affairs. In a garden, you don't have carrots imitating cabbages and growing big leaves. You don't have onions making war on parsnips and forcibly converting them into pseudo-onions. Eggplants never dominate tomatoes and rob them of their heritage through cultural imperialism. Biological organisms follow a fixed line of development without changing their traits along the way. But human societies borrow cultural traits from each other. This means that they can skip whole stages of development. The technology of the Australian tribesmen, for example, is moving straight from the stone age into the industrial age as a result of European influence. This cultural borrowing is called *diffusion.* You can trace on a map the spread of a given trait. Ways of building canoes, the use of writing, the habit of smoking tobacco—examples of diffusion are countless. How many nations can build atomic bombs? Most of them learned how through diffusion.

Not all diffusion moves ideas from technologically advanced societies to backward ones, though this happens quite often. Actually, the distinction between "backward," or "primitive," and "advanced" assumes a unilinear view of social change; by using such terms we implicitly claim that one society is "ahead" and one is "behind". But "advanced" nations also borrow cultural ideas from "backward" ones—so which society is ahead? Diffusion challenged evolutionary theory, and caused many sociologists to give up the whole idea of evolutionism and turn to other topics.

That decision, however, also proved awkward. Although there were problems with evolutionism, there was *something* to it. Therefore, during the past 15 years of so, sociologists have been developing a new version of evolutionism.

Evolutionary theory today

What can be said for the idea of social evolution? Certainly, some things have to happen in a fixed order. For example, no hunting-and-gathering society could have discovered atomic energy. No preliterate society could have put together a large political empire. No society with a barter economy could have developed capitalism. *Some historical developments are necessary in order to make other developments possible.* This is why it

Much of the technology used around the world has been transmitted by diffusion. People don't have to invent sewing machines and motor scooters for themselves—they can borrow the ideas.

Rebecca Busselle/DPI   Fujihira/Monkmeyer

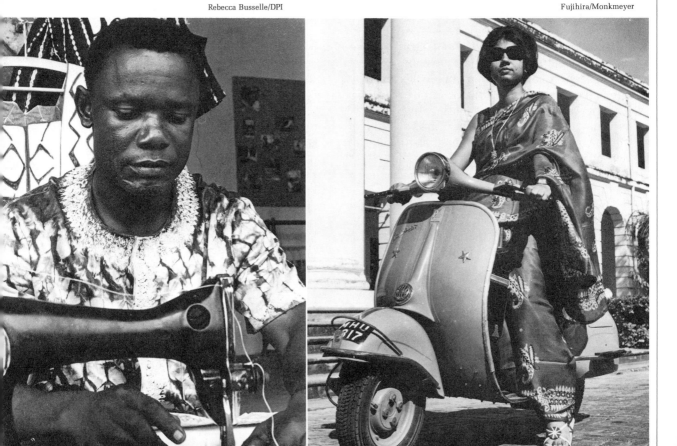

makes sense to call some societies more "advanced" than others. Bows and arrows are less advanced than atomic bombs because they developed first. Certain innovations are crucial to further development. For example, only a society that grasps the concept of zero can make further advances in mathematics, as well as in the sciences that depend on mathematics.

This is what we mean by "progress." Humankind can develop ideas and institutions in later stages that would have been impossible in earlier stages. Thus modern theories of social evolution are attempts to explain the sequence in which such developments occur. However, it is also important to recognize what evolutionism does *not* imply. In order to make evolutionism stand up against criticism, theorists have had to make certain changes, which are as follows:

1. *Evolution is not inevitable.* Progress may take place—or it may not. A society that grasps a concept that *might* lead to further development may not see the implications of that concept. Thus the Mayan Indians understood the concept of the wheel (pottery toys with wheels have been found in their tombs), but they didn't recognize the usefulness of wheels for vehicles and machinery. Discovery of the wheel made further evolution possible, but obviously this didn't make it inevitable. Because it didn't always happen.

2. *Evolution is not unilinear.* There is no single sequence of steps through which all societies must pass as they become more advanced. For that matter, some societies *don't* advance. They may stay about the same for thousands of years, or they may decline instead of progressing. Others borrow from other cultures and skip many stages of development. Cultural change does not follow a fixed order, as the growth of an organism does. We can predict that an acorn will become an oak tree, not a willow. But we can't predict what system of government India will have 50 years from now.

3. *Evolutionism is not social Darwinism.* Spencer thought human progress depended on raw competition between individuals or societies. We know better! Progress depends on cooperation more than competition. Through cooperation we can increase the total amount of resources available so that everyone benefits. We don't have to fight over the limited available food or water. By working together we can produce *more* food, build canals to bring in *more* water, and so on. One group does not have to wipe out other groups in order to survive.

4. *Evolutionism does not imply a final goal.* The word *progress* implies progress toward a goal, but we do not necessarily have to agree on all our goals to know whether we are getting ahead or going downhill. Your idea of progress may not be the same as mine, and therefore we won't always agree about whether a given change is an improvement or a step backward. Still, we often do agree. We all agree, for example, that the introduction of writing or voting is progress.

5. *Progress in one area may not be progress in another area.* For example, a technological advance may not be an aesthetic or moral advance. Our century has seen dramatic technological progress, but it has also seen more cruelty than any previous century. Often an evolutionary breakthrough increases justice or raises living standards, but that is not always so. Thus an advance in social organization made it possible to build the pyramids, but the poor fellows who had to haul the blocks of stone probably didn't think they were getting a better deal. Likewise, landing on the moon was a fantastic technical achievement, but later generations may think of it as a huge waste of money. What society calls progress depends on what it values. We value rocket research, but whether it is necessary for further development is not yet known. An **evolutionary breakthrough** is an innovation that makes further advances possible. It may be an immediate blessing to all or it may cause suffering instead, just as the Industrial Revolution initially brought deprivation and disorder for many people. Thus, progress on one front is not necessarily progress on all fronts.

FUNCTIONALISM

As mentioned earlier, sociologists dropped the idea of evolutionism because it was unable to account for the phenomenon of diffusion, and it has only recently been revived. Meanwhile scholars turned their attention to several other theories of social change. Among these was functionalism. Instead of asking what stages of development societies go through in developing their family patterns, their political systems, or their economies, the functionalists focused on the part these arrangements play in the societies in which they are found.

Functionalism is the belief that a social pattern is best understood not in terms of its past historical development but in terms of its current consequences for the society in which it is operating. We have already looked at a number of functionalist theories. For example, we saw that stratification has certain effects (functions) in terms of getting well-qualified people to fill key occupational roles. We saw that religion has certain functions in terms of integrating a person into his or her group, and that the family has many functions—such as regulating sexual activity, socializing children, and providing emotional support.

In all of these examples, the institution in question is assumed to serve a *positive* function for the group. This is where functionalism is biased. It tends to be conservative, suggesting that whatever exists is good. It supports reasoning like this: "Whatever exists must exist because it serves some function. And if it serves a function, it shouldn't be changed." Naturally, nobody *says* such a thing. It sounds so obviously naive. Nevertheless, I think functionalist theories tend to run along those lines.

You may have noticed something else. Functionalist theories explain why things are the way they are; they don't explain change. They are *static*, not *dynamic*. Despite this drawback, functional explanations are often interesting, and when functionalism is linked to evolutionism it becomes quite useful. We will discuss this combination in the next section. First it is necessary to describe how functionalism has been modified in recent years.

1. *Societies are not "integrated" systems in which every part is necessary for the whole to function.* This is obvious. Often we just limp along, surviving in spite of, not because of, certain social practices. Some social customs are dysfunctional. And some customs serve no function at all; they are neither functional nor dysfunctional, neither good nor bad. For example, no functional explanation is possible for the buttons on men's coatsleeves. To explain their presence, we must point out that they survive from the time when they were used to fasten on gauntlets. (Some of my students hold to a different, more interesting explanation—that they were sewn on by order of a general to keep soldiers from wiping their runny noses on their sleeves!)

2. *A custom may be helpful to a segment of the social system and harmful to the system as a whole.* For example, a code of honor among thieves is helpful to professional criminals but does nothing for the society of which those criminals are a part.

3. *Elements that are suitable are not necessarily essential.* Substitutes are possible. For example, parliamentary democracy is suitable to an industrialized economy, but it is not essential. Some industrial societies have other forms of government.

4. *The components of a social system do not always fit together harmoniously.* Indeed, society can be viewed as a "tension management system."4 There are strains, contradictions, and a never-ending series of problems in every society. When one problem has been solved, a new one pops up to take its place. Some problems don't get solved. We simply cope, with varying success, sometimes for centuries.

After all this, what is left of functionalism? Well, the idea of functional requisites still seems useful. There are certain requirements that all societies must meet, at least at a minimum level. Socialization is an example. Child-rearing systems vary—but if a society completely fails to train its young for adult roles, that society will not survive.

The concept of functional requisites is useful in combining evolutionism and functionalism. Societies that meet their functional requisites very well are more likely to survive than other social groups. And this is one basis for evolution. Let's see how well functionalism and evolution fit together.

A functionalist theory of social evolution

Let's start with evolutionism. Our theory resembles Darwin's in that it accounts for change in terms of *variation* and *challenge.* In biology, mutation is a constant source of variation: Every so often a gene changes, for some mysterious reason, and a new trait crops up in a given organism. For example, variation in the length of horses' legs is due to mutation. Long ago horses were small—about the size of foxes. And there were challenges for them to face—meat-eating enemies, such as tigers. Whenever tigers chased horses, more of the short-legged ones were caught. Hence, more long-legged than short-legged horses survived to reproduce. This explains why, over many generations, the whole species changed.

In human affairs, there are many other explanations besides mutation for the varia-

tions in the ways that different groups and individuals do things. The notion of *challenge* is important, however. In Darwinian theory, tigers challenged horses. In social theory, human relationships and natural events challenge human beings, and human beings adapt. Whenever a group finds a solution to a challenge to its survival, it probably prizes that solution and passes it along through its culture. Indeed, other groups, recognizing that it is a nifty trait, may borrow it. So a challenge fosters innovation, and an innovation, if useful, diffuses to other populations. (In biological evolution, genes cannot be transmitted except through reproduction, so traits remain within a given population.)

Of course, not *all* useful innovations are recognized. There is nothing inevitable about this process. Some terrific ideas have been ignored or forgotten. Evolutionists simply claim that, on the average, a good idea stands a fair chance of being adopted and kept— especially if it appears just when people most need it.

Good ideas do tend to arise when they are needed and not otherwise. This is why challenge is an important element in our theory. Challenge stimulates people to search for new ideas. With no challenge, there is no innovation. People will stick to custom as long as it works even moderately well. As a result, most human societies have remained primitive. According to the historian Arnold Toynbee, only 21 one of them have progressed to becoming genuine civilizations. When people are faced with a problem that demands adaptation, they may change—or they may not. If they do, the change may work—or it may not. If it doesn't, the group may vanish, just as short-legged horses vanished, thanks to the fast tigers. Institutions that survive may be those of the surviving groups. We forget the others that didn't survive.

But innovation poses new challenges too. Once a group starts changing it may be unable to stop for a long time. Society is not a stable, harmonious, well-integrated system—

or at least Western society is not. Some primitive societies may be. But modern societies are, at best, "tension-management systems." For example, if we cure malaria by eliminating mosquitoes, we can rejoice for a few years. Then we find out that the DDT we're using has problems of its own—problems that may be worse than mosquitoes. New problems arise as fast as old ones are solved. Modern society has an endless supply of new challenges.

The sources of change may be technology or unexpected ideas. In modern society, technology changes rapidly. Whenever some new machine or medicine diffuses throughout the world, it affects other social institutions. In Chapter 3, I mentioned *cultural lag*,[5] the tendency of social institutions to fall behind

Human beings are very stimulated by challenges and one of the greatest challenges has been to travel and live in outer space. Shown here is a 10,000 inhabitant space colony proposed by the NASA—Ames/Stanford study. Scientists say such a colony might be built with existing technology by 1995.

NASA

technological change. Cultural lag produces a variety of social problems. Pollution is an example. Until recently, our laws have allowed industry to exploit the environment almost unhindered. We have assumed that Mother Nature could heal her own wounds. Now she is gasping and moaning, but by the time we come to her aid with some new laws, she may be mortally wounded.

Ideas are another source of challenge. Many ideas come from confronting other people who think in different ways. The most stable, unchanging societies are almost always those that are isolated from contact with foreigners; strange beliefs and practices tend to unsettle one's habitual outlook and require re-thinking. When you have to deal with foreigners, especially face to face, you must either adopt their ways or at least try to reconcile them with your own. And doing this stimulates discovery and new solutions. For example, when the American journalist James Reston was in China he had appendicitis. His surgeons used acupuncture to anesthetize him. When he wrote about this in his column, thousands of Americans asked their own doctors about acupuncture. The American doctors were unable to ignore the challenge, so they began studying acupuncture. No one fully understands how acupuncture works—at least no one in the West. Hence, if we arrive is an explanation, it will have to be one that reconciles Chinese medical theory with Western science. Such a challenge would not have arisen without contact between the two societies.

When cultures meet, as, for example, during migrations, some people find themselves in an ambiguous position. They belong partly to one tradition and partly to another. These people are "marginal."[6] Their situation is both uncomfortable and stimulating. Because they have to reconcile two ways of life, they often come up with creative innovations. For example, the Jews have been very creative—possibly because they have often been marginal.

Wide World

American doctors didn't believe in acupuncture until an American journalist described his own surgery in China. Now they are studying it too. This boy is being treated for deafness and his hearing has improved.

Suppose you want to stimulate social change and innovation. How will you do it? One way might be to gather a lot of incompatible ideas and ask people to sort them out. Some of our most vital social institutions do just that. Universities do it. Libraries do it. Science does it. All of these institutions have built-in sources of social change. They challenge people simply by bringing dissimilar ideas together. Scientists, for example, are paid to conduct studies, publish their results, and read the findings that other scientists publish. Naturally, they criticize one another's work, and this criticism leads to scientific discovery.

Social evolution, therefore, is mainly a response to challenge. Functionalists can contribute quite a bit to our understanding of this process by identifying evolutionary (or cultural) breakthroughs. That is, functionalism helps us analyze the effects of a given

NFB Photothèque/Pearce

Modernization is not all positive. This Inuit family's diet includes too much sugar and processed food to be wholesome.

social pattern on other aspects of the social system.

Functionalists point out that all societies have certain functional requisites. They all have to meet certain basic problems, such as feeding and sheltering their populations, reproducing and socializing their children, giving emotional support to their members, settling disputes in an orderly way, and so on. Some societies solve some of these problems better than others do. Functionalism helps us understand how a given society solves its problems. To understand whether an innovation is a terrific idea or a terrible one, we have to look at it along with other arrangements in the society and see whether they will fit together or not. This is functional analysis.

Successful innovations are those that move societies forward and make them better able to cope with a wide range of problems. For example, a literate society can do many things that a preliterate society cannot do. So writing is an evolutionary breakthrough. Through the creation and diffusion of cultural breakthroughs, human society has moved from one stage of evolution to another. Talcott Parsons provides some examples of this process.

Parsons: cultural breakthroughs and evolution

Parsons was both an evolutionist and a functionalist. He showed how certain civilizations solved problems better than other civilizations, thereby enabling further advances to take place. Two of the most important cultural breakthroughs described by Parsons were writing and the development of formal rational law.

Parsons classified human societies into three main levels of development—primitive, intermediate, and modern. In his view, it was writing that moved human society from the primitive level to the intermediate level. It was primarily rational, formal law that moved society from the intermediate level to the modern level.

The invention of writing makes possible a great increase in cultural diffusion, both in space and in time. It enables one to "broadcast" messages to anyone who is literate and happens to come across the document. And a literate society can have a *history*. It can record events that are beyond the memories of living people. We discussed the importance of writing in Chapter 3. Parsons claimed that it was one of human society's greatest breakthroughs. It led to major developments in many other areas. Written documents are *cumulative* in impact. This means that a literate society possesses enormously greater cultural capacity than a preliterate one. Accordingly, Parsons classified literate societies as "intermediate" in their evolutionary development—a giant step ahead of primitive societies. Examples of such "intermediate" societies are: the Egyptians; the Mesopotamians; the Incas; the Islamic, Chinese, Indian, and Roman empires; and the cultures of the Greeks and the Hebrews.

Parsons dated "modern" society from the Protestant Reformation of the seventeenth century. Several important evolutionary breakthroughs took place at that time. One of these was the development of formal law. Of course the Romans had a highly developed legal system; in fact, English common law was Roman law adapted to English life. However, a very special development took place in England in the seventeenth century: The law became independent of the crown. The legal profession began to protect private rights *in opposition to the crown*. The British government thus was put in the position of both defining and enforcing restrictions on its own power.

The development of formal law gave citizens a way of using the government to protect themselves *from* the government and using the law to protect themselves from the legal system. Parsons believed that the development of formal rational law was a cultural breakthrough because it provided for social order, for predictability, for security of private rights, and personal freedom, all at once. This social context encouraged additional cultural progress. Parsons considered the law to be one of the great achievements of Western civilization.

Conflict theory and social change

I often have imaginary conversations with Karl Marx. In my fantasy he has a bushy white mane and beard and is almost handsome, but he is a fierce critic. I never win arguments with him, so I had hoped to tiptoe past him in this chapter and not discuss social change with him at all. No such luck. He hailed me in his usual manner, by bellowing, "Bourgeois ideologist!" I knew I was caught. I'd have to discuss the functionalist theory of evolution with him.

For a while the discussion didn't go too badly. Marx seemed to agree with the concept of evolution. His own theory, historical materialism, was in a way an evolutionary account of social change throughout history. Remember how he said that capitalism "contains the seeds of its own destruction"? This is clearly a theory of social change that points to a better future.

We also agreed on the importance of technological change in creating changes in social relationships. To be sure, Marx said that the productive system of a society would determine its social classes—the working class and the ruling class. And he said that clashes between those groups would lead to social change. Moreover, he argued that competition between the bourgeois industrialists would force them to improve their technologies and that in the long run this would cause their own downfall. Thus Marx believed that the future of human history was predictable, even inevitable.

When I mentioned the importance of challenges and contradictions as a source of innovation, he nodded. I mentioned how new ideas usually develop from the clash of opposing points of view. "Of course," he interrupted. "That's called the dialectic! But it isn't just *ideas* that clash. It's the interests of different social classes!"

I thought about this for a while and realized that what I had described as the challenge of being marginal was very similar to an idea that Marx had picked up from Hegel. Hegel had suggested that ideas always work themselves out by being challenged by opposing views. In time these pairs of opposites (which he called "thesis" and "antithesis") are reconciled in some new idea (or "synthesis") that uses whatever is valid in each of the opposing views but improves on both of them. This moves thought in a progressive direction. In time, the synthesis would itself become a thesis, would be opposed by a new antithesis, and finally would be replaced by another, more advanced synthesis. This whole process Hegel called "the dialectic."

Marx turned Hegel's dialectic into a theory of history, saying that instead of *ideas* fighting it was *social classes* that did so. Hence, Marx's theory of social change is called "historical materialism" or "dialectical materialism."

I was beginning to feel rather pleased by my success in winning Marx's approval as we discussed the concept of evolution. However, when I turned to functionalism and evolutionary breakthroughs my luck ran out.

I said that societies probably tend to maintain the social practices that have been most useful in helping them meet their functional requisites. He frowned and called me a "lackey of the ruling class." Then he launched a major attack on functionalism, calling it a conservative ideology. The main point in his argument seemed to be this: It is not whether something is *useful*, not whether it is *functional*, that determines whether it will be kept by a society. What determines that is power, sheer *power!* The group that has enough power to get its way determines what institutions are maintained. Is capitalist exploitation of workers "functional"? Is it "useful?" Of course not! Exploitation continues because the capitalists still have power. When the workers have enough power to stop them, it will stop. You don't have to believe that everything that exists does so for a good reason.

He had won again. I had to agree with him on that point. Social practices that exist at any one time may indeed be harmful, not helpful. They may be maintained, not because they have proved valuable as solutions to the problems and challenges of the society, but simply because an oppressive group has the power to keep them going.

"So remember that! And tell your students to remember it too!" he growled.

"Yes, Karl, I will. I promise," I replied.

So you remember it too. This is your final lesson in conflict theory.

SOCIAL RESEARCH: Sociologists at Work

So far we have discussed social change at the societal level. We have seen how ancient literate empires differed from primitive hunting-and-gathering bands and how seventeenth-century England differed from other European societies of the time. We have talked about changes taking place across the centuries, changes involving all of humankind.

Now we're going to look at the social changes that are happening *within the individual* and *in our own time.* Throughout the world, billions of human beings are changing their outlook, behavior, and expectations and adjusting to their fast-changing societies. What happens to the personalities of traditional people as they become modern people? This is the subject of a book by Alex Inkeles and David H. Smith entitled *Becoming Modern,*[7] a detailed survey conducted in 1964 of the attitudes and behavior of thousands of men working in six developing societies: Argentina, Chile, East Pakistan, India, Israel, and Nigeria. (Women's work experiences couldn't be compared easily so they were not included.)

Inkeles and Smith were interested, first of all, in finding out whether there is any general set of attitudes or behaviors that can be considered *modern* as distinct from *traditional.* For example, our discussion of evolution assumes that humankind is moving in a certain direction, toward modernity—whatever that may be. But we may be mistaken. After all, traditional societies vary greatly.

A traditional man herding sheep in North Africa is very different from a traditional man fishing on an outrigger canoe off Fiji or Samoa. And both of them are different from a traditional Siberian shaman curing a sick nomad with magical incantations.

If traditional people differ so much, may not modern people differ just as much? An office worker in Japan is obviously quite different from an office worker in Stockholm or Leningrad. Does it even make sense to call them all "modern," as if they all had some basic traits in common? Doesn't this amount to assuming unilinear evolution toward a single life style?

Inkeles didn't think so. While he recognized the great diversity that exists among industrial societies, he was also struck by certain similarities among the people of those societies. And he believed that modern people differ in consistent ways from traditional people. So he set out to see

Modernity is coming to places like Kuwait. Except for the robed shopper, this market could be almost any place in the world.

Omar Bessim/Monkmeyer

TABLE 19.2

Simplified OM scale

PURELY ATTITUDINAL ITEMS[a]

1. Have you ever (thought over so much) gotten so highly concerned (involved) regarding some public issue (such as . . .) that you really wanted to do something about it?
   Frequently / Few times / Never

2. If schooling is freely available (if there were no kinds of obstacles) how much schooling (reading and writing) do you think children (the son) of people like yourself should have?

3. Two 12-year-old boys took time out from their work in the corn (rice) fields. They were trying to figure out a way to grow the same amount of corn (rice) with fewer hours of work.
   The father of one boy said: "That is a good thing to think about.
   Tell me your thoughts about how we should change our ways of growing corn (rice)."
   The father of the other boy said: "The way to grow corn (rice) is the way we have always done it. Talk about change will waste time but not help."
   Which father said the wiser words?

4. What should most qualify a man to hold high office?
   Coming from (right, distinguished, or high) family background
   Devotion to the old and (revered) time-honored ways
   Being the most popular among the people
   High education and special knowledge

5. Which is most important for the future of (this country)?
   The hard work of the people
   Good planning on the part of the government
   God's help
   Good luck

6. Learned men (scholars, scientists) in the universities are studying such things as what determines whether a baby is a boy or girl and how it is that a seed turns into a plant. Do you think that these investigations (studies) are:

   All very good (beneficial) / All somewhat good (beneficial)
   All somewhat harmful / All very harmful
   Some people say that it is necessary for a man and his wife to limit the number of children to be born so they can take better care of those they do have (already have).
   Others say that it is wrong for a man and wife purposely (voluntarily) to limit the number of children to be born.
   Which of these opinions do you agree with more?

7. Which one of these (following) kinds of news interests you most?
   World events (happenings in other countries)
   The nation
   Your home town (or village)
   Sports
   Religious (or tribal, cultural) events (ceremonies) or festivals

8. If you were to meet a person who lives in another country a long way off (thousands of kilometers / miles away), could you understand his way of thinking?
   Yes / No

9. Do you think a man could be truly good without having any religion at all?
   Yes / No

BEHAVIOR-INFORMATION ITEMS

10. Do you belong to any organization (associations, clubs), such as, for example, social clubs, unions, church organizations, political groups, or other groups? If "Yes," what are the names of all the organizations you belong to? (Scored for number of organizations.)

11. Would you tell me what are the biggest problems you see facing (your country)? (Scored for number of problems or words in answer.)

12. Where is (in what country is the city of) Washington / Moscow? (Scored correct or incorrect.)

13. How often do you (usually) get news and information from newspapers?
    Everyday / Few times a week
    Occasionally (rarely) / Never

[a]Words in parentheses are alternative phrasing for aid in translation. In every case the items should be adapted to make sense in the particular culture.

Source: Alex Inkeles and David H. Smith. *Becoming Modern.* Cambridge, Mass.: Harvard University Press, 1974. Copyright © 1974 by the President and Fellows of Harvard College.

whether certain experiences that occur in industrialized settings encourage the orientation that he calls "modern."

Inkeles and Smith organized a large team of researchers that included social scientists from all the nations that they planned to study. Then they developed a questionnaire containing nearly 500 items. (It took an interviewer several hours to question a single respondent.) The questions dealt with a variety of habits, beliefs, and opinions. The family was discussed, and such issues as women's rights and birth control were covered. Religion, politics, the position of the aged in society, the communications media, social stratification, and consumerism were all explored.

In each society, respondents were chosen in such a way as to permit comparisons between people in three main job categories: (1) farmers, (2) factory workers, and (3) urban nonindustrial workers (barbers, cab drivers, street vendors, and so on). Inkeles suspected that working in a factory generally had a strong modernizing influence on people. He also wanted to consider the impact of other factors—urban living, education, exposure to mass media, and so on. But the first task was to decide how to measure modernity.

MEASURING MODERNITY

How would you arrive at a single "test" by which to classify men in terms of modernity or traditionalism? Inkeles and Smith did what psychologists often do when they are inventing an intelligence test: They looked at the correlations between the various items that they had included in their questionnaire. They started out with a set of items that had some bearing on modernity, and they refined their test by choosing items that were generally related. That is, a person who scored high on one item in this group might be expected to score high on others as well. Items that were not correlated with the others were tossed out.

The advantage of the Inkeles-Smith scale is that it can be used cross-culturally. No matter what society you are visiting, it is probably correct to say that it measures modernity there as well as it does in the six nations where it was originally developed. Inkeles argues that it applies to people in socialist societies as well as to people in the Third World and in more modern countries. Using this scale (which has been simplified since Inkeles and Smith be-

gan), a researcher can give each respondent a score that indicates how modern or how traditional he is compared to people in other areas of the world.

EXPLAINING HOW MEN BECOME MODERN

As soon as they had perfected their scale (called the OM scale, for "overall modernity"), Inkeles and Smith set to work comparing the average scores of workers in different categories. They looked at the effects of several variables, and, on the whole, they were not surprised by the results. Education was by far the most important variable. Men who had been educated had higher OM scores for each year of schooling, and the differences were marked. In fact, the impact of education on modernity was two or three times as great as that of any other variable.

Next in influence were a number of other variables. Job experience and exposure to the mass media were similar in degree of impact. Men who worked in factories had higher scores than urban nonindustrial workers, who in turn had higher scores than farmers. The differences between the factory and the urban non-industrial workers were not as great as the researchers had expected, however. It seems that people learn modern values and life styles by driving a cab or sweeping streets, though in general the factory is a somewhat better "school for modernity." The longer men had worked in these modern settings, the higher their scores tended to be.

However, under certain circumstances, nonurban workers could also develop more modern attitudes. The researcher found this out when studying a co-operative in East Pakistan. Most of the farmers surveyed were peasants working in the situations in which peasants work throughout most of the Third World. Their modernity was quite limited. But one group of farmers in East Pakistan belonged to a farm co-operative. These workers did not rely much on new machinery, but they had increased their production greatly, chiefly by reorganizing their methods of working. Inkeles and Smith found that their OM scores were markedly higher than those of other workers. Their experience in self-help and new interpersonal relationships had changed their attitudes.

Inkeles and Smith had expected to find that urban residence, as opposed to rural residence, influences modernity, but this is not the case.

Of all the influences that modernize people, education is the most powerful. Schooling can go on in all kinds of settings.

Living in a city does not, *in itself*, bring about more modern attitudes than living in a village or in a rural farm setting. To be sure, urban men do, on the average, differ from country people. But their greater modernity results not from living in a city but from other factors that often, but *not necessarily*, go with city life. City people are more often educated, are more likely to work in factories, and are exposed to the mass media more often than rural people. However, it is important to realize that *if* rural people were exposed to the same influences, they would probably adopt modern views as much as city people do. This fact may be an important consideration when determining, for example, whether it is desirable to locate more factories in the countryside to link up with agriculture more effectively.

WHAT ARE MODERN PEOPLE LIKE?

By now we know something about how people become modern. But what are modern people like? How do they differ from traditional people in the same society?

Modern man is well informed. In all six countries studied by Inkeles and Smith, modern respondents were far more likely than others to be able to answer questions about geography, political affairs, consumer items, books, and the like.

Modern people also tend to have a high sense of *personal efficacy.* For example, they believe that a person's position in life depends more on his own efforts than on fate. They believe that a job with more responsibility and more opportunity to exercise control is better than a job with little responsibility. They believe that scientific research is beneficial. And at times they become so concerned about a public issue that they want to do something about it. (Traditional people, in contrast, are likely to take the opposite views on such matters. For example, they are likely to believe that fate or God's will is more important in solving a nation's problems than anything the people or the government can do.)

In a number of other areas, modern people tend to frequently believe that they are able to control their own situations. They tend to have more ambition, for example. They believe that preventing accidents is more a matter of care than of luck. They believe that medicine is more effective in curing the sick than prayers. They want to make their own job and marital choices instead of allowing their family to decide these matters for them. They like to meet people and to make plans, they belong to more organizations, and so on.

The modern person more broadly identifies with a wider, more modern collectivity than does the traditional person. For example, modern men said they would take the advice of the government instead of the church. They would identify with the nation, not with the ethnic group, the religion, or the village. They believed in giving to charity, not because of fear of God, but because of generosity.

On the other hand, Inkeles and Smith had expected that modern men would be, in general, more trusting (e.g., when dealing with merchants or relatives) than traditional people. But this is not the case. Nor are modern people more likely than traditional people to believe that kinship ties aren't

very important. Inkeles and Smith had expected that, as people modernize, they come to think it is less important to support their kin and keep in touch with them. But this was not supported by the evidence. Another theory that did not hold up was that modern people are somehow more materialistic—that they are more likely to believe that money and goods bring happiness.

What does hold up, very clearly, is the image of modern people as *active, well-informed, participating citizens.* And their activism is oriented in a generally more liberal direction. They are more likely, for example, to support women's rights, birth control, scientific research, government planning, education, and so on. These traits occur among modern men all around the world, however they may differ otherwise.

Finally, though modernizing must involve some stress, the study did not find that modern people suffer more than traditional people from psychological problems. This was determined by asking whether the respondent had trouble sleeping at night, whether he often showed various symptoms of anxiety, and so on. It seems that people who modernize must cope with changes all around them, but that life in a rural village has its own problems. The two social environments do not result in markedly different degrees of psychological or emotional distress, at least as measured by the Inkeles-Smith questionnaire.

What conclusions can we reach? That the world is changing. That humankind is becoming modern. That modern people have different personalities than traditional people. And, so far as we can judge, that's fine. Just fine.

SOCIAL POLICY:
Issues and Viewpoints

In Chapter 1, I brought up a question that often troubles sociologists: To what extent should sociologists keep their personal values from affecting their research? Is it possible to separate one's ethical, political, aesthetic, or emotional judgments from factual descriptions of society's institutions?

By now you may have formed your own views on this question.

This book has not been oriented toward particular policies, nor has it tried very hard to keep a neutral point of view. A policy-oriented book might discuss how much various programs cost, how effective they have been, which lobbies are backing them, and so on. You may want to work with social policies, possibly by serving as an administrator or by going into politics. But even if you do not become involved in practical social-action programs, you will have to make judgments that somehow relate to issues that have been discussed, in a general way, in this book. It seems to me that the framework within which we interpret and understand the society around us strongly affects the particular policies we support. The purpose of this book has been to examine our assumptions and then to see how our values are affected by those assumptions. Let's go back and take another look at those assumptions.

In our discussion of culture we ran across the issue of cultural relativism. If you have to make policies that affect the life style of cultural groups other than you own, this issue is an important one. As an administrator, perhaps, or as a social worker, you may face the question of whether or not you should encourage people to give up their traditional customs in favor of your way of life. What standards would you use in deciding such matters? Would you willingly work for, say, a relief agency or family planning program that tries to get people to change their way of life? I have pointed out in this book that foreign customs often make good sense in other societies, while they would be impractical in our own. Nevertheless, it is possible to show proper respect for the customs of others and still try to influence others in ways that you believe are beneficial. If you want to help others, you must have some effect on them. Respect for the ways of others does not require you to keep silent about the issues that affect them. You can share your point of view. As long as you also listen to their views as well, people will recognize that you mean well.

When we discussed culture, we dealt with several problems that you will encounter as a Canadian. Should Canada place a high priority on developing the distinctiveness of its culture? How important is this goal as compared to other objectives? Should stronger laws be passed to support Canadian plays, movies, art, and music, and to protect these cultural products from foreign competition?

We have also discussed government control of the mass media. Should the government support excellence in the arts even if box office receipts are low? Should the government back popular culture or should it support a greater variety of cultural offerings for small ethnic communities, for people with off-beat artistic tastes, and so on. I don't have a firm opinion on this question, but I lean toward pluralism. Do you?

In our discussion of socialization, we considered some of the issues involved in the psychological development of children. Parents always

have to decide how best to support the security and well-being of their children. In traditional societies, such decisions are dictated by long-established customs. In ours, however, there are conflicting opinions on questions such as who should care for children while their parents work. Because the government is involved in planning day care facilities, this question is also a political issue for public debate. You may have to consider problems of childcare both privately, as a parent, and publicly, as a politically active citizen.

When discussing social groups, we raised questions about our tendency to comply to authority. This is an issue of enormous importance. You may never be asked by an impressive-looking scientist to torture another human being, but you will be asked every day of your life to conform unthinkingly to someone else's idea of how you should behave. It is often hard to decide on a correct course of behavior, especially when you are in an unfamiliar situation and confronted by the advice of "experts." Therefore, it is useful to be aware of the tendency of all human beings to follow orders and to avoid taking responsibility for their actions. Harry Truman kept a sign on his desk that said "The buck stops here." He was the president of the United States, but no matter what your rank, you can live by that motto at all times, if you decide to. That is what it means to be responsible.

In touching on the subject of deviance, we raised a number of issues. Theories of what causes deviance *determine* policy in this area. For example, a commonly accepted explanation of delinquency is the "labeling" theory, which is based on role-self theory. If the labeling explanation is correct, then policy derived from it should be very effective. This is a policy of "hands off," which claims that the less one does to define a youth as delinquent, the more likely he is to think of himself as a lawful person and to live up to that self-image. According to this view, punishing criminals would be more harmful than helpful. I would feel uncomfortable with such a policy, however. If you would too, you may want to think about it in greater detail.

What about the more general question of whether to allow people to pursue their private vices as long as they do not hurt anyone else? Legalization of gambling, sexual deviance, drug use, and other forms of behavior that most people disapprove of would follow from this policy.

When we turn to formal organizations, we come to a subject that affects everyone. But there is no particular public policy toward organizations. You will have to decide whether to take a job in a large organization or whether that would turn you into some sort of robot, unable to take responsibility or to respond with feeling to the people you know. Hence, your view of bureaucracy may determine your career.

Not all writers view bureaucrats in the same

way. My own view is that bureaucracies are only as irresponsible as people allow them to be. I have seen organizations in which every member was fully responsible for the entire operation. Every participant supported every other one in getting the job done. A person who questioned something he saw happening did not go on following orders and muttering misgivings under his breath, but went to

TABLE 19.3

Predictions for the year 2000

VERY LIKELY POSSIBILITIES

1. The application of lasers for sensing, measuring, communication, cutting, welding, power transmission, defense, and other purposes (already partially achieved)
2. Worldwide use of high-altitude cameras for mapping, prospecting, census, land use, and geological investigations (achieved)
3. Major reductions in hereditary and congenital defects (partially achieved)
4. Three-dimensional photography, films, and television (partially achieved through holography)
5. Use of nuclear explosions for excavation and mining, for the generation of power, and as a source of neutrons (partially achieved)
6. New techniques for inexpensive, convenient, and reliable birth control (achieved)
7. Control of weather and climate
8. General and substantial increase in life expectancy, postponement of aging, and limited rejuvenation
9. Chemical methods for improving memory and learning
10. Artificial moons for lighting large areas at night

LESS LIKELY POSSIBILITIES

1. Artificial intelligence (partially achieved with computers)
2. Artificial growth of new limbs and organs
3. Major use of rockets for commercial or private transportation
4. Effective chemical or biological treatment for most mental illnesses
5. Suspended animation for years or for centuries
6. Automated highways
7. Direct augmentation of human mental capacity by interconnection of the brain with a computer
8. Verification of some extrasensory phenomena
9. Practical laboratory conception and nurturing of human fetuses
10. Substantial manned lunar or planetary installations

REMOTE POSSIBILITIES

1. Life expectancy extended to substantially more than 150 years
2. Almost complete genetic control
3. Interstellar travel
4. Practical and routine use of extrasensory phenomena
5. Laboratory creation of living plants and animals

Source: Herman Kahn and Anthony Wiener. *The Year 2000.* New York: Macmillan, 1967.

the person who could do something about it and expressed his objections. In this way he took responsibility for his own activity and the activity of his group. This let him work toward a goal he could feel good about serving. A subordinate in an organization can be as fully responsible as the top executive.

In a later chapter, we considered the issue of ethnic relations in Canada and around the world. You may be sure that this issue will face you many times in your personal and political life. For example, you may have to decide what language should be used in your neighborhood schools and your decision may have important consequences. How will you weigh the various important considerations that must affect your decision?

Our discussion of collective behavior and social movements raised the question of whether to allow press coverage of behavior that may be imitated. Does such coverage promote the idea of kidnapping, terrorism, hijacking, or rioting to people who otherwise might not think of doing these things? If so, how can we overcome the problem without endangering freedom of the press? Personally, I think crime is becoming a way of life today, largely because the public is so fascinated by it. Why else do people watch programs about gunmen, or buy papers that focus on murders, the latest fads in narcotics, and other destructive activities? I am just about ready to support laws requiring the mass media to "change the subject," though I fully understand the reasons why such laws may be dangerous. What do you think about this?

Coming closer to home, you will have to make personal decisions about the proper roles and duties of family members. And you will also probably have to make decisions collectively, with other members of your church, your school board, or your government, about matters related to family life. Should homosexuals be allowed to hold a dance in a public auditorium? Should welfare mothers not be supported if they live with their boyfriends? Should divorce be granted freely upon request, or should spouses have to prove that one partner is at fault before a divorce is granted? Issues like these arise on a regular basis. They have to be answered in the light of both factual information and informed, well thought-out values based on some understanding of the functions of families.

Policies toward matters of religion come up from time to time. Even though we live in a political system that guarantees freedom of religion, sometimes that freedom contradicts certain other guaranteed rights. The courts then have to decide which set of rights takes precedence. For example, many religious groups use strongly persuasive techniques of social control on their members. They threaten their members with eternal damnation or with some earthly exclusion that is only slightly less upsetting. Such practices as chanting, fasting, limitation of sleep, physical exhaustion, and other extreme exercises have been routine aspects of both Christian and Asian communities for hundreds of years. However, they are noteworthy today because they are employed by certain new religious groups that seem alarming to many, especially after the dreadful events that occurred in the People's Temple in Guyana. Is there any way of guarding participants against the possibly harmful effects of such practices without interfering with their basic rights to freedom of religion? I don't know of any way to do so.

The field of education, perhaps more than any other area of sociological study, is linked to public policy. For one thing, education is controlled almost entirely by the state. Therefore it is impossible for the government to be completely separate from it and to allow schools and universities to set their own policies. The state pays the bills and decides what will be taught and what research will be funded. It supplies people with certain skills in response to demands by industry and the professions. Almost everyone has ideas about what courses should be taught and what methods of instruction are most desirable. You probably do too.

In the chapters on economic life and population we considered some of the giant issues of our generation—the problems created by the need to feed a rapidly increasing world population. I have suggested that the basic problem must be seen within the framework of the global economy—particularly the international market for food and agricultural products. How can we free people in the Third World to feed themselves? How can we help them achieve self-sufficiency as soon as possible? World hunger is the greatest policy issue of our lifetime. On it will depend the solution to the population explosion and all the misery and problems that it brings.

In our discussion of politics we have mentioned Canada's position in the increasingly interdependent world of corporate capitalism. How much more decision-making power is realistically available to Canadians and people elsewhere in matters that affect their own lives? If dependency theory is correct, what can Canadians or anyone else do to reverse the increasing oppression of the underdeveloped Third World?

Finally, in the chapter on urban living we touched briefly on city planning and development. I have suggested that policies aimed at correcting social problems in slums depend on the policy makers' definition of a slum and their opinions on how slums come into existence. Such matters as the tax system, mortgage interest rates, freeway or subway construction, and zoning ordinances can affect the life of the city for years or even generations. By choosing between, say, urban apartment living and suburban split-level houses, we not only choose a way of life for ourselves but also affect the future of the community we live in.

Thus sociology can never be separated from our values. We can be fair in representing various points of view without bias. We can be honest in considering evidence presented by people whose views differ from our own. We can respect one another and our right to hold opposing opinions. But we can never leave our values wholly to one side.

The world is an interdependent system. Your map may show nations in different colors with lines around them, but those lines and colors are misleading. Our deepest loyalty should be to humanity, not to our tribe, our nation, or to any other collectivity. I think the political goal of sociologists should be to create a world government that features justice and freedom. I do not expect to see it in my lifetime, but I hope you do in yours.

We have discussed a number of problems in this book, and you will face many others. May sociology be of service to you as you respond to those problems and search for solutions.

SUMMARY

1. Some theorists have assumed that social change is cyclical, but the evolutionary view has been more common. Comte and Spencer were evolutionists in that they believed that social progress was normal.

2. Modern evolutionists hold that some developments are necessary in order to make other developments possible. However, progress from one stage to another is not inevitable, nor is there any single line of development through which all societies must pass. Diffusion allows some societies to skip certain stages. An *evolutionary breakthrough* is an innovation that makes further advances possible.

3. Functionalists look for the effects of social patterns instead of for their origins. Functionalism can be accepted today with modification, just as evolutionism requires modification. Societies are not integrated systems. They contain some elements that do not fit well with others. The solution to one problem may cause a new one. However, some societies meet their functional requirements better than others do, and over time their social patterns tend to win out over those of less successful societies. This is one basis for social evolution.

4. Challenge leads to innovation. The challenge may be technological or may consist of people confronting others with new ideas, as marginal people often do.

5. Parsons classifies human societies as primitive, intermediate, or modern. He believes that the invention of writing moved societies from the primitive level to the intermediate level and that the introduction of formal law, along with other cultural breakthroughs, enabled them to move into the modern period.

6. Conflict theories of social change are similar in some ways to evolutionary theories. Marx expected change to result from conflict between social classes. He based his theory of historical materialism on Hegel's "dialectic," which stressed the conflict of opposites and the resulting synthesis.

KEY TERMS

evolutionary (cultural) breakthrough an innovation that makes further advances possible.

evolutionism the belief that every society progresses toward perfection through stages of increasing complexity.

functionalism the belief that a social pattern is best understood not in terms of its past historical development but in terms of its current consequences for the society in which it is operating.

functional requisites the requirements that all societies must meet, at least at a minimum level.

multilinear evolutionism the belief that various societies follow different lines of development.

unilinear evolutionism the belief that there is a single set of stages through which every society must proceed.

FOR FURTHER READING

BELL, DANIEL. *The Coming of Post Industrial Society: A Venture in Social Forecasting.* New York: Basic Books, 1973. This is a weighty book in every sense of the word, and an important one.

CHIROT, DANIEL. *Social Change in the Twentieth Century.* New York: Harcourt Brace Jovanovich, 1977. This book is having a strong impact on Canadian sociologists, particularly Marsden and Harvey, whose book is listed below.

GAGNE, W., ed. *Nationalism, Technology and the Future of Canada.* Toronto: Macmillan, 1976. This is a collection of papers on a topic which affects the fate of us all.

DEWITT, ROBERT L. *Public Policy in Community Protest.* Toronto: University of Toronto Press, 1970. This deals with how an isolated group of Newfoundland fishermen adapt to industrialization and respond to political policies.

ETZIONI, AMITAI. *The Active Society.* New York: Free Press, 1968. Another heavy book. Etzioni is committed to applied research and in this work discusses the issues concerning how, when, and to what extent we can control social change through rational planning.

MALINOWSKI, BRONISLAW. *The Dynamics of Cultural Change.* New Haven, Conn.: Yale University Press, 1945. Malinowski was a functionalist anthropologist who mostly studied South Sea Island societies. In this book he develops his theory of social change.

MARSDEN, LORNA R. and EDWARD B. HARVEY. *Fragile Federation: Social Change in Canada.* Toronto: McGraw-Hill Ryerson, 1979. The authors tackle some important theoretical problems, ranging from questions about population to the future of the women's movement. Stimulating and readable.

TOFFLER, ALVIN. *Future Shock.* New York: Bantam, 1971. This was a best-seller and deserved to be. It deals with the personal adjustments that are necessary for people living in fast-changing societies like ours. More exciting than science fiction to read.

WHITE, LESLIE A. *The Evolution of Culture: The Development of Civilization to the Fall of Rome.* New York: McGraw-Hill, 1959. White is an anthropologist who was arguing in favor of evolutionism when the idea was unpopular. Now it is quite popular.

YELADA, SHANKER A., ed. *Canadian Social Policy.* Waterloo: Wilfred Laurier Press, 1978. This is a fairly successful discussion of policies relating to such social problems as unemployment, poverty, inflation, and the oppression of women, children, and native people.

THE REFERENCE PAPER

FINDING YOUR TOPIC

The secret of a successful term paper is the argument it develops. No matter how interesting your topic is, your paper will sound dull unless it generates a little suspense. So your first job is to find—or invent—a problem or puzzle to work on in your paper. Later you will have to think of how to "sell" the reader on your problem. A vacuum cleaner salesperson, for example, tries to make you believe that you *need* the machine, that you can hardly get along without it. It's the same with a term paper. Don't freely give your findings away to the reader. Convince us first that we *need* the information that you can provide. Show us how some problem exists that is absolutely crying out for a solution. Selling the problem is actually as important in a term paper as providing the answer. Set up an argument, show the confusion that exists because of the problem, and then if you can't solve it completely by yourself, that's all right. You can just modestly claim to have advanced sociology a tiny bit toward solving this important question.

For these reasons, I suggest that you pay a lot of attention to finding your topic. If your teacher hands out lists of suggested topics, don't just pick one passively; it may be too vague and broad for your purpose. You must narrow it down to a more specific question and built up suspense about its answer. Suppose your instructor suggests that you write on drug abuse or divorce. Fine! What *about* drugs or divorce? You have to make the question your own. Maybe you will want to show that rates of drug use or divorce are increasing or decreasing more than people generally realize, and that you know why this is going on. Or maybe you will want to evaluate the various treatment programs for drug addiction to discover which ones, if any, work successfully. Or maybe you will want to point out some effects of divorce on the emotional adjustment of the couple's children.

Try to show that your evidence corrects a widespread mistaken belief. Set up your argument before you try to settle it.

GATHERING INFORMATION

The material you use in a paper can vary greatly. You can write a fine paper just defining a single word (such as "culture" or "power") that is widely used in the social sciences. But don't do this unless you can show that there is some confusion about the meaning of this particular word, and that your definition will straighten out problems that have confronted various writers. Of course, you will need to read a lot before tackling such a problem, if only to locate such problems in the writings of various scholars.

In general, however, you will write papers that deal with empirical, factual topics; for such papers you need evidence. Chapter 2 suggests sources of evidence, such as historical documents, government statistics, public opinion polls, and the like. You may decide to do a survey of your own, possibly by telephoning a sample of respondents and interviewing them. Or you may decide to do field research—such as, say, sitting in a singles bar several nights to note what people say first when getting acquainted. In any case, you must be sure that your information will point toward a solution to a definite question.

USING THE LIBRARY

Before writing your paper, spend time reading what other people have written on your chosen subject. The trick is to be able to find the most useful written material quickly and to keep track of what you learn from reading it. Fortunately, scholars will help you. They cite the sources of their information in footnotes and bibliographies, just as you will do when you write your own paper. Thus, all you may need is one good reference to start your research. After that, you can work your way backward by tracking down the sources that are mentioned by that author, and then sources that *they* mention in turn, and so on. Pretty soon you will have more references than you can read, and you will have to skim through them and select the best ones for your purpose.

However, this way of searching won't help you find recent articles. Suppose you start with a fairly old book. Any references in it will be even older. But you may need up-to-date publications, so you will have to look for additional sources in current journals and other recent sources of data. How should you proceed? I suggest that you take along a batch of index cards and record each of your references on a separate card, noting the author, title, place and date of publication, name of publisher, and relevant pages. Below that, jot down whatever impressions you gain from reading the article or book that you may want to recall later.

The card catalog

First go to the card catalog. This is probably located in a big wooden filing case near the middle of the room, although many libraries are now switching over to a microfilm system. In either case, the catalog has two separate file systems, one that is organized alphabetically by the authors' surnames, followed by their book titles, and another that is organized by subject category. If you know the author's name, you should refer to the author/title catalog. Many libraries have an additional file system that lists books by their titles, which is useful if you know the title but not the author's name.

The file card will show the call number assigned to that particular book. Most libraries use the Library of Congress numbering system, in which sociology books have call numbers beginning with HM. Books are assigned to the shelves according to these numbers, so once you know its number, you can probably trot right over and pull your chosen book off the shelf.

Your library will probably have special shelves for reserved books—ones that are in high demand and therefore loaned for shorter periods. Some of your library's holdings may also be in special libraries around the campus. Reference books are always kept in a particular section, usually on the main floor. The catalog will show you how to find the book you need.

If you don't yet have a reference to a particular book, you may start with the subject card catalog. Material on sociology will include such headings as *social surveys, deviant behavior*, and *demography*. Various books and journals are listed under each heading.

Suppose you decide to look for a general overview of the topic that you want to study. You may then begin with an article in the *International Encyclopedia of the Social Sciences*. Your card catalog may list it as REF H 40 A215; the REF indicates that it is filed in the reference section of the library. In this encyclopedia are articles with bibliographies at the end. You should also become familiar with other reference books filed near it; these include *A Modern Dictionary of Sociology* and a more recent book, the *Encyclopedia of Sociology*.

Journals and abstracts

Suppose you want to find some up-to-date research on a topic. You may want to go straight to the journals. Your library probably subscribes to several sociology journals. The most widely used are the *American Sociological Review*, the *American Journal of Sociology*, *Social Forces*, the *British Journal of Sociology*, and the *Canadian Review of Sociology and Anthropology*.

There are so many journals that it is inefficient for you to just leaf through them, hoping to stumble across what you need. You should look first at a periodical index, the most useful one being *Sociological Abstracts*. These are big bound volumes, usually kept in the reference department, that summarize articles from many different journals. You may need some help in learning to use *Soc Abstracts*, as they are called. Near the end of the final volume for each year, you will find a subject index. Abstracts on "immigration," for example, may be found in Section 20 (Sociology of the Occupations), Section 37 (Demography), and Section 21 (Industrial Sociology). The subject index will list all the abstract numbers for articles on these various aspects of immigration.

EXAMPLE: ABSTRACTS

Immigration
Aspects of immigration. 74G6984
Attitudes of white South Africans toward South Africa's immigration policy. 74G6982.

This last number indicates that you should turn to G6982 in the volumes for 1974 to find the abstract of the article on white South Africans.[1]

Suppose, on the other hand, that you want to find abstracts on a wide subject area, not a narrow topic like immigration. You may then begin by looking at the table of contents at the front of each issue of *Soc Abstracts*. In either case, when you have found the abstract number, turn to the main body of the issue or volume to find the abstract. Then, if an abstract seems particularly important to your research, go find the original article in the journal elsewhere in the library.

Most libraries stock recent journals in little cubbyholes along a wall, but older copies will be bound and shelved with the other books in the stacks. For those older issues, you need to use the card catalog in the ordinary way to find the call number. Journal titles are listed in the author/title catalog.

If you are doing research on a general topic, before narrowing your topic down you may want to read a few book reviews to find some good leads to recent books. The last half of each issue of the *American Journal of Sociology* and of the *Canadian Review of Sociology and Anthropology* is devoted to

book reviews. Another source is *Contemporary Sociology*, published by the professional organization of sociologists, the American Sociological Association, entirely for reviewing books. The tables of contents classify reviews according to subject matter.

A final suggestion: Feel free to ask your librarians for help. That's what they are there for.

WRITING YOUR REPORT

By the time you have finished reading, you will have found references to more articles and books than you can handle. Research can never be "complete," because everything you read leads you to something else. But you must eventually put a stop to your reading and spend time by yourself, letting everything jell until you know what you want to tell people about your investigation. (During this period I wander around the house moaning and drinking tea.) Then you must seat yourself firmly in front of your typewriter and stay there for a long time, no matter what exciting or distracting things you have a chance to do instead.

This is the time to "sell" your problem to the reader, so make a strong case for its importance. Then go on to tell your findings. Eventually you can wrap it up with a conclusion, reviewing the whole argument again briefly and pointing out what you think are unfinished pieces of the puzzle that somebody else should work on next.

I can't tell you *what* to say in your paper, but I have six suggestions about *how* to say it:

1 *Don't be wordy.* Cut excess phrases out, so every word counts.
2 *Don't be roundabout.* It is fine to say, "I think that ..." instead of "It is the opinion of this writer that ..."
3 *Nail down your claims.* If you say something that might be questioned, say how you know it is so. Where did you read it? Who told you?
4 *Respect your reader's point of view.* If you want to make a case for a particular church, or

political party, or value (for example, the right to have free abortions, or the "immorality" of homosexual behavior), be aware that your reader may have a different opinion. Don't assume that all reasonable human beings *must* see things your way. I'm not saying that you must never let your own values show (though your instructor may say that, so check it out with him or her before you start), but I am saying that you don't want to seem insulting or naive or preachy. Do your soapbox act someplace else, not in your term paper. If you do show your personal biases, it is a good idea to label them as such, so the reader sees that you *know* you are going beyond the facts and expressing an opinion or judgment.

5 *Cite your sources.* It is fine to borrow other people's ideas, but say that you are doing so in a footnote. This is an easy place to slip up badly, and it can cost you a terrible price to do so. Plagiarism is regarded as a serious crime by scholars. If you are using somebody else's words, put them in quotation marks and use a footnote to say where the words were originally published. If you are using ideas suggested verbally, you can say in the text, "As Susan Jones has pointed out . . .," or you can say in a footnote, "Susan Jones, personal communication." Or you can have a special section thanking people for their criticism of your paper, and include Susan's name on that list.

6 *Try your paper out on a reader.* Before you type your final draft, it is a good idea to have a friend read what you have written and suggest ways of improving it. Though your draft will be messy at this point, you want your reader to look for spelling or punctuation errors, awkward style, and errors of fact. Every book that is published is read by a copy editor. You will do yourself a favor by finding a free copy editor in your family or dormitory. You want someone who will be super-critical, not someone who adores every word you say. However, in the long run it is your own paper, and if your reader offers suggestions that you don't like, you are certainly free to disregard them.

Footnoting

For the most part, you will be citing publications, and you can choose between two different forms of footnoting.

The first system is the one used in this

book. You insert a number at the point in your paper that is drawn from a particular reference. Then, either at the bottom of the page or at the end of your paper, you list those numbers in order and give the particular publication that each one refers to. Examples are shown below. Notice the order of the items and punctuation of these examples so you can follow the pattern in your own paper. Other variations are sometimes used, but the one below will work quite well. Whatever style you adopt, be consistent in using it.

EXAMPLE: FOOTNOTES

1. Herbert Marcuse, *Eros and Civilization* (Boston: Beacon Press, 1965), p. 97.
2. Marcuse, p. 202.
3. R. Stephen Warner, "Toward a Redefinition of Action Theory," *American Journal of Sociology,* 83(6), May, 1978, pp. 1317-1347.
4. R. Stephen Warner, "Sociological Theory in Historical Context," in *Sociological Theory: Historical and Formal,* by Neil J. Smelser and R. Stephen Warner (Morristown, N.J.: General Learning Press, 1976), pp. 1-133.
5. Warner, "Toward a Redefinition . . .," p. 1322.
6. Not all cases are presented here because too few interviews were completed by Japanese respondents to give a reliable estimate about the opinions of the Japanese community in Salem.
7. Mary Haywood Metz, *Classrooms and Corridors* (Berkeley: University of California Press, 1978), pp. 99-101.

Let me draw attention to a few features of this footnoting system. First, notice that the authors' first names appear first, followed by their last names. Some students mistakenly put the surnames first, which is proper for bibliographies, but not for footnotes of this kind. Notice too that the book or journal title is underlined. If your paper is published, underlined material will be set in italics, but when you type, underlining is used in place of italics. The title of an article or chapter within a book or journal is not underlined but enclosed in quotation marks.

In footnote 2, since I repeated a reference to the Marcuse book that had previously been cited, I didn't repeat the whole story, but just the author's surname and the page. In footnote

5, I was also referring to a source previously cited, but I gave a little more information than in footnote 2. This is because there were two Warner articles footnoted previously, and I must make it clear which one I am referring to in this note. Finally, in footnote 6 I was not citing any publication but was explaining some small point about my research. Side remarks such as this one should be inserted in footnotes to avoid disrupting the flow of the discussion in the paper itself.

Let's consider the second system of footnoting. It has become more popular recently in journal articles than the first system. It does not use numbered footnotes at all, but refers to the items in the bibliography with a short parenthetical notation. Thus, at the end of a sentence you may simply put: (Warner, 1978). This informs the reader that you are referring to a 1978 article by Warner that is to be referenced in the bibliography. Suppose Warner has written two articles in 1978, and you refer to both of them. You label one "a" and the other "b", both in the parentheses and in the bibliography. Thus, you might insert: (Warner, 1978b).

Bibliography

Whichever system of footnoting you use, you always supply a bibliography on a separate sheet at the end of your paper. It should list all the articles and books to which you have referred. This bibliography organizes the references in alphabetical order, according to the first letter in the authors' *surnames*, which are placed *before* the given names in this case. If a particular author's work is listed more than once, the early publications come first and subsequent ones follow in chronological order. You need not repeat the author's name each time, but draw a line in its place after it has appeared once. Page numbers are shown in the bibliography only to indicate where whole articles are located in a given book or journal. The particular pages that you cite for your own reference should be shown in the footnotes, not in the bibliography.

EXAMPLE: BIBLIOGRAPHY

MARCUSE, HERBERT. *Eros and Civilization.* Boston: Beacon Press, 1965.

METZ, MARY HAYWOOD. *Classrooms and Corridors.* Berkeley: University of California Press, 1978.

WARNER, R. STEPHEN. "Sociological Theory in Historical Context," in Neil J. Smelser and R. Stephen Warner, *Sociological Theory: Historical and Formal.* Morristown, N.J.: General Learning Press, 1976.

————. "Toward a Redefinition of Action Theory," *American Journal of Sociology,* 83 (6), 1978, pp. 1317-1347.

This summary on citations may not be adequate to answer all the problems about details that arise while you are writing your paper. For further advice, consult a handbook of style, such as Kate L. Turabian's *The Student Guide for Writing College Papers,* University of Chicago Press, 1976.

NOTES

Chapter 1
What is sociology

1. Seymour Martin Lipset, "Political Sociology," in Robert K. Merton, Leonard Broom, and Leonard S. Cottrell, Jr., eds., *Sociology Today: Problems and Prospects* (New York: Basic Books, 1959), p. 83.
2. Solomon Asch, *Social Psychology* (Englewood Cliffs, N.J.: Prentice-Hall, 1952), pp. 450-501.
3. Morris Janowitz and Dwaine Marvick, "Authoritarianism and Political Behavior," *Public Opinion Quarterly*, 17 (1953), pp. 185-201.
4. Emile Durkheim, *The Rules of Sociological Method*, 8th ed., ed. G. Catlin and trans. S. Solovay and J. Mueller (Chicago: University of Chicago Press, 1938), p. 139.
5. Some contributions from the Chicago school of sociologists are: Robert Park, Edward W. Burgess, and R.D. McKenzie, *The City* (Chicago: University of Chicago Press, 1925); Nels Anderson, *The Hobo: The Sociology of the Homeless Man* (Chicago: University of Chicago Press, 1929); Harvey Zorbaugh, *The Gold Coast and the Slum* (Chicago: University of Chicago Press, 1929); William I. Thomas, *The Unadjusted Girl* (Boston: Little, Brown, 1931); Clifford Shaw, *The Jack-Roller* (Chicago: University of Chicago Press, 1930): Frederic Thrasher, *The Gang* (Chicago: University of Chicago Press, 1927).
6. James E. Curtis, Desmond M. Connor, and John Harp, "An Emergent Professional Community: French and English Sociologists and Anthropologists in Canada," *Social Science Information*, 9(4), 1970, pp. 113-36.
7. S.D. Clark, *Canadian Society in Historical Pespective* (Toronto: McGraw-Hill Ryerson, 1976), pp. 1-19.
8. For further discussion of trends in contemporary research, see Lorne Tepperman, "Sociology in English-Speaking Canada: The Last Five Years," *Canadian Historical Review*, LIX, 4, 1978, pp. 435-46.
9. Emile Durkheim, *The Division of Labor in Society*, trans. G. Simpson (Glencoe, Ill.: Free Press, 1933).
10. Leslie White, *The Science of Culture* (New York: Farrar, Strauss, 1949).
11. David F. Aberle et al., "The Functional Prerequisites of a Society," *Ethics*, 60 (1950), pp. 100-11.
12. Peter McHugh, Stanley Raffel, Daniel C. Foss, and Alan F. Blum, *On the Beginning of Social Inquiry*, (London: Routledge and Kegan Paul, 1974).

Chapter 2
Methods of social research

1. Richard H. Franke and James D. Kaul, "The Hawthorne Experiments: First Statistical Interpretation," *American Sociological Review*, 43, (Oct. 1978), pp. 623-43.
2. Cyril Burt's cheating was recently reported in newspapers and magazines everywhere.
3. Rex A. Lucas, *Men in Crisis: A Study of a Mine Disaster* (New York: Basic Books, 1969).
4. See Andrew F. Henry and James F. Short, Jr., *Suicide and Homicide* (New York: Free Press, 1954).
5. Martin Schiff, "Sexual Liberation, The Welfare State and Sexual Malaise in Sweden: An Analysis of Popular Myths Concerning the Swedish Way of Life," *Sociological Analysis and Theory*, Vol. 5 (3) October 1975, pp. 359-79. Unless otherwise indicated, all the statistics in "The truth about Sweden" are drawn from this paper.
6. *Canada Year Book 1975-76*, (Ottawa: Minister of Industry, Trade and Commerce), p. 217.
7. P.J. Giffen, "Official Rates of Crime and Delinquency, in W.T. McGrath, ed., *Crime and Its Treatment in Canada* (Toronto: Macmillan, 1976), p. 108.
8. Donald J. Mulvihill and Melvin M. Tumin, *Crimes of Violence, Vol. II* (Washington, D.C.: United States Government Printing Office, 1969), p. 124.
9. Alice M. Rivlin, *Systematic Thinking for Social Action* (Washington, D.C.: The Brookings Institution, 1971).
10. William F. Whyte, *Street Corner Society* (Chicago: University of Chicago Press, 1943).
11. Hubert M. Blalock, Jr., *An Introduction to Social Research* (Englewood Cliffs, N.J.: Prentice-Hall, 1970), pp. 57-58.
12. W.I. Thomas and Florian Znaniecki, *The Polish Peasant in Europe and America* (New York: Octagon Books, 1971), first published in 1919.
13. David McClelland, *The Achieving Society* (New York: Van Nostrand, 1961).
14. Philippe Aries, *Centuries of Childhood* (New York: Knopf, 1962).
15. J. Mabley, "Mabley's Report," *Chicago American*, January 22, 1963, pp. 62-63.
16. J. Durand, "Mortality Estimates from Roman Tombstone Inscriptions", *American Journal of Sociology*, 65 (1960), pp. 365-73.
17. W. Lloyd Warner, *The Living and the Dead* (New Haven, Conn.: Yale University

Press, 1959).

18. Claire Selltiz, Marie Jahoda, Morton Deutsch, and Stuart W. Cook, *Research Methods in Social Relations*, rev. ed. (New York: Holt, Rinehart and Winston, 1959), p. 241.
19. Alan Listiak, "'Legitimate Deviance' and Social Class: Bar Behavior during Grey Cup Week," *Sociological Focus*, vol. 7. (1974), 3.
20. Craig Haney, W. Curtis Banks, and Philip G. Zimbardo, "Interpersonal Dynamics in a Simulated Prison", *International Journal of Criminology and Penology*, vol. 1 (1973), pp. 69-97.
21. Alice M. Isen, T.E. Shalker, M. Clark, and L. Karp, "Affect, Accessibility of Material in Memory, and Behavior: A Cognitive Loop?", *Journal of Personality and Social Psychology*, 1978, vol. 36, no. 1, pp. 1-12.
22. Anthony N. Doob and Alan E. Gross, "Status of Frustrator as an Inhibitor of Horn-Honking Responses," *Journal of Social Psychology*, vol. 76 (1968), pp. 213-218.
23. Jeffrey H. Goldstein and Robert L. Arms, "Effects of Observing Athletic Contests on Hostility," *Sociometry*, vol. 34 (1971), pp. 83-90.
24. S.W. Pyke, "Children's Literature: Conceptions of Sex Roles", from *Socialization and the Values in Canadian Society*, vol. 2, by Robert M. Pike and Elia Zureik, (Toronto: McClelland and Stewart, 1975).

Chapter 3
Culture

1. E.B. Tylor, *Primitive Culture*, 7th ed. (New York: Brentano's, 1924), p. 1.
2. Seymour Martin Lipset, *The First New Nation: The United States in Historical and Comparative Perspective* (Garden City, N.Y.: Doubleday, 1967), pp. 240-42, 284-85.
3. William Graham Summer, *Folkways* (Boston: Ginn, 1940).
4. For a good discussion of the cow slaughter issue, see Marvin Harris, *Cows, Pigs, Wars and Witches* (New York: Random House, 1974).
5. William F. Ogburn, *Social Change* (New York: Viking, 1950), pp. 200-13.
6. R.L. Sharp, "Steel Axes for Stone Age Australians," *Human Organization*, 11 (1952), pp. 17-22.
7. Ellsworth Huntington, *Mainsprings of Civilization* (New York: Wiley, 1945).
8. See Karl Marx, *Selected Writings in Sociology and Social Philosophy*, ed. T.B. Bottomore (New York: McGraw-Hill, 1956).

9. Harold Innis, *The Bias of Communication* (Toronto: University of Toronto Press, 1971).
10. Marshall McLuhan, *The Gutenberg Galaxy* (Toronto: University of Toronto Press, 1962).
11. Marshall McLuhan, *Understanding Media* (New York: McGraw-Hill, 1964).
12. S.M. Crean, *Who's Afraid of Canadian Culture?* (Don Mills, Ont.: General Publishing Co., 1976).
13. Ibid., p. 186.
14. Ibid., p. 203.
15. Herbert Gans, *Popular Culture and High Culture* (New York: Basic Books, 1974), p. 37.
16. Maxwell McCombs and Donald Shaw, "The Agenda-Setting Function of Mass Media," *Public Opinion Quarterly*, 36 (Summer 1972), pp. 176-87.
17. *Report of the Commission on Obscenity and Pornography* (New York: Bantam Books, 1970), esp. pp. 169-309.
18. Surgeon General's Advisory Committee, *Television and Growing Up: The Impact of Televised Violence* (Washington: Government Printing Office, 1972), 5 vols. See also J.C. Thatcher, Queen's Printer for Ontario, *Report of the Royal Commission on Violence in the Communications Industry*, 6 vols. (Toronto: Queen's Printer, 1977).
19. Daniel Bell, "The Myth of Crime Waves," in *The End of Ideology* (Glencoe, Ill: Free Press, 1960), chap. 8; and Theodore N. Ferdinand, "The Criminal Patterns of Boston Since 1849," *American Journal of Sociology*, 73 (July 1967), pp. 84-99.

Chapter 4
Socialization

1. S.K. Escalona, "Feeding Disturbances in Very Young Children," *American Journal of Orthopsychiatry*, 15 (1945), pp. 78-80.
2. Bruce Eckland, "Genetics and Sociology: A Reconsideration," *American Sociological Review*, 32, No. 2 (April 1967), pp. 173-93.
3. J.W.B. Douglas, *The Home and the School: A Study of Ability and Attainment in the Primary School* (London: MacGibbon and Kee, 1964).
4. John Clausen, "Family Structure, Socialization, Personality," in Lois Hoffman and Martin L. Hoffman, eds., *Review of Child Development Research* (New York: Russell Sage, 1966), p. 14.
5. Glen H. Elder, Jr., and C. E. Bowerman, "Family Structure and Sex Composition," *American Sociological Review*, 28 (1963), pp. 891-905.

6. J. K. Bossard and E. S. Boll, "Personality Roles in the Large Family," *Child Development*, 26 (1955), pp. 71-78.

7. Clausen, p. 18.

8. Douglas, p.84.

9. Susan Ervin-Tripp, "Language Development," in Lois Hoffman and Martin Hoffman, eds., *Review of Child Development Research* (New York: Russell Sage, 1966), II, p. 92.

10. H. Hartshorne and M.A. May, *Studies in the Nature of Character* (New York: Macmillan, 1928-1930), 3 vols.

11. Minako Kurokawa, "Mennonite Children in Waterloo County" in Jean Leonard Elliott, ed., *Immigrant Groups* (Scarborough, Ont.: Prentice-Hall, 1971) pp. 33-46.

12. Howard S. Becker, *Boys in White* (Chicago: University of Chicago Press, 1963).

13. Erving Goffman, *Asylums: Essays on the Social Situation of Mental Patients and Other Inmates* (Garden City, N.Y.: Doubleday, 1961).

14. Emile Durkheim, *Education and Sociology* (New York: Free Press, 1965), p. 87.

15. Ibid., pp. 85-86.

16. Ibid., p. 88.

17. Jean Piaget, *The Moral Judgment of the Child* (New York: Free Press, 1965).

18. Sigmund Freud, *Civilization and Its Discontents* (New York: Norton, 1961).

19. Ibid., p. 42.

20. Ibid., pp. 26-27.

21. Herbert Marcuse, *Eros and Civilization* (New York: Vintage, 1962). For a good, short introduction to Marcuse's analysis, see Theodore Roszak, *The Making of a Counterculture* (Garden City, N.Y.: Doubleday, 1969), chap. 3.

22. Sherryl Kleinman, "Female Premarital Sexual Careers," in Jack Haas and William Shaffir, *Shaping Identity in Canadian Society* (Scarborough, Ont.: Prentice-Hall, 1978), pp. 101-17.

23. Ira Reiss, "Premarital Sex as Deviant Behavior: An Application of Current Approaches to Deviance," *American Sociological Review*, 35 (Feb. 1970), p. 80.

24. J.W. Atkinson and D.C. McClelland, "The Projective Expression of Needs," *Journal of Experimental Psychology*, 38 (1948), p. 405.

25. Matina S. Horner, "Toward an Understanding of Achievement Related Conflicts in Women," *Journal of Social Issues*, 28, no. 2 (1962), pp. 157-76.

26. Ibid., pp. 162-63.

27. Ibid., p. 171.

28. Ibid., p. 172.

29. Adelina Levine and Janice Crumrine, "Women and Fear of Success: A Problem in Replication," *American Journal of Sociology*, 80 (January 1975), pp. 964-74.

30. John Bowlby *Attachment and Loss, Vol. I: Attachment* (New York: Basic Books, 1969), p. 209.

31. Especially Jerome Kagan. See his *Understanding Children* (New York: Harcourt Brace Jovanovich, 1971).

32. Greta Fein and Alison Clarke-Stewart, *Day Care in Context* (New York: Wiley, 1973).

33. Laura C. Johnson, and Eric Leightman, *Child Care Patterns in Metropolitan Toronto* (Toronto: Social Planning Council, 1978). Findings from this source did not entirely agree with findings of other researchers on the subject.

Chapter 5
Sex roles

1. John Money and Anke A. Ehrhardt, *Man and Woman, Boy and Girl* (Baltimore: Johns Hopkins Press, 1972), p. 293.

2. Margaret Mead, *Sex and Temperament in Three Primitive Societies* (New York: Dell, 1935).

3. Randall Collins, *Conflict Sociology: Toward an Explanatory Science* (New York: Academic Press, 1975). pp. 228-49.

4. Eleanor E. Maccoby and Carol Nagy Jacklin, *The Psychology of Sex Differences* (Palo Alto, Calif.: Stanford University Press, 1974).

5. Alice Rossi, "A Biosocial Theory of Parenting," *Daedalus*, Spring 1977. My discussion follows Rossi's closely.

6. Jerome Kagan, "The Child in the Family," *Daedalus*, Spring 1977, p. 36.

7. Jean Lipman-Blumen and Ann R. Tickamyer. "Sex Roles in Transition," in Alex Inkeles, James Coleman, and Neil Smelser, eds., *Annual Review of Sociology* (Palo Alto, Calif.: Annual Reviews, 1975), I. p. 298.

8. Martin Meissner, Elizabeth W. Humphreys, Scott M. Meis, and William J. Scheu, "No Exit for Wives: Sexual Division of Labour," *Canadian Review of Sociology and Anthropology*, 12, no. 4 (November 1975), p. 432.

9. Hugh Armstrong and Pat Armstrong, "Women in the Canadian Labour Force, 1941-1971," *Canadian Review of Sociology and Anthropology*, 12, no. 4 (November 1975), p. 370.

10. Lorna Marsden, Edward Harvey, and Ivan Charner, "Female Graduates: Their Occupational Mobility and Attainments," *Canadian Review of Sociology and Anthropology*, 12, no. 4 (November 1975), pp. 385-403.

11. Saul D. Feldman, *Escape from the Doll's House: Women in Graduate and Professional School Education* (San Francisco: Jossey-Bass, 1974).

12. Ronald Lambert, *Sex Role Imagery in Children: The Social Origins of Mind*, Studies of the Royal Commission on the Status of Women in Canada, no. 6 (Ottawa: Queen's Printer, 1969).

13. Susan Russell, *Sex Role Socialization in the High School: A Study of the Perpetuation of the Patriarchal Culture*. Unpublished Ph.D. Dissertation, Department of Sociology, University of Toronto, 1978.

14. Jo Freeman, "The Origins of the Women's Liberation Movement," *American Journal of Sociology*, 78, no. 4 (Jan. 1973), pp. 792-811. See also Jo Freeman, *The Politics of Women's Liberation* (New York: McKay, 1975).

15. Lynn MacDonald, "The Evolution of the Women's Movement," *Branching Out*, vol. VI, no. 2, 1979, pp. 31-39.

16. Lorna Marsden and Edward B. Harvey, *Fragile Federation: Social Change in Canada* (Toronto: McGraw-Hill Ryerson, 1979), pp. 189-98.

17. Freeman, *The Politics of Women's Liberation*, p. 20.

18. Alice Rossi, "Equality Between the Sexes: An Immodest Proposal," in Robert J. Lifton, ed., *The Woman in America* (Boston: Beacon Press, 1964), p. 106.

19. Freeman, "Origins of Women's Liberation," p. 799.

20. Marsden & Harvey, p. 195.

21. Based on *Men and Women of the Corporation*, by Rosabeth Moss Kanter, ©1977 by Rosabeth Moss Kanter, Basic Books, Inc., Publishers, New York.

22. Amitai Etzioni, *A Comparative Analysis of Complex Organizations* (New York: Free Press, 1975).

Chapter 6
Social groups

1. Kingsley Davis, "Extreme Isolation of a Child," *American Journal of Sociology*, 45 (1940), pp. 554-565, and "Final Note on a Case of Extreme Isolation," *American Journal of Sociology*, 52 (1947), pp. 432-37.

2. Jean Marc Itard, *The Wild Boy of Aveyron* (New York: Appleton-Century-Crofts, 1962). See also J.A.L. Singh and R.M. Zingg, *Wolf Children and Feral Man* (New York: Harper, 1942).

3. Bruno Bettelheim, "Feral Children and Autistic Children," *American Journal of Sociology*, 54 (March 1959), p. 458.

4. Rene Spitz, "Hospitalism, An Inquiry Into the Genesis of Psychiatric Conditions in Early Childhood," in A. Freund et al., eds., *Psychoanalytic Study of the Child*, 3rd ed. (New York: International Universities Press, 1958), vol. 1.

5. Harry F. Harlow, "The Nature of Love, *American Psychologist*, 13, no. 12 (December 1958), pp. 673-85, and "The Affectional Systems," in Allen M. Schrier, Harry F. Harlow, and Fred Stollnitz, eds., *Behavior of Nonhuman Primates* (New York: Academic Press, 1965).

6. W.N. Kellogg and L.A. Kellogg, *The Ape and the Child* (New York: McGraw-Hill, 1933).

7. R.A. Gardner and B.T. Gardner, "Teaching Sign Language to a Chimpanzee," *Science*, August 15, 1969, pp. 664-66.

8. David Premack, "Language in Chimpanzee?" *Science*, May 21, 1971, pp. 808-21.

9. Boyce Rensberger, "Talking Chimpanzee Asks for Names of Things Now," *The New York Times*, Dec. 4, 1974.

10. Desmond Morris, *The Naked Ape* (New York: McGraw-Hill, 1969).

11. Lionel Tiger, *Men in Groups* (New York: Random House, 1969).

12. See, for example, Erving Goffman, *Relations in Public* (New York: Basic Books, 1971).

13. Ibid., p. 7.

14. Robert Sommer, *Personal Space* (Englewood Cliffs, N.J.: Prentice-Hall, 1969), p. 50.

15. Ibid., p. 53.

16. See Marvin Scott and Stanford Lyman, "Territoriality, A Neglected Sociological Dimension," *Social Problems*, 15 (Fall 1967), pp. 243-44. See also C.R. Carpenter, "Territoriality: A Review of Concepts and Problems," in A. Roe and G.G. Simpson, eds., *Behavior and Evolution* (New Haven, Conn.: Yale University Press, 1958).

17. Jane van Lawick-Goodall, *My Friends, the Wild Chimpanzees* (Washington, D.C.: National Geographic Society, 1967), p. 140.

18. Goffman, *Relations in Public*, p. 84.

19. See Ray Birdwhistell, *Kinesics and Context* (Philadelphia: University of Pennsylvania Press, 1970).

20. Paul Ekman and Wallace V. Friesen, "The Repertoire of Nonverbal Behavior: Categories, Origins, Usage, and Coding," *Semiotica*, 1 (1969), pp. 49-98.

21. Paul Ekman and Wallace V. Friesen, "Nonverbal Leakage and Clues to Deception," *Psychiatry*, 32 (1969), pp. 88-108.

22. Charles Horton Cooley's best-known books are *Human Nature and the Social Order* (Glencoe, Ill.: Free Press, 1956), first published in 1909, and *Social Organization* (New York: Scribner's, 1909).

23. Cooley, *Social Organization*, p. 357.

24. Ibid., p. 359.

25. For a glimpse of John Dewey's ideas on education, see *Experience and Education* (New York: Collier, 1972), first published in 1938.

26. George Herbert Mead, *Mind, Self and Society*, ed. Charles W. Morris (Chicago: University of Chicago Press, 1934).
27. Herbert Blumer's influence has been, like Mead's, transmitted primarily through his role as a teacher. However, his book *Symbolic Interactionism* (Englewood Cliffs, N.J.: Prentice-Hall, 1969) contains a few of his important essays. This chapter was deeply influenced by Blumer's lectures, as no doubt his many former students will recognize.
28. Sheldon Glueck and Eleanor Glueck, *Unraveling Juvenile Delinquency* (Cambridge, Mass.: Harvard University Press, 1955).
29. Gresham M. Sykes and David Matza, "Techniques of Neutralization: A Theory of Delinquency," *American Sociological Review*, 22 (December 1957), pp. 664-70.
30. Mark Granovetter, "The Strength of Weak Ties," *American Journal of Sociology*, 78 (May 1973), pp. 1360-80.
31. Barry Wellman, "The Community Question: The Intimate Networks of East Yorkers," *American Journal of Sociology*, 84 (5) March 1979, pp. 1201-31.
32. Norman Shulman, "Network Analysis: A New Addition to an Old Bag of Tricks," *Acta Sociologica*, 19 (December 1976), pp. 307-23.
33. Stanley Milgram, "Behavioral Study of Obedience," *Journal of Abnormal and Social Psychology*, 67 (1963), pp. 371-78.
34. Solomon Asch, "Effects of Group Pressure Upon the Modification and Distortion of Judgments," in Harold S. Guetzkow, ed., *Groups, Leadership, and Men* (Pittsburgh: Carnegie Press, 1951).
35. Jonathan L. Freedman, J. Merrill Carlsmith, and David O. Sears, *Social Psychology*, 2nd ed. (Englewood Cliffs, N.J.: Prentice-Hall, 1970), pp. 217-20.
36. Hannah Arendt, *Eichmann in Jerusalem* (New York: Viking Press, 1963).
37. William Shakespeare, *Henry V*, Act IV, Scene i.

Chapter 7
Deviance and control

1. Emile Durkheim, *Sociology and Philosophy* (Glencoe, Ill.: Free Press, 1963), p. 45.
2. Gwynn Nettler, *Explaining Crime* (New York: McGraw-Hill, 1974), p. 66. Other estimates place the discrepancy at between one out of three and one out of ten crimes.
3. P.J. Giffen, "Official Rates of Crime and Delinquency," in W.T. McGrath, ed., *Crime and Its Treatment in Canada*, 2nd ed. (Toronto: Macmillan, 1976), p. 73.
4. John Hagan, "The Labelling Perspective, the Delinquent, and the Police: A Review of the Literature," *Canadian Journal of Criminology and Corrections*, vol. 14 (April 1972), pp. 150-65.
5. See Edwin M. Schur, *Crimes without Victims* (Englewood Cliffs, N.J.: Prentice-Hall, 1965).
6. Lorenne Clark and Debra Lewis, *Rape: The Price of Coercive Sexuality* (Toronto: The Canadian Women's Educational Press, 1977).
7. Maureen McTeer, "Rape and the Canadian Legal Process," in Mary Alice Beyer Gammon, ed., *Violence in Canada* (Toronto: Methuen, 1978).
8. M.C. Courtis, "Victimization in Toronto," in Robert A. Silverman and James J. Teevan, Jr., eds., *Crime in Canadian Society* (Toronto: Butterworth, 1975), pp. 119-26.
9. Giffen, pp. 108-10.
10. James S. Wallerstein and Clement J. Wyle, "Our Law-Abiding Law-Breakers," *Probation*, 25 (Mar.-Apr. 1947), pp. 107-12.
11. E. W. Vaz, *Aspects of Deviance* (Scarborough, Ont.: Prentice-Hall, 1976), p. 118. See also Lorne Tepperman, *Crime Control* (Toronto: McGraw-Hill Ryerson, 1977).
12. Edmund W. Vaz, "Delinquency among Middle-class Boys," *Canadian Review of Sociology and Anthropology*, 2 (1965).
13. James F. Short, Jr., "The Study of Juvenile Delinquency by Reported Behavior: An Experiment in Method and Preliminary Findings." (Paper presented at Annual Meetings of the American Sociological Society, 1955); Austin L. Porterfield, *Youth in Trouble* (Forth Worth: Leo Potishman Foundation, 1946); Edward E. Schwarz, "A Community Experiment in Measurement of Delinquency," *National Probation and Parole Association Yearbook* (1945), pp. 157-81; Fred J. Murphy, Mary M. Shirley, and Helen L. Witmer, "The Incidence of Hidden Delinquency," *American Journal of Orthopsychiatry*, 16 (1946), pp. 686-96; Maynard L. Erickson and LaMar T. Empey, "Court Records, Undetected Delinquency, and Decision Making," *Journal of Criminal Law, Criminology and Police Science*, 54 (1963), pp. 456-69.
14. Short, "The Study of Juvenile Delinquency by Reported Behavior."
15. Peter Chimbos, "Some Trends of Organized Crime in Canada: A Preliminary Review," in Silverman and Teevan, p. 340.
16. Ibid., p. 340.
17. Benjamin Schlesinger, ed., *Sexual Behavior in Canada: Patterns and Problems* (Toronto: University of Toronto Press, 1977), p. 150.
18. Ibid., p. 153.
19. Alfred C. Kinsey et al., *Sexual Behavior in*

the Human Male (Philadelphia: Saunders, 1948).

20. Statistics Canada, *Vital Statistics, Vol. III, Deaths* (Ottawa: Supply and Services Canada, 1976), p. 28.

21. Emile Durkheim, *Suicide: A Study in Sociology*, trans. John A. Spaulding and George Simpson (New York: Free Press, 1951).

22. J.D. Armstrong and R.E. Turner, "Special Problem Offenders: Alcoholics, Drug Abusers, Sex Offenders," in McGrath, p. 508.

23. Ibid., p. 507.

24. Statistics Canada, Justice Statistics Division, Paul Reed, Teresa Blexzynski, and Robert Gaucher, "Homicide in Canada: A Statistical Synopsis," in Gammon, p. 203.

25. Paul C. Whitehead, *Alcohol and Young Drivers: Impact and Implications of Lowering the Drinking Age* (Ottawa: Dept. of National Health and Welfare, 1977).

26. Don Cahalan, *Problem Drinkers* (San Francisco: Jossey-Bass, 1970), p. 142.

27. G. Lolli, quoted in Israel Zwerling and Milton Rosenbaum, "Alcoholic Addiction and Personality," in Silvano Arieti, ed., *American Handbook of Psychiatry* (New York: Basic Books, 1959), p. 627.

28. David McClelland, William N. Davis, Rudolf Kalin, and Eric Wanner, *The Drinking Man* (New York: The Free Press, 1972), p. 334.

29. L. Kaiij, *Alcoholism in Twins: Studies on the Etiology and Sequels of Abuse of Alcohol* (Stockholm: Alcuquist and Wiksell, 1960).

30. D.A. Rodgers and G.E. McClearn, "Mouse Strain Differences in Preference for Various Concentrations of Alcohol," *Quarterly Journal of Studies on Alcohol*, 23 (1962), pp. 26-33.

31. John Clausen, "Mental Disorders," in Robert Merton and Robert Nisbet, eds., *Contemporary Social Problems* (New York: Harcourt, Brace, 1971), p. 29.

32. See Thomas Scheff, *Being Mentally Ill: A Sociological Theory* (Chicago: Aldine, 1966), and Thomas S. Szasz, *The Myth of Mental Illness* (New York: Harper, 1961).

33. For a discussion of moral responsibility and mental illness, see Helmut Schoeck and James Wiggins, eds., *Psychiatry and Responsibility* (New York: Van Nostrand, 1962).

34. Donald Mazer, "Mental Illness and the Law," in W.K. Greenaway and S.L. Brickey, eds., *Law and Social Control in Canada* (Scarborough, Ont.: Prentice-Hall, 1978), p. 95.

35. John Hagan, *The Disreputable Pleasures* (Toronto: McGraw-Hill Ryerson, 1977), p. 63.

36. Kenneth Westhues, *Society's Shadow: Studies in the Sociology of Countercultures* (Toronto: McGraw-Hill Ryerson, 1972), pp. 15-17.

37. Howard Becker, *Outsiders: Studies in the Sociology of Deviance* (New York: Free Press of Glencoe, 1963), pp. 19-22.

38. Shirley Small, "Canadian Narcotics Legislation, 1908-1923: A Conflict Model Interpretation," in Greenaway and Brickey, pp. 28-41.

39. John Hagan, A.R. Gillis, and Janet Chan, "Explaining Official Delinquency: A Spatial Study of Class, Conflict and Control," *Sociological Quarterly*, 19 (Summer 1978), pp. 386-398. See also Lynn McDonald, *The Sociology of Law and Order* (London: Faber, 1976).

40. Hagan, Gillis, and Chan, p. 396.

41. Gary T. Marx, "Civil Disorder and the Agents of Social Control," *Journal of Social Issues*, 26 (Winter 1970), pp. 19-58.

42. Edwin H. Sutherland, *White Collar Crime* (New York: Dryden, 1949).

43. Laureen Snider, "Corporate Crime in Canada: A Preliminary Report." (Paper presented at the Canadian Sociology and Anthropology Association Meetings, Quebec City, 1976.)

44. Colin H. Goff and Charles E. Reasons, *Corporate Crime in Canada: A Critical Analysis of Anti-Combines Legislation* (Scarborough, Ont.: Prentice-Hall, 1978).

45. Erving Goffman, *Stigma: Notes on the Management of Spoiled Identity* (Englewood Cliffs, N.J.: Prentice-Hall, 1963).

46. See David Rosenthal and Seymour Kety, eds., *The Transmission of Schizophrenia* (London: Pergamon, 1969), pp. 175-266.

47. See James S. Coleman, *The Adolescent Society: The Social Life of the Teenager and Its Impact on Education* (New York: The Free Press of Glencoe, 1961).

48. See Robert Martinson, "What Works? Questions and Answers about Prison Reform," *The Public Interest*, 35 (Spring 1974), pp. 22-54.

49. James C. Hackler, *The Prevention of Youthful Crime: The Great Stumble Forward* (Toronto: Methuen, 1978).

50. See Norman Jaspan, with Hillel Black, *The Thief in the White Collar* (Philadelphia: Lippincott, 1960), pp. 223-34.

51. U.S. Congress, Senate Committee on Government Operations, *Gambling and Organized Crime: Report of the Permanent Subcommittee on Investigations*, 87th Cong., 2nd sess., 1962, S. Rept. 1310, pp. 13-16.

52. See Kingsley Davis, "The Sociology of Prostitution," *American Sociological Review*, vol. 2 (October 1937), pp. 744-55; and "Prostitution," in Robert K. Merton and Robert Nisbet, eds., *Contemporary Social Problems* (New York: Harcourt, Brace,

1952), pp. 262-288.

53. Compare with Kai T. Erikson, "Notes on the Sociology of Deviance," *Social Problems*, 9 (Spring 1962), pp. 307-14.

54. See George Herbert Mead, "The Psychology of Punitive Justice," in Lewis A. Coser and Bernard Rosenberg, eds., *Sociological Theory: A Book of Readings*, 2nd. ed. (New York: Macmillan, 1964), p. 596.

55. See Robert A. Dentler and Kai T. Erikson, "The Functions of Deviance in Groups," *Social Problems*, 7 (Fall 1959), pp. 98-107.

56. See Lewis A. Coser, "Some Functions of Deviant Behavior and Normative Flexibility," *American Journal of Sociology*, 68 (September 1962), p. 174.

57. Albert K. Cohen, "The Sociology of the Deviant Act: Anomie Theory and Beyond," *American Sociological Review*, 30 (February 1965), p. 10. Based on William J. Chambliss, "The Deterrent Influence of Punishment: A Study of the Violation of Parking Regulations," (M.A. diss., Indiana University, 1960).

58. Emile Durkheim, *The Rules of Sociological Method*, 8th ed., trans. Sarah Solovnay and John H. Mueller, ed. George E.H. Catlin (New York: Free Press, 1950), pp. 68-69.

59. Kai T. Erikson, *Wayward Puritans* (New York: Wiley, 1966), p. 6.

60. See Samuel A. Stouffer's classic study, "An Analysis of Conflicting Social Norms," *American Sociological Review*, 18 (December 1949), pp. 707-17.

61. Cesare Lombroso, *Crime: Its Causes and Remedies* (Boston: Little, Brown, 1918, translated from French edition of 1899), p. 376.

62. Charles Goring, *The English Convict* (London: His Majesty's Stationery Office, 1913).

63. William H. Sheldon, in collaboration with Emil H. Hartl and Eugene McDermott, *Varieties of Delinquent Youth* (New York: Harper, 1956).

64. Sheldon Glueck and Eleanor Glueck, *Physique and Delinquency* (New York: Harper, 1956).

65. Kennedy McWhirter, "XYY Chromosomes and Criminal Acts," *Science*, June 6, 1969. See also Amir J. Berman, "Chromosomal Deviation and Crime," *Federal Probation*, June 1970, pp. 55-62.

66. One of the most careful and systematic studies in this vein is Albert Bandura and Richard H. Walters, *Adolescent Aggression* (New York: Ronald Press, 1959), especially Chap. 6.

67. John Dollard, Leonard W. Dobb, Neal E. Miller, O.H. Mowrer, and Robert R. Sears, *Frustration and Aggression* (New Haven, Conn.: Yale University Press, 1939). See also Elton B. McNeil, "Psychology and Aggression," *The Journal of Conflict Re-*

solution, 3 (September 1959), pp. 195-294; O.H. Mowrer, "Frustration and Aggression," in *Encyclopedia of Criminology* (New York: Philosophical Library, 1949), pp. 176-86.

68. Andrew F. Henry and James F. Short, Jr., *Suicide and Homicide* (Glencoe, Ill.: Free Press, 1954); "The Sociology of Suicide," in Edwin S. Schneidman and Norman L. Farberow, eds., *Clues to Suicide* (New York: McGraw-Hill, 1957), pp. 58-69.

69. For an alternative interpretation of the causes of suicide, see Jack P. Gibbs and Walter T. Martin, *Status Integration and Suicide* (Eugene: University of Oregon Books, 1964).

70. Albert K. Cohen, *Delinquent Boys: The Culture of the Gang* (Glencoe, Ill.: Free Press, 1955).

71. Emile Durkheim, *The Division of Labor in Society* (New York: Free Press of Glencoe, 1964), vol. 3, pp. 353-73.

72. Robert K. Merton, "Social Structure and Anomie," *American Sociological Review*, 3 (October 1938), pp. 672-682. Revised and enlarged in R.K. Merton, *Social Theory and Social Structure* (Glencoe, Ill.: Free Press, 1957), pp. 131-194.

73. Clifford R. Shaw, *The Jack-Roller* (Chicago: University of Chicago Press, 1930), *The Natural History of a Delinquent Career* (Chicago: University of Chicago Press, 1931), and *Brothers in Crime* (Chicago: University of Chicago Press, 1938); Clifford R. Shaw and Henry D. McKay, *Social Factors in Juvenile Delinquency*, Vol. 2 of National Committee on Law Observance and Law Enforcement, *Report on the Causes of Crime* (Washington, D.C.: Government Printing Office, 1931), and *Juvenile Delinquency and Urban Areas* (Chicago: University of Chicago Press, 1942).

74. Shaw and McKay, *Social Factors in Juvenile Delinquency*, p. 387.

75. See Edwin H. Sutherland and Donald R. Cressey, *Principles of Criminology*, 6th ed. (Philadelphia: Lippincott, 1960), chap. 4; Alfred Cohen, Alfred Lindesmith, and Karl Schuessler, eds., *The Sutherland Papers* (Bloomington: Indiana University Press, 1956), pp. 5-43; and Donald Cressey, *Delinquency, Crime and Differential Association* (The Hague: Martinus Nijhoff, 1964). See also the commentaries by Daniel Glaser: "Differential Association and Criminological Prediction," *Social Problems*, 7 (Summer 1960), pp. 2-6; "The Sociological Approach to Crime and Correction," *Law and Contemporary Problems*, 23 (Autumn 1958), pp. 683-702; and "The Differential Association Theory of Crime," in Arnold M. Rose, ed., *Human Behavior and Social Processes: An Inter-*

actionist Approach (Boston: Houghton Mifflin, 1962), pp. 425-42.

76. See Erving Goffman, *Stigma* (Englewood Cliffs, N.J.: Prentice-Hall, 1963).

77. George Grosser, "Juvenile Delinquency and Contemporary American Sex Roles," (Ph.D. diss., Harvard University, 1952).

78. Cohen, "The Sociology of the Deviant Act," p. 13.

79. One important effort to integrate cultural-transmission and anomie theory is the work of Richard A. Cloward and Lloyd B. Ohlin, *Delinquency and Opportunity: A Theory of Delinquent Gangs* (Glencoe, Ill.: Free Press, 1960).

80. Edward Mann and John Alan Lee, *RCMP Vs. the People* (Don Mills, Ont.: General Publishing, 1979).

81. Ibid., p. 163.

82. Ibid., pp. 157-8.

83. Ibid., p. 163.

84. Ibid., pp. 158-61.

85. Ibid., p. 38.

86. Ibid., p. 53.

87. Ibid., p. 165.

88. Ibid., pp. 168-9.

89. Ibid., p. 171.

90. Ibid., p. 173.

91. Ibid., p. 176.

92. Richard L. Henshel, "Will police disruptive tactics leave only the facade of democracy?" *Canadian Journal of Sociology*, 4 (2), pp. 167-171. See also his article, "Controlling the Police Power," *Canadian Forum*, Nov. 1977.

Chapter 8
Organizations

1. See Robert Presthus, *The Organizational Society* (New York: Knopf, 1962).

2. Talcott Parsons, *Structure and Process in Modern Societies* (Glencoe, Ill.: Free Press, 1960), p. 17.

3. For a thorough discussion of who does and does not join and for the information on which this paragraph is based, see Nicholas Babchuk and Alan Booth, "Voluntary Association Membership: A Longitudinal Analysis," *American Sociological Review*, 34, no. 1 (February 1969), pp. 31-45, and James Curtis, "Voluntary Association Joining: A Cross-National Comparative Note," *American Sociological Review*, 36, no. 5 (October 1971), pp. 872-880.

4. Curtis, p. 874.

5. Presthus, p. 74.

6. Max Weber, *The Theory of Social and Economic Organization*, trans. by A.M. Henderson and Talcott Parsons (New York: Macmillan Publishing Company,

Inc., 1947). © 1947, 1975, by Talcott Parsons.

7. This discussion draws upon Amitai Etzioni, *A Comparative Analysis of Complex Organizations* (New York: Free Press, 1961).

8. K.J. Scudder, "The Open Institution," *Annals of the American Academy of Political and Social Science*, 293 (1954), pp. 80-82.

9. See H.A. Simon, *Administrative Behavior* (New York: Macmillan, 1945), for a full discussion of socialization as a means of control.

10. Frederick W. Taylor, *Scientific Management* (New York: Harper, 1911).

11. See, for example, Luther Gulick and L. Urwin, eds., *Papers on the Science of Administration* (New York: Columbia University, Institute of Public Administration, 1937).

12. For a summary of the Hawthorne studies see F.J. Roethlisberger and W.J Dickson, *Management and The Worker* (Cambridge, Mass.: Harvard University Press, 1939).

13. Alex Carey, "The Hawthorne Studies: A Radical Criticism," *American Sociological Review*, 32 (June 1967), pp. 403-16.

14. Richard Herbert Franke and James D. Kaul, "The Hawthorne Experiments: First Statistical Interpretation," *American Sociological Review*, 43 (5) October 1978, pp. 623-42.

15. Reinhard Bendix and Lloyd Fisher, "Perspective of Elton Mayo," in Amitai Etzioni, ed., *Complex Organizations* (New York: Holt, Rinehart and Winston, 1961).

16. Robert Dubin, "Industrial Workers' Worlds: A Study of the Central Life Interests of Industrial Workers," *Social Problems*, 4 (1956), p. 136.

17. D.R. Walker and R.H. Guest, *The Man on the Assembly Line* (Cambridge, Mass.: Harvard University Press, 1952).

18. Ibid., p. 91.

19. Edward Harvey, "Technology and the Structure of Organizations," *American Sociological Review*, 33 (April 1968), p. 255.

20. Charles Perrow, *Organizational Analysis: A Sociological View* (Belmont, California: Wadsworth, 1970).

21. Christopher Beattie, *Minority Men in a Majority Setting* (Ottawa: Carleton, 1975).

22. Ibid., p. 163.

23. Rex. A. Lucas, *Minetown, Milltown, Railtown: Life in Canadian Communities of Single Industry* (Toronto: University of Toronto Press, 1971).

24. Ibid., p. 392.

25. Oswald Hall, "The Canadian Division of Labour Revisited," in Richard J. Ossenberg, ed., *Canadian Society: Pluralism, Change, and Conflict* (Scarborough, Ont:

Prentice-Hall, 1971), pp. 89-100.

26. Hall cites P. Briant, "The Construction Industry in Montreal," an unpublished report for the Royal Commission on Bilingualism and Biculturalism.

27. Hall, p. 93.

28. Theodore Roszak, *The Making of a Counterculture* (New York: Doubleday, 1969).

29. Charles A. Reich, *The Greening of America* (New York: Random House, 1970).

30. William H. Whyte, Jr., *The Organization Man* (New York: Simon & Schuster, 1956).

31. Robert Merton, *Social Theory and Social Structure*, rev. ed. (Glencoe, Ill.: Free Press, 1957), chap. 6.

32. Melvin Kohn, "Bureaucratic Man: A Portrait ad an Interpretation," *American Sociological Review*, 36 (June 1971), pp. 461-74.

Chapter 9
Social stratification

1. For details see J. Richard Udry, "The Importance of Being Beautiful: A Reexamination and Racial Comparison," *American Journal of Sociology*, 83, no. 1 (July 1977), pp. 154-60.

2. Saul Feldman, "The Presentation of Shortness in Everyday Life: Height and Heightism in American Society: Toward a Sociology of Stature." (Paper presented at the American Sociological Association Convention in Denver, 1971.)

3. Gerald Berreman, "Caste in India and the United States," *American Journal of Sociology*, 64 (September 1960), pp. 120-27.

4. Gerhard Lenski, *Power and Privilege* (New York: McGraw-Hill, 1966).

5. J.H. Thompson, "The Beginning of Our Regeneration: The Great War and Western Canadian Reform Movements," in Samuel Clark, J. Paul Grayson, and Linda M. Grayson, eds., *Prophecy and Protest: Social Movements in Twentieth Century Canada* (Toronto: Gage, 1975).

6. S.D. Clark, "Movements of Protest in Postwar Canadian Society," in Clark, Grayson, and Grayson, pp. 409-11.

7. See, for example, Marvin E. Olsen and Judy Corder Tully, "Socioeconomic-Ethnic Status Inconsistency and Preference for Political Change," *American Sociological Review*, 37 (October 1972), pp. 560-74.

8. Thorstein Veblen, *The Theory of the Leisure Class* (New York: New American Library, 1954).

9. See Gunnar Myrdal, *Asian Drama* (New York: Twentieth Century Fund, 1968).

10. Leo A. Johnson, "Precapitalist Economic Formations and the Capitalist Labor Market in Canada, 1911-71," in James E. Curtis and William G. Scott, eds., *Social Stratification: Canada*, 2nd ed. (Scarborough, Ont.: Prentice-Hall, 1979).

11. Ibid., p. 143.

12. Jenny Podoluk, *Incomes of Canadians* (Ottawa: Dominion Bureau of Statistics, 1968), p. 185.

13. Dennis Forcese, *The Canadian Class Structure* (Toronto: McGraw-Hill Ryerson, 1975), p. 54.

14. National Council on Welfare, *The Working Poor* (Ottawa: Supply and Services Canada, 1977), p. 1.

15. Ibid., p. 12.

16. Ibid., p. 29.

17. Wilfred B.W. Martin and Allan J. Macdonell, *Canadian Education: A Sociological Analysis* (Scarborough, Ont.: Prentice-Hall, 1978), p. 248.

18. *Canada Year Book, 1975* (Ottawa: Minister of Industry, Trade and Commerce), p. 236.

19. Martin and Macdonell, p. 245.

20. Pat Armstrong and Hugh Armstrong, *The Double Ghetto: Canadian Women and Their Segregated Work* (Toronto: McClelland and Stewart, 1978), p. 38.

21. Ibid., p. 38.

22. C.M. Lanphier and R.N. Morris, "Structural Aspects of Differences in Income Between Anglophones and Francophones," *Canadian Review of Sociology and Anthropology*, 11 (Feb. 1974), pp. 53-66.

23. *Royal Commission on Bilingualism and Biculturalism, Vol. III, The Work World* (Ottawa: Information Canada, 1969), p. 35.

24. David Caplovitz, *The Poor Pay More: Consumer Practices of Low-Income Families* (New York: Free Press, 1963).

25. National Council of Welfare, *The Hidden Welfare System* (Ottawa, Ontario: National Council of Welfare, November, 1976).

26. Statistics Canada: Vital Statistics, Vol. II., *Marriage and Divorce* (Ottawa, Statistics Canada, 1976), p. 39.

27. Warren E. Kalbach and Wayne W. McVey, *The Demographic Bases of Canadian Society*, 2nd. ed. (Toronto: McGraw-Hill Ryerson, 1979), pp. 110, 112.

28. J. Lorimer and M. Phillips, *Working People: Life in a Downtown City Neighborhood* (Toronto: James Lewis and Samuel, 1971), p. 40.

29. Forcese, p. 92.

30. International evidence on the relation of mortality to socioeconomic status is reviewed by Samuel H. Preston, "Mortality Trends," in Alex Inkeles, ed., *Annual Review of Sociology*, vol. 3 (Palo Alto: Annual Review, 1977), pp. 168-69.

31. Forcese, pp. 84-85.

32. Melvin Tumin and W. Arnold Feldman, *Social Class and Social Change in Puerto*

Rico (Princeton, N.J.: Princeton University Press, 1961).

33. James Curtis, "Voluntary Associations Joining: A Cross-National Comparative Note," *American Sociological Review*, 36, no. 4 (October 1971), pp. 872-880.

34. Stewart Crysdale, *The Changing Church in Canada* (Toronto: Board of Evangelism and Social Service, 1965). I refer also to James L. Teevan, Jr. and J.E. Jackson, "Religion and Social Class in Toronto." (Unpublished paper presented at Canadian Sociological and Anthropological Meetings, Montreal, 1972.)

35. John Porter, *The Vertical Mosaic* (Toronto: University of Toronto Press, 1965).

36. Liston Pope, "Religion and the Class Structure," *Annals of the American Academy of Political and Social Science*, March 1948, pp. 84-91.

37. John F. Myles, "Differences in the Canadian and American Class Vote: Fact or Pseudo-fact?" *American Journal of Sociology*, 84 (5) March 1979, pp. 1232-36.

38. William A. Rushing and Suzanne T. Ortega, "Socioeconomic Status and Mental Disorder: New Evidence and a Sociomedical Formulation," *American Journal of Sociology*, 84 (5) March 1979, pp. 1175-200.

39. Robert M. Hauser and David L. Featherman, "Trends in the Occupational Mobility of United States Men, 1962-70," *American Sociological Review*, 38 (June 1973), pp. 302-10.

40. On this point see Natalie Rogoff, *Recent Trends in Occupational Mobility* (Glencoe, Ill: Free Press, 1953).

41. S.M. Lipset and Reinhard Bendix, *Social Mobility in Industrial Society* (Berkeley: University of California Press, 1960).

42. Peter M. Blau and Otis Dudley Duncan, *The American Occupational Structure* (New York: Wiley, 1967).

43. See, for example, P.C. Pineo, "Social Mobility in Canada: The Current Picture," *Sociological Focus*, 9 (April 1976), pp. 109-23. See also Carl J. Cuneo and James E. Curtis, "Social Ascription in the Education and Occupational Status Attainment of Urban Canadians," *Canadian Review of Sociology and Anthropology*, 12, (1975). Also, an unpublished paper by A.H. Turrittin is discussed in Lorne Tepperman, *Social Mobility in Canada* (Toronto: McGraw-Hill Ryerson, 1975). Tepperman's own research and informed speculation supports the Lipset-Bendix conclusions.

44. Lipset and Bendix, p. 73.

45. Tepperman, pp. 48-49.

46. Christopher Jencks et al., *Who Gets Ahead? The Determinants of Economic Success in America* (New York: Basic Books, 1979).

47. John C. Goyder and James E. Curtis, "Occupational Mobility in Canada over Four Generations," *Canadian Review of Sociology and Anthropology*, 14 (3), Aug. 1977, pp. 303-17.

48. Harold Wilensky and Hugh Edmonds, "The Skidder: Ideological Adjustments of Downwardly Mobile Workers," *American Sociological Review*, 24 (April 1949), pp. 215-31.

49. Andrew Hopkins, "Political Overconformity by Upwardly Mobile American Men," *American Sociological Review*, 38 (February 1973), pp. 143-47.

50. August Hollingshead, R. Ellis, and E. Kirby, "Social Mobility and Mental Illness," *American Sociological Review*, 19 (October 1954), pp. 577-83.

51. Peter M. Blau, "Occupational Bias and Mobility," *American Sociological Review*, 22 (August 1957), pp. 393-99.

52. Hans Gerth and C.W. Mills, *From Max Weber* (New York: Oxford University Press, 1958), p. 194.

53. Ibid., p. 94.

54. W. Lloyd Warner, *The Social Life of a Modern Community* (New Haven, Conn.: Yale University Press, 1955).

55. Kingsley Davis and Wilbert E. Moore, "Some Principles of Stratification," *American Sociological Review*, 10 (April 1945), pp. 242-49.

56. Ibid., p. 244.

57. Wlodzimierz Wesolowski, "Some Notes on the Functional Theory of Stratification," in Lipset and Bendix, op. cit.

58. Bernd Baldus and Verna Tribe, "The Development of Perceptions and Evaluations of Social Inequality Among Public School Children," *Canadian Review of Sociology and Anthropology*, 15(1), Feb. 1978, pp. 50-60.

Chapter 10
Racial and ethnic groups

1. This definition is drawn largely from Frederick Barth, "Introduction," in Frederick Barth, ed., *Ethnic Groups and Boundaries* (Boston: Little, Brown, 1969), pp. 10-11.

2. See Harald Eidheim, "When Ethnic Identity Is a Social Stigma," in Barth, pp. 39-57.

3. Herbert Blumer, "Race Prejudice as a Sense of Group Position," in J. Masuoka and P. Valien, eds., *Race Relations: Problems and Theory* (Chapel Hill: University of North Carolina Press, 1961), pp. 217-27.

4. Gertrude J. Selznick and Stephen Steinberg, *The Tenacity of Prejudice* (New York: Harper & Row, 1969).

5. See, for example, Madison Grant, *The Passing of the Great Race* (New York: Scribner's, 1916).

6. M.F. Ashley Montagu, *Man's Most Dangerous Myth: The Fallacy of Race*, 4th ed. (Cleveland; World, 1964).
7. Ronald D. Lambert and James E. Curtis, "The French- and English-Canadian Language Communities and Multicultural Attitudes," unpublished manuscript, University of Waterloo, 1980.
8. Karl Deutsch, *Nationalism and Its Alternatives* (New York: Knopf, 1969).
9. Wolfram Eberhard, *Conquerors and Rulers: Social Forces in Medieval China* (Leiden: Brill, 1965), pp. 1-11.
10. Raymond Breton, "Institutional Completeness of Ethnic Communities and the Personal Relations of Immigrants," *American Journal of Sociology*, LXX (2) Sept. 1964, pp. 193-205.
11. Warren E. Kalbach and Wayne W. McVey, *The Demographic Bases of Canadian Society*, 2nd ed. (Toronto: McGraw-Hill Ryerson, 1979), p. 176.
12. Ibid., p. 176.
13. J.S. Frideres, *Canada's Indians: Contemporary Conflicts* (Scarborough, Ont.: Prentice-Hall, 1974), p. 88.
14. Ibid., p. 25.
15. Ibid., p. 30.
16. Ibid., p. 54.
17. Ibid., p. 57.
18. Ibid., p. 180.
19. See Frank G. Vallee, "Eskimos of Canada as a Minority Group," in Jean L. Elliot, ed., *Native Peoples* (Scarborough, Ont.: Prentice-Hall, 1971).
20. W.L. Morton, *The Kingdom of Canada* (Toronto: McClelland and Stewart, 1972), p. 151.
21. Raymond N. Morris and C. Michael Lanphier, *Three Scales of Inequality: Perspectives on French-English Relations* (Don Mills, Ont.: Longman's, 1977), p. 101.
22. Ibid., p. 137.
23. See Stanley Lieberson, *Language and Ethnic Relations in Canada* (New York: Wiley, 1970).
24. Richard J. Joy, "Languages in Conflict: Canada, 1976," in James E. Curtis and William G. Scott, eds., *Social Stratification: Canada* (Scarborough, Ont.: Prentice-Hall, 1979), pp. 295-305.
25. Danielle Juteau Lee and Jean Lapointe, "The Emergence of Franco-Ontarians: New Identity, New Boundaries," in Jean L. Elliot, ed., *Two Nations, Many Cultures: Ethnic Groups in Canada* (Scarborough, Ont.: Prentice-Hall, 1979), pp. 99-113.
26. Kalbach and McVey, p. 127.
27. Alan B. Anderson, "Ukrainian Ethnicity: Generations of Change in Rural Saskatchewan," in Elliot, *Two Nations, Many Cultures*, pp. 251-265.
28. John Porter, *The Vertical Mosaic* (Toronto: University of Toronto Press, 1965).
29. See Anthony H. Richmond, "Immigration and Racial Prejudice in Britain and Canada," in Elliot, *Two Nations, Many Cultures*, pp. 290-307.
30. Jeffrey Reitz, *The Survival of Ethnic Groups* (Toronto: McGraw-Hill Ryerson, 1980).
31. K.G. O'Bryan, Jeffrey Reitz, and O.M. Kuplowska, *Non-official Languages: A Study in Canadian Multiculturalism* (Ottawa: Supplies and Services Canada, 1976).
32. Harold Garfinkel, *Studies in Ethnomethodology* (Englewood Cliffs, N.J.: Prentice-Hall, 1967), chapter 2.

Chapter 11
Collective behavior and social movements

1. Neil J. Smelser, *The Theory of Collective Behavior* (New York: Free Press, 1962).
2. Gustave Le Bon, *The Crowd* (New York: Viking, 1960). This study was first published in 1895.
3. Sigmund Freud, *Group Psychology and the Analysis of the Ego* (New York: Liveright, 1951).
4. See Herbert Blumer's articles in Robert R. Evans, ed., *Readings on Collective Behavior* (Chicago: Rand McNally, 1969).
5. For a more ample critique of these theories, see Richard A. Berk, *Collective Behavior* (Chicago: William Brown, 1974).
6. E.D. Martin, *The Behavior of Crowds* (New York: Harper, 1920), p. 37.
7. Floyd H. Allport, *Social Psychology* (Boston: Houghton Mifflin, 1924), p. 295.
8. For a fuller discussion of convergence theory, see Ralph H. Turner, "Collective Behavior," in Robert E.L. Faris, ed., *Handbook of Modern Sociology* (Chicago: Rand McNally, 1964).
9. Ibid., p. 395.
10. Ralph H. Turner and Lewis M. Killian, *Collective Behavior*, 2nd. ed. (Englewood Cliffs, N.J.: Prentice-Hall, 1972), p. 23.
11. Roger Brown, *Social Psychology* (New York: Free Press, 1965). See also Berk, pp. 67-74.
12. Gordon Allport and L. Postman, *The Psychology of Rumor* (New York: Holt, 1947).
13. H. Taylor Buckner, "A Theory of Rumor Transmission," in Evans, pp. 120-134.
14. Turner and Killian, p. 179.
15. Elihu Katz, "The Two-Step Flow of Communication: An Up-to-Date Report on an Hypothesis," *Public Opinion Quarterly*, 21 (Spring 1957), 61.
16. W. Schramm, J. Lyle, and E.B. Parker, *Television in the Lives of Our Children* (Palo Alto, Calif.: Stanford University Press, 1961).
17. Walter Weiss, "Effects of the Mass Media

of Communication," in Gardner Lindzey and Elliot Aronson, eds., *The Handbook of Social Psychology*, 2nd ed. (Reading, Mass.: Addison-Wesley, 1969), p. 133.

18. David P. Phillips, "The Influence of Suggestion on Suicide: Substantive and Theoretical Implications of the Werther Effect," *American Sociological Review*, 39 (June 1974), pp. 340-54.

19. Martin F. Herz, "Some Psychological Lessons from Leaflet Propaganda in World War II," *Public Opinion Quarterly*, 13 (Fall 1949), pp. 471-86.

20. Hadley Cantril, Hazel Gaudet, and H. Herzog, *Invasion from Mars* (Princeton, N.J.: Princeton University Press, 1940).

21. Donald M. Johnson, "The Phantom Anesthetist of Mattoon: A Field Study of Mass Hysteria," *Journal of Abnormal and Social Psychology*, 40 (April 1945), pp. 175-86.

22. This is Herbert Blumer's definition in A.M. Lee, ed., *Principles of Sociology*, 2nd. ed. (New York: Barnes and Noble, 1964), p. 199.

23. Alain Touraine, *Sociologie de l'action* (Paris: Editions du Seuil, 1965). For a brief summary of Touraine's position in English, see Guy Rocher, *A General Introduction to Sociology: A Theoretical Perspective* (Toronto: Macmillan, 1972), pp. 442-447.

24. Norman Cohn, *The Pursuit of the Millennium* (New York: Oxford University Press, 1970).

25. See Rocher, pp. 445-447, for a discussion of these functions.

26. Carl A. Dawson and Warner E. Gettys, *Introduction to Sociology*, rev. ed. (New York: Ronald Press, 1934), pp. 708-9.

27. Samuel Clark, J. Paul Grayson, and Linda M. Grayson, eds., *Prophecy and Protest: Social Movements in Twentieth-Century Canada* (Toronto: Gage, 1975).

28. J.H. Thompson, "'The Beginning of our Regeneration': The Great War and Western Canadian Reform Movements," in Clark, Grayson, and Grayson, op. cit., p. 87.

29. Ibid., p. 90.
30. Ibid., p. 91.
31. Ibid., p. 92.
32. Ibid., p. 97.
33. Ibid., p. 99.

Chapter 12
The family

1. George P. Murdock, *Social Structure* (New York: Macmillan, 1949), pp. 213-14.

2. William J. Goode, *The Family* (Englewood Cliffs, N.J.: Prentice-Hall, 1964), p. 218.

3. David A. Schulz, *The Changing Family* (Englewood Cliffs, N.J.: Prentice-Hall, 1972), pp. 54-55.

4. Louis M. Terman, *Psychological Factors in Marital Happiness* (New York: McGraw-Hill, 1938).

5. See Kenneth L. Cannon and Richard Long, "Premarital Sexual Behavior in the Sixties," in Carlfred B. Broderick, ed., *A Decade of Family Research and Action* (Washington, D.C.: National Council on Family Relations, 1972), pp. 25-38.

6. Ibid., p. 37.

7. C.W. Hobart, "Changing Orientations to Courtship: A Study of Young Canadians," in W.E. Mann, ed., *Social and Cultural Change in Canada, Vol. 2* (Vancouver: Copp Clark, 1970).

8. E.B. Luckey and G.D. Nass, "A Comparison of Sexual Attitudes and Behavior in an International Sample," *Journal of Marriage and the Family*, 31, 1969, pp. 364-79.

9. R.R. Wake, "Attitudes of Parents Towards the Premarital Sex Behavior of Their Children and Themselves," *Journal of Sex Research*, 5 (1969), pp. 170-71.

10. See Alfred Kinsey, Wardell B. Pomeroy, and Clyde E. Martin, *Sexual Behavior in the Human Male* (Philadelphia: Saunders, 1948).

11. Mary E. Heltsley and Carlfred B. Broderick, "Religiosity and Premarital Sexual Permissiveness," *Journal of Marriage and the Family*, 31 (1969), pp. 441-43.

12. Shere Hite, *The Hite Report: A Nationwide Study on Female Sexuality* (New York: Macmillan, 1976).

13. Wardell B. Pomeroy, "Homosexuality," in Ralph W. Weltge, ed., *The Same Sex: An Appraisal of Homosexuality* (Philadelphia: Pilgrim Press, 1969), p. 8.

14. "The Weekend Poll," *Weekend Magazine*, December 3, 1977, p. 3.

15. Evelyn Hooker, "The Adjustment of the Male Overt Homosexual," *Journal of Projective Techniques*, 21 (February, 1957), pp. 18-31.

16. Martin S. Weinberg and Colin J. Williams, *Male Homosexuals: Their Problems and Adaptations* (New York: Oxford University Press, 1974), pp. 235-40.

17. James J. Lynch, *The Broken Heart* (New York: Basic Books, 1977).

18. Schulz, *Family*, pp. 227, 228.

19. Eleanor B. Luckey, "Perceptual Congruence of Self and Family Concepts as Related to Marital Interaction," *Sociometry*, 24 (September 1966), pp. 234-50. See also Eleanor Braun Luckey and Joyce Koym Bain, "Children: A Factor in Marital Satisfaction," *Journal of Marriage and the Family*, 32 (1970), pp. 43-44.

20. Matilda White Riley and Anne Foner, *Aging and Society* (New York: Russell Sage, 1968), I, p. 169.

21. Michael Young and Peter Wilmott, *Family and Kinship in East London* (Glencoe, Ill.:

Free Press, 1957).

22. Peter C. Pineo, "The Extended Family in a Working-Class Area of Hamilton," in Bernard Blishen et al., eds., *Canadian Society* (Toronto: Macmillan of Canada, 1971), pp. 115-25.

23. These data are summarized by Bert N. Adams, "Isolation, Function and Beyond: American Kinship in the 1960's," in Broderick, op. cit. See also Bert N. Adams, *Kinship in an Urban Setting* (Chicago: Markham, 1968).

24. K. Ishwaren, *The Canadian Family* (Toronto: Holt, Rinehart and Winston, 1971).

25. Philippe Garigue, "French Canadian Kinship and Urban Life," *American Anthropologist*, 58 (1956), pp. 1090-101.

26. William J. Goode, "Illegitimacy, Anomie, and Cultural Penetration," *American Sociological Review*, 26 (December 1961), pp. 910-25.

27. Judith Blake, *Family Structure in Jamaica* (Glencoe, Ill.: Free Press, 1961).

28. J.E. Veevers, *The Family in Canada* (Ottawa: Statistics Canada, Bulletin 5.3.3., 1977), p. 35.

29. Ibid., p. 35.

30. William J. Goode, "Family Disorganization," in Robert K. Merton and Robert Nisbet, eds. *Contemporary Social Problems* (New York: Harcourt, Brace and World, 1961), p. 404.

31. Veevers, p. 40.

32. Ibid., p. 46.

33. Ibid., p. 44.

34. Mary Jo Bane, *Here to Stay: American Families in the Twentieth Century* (New York: Basic Books, 1976), p. 32.

35. Ibid., p. 80.

36. Veevers, p. 44.

37. Robert N. Whitehurst, Gerald Booth, Mohammed Hanif, "Factors in Marital Breakup: Separation and Divorce Decision-Making," in *Sociological Footsteps*, Leonard Vargan and Jeanne Ballentine, eds. (New York: Houghton Mifflin, 1979).

38. Robert N. Whitehurst, "A Comparison of Canadian and Israeli Separation and Divorce," in *International Journal of Family Therapy*, vol. 1, (4) 1979.

39. See Judson T. Landis, "A Comparison of Children from Divorced and Nondivorced Unhappy Marriages," *Family LIfe Coordinator*, 11 (July 1962), pp. 61-65.

40. Gerald R. Leslie, *The Family in Social Context* (New York: Oxford University Press, 1967), p. 619.

41. Murdock, chap. 1.

42. E. Kathleen Gough, "The Nayars and the Definition of Marriage," *Journal of the Royal Anthropological Institute*, 89 (1954), pp. 23-24.

43. M.E. Spiro, "Is the Family Universal?" *American Anthropologist*, 56 (1954), pp. 839-46.

44. Professor Brandenburgsky, as cited by Vladimir Gsovski, "Family and Inheritance in Soviet Law," in Alex Inkeles and Kent Geiger, eds., *Soviet Society* (Boston: Houghton Mifflin, 1961), p. 533.

45. Friedrich Engels, *Origin of the Family, Private Property, and the State*, ed. Eleanor B. Leacock (New York: International Publishers, 1971).

46. Karl Marx, *Capital* (New York: Modern Library), pp. 432-39.

47. Engels, p. 145.

48. See Talcott Parsons, *The System of Modern Societies* (Englewood Cliffs, N.J.: Prentice-Hall, 1971), esp. p. 26.

49. Neil J. Smelser, *Social Change in the Industrial Revolution* (Chicago: University of Chicago Press, 1959).

50. William J. Goode, *World Revolution and Family Patterns* (New York: Free Press, 1971).

51. Peter Laslett, *Family and Household in Past Time* (Cambridge: University of Cambridge Press, 1973).

52. Talcott Parsons and Robert Freed Bales, *Family: Socialization and Interaction Process* (Glencoe, Ill.: Free Press, 1955).

53. For an excellent survey of this topic see Lillian E. Troll, "The Family in Later Life," in Broderick, op. cit.

54. *Perspective Canada II: A Compendium of Social Statistics 1977* (Ottawa: Statistics Canada, 1977), p. 36.

55. See Harold Feldman, "Development of the Husband-Wife Relationship," Preliminary Report, Cornell Studies in Marital Development, 1964.

56. See Elliott Feigenbaum, Marjorie F. Lowenthal, and Mella L. Trier, "Sexual Attitudes in the Elderly," paper presented at Gerontological Society meeting, New York, 1966.

57. *Perspective Canada II*, p. 36.

58. Troll, p. 202.

59. Ethel Shanas et al., *Older People in Three Industrial Societies* (New York: Atherton, 1968), p. 166.

60. For a good discussion of a retirement village for welfare recipients, see Arlie R. Hochschild, *The Unexpected Community* (Englewood Cliffs, N.J.: Prentice-Hall, 1973).

61. Bane, op cit.

62. Veevers, op. cit.

63. Bane, p. 19.

64. Veevers, p. 58.

65. Bane, p. 9.

66. Veevers, p. 59.

67. Bane, p. 25.

68. Ibid., p. 10.

69. Kate Millett, *Sexual Politics* (New York: Doubleday, 1970).

70. R.D. Laing, *The Politics of the Family* (New York: Pantheon, 1971).
71. Frederick H. Stroller, "The Intimate Network of Families as a New Structure," in Herbert A. Otto, ed., *The Family in Search of a Future: Alternate Models for Moderns* (Englewood Cliffs, N.J.: Prentice-Hall, 1970).

Chapter 13
Religion

1. David E. Sopher, *Geography of Religions* (Englewood Cliffs, N.J.: Prentice-Hall, 1967), p. 7.
2. Max Weber, *Theory of Social and Economic Organization*, trans. A.M. Henderson and Talcott Parsons (New York: Oxford University Press, 1947), pp. 358-59.
3. Ibid., p. 364.
4. Susanne K. Langer, *Philosophy in a New Key* (Cambridge, Mass: Harvard University Press, 1957), p. 40.
5. See Max Weber, *The Sociology of Religion*, trans. E. Fischoffs (Boston: Beacon Press, 1964).
6. Joaquim Wach, *The Sociology of Religion* (Chicago: University of Chicago Press, 1944), p. 111.
7. This conflict is spelled out in a book by Charles Y. Glock, Benjamin Ringer, and Earl R. Babbie, *To Comfort and to Challenge* (Berkeley and Los Angeles: University of California Press, 1967).
8. Luke M. Smith, "The Clergy: Authority, Structure, Ideology, Migration," *American Sociological Review*, 28 (June 1953), pp. 242-248.
9. Kingsley Davis, *Human Society* (New York: Macmillan, 1948), p. 531.
10. Emile Durkheim, *The Elementary Forms of Religious Life*, trans. Joseph Ward Swain (Glencoe, Ill.: Free Press, 1954).
11. Bronislaw Malinowski, *Magic, Science, and Religion* (Glencoe, Ill.: Free Press, 1954), pp. 39-40.
12. Ibid., pp. 28-29.
13. This discussion of witchcraft and sorcery owes much to an unpublished paper by Dward E. Walker, Jr.
14. Weber, p. 97.
15. Ibid., pp. 80, 97.
16. Ibid., p. 97.
17. Ibid., p. 90.
18. Ibid., p. 107.
19. Ibid., pp. 97, 104.
20. Canadian Institute of Public Opinion, *Report*, Wed. July 4, 1979.
21. Harry H. Hiller, *Canadian Society: A Sociological Analysis* (Scarborough, Ont.: Prentice-Hall, 1976), p. 26.
22. Kenneth Courtis's research in political science, conducted at Laval University, was reported by William Johnson in his column on Quebec on Aug. 15, 1979, in *The Globe and Mail*, Toronto.
23. Harry H. Hiller, "Continentalism and the Third Force in Religion," *Canadian Journal of Sociology*, vol. 3, no. 2, Spring 1978.
24. See Charles Y. Glock and Rodney Stark, *Religion and Society in Tension* (Chicago: Rand McNally, 1965); also Michael Argyle, *Religious Behavior* (London: Routledge and Kegan Paul, 1958), pp. 130-131.
25. See Courtis, as reported by Johnson, *The Globe and Mail*, Aug. 15, 1979.
26. James J. Teevan Jr. and J.E. Winston Jackson, "Religion and Social Class in Toronto." (Paper presented at Meetings of the Canadian Sociology and Anthropology Association, Montreal, 1972.)
27. Dennis Forcese, *The Canadian Class Structure* (Toronto: McGraw-Hill Ryerson, 1975), p. 107.
28. William Johnson, *The Globe and Mail*, Aug. 15, 1979.
29. Canadian Institute of Public Opinion, *Report*, Feb. 28, 1979.
30. Durkheim, p. 416.
31. Sigmund Freud, *The Future of an Illusion*, trans. W.D. Robson-Scott (Garden City, N.Y.: Doubleday, 1957), p. 3.
32. Ibid., p. 45.
33. Ibid., p. 88.
34. Max Weber, *The Protestant Ethic and the Spirit of Capitalism*, trans. Talcott Parsons (New York: Scribner's, 1930).
35. Max Weber, *General Economic History* (New York: Free Press, 1961).
36. Quoted by Weber in *The Protestant Ethic*, p. 175.
37. N.J. Demerath III and Phillip E. Hammond, *Religion in Social Context* (New York: Random House, 1969), p. 90.
38. Ibid., p. 98.
39. Peter Worsley, *The Trumpet Shall Sound* (London: MacGibbon, 1967), p. 224.
40. See Norman Cohn, *The Pursuit of the Millennium* (New York: Harper & Row, 1961).
41. Ibid., p. 315.
42. See Vittorio Lanternari, *The Religions of the Oppressed* (New York: Knopf, 1963).
43. Worsley, pp. 227-28.
44. Lanternari, p. 312.
45. Cohn, p. 310.
46. Robert Wuthnow, "The New Religions in Social Context," in Charles Y. Glock and Robert Bellah, eds., *The New Religious Consciousness* (Berkeley: University of California Press, 1976), pp. 267-94.
47. Ibid., p. 274.
48. Harvey Cox, *Turning East; The Promise and Peril of the New Orientalism* (New York: Simon and Schuster, 1977).
49. Ibid., p. 96.

50. Ibid., pp. 100-1.
51. Max Heirich, "Change of Heart: A Test of Some Widely Held Theories about Religious Conversion," *American Journal of Sociology*, 83, no. 3 (November 1977), pp. 653-77.
52. See Thomas Kuhn, *The Structure of Scientific Revolutions* (Chicago: University of Chicago Press, 1970).

Chapter 14
Education

1. Jean Jacques Rousseau, *Emile*, trans. and ed. by William Boyd (New York: Columbia University Press, 1956).
2. A. Wolfgang, ed., *Education of Immigrant Students: Issues and Answers* (Toronto: Ontario Institute for Studies in Education, Symposium Series 5, 1975).
3. John Porter, *The Vertical Mosaic* (Toronto: University of Toronto Press, 1965).
4. Talcott Parsons, "*The School Class as a Social System*," in A.H. Halsey, Jean Floud, and C. Arnold Anderson, eds., *Education, Economy, and Society* (New York: Free Press, 1961).
5. Wallace Clement, *Continental Corporate Power: Economic Linkages between Canada and the United States* (Toronto: McClelland and Steward, 1977), p. 240.
6. M. Swain, *Bilingual Schooling: Some Experiences in Canada and the United States* (Toronto: Ontario Institute for Studies in Education, Symposium Series 1, 1972).
7. Wilfred B. W. Martin and Allan J. Macdonell, *Canadian Education: A Sociological Analysis* (Scarborough, Ont.: Prentice-Hall, 1978).
8. Ibid., p. 273 and passim.
9. Ibid., p. 276, referring to Statistics Canada information.
10. Ibid., p. 248.
11. Randall Collins, "Functional and Conflict Theories of Educational Stratification," *American Sociological Review*, 36 (December 1971), pp. 1002-18.
12. Ivar Berg, *Education and Jobs: The Great Training Robbery* (New York: Praeger, 1970).
13. Porter, *The Vertical Mosaic*.
14. M.R. Porter, John Porter, and Bernard R. Blishen, *Does Money Matter? Prospects for Higher Education* (Toronto: Institute for Behavioural Research, York University, 1973).
15. Clement, *Continental Corporate Power*, p. 237.
16. Carl J. Cuneo and James E. Curtis, "Social Ascription in the Educational and Occupational Status Attainment of Urban Canadians," *Canadian Review of Sociology and Anthropology*, 12 (1) 1975, pp. 6-24.
17. Christopher Jencks et al., *Inequality* (New York: Basic Books, 1972).
18. Edward B. Harvey and I. Charner, "Social Mobility and Occupational Attainments of University Graduates," *The Canadian Review of Sociology and Anthropology*, 12(2), 1975, pp. 134-49.
19. See Gunnar Myrdal, *Asian Drama* (New York: Pantheon, 1968), especially chapter 32.
20. Ivan Illich, *Deschooling Society* (New York: Harper & Row, 1971).
21. H. Zeigler and W. Peak, "The Political Functions of the Educational System," *Sociology of Education*, 43 (1970).

Chapter 15
Politics and society

1. Talcott Parsons, "The Political Aspect of Social Structure and Process," in David Easton, ed., *Varieties of Political Theory* (Englewood Cliffs, N.J.: Prentice-Hall, 1966), p. 72.
2. See R.D. Laing, *The Politics of the Family and Other Essays* (New York: Pantheon, 1971).
3. Kate Millett, *Sexual Politics* (Garden City, N.Y.: Doubleday, 1970).
4. For a review of this crisis, see Abraham Rotstein, *Power Corrupted* (Toronto: New Press, 1971).
5. Robert Nisbet, *The Sociological Tradition* (New York: Basic Books, 1966).
6. Alexis de Tocqueville, *Democracy in America* (New York: Vintage Books, 1945).
7. Ibid., vol. 2, chap. 7.
8. Emile Durkheim, *Professional Ethics and Civic Morals*, trans. Cornelia Brookfield (Glencoe, Ill.: Free Press, 1960).
9. Joseph R. Gusfield uses the phrase "linked pluralism" to refer to what we call "criss-crossing divisions." See Gusfield, "Mass Society and Extremist Politics," *American Sociological Review*, 27 (February 1962), pp. 19-30.
10. David Riesman, *The Lonely Crowd* (New York: Doubleday, 1953). See also William Kornhauser, "Power Elite or Veto Groups," in S.M. Lipset and Leo Lowenthal, eds., *Culture and Social Character* (Glencoe, Ill.: Free Press, 1961).
11. Robert Michels, *Political Parties* (New York: Crowell and Collier, 1962).
12. S.M. Lipset, Martin Trow, and James Coleman, *Union Democracy* (New York: Dover, 1935).
13. Vilfredo Pareto, *The Mind and Society*, trans. Arthur Livingstone (New York: Free Press, 1956).
14. Karl Mannheim, *Man and Society in an*

Age of Reconstruction (New York: Harcourt Brace, 1940).

15. Suzanne Keller, *Beyond the Ruling Class* (New York: Random House, 1963).

16. E. Digby Baltzell, *The Philadelphia Gentlemen: The Making of a National Upper Class* (New York: Free Press, 1958).

17. C. Wright Mills, *The Power Elite* (New York: Oxford University Press, 1956).

18. John Porter, *The Vertical Mosaic* (Toronto: University of Toronto Press, 1965).

19. Wallace Clement, *The Canadian Corporate Elite: An Analysis of Economic Power* (Toronto: McClelland and Stewart, 1977).

20. For a useful comparison between the views of Porter and Clement, see Kuola Mellos, "Critical Remarks on Critical Elite Theory," *Journal of Canadian Studies*, 13(4), Winter 1978, pp. 72-88.

21. Wallace Clement, *Continental Corporate Power: Economic Linkages Between Canada and the United States* (Toronto: McClelland and Stewart, 1977), p. 24.

22. Marc Pilisuk and Thomas Hayden, "Is There a Military-Industrial Complex Which Prevents Peace? Consensus and Countervailing Power in Pluralistic Systems," *Journal of Social Issues*, 21, no. 3 (1965), pp. 67-117.

23. John Kautsky and Roger Benjamin, "Communism and Economic Development," in John Kautsky, ed., *Communism and the Politics of Development* (New York: Wiley, 1968), pp. 184-206.

24. See Ralf Dahrendorf, *Class and Class Conflict in Industrial Society* (Palo Alto, Calif.: Stanford University Press, 1959).

25. See John Child, *The Business Enterprise in Modern Society* (London: Collier-Macmillan, 1970).

26. Peter Newman, *The Canadian Establishment*, Vol. 1 (Toronto: McClelland and Stewart, 1975).

27. Leo Johnson, *Poverty in Wealth: The Capitalist Labour Market and Income Distribution in Canada* (Toronto: New Hogtown Press, 1974).

28. Andre Gunder Frank, "The Development of Underdevelopment," in Robert I. Rhodes, ed., *Imperialism and Underdevelopment: A Reader* (New York: Monthly Review Press, 1970).

29. G. William Domhoff, *Who Rules America?* (Englewood Cliffs, N.J.: Prentice-Hall, 1967).

30. Among Harold Innis's works are the following: *The Fur Trade in Canada* (Toronto: University of Toronto Press, 1930); *The Cod Fisheries* (Toronto: University of Toronto Press, 1940); and *Empire and Communications* (Toronto: University of Toronto Press, 1950). Innis's ideas have been elaborated and revised by various writers, including Gilles Paquet, "Some Views on the Patterns of Canadian Economic Development," in T.N. Brewis, ed., *Growth and the Canadian Economy* (Toronto: McClelland and Stewart, 1968).

31. See Arthur K. Davis, "Canadian Society as Hinterland Versus Metropolis," in Richard Ossenberg, ed., *Canadian Society: Pluralism, Change, and Conflict* (Scarborough, Ont.: Prentice-Hall, 1971), pp. 6-32.

32. Andre Gunder Frank, *Latin America: Underdevelopment or Revolution* (New York: Monthly Review Press, 1969), and *Capitalism and Underdevelopment in Latin America* (New York: Monthly Review Press, 1977). For the work of another Dependency Theorist, see Johan Galtung, "Structural Theory of Imperialism," *The African Review*, 1(4), 1972, pp. 93-138.

33. Harriet Friedmann and Jack Wayne, "Dependency Theory: A Critique," *Canadian Journal of Sociology*, 2(4), Fall, 1977, pp. 399-416.

34. Lorna R. Marsden and Edward B. Harvey, *Fragile Federation: Social Change in Canada* (Toronto: McGraw-Hill Ryerson, 1979).

35. Hubert Guindon, "The Modernization of Quebec and the Legitimacy of the Canadian State," *Canadian Review of Sociology and Anthropology*, 15 (2), 1978, pp. 227-45.

36. Michael D. Ornstein, H. Michael Stevenson, and A. Paul M. Williams, "Public Opinion and the Canadian Political Crisis," *Canadian Review of Sociology and Anthropology*, 15(2), 1978, pp. 158-205.

37. Peter Bachrach, *The Theory of Democratic Elitism* (Boston: Little, Brown, 1967).

38. Robert L. Heilbroner, *An Inquiry into the Human Prospect* (New York: Norton, 1974).

Chapter 16
Economic life

1. Roger Revelle, "Food and Population," *Scientific American*, September 1974, p. 166.

2. Marcel Mauss, *The Gift* (Glencoe, Ill.: Free Press, 1954), p. 66. Originally published in 1925.

3. Bronislaw Malinowski, *Argonauts of the Western Pacific* (London: Routledge, 1922).

4. Karl Polanyi, *Primitive, Archaic, and Modern Economies*, ed. George Dalton (Garden City, N.Y.: Doubleday, 1968), p. 9.

5. Richard Lee and I. DeVore, *Kalahari Hunter-Gatherers* (Cambridge, Mass.: Harvard University Press, 1975).

6. Ester Boserup, *The Conditions of Agricultural Growth* (Chicago: Aldine, 1965).

7. Joan Robinson, *Freedom and Necessity* (New York: Random House, 1970), p. 43.

8. N.S.B. Gras, *An Introduction to Economic History* (New York: Kelley, 1969), p. 82.
9. See Polanyi, chap. 2.
10. Robinson, p. 54.
11. Gras, p. 163.
12. Robinson, p. 57.
13. Karl Polanyi, *The Great Transformation* (Boston: Beacon Press, 1957), p. 37.
14. Robinson, p. 64.
15. Ibid., p. 67.
16. A.A. Berle and Gardiner Means, *The Modern Corporation and Private Property* (New York: Macmillan, 1934).
17. Eugene V. Rostow, "To Whom and For What Ends Is Corporate Management Responsible?" in Edward S. Mason, ed., *The Corporation in Modern Society* (Cambridge, Mass.: Harvard University Press, 1959), pp. 53-56.
18. Paul A. Baran and Paul Sweezy, *Monopoly Capital* (New York: Monthy Review Press, 1966), p. 36.
19. John K. Galbraith, *The New Industrial State* (Boston: Houghton Mifflin, 1967).
20. See C. Wright Mills, *The Power Elite* (New York: Oxford University Press, 1956).
21. Baran and Sweezy, p. 63.
22. Clark Kerr, John T. Dunlap, Frederick H. Harbison, and Charles A. Myers, *Industrialism and Industrial Man* (Cambridge, Mass.: Harvard University Press, 1960), pp. 209-10.
23. For accounts of Canadian labor history and the On to Ottawa Trek, see Irving Abella, *Nationalism, Communism, and Canadian Labour* (Toronto: University of Toronto Press, 1973); James Gray, *The Winter Years* (Toronto: Macmillan of Canada, 1966); A. Balawyder, *The Winnipeg General Strike* (Toronto: Copp Clark, 1967); Dennis Forcese, *The Canadian Class Structure* (Toronto: McGraw-Hill Ryerson, 1975).
24. M. Patricia Marchak, *Ideological Perspectives on Canada* (Toronto: McGraw-Hill Ryerson, 1975), p. 44.
25. Wallace Clement, *Continental Corporate Power: Economic Linkages Between Canada and the United States* (Toronto: McClelland and Stewart, 1977), pp. 296-97.
26. Kari Levitt, *Silent Surrender* (Toronto: Macmillan, 1971).
27. Paul A. Samuelson, *Economics*, 9th ed. (New York: McGraw-Hill, 1973), p. 881.
28. Majdan Pasic, "Self-Management as an Integral Political System," in M.J. Brookmeyer, ed., *Yugoslav Workers' Self-Management* (Dordrecht, Holland: D. Reidel, 1970).
29. Robinson, pp. 100-1, 107.
30. Warren E. Kalbach and Wayne W. McVey, *The Demographic Bases of Canadian Society*, 2nd ed. (Toronto: McGraw-Hill Ryerson, 1979), p. 266.

31. Ibid., pp. 273-75.
32. Ibid., p. 277.
33. Ibid., p. 279.
34. Andree Michel, "Working Wives and Family Interaction in French and American Families," *International Journal of Comparative Sociology*, 11, no. 2 (June 1970), pp. 157-65.
35. Gertrude Bancroft McNally, "Patterns of Female Labor Force Activity," *Industrial Relations*, 7, no. 3 (May, 1968), pp. 205-6.
36. Bernard Blishen, "Social Class and Opportunity in Canada," *Canadian Review of Sociology and Anthropology*, 17 (1970), pp. 110-27.
37. Cited by Dennis Forcese, *The Canadian Class Structure* (Toronto: McGraw-Hill Ryerson, 1975), p. 48.
38. John Porter, *The Vertical Mosaic* (Toronto: University of Toronto Press, 1965).
39. Robert Blauner, *Alienation and Freedom* (Chicago: University of Chicago Press, 1964).
40. Michael Fullan, "Industrial Technology and Worker Integration in the Organization," *American Sociological Review*, 35, no. 6 (December 1970), pp. 1028-29.
41. Arthur Kornhauser, with the collaboration of Otto M. Reid, *Mental Health of the Industrial Worker: A Detroit Study* (New York: Wiley, 1965), pp. 260-62.
42. John K. Goldthorpe, "Attributes and Behavior of Car Assembly Workers: A Deviant Case and a Theoretical Critique," *British Journal of Sociology*, 17, no. 3 (September 1966), pp. 228-30.
43. See Arthur M. Ross, "Introduction: The Problem of Unemployment," in Arthur M. Ross, ed., *Unemployment in the American Economy* (New York: Wiley, 1964).
44. See Jon M. Shepard, *Automation and Alienation: A Study of Office and Factory Workers* (Cambridge, Mass.: MIT Press, 1971).
45. Gerald I. Susman, "Process Design, Automation, and Worker Alienation," *Industrial Relations*, 11, no. 1 (February 1971), pp. 34-35.
46. See Eugene V. Schneider, *Industrial Sociology*, 2nd ed. (New York: McGraw-Hill, 1969), pp. 146-50.
47. See Robert L. Kahn et al., *Occupational Stress* (New York: Wiley, 1964); Delbert C. Miller and William H. Form, *Industrial Sociology*, 2nd ed. (New York: Harper & Row, 1964), pp. 480-86.
48. Harold L. Wilensky, "The Professionalization of Everyone?", *American Journal of Sociology*, 70, no. 2 (September 1964), pp.137-58.
49. See Richard H. Hall, *Occupations and the Social Structure* (Englewood Cliffs, N.J.: Prentice-Hall, 1969), pp. 218-19.
50. Ely Chinoy, "Manning the Machines: The

Assembly Line Worker," in *The Human Shape of Labor* (New York: Oxford University Press, 1968).

51. Daniel Bell, *The Coming of Post-Industrial Society* (New York: Basic Books, 1973).

52. Abraham Rotstein, ed., *Beyond Industrial Growth: The Massey College Lectures, 1974-75* (Toronto: University of Toronto Press, 1976).

53. Vivian Rakoff, "Perennial Man and the Slowed Machine," in Rotstein, pp. 99-116.

54. Ragnar Nurkse, *Problems of Capital Formation in Underdeveloped Areas* (New York: Oxford University Press, 1962), especially chapter 1.

55. Jan Tinbergen, "Self-Management and the Optimum Order," in Brookmeyer, p. 119.

56. Ta-Chung Liv and Kung-Chia Yeh, "Chinese and other Asian Economies: A Quantitative Evaluation," *American Economic Review*, 63 (May 1973), pp. 215-23.

Chapter 17
Population and ecology

1. See Moni Nag, *Factors Affecting Human Fertility in Nonindustrial Societies: A Cross-cultural Study* (New Haven, Conn.: Yale University Press, 1962).

2. See Joseph Eaton and Albert J. Mayer, "The Social Biology of Very High Fertility Among the Hutterites: The Demography of a Unique Population," *Human Biology*, 25 (1953), pp. 206-65.

3. See W. James, "The Effect of Altitude on Fertility in Andean Countries," *Population Studies*, 20 (July 1966), pp. 97-101, and Ancel Keys et al., *The Biology of Human Starvation: I* (Minneapolis: University of Minnesota Press, 1950), pp. 749-63.

4. Robert G. Potter, Jr., "Birth Intervals: Structure and Change," *Population Studies*, 17 (November 1963), pp. 155-56, and Robert G. Potter, Jr., et al., "A Case Study of Birth Interval Dynamics," *Population Studies*, 19 (July 1965), pp. 81-96.

5. Ibid., pp. 155-66.

6. Geoffrey Gorer, *Death, Grief, and Mourning* (Garden City, N.Y.: Doubleday, 1965).

7. Statistics Canada, *1971 Census of Canada*, Bulletin 1.2 - 7 (Ottawa: Information Canada, 1974, Table 2a).

8. Leroy O. Stone and Susan Fletcher, *Migration in Canada, 1971 Census of Canada Profile Study*, Bulletin 5.1 - 5 (Ottawa: Supply and Services Canada, 1977), p. 40.

9. Jacques Henripin, *Immigration and Language Imbalance*, Canadian Immigration & Population Study (Ottawa: Information Canada, 1974), pp. 37-39. See also Warren Kalbach and Wayne W. McVey, *The Demographic Bases of Canadian Society*, 2nd ed.

(Toronto: McGraw-Hill Ryerson, 1979), p. 57.

10. Edward S. Deevey, Jr., "The Human Population," *Scientific American*, 203 (September 1960), pp. 195-204.

11. United Nations Population Division, *The Determinants and Consequences of Population Trends* (New York: United Nations, 1953), p. 8.

12. Ansley Coale, "The History of the Human Population," *Scientific American*, 231 (September 1974), p. 51.

13. See Thomas Malthus, "A Summary View of the Principle of Population," in Thomas Malthus et al., *Three Essays on Population* (New York: Mentor, 1960), pp. 13-59.

14. Joseph J. Spengler, "Values and Fertility Analysis," *Demography*, 3 (1966), pp. 109-30.

15. Susan George, *How the Other Half Dies: The Real Reasons for World Hunger* (Baltimore: Penguin Books, 1976), pp. 299-300.

16. Ibid., p. 300.

17. Sir Harold Hartley, "World Energy Prospects," in Nigel Calder, ed., *The World in 1984*, I (Baltimore: Penguin Books, 1965), p. 71.

18. See George, op cit.

19. Frances Moore Lappe and Joseph Collins, *Food First: Beyond the Myth of Scarcity* (Boston: Houghton Mifflin, 1977).

20. Ibid., pp. 310-19.

21. See George, p. 29.

22. Ibid., p. 58.

23. Lappe and Collins, p. 214.

24. Ibid., p. 214.

25. Ibid., p. 215.

26. Ibid., p. 215.

27. Ibid., p. 324.

28. Ibid., p. 324.

29. Ibid., p. 324.

30. S.M. Keeny, ed., "East Asia Review, 1972," *Studies in Family Planning*, vol. 4, no. 5, p. 119.

31. Phyllis Tilson Piotrow, *World Population Crisis: The United States Response* (New York: Praeger, 1973), p. 178.

32. George, p. 273.

33. Ibid., p. 273.

34. Andrew Malleson, *The Medical Runaround* (New York: Hart, 1973).

35. *Population Bulletin, International Migration*, 32, no. 4 (September 1977), pp. 19-21.

Chapter 18
Urban living

1. *Gallup Opinion Index*, 1973, no. 94:31; Canadian Institute for Public Opinion, #366, (1974).

2. William Michelson, *Environmental Choice, Human Behavior, and Residential Satis-*

faction (New York: Oxford University Press, 1977).

3. Norton Ginsburg, "The City and Modernization," in Myron Weiner, ed., *Modernization* (New York: Basic Books, 1966), p. 126.

4. Gideon Sjoberg, "The Rise and Fall of Cities: A Theoretical Perspective," *International Journal of Comparative Sociology*, 4 (1963), pp. 107-20.

5. For a fuller discussion of the differences, see O.C. Cox, "The Preindustrial City Reconsidered," in Paul Meadows and Ephraim Mizruchi, eds., *Urbanism, Urbanization, and Change: Some Perspectives on Urban Life* (Reading, Mass.: Addison-Wesley, 1969).

6. Max Weber, *The City* (New York: Free Press, 1958).

7. Ginsburg, p. 127.

8. Kingsley Davis, "The Urbanization of the Human Population," in Sylvia Fleis Fava, ed., *Urbanism in World Perspective: A Reader* (New York: Crowell, 1968), p. 44.

9. S.D. Clark, *The Suburban Society* (Toronto: University of Toronto Press, 1966), p. 223.

10. Robert Redfield, *The Folk Culture of Yucatan* (Chicago: University of Chicago Press, 1941).

11. Louis Wirth, "Urbanism as a Way of Life," *American Journal of Sociology*, 44 (July 1938), pp. 3-24.

12. Claude S. Fischer, *The Urban Experience* (New York: Harcourt, Brace, Jovanovich, 1976), pp. 29-39.

13. Quoted by Harvey Molotch, "Urban Society," in Jack D. Douglas, ed., *Introduction to Sociology* (New York: Free Press, 1973), p. 508.

14. Claude S. Fischer, "On Urban Alienation and Anomie: Powerless and Social Isolation," *American Sociological Review*, 38 (June 1973), p. 323.

15. Jack Wayne, "The Case of the Friendless Urbanite," in Alan Powell, ed., *The City: Attacking Modern Myths* (Toronto: McClelland and Stewart, 1972), pp. 90-92. See also Barry Wellman, "Who Needs Neighborhoods?" in Powell, pp. 94-100.

16. Ernest W. Burgess, "The Growth of the City: An Introduction to a Research Project," in George A. Theodorson, ed., *Studies in Human Ecology* (Evanston, Ill.: Row, Peterson, 1961).

17. Avery M. Guest, "The Applicability of the Burgess Zonal Hypothesis to Urban Canada," *Demography*, vol. 3 (Aug. 1969), pp. 271-77.

18. Homer Hoyt, *The Structure and Growth of Residential Neighborhoods in American Cities* (Washington, D.C.: Federal Housing Administration, 1939).

19. Chauncy D. Harris and Edward L. Ullman, "The Nature of Cities," *Annals of the American Academy of Political and Social Science*, 242 (November 1945), pp. 7-17.

20. William Michelson, *Man and His Urban Environment* (Reading, Mass.: Addison-Wesley, 1970).

21. Oscar Newman, *Defensible Space* (New York: Collier, 1973). See also A.E. Gillis, "Population Density and Social Pathology," *Social Forces*, 53 (December 1974), pp. 304-14.

22. William Michelson, "The Reconciliation of 'Subjective' and 'Objective' Data on Physical Environment in the Community," *Sociological Inquiry*, 43 (1973), pp. 147-73.

23. Fischer, p. 48. See also Warren E. Kalbach and Wayne W. McVey, *The Demographic Bases of Canadian Society*, 2nd. ed. (Toronto: McGraw-Hill Ryerson, 1979), p. 363.

24. Michelson, *Environmental Choice, Human Behavior, and Residential Satisfaction*.

25. Jane Jacobs, *The Death and Life of Great American Cities* (New York: Random House, 1961).

26. Herbert Gans, *People, Planning, and Politics* (New York: Basic Books, 1968).

27. *Urban Renewal Study for the City of Edmonton*, Edmonton City Planning Department, 1963-64.

28. Kalbach and McVey, p. 365.

29. Ibid., p. 367.

30. Michelson, *Environmental Choice, Human Behavior, and Residential Satisfaction*, Chap. 10.

Chapter 19
Social change

1. Oswald Spengler, *The Decline of the West*, trans. Charles F. Atkinson (London: Allen and Unwin, 1926-1929), 2 vols.

2. Auguste Comte, *Cours de Philosophie Positive* (Paris: Rouen, 1830-1842).

3. Herbert Spencer, *First Principles* (New York: Appleton, 1890); also *Principles of Sociology* (New York: Appleton, 1898-1899), 3 vols.

4. See Wilbert E. Moore and Arnold S. Feldman, "Society as a Tension-Management System," in George Baker and Leonard S. Cottrell, Jr., eds., *Behavioral Science and Civil Defense Disaster Research Group* (Washington, D.C.: National Academy of Sciences, National Research Council, 1962), pp. 93-105.

5. William F. Ogburn, *Social Change* (New York: Viking, 1922), pp. 200-13.

6. Robert E. Park, *Race and Culture*, (Glencoe, Ill.: Free Press, 1950).

7. Alex Inkeles and David H. Smith, *Becoming Modern: Individual Change in Six Developing Countries* (Cambridge, Mass.: Harvard University Press, 1974).

GLOSSARY

achieved status status assigned on the basis of standards over which a person has some control.

act the basic unit of human conduct.

acting crowd a potentially violent mob that chooses a course of action on the spot.

alienation the frustration and unhappiness of workers who have no control over how their labor is used.

amalgamation the blending of racial types through long interbreeding.

annihilation destruction of the entire population of one ethnic community by another.

anomie normlessness or deregulation.

anticipatory socialization trying out a role in one's imagination because one may play that role at some time in the future.

ascribed status status assigned on the basis of standards over which a person has no control.

assimilation the process by which a group integrates itself into the culture around it.

authority power that is regarded as legitimate by the members of the group.

bilateral descent a system that reckons descent from both the mother's side and the father's side.

boundaries the codes and customs that define a person as a member or nonmember of a particular group.

bureaucracy an organization with a hierarchy of offices set up to do work.

bureaucratic authority authority that is seen as legitimate if its rulings are consistent with a set of abstract rules with which the members of the group agree.

case study an in-depth investigation of a single case of a given phenomenon.

caste system a closed stratification system.

census metropolitan area (CMA) a metropolitan region consisting of a large central city surrounded by smaller, dependent cities.

charismatic authority authority that is seen as legitimate because of the leader's magnetic personality.

city a large, permanent, densely populated settlement.

code a grammar or set of rules that may be passed along from one generation to the next.

coding the process by which raw answers are sorted into categories that can be tallied and counted.

coercive power power based on physical means of control.

collective behavior spontaneous, transitory, non-institutionalized group action.

composite family a number of nuclear families living together in a single household.

conflict model the belief that societies are usually in a state of conflict and that the basic condition of life is competition for power and status.

congregational organization a religious organization that hires and fires its own leader and in which there is no church hierarchy.

content analysis the study of representative samples of writing from a given period or by particular individuals in order to discover common or repeated themes.

control a variable that is held constant in order to check the apparent cause-and-effect relationship between two other variables.

counterculture the subculture of hippies and dropouts of the late 1960s and early 1970s.

covert phase the phase during which one is preparing to act but has not yet begun to do so.

craze a fad or fashion that becomes so important to people that they spend a great deal of money and emotion on it.

crisis of legitimacy the situation in which large numbers of people withdraw their support from a regime.

crowd a large, temporary group of people who have some common goal or interest.

crude birthrate the number of births per year per 1000 people.

crude death rate the number of deaths per year per 1000 people.

cultural lag a term used to explain social problems that arise because there is a time lag between a technological change and the social and cultural changes required by that change.

cultural relativism the assumption that all cultures are equally valid and that any culture deserves respect.

culture a system of ideas, values, beliefs, knowledge, and customs transmitted from generation to generation within a social group.

cultural goals the wants and ambitions that people are taught by their society.

culture trait the smallest unit of culture.

demographic-transition model a model used to describe the process by which preindustrial societies with high rates of fertility and mortality are transformed into modern societies with low rates of fertility and mortality.

demography the study of human populations.

dependency ratio the ratio of people in dependent age groups to people in economically productive age groups.

dependent variable a variable that is assumed to be the effect of an independent variable.

detached observation observation in which the researcher watches what is going on without getting involved.

deviance any form of behavior that violates the norms of a social group.

discrimination the process by which a dominant group informally deprives a minority group of equal access to privileges and opportunities.

ecology the relationship between the physical environment and the human population that lives in that environment.

economics the social science that deals with the production, distribution, exchange, and consumption of scarce goods and services.

education a set of processes designed to transmit knowledge and skills and to develop mental abilities.

elite theory the belief that some group always gets the upper hand and rules the masses.

endogamy a rule requiring a person to marry someone within his or her own group.

episcopal organization a religious organization in which there is a well-defined hierarchy of authority.

esteem appreciation of a person regardless of his or her rank.

ethnic group a large collectivity in which membership is generally inherited and whose members share a feeling of identification with the group.

ethnic group cohesion the degree to which members act and identify themselves as a group distinct from the mainstream culture.

ethnic pluralism the situation in which ethnic groups are equal and live together on good terms.

ethnic religion a religion that is tied to a specific place and people.

ethnic stratification the situation in which ethnic groups form a hierarchy of dominance.

ethnocentrism the tendency to judge other ways of life by the standards of one's own group.

evolutionary (cultural) breakthrough an innovation that makes further advances possible.

evolutionism the belief in a law of historical progress; in sociology, that all societies go through stages of increasing complexity.

exogamy a rule requiring a person to choose a mate from a different group.

expressive crowd a group that shows especially strong feelings.

expulsion the sending of minority group members to another country.

extended family (consanguine family) a household made up of a nuclear family plus other relatives.

fad a culture trait that suddenly becomes popular and then disappears.

fashion a culture trait that is popular for a short time and is gradually replaced.

fecundity a woman's capacity to bear children.

fertility the rate at which a population gives birth.

fiscal policy a governmental policy of spending or not spending on goods and services.

folklore a society's collection of jokes, superstitions, lullabies, old wives' tales, slang words, ghost stories, etc.

folk society a small, isolated, homogeneous society; a peasant society.

folkway the trivial norms or conventions shared by members of a society.

frequency a number that shows the total of items in a given category.

functionalism the belief that a social pattern is best understood in terms of its functions in a given society.

functional requisites the requirements that all societies must meet, at least at a minimum level.

game stage the stage at which a child can understand a set of roles as a system.

gemeinschaft a society held together by a set of stable, secure bonds; a community.

gender the awareness of being a member of one sex or the other.

gender identity (sexual identity) the sex of which one considers oneself to be a member.

gender role (sex role) the culturally defined set of behaviors that are considered sex-appropriate within a given society.

generalization a statement that applies to a whole class of similar events.

generalized other an abstract role that stands for a set of particular roles.

gesellschaft a society in which relationships are impersonal or associational.

hierarchy a chain of command in which each person has authority over several other people.

homogamy the tendency to choose a spouse similar to oneself.

horizontal mobility social mobility that does not involve a gain or loss of status.

hypothesis a specific prediction that may be verified by empirical findings.

ideology a doctrine used to justify a group's actions in pursuing its own interests.

illegitimacy the birth of a child to an unmarried woman.

independent variable a variable that is assumed to be the cause of a dependent variable.

indicator a concrete representation of an abstract variable.

institution a complex structure of roles organized around a central activity or social need.

institutional completeness the maintenance by an ethnic group of a complete set of distinct institutions to meet the everyday needs of its members.

institutionalization the process through which culture influences the social system.

institutionalized means the resources available to the individual to pursue his or her goals.

integration the situation in which equality is achieved by reducing the separation between ethnic groups and encouraging them to participate in the same activities.

interest group a unified group that tries to influence the state in its favor.

internalization the process by which one makes the society's values part of one's personality.

joint family a type of extended family in which brothers share property but do not always live in a single household.

kin people who are related either by birth or by marriage.

labeling the social definition of a person as deviant.

laissez faire the belief that the state should not regulate the economy but should allow it to regulate itself.

legitimacy the state in which actions are generally regarded as lawful and proper.

legitimation acceptance of the use of power by the leaders of a group because it is in line with the values of the members of the group.

life chances patterns of infant mortality, physical and mental illness, childlessness, marital conflict, separation, divorce, etc.

life style patterns of eating and dressing, cultural and recreational activities, relationships between parents and children, etc.

looking-glass self the self-image that a person acquires from the opinions of others.

magic practices directed toward the control of spirits or other forces beyond the reach of ordinary human powers.

marginal person a person who belongs to two or more groups that are supposedly mutually exclusive.

market exchange a system in which goods and services are exchanged in a market context.

Marxism any doctrine that is supposedly derived from the teachings of Karl Marx.

matriarchy a society in which women are dominant over men.

matrilineal descent system a descent system in which a person belongs to his or her mother's line of descent.

matrilocal residence a rule requiring a newly married couple to live with the wife's family.

mechanical solidarity the pattern in which people get along by being alike in their backgrounds, religious practices, ideas about morality, and so forth.

median age the age that divides any population equally, so that half are older and half are younger.

megalopolis a supercity in which several cities

merge together to form an extended urbanized region.

mercantilism the belief that the best way to increase national power is to increase national wealth (i.e., the nation's supply of gold and silver).

migration the movement of people into or out of an area.

minority group an ethnic group that is subordinate to another group.

model a mental map of a subject that may be incomplete or misleading but cannot be proved wrong.

monetary policy a governmental policy of manipulating the prime lending rate of the total money supply.

morality of cooperation the view that rules and obligations are rational agreements rather than fixed principles.

moral realism the view that rules have existed forever or were laid down by God or some other authority figure.

mores a society's important ethical rules.

mortality the rate at which a population dies.

multilinear evolutionism the belief that various societies follow different lines of development.

myth a nonhistorical story known by almost everyone in a group and symbolizing great truths to the group's members.

nationalism ethnic-group chauvinism.

neolocal residence a rule requiring newly married couples to set up housekeeping on their own.

neo-Marxism the Marxist view of capitalism, updated to correspond with developments since Marx's time.

norm a rule that tells members of a society how to behave in particular situations; a rule that prescribes legitimate means of pursuing one's goals.

normative power power based on symbolic means of control.

nuclear family (conjugal family) a husband, his wife, and their unmarried children.

organic solidarity the pattern in which people are interdependent even though they are very different in experience, opinions, habits, and so forth.

organization a social unit deliberately constructed and reconstructed to pursue specific goals.

overt phase the phase during which an action is actually performed.

participant observation observation in which the researcher takes some role within the group being observed.

particularism bending rules or making special ones to fit special persons or groups.

patriarchy a society in which men are dominant over women.

patrilineal descent system a descent system in which a person belongs to his or her father's line of descent.

patrilocal residence a rule requiring a newly married couple to live with the husband's family.

peer group a group of people of similar status.

play stage the stage at which a child does not coordinate his or her activities with those of others.

pluralism the view that the best way to preserve freedom in a society is to have within it a number of powerful groups that represent various interests.

politics any action involving the collective pursuit of collective goals.

polyandry the marriage of a woman to more than one husband.

polygamous family a family in which there are several wives or husbands.

polygyny the marriage of a man to more than one wife.

population the whole number of units from which a sample is drawn.

population pyramid a diagram that shows the age-sex composition of a population at a given time.

power the ability to get one's orders obeyed despite opposition; the ability to achieve one's goals even in the face of opposition.

prejudice prejudging against individuals on the basis of characteristics believed to be shared by all members of their ethnic group.

presbyterian organization a religious organization in which authority is in the hands of an elected regional board of ministers and lay members.

prestige social honor attached to particular roles.

primary group a group whose members interact in a personal, intimate, and emotional way.

propaganda the planned use of mass media to influence the beliefs and opinions of a population.

property rights or control over goods and services.

public a group of people who share a particular code; a scattered group of people who have different opinions about an issue and are involved in a discussion of that issue.

questionnaire a printed list of questions given to respondents to answer themselves.

quota sampling sampling in which the percentage of people with a given characteristic is equal to the percentage of such people in the whole population.

racial group an ethnic group to which members are assigned on the basis of inherited biological traits.

racism the belief that ethnic and racial groups are based on genetic similarities rather than on social agreements.

random sampling sampling in which every member of the population has an equal chance of being chosen as part of the sample.

rational-legal authority power based on the rules of the constitution under which the leader has been elected or appointed.

reaction formation a mechanism for denying an unacceptable element of the personality.

reciprocity two-way exchange of goods or services.

redistribution a system in which goods and services are brought to a central source and then redistributed throughout the population.

reference group the group to which one compares oneself when judging one's own status.

reliability the degree of consistency obtained by repeated measurements.

religion the relationship of humankind to some ultimate reality.

representativeness the extent to which the objects studied are typical of a whole class of similar cases.

repression the effort to restrain certain impulses within the personality.

resocialization the process by which an adult whose previous socialization was inadequate is made to behave in ways that the society approves of.

role the part each person must play to create a collective activity.

role conflict the situation in which a person occupies two roles that are regulated by incompatible norms.

role taking the ability of a person to imagine the role of another person with whom he or she interacts.

rumor a piece of information that is passed from one person to another throughout a group without being checked for accuracy.

sanction a reward for desirable behavior or a punishment for undesirable behavior.

secondary group a group whose members interact in an impersonal, unsentimental, and business-like way.

segmental religion a religion that is an offshoot of a universalizing religion or a new religious system that integrates small groups into larger communities.

segregation forcing minority group members to work or live in separate areas whenever possible and to use facilities separate from those used by the dominant group,

self-reflexive behavior interaction with the self.

sex the biological fact of being male or female.

sex ratio the number of males per 100 females in a population.

significant other a person whose opinions are important to one; usually a family member.

social class a set of people with similar socio-economic status.

social control the process by which members of a group support desired forms of behavior and discourage undesired forms.

socialization the process of learning the rules of behavior for a given social group.

social mobility movement from one status or occupation to another.

social movement a collective effort to bring about a new order of life.

social stratification a hierarchy of layers or strata that are unequal in terms of property, power, and prestige.

social system the interactions among two or more people; the roles and actual practices that exist among members of a social group.

society a large, permanent, self-sufficient, self-perpetuating group of interacting people.

sociology the study of human group life.

state the organization that has a monopoly on the legitimate use of force in a given territory.

status a person's rank based on income, prestige, education, or power.

status inconsistency the situation in which a person ranks higher by one standard than by another.

stereotype a mental cartoon that exaggerates the traits of the typical member of a particular group.

stigma the mark of disgrace that is attached to people in disvalued roles.

stratified sampling random sampling within particular groups of individuals.

structured interview an interview that uses a standard list of questions.

subculture a group whose members share values and ideas that differ from those of the wider society.

sublimation the process by which energy is channeled away from sexual concerns and into more refined concerns.

suburbanization the movement of people from central cities to smaller communities in the surrounding area.

surplus repression repression in excess of what is necessary for people to live together in a civilized way.

symbol anything that represents something else, i.e., anything that has meaning.

symbolic interactionism the belief that social relationships are built up through social interactions on a symbolic level.

technology the institutionalized application of knowledge to control nature for human uses.

territoriality the establishment of a certain zone or space that may not be occupied by any other person or animal.

theology the organization of religious beliefs into a unified doctrine.

theory a statement based on observed facts that explains what is supposed to be a causal relationship between those facts.

traditional authority authority that is seen as legitimate because it has existed for a long time; power based on the customs under which a leader gains his or her position.

transsexual a person whose sex has been changed through surgery and hormone treatment.

transvestite a person whose gender identity differs from his or her sex.

unilinear descent a system that reckons descent from either the male blood line or the female blood line.

unilinear evolutionism the belief that there is a single set of stages through which every society must proceed.

universalism adhering to the same rules in dealing with all people.

universalizing religion a religion that is not tied to any particular region or ethnic group and whose members consider their beliefs to be right for all humankind.

unstructured interview an interview in which the respondent is asked questions that lead to an open discussion of the topic.

urbanization the movement of people from rural areas to cities and from small cities to larger ones.

urban society a large-scale, heterogeneous society located in a city.

utilitarian power power based on material means of control.

validity the ability of an indicator to genuinely and accurately represent the variable that it is meant to represent.

value a standard used by members of a society to judge behavior and to choose among various possible goals.

variable a characteristic that differs among situations, individuals, or groups and can be measured.

vertical mobility social mobility that involves movement toward higher or lower status.

veto group an interest group that can prevent any action that conflicts with its values and interests.

voluntary association a group that people join because they support its goals and values.

zero population growth (ZPG) the point at which there is no natural increase in population.

NAME INDEX

Marx, Gary T., 595
Marx, Karl, 9, 10, 16, 17, 18, 21, 79-80, 109, 126,
    235, 246-47, 252, 270, 271, 272, 273-74,
    284, 336, 362-63, 393, 394-95, 419, 447,
    448, 449-50, 451, 471, 476, 477, 482-84,
    486, 487, 490, 492, 571-72, 591, 602
Mason, Edward S., 606
Masuoka, J., 599
Matisse, Henri, 76, 170, 594
Mauss, Marcel, 468, 605
May, M.A., 592
Mayer, Albert J., 607
Mayo, Elton, 233
Mazer, Donald, 595
Mead, George Herbert, 12, 160, 161, 162, 163-65,
    166-67, 168-69, 208, 594, 596
Mead, Margaret, 125-26, 153, 371, 592
Meadows, Paul, 608
Means, Gardiner, 606
Meis, Scott M., 592
Meissner, Martin, 592
Mellos, Kuola, 605
Merton, Robert K., 12, 205, 206, 209, 210, 213,
    240, 595, 596, 598, 602
Michel, Andrée, 606
Michels, Robert, 442, 443, 450, 604
Michelson, William, 550-52, 555, 607
Milgram, Stanley, 42, 174-75, 177, 594
Miller, Delbert C., 606
Miller, Neal E., 596
Millett, Kate, 603, 604
Mills, C. Wright, 446, 451, 599, 605, 606
Mizruchi, Ephraim, 608
Molotch, Harvey, 608
Money, John, 592
Montagu, M.F. Ashley, 290, 600
Moore, Wilbert E., 12, 270, 274, 421, 423, 599,
    608
Morris, Desmond, 150, 593
Morris, Raymond N., 598, 600
Morton, W.L., 600
Moses, Anna Mary Robertson (Grandma), 72
Mowrer, O.H., 596
Mulvihill, Donald J., 185, 590
Murdock, G.P., 359, 362, 601, 602
Murphy, Fred J., 594
Myers, Charles A., 606
Myles, John F., 599
Myrdal, Gunnar, 598, 604

Nag, Moni, 607
Napoleon (Bonaparte), 436
Nass, G.D., 601
National Council on Welfare, 598
Nettler, Gwynn, 594
Newman, Oscar, 608
Newman, Peter, 450, 451, 605
Newton, Isaac, 31
Nisbet, Robert, 595, 602, 604
Nurkse, Ragnar, 607

O'Bryan, K.G., 309, 600
Ogburn, William F., 76, 591, 608
Ohlin, Lloyd B., 597
Olsen, Marvin E., 598
Ornstein, Michael D., 454, 457, 605
Ortega, Suzanne T., 599
Ossenberg, Richard J., 596, 605
Otto, Herbert A., 603

Paquet, Gilles, 605
Pareto, Vilfredo, 444, 446, 604
Park, Robert E., 12, 538, 545, 590, 608
Parker, E.B., 600
Parsons, Talcott, 12, 18, 20, 74, 363, 364, 365,
    412, 570-71, 597, 602, 604
Pasic, Majdan, 606
Peak, W., 604

Pearson, Lester B., 139
Perrow, Charles, 597
Phillips, David P., 601
Phillips, M., 598
Piaget, Jean, 105, 106-8, 162, 592
Picasso, Pablo, 76
Pilisuk, Marc, 605
Pineo, Peter C., 599, 602
Piotrow, Phyllis Tilson, 607
Podoluk, Jenny, 598
Polanyi, Karl, 605, 606
Pollock, Jackson, 72
Pomeroy, Wardell B., 601
Pope, Liston, 599
Porter, John, 15, 263, 308, 310, 411, 422, 423, 446,
    451, 486, 599, 600, 604, 605, 606
Porter, Marion R., 423, 604
Porterfield, Austin L., 594
Postman, L., 600
Potter, Robert G., Jr., 607
Powell, Alan, 608
Premack, David, 593
Presthus, Robert, 597
Preston, Samuel H., 598
Pyke, S.W., 56, 591

Raffel, Stanley, 590
Rakoff, Vivian, 490, 607
Reasons, Charles E., 195, 595
Redfield, Robert, 8, 538, 539-40, 542, 544
Reed, Paul, 595
Reich, Charles A., 240, 598
Reid, Otto M., 606
Reiss, Ira, 592
Reitz, Jeffrey, 309-12, 600
Rensberger, Boyce, 593
Reston, James, 569
Revelle, Roger, 605
Rhodes, Robert I., 605
Richmond, Anthony H., 308, 486, 600
Riel, Louis, 199, 300, 304
Riesman, David, 604
Riley, Matilda White, 601
Ringer, Benjamin, 603
Rivlin, Alice, 599
Robinson, Joan, 605, 606
Rocher, Guy, 601
Rodgers, D.A., 595
Roethlisberger, F.J., 597
Rogoff, Natalie, 599
Romulus and Remus, 148
Roosevelt, Eleanor, 139
Rose, Arnold M., 596
Rosenbaum, Milton, 595
Rosenberg, Bernard, 596
Rosenthal, David, 595
Ross, Arthur M., 606
Rossi, Alice, 131-32, 592, 593
Rostow, Eugene V., 606
Roszak, Theodore, 240, 592, 598
Rotstein, Abraham, 604, 607
Rousseau, Jean Jacques, 410, 604
Royal Commission on Bilingualism and
    Biculturalism, 598
Royal Commission on Violence in the
    Communications Industry, 591
Rushing, William A., 599
Russell, Susan, 593
Ryan, Claude, 390

Samuelson, Paul A., 606
Scheff, Thomas, 595
Scheu, William J., 592
Schiff, Martin, 37, 590
Schlesinger, Benjamin, 594
Schneider, Louis, 606
Schneidman, Edwin S., 596
Schoeck, Helmut, 595
Schramm, W., 600

Schulz, David A., 601
Schuessler, Karl, 596
Schur, Edwin M., 594
Schwarz, Edward E., 594
Scott, Marvin, 593
Scott, William G., 600
Scudder, K.J., 597
Sears, David O., 594
Sears, Robert R., 596
Sellitz, Claire, 591
Selznick, Gertrude J., 599
Shakespeare, William, 95, 177, 200, 594
Shalker, T.E., 591
Shanas, Ethel, 602
Sharp, R.L., 591
Shaw, Clifford R., 207, 590, 596
Shaw, Donald, 591
Sheldon, William H., 202-3, 596
Shepard, Jon M., 606
Shirley, Mary M., 594
Short, James F., Jr., 203-4, 590, 594, 596
Shulman, Norman, 594
Sifton, Clifford, 306
Simmel, George, 12
Simon, H.A., 597
Singh, J.A.L., 593
Sjoberg, Gideon, 530, 531, 608
Small, Shirley, 193, 595
Smelser, Neil J., 12, 320, 321, 363, 600, 602
Smith, Adam, 231, 482, 484, 485
Smith, David H., 573-77, 608
Smith, Luke M., 603
Snider, Laureen, 595
Sommer, Robert, 151, 593
Sopher, David E., 376, 603
Sorokin, Pitrim, 12, 561
Spencer, Herbert, 9-10, 17, 18, 418-19, 429, 561,
    563, 608
Spengler, Joseph J., 512, 607
Spengler, Oswald, 561, 608
Spiro, M.E., 602
Spitz, Rene, 593
Stalin, Joseph, 523
Stark, Rodney, 603
Statistics Canada, 595, 607
Steinberg, Stephen, 599
Stevenson, H. Michael, 454, 457, 605
Stone, Leroy O., 607
Stouffer, Samuel A., 596
Stroller, Frederick H., 603
Sumner, William Graham, 69, 591
Surgeon General's Advisory Committee, 591
Susman, Gerald I., 606
Sutherland, Edwin H., 195, 204, 205, 206, 207-8,
    210, 595, 596
Swain, M., 604
Sweezy, Paul, 606
Sykes, Gresham M., 170, 594
Szasz, Thomas, 191, 595

Taylor, Frederick W., 231, 232, 233, 597
Teevan, James, Jr., 599, 603
Tepperman, Lorne, 268, 590, 594, 599
Terman, Louis M., 601
Theodorson, George A., 608
Thomas, W.I., 12, 47, 590
Thompson, J.H., 598, 601
Thrasher, Frederick, 590
Tickamyer, Ann R., 592
Tiger, Lionel, 150, 593
Tinbergen, Jan, 607
Tocqueville, Alexis de, 438-39, 440, 443, 604
Tönnies, Ferdinand, 174
Touraine, Alain, 335-36, 601
Toynbee, Arnold, 567
Trew, Peter, 211
Tribe, Verna, 275, 276, 599
Trier, Mella L., 602
Troll, Lillian E., 602
Trow, Martin, 604

SUBJECT INDEX

Utilitarian power, 228, 229, 230, 243, 615
Utopian movement, 337

Validity, 43-44, 62, 199, 615
Values, 24-25, 67-68, 74, 90, 100-1, 142, 270, 335, 336, 352, 393, 395, 396, 410, 412-13, 615
Variables, 34, 58-60, 62, 169, 615
Vasectomy, 500
Verbal ability, sex differences in, 130
Vertical mobility, 266, 280, 615
Vertical Mosaic (Porter), 15, 308, 446
Veto groups, 441, 462, 615
Vices, 578
Vietnam War, 446, 447, 448, 474
Violence, 54-55, 86-87, 340
Violent resistance, 298, 299-300
Visual-spatial ability, sex differences in, 130
Voluntary associations, 221-22, 243, 438, 439, 615

Wales, 185
War Measures Act, 437
War of the Worlds (Wells), 334
WASP, 285
Water supplies, world, 515-16
Watergate scandal, 210, 435, 447
Wealth of Nations, The (Smith), 231, 482, 484
"We-feeling", 162, 171, 172
"We-ness", 162, 170
Welfare state, 474-75
Werther effect, 332
West Germany, 222, 223
White-collar crime, 195, 203
Wild Child, The, 148
Winnipeg General Strike, 338, 473
Witchcraft, 387
Withdrawal, passivity and, 298-99
Women:
    socialization for sexuality, 110-12

in work force, 485-86
Women's Christian Temperance Union, 136
Women's Institutes, 139
Women's movement, 112, 114, 135-40, 334-35, 337, 369, 370
Women's suffrage, 338, 339-40
"Wonder drugs", 522
Work, 488-90 (see also Jobs; Labor)
"World system" model, 454
Writing, as cultural breakthrough, 570-71

"Yankee City", 273
Yerkes Primate Research Center, 149
Yucatan, 539, 540, 542
Yugoslavia, 476, 478, 492

Zero population growth (ZPG), 511, 525, 615